7.95 p
T
S-GS

Psychology of Learning and Teaching

PSYCHOLOGY OF LEARNING AND TEACHING

second edition

HAROLD W. BERNARD, Ph.D.

Division of Continuing Education
and University of Oregon
Oregon State System of Higher Education

McGRAW-HILL BOOK COMPANY

New York   St. Louis   San Francisco
Toronto   London   Sydney

To Wright, Rodger, and Richard

Preface

Like many other areas of study, educational psychology is changing and developing rapidly. Since the first edition of *Psychology of Learning and Teaching* was published, machine teaching and programmed learning have become important topics to be investigated and practiced. A surge of interest in group dynamics as a factor in learning and as a phase of motivation has resulted in an emphasis that was touched on only lightly in the first edition. The impact of cultural influences on motivation and learning receives additional emphasis here. Continuing studies, particularly longitudinal ones, on the nature and development of intelligence have tended to give additional weight to the role and importance of motivation—these studies are recognized in the second edition. Rapid social and technological changes have stimulated a revival of interest in problem solving and creativity. These developments, plus the solid core of learning theory, transfer of training, and individual differences and their assessment, which have long been the focuses of interest in educational psychology, are the emphases in this second edition.

Just how to combine developments with the historically significant aspects of educational psychology to form an integrated presentation was, and is, a problem. I have not divided the book into parts as I did in the first edition because individual chapters relate directly to more than one chapter. Instructors will, I think, find it easier to develop their own sequences if the parts division is omitted.

I can conceive of Chapters 2 to 6 (dealing with learning theory, transfer, problem solving, habit formation, and factors that facilitate learning) as one part, devoted largely to the theoretical underpinnings of educational psychology. However, in these chapters applications to classroom problems are emphasized and illustrated. This is especially true in Chapter 5 on habit formation, in which theory is directly related to the study habits that prospective teachers can use now and later communicate to their pupils.

Chapters 7 to 15 could well be considered a second major part, in which the nature of the individual is the focus. The individual—how he grows, the part language plays in his development, how intelligence and motivation combine to shape his personality—is the major emphasis. This part also includes an examination of specific aspects and principles of child and adolescent development as they relate to problems of learning and teaching.

Chapters 16 to 21 might well be considered part three. Here the emphasis is on the larger setting of learning—cultural influences, group dynamics, and the role of the teacher—within which the boy or girl lives and works as a school pupil. But here the part conception tends to break down, because Chapters 18, 19, and 21 reflect back upon, summarize, expand, and illustrate material presented in earlier chapters. Specifically, programmed learning refers back to learning theory and motivation; mental hygiene refers back particularly to motivation and cultural influences; and evaluation must be made in terms of the many facets of growth that are a part of learning, and it must also include reference to the future. The book concludes with a discussion of the responsibility the teacher has for interpreting and implementing all the influences that bear on learning and teaching.

Throughout the text I have tried to bring into clear perspective the psychological principles that have been derived from experimental investigations. Additional tentative principles have been derived from empirical studies. Finally, an attempt has been made to draw on other fields of study—sociology, cultural anthropology, and philosophy—to make the generalizations pertinent to our times. These principles are often stated as generalizations, which are then left to the teacher to apply. The case study is used sparingly because of the tendency to limit the application of the generalizations to that specific case, rather than to think of them in terms of the many situations to which they can and should apply. The reader is asked to project and visualize his own probable teaching assignment in terms of the principles given. The Problems and Exercises section at the end of each chapter will assist him in doing so.

The studies used in preparation of the various chapters are listed in the Bibliography at the end of the book. The Suggested Additional Readings section at the end of each chapter contains a few references; they are presented for the benefit of students who want to have some selected readings rather than to be "snowed under" by vague possibilities. The author has found these works very readable. They may serve to further speculation and offer some applications, as well as to provide further theoretical understanding.

Some readers of the first edition and advisers on the manuscript of this edition have suggested that I briefly present my own orientation toward the teaching-learning focus that is used. Here it is:

1. I conceive of the pupil as a dynamic system, very responsive to his environment. His response is unique because of each person's varied potential for responding; thus, each pupil selects different aspects of the total milieu to which he responds. For example, intelligence is regarded as a potential; it determines or influences the selection of op-

portunities to which the individual responds; in turn, intelligence is developed by the response to these opportunities—vigorous participation in school is a result of intelligence, and (I think) in turn develops or enlarges intelligent behavior. Similarly with motivation, personality, skill development, socialization.

2. Although I did my graduate work in psychology in the functional orientation, I find that I cannot consistently subscribe to one school. It seems to me that drill and repetition have their place in much effective learning, especially in language and the fundamental processes of arithmetic. Insight is also necessary as we study the meaning—not just the facts—of history; it is necessary in the higher mathematics and in art, esthetics, literature, and social studies.

3. The socioeconomic class of the learner—and this involves both parental and peer group relationships—affects what he brings to the school in terms of attitude or motivation and in terms of a background to which the new is attached. Hence, this area receives much and frequent attention in this book. The teacher should understand group dynamics and the broad personal orientation provided by social class functionally, as well as academically. This has additional import as the guns are trained in the war on poverty.

4. I believe the teacher is exceedingly important in what the pupil learns. The teacher is, at least in part—but only in part—responsible for the vigor with which pupils pursue academic tasks. Some teachers stultify growth; others greatly enhance it. There is no evading the fact that some pupils will emulate the teacher; it is therefore an inescapable responsibility that all teachers worthy of the name themselves be active learners.

Gratitude for the permission to quote from studies, reports, or illustrative examples is expressed in footnotes. Special thanks are also due to Dr. Leroy Pierson, Division of Continuing Education, Oregon State System of Higher Education, who read the chapters as they were written and suggested ideas to be incorporated and ways to increase the pertinency of the total outline. Thanks are also due to Dr. M. Benimoff, Glassboro (New Jersey) State College, who read and criticized the first edition point by point and suggested deletions, additions, and bibliographical references that have been carefully attended to in the preparation of the second edition. Thanks are also merited by Anneva Lenz, who typed and retyped the manuscript, called my attention to awkward sentences, and on many occasions, checked references.

Harold W. Bernard

Contents

The Field of Educational Psychology

The speed, accuracy, and complexity of computer operations serve to emphasize the alertness, perceptiveness, and sheer power of man's brain. The potential of man's mind has been likened to a mechanical brain huge enough to fill San Francisco's Cow Palace (Kubie, 1956).[1] The potential, however, is often blocked because of impairing, and often destructive, emotional conflicts. It would seem easy to agree with Landsman (1962) that probing an inch into human nature would be worth the exploration of thousands of miles of space. Yet, while millions of dollars and the energies of armies of men are spent on physical sciences, comparatively minute amounts of time and money are devoted to probing the mysteries of man himself.

The life sciences—e.g., sociology, anthropology, psychiatry, and ethics—are making contributions to the understanding of man, and as progress is made, it becomes clear that sharp lines cannot be drawn between human sciences and the physical and biological sciences. Chemistry, physics, biology, genetics, medicine, and the like also make their contributions to the use, misuse, and disuse of man's potential. It is quite clear that the great challenge of this and all other ages is to bring all interrelated sciences together in the single mind of man (Barzun, 1961, p. 21).

Psychology is one of the sciences engaged in the study of man. The area and delimitations of psychological study are different from those of other human sciences largely in terms of degrees of emphasis. Psychology, with due respect for its overlapping with other sciences, may be defined as the study of man's behavior, experience, and his conscious and subconscious life. Psychology is concerned with the whole man; hence biology, endocrinology, and pathology have bearing, but their focus is on how they influence behaving, experiencing, thinking, and feeling. Psychology must be concerned with the physical and social environment because these also help to shape man's behavior, experience, and conscious and subconscious life. Educational psychology—the subject of this book—is the study of how,

[1] Full data for published works referred to in parentheses may be found in the Bibliography at the end of the book.

why, and under what conditions individuals learn. It is concerned with the application of psychology and psychological research to all aspects of educational practice. Representative topics with which educational psychology deals can be seen by examining the table of contents of this book. Because the school is society's specific institution for learning, we are here *primarily* concerned with learning in the school.

Relationships of psychology to education

The Meaning and Aims of Psychology   As one searches for understanding, he quickly discovers that seemingly simple behavior is actually extremely complex. For example, we have not always realized how important it is to love, cuddle, and fondle a baby. In fact, the behaviorists[2] of the early twenties advised against cuddling and fondling. Today we readily appreciate that love affects the baby's development of social response, rate of physical and mental development, and establishment of emotional patterns. It is less readily perceived that early love experiences affect the child's response to peers and teachers in the school. It is still more difficult to see that the adolescent's self-esteem and his idealized models (not necessarily actual persons) are still being influenced by the early limitation or abundance of love (Kagan, 1963). All through adulthood, in either extreme mental illness or exceptional creativity, love —and its complex ramifications—*along with many other experiences* must be recognized as a force that molds behavior. The effects of love are mentioned here only as an example of the complexity of behavior. We could have used conditioning, social class influences on behavior, peer influences, or teacher personality to indicate the ramifications of a single factor in behavior. This attention to the minute and specific (sometimes called the "molecular approach") is a step toward understanding man's total behavior. (Considering the total—the man—is called the "molar approach.")

It has been shown that a major function of psychology is to improve our understanding of behavior—partial, incomplete, and tentative though our understanding may be. Another function is to predict what behavior will be under given circumstances and thus lay the groundwork for controlling and shaping responses so that optimum development will occur. Psychology is also concerned with developing theory; that is, as ideas are disclosed, then evaluated by many minds and tested in various

[2] Behaviorists actually include persons who have quite a variety of psychological orientations; hence, one may see the terms "extreme behaviorist," "behavioristic associationist," or "descriptive behaviorist" as indicating differences. Basically, "behaviorist" refers to a psychologist who emphasizes the objective study (observation or measurement) of responses and is less concerned with, or even ignores, conscious processes.

situations, a theory is evolved and then further tested. Finally, if that theory withstands further testing, psychologists may formulate principles of behavior and development that guide the application of psychology to daily living. At this point, we can only guess about and hope for things to come. But in it all, we hope to see the vast potentialities of individual minds come much closer to complete realization.

Man, as a physical organism, is an exceedingly intricate phenomenon, consisting of heart, brain, spinal cord, muscles, bones, glands, blood, sensory organs, and so on without end.[3] The actions and interdependencies of these components add another dimension of complexity. Adjustments and the processes of adjusting, in continuous operation from conception to death and often referred to as "homeostatic" (see Glossary) processes, are a focus of psychology (Stagner and Karowski, 1952, p. 19). Still another complexity in psychology develops from the ramifications of environment, which includes social, economic, geographical, institutional, physical, and perceptual factors that affect different persons in various ways. Thus there can be no satisfactory simple capsule assertion of what psychology is or what it does. At all times there is great danger of oversimplification, but with due regard for the many possible interpretations of each word we will say: Psychology is mainly concerned with the study of continuing processes (adjustments) through which inherent potentialities (of the organism) are affected by circumstances (environment) in order to produce new and, we hope, better ways of living. This inclusive aim is more meaningful when divided into subordinate aims that embrace the various elements involved in behavior, i.e., the stimulating situation, the organism, and the response. Thus the aims may be stated as follows:

1. Psychology aims to understand the combinations of stimuli that evoke responses—both adequate and inadequate—with the ultimate goal of controlling the situation to obtain better responses. Thus the family, the neighborhood, the culture, and indeed, the universe are areas of concern.

2. Stimuli are internal as well as external, so psychology seeks to know the nature of the individual. This includes his inherited equipment —glands, reflexes, sense organs, appetites, etc. It also includes the residue of his previous experiences. Generalizations are formed regarding the characteristics, qualities, and experiences of childhood, adolescence, and maturity.

3. Psychology aims to formulate tentative principles of behavior— descriptions of how successful responses are selected and consolidated into behavior patterns. Descriptions of the pervasive elements of many

---

[3] The words "without end" are used advisedly, since we do not know all there is to know about any one of the constituents, e.g., blood.

similar situations are then summarized in an inclusive generalization. Theories must necessarily be postulated so that the tentative principles may be tested and refined.

4. Psychology seeks to take improved knowledge of the three foregoing factors—situations, the individual, and responses—and develop new questions for which new answers must be found. Thus there is an assumption of responsibility for new thrusts for integrated knowledge.

Branches of Psychology   All man's activities have psychological implications. It has become necessary, as knowledge has increased and the avenues for more investigations have been opened, to make many divisions of psychology. These divisions single out of the entire realm of psychology particular groups of phenomena for study. However, the divisions are not sharp, because phenomena that function in one area have bearing on others. Thus Stephens asserts that the educational psychologist will find his most useful materials in such areas as developmental psychology, learning theory, techniques of assessment, individual differences, personality, social and group processes, problem solving, and counseling (Stephens, 1959, p. 109). The distinctions are made primarily for the sake of convenience in academic discussion and for ease in following the themes of one's major interests. Lines of demarcation become less clear as one attempts to apply psychology, as can be seen from a listing of the divisions that comprise the American Psychological Association.

Autonomous divisions, having their own by-laws, officers, and often their own publications are:

General Psychology
Teaching of Psychology
Experimental Psychology
Evaluation and Measurement
Physiological and Comparative Psychology
Developmental Psychology
Personality and Social Psychology
Esthetics
Clinical Psychology

Consulting Psychology
Industrial and Business Psychology
Educational Psychology
School Psychologists
Counseling Psychology
Psychologists in Public Service
Military Psychology
Maturity and Old Age
Consumer Psychology
Philosophical Psychology

The Division of General Psychology cuts across lines and embraces persons who may also be interested in other divisions. Three areas of interest that have not become autonomous but operate within the framework of the American Psychological Association are (1) Society for the Psychological Study of Social Issues, (2) Society of Engineering Psychologists, and (3) the National Council on Psychological Aspects of Disability.

Twelve psychological journals are published by the American Psychological Association, or certain of its divisions. One of them is the *Journal of Educational Psychology*, with six issues a year devoted to various studies of learning and teaching.

Students are probably more familiar with the division of psychology into areas such as child psychology and psychology of adolescence. These are simply aspects of developmental psychology and deal with such things as heredity, prenatal influences, family relationships, play groups, and community factors as they influence growth and development in the early years. These concerns, it can readily be seen, are also of intimate interest to the study of teaching and learning.

Psychology of education

The Meaning of Educational Psychology Educational psychology is one of the branches of psychology—parallel to social, abnormal, or industrial psychology. It has both applied and theoretical emphases. Its areas of concern relate to learning and teaching, and they may be listed as follows: (1) the nature and characteristics of the learner, including growth and development, (2) the internal and external factors involved in learning processes, (3) the manner in which these processes may be facilitated by the teacher, including (4) the total personality and techniques of the teacher, and (5) the formulation of scientific principles that can point the way to the most effective procedures to be used in formal education. In short, the pervasive function of educational psychology is to encourage the use of inclusive principles that will allow for effectively adapting procedural applications to the pupil, the teachers, and the immediate situation. The "how-to-do-it," hortatory approach that stems from the experience of one or two persons is avoided.

Further discussion of these primary concerns will more clearly describe the field of educational psychology. The nature of the learner will be revealed through a study of individual differences in intelligence, past experiences, bodily vigor, and mental health. Increased attention has recently been given to noncognitive aspects of learning, as evidence accumulates that individuals use intellective capacities in vastly different directions and with vastly different strength. The nature of the learner is also approached through study of the salient characteristics of childhood and adolescence. What can and should be learned is investigated through study of the relative difficulty of school subjects for individuals because of their age and readiness to master difficult problems. The meaning that material has for the individual, the situation in which material is presented, the concreteness or abstractness of the material, and the degree to which material satisfies a need or desire of the learner are also involved in learning processes. Study of these and other areas of concern lead to the formulation of scientific principles of effective learning, such as the following:

The desire to learn facilitates the learning process.

One learns more rapidly when the new has meaning related to the old.

Past experiences affect what one perceives in the present. The facts than an individual learns in the classroom are determined by both his own and the teacher's attitudes.

The feelings that pupils have for peers and teacher and the feelings teachers have toward pupils influence both the content and the speed of learning.

The Purpose of Educational Psychology Basically, the aim of educational psychology is to understand how learning processes may be most effectively guided. The ultimate test is the extent to which the study of educational psychology makes a difference in your own learning, teaching, and living. Improved insights and techniques are too readily available today for teachers to be satisfied with teaching as they were taught. Social psychological knowledge, insights into learning processes, and analyses of motivation that have been made in the last few decades present a challenge to teachers. This new knowledge has important implications for teachers—implications that cannot be implemented without considerable effort and some strife—but there are some who will succeed (Jensen, 1960, p. 4).

Marked changes in educational practice have only begun to be made, but they will come more rapidly. It has been said that technological progress from 1850 to 1950 equaled that of all previous history; progress from 1950 to 1960 equalled that of the previous hundred years; today, progress in one year equals that made from 1950 to 1960. Today, there is a shorter and shorter time lag between the inception of an idea and its application. Progress in the human sciences may not be quite so startling, but there are indications that progress is accelerating. Recently we have seen gratifying gains made in the implementation of individual instruction, challenging the able student, provision for counseling and guidance, and understanding and using group dynamics. It is imperative that today's teacher be deeply involved in his own learning processes if he is to keep abreast of educational change or be instrumental in it.

An Illustration of the Functioning of Educational Psychology More frequently than any other subject, with the exception of student teaching, educational psychology is a required course for certification of public school teachers. Its recognized importance can be explained by citing an example of how it functions in a particular case—a fifth-grade boy who cannot read so well as his peers and for whom reading is an unwelcome part of the school day.

Test results may provide *clues*, not conclusions, that lead to insights into the boy's potentialities and responses. Scholastic ability tests indicate something about his aptitude for academic tasks. Achievement tests reveal whether or not he is doing fifth-grade work in arithmetic, spelling, and social studies. Should these two types of tests suggest normal ability and progress, the teacher has an indication that reading is a *specific* difficulty. If he is below grade in all subjects and has less than normal ability, then it may be that too much is expected and that his frustration arises from inability to live up to unrealistic expectations. Diagnostic tests may be given to see if word analysis (phonics), vocabulary, or paragraph meaning would be likely to respond to remedial teaching. Specific aptitude tests in art, music, or mechanics may suggest that relating reading to an area in which he achieves success more readily might serve as a motivating device.

It may be that the boy does not hear well, is visually handicapped, or has some glandular dysfunction that limits his energy or even causes pain. There may be many contributing physical factors that bear on ability and/or endeavor. Usually it is not a single factor but a pattern of causes and responses to them that must be understood by the practical educational psychologist. Understanding these and other factors would improve not just the boy's school work but his whole life because he would be also getting a more wholesome evaluation of himself as a person.

Motivation, exclusive of the above, may be the source of the boy's difficulty. He may not see the importance of reading the "stuff" he is given, and therefore he may not have accepted reading as his personal goal. This happens frequently in two common situations. In one, the pupil comes from a home of low socioeconomic status, and the parents are not convinced of the value of schooling—he does not live in a *total* situation in which reading is important. In the other case, a youngster may be subjected to too much pressure and refuse to make further attempts to conform to parental expectations, since nothing he has done has seemed to satisfy them. In still other instances of inadequate motivation, tensions in the home may be keeping a child from applying himself to school tasks. Sickness of his mother, unemployment of his father, the marriage of a sister, or his older brother's departure for college worry him. In many instances, poor motivation may stem from a child's inability to see a relationship between reading and his ambition to be a truck driver, cowboy, circus performer, baseball player, or even a scientist or lawyer. Each of these possibilities suggests a different approach. And again, the remedy may affect a pupil's entire existence.

Perhaps none of the above suggestions is fruitful for our fifth grader who has difficulty in reading. The problem may lie in the relationship that exists between the pupil and his teacher. If there is hostility, suspicion, or a feeling of unfriendliness, the youngster will not be inclined to put forth his best effort. The teacher is responsible for evidencing an interest in the child despite his reluctance to learn or his objectionable behavior. The teacher, as the adult in the situation, should reveal friendliness and indicate a tolerance for shortcomings and personal deficiencies. Many feelings of dislike or indifference on the part of the teacher will be overcome when he gains a genuine understanding of the nature of the child and his difficulties.

Much of the foregoing can be further illustrated by a case reported by a school superintendent:

> Timothy was a talented youth, although as his English teacher I must confess that the mark I gave him at the end of each of the first two marking periods did not in any way reflect his inherent ability.
>
> In the comments I penned on his report card, opinions were expressed concerning his indifference, his uncooperative attitude, and his lack of effort. When Tim's second report was returned to me, I noticed that Tim's father had written on the space reserved for parents' reactions the pithy comment, "I am dissatisfied, too."
>
> But the situation changed markedly in February. By chance I learned that Tim was interested in tennis. I asked him to stay after school, and in the conversation I mentioned some of the major tournaments I had seen.
>
> Because of his interest, I invited him to my home on a Saturday afternoon to meet my eldest son, who had acquired some prominence as a local net star. When Tim left my home, after a demonstration of tennis strokes, he took with him a half-dozen books on court technics and strategy.
>
> Frequently thereafter he stayed after school to talk to me about his reading. He developed an eagerness to give expository talks to his classmates on his hobby. He wrote several papers on tennis ethics and the lessons taught by the lives of great net stars. His paper on tennis ethics he must have rewritten at least a dozen times before it was accepted by the school literary magazine.
>
> I believe no one in the class read or wrote more than he did during the next six weeks. His classmates obtained a liberal education in the romance of tennis.
>
> When I totaled his grades for the next report card, I was surprised to see the great advances he had made in his knowledge of and skill in English. When I inscribed his mark on his card, I wrote:
>
> "Timothy has made rapid advances recently as a student, and I congratulate him."
>
> Back came the father's response. "You give my son too much credit, sir. It is you who should be congratulated, for the rapid advances you have made recently as a teacher." [4]

[4] Thomas E. Robinson, "His Teacher Improved, Too," *NEA Journal*, 41:54, 1952.

This, then, is the reason for our study of educational psychology—to understand the many factors that impinge on learning so that they can be manipulated to produce the most effective teaching and learning situation.

Educational Psychology and the Curriculum   The material to be taught (involving educational philosophy and the current culture) must be continuously examined with the view to its making maximum contributions to the learning milieu. Some content may involve abstractions that are beyond the comprehension of the entire class—including that of the youngster with reading difficulty or the lad who is indifferent to English composition. Everyday examples, concrete illustrations, the display of specific objects, and pupils' discussion of personal experiences can give meaning to material. Whatever is taught should have meaning for the student—though some will learn what is—to them—nonsense material (algebra, in some cases) because that is desired by teachers or parents. Principle: *Curricular content must make sense and be understandable in terms of the intellectual maturity and experience of individual students.*

It may appear to be difficult to study each child in terms such as those described above. Actually, it is only the exceedingly difficult and relatively rare pupil who will require intensive study. The generalizations of educational psychology come to the rescue. All pupils learn as individuals, and despite outward appearances of conformity and attentiveness, each one is learning different values, attitudes, and facts and is achieving different perceptions. Some responsibility for the lives of pupils is unavoidable, and the teacher, like the construction engineer, must know the broad plans, the specific framework, the stresses, time factors, and present skills of workmen if his project is to succeed. The principles of educational psychology narrow the range of factors that should have priority in investigation. Educational psychology should teach one what to look for, e.g., intelligence level, motivation, meaningfulness of curriculum, etc. It provides clues to the solution of learning problems, e.g., finding appropriate levels of curricular difficulty, stimulating a sense of security or importance, selecting material related to pupils' background, etc. Educational psychology should suggest appropriate challenges, e.g., achievement of personal prestige, performance of socially oriented service, growth from the current to a higher level of performance or understanding, etc. It should help the teacher to formulate tentative procedures (in light of the above) that have generally been effective, e.g., simply describing something, showing models, providing for experimentation, involving students as coteachers, etc.

The Teacher as an Educational Engineer   The role of psychology in teaching can be described in terms of engineering concepts, as Bernays did in *The Engineering of Consent* (1955). Bernays has described how public relations—information, persuasion, and adjustment—can be used to gain support for a cause, activity, or institution. Instead of dealing with prescriptions of minutiae, Bernays describes the underlying processes that can be adapted to specific situations. The headings he uses can be readily transferred to the use of psychology in teaching.

Define your objectives. This is the first task of a teacher as he studies the broad purposes of education, the courses of study, and the parts of the curriculum for which he is responsible. It has been done [for this volume] in the section above in broad terms, and it is done in terms of behavioral objectives in the next section (see Aims of Educational Psychology as Behavioral Outcomes).

Research your public. In part, this is accomplished in college courses in child, adolescent, and educational psychology, in which the general nature of pupils is studied. Research is continued as individuals are studied through test data, sociometric ratings, questionnaires, school records, and observation.

Modify objectives to reach goals that research shows are attainable. This is done in part by curricular allocations, studying the phenomena of readiness, and knowing the status of one's pupils. In part, it is a matter of modifying objectives as the status of the class changes from day to day.

Decide on strategy. The strategies of teaching can be derived directly from the strategies of public relations, which include timing, forbearance, teaching techniques, surprise, participation, and association (hero worship and the use of ideals).

Set up themes, symbols, and appeals. This could include appeals to the pupils' desires for health, achieving good grades, learning how to get along with peers, and vocational choice and preparation. It would seem that meeting children's needs (see Chapter 14) could provide themes, symbols, and appeals appropriate to educational motivation.

Blueprint an effective organization. Two approaches are of outstanding importance in educational planning. One is to capitalize on pupil skills and interests to carry out democratic participation in student activities and academic work. The other is to chart the daily and monthly lesson plans, including library resources, audio-visual equipment, and laboratory and field activities.

Chart the plan for timing and tactics. The sequence of studies, the successive skills and knowledges to be acquired, and the techniques used to evaluate progress are included in this step. The tactics are the tools and methods used to convey thought—lecture, discussion, demonstration and testing are among the tactics of communication.

Carry out the tactics. Here the problem is one of adjusting the foregoing steps to the exigencies of the moment. One cannot expect immediate results, but in education, as in public relations, there must be trust in the cumulative effect. Education is a slow process, and faith in sound planning and sound techniques must be maintained.

Examination of the above eight points suggests that educational effort, like public relations, can become more effective when carefully engineered. The role of psychology is not that of detailing those methods but that of providing a sound rationale for developing flexible and workable techniques.

Aims of Educational Psychology as Behavioral Outcomes If we now state the aims of our study in terms of behavioral outcomes, the list will include:

The teacher understands the nature of children and adolescents in general and knows how to evaluate the motives and ability of individuals.

The teacher can devise learning situations that take account of the individual differences among pupils.

The teacher knows how to study, evaluate, and make adjustments to the conditions of home and community that bear on pupils' behavior in school.

Emotionally and intellectually, the teacher reacts appropriately to the emotions, feelings, and attitudes revealed by pupils.

The teacher recognizes that pupils respond to the whole school climate —philosophy, curriculum, and student body—and can react impersonally to deviating behavior in the classroom.

The teacher can clearly formulate the objectives of schoolwork and can communicate them to his pupils so that they have personal meaning.

The teacher acts on the realization that the pupil as a whole—emotionally, physically, and intellectually—responds to the school as an integral unit, not just to the curriculum or teacher or his peers.

The teacher acts on the assumption that a course in educational psychology is effective only when it begins to affect his own teaching, learning, and living. Moreover, an introductory course should be the beginning of a lifelong pursuit of more knowledge about educational psychology and its application.

The teacher appreciates his role in extending knowledge about learning and teaching and is most creative when he contributes to the expansion and application of educational psychology.

The above listing of behavioral outcomes is partial and tentative. One might well begin his study of educational psychology by projecting and stating other outcomes in terms of what he now thinks should accrue from the study.

Aims of Education in Relation to Psychology All behavior is either purposeful or purposive (see Appendix). *The more clearly the goals of learning are perceived, the more effectively learning will proceed.* An early step in the study of educational psychology should be to review the purposes of education. The late John Dewey asserted that education "is that reconstruction or reorganization of experience which adds to the meaning of experience, and which increases ability to direct the course of subsequent experience" (Dewey, 1928, p. 90). Mayer has more recently emphasized that educational psychologists should regard the mind not merely as a reacting function but also as a creative and reconstructive function (Mayer, 1958, p. 115). According to these and other concepts, education is a growth and developmental process. Education is a way of thinking, doing, and living—a dynamic forward movement rather than a static achievement. Educational psychology, teaming up with other life sciences, is designed to facilitate movement in these processes of thinking, doing, and living.

Education is too frequently thought of as a product—as is attested to by degrees, diplomas, and certificates—a product consisting of knowledge, skills, attitudes, habits, and ideals. An earlier statement of the objectives of education stressed acquisitions and concerned (1) language adaptation—social communication, (2) health, (3) citizenship, (4) social adaptation, (5) leisure-time activities, (6) mental fitness, (7) religious activities, (8) family relationships, (9) nonvocational practical activities, and (10) vocational competence (Bobbitt, 1934, p. 86). A recent statement gives more explicit recognition to education as a process and is couched in dynamic terms. French includes four areas of behavioral competence, each of which involves three directions of growth toward maturity (French, 1957, pp. 88–89).

1. Attaining maximum intellectual growth and development
2. Becoming culturally oriented and integrated
3. Maintaining and improving physical and mental health
4. Becoming economically competent

Each of these areas has the following three subdivisions:

a. Self-realization
b. Desirable interpersonal relations with family, school peers, and community groups
c. Effective membership or leadership in larger religious, cultural, social, political, and economic groups

An examination of such educational objectives as the above—and there are other similar statements—indicates that if psychology is to contribute to education, there must be concern for much more than problems of mastering the fundamental processes of reading, writing, and arithmetic. There must also be concern for procedures that will produce certain attitudes and ideals, lead to the continual seeking of information and skills, develop healthful habits, and in all these ways contribute to effective living. Thus the province of educational psychology, like education itself, is the "whole child," i.e., the major facets of his personality, consisting of the mental, physical, emotional, and spiritual aspects and the impact of the school on them all (Stephens, 1959, p. 110).

Each of you will be effective teachers, practical educational psychologists, to the extent to which you realize and act upon the basic fact that *the child grows as a complex, but unified, entity.* You are more than teachers of reading, arithmetic, geometry, algebra, chemistry, or biology. You are teachers of individual children—children who have physical energy, dissimilar interests, divergent abilities, varied home and community backgrounds, and unique emotional problems.

The Data of Educational Psychology   The aims and outcomes of educational psychology can be realized only through the accumulation and use of reliable data. There are many ways in which the basic information is acquired.

Valuable data are derived from teaching experience. Teachers and psychologists have evaluated their work in terms of recurrent phenomena and have drawn tentative conclusions regarding what effective procedures might be in the future. A teacher might, for instance, reflect upon his experiences to formulate some generalizations about a more effective method for teaching spelling or arithmetic. Psychologists call such an approach "uncontrolled observation," because influential items (intellectual level, age, time of day, or materials) may not be called to strict account ("controlled"). Thus, there are some relative dangers that must be recognized, and one must be on guard against the subjective element (the teacher's enthusiasm with the project) as interpretations are made. Actually, some of the empirical data (see Glossary) thus gathered have been disproved by careful experimentation; other such data have been verified. One should not discount the everyday experiences that provide hypotheses for setting up the more precise methods of experimentation that may result in the development of valid principles.

Controlled observation utilizes several techniques and is midway between daily experience and that gathered by experimentation. A questionnaire may serve to focus attention upon some particular aspects of behavior—for instance, the ways in which children act in the classroom when an adult visitor is present or when arithmetic problems are presented as games. A clinical investigation may be made. A child who is caught stealing the possessions of his classmates is studied in terms of his health, his home background, his past school success, his aptitudes, his social competence, and his out-of-school activities. Genetic studies consisting of a continual recording of behavior and growth for a prolonged period are sometimes made of his life and development. Often genetic studies are made by watching babies in cabinets or in rooms that have a one-way glass in one wall. An observer makes detailed notes on what is observed. Thus details of the observation that are deemed of significance are controlled and systematic. The statement that controlled observation is midway between daily experience and experimentation implies no criticism. The method is, in fact, highly respected and widely used. It has the advantage of enabling the teacher to see the whole child in a whole situation.

Experimentation is used both to discover and to refine the data of educational psychology. Experimentation places much emphasis on what is known as the single variable. That is, two or more situations are studied, and all elements in the situations are kept as closely identical as possible except for the one thing that is being studied. The experimenter might wish to determine the relative merits of teaching social studies on an assign-study-recite basis and with a problem approach. The age, intelligence, sex, educational background of the pupils and teacher and the materials are kept as much alike as possible in the two situations. Only the method of presentation is varied. The relative gain in knowledge of the two groups at the end of the experiment is made the basis for evaluation of the two techniques. There are many variations of the experimental technique, but the focal point is always an attempt to control contingent factors and vary only one element in the two situations. Actually, control is extremely difficult to effect, and obtaining it is one of the more persistent problems of psychologists. There are so many variables in a situation and equating individuals is so complex—in addition to the fact that individuals are growing and changing—that control is a relative matter. It is hazardous to assume that one element (intelligence or motivation) will stay put during the progress of study (Scheier, 1959). The complexity of behavior is such that some believe that much educational research is concerned with a "bittiness" that limits fruitful conclusions. Despite limitations in experimental control, many valuable data have been derived from experimental techniques, and they will remain one of the major sources of information.

Many of the data of educational psychology will be borrowed from related fields. The fact of dependence upon psychological specialties such as motivation, individual differences, personality, and especially social and group psychology has led Symonds (1957) to recommend a coordinating council for educational research. Many recent studies have pointed out the influence of socioeconomic status on pupil behavior. School attendance, participation in school affairs, attitudes toward courses, relations with teachers, and belief in the value of education are strongly influenced by social class factors (Costar, 1959). Accordingly, one of the important studies for teachers is provided under the rubric of cultural anthropology. This forthright borrowing from other disciplines is probably one of the more important recent developments in the field of educational psychology.

No one of these sources of information may safely be ignored. Everyday experience may later be substantiated and will always have the advantage of presenting hypotheses that can be tested by controlled observation, experimentation, and data from related disciplines. Controlled observation has the advantage of naturalness; experiments have the advantage of isolating the more significant aspects of a situation; and related disciplines reduce the bias of the limited school setting.

Purpose and organization of this book

The purpose of this book is to review and clarify the fundamentals of psychology that have most direct bearing on learning situations in the school. The direct implications of these fundamentals for teaching practice will be pointed out as cogently as possible. An attempt is made to bring together recent findings from research, especially findings that are related to novel areas such as programmed learning, machine teaching, creativity, and group processes. Throughout, there is a studied attempt to unite psychological theory with classroom procedures.

Study of this book should facilitate transfer of learnings from the college classroom to the classroom in which you will work as a teacher. This objective will be implemented by pointing out *some* of the ways in which theory may be applied. For example, the things that you, as a teacher, will see to do in the classroom will be determined by your personality and background experiences. Your motivation and the knowledge and attitudes you bring to and develop in this course will, in turn, provide part of the background experiences that will later influence your classroom perceptions. How you view your pupils may be influenced, for example, by your beliefs in the modifiability or immutability of pupils' intelligence, by your perceptions of peer influences, by your understanding of social class influences, or by your appreciation of your classroom influence as a person. An understanding of educational psychology is something like providing corrective lenses for a myopic traveler.

Transfer of psychological principles to classroom situations will be further implemented by formulating generalizations that can be used in a variety of situations. There is a danger in this approach that the student must avoid; i.e., the suggested practices do not exhaust the possibilities of sound educational application. You will do well therefore to consider the suggestions as *indicative* and *exploratory* rather than conclusive and inclusive. Actually, the generalizations are probably more important than the suggestions because they should form the basis for your adaptation of procedures in effective teaching.

Interspersed throughout the book are a number of statements, which are principles, hypotheses, or generalizations derived from the field of educational psychology or from psychological fields that have direct pertinency for education. The discussions leading to and following the statement of principle are designed to justify, explain, and illustrate the principle. Because learning is an active process, you can profit most from the study of this book by formulating your own additional applications and illustrations of the principle being studied.

Summary

There is some consensus that man's potential for development is relatively untapped and that we are merely on the threshold of appreciating that potential. Many sciences are devoted to studying man's capacity for development, and psychology is foremost among them. Psychology is the study of man's behavior or adjusting processes. Actually, there are many branches of psychology; the American Psychological Association lists about twenty, with major subdivisions.

The aims of psychology are to understand, predict, control, and improve behavior, as well as to discover new data and develop more accurate descriptions of behavior. Educational psychology, one of the major divisions of the broad study, deals with learning and teaching, especially in the school, which is society's formal institution for facilitating learning. The major problems of educational psychology center about (1) the nature of the individual, (2) the nature and content of the material to be learned, (3) the economy of learning, (4) the formulation of psychological principles of education, and (5) the quest for the extension of knowledge of behavior. The learning that we, as teachers, hope to facilitate includes all those things that are considered the objectives of education. These can be stated both as the acquisition of certain knowledges and skills and as dynamic behavioral patterns that have bearing on future growth toward maturity.

Data for the solution of the many problems raised in educational psychology are derived from (1) practical experience, (2) controlled observation, (3) experimentation, and (4) the facts and principles borrowed from various branches of psychology and disciplines related to psychology. These data lead to the formulation of generalizations that are helpful in solving the particular and specific problems of individuals whom we meet in the classroom. The extent to which you receive help on such problems depends largely on the degree to which your study of educational psychology makes a difference in your own living, learning, and teaching.

Problems and exercises

1 Before studying subsequent chapters, describe what you expect to learn as you pursue your study of educational psychology.

2 Which three of the various branches of psychology would you expect to make the greatest contributions to understanding learning and teaching in the school?

3 Reformulate in your own words the aims of educational psychology as

expressed in behavioral outcomes. Do you think some important ones have been omitted?

4 Cite some examples from your own school experience that seem to indicate a lack of knowledge of psychology on the part of the teacher. Cite some instances that indicate a functional knowledge of educational psychology on the part of the teacher.

5 Discuss the appropriateness of describing the teacher's work as educational engineering.

6 What are the implications of the statements "Where there is no learning, there is no teaching" and "As the teacher, so is the school"?

Suggested additional readings

Biderman, Albert C., and Herbert Zimmer: *The Manipulation of Human Behavior,* New York: John Wiley & Sons, Inc., 1961.
    This unusual book describes a negative approach to control behavior—brainwashing. The use of environmental manipulation, hypnosis, torture, and drugs are dealt with. It suggests some of the ways in which means for changing behavior might be used for more humanitarian purposes.

Eiseley, Loren: "An Evolutionist Looks at Modern Man," in Richard Thruelson and John Kobler (eds.), *Adventures of the Mind,* First Series, New York: Alfred A. Knopf, Inc., 1961, pp. 3–16.
    The author relates evolution to man's plasticity and indicates that the future will depend more on our knowing man better than on flights to the moon.

Hilgard, Ernest R.: *Introduction to Psychology,* 3d ed., New York: Harcourt, Brace & World, Inc., 1962, pp. 581–612.
    The chapter "Vocational and Professional Applications of Psychology" shows how psychology may function in vocational choice and adjustment. A short section is devoted to psychology and education.

Mednick, Sarnoff A.: *Learning,* Englewood Cliffs, N.J.: Prentice-Hall, Inc., 1964. (Paperback.)
    This short book is recommended because (1) it describes learning in worms and animals and thus indicates man's infinite potential as a learner; (2) it introduces the important concepts of learning—conditioning, motivation, habit formation, remembering, etc.; and (3) it refers to some leaders in learning theory—Guthrie, Hull, Skinner, and Watson.

Ross, Sherman, and Robert F. Lockman: *A Career in Psychology,* Washington: American Psychological Association, Inc., 1963.
    This brochure indicates the problems attacked by psychology and defines the areas of concern, kinds of work, and preparation of psychologists.

Thelen, Herbert A.: *Education and the Human Quest,* New York: Harper & Row, Publishers, 1960.
    The author claims that we know a great deal about the nature of man, learning, and social action, but that educational practice makes too little use of the knowledge. He suggests some ways in which our knowledge can be made more functional.

The Nature and Course of Learning

2

The major concern in the study of educational psychology is the matter of the nature and conditions of learning. Learning is an exceedingly complex affair, including—as it does—not only the acquisition of subject matter but also habits, attitudes, perceptions, preferences, interests, social adjustments, skills of many types, and ideals. Even such seemingly simple things as learning to spell and add involve these varied forms of learning. Because of this complexity, it is desirable that the many aspects of learning be brought into some encompassing system—some embracing explanation that will account for the various modes and nuances of learning. The task of formulating such comprehensive statements has occupied the time and attention of psychologists for centuries, but in the last half century the effort seems to have been intensified. Helpful statements that are somewhat inclusive but definitely not conclusive have been postulated. More is being discovered daily, and the frontiers appear to be wide open—as witness the surge in programmed learning, group involvement, and enrichment and acceleration.

In this chapter, theories regarding the nature and conditions of learning will be briefly reviewed. The generalizations formulated here are threads that run through the remaining chapters. For example, entire chapters will be devoted to such matters as motivation, habit formation, transfer of learning, personality (individual perceptions), reinforcement (programmed learning), and intelligence—to mention but a few. You may enhance your own learning of educational psychology by reviewing this chapter periodically as you read other chapters, so that basic theory will be contiguous to detailed explanations.

The nature and implications of the learning process

What Learning Is We do not know for certain what happens physiologically—the possible changes in nerve or cell structure or in electrical potential and movement—when learning takes place. We do know, however, a great deal about the conditions

18

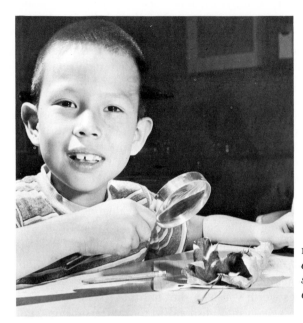

FIGURE 1. *Stimulation of a love of learning should be a major goal of all teachers.*

under which learning takes place most effectively. These conditions and the ways in which they may be improved are, at least in part, subject to the control of teachers. Knowing what these conditions are will make it possible for the teacher to perform effectively the role that is assigned to him by society.

We may begin by stating that learning involves the modification of perception and behavior. Improvement of behavior, i.e., the more complete satisfaction of the needs of society and self, is usually implied. Even when behavior is maladaptive in the eyes of society, the individual perceives that his behavior will satisfy his own needs. But typically, learning expands the possibilities of adaptive behavior; that is, behavioral modifications occur in meeting changed conditions so that obstacles are overcome or so that homeostasis may be maintained. It should also be observed that not all behavior change is learning. Without learning anything new, one may be able to lift heavier weights because of muscular development. A child comes to eat more because his stomach enlarges and because his energy needs increase, but the changed behavior is not learning. He may, however, *learn* to eat more because of parental example or because of psychological needs that appear to be satisfied through food. The loss of an arm through accident modifies behavior, but the loss itself is not learning. The person may, though, learn to compensate for the loss of his arm by learning new skills.

Modification does not necessarily result in improvement—at least in terms of societal values. Pupils may learn to dislike school, but their adjustment is not improved thereby. Criminals learn to violate legal and moral codes and may become experts at it, but their behavior, from a social viewpoint, is not improved. With these and many other considerations, we may define learning as change in performance through conditions of activity, practice, and experience (McGeoch and Irion, 1952, p. 5). This is an operational definition, and it is derived in part from scientific investigations. The particular conditions that receive most emphasis depend somewhat upon the psychologist's orientation, as will be seen in subsequent sections where learning theories are discussed. In the classroom, the activities and experiences that lead to change in performance involve telling and listening, judging, reading, reciting, observation of demonstrations, and experimenting. We trust that sporadic practice and formalized drill in reading, speaking, and writing will change performance. Living and working with others and the evaluation that comes from reflecting and discussing while engulfed in classroom learning will, we hope, lead to changed performance beyond school confines.

The Physical Basis of Learning   Learning, defined in the previous section, is a result of activity which begins with the organism. You, for instance, may listen to the speaker's word; you may shut out that sound and reflect on last night's discussion; or you may respond to the warm sunshine and plan this afternoon's golf game. Your learning may be conditioned by your ability to see what is written on the board, the fact that the battery to your hearing aid has run down, or by the misery of a cold you have just caught. Learning is influenced by the functioning of the endocrine system, the state of one's general health, the physiology of one's emotions (being angry or in love does not enhance learning the results of Mycenaean excavations). There can be no doubt that pupils' learning abilities are affected by the speed with which nerve messages move, are sorted and combined, and by the degree of permanence of the impression they make. These physical bases may be hereditary, congenital, or developmental in origin and in functioning, but they do influence the nature and speed of learning. Without going into a detailed description of sense organs, response mechanisms, and nervous system, which are of only indirect import to the classroom teacher, we will simply say that learning depends on the inclination and ability to receive and respond to stimulation from the environment.

> If the curriculum is to be made more adequate from an intellectual standpoint, it is necessary that the logical operations possible for the individual, at each stage, be identified and adequately catered to by instruction. This also means that content should be properly selected, with emphasis upon more important elements of it, for the purpose of highlighting operational excellence.[1]

[1] Harry S. Broudy, B. Othanel Smith, and Joe R. Burnett, *Democracy and Excellence in American Secondary Education,* Chicago: Rand McNally & Company, 1964, p. 103.

There are physical aspects of learning that cannot be ignored by the teacher, e.g., vision and hearing. Biochemical factors influence the amount of energy that can be brought to bear on learning, and they also affect the comfort and satisfaction that an individual derives from the pursuit of learning (Eichorn, 1963). Such influences bear heavily on personality orientation and are therefore dealt with in Chapter 13, "Personality and Its Development."

Certainly learning depends on the retentivity and plasticity of the central nervous system. This too will be considered from an operational viewpoint, rather than in terms of biological description—*functional* intelligence is dealt with in Chapter 10, "The Nature and the Nurture of Intelligence."

Educational practice and the physical basis of learning Both the man on the street and the scientist recognize that differences exist among individuals in innate ability to learn. A cretin, a mongoloid, or a microcephalic does not learn with the facility of a normal individual. Less obvious, but nonetheless certain, is the fact that among children who *appear* to be normal, there are also enormous differences in degrees of ability. These differences, which cannot be traced to environment or opportunity, are attributed to basic physiological differences.

Teachers must recognize these basic differences; otherwise, they may try to force all children to learn at a uniform rate and berate youngsters who do not keep up with the class. On the other hand, a child who learns more rapidly than the group may become a troublemaker to offset his boredom. Hence teachers should become aware of symptoms (indifference, failure, boredom, inattention, tantrums, and the like) which indicate that they are expecting too much or too little of their pupils. Pressure can mean trying to make a pupil go more rapidly or more slowly than is comfortable for him.

Although it is not the function of the teacher to conduct medical examinations, he should be on guard for symptoms that indicate the need for them. For example, visual difficulty may be evidenced by squinting, rubbing the eyes, leaning forward to see the board, tilting the head, brushing material off the printed page, holding a book very close to the eyes, reddened or watering eyes, and frowning. Hearing difficulty may be manifested by turning one side of the head toward the source of sound, asking that questions be repeated, failure to respond or belated response to questions or remarks, speech defects, difficulty in group discussions, inattention, and listlessness.

There is evidence that the role of physical disability in learning has not been sufficiently recognized. It is estimated that 50 per cent of the schoolchildren in the United States who have such disability are not receiving the necessary attention (Voelker and Mullen, 1963). This condition exists despite knowledge and experience that show that many deficiencies can be prevented, remedied, or compensated for.

Besides sensory disability, there are many limitations imposed on learning by virtue of glandular dysfunction and dietary deficiency. Hypofunctioning (underactivity) of the thyroid is accompanied by listlessness, lethargy, and varying degrees of dullness. A certain teacher noticed that one pupil had a tendency to be somewhat pudgy, appeared to be sleepy much of the time, and had some difficulty in learning. He suggested that the child be given a metabolism test. A slight thyroid deficiency was found, and appropriate treatment was instituted. After a period of time, the child became more active and interested in what was going on and made better progress in his schoolwork. Of course, not all learning difficulties will be removed by glandular treatment. Teachers should not attempt to be diagnosticians, but they should be aware of the role of physiological conditions. In this respect, they have the advantage of being able to observe and compare many children.

The Individual's Response   Learning is a response on the part of the individual, but pupils respond with varying degrees of vigor and purposefulness. This vigor derives only in part from physical conditions, so we move on to consider responses in terms of perceptions and motivations. One pupil may perceive that succeeding academically will place him in positions of prestige or leadership that he wishes to avoid (Kagan, 1963). Another may perceive academic success as constituting submission to power beings whose authority he resists. It is the author's belief, based on contacts with high school pupils in counseling situations, that this occurs much more frequently than is commonly supposed. Just how one perceives any situation is itself subject to change through instruction. Abercrombie (1960) has described in detail how perception may be changed through discussion in which students are given responsibility rather than depending on authority.

Fortunately, most youngsters wish to please authority figures, they cherish the prestige of leadership, and they are willing to try to achieve the academic task—not because they see it as serving their personal needs directly but because they wish to get along with and please others. Should these pupils not meet the experience of failure too frequently or too consistently, they will continue to give vigorous responses to their school learnings.

The individual's response is partially dependent on the nature of his social relationships with his peers, parents, siblings, and teachers. Response is also conditioned by interest, goals, abilities, and social expectation. These will be dealt with in later chapters on motivation, group processes, creativity, and personality formation. Part of the task of educational psychology is to define and illustrate the response-influencing factors.

Educational practice and the individual's response   Even at the college level, and for some time in elementary and secondary schools, the teacher's attitude of "Here it is, you learn it" has been shifting to one of responsibility for trying to make the learner receptive. Many things can be and are being done to arrange the physical environment so that it is most conducive to learning. If the teacher is cognizant of the ways in which different pupils respond to ostensibly the same situation, he can change the nature or pattern of physical stimulation; e.g., present material through a demonstration rather than via printed description. A second approach is to attempt to alter the pupil's perception. This can be done through explanation in class, but success is more probable if the pupil is approached in a person-to-person conversation (not a lecture). Success is still more likely if the attempt is made through peer-group discussion.

The point here is that the teacher's job is much greater than the mere presenting of materials. The real teaching will occur when both teacher and pupil are actively involved in the fluid process of learning.

The Learning Environment The aspect of learning that is most readily accessible to modification is the environment. The creation of a favorable environment for learning is the basic function of our system of formal education. For example, at the national level a pressing problem is that of racial integration. Increasingly, this is perceived as a question of educational opportunity—substituting a richer learning environment for the cultural impoverishment experienced by many colored children (Dodson, 1963). Similarly, fuller employment and technological progress are perceived as resting heavily on extended educational opportunities for all citizens. Thus, national welfare as well as the welfare of the individual is based on an abundant and approprite learning environment (Johnson, 1964). Many changes are currently being discussed and experimented with, examples of which are the year-round schools (Lipson, 1962) and the extension of the school beyond the confines of the physical plant, e.g., work experience education, "higher horizons" (see Chapter 13, section on The Effect of the Total School Atmosphere), and foreign exchange students. In addition, many modifications of the learning environment have been in progress for years (methods for improving instruction, raising the preparation level of teachers, providing better instructional aids). These points need not be expanded here because the bulk of this volume deals in detail with psychological factors of such facets of the learning environment.

Forms of learning

There are numerous ways in which the behavior changes involved in learning may be manifested. While the following forms are not mutually exclusive, they may serve to show the complexity of the problems with which the teacher must deal.

Sensorimotor Skills These skills become so automatic that other learned activities may be carried on simultaneously without interference. Walking, riding a bicycle, using eating utensils, getting dressed (except when choice is involved), dancing, and, for some persons, such things as plain knitting are examples. The stimulus for these acts comes from pressures and impulses from joints and muscles, and outside stimulation may actually interfere—as, for example, when a person tries to analyze or explain just how he performs a certain dance step or ties his shoelace. The teacher's contribution to the learning of sensorimotor skills resides in the early detection of gross errors (posture, holding a pencil) and setting a good example.

Perceptual Motor Skills A perceptual pattern or stimulation is added to the behavior when these skills are used. In typing, for example, the same finger is used consistently to strike given letters, but the sequence of letters and spacing depends on what is being typed from copy, memory, or thought. These skills therefore, depend on association (see section on Associational Learning). Teachers aid in the learning of perceptual motor skills by watching the form of sensorimotor skills, by clarifying understanding of the associations to be formed, by acting calmly and slowly so that there is no unnecessary interference with early acts, by providing drill in various situations, and by providing alternate periods of drill and rest or change.

Perceptual Learning What one hears and sees is not solely the result of physical stimulation. Percepts are the mental modifications that come into existence when one perceives; they must not be mistaken for the physical thing that is objectively present. Perception depends, too, on what the individual has been conditioned to perceive. Thus, experiments indicate what a person has been conditioned to perceive. A medical doctor, for example, can perceive accurately and derive meaning from shadows on an X-ray; an outdoorsman can readily see forms in grass and brush that are birds or animals. The uninitiated would have to have these pointed out specifically and would probably miss them on the next trial. Similarly, experiments indicate that potentiality for learning a language declines after the age of nine because perceptual ability has not been exercised when the neural connections are ready (Penfield and Roberts, 1959, p. 236), and the capacity for developing nuances in pronunciation becomes more limited. The "foreigner" simply does not hear, because he has not been conditioned to listen for the shadings of pronunciation that are meaningful to the person using the "foreign" language. Moreover, the muscles of the throat and tongue that are needed to pronounce the "foreign" word correctly have not been exercised with the appropriate coordination and quite possibly have atrophied or lost their plasticity. Perceptual ability (as suggested in the cases of the doctor and the outdoorsman) depends on exposure to patterned stimulations in the early environment (Hebb, 1958, p. 123) as well as upon the intellectual aptitude of the learner.

Throughout this book, the reader will note frequent references to self-perceptions. How one perceives a situation is influenced by how he perceives himself. Kathy may anticipate that the tasks suggested are too difficult for her to perform; she approaches them hesitantly and interprets the first difficulty as an insurmountable obstacle. Rick seems to believe that nothing is too difficult and sees failure (which is frequent, in view of his numerous ventures) as only a temporarily inadequate approach that needs some modification. Combs and Snygg (1959, p. 240) describe the seeing of oneself in a positive (being wanted, liked, acceptable worthy, able) manner as being the basic need of every one of us.

Associational Learning Vocabularly is a good example of the result of associational learning—certain sequences of letters become so related to given objects, concepts, or situations that one tends to recall the other. When we speak of "meaning" in teaching-learning settings, we refer to the power of words to recall real, tangible situations or objects *to the learner*. Such learning depends on experiencing the words and their related objects or situations together. Facilitation of associational learning is accomplished by preliminary surveys, classifications, relating the new to the known, review for the purpose of emphasizing the new associations, and explanation of the reasons for certain steps and processes in study habits (see Chapter 15).

Conceptual Learning Concepts are general or abstract mental representations of situations or conditions. While simple associations are a one-to-one affair, concepts involve many interrelationships and conditions; several percepts are combined in terms of some cogent relationship or common theme to form a concept. Democracy may be used as an example —others are motherhood, communism, Negro, salesman, etc. The concept of democracy grows beyond the idea of equality, if that should be the initially thought-of factor, to include the supreme importance of the individual, responsibility for one's own conduct, institutions as the servants of man, common consent and voluntary cooperation, devotion to truth, equitable moral and ethical standards, pursuit of happiness, brotherhood, freedom to develop individuality, and justice (Educational Policies Commission, 1951, pp. 18–29). This example suggests that concepts are constantly evolving through home, school, work, leisure, community, and experiences.

Perhaps one of the more common errors in teaching is the teacher's assumption that one child has the same conceptual grasp of a situation as another and that both are similar to his own. A more accurate assumption would be that the concepts differ widely—if, indeed, the concept exists at all in the child (see Chapter 17). Teachers may aid in the development of concepts by providing a variety of direct experiences, by encouraging discussion (Abercrombie, 1960), by trying to speak in terms of the pupils' level of maturity, and by having the children give summaries and formulate definitions and by doing so themselves.

Briefly, the teacher's role is to provide a wide variety of experiences, call attention to details that initially escaped attention, reiterate the most essential features of a situation, and lead in the discovery of characteristics that are common and pervasive. In addition to pointing out the "facts" of the situation, he must give attention to the roles played by individual pupils. A person's ability to act as an individual or as one within a group is limited by his personal development—his tolerance for stress and strain, the quality of his interpersonal relations, and the recognition of his competencies and limitations (Lynton, 1960, p. 89). The teacher must be deeply concerned with really knowing his pupils and strengthening their self-concepts.

Learning of Ideals and Attitudes   One of the big problems of the world is based on the difficulty that people from different cultures have in really understanding one another. To us, pork and chicken are delightful foods—to others, the thought of eating them is nauseating. In some cultures, women with large buttocks are admirable; to us, such development is equivalent to deformity. Countless other examples could be given, but the point is that one is is not born with tastes and preferences—they are acquired through learning processes. Learning ideals, attitudes, tastes, and preferences is most probably a result of conditioning processes, which will be examined in some detail in the next section. Some men do prefer "overweight" women, but others wonder why in the world there is such preference. Some persons "turn green" at the sight of pork. Tracing back their personal histories, it is usually found that the first contact, or first series of contacts, with large women or with pork was in a distinctly pleasant or unpleasant situation. If the first contact was pleasant, the response was liking, accepting, seeking to prolong contact. If unpleasant, then dislike and aversion resulted. The reason why there are national likes and dislikes is that any society tends to create emotional atmospheres around given situations. The reason why there are unusual personal preferences is that initial experiences may be unique.

The teaching of tastes, preferences, ideals, and attitudes is an important function of formal education that is too frequently overlooked or slighted. One is tempted to say that these learnings are the most important outcomes of education because they are so likely to inhibit or foster the continued learning that is essential for growth and development beyond the school years. Let us take the example of reading good literature. If literature is presented by a gruff taskmaster with the aim of covering so many pages or getting through the syllabus or course of study, then the probable results will be dislike and avoidance. On the other hand, a teacher who can communicate his own liking and interest, who takes the time to prepare an attractive physical setting and to maintain a pleasant atmosphere, and who relates the literature to events in the pupils' lives is most likely to get the immediate lesson across and, in addition, is more likely to create an attitude that will lead to the continued pursuit of reading. The student seeks to recapture the pleasant associations after the school lessons become history.

Problem-solving Learning [2]   This is considered by some authorities to be the highest type of learning because responses are not dependent simply on past associations and conditionings; rather response is dependent upon the ability to manipulate abstract ideas, to use aspects and modifications of previous learnings, and to perceive small differences. Problem solving demands the creation, not the repetition, of responses when a situation arises that is of such complexity that initiative and mental synthesis are required to adjust to it.

Problem solving demands enough mental maturity to perceive the problem. This perception involves the ability to guess what kind of data are required for its solution. Action must be delayed in order to gather information and give the solution an imaginary or actual trial. The culmination of problem solving may extend beyond the resolution of the actual difficulty to the formulation of a generalization, or concept, that will aid in future problem situations.

Teachers may facilitate problem-solving behavior (see Chapter 4) in many ways. The provision of broad experiences is one of them. Certainly, because the first step in problem solving is recognition of the problem, problems must be suited to the maturity level of pupils. This also involves taking the problem from the life experiences of children. When students are encouraged to participate in the life of the school and community, they are being provided with excellent opportunities for exercising problem-solving ability (Aiken, 1963). Time must be allotted for exploration, discussion, and experimentation. A teacher who feels that a certain number of pages should be covered in the textbook, who considers the syllabus as a prescription rather than a guide, and who is afraid to "get off the subject" is not likely to foster problem-solving ability. Several hazards must be avoided by the teacher if he is to contribute to problem solving by pupils. He must avoid the temptation to believe that his own conclusions are necessarily the right ones. He must hesitate to give his answers even when he knows the correct ones. He must avoid haste so that the pupil will have time to explore possibilities and "incubate" ideas.

[2] Problem solving is considered in more detail in Chap. 4.

The foregoing description of various forms or results of learning should make it clear that many factors are involved in the dynamics of learning. Certain theories or viewpoints of learning have evolved. These theories differ very largely in the relative emphasis that is made in each theoretical formulation; i.e., one emphasizes the relationship between and repetition of stimulus and response (emphasizes success and/or reward), while another emphasizes perception, insight, and understanding. Hilgard (1956) describes ten major theories; but in certain theories he has included two or more that have been treated as one viewpoint in other descriptions. For classroom teachers, the three theories described below—simple conditioning, reinforcement, and insight—may be sufficient as an introduction.

Simple Conditioning—Contiguity Theory Conditioning consists of eliciting a response by means of a previously neutral or inadequate stimulus. Through contiguity of stimulus and response, a stimulus that was inadequate to arousing a response becomes capable of doing so.

The pioneer in the field was Ivan Pavlov (1927), a Russian physiologist, who provided some of the basic terms that are commonly used in conditioning theory. His basic experiments consisted of cutting small holes in the cheeks of dogs so that their secreted saliva could be collected and measured. The dogs were placed in soundproof rooms (to reduce the number of stimulus variables) and observed through small windows. A tuning fork was sounded, and seconds later meat powder was presented to the subject dog. Originally, the tuning fork did not cause the flow of saliva, but the meat powder did. The meat powder was called the "unconditioned stimulus." As the experiment was repeated, the tuning fork did come to cause the flow of saliva—it was called the "conditioned stimulus." The flow of saliva, when caused by meat, was called the "unconditioned response"; but when caused by the tuning fork, it was called the "conditioned response." If, after conditioning, the tuning fork was sounded and reinforcement with meat did not occur, the amount of saliva progressively lessened—this process was called "extinction."

Conditioning includes two main types: *classical* and *instrumental*. The classical type can be illustrated by Pavlov's pioneering experiment. When the sound of a bell causes a dog to salivate, the iris of a human eye to contract, or a chicken to turn twice to the right (all of which have been accomplished), we say that an inadequate stimulus (one not normally attached to the unconditioned response) has become adequate —it does elicit the response. This type of simple learning—simple because the organism enters the situation only in a highly mechanical or automatic way—is also called "associative shifting," "substitute stimulus," "conditioned reflex," and "redintegration." Basically, conditioning may be defined as the automatization of a response by repetition of a stimulus that *accompanies* a given response and ultimately becomes a cause for behavior that formerly it merely accompanied.

An outstanding aspect of simple conditioning is association, the principle of which may be stated as follows: "Patterns of stimuli which are acting at the time of a response tend, on their recurrence, to occasion that response."[3] Association is facilitated by contiguity, which means that the substitute stimulus must occur at virtually the same time as the adequate stimulus.

Simple conditioning is an important means of learning in childhood. Thus, the infant stops crying when picked up instead of continuing until he is actually fed. The fact that he has been conditioned is demonstrated by the fact that he will resume crying if not fed soon after being picked up. Babies learn through "No, no" to avoid touching the hot stove, to keep away from kitchen knives, or to stay on the curb. Some school learning comes through simple conditioning; and repetition, drill, and practice are important learning avenues. It is essential that the pupil be

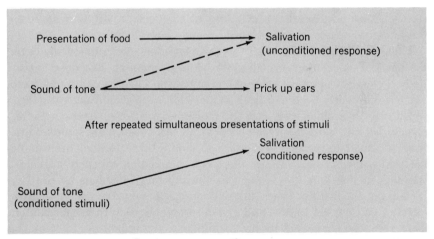

FIGURE 2. *Diagrammatic illustration of classical conditioning. The solid lines represent functional (natural) connections; the broken line represents a potential connection.*

[3] E. R. Guthrie, "Conditioning: A Theory of Learning in Terms of Stimulus, Response, and Association," *The Psychology of Learning*, Forty-first Yearbook of the National Society for the Study of Education, Chicago: The University of Chicago Press, 1942, part II, p. 58.

led to do what he is to learn; examples are spelling, learning number combinations, chemical symbols and formulas, foreign vocabulary, etc. The fundamental implication of contiguity conditioning for education is the principle of learning through making and doing (Thorpe and Schmuller, 1954, p. 116). But we do not want pupils to become mere automatons. Additional learning theories have, therefore, been developed to provide understandings of more complex learnings.

Instrumental Conditioning—Reinforcement Theory Instrumental conditioning involves the *active* participation of the organism to a much greater extent than does classical conditioning. Reward, or reinforcement, is an integral part of instrumental conditioning; need satisfaction and relief from tension, or avoidance of punishment, are all part of the total process.

A dog in a box is given an electric shock in his foot, upon which he yelps, moves his foot, puts his tail between his legs, or snaps at some object. If each time, just before the shock is applied, the dog hears a bell, he will soon react diffusely to the bell alone; but as the process continues, the useless parts of the diffuse response are dropped, and he simply lifts his foot at the sound of the bell and avoids the shock (see Figure 3). He *anticipates* from the bell the imminence of shock and is rewarded, or reinforced, by avoiding it. Similarly, a cat may learn to press a bar to be released from a cage or get a bit of food.

There is much evidence that the organism does not respond solely on the basis of association or contiguity—as a mechanism. Response is partially dependent upon the state of the organism. Pavlov's dog might have reacted differently if he had been so sick that meat would not cause him to salivate. If a child feels that the multiplication tables have no significance, he will learn them slowly, if at all. There must be some ability, however small, to respond to the task at hand. Further, stimuli are usually not purely mechanical because there is a cumulative effect. A schoolgirl standing in line may not respond to the tug given her hair by the boy behind her the first five times; but one more tug may have the cumulative effect of causing her to turn and give a resounding slap to her tormentor. Thus response is affected by the condition of the organism.

It can be seen that responses are not purely mechanical when one considers the phenomenon of forgetting, which may be explained in terms of the weakening of old responses *or* by the learning of new ones. New associations destroy, weaken, or overlap the connection between original stimuli and responses. Forgetting is thus not necessarily the loss of a function but may be due to the addition of more recent responses (Guthrie, 1942, p. 29).

Conditioning theory has the advantage of dealing with factors that are highly tangible—teachers can work with them. We do not expect the theory to explain all learning phenomena, but there are several ways in which teachers may take advantage of the theory. First, it is well for teachers to realize that pupils will learn what they do. Their diligence and sincere efforts carry over into habit patterns. This does not mean that work should be so rigorous as to be burdensome. Rather, the teacher should encourage application, industry, and studiousness by seeing that the material fits the child's needs or wants; thus, study will bring him satisfaction (reinforcement).

Repetition is of substantial value in learning. Admittedly, mere repetition is not all there is to learning. But the fact remains that pupils may understand a poem, the multiplication tables, or formulas in algebra or chemistry without knowing them well enough to repeat them. Practice, drill, or repetition is necessary to consolidate such knowledge. Drill should involve practice in various settings and orders. For instance, drill should be sufficiently effective so that a pupil can give the product of 7×8 without having to repeat $7 \times 5, 7 \times 6$, and 7×7 before he arrives at 56. Moreover, the drill should be motivated and meaningful, varied and periodic.

Closely allied to drill is review. Review will prevent the initially rapid forgetting that often accompanies learning. The word "review" means "taking another view"—placing the material in a different perspective, relating the facts learned to another problem, and attaching them to the present lessons. Review should serve the purposes not only of sustaining

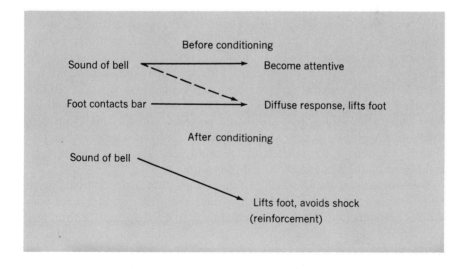

FIGURE 3. *Diagrammatic representation of instrumental conditioning.*

learning but of attaching new meanings to what has been learned and to providing a transition to new subject matter.

Finally, the teacher must be aware of the existence of conflicting and competing stimuli in the classroom situation. For example, a child may scarcely be aware of a clear, colorful, and impressive situation that the teacher has attempted to create because he is concerned about the illness of his mother. His father may be unnecessarily strict with him. High school pupils may be concerned about making the basketball team, getting a part in the class play, holding a part-time job, or solving some problem in peer relationships. Books and articles on mental health emphasize that all too often such conflicting stimuli are not properly evaluated by teachers. Some teachers take the attitude that the pupil's inattentiveness is a personal insult and reprimand him accordingly. Though conditioning may be reduced to one stimulus in the laboratory, in the classroom there are always multiple stimuli.

Stimulus-response, or reinforcement theory, has been elucidated by E. L. Thorndike, who holds that learning consists of forming bonds or connections between stimuli and responses. The involvement of the organism (learner) is basic and significant. New bonds are formed through experience, and the formation of these bonds is influenced by frequency, recency, intensity, and vividness of the experience, mood and capacity of the subject, similarity of situations, *and resulting satisfaction,* or reinforcement, which is basic in conditioning theory. These conditions are summarized in the "laws of learning," which are presented in the following paragraphs.

1. *The law of effect* Thorndike's early formulation of the law of effect was that when a modifiable connection between a stimulus and a response has been made, it is strengthened if it results in satisfaction (is reinforced) and weakened if it leads to annoyance. This statement was criticized, and his own experiments indicated that annoyance did not seem to be an adequate explanation for weakening responses. Thorndike modified his position in 1932 (267, p. 311). Satisfaction, according to his later statement, strengthens the bond between stimulus and response, but annoyance does not weaken it. Rather, annoyance aids learning in that it encourages the learner to try something else. A child may be reinforced by the recognition of inappropriate acts.

Some classroom implications of this law are that a pupil should have the following conditions for obtaining reinforcement: (a) a teacher who enjoys his work and his pupils and who has good mental health; (b) schoolwork and activities that are understandable and meaningful in terms of his personal life; (c) schoolwork and activities in which he can have some degree of success; (d) schoolwork that is progressive in nature and builds on earlier work, thereby giving him an awareness of growth; (*e*) presentation of material with varied approaches so that novelty is provided; (*f*) guidance, praise, and encouragement that bring him the satisfaction of knowing that he is on the right path.

2. *The law of exercise* This law is made up of two parts: the law of use and the law of disuse. The law of use asserts that, other things being equal, the more frequently a modifiable connection between a situation and a response is made, the stronger that connection will be. The law of disuse asserts that, other things being equal, when a modifiable connection between a situation and a response is not made over a period of time, the strength of that connection is weakened.

This "law" has a number of implications, such as the following: Pupils should be given every opportunity to use what they know. Examinations have their place in providing exercise—though they should not be regarded as the sole objective of classroom instruction. Oral quizzes can serve to diagnose weaknesses in teaching procedures and at the same time provide pupils with an opportunity to display their knowledge. Review provides an opportunity for repetition (exercise) and at the same time places knowledge in new settings. Provided understanding accompanies repetition, the law of exercise justifies the use of drill in various forms. But drill must lead somewhere—it must not pass from isolated fact to isolated fact. Instead of rote recitation, discussions should encourage pupils to bring their own experiences to class for interpretation in terms of the content being presented. Recent professional literature places much emphasis on discussion, pupil contributions, and the conversational method. Mathematics instruction, for example, is enhanced by discussion immediately following presentation (A. M. Jones, 1959). Even at the college level, where the lecture method is most firmly entrenched, it is estimated that dependence on lectures during the past few years has decreased from about 90 per cent to slightly over 50 per cent. Increasing emphasis has been placed on student reports, individual research, group projects, and class participation. It is considered important that all pupils have a chance to contribute; therefore, physical and intellectual freedom have been encouraged. The emphasis on mere memorization of facts has given way to the use, cross-use, and interpretation of those facts. This practice accords with the findings of research, which indicate that the ability to apply principles or interpret new experiments is not lost over a period of one year, but that the ability to recall memorized items or information is largely lost in the same period of time (M. Brown, 1961). Drill should not be repudiated, but it should have a purpose that pupils comprehend. Thus, in summary, the law of exercise is supported by both educational philosophy and educational experience.

3. *The law of readiness* When a modifiable connection is ready to act, to do so is satisfying; when it is not ready, to do so is unsatisfying.

Readiness is dependent upon both maturation and experience. This statement may be clarified by reference to the concept of reading readiness. It has been found that if, among other requisites, a child has reached the mental age of 6½ years, he is mentally capable of learning to read. If he does not have the requisite maturation, the experience of trying to learn to read will be annoying and frustrating. But he must also have the mental set, the desire, to learn to read. The more or less permanent condition of readiness should not be confused with the temporary condition of mental set, which is dependent upon interest, pertinency, or timeliness.

All too often, the classroom implications of readiness are overlooked. This is demonstrated by teachers who ask, "How can I teach numbers (or spelling, algebra, or history) to pupils who have low IQs?" "How can I bring up the slow learners to the class average?" At least part of the answer is to be found in the concept of readiness. Teachers must either wait for readiness, accept the present level of readiness and be satisfied with a slower learning rate, or provide experiences that will enhance readiness. It must be realized that some students may never reach the level of readiness that will enable them to comprehend the abstractions involved in certain school subjects.

Educators are today strongly advising that a child not be forced "beyond his depth" in reading, arithmetic, or social activities or that too much be expected of him in moral development (Kohlberg, 1963, p. 323). No doubt some children are taught to swim by being tossed into the deep end—but frequently at the expense of their desire to swim. A pupil who is forced to read before all elements of readiness converge may acquire some degree of reading skill, but he may also decide that he will read only when forced to do so. Very recently an experienced teacher said, "But I just can't let him go on this way in reading any longer—he's eight years old." This nonreading lad had a mental age of about five years on a group test of intelligence—eighteen months below the mental age considered necessary for reading readiness. It is difficult for teachers to recognize the wide differences in readiness, but failure to do so will result in futile effort.

Capitalizing on the principle of readiness is not necessarily a matter of passive waiting. Preparatory experience that will hasten the growth of readiness can be provided. Thus the primary teacher reads and tells stories to his pupils, encourages them to look at picture books and tell stories about what they see, and takes them on excursions and records the results on experience charts. Because readiness for reading consists of more than book experiences, he encourages group play and the exercise of independence and praises emotional control.[4]

[4] See Chap. 8, "Growth and Its Relationships to Learning and Teaching," for further discussion of readiness.

Aptitude tests in various subjects can be helpful to teachers in determining the thoroughness of pupils' preparation for those subjects. For example, there are mathematics, English, chemistry, language, and mechanical aptitude tests and, of course, general intelligence tests—all of which will provide partial answers concerning the probable success of students. Correctly used, such tests should help the teacher avoid the bewilderment and frustration that result from starting students in various subject areas simply because they have reached a certain grade or chronological age.

Five supplementary principles, in addition to the three above-mentioned primary laws of learning, are included in Thorndike's formulation of stimulus-response, reinforcement theory.

1. *The principle of multiple response* This principle, also known as trial-and-error learning or the principle of varied reaction, means that many responses may be tried before a satisfying one is hit upon. As learning takes place, useless parts of an act are dropped, and efficient, coordinated action ensues. This is one of the justifications for guidance of learning experiences—the teacher can point out pertinent clues and indicate the probable futility of some responses. There are several factors involved in trial-and-error learning: a need or motive; a difficulty (problematic situation) or obstacle; random, experimental, sometimes almost aimless attempts to achieve the goal; a successful trial; elimination of unproductive responses and consolidation of successful (reinforced) ones; and finally, the coordination of selected activities into large, unified patterns of behavior (see Figure 4).

The significance of trial-and-error learning for education is that it allows pupils an opportunity for wide experience, a chance to experiment for themselves, to learn from their own errors. Art teachers, for example, are moving away from stereotyped methods and encouraging children to select their own art media, to choose their own subjects, and to experiment with their own techniques. Help is provided when it is requested or when a pupil makes a gross error; but there is an increasing realization that experience, including the making of errors, is educative.

2. *The principle of mental set* This refers to the more or less temporary attitudes, feelings, and interests of the learner. A pupil may be *ready* (in terms of maturation) for the experience of reading, but not have the *anticipatory adjustment* that causes him to seek the learning goal. "Mental set" refers to the predisposition to act in a given way. Without conditioning pupils to expect to learn to read and write, to accept the teacher in his role, and to adopt school behavior, both the pupils' and the teacher's tasks would be most difficult. Mental set is seen to operate in a negative and alarming manner in school dropouts. For the most part, the parents of these youngsters have little schooling and are indifferent toward education. The youngsters, for the most part, do

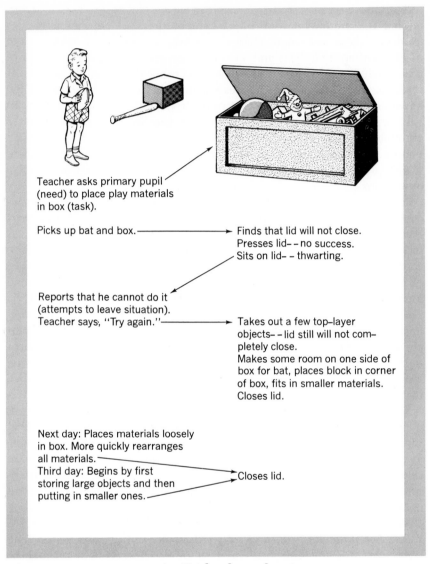

FIGURE 4. *Trial-and-error learning.*

not participate in school activities; they are discouraged with their past performance; and, even when they have the requisite ability, they are not predisposed to apply themselves to school tasks (Schrieber, 1963).

One of the effective ways to utilize the principle of mental set is to relate school activities to the lives of the pupils. Teachers can capitalize on school events, anniversaries, and outstanding community events to orient students to the daily lesson or the new unit. Pupils of high school age (and often younger) are likely to be reading at least the newspaper headlines. Events encountered thus, which are often discussed in the home, can provide a convenient orientation point for learning activities. For example, one elementary school teacher used the community dairy industry, which was being discussed in the state legislature, as the point of departure in teaching geography and social studies.

It has been shown that the emotional atmosphere of the classroom is an important factor in mental set. If the teacher is happy and congenial, the attitude of his pupils is likely to be positive. An attempt should be made to encourage congenial attitudes and cooperative relationships between pupils. This can be done by openly discussing strong and weak points in such relationships. The meaningfulness of the schoolwork is a powerful determinant of mental set. Even youngsters in the elementary grades have criticized the meaninglessness of preparing scrapbook after scrapbook when the only result they can foresee is a grade.

Mental set is a problem for individuals as well as for the class as a whole. The temporary disappointments that every individual suffers have a negative effect upon the mental set for learning. A junior high school girl with an IQ that placed her in the superior classification was failing in part of her work and causing disturbances by fighting with boys. Her mental set was changed by a teacher who sought the cause of her difficulty. The teacher, in talking with the girl, discovered that she was embarrassed by the lack of one front tooth and a protruding abdomen. Help was secured from a charitable organization to defray the cost of a new tooth, better clothes were obtained, and the teacher taught the girl some pertinent aspects of personal grooming. The girl was objective and accepted the teacher's explanation that a protruding abdomen was normal in preadolescence. The transformation of attitude seemed miraculous. The girl's grades quickly improved; she was able to laugh at the boys who made fun of her; and soon she had a substantial group of friends. Pupils have been known to develop favorable attitudes toward learning merely on the basis of knowing that the teacher is concerned about them and desires to be of assistance.

3. *The principle of partial activity* A response is made only to parts or aspects of a total rather than to the totality, according to this principle. Part of a total situation may be prepotent in the determination of a response. For example, a baby will respond to its mother whether she is in night clothes or evening dress, whether she is at home, on the street, or visiting with friends. A pupil will respond to the number combination 3×4—if he has learned it—whether he sees it in a book or is asked for the product by his teacher or his father. This is an economical factor in learning because it means that appropriate responses can be made without

exact duplication of an entire situation. Words are perhaps the most widespread means by which part of a situation serves to recall a larger total (Rosenzweig, 1958).

4. *The principle of analogy, or assimilation*   This means that when an individual is faced with a new situation for which he has no natural or learned response, the response he makes will resemble an earlier response to a similar situation. The new situation tends to arouse more or less the same structure as that activated by the previous one (Gewirtz, 1959).

Classroom implications of the principle of analogy include the need for pointing out similarities between the new and the old, the importance of leading from the known to the unknown, and the usefulness of bringing textbook abstractions to life by relating them to the experiences of the learner. Schools cannot hope to prepare pupils for all future experiences, but they can be given some basis for assimilating later experiences if equivalents, similarities, and parallels are indicated in the course of instruction. Teachers who point out similarities between historical events and present-day happenings are helping to produce understanding and responsible citizens. Parallels between the special economic and social problems of the community, for example, and those described in texts and references should be presented to the student.

The principle of analogy gives psychological support to the unit approach in teaching,[5] the basic purpose of which is to draw related knowledge from various fields. The unifying factor may be a problem, an era of history, or a trend in scientific development. At any rate, it is the common point of reference that gives cohesiveness to the study. The unit generates a large, related body of subject matter that cannot be covered in a day or in one lesson. It is therefore of increasing importance that relationships be perceived by the pupils. Our daily problems are resolved in this same assimilative and integrative manner. For example, taxation problems are not solved simply by a study of road construction or school support; understanding of the problems in terms of economics, sociology, philosophy, and politics is also required. There is a dual need for seeing a situation in its larger perspective and studying the contributions that can be made by separate subjects. This is the aim of the unit method. The principle of analogy is simply the psychological explanation of what has been pragmatically tested. It has been shown, for instance, that pupils learn to make wise choices, render decisions, evaluate consequences, and in general, become better citizens when they participate in student activities and government (Nimmo, 1958).

The experience unit recognizes that for every individual, the only reality lies in what he sees in the objects about him. These objects have

[5] An experience, or teaching, unit is a plan by which the teacher focuses many skills and knowledges around some central theme; e.g., transportation may become the focus of teaching language, writing, history, geography, etc. See Chap. 6.

different meanings for different persons (White, 1963, pp. 203ff). It is recognized that superior learning takes place when the task contributes to ends that have value for the learner. And finally, from the democratic point of view, personal growth, i.e., an individual's pursuit of his own goals, is synonymous with social progress. The experience unit, then, is psychologically sound—from the standpoints of learning efficiency, appeal to the individual (motivation), and productiveness of social values. Thus in many ways—by promoting perception of cross relationships, encouraging the observation of parallels, and capitalizing on individual experiences —the unit approach illustrates the principle of analogy. (Incidentally, your own study of educational psychology will be more interesting and meaningful if you trace parallels between your school experience and the textbook and class discussions and if you make frequent visits to classrooms to test the validity of what you have learned.)

5. *The principle of associative shifting* Actually, this is a formal statement of the phenomenon of conditioning—it means that any response of which a learner is capable may be attached to any stimulation to which he is sensitive. The most common school example would be reading, where certain combinations of letters—through practice, repetition, and reinforcement—call to mind highly specific things. The letters *h, o, r, s, e,* in that sequence, are attached to a large solid-hoofed grass-eating animal. Associative shifting may then cause these same letters to mean a device on which wood may be held while it is being sawed, to move an object by brute power, or to engage in tomfoolery.

Among the important implications of associative shifting must be included the pupil's attitude toward school and continued learning. The habits, attitudes, and interests that children develop in the school inevitably form the working equipment with which they will perform their functions as adults in society. Everything the teacher can do to make learning both successful and gratifying will contribute to this desirable type of associative shifting. A respect for objective viewpoints, the search for reliable data, systematic methods of problem solving, concern for others, and effective work habits will more readily become part of adult behavior patterns if they have been practiced in school.

Associative shifting does not operate independently of other principles of learning. Some of the factors that work together to produce effective learning and desirable conditioning are pleasurable aftereffects, consistency in the program, recognition of the necessity for readiness, guided activity, attention to temporary mental set, knowledge of the most compelling aspects of a situation, and indication of similarities.

It can be seen that stimulus-response, reinforcement theory has very practical implications for teaching. Whether or not teachers are acquainted with the term "connectionism," which identifies Thorndike's interpretations, the fact remains that this viewpoint has played a dominant part in our educational practice for the first half of the twentieth century. Refinements of the theory are still being developed, but currently much attention is given to a more global approach (Warburton, 1962, pp. 372ff).

Conditioning Theory and Learning Several theorists and experimenters, in addition to Pavlov, have made contributions to our understanding of learning by means of conditioning. Some of these are mentioned here. E. R. Guthrie, noted for his emphasis on contiguity (the simultaneous occurrence of stimuli and responses), and E. L. Thorndike, noted for his formulation of principles that may be applied in the classroom, have been mentioned in the foregoing material as leaders in conditioning theory. There are others whose names and contributions should be familiar to the student of educational psychology. Some of them are alive today and continuously adding to both learning theory and educational implications of that theory.

Clark R. Hull (1943) has emphasized the importance of acquired drives and acquired rewards as contrasted to the primary drives such as those emphasized in classical conditioning. These motives and rewards are learned, but they are, nevertheless, important means of influencing behavior. Inasmuch as rewards and punishments are administered by people, social learnings are better understood if culture and society are recognized as providing the locus of acquired drives. This emphasis on acquired drives and social rewards receives particular emphasis in Chapter 15, where adolescence is conceptualized as a cultural phenomenon. The significance of acquired drives may be seen in the school and in life in general as students and adults strive for grades, honors, prestige, and monetary reward.

Dollard and Miller (1950, pp. 25–47) have given a succinct summary of fundamentals of learning that are related to conditioning. They emphasize the fact that learning involves the following: (1) drive, the stimuli that impel action, the motivation to achieve a goal, including both primary and secondary, or learned, drives (Hull, 1943); (2) cues that elicit responses and determine if, when, where, and how a response will be made, including the physical classroom, classmates, the teacher, and the learning media as they provide the setting for a response; (3) the response, which must be made before it can be rewarded; and (4) reward for the individual's correct response, or reinforcement. Because planned techniques of reinforcement have been discussed elsewhere, it might be well to mention here that reinforcement may come from unplanned sources. Thus a slow reader might receive reinforcement from the attention he gets from being able to be with the "special" reading teacher. He knows that if he learns to read at grade level, he will no longer be sent to these enjoyable sessions. The misbehaving girl might be getting reinforcement from her peers as well as from the teacher's obvious displeasure. Neither the slow reader nor the misbehaving girl would have much desire to change in the direction that adults would have planned.

B. F. Skinner (1958) has emphasized some things about reinforcement, and supported his views with experiments that appear to be extremely important and made motion pictures about them. Rats, chickens, pigeons, and other animals were trained to do some rather amazing things—bowl, play table tennis, shoot baskets—by using instantaneous reinforcement of crude approximations of the desired final result. Skinner believes that we do not know nearly enough about human learning—that we have pictured the results, but not the "how," the operation of learning. For instance, behavior is almost never invariably reinforced in natural situations, yet new patterns of behavior are constantly being acquired. We must therefore consider that intermittent reinforcement is effective. Witness the fisherman who only occasionally catches a fish yet keeps at it and will return after failure—provided he is reinforced (lands a fish) now and then. However, if there is a schedule of reinforcement [6]—regular reinforcement for small acts, such as is provided in programmed learning—then the rate of responding becomes maximal.

> As a result of careful scheduling, pigeons, rats, and monkeys have done things during the past five years which members of their species have never done before. It is not that their forebears were incapable of such behavior; nature had simply never arranged effective sequences of schedules. . . .
>
> A program of cultural design in the broadest sense is now within reach. Sociologists, anthropologists, political scientists, economists, theologians, psychotherapists and psychologists have long tried to reach an understanding of human behavior which would be useful in solving practical problems. In that technological race a dark horse is coming up fast. The new principles and methods of analysis which are emerging from the study of reinforcement may prove to be among the most productive social instruments of the twentieth century.[7]

O. H. Mowrer (1947) has developed a two-factor theory that includes both classical (associational) and reinforcement conditioning. He emphasizes significant differences between the two learning processes instead of trying to consolidate them. He regards them as two distinctly different avenues of learning. One involves the central nervous system and skeletal muscles: it is a process of need reduction, and thus reinforcement, through successful action. The needs may be innate (hunger, sex)

---

[6] Schedules of reinforcement may be predetermined, e.g., reinforcement at fixed intervals (every two or ten minutes), at variable intervals (first at one minute, second at three minutes, third at forty seconds, etc.), or in proportion to the number of responses—which may be fixed (every tenth response) or variable (after second, seventh, tenth, sixteenth, etc.).

[7] B. F. Skinner, "Reinforcement Today," *The American Psychologist*, 13:96, 99; 1958.

or learned (prestige, security). The law of effect takes precedence over, but does not eliminate, the association between stimulus and response.

The other takes place at the level of the autonomic nervous system and involves visceral and vascular changes. Rather than solving problems (as does successful action as described in the preceding paragraph), these visceral (or emotional) changes are problem-creating. They are unconscious responses of love, fear, anxiety, etc. These responses are usually neither pleasant nor need-satisfying, and they cannot, according to Mowrer, be acquired in the same way (through reinforcement) as the responses that successfully reduce tension. What the organism learns is not a response, but the anticipation of a response, a motivation that predisposes him to an action (Travers, 1963, p. 13). Thus in a conditioning experiment, the immediate learning is that the bell is cause for fear (not the direct raising of the foot to avoid shock), which then becomes the drive for avoidance behavior. Mowrer has lately suggested that in both avoidance and approach behavior, the emotion, the drive state is conditioned—which, in turn, leads to the avoidance or approach responses (Mowrer, 1960, pp. 4ff).

Mowrer's theory explains some classroom phenomena that were difficult to interpret prior to his presentation; namely, why children learn in unenjoyable classrooms or when the need for security or recognition has not been satisfied. Many attempts have been made to make learning pleasant, need-satisfying, or nonthreatening because of the assumption that learning demands reinforcement. Yet we know that many pupils have learned, and learned effectively, under threat. Thus it is effective to tell some youngsters to work hard, to do their lessons, to score high on tests because if they do not their later employment will be uncertain. The threat that it will be hard to find and easy to lose a job if scores are low provides impetus for schoolwork—avoidance of the unpleasant.

Field Theories and Learning—The Molar Emphasis   Field theories have been formulated in reaction to what is sometimes considered to be the atomistic (i.e., concerned with supposedly isolated details) nature or so-called "molecular view" of conditioning and reinforcement theory. Field theories endorse the molar view, which maintains that all parts are intimately interrelated and interdependent. Emphasis is placed on the total organization of the "field," which is made up of (1) the occurrence of many stimuli, (2) these stimuli assembled into a meaningful pattern, (3) the reaction of the organism, which alters both the external situation and the organism, and (4) the changing nature of the organism itself. These differences are schematically illustrated in Figure 5.

Field theories emphasize the phenomena of perception and organization. They stress the fact that a stimulus never occurs in simple isolation —there are always competing stimuli and shifting conditions. Thus, in Figure 5, the double arrows indicate that the organism selects out of

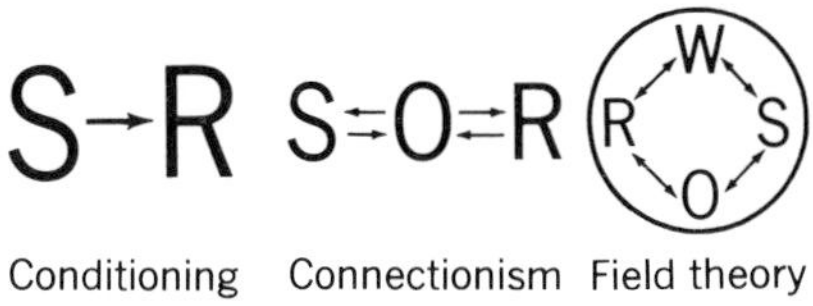

S→R   S⇋O⇋R

Conditioning   Connectionism   Field theory

FIGURE 5.   *Schematic representation of major learning theories. (S indicates stimulus, R, response; O, organism; and W, world.)*

the total situation certain stimuli to which it will react, that what it selects changes the organism, and that a reaction not only is a product but becomes a force in changing the world.

Field theories offer no simple explanation of learning processes. In fact, oversimplification in explaining them disturbs the field theorist. Learning, according to him, is the organization and reorganization of behavior that results from the many interacting influences on the developing organism acting in its shifting environment.

One of the leading field theories is gestalt psychology. The word "gestalt" means shape, form, or configuration. In this context, it implies that a set of stimulating circumstances takes shape according to the relative values of various stimuli acting at the same time. A musical pattern is not dependent upon c, d, e, f, etc., alone, but also upon the relationship in time and sequence that the notes bear to one another. The same notes may be used in "Annie Laurie" and "Yankee Doodle," but the timing and sequence of the notes give each piece its distinction and configuration. Identity resides in the total organization.

Configuration is partially dependent upon the phenomenon of "figure-ground." Typically, the figure in a perceptual field is clearly outlined, small, and well shaped, while the ground is vague, relatively massive, and amorphous. Figure-ground simply recognizes that some stimuli are prominent, while others constitute the fringe or background. Thus in a large landscape painting, the red barn, though comparatively small, is the "figure," while the fence, sky, hills in back, and field in front are the "ground." The organism also plays a part in the perception of a figure. The professor's words regarding operant conditioning, despite their clarity and brilliance, may not be the "figure" for the young man who is concerned about a date for Friday as he eyes the girl with jet-black hair two rows in front and two seats to the right.

Field theory places much emphasis on the organism, the learner, as does the concept of reinforcement. Action begins with the organism, and pupils must have a desire or need to achieve learning goals. This creates tension that causes action. In diagraming learning, Lewin (1942, pp. 215ff), represents the person as central in the learning configuration and by arrows and crosshatching shows the existence of tension. After the goal has been achieved, the organism returns to a state of repose until a new desire or need creates another condition of tension. Thus in field theory, the organism is quite as important a part of the total configuration as is the patterned set of stimulating conditions.

"Insight" (see Glossary), another of the major emphases in field theory, is the mental process by which new and revealing combinations of data are perceived; it is sometimes defined as the sudden perception of the relationships in a total situation, i.e., the relationships between the organism, the goal, and the intervening obstacles. Even though we admit that the moment of insight itself may be sudden, it is important to realize that it is preceded by more or less gradual development, growth, or progression toward a goal. It is necessary in learning to take preparatory steps. Thus insight is related to motivation and the acquisition of information, as well as to the phenomenon of readiness. Hilgard (1956, pp. 234ff) has summarized the factors that contribute to insight into four characteristics—to which educational principles may readily be attached.

1. Insight depends on capacity. Here the problem of readiness applies. Teachers must recognize age and differences in capacity.

2. Previous experience conditions insight. This indicates the necessity for preliminary steps, for basic vocabulary, for familiarity with cause-effect relationships.

3. Arrangement of the elements in the situation conditions insight. In general, this means that teachers should study pupil reactions in order to determine the methods and order of presentation that will prove most helpful.

4. Fumbling and search are preliminary to insight. This is more than trial-and-error procedure. It is purposeful experimentation that emphasizes the educational value of freedom to make mistakes. The teacher should seek to overcome impatience because the moment of insight is unpredictable.

Educational implications of field theory   The figure-ground concept stresses the importance of clear explanation and demonstration to make the most significant points stand out. Distinctive, understandable vocabulary, pictorial and auditory aids, and direct experience are necessary. Broad generalities have their place in an introduction to the subject area, but out of them should come preciseness and exactitude of description. The figure-ground concept shows the need for seeing the whole, but also for observing the details. Thus in reading, word analysis and phonetics are subordinate to getting the idea; they are significant only as they contribute to better understanding. Experienced teachers know that there are many pupils who can read the words but fail to grasp the meaning. It must not be forgotten that the figure perceived depends partially upon the experience and background of the learner.

Because the organism is an integral part of the learning configuration, certain implications derive from the phenomenon of tension:

1. The teacher must help the pupil to perceive, at least partially, the goal and the intervening obstacles.

2. If the goal is too difficult in terms of the pupil's present development, it must be made easier or its pursuit must be delayed. Otherwise, the pupil will develop symptoms of recessiveness (fleeing) or aggressiveness (fighting). Partial insight means a partial relief from tension.

3. Teachers should not be disturbed because all problems are not solved. It is stimulating to the pupil to know that some progress has been made and that there are approaches to the remaining problems.

The major classroom implications of the phenomenon of insight focus about ways of contributing to understanding. One of these relates to the necessity of building step by step—be it in history, geometry, or skill in playing a musical instrument. Some insight is sudden—like the moment at which the mountain climber achieves the peak and sees before him a vast panorama of other peaks, valleys, rivers, fields, and forests. But he had partial glimpses (insights) of the scene before he reached the peak. So too, the learner has partial glimpses of the total. The culminating step toward total insight may take place suddenly, but there are many preparatory steps—perhaps even some wanderings from the most fruitful paths—before the goal is reached. A teacher must bear in mind that although there is a final moment of triumph, there are also many individual steps, many partial understandings, and many experiments that must be made. Much patience must be exercised before the final insight is achieved.

The definition of insight as a restructuring of the perceptual field is enlightening—previously unseen relationships and patterns are perceived, and all elements of the situation appear to be unified in some way. A rabbit crouching in a field may at first be unobserved. When an experienced naturalist points to the animal, the tyro will exclaim, "Oh, I see it now." The student who has been laboring over an algebra problem expresses the same thought when he says that he "sees" the answer. In fact, insight is the factor that distinguishes the student who perceives the principle or pattern in geometry from the one who, having memorized the theorem, is upset because the teacher places a new set of letters at the corners of the geometrical shapes. Learning to repeat a set of figures, such as 6, 7, 9, 12, 16, 21, 27, 34, etc., or 8, 7, 9, 6, 10, 5, 11, 4, is more readily accomplished when the pupil sees the pattern or relationship of the numbers. In fact, if insight is achieved immediately, there is no need for repetition. Obviously, maturation is a factor in the ability to perceive clearly the figure-ground pattern and thus achieve insight. A child who knows numbers but not the concept of addition may learn to repeat the series of numbers, but a child who knows how to add (a matter of maturation and experience) can learn the series more readily.

If insight is to be achieved, school tasks must be appropriate to the understanding of the child. This emphasis is one of the more significant contributions of field theory to the interpretation of learning. The frequency of failure in grade school and poor work in academic subjects in high school is evidence that either (1) the work is too difficult for pupils to achieve insight, or (2) explanations by the teacher and/or textbooks are not sufficiently clear to foster insight.

In the concept of insight, emphasis is again placed on motivation. Development of insight is more likely if goals are clearly defined and if they are significant to the learner. When the learner accepts the goal, he will exert energy to achieve that goal.

The teacher who trusts in the slow processes of growth will not despair when pupils state or otherwise indicate that they do not understand a particular problem. In such cases, smaller steps may be taken or intermediate goals may be pursued. An experiment in insight made on monkeys has shown that the animals initially required a long time to solve problems, but that as they were trained in a large number of situations requiring discrimination, they began to solve new problems more readily (Harlow, 1949).

The concept of insight can be helpful to the teacher when he realizes that insights are partial and dependent upon the development level and experience background of the learner, that goals tend to consolidate energy, and that even attempts to solve problems (though they may not really be solved) are educative. Some ways in which insight may be fostered are schematically shown in Figure 6.

The classroom implications of field theory as a whole include the importance of seeing the total situation at the beginning. This is accomplished by having pupils discuss both the immediate and ultimate goals of learning. Questions that will be answered during the study of the subject should be raised. The teacher should preview the activities involved and the problems to be encountered. However, details should not be ignored; they are important as *aspects* of the larger problem. For example, in primary reading, the teacher will tell briefly what the story is about, describe the characters, and relate the story to the pupils' experience. At the high school level, instead of introducing the study of chemistry with a detailed analysis of a given element, the teacher should first discuss the operation of chemistry in daily living, the overall field, and the problems to be considered.

The pupil, the teacher, the school, and the peer group are all parts of the total situation, which also includes the present and previous reactions of every individual in the class. Thus the pupil's intelligence, his background, and his interest in the subject must be known before the total situation is comprehended.

We may summarize by saying that learning is characterized by changed

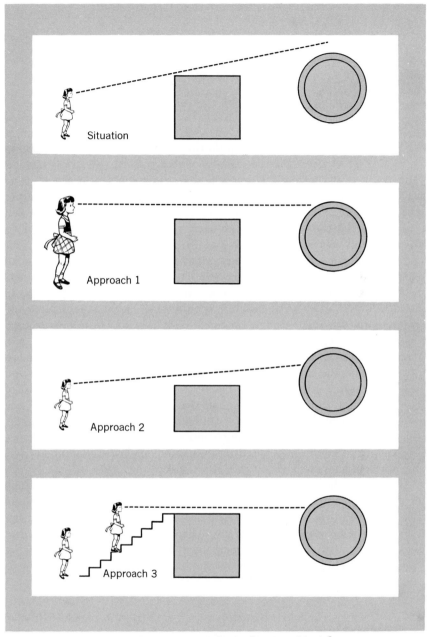

FIGURE 6.   *Schematic representation of the facilitation of insight.*

Situation: The need for insight—an obstacle (difficulty) blocks the perception or achievement of the goal.

Approach 1: Permit the pupil to grow by waiting or by providing preparatory experiences and knowledge that will increase her power.

Approach 2: Make the problem less difficult. Get an easier textbook. Use more immediate goals. Find more concrete problems.

Approach 3: Give the pupil some help. Offer suggestions, hints, clues. Show her how to take a specific step. Arrange a sequential approach.

perception, improved reactions, differentiation of stimuli and response, integration of stimuli and response, and achievement of understanding, or insight. Factors that condition learning are the state of the organism, the appropriateness of stimulation, and the existence of goals.

Reconciliation of the viewpoints of learning

The purpose of presenting representative viewpoints of learning is to emphasize that there are various and multiple explanations for the nature and conditions of learning. No one theory presents all the answers. But each has a contribution to make in terms of understanding the total field of psychology and educational psychology.

There are some who are concerned that psychologists have not reached common agreement and that there is so much apparent dissension. Others feel that the disagreement is healthy and serves to bring attention to various important aspects. Both viewpoints have merit. It is unfortunate that we do not have enough precise information to be able to discard doubtful theories. Yet it is fortunate that such stimulation by disagreement keeps psychological knowledge growing. Deese (1958, p. 302) has observed that the arguments between theories has been greatly reduced and that arguments are more likely to occur regarding methods of investigation. Certainly, most psychologists today are not disciples of any one or another of the major schools (Hilgard, 1956, p. 325). Most scholars can find merit in the outstanding contributions of the various schools. Finally, it must be remembered that much of our knowledge about psychology is independent of any particular school.

It has been shown that the nature of learning and its various theoretical explanations can be utilized to make the work of the teacher more effective. It is up to the teacher to use all available knowledge in attempting to solve specific classroom problems. The teacher must also continue to seek better answers from contemporary literature. Only the growing teacher can stimulate optimum growth in his pupils.

Summary

Learning is an extremely complex phenomenon, and it is not surprising that new discoveries as to its nature are being gained constantly. We do know that learning depends on biochemical factors, on opportunity, and on the individual's response to his physical makeup and opportunity.

Learning occurs in many ways and has many types of outcome. These may conveniently be classified as sensorimotor skills, perceptual motor skills, associational learning, conceptual learning, perceptual learning, the learning of attitudes and ideals, and problem-solving skill.

Because learning is so important and complex and occurs in so many forms, inclusive and conclusive theoretical descriptions are extremely difficult. In fact, no such formulation that is acceptable to all has been accomplished to date. Three viewpoints have been described in this chapter—though another author might describe five or ten or even omit any "naming" of a viewpoint.

Simple conditioning or contiguity theory emphasizes the virtually simultaneous occurrence of a stimulus and response. Repeated occurrences result in the organism's responding to stimuli that really have no natural or inherent connection. Drill, practice, repetition, and consistency in the classroom can be justified in terms of conditioning theory.

Reinforcement theory involves the participation of the learner in a vigorous and vital manner. Simple repetition must be supplemented by reinforcement— in fact, in the presence of reinforcement, the number of repetitions can be reduced to almost the point of disappearance. E. L. Thorndike has elucidated reinforcement theory with his primary and secondary laws of learning; these laws have for almost half a century been used to justify much current practice.

Field theory places emphasis upon the unity rather than the units of a learning situation. All parts of the total pattern—the nature, size, and structure of figure-ground, the learner's perception, and the learner's insight—are important focuses in field theory.

The various viewpoints on learning have values in that each stresses some factor that another viewpoint either overlooks, takes for granted, or includes as a minor emphasis. Together, they provide a basis that enables teachers to adapt to the unique problems of their own classroom situations rather than depending on a prescription derived from a learning situation that is somewhat different.

Problems and exercises

1 Can you derive from this chapter any direct applications of theory to your own study of educational psychology?

2 To what extent is the individual "free" to determine his response—or is he bound by hereditary equipment and environmental surroundings to make the responses he does?

3 Defend or criticize the following statements from the standpoint of educational psychology:

"You can lead a horse to water but you can't make him drink."

"Necessity is the mother of invention."

"Practice makes perfect."

"We learn to swim in the winter and to skate in the summer."

"You can't teach an old dog new tricks."

"You can't change human nature."

"When reason is against a man, he will soon turn against reason."

4 Why do we tend to forget the content of a history lesson or a memorized poem sooner than we forget how to swim?

5 Cite a number of theoretical considerations that support the use of the

unit approach to learning. What are the theoretical shortcomings of such a method?

6 What stand would you take on a year-round school calendar?

7 Visit an elementary classroom and record every evidence you see of the use of the principles of reinforcement theory.

8 Visit a high school class and record any evidences of the operation of field theory. What additional uses might have been made of the theory?

9 Could you argue successfully that school learning should always seek insight for pupils?

Suggested additional readings

Bruner, Jerome S.: *On Knowing: Essays for the Left Hand,* Cambridge, Mass.: Harvard University Press, 1962.

The author expresses a feeling that current psychological theories are incomplete—that they are "lock-step." His essays suggest the need for examination of myths, learning more about intuition and creativity, breaking the hold of the tradition-bound right hand.

Hilgard, Ernest R.: *Theories of Learning,* 2d ed., New York: Appleton-Century-Crofts, Inc., 1956.

This is not always easy reading, but the serious student will gain much understanding from seeing the emphases that are made in ten major theories of learning.

Klausmeier, Herbert J.: *Learning and Human Abilities,* New York: Harcourt, Brace & World, Inc., 1961, pp. 3–33.

Purposeful, imitative, and conditioned learning are discussed. A major emphasis is on how the teacher may promote each of these kinds of learning.

Sawrey, James M., and Charles W. Telford: "Learning: Some General Considerations," in *Dynamics of Mental Health,* Boston, Mass.: Allyn and Bacon, Inc., 1963, pp. 141–165.

The authors present a brief summary of classical conditioning, instrumental conditioning, a discussion of reinforcement, and materials on trial-and-error and imitative learning.

Theories of Learning and Instruction, Sixty-third Yearbook of the National Society for the Study of Education, Chicago: The University of Chicago Press, 1964, part I.

Chapters by outstanding scholars cover a wide range of topics that are pertinent for the student of educational psychology—theory, motivation, readiness, learning specific subjects, and auto-instruction.

Educational Implications of Transfer

If it were not for the phenomenon of transfer of learning, there would be little point in formal education. Without transfer, the preparation of children for adult life would be as limited as teaching animals to perform tricks. Without transfer, man's repertoire of behavior would be extremely limited and highly specific. The difference between training and education resides in the fact that in education there is transfer of learning, which means that learning in one area or of one kind can facilitate learning in another area. Virtually all our educational efforts are directed to learnings that can be transferred to other and new areas and from the present to the immediate and remote future. Transfer is the ubiquitous, pervasive factor in the study of educational psychology, and it is essential to the success and value of education.

Education is concerned with preparing persons to meet, with increasing effectiveness, the problems of life. Some of these problems can be anticipated with a degree of accuracy, but others can be anticipated only approximately. The application of transfer is this: If problems cannot be specifically prepared for in advance, they should be prepared for in general. If a solution cannot be reached now, an approach to a solution, a system of attack, and a set of guiding principles should be highly practicable. Because life is so complex and evolving so rapidly, it is not possible to provide answers ahead of time. We teach some things in order that they may be adopted, modified, or transferred to other similar situations.

The student of educational psychology is concerned with these questions: How can we get more transfer values? What subjects are most likely to stimulate transfer? What teaching methods facilitate the occurrence of transfer? This chapter deals with data concerning these questions. Any answers must be considered suggestive and illustrative. You must apply (transfer) the generalizations presented here to your own problems.

3

Mental Discipline   The theory of transfer of learning can more readily be understood if it is contrasted with its historical forerunner, mental discipline (also called "formal discipline"). At one time, it was thought that the mind was made up of certain faculties or compartments. It was believed, for instance, that there was a faculty for memory, a faculty for reasoning, a faculty for aesthetic appreciation, and a faculty for judgment. This element of the earlier theory was not completely erroneous, as contemporary experiments indicate. There are *generalized* areas of the brain that function primarily in certain mental activities. Another aspect of the theory was questionable, namely, that these faculties are sharpened by exercise or by mental discipline, just as the muscles of the arm or leg are strengthened by exercise.

Educational practice based on the theory of mental discipline stressed the necessity for developing the "sinews of the mind" by rigorous exercise. The harder the exercise, the more the faculties were disciplined. The more difficult the schoolwork, the more it was favored by teachers. Subjects that had proved to be particularly arduous were Greek, Latin, mathematics, and science. These subjects were rigorously taught for their disciplinary value. Memorizing multiplication tables was thought to develop the power of reasoning. Learning about the saints was thought to develop moral capacity. There was no attempt to make schoolwork pleasant or interesting; in fact, more "discipline" was engendered if the tasks were unpleasant and burdensome. Little consideration was given to the utility of a subject, so long as it provided strenuous mental activity.

The concept of mental discipline is today unpopular with psychologists and educators. Experimental studies indicate, for example, that memory as a general function is not improved simply by memorizing stanzas of poetry. In fields other than mathematics, reasoning is not automatically improved by studying algebra and geometry or by memorizing the mutiplication tables. Morality can be taught, but not simply by reciting the lives of saints. However, the past cannot be cavalierly cast aside. There are still parents, school patrons, and teachers who are convinced that Latin, Greek, and mathematics should be included in the school curriculum because it is "good for the student." (Let it be said emphatically at this point that there is no objection to these subjects or to any others, provided they are taught with transfer values in mind.) Educators who teach as if the subject were all important are apparently concerned with the disciplinary function of learning.

Transfer of Learning   There is no doubt that learning in one situation has an effect on learning in or adaptation to another situation. The methods of solving and the symbols for presenting problems in arith metic may readily be transferred to the study of algebra. Latin may facilitate learning English words and does greatly facilitate such study *when teachers have pointed out and illustrated the relationship between the languages* (Hamblen, 1925). Transfer of learning means that if certain habits, skills, ideas, or ideals are acquired, learning other habits, skills, and ideas is facilitated or inhibited. If transfer is inhibited, it is called "negative transfer"; if facilitated, it is called "positive." Of course, there are many times when something learned has little or no measurable effect —either positive or negative—upon another learning situation.

An example of the way transfer functions in a positive direction and an illustration of the theory of generalization in transfer are given in the following report of a pioneer experiment that involved shooting at a target under water:

> One group of boys was given a full theoretical explanation of refraction. The other group of boys was left to work out experience without theoretical training. These two groups began practice with the target under twelve inches of water. It is a very striking fact that in the first series of trials the boys who knew the theory of refraction and those who did not gave about the same results. That is, a theory seemed to be of no value in the first tests. All the boys had to learn how to use the dart, and theory proved to be no substitute for practice. At this point the conditions were changed. The twelve inches of water were reduced to four. The differences between the two groups of boys came out very strikingly. The boys without theory were very much confused. The practice gained with twelve inches of water did not help them with four inches. Their errors were large and persistent. On the other hand, the boys who had the theory fitted themselves to four inches very rapidly.[1]

Negative transfer Learning in one situation may interfere with learning (be negative) in another situation. In the field of sports, for example, some baseball coaches do not like to have their players engage in leisure-time golf because they feel that swinging a bat is so different from swinging a golf club that the player's batting may suffer. Swimming is sometimes frowned upon by football coaches because swimming develops soft, fluid muscles, while football requires hard, powerful muscles. In the school situation, teachers are justifiably concerned that school requirements and expectations may cause the student to avoid books, disdain education, and disrespect authority. Feelings of academic inadequacy may transfer to out-of-school performance and have a negative effect on work and marital adjustment (Andrews and Cronbach, 1962). The same thing applies to languages. An American Field Service exchange student to Germany reported that he had reached the point

[1] Charles H. Judd, "The Relation of Special Training to General Intelligence," *Educational Review*, 36:37, 1908.

where he had to translate his German thoughts into English before he could write home. Learning the placement of words and the endings used in German resulted in a deterioration of his English. This phenomenon has been verified by an experimental investigation that revealed that students studying Latin wrote English compositions inferior to those written by control groups who had no Latin (Woodring, 1925). Negative transfer, like positive transfer, is dependent on the method of teaching and the individual's response as much as it is on the subject.

Many of you may have encountered in college an example of one learning that interferes with another. The two conflicting skills are reading and studying. Despite the fact that he does a great deal of reading in college, the typical student does not improve in either rate or comprehension. Many, in fact, are known to deteriorate in reading skills from the senior year in high school to the senior year in college. One explanation is that college students literally stop reading and spend all their time studying. Interrupting reading to underline and take notes and trying to make sure all details have been grasped interfere with the rhythmical, steadily progressing pace that results in speed and global comprehension.[2]

Experimental studies indicate that it may be well to avoid attempting to learn two very similar skills at the same time (Nelson, 1957). Confusions are likely to result if a pupil practices on a certain typewriter at school, but uses another typewriter with a somewhat different keyboard at home. Attempting to learn two foreign languages at the same time is subject to similar criticism. In French class, a student is likely to substitute a German word for a French word, for example. Many studies have been made on pupils with a bilingual background (two languages spoken in the home). And while children with a bilingual background are not consistently slow in learning correct English usage, difficulty does occur frequently.

These observations have pertinence for all teachers. It will help them better to understand children from neighborhoods where languages other than English are spoken. It may be helpful, in situations where the child is experiencing difficulty in language development, to explain to parents the handicap they are imposing by *alternately* [3] speaking two languages. As will be shown later, pupils with high intelligence experience relatively little difficulty because high intelligence facilitates positive transfer. But

[2] This is not to say there is no place for detailed, analytical reading for certain purposes. It does imply that *part* of the college student's reading should be free reading, designed, in part, to maintain and improve speed and comprehension. See Francis P. Robinson, *Effective Study*, rev. ed., New York: Harper & Row, Publishers, 1961, pp. 137–159.

[3] If one parent speaks only one language in the presence of the young child, he learns to distinguish between it and the language spoken by the other parent. For children beyond the primary years, the hazard declines.

for those of less intelligence, the chances for confusion are sufficient to warrant informing parents about the phenomenon of negative transfer.

   The practical import of transfer   If we agree with the statement that "beauty is its own excuse for being," then some school subjects need no further justification. Art, music, and literature can be justified on the basis of their enrichment of daily living, and perhaps we need not be concerned about the transfer value of such subjects. Art and literature provide satisfaction and enjoyment quite apart from any bearing that they may have on other aspects of living. However, if they are taught with transfer values in mind, *their worth is enhanced.* While a student may derive satisfaction from working with color, there is no reason why he should not apply his knowledge to everyday matters of dress and decoration. The present values of a particular pursuit need not be repudiated because the pursuit has future implications.

   When it comes to other subjects in both the elementary grades and high school, the importance of teaching for transfer is still more evident. Consider the areas of mathematics, social studies, and science. A few bright pupils may get so much fun out of solving mathematical problems that the subject constitutes an avenue for creativity. A few others may involve themselves in social studies or science just for the fun of knowing and learning. But for the balance of the students who do not derive such enjoyment from the subjects—to believe that mathematics or science improves "thinking ability" is to subscribe to the erroneous notion of mental discipline. In general, students who take mathematics and science tend to earn better-than-average achievement scores, but it has been suggested that those who choose these subjects are likely to have been better students originally. It is their innate superiority, not the discipline of the courses, that is reflected in the high scores (Wesman, 1945). Thus it is safe to say that school subjects have additional merit to the extent to which they are taught by methods that enhance transfer. The subject per se does not automatically ensure transfer. Furthermore, one cannot assume automatic transfer of anything from the curriculum until experimental evidence confirms the existence of transfer effects.

   Inclusion of certain subjects in the curriculum just because they are difficult is not justifiable. Much of the truth about transfer and mental discipline has been known for years, so it is disturbing to see the persistence of fallacious reasoning and the resistance to translating psychological findings into school practice. Some of the high school curriculum is still taught because it will "improve the mind"—at least, this is the explanation given by some teachers and parents. The development of intercultural understanding is a very good reason for teaching foreign languages. It is foolish to justify them on the basis of their value in disciplining the mind. Some students will use mathematics as an important professional tool, but those who teach mathematics often call it good "general training."

The fact that education per se does not make a person "smarter" outside his line of specialty is a lesson that both teachers and laymen seem to resist learning. However, let it be emphasized that mental discipline must be distinguished from intellectual development. One develops intellectually by "disciplining" and systematizing his learning procedures and by increasing his fund of data (Kolesnik, 1958).

Many factors enter into good teaching—enthusiasm, knowledge of subject matter, communication skills—and one of the most important of them is the deliberate attempt to teach for transfer. As schoolchildren, pupils are better prepared for new subjects if transfer has been emphasized. As adults, they will be able to relate one activity to another. All America has been alarmed by the accusation that atomic scientists have not studied the import of their work on human lives. That scientists are any more guilty than the proponents of other disciplines is questionable. That cross-fertilization of philosophy and science is needed is a readily accepted idea. Even the names of recently developed courses and disciplines suggest recognition of the great need for transfer, e.g., biochemistry, psychosomatic medicine, psychosocial development. One of the reasons for the fact that "outside his field he is no more capable than others" is that as a student, he studied specialized, isolated subjects. Teachers are often incensed that the pupil who earns an A in English composition writes poorly constructed papers in social studies or the natural sciences (Beck, 1962, p. 43). Transfer is being sought in correlated or integrated courses, where social studies, English, science, and mathematics are combined into larger amalgamations of subject matter. Too often pupils have studied from a textbook without being shown its implications for other fields and daily living, present and future. The inadequacy of the theory of mental discipline and the efficacy of transfer of learning provide a psychological basis for curricular organization that stresses the correlation of subject matter and the relation of subject matter to problems of daily living.

Basic principles involved in transfer

How can we get maximum benefit from transfer? We all are concerned with making learning more effective, and transfer is another way of viewing the learning process. Teachers should, therefore, be interested in the conditions that make for optimum transfer. Several explanations have been offered of the way in which transfer occurs. Each of these theories has very direct teaching and learning implications.

The Theory of Common Components This theory may be stated as follows: Learning is facilitated in a second situation to the extent to which it possesses factors that were present in the first situation (Thorndike, 1924). As presently modified, the theory states that the extent of transfer from one situation to another depends on the degree to which the new situation *resembles* and *is recognized* as the practiced one (Gibson, 1941). The similarity of the two situations may be in content, likeness of method or procedure, or commonness of aims. Thus the study of Latin may promote the learning of English vocabulary to the extent that similar or identical roots are a planned part of teaching and are recognized by the student (Maltzman, Eisman, and Brooks, 1956). Tennis experience and learnings—keeping away from the middle of the court and keeping the feet parallel, for example—facilitate learning to play handball.

This disarmingly simple explanation makes it seem that there is something within the situation itself that causes transfer. Actually, of course, it is something within the individual that causes transfer. If he has learned the habits involved so well that they have become a part of his reaction pattern, then transfer will be relatively great. Thus it appears that overlearning (see Glossary) is generally advantageous to transfer— overlearning an error will, of course, reduce positive transfer. But again taking Latin and English vocabulary as an example, *transfer depends in part upon the extent to which the learner perceives similarities between it and English.* This perception is most likely to occur if the teacher makes an effort to indicate what the common components are. He can prompt students to discover and enumerate the common components and the similarities between two situations. Problems that call for the use of previously learned facts in their solution may be presented.

Some transfer is automatic and will take place in spite of defective teaching. But maximum transfer is largely dependent upon effective teaching methods. The relatively intelligent pupil will see many similarities without help from the teacher. But the less intelligent will not perceive the similarity unless he receives some assistance, and even the bright pupil will probably see more relationships if the teacher gives some assistance. Knowledge of algebra as a technique for solving problems does not automatically carry over into the solution of political and social problems. Yet mathematics has been successfully taught as a method of problem solving in general. Fawcett (1938) reports that students were led to see that mathematics and problem solving have these elements in common: making assumptions, forming precise definitions, breaking the major problem into steps, and seeking proof of the derived conclusion. The experiment showed that the students who had studied geometry as a method of problem solving not only were superior in a statewide geometry test, but were able to transfer the techniques of practical reasoning to other areas. Those who defend the place of mathematics in the improvement of reasoning should realize that it is not mathematics that should be credited, but the method by which it is taught.

Transfer of Learning through Generalization If two learning situations have a high degree of similarity, the theory of common elements seems to provide an adequate explanation for transfer of learning. If, however, the degree of similarity is slight, transfer by generalization appears to be a more adequate explanation.

Stated briefly, the theory is that the degree of transfer depends upon the extent to which experiences in one situation are consolidated into generalizations. This theory is supported by memory experiments which have demonstrated that forgetting memorized nonsense syllables, meaningless numbers, and isolated words is most rapid, while forgetting prose or poetry is comparatively slow. Meaningful materials show the highest rates of retention because of the interrelationships, or generalizations, that bind ideas together. Thus there is greater likelihood of transfer from one situation to the next when generalizations, or principles, are mastered (Gibson, 1953).

Even though generalizations are stressed in the learning process, it is necessary for the learner to realize that the possibility of further application exists. If you want transfer, you must teach for it. For example, a student can memorize the growth principles (see Chapter 8), but if maximum transfer is to be made, he should be given numerous examples of the principle—in physical growth, mental development, the acquisition of knowledge, the evolution of personality, and the gaining of skill. Such generalization enhances the possibility of application of the principles to new learning conditions. Direct application, such as suggested below, will enhance both the likelihood of application and generalization of knowledge.

> There are plenty of educative opportunities: improving 50,000 ugly small towns; youth work camps in conservation and urban renewal; countervailing mass-communications with hundreds of little theaters, little radio, local paper; technical apprenticeships *within* the industries, paid by public and corporation, with the aim of making workmen who understand what they are doing and can be inventive; subsidizing small farms, to make them economically feasible and reverse the rural ratio to something nearer 30 per cent, instead of the present absurd 8 per cent; community service like Friends Service and Peace Corps. In such concrete activities, directly useful in society, millions of youth could find educational opportunity more tailored to their needs. Are they less cultural than the average classroom for the non-bookish kid? [4]

The theory of generalization stresses the importance of learning materials so that they may be related to subsequent experiences. In the target-shooting exercise described earlier, the principle of the refraction

[4] Paul Goodman, "Why Go to School?" *New Republic*, 149 (2550):14, 1963.

of light enabled the boys to adjust more readily to a change of depth. Since it is impossible to educate youth for specific future situations, learning that encompasses principles and broad generalizations is more productive than the memorization and recitation of isolated fact (Haselrud, 1958). And furthermore, if the student formulates his own version of the principle, this is superior to having the teacher give it (Kersh, 1958).

Your study of educational psychology illustrates the value of generalization in facilitating transfer. It should be obvious that this course will not give a direct answer to the problems you will encounter in teaching. But generalizations obtained through this course will help narrow your search for the appropriate key to a specific teaching situation, and the details of educational psychology will be quickly forgotten, except for the parts that can be related to your own *real* problems. In addition, your chances for success will depend partially on your appreciation of the import of generalization to your students. You will see that arithmetic teaching is most effective when the pupil understands the principles involved. In English composition, you will find that he writes more effectively when he comprehends the rules of grammar. Geometry problems can be solved—even when the letters on the figures are shifted—when the pupil "sees" the theorem.

Actually, explanation of transfer on the basis of common elements is not so different from explanation on the basis of generalization. The efficacy of generalization depends upon similarity between two situations, and pointing out common elements is in itself a concern of generalization. Further, the basic teaching consideration is the same in both. Transfer must be a planned objective.

Another explanation of transfer was postulated by W. C. Bagley (1911, p. 118), who felt that transfer is dependent on the formation of ideals. Pupils who have been encouraged to be neat and accurate on their arithmetic papers are not equally neat in presenting their spelling lessons. One principal found that emphasizing order on papers had small effect on litter in the classroom and hallways until neatness was emphasized as an ideal. This can also be interpreted as indicating the need for pointing out functional applications of what is studied (Capoferi, 1956).

Neatness is a relatively minor ideal; but love of learning, desire for knowledge, tolerance for differences of opinion, and eagerness to grow are ideals, or generalizations and principles, of continuing importance. These should be made conscious objectives of the teacher who seeks maximum values from the phenomenon of transfer.

Generalizations usually involve some inductive or analytic processes; they are formed from several specifics. All too typically, generalizations are formed from limited specifics. This can be tested in the classroom by an examination of racial stereotypes: "Negroes have no ambition,"

"You can't insult a Jew." [5] Instances are cited; counter instances are offered. In dealing with such situations, questions can be asked about the relator's experience. Other equally erroneous stereotypes can be offered—for example, Missourians and Idahoans, city children and country children, Presbyterians and Baptists. The question of what accurate generalizations can be made about any people may be asked.

The Gestalt View of Transfer   Gestalt psychology places emphasis on total patterns of behavior. Wholeness, or unity of response, is stressed. Strenuous objection is made to the notion of *parts* functioning in isolation. According to this view, transfer from old to new situations occurs when the individual recognizes them as being similar or when the common principles (generalizations) are understood (Andrews and Cronbach, 1962, p. 456). It is not just the presence of common components or the existence of encompassing generalizations, but also the response of the individual that constitute the integral whole of functional transfer.

One gestalt psychologist claims that what is called "transfer" consists essentially of some degree of duplication of response in two situations. Such duplication takes place under three possible conditions: (1) when the content is similar, (2) when there is a similarity in method, and (3) when attitudes (set) are comparable. Transfer occurs only when the similarity of the two tasks is such that the subject perceives them as a whole (Wheeler, 1940, pp. 264ff). Thus the intelligence of the subject, his perception, and the simplicity or complexity of the situation all combine to determine the amount of transfer. The combination of common elements, teaching methods, and the learner's response determines the amount and kind of transfer that occurs. Pupils who learned neatness in arithmetic did not transfer neatness to another situation because they did not perceive the similarity between situations. Obviously, they could not have had such perception if there had been no similarity. There can be little quarrel with the gestaltists that behavior patterns are the result of configurations of learnings. These configurations include the organism (emotions, mentality, physical makeup), the situation (teaching methods, school climate), and the response (particularly insight) of the organism to the situation. This view does not differ essentially from others—it does add materially to the needed emphasis on understanding as an aspect of transfer.

Intelligence and Transfer   Since transfer is dependent upon perception of relationships between situations, it is obvious that greater transfer will occur with more intelligent individuals (Blair, Jones, and Simpson, 1962, p. 285). To the extent that transfer takes place without teacher interven-

[5] See Boris M. Levinson, "Some Research Findings with Jewish Subjects of Traditional Background," *Mental Hygiene*, 47:129–134, 1963, for an examination of some culturally induced attitudes and self-concepts of the Jew.

tion and planning, it does so because the student can, by himself, see the relationships and common elements and pervasive principles.

Actually, the role of intelligence in transfer gives further justification to the admonition that we must teach for transfer. Let us assume that intelligence is a relatively fixed aspect of personality. Teachers are responsible for helping *all* pupils increase their ability to see the opportunities for greater transfer, and this includes directing their discovery of principles (Rowlett, 1960). You may ask, "How can I make transfer work for me right now?" Remember that both the student and the instructor are part of the teaching-learning situation. The student's desire to learn effectively, to secure maximum transfer, is as important as the skill of the teacher who points the way; the more completely he learns in situation A, the greater the likelihood that he will perceive its relationships to situation B. Learning something thoroughly facilitates transfer, so material should be reviewed and reflected upon by the student, generalizations should be sought, and attitudes should be examined. Lack of interest may reduce the drive devoted to a particular task (Kausler, 1951). Persons who are interested enough to organize their work gain better results; in turn, they gain a feeling of success and greater confidence. Increased confidence improves the chance for coping with the next situation. Hence, a chain of helpful circumstances stem from interest grounded in attitudes, ideals, and experiences. Transfer can no more be reduced to one or two factors than can learning in general.

Repudiation of the theory of mental discipline means that we no longer depend on the idea that the mind is improved by rigorous exercise. But the use that we make of the mentality we possess is influenced by our particular level of aspiration. We can seek through steady application to gain the common elements that make for transfer. We can analyze the source of our attitudes and try to improve attitudes that hinder maximum effectiveness. We can actively seek to perceive relationships. We can ask ourselves questions that will stimulate active response instead of passively accepting new experiences. The mistake made by both teachers and pupils in learning material verbatim and without comprehension should be avoided.

Teaching for the transfer of learning

You are encountering in the study of transfer one of the most important phenomena affecting your future vocation. Practical questions have been raised about the circumstances in which maximum transfer will take place: What teaching methods will be most productive of transfer? What subjects will contribute most to transfer? What do we want to transfer, and to what should it be transferred? This section is devoted to representative and suggestive answers to these basic questions.

Teaching Methods and Transfer The questions above pertain to methods of teaching. Subjects that seem to have great transfer value may actually have relatively little such value because of the methods by which they are taught. Subject matter must, of course, be learned *before* it can be transferred, and is therefore important. But subject matter without transfer is, at best, of transitory value. What is to be transferred and to what must be a consideration in determining instructional techniques.

1. *Significance of aims* Clearly defined aims are conducive to effective learning: The learner must know where he is going, and—even more important—so must the teacher, because he must aid the learner in gaining a clear perception of the objectives of his study. The attitudes the learner develops are a concern in all schoolwork—he should be confident, open minded, and eager to gain new knowledge; he should feel that he is a worthy and able person. Good work habits, such as system, thoroughness, perseverance, and determination, should be emphasized. An additional aim is a practical emphasis—knowledge and attitudes that will help to solve problems of adjustment both in and out of school—that is not restricted to immediate personal and social use but is related to the remote future as well. You will have the opportunity to see this, after a period of teaching experience when you review your text and notes for this course. Review your notes on motivation when one of your pupils submits some obviously cursory work. Read again about social class when a boy is sincere in jeering academic achievement. A year from now, select a chapter at random from your text and read it when you are on the job in a seventh grade to see if it has additional pertinence. Study again the discussion of individual differences when one of your pupils does the problem before you finish making the assignment, while another does not know which page you are on.

2. *The role of understanding* We have seen that transfer is greater with pupils of higher intelligence. It is important for the teacher to realize that intelligence is not indicated by the IQ, which is an indication of the present rate of mental growth, but by mental age (MA). The younger the pupil and the lower the MA, the more necessary it is to clarify principles, to help in the formulation of generalizations, and to indicate common factors in various situations. Students of the same chronological age vary greatly in their need for specific examples, concrete illustrations, and precise explanation.

At the elementary level particularly, pupils need to see models, mock-ups, and illustrations, to visit places and people and later discuss what they have seen. Such features make the "higher-horizons" program an educative experience (Schreiber, 1960). Of course, it must be remembered that verbalization is not equivalent to understanding, and testing verbalization occasionally is informative. At the secondary level, it will be well to see if the student can discuss and explain the report on crustaceans that he has written (often by copying with little alteration from a textbook or encyclopedia). Student discussion periods can do much to transfer verbalization to conceptualization—and test the transfer.

Understanding is improved by dealing with real problems. Many school patrons and some teachers who know techniques but are not well grounded in theory may object to the minimizing of drill in the classroom. But it must be emphasized that understanding is incomplete without application. But learning by doing has greater transfer value than learning by drill, and time spent in building birdhouses, making cookies for the school bazaar, visiting a museum, or discussing student government are productive of understanding—especially when transfer is emphasized. And arithmetic, language, and historical data can be related to problems close to the life of the student. But learning by doing can be as meaningless as drill. A teacher may decide that activity projects, field trips, and motion pictures are ways to prevent "mere verbalization," but these can be as fruitless as memorizing for mental discipline. The method of presenting material must be justified in terms of its facilitating transfer: Common elements between the movie and other school learnings and the child's life must be indicated; generalizations developed through discussion should follow the field trip or activity project.

3. *The role of process* It is not enough that pupils can verbalize the right answers to factual questions or give acceptable solutions to problems that are posed. Teachers should seek to have their pupils explain why they gave the answers they did. Pupils should be able to discuss the steps that led them to their answers—correct or incorrect. The skills of outlining, reading for varied purposes, making a written paragraph complete, taking tests, and techniques of study can be shown to be useful in many subjects. Similarly, if the process of logical thinking were made a constant focus in teaching (rather than emphasis only on outcome), as much could be accomplished as by changing the curriculum (Broudy, Smith, and Burnett, 1964, p. 101).

4. *The role of relationships* The author had two years of Latin in high school. The study was confined to declensions, conjugations, and translations. No attempt was made by the teacher to relate the study to English vocabulary. Today, few words "come through" as having Latin origins. Those who can define newly encountered English words in terms of such derivation are looked upon with a degree of jealousy. It is worth noting that such persons report that their teachers made a point of indicating relationships.

Recently an experienced teacher attended an advanced educational psychology class in which the importance of relating mathematics to everyday life was discussed. Later, in her own class, she departed from the text to discuss the practical applications of algebraic processes to bridge building, the timing of traffic lights, and the construction of water towers. After the class she remarked, "I felt that I was stealing time from the students because we did not work any of the supplementary exercises on pages 97 to 101." She failed to see that teaching algebra in connection with real-life situations was far more effective in both process and content than doing ready-made exercises. Despite her skill in showing the relationships of algebra to commerce and industry, she felt guilty about not covering the text.

These anecdotes are not intended as a plea for abandoning Latin and algebra because they are sterile for some. The point is that unless the teacher can find and explain common elements in various types of subject matter, then he certainly needs to refresh and refurbish his knowledge of his subject. A little practice and experience soon reveal that the burden of teaching can be lightened and the joy of learning increased by emphasizing transfer values.

5. *Thorough learning aids transfer* Thorough learning includes seeing what has been learned in several settings. It includes rote repetition. Citing many examples and relating older learnings to more recent acquisitions consolidates learning. Maximum transfer is thus obtained from thorough instruction (Hendrickson and Schroeder, 1941).

The teaching implications are clear. Time spent on thorough learning is profitable in terms of the wider ramifications of learning. Review, drill, discussion of pertinent problems, and the presentation of examples—whether in arithmetic, social studies, or science—increase the degree of learning and thus foster transfer. We need not reflect very deeply on our own educational experiences to realize that the anxiety of teachers to "cover" subject matter has often resulted in our own superficial and incomplete learning. Teachers at all levels, from the primary grades to college, become concerned about completing the lesson. They "cover ground" by resorting to lectures that leave the students bewildered. More time spent in elaborating on the materials that are covered leads to better understanding and to overlearning (see Chapter 6, section on Overlearning) and increases the amount that will be retained. In the final analysis, you cannot teach it all in any event. Let the pupils discover some of it themselves; it has been found that independent discovery shows transfer that is superior to instruction in which the teacher gave the rules, facts, and principles (Kersh, 1958).

6. *Emphasis on principles* The statement of a principle is a means of compressing many factors and conditions. A principle may consolidate a number of apparently discrete instances or practices into a single generalization. Because of the nature of the principle, it is not sufficient simply to state it, memorize it, or read it from a book. It is necessary to understand the many factors and instances that have gone into its formulation.

As educators, we hope to see our instruction extend beyond the schoolhouse walls. An approach to this goal is to take advantage of the phenomenon of transfer by emphasizing the formation of generalizations. The pupil must see a number of situations to which a particular principle may be applied. The use of numerous examples helps. A variety of approaches helps. Exceptions to the generalization may be noted. However, teachers must avoid giving too much direction in what the basic principles are. It has been found that more is retained and transferred when there is an intermediate amount of direction (Kittell, 1957).

The importance of stressing principles has immediate implications for you. Instead of studying to learn facts, seek and master the basic principles and generalizations that govern those facts. Develop a healthy respect for the so-called "theory courses." Thus the study of educational psychology should find its major justification in terms of underlying principles that will be operative in many and different situations. By attuning yourself now to the importance of this "representative" approach, you will find it easier to direct your subsequent teaching to the significant items in learning.

7. *Emphasis on attitudes and ideals* A sharp line of distinction cannot be drawn between principles and ideals. Ideals are principles, or generalizations, that tend to shape the individual's course of activity. The teacher's work includes modifying ideals that extend beyond a particular subject area. Thus many teachers draw up both tentative and final units of study and state precisely what attitudes and ideals they hope to promote. Such a statement may include the following:

   a. Inculcating ideals of social cooperation
   b. Increasing appreciation of music, art, drama, and literature
   c. Developing a respect for methods of critical thinking
   d. Establishing effective work habits and study skills
   e. Expanding the pupil's range of constructive interests
   f. Respecting differences of opinion and conflicting information
   g. Learning to appreciate conditions of mental and physical health
   h. Developing a wholesome philosophy of life

The statement of ideals and attitudes is only a beginning step. It is necessary that each ideal be broken down into precise and specific acts. Thus ideals of social cooperation might be thought of in terms of specific acts, such as courteous listening, working as a chairman or participant in a small group, keeping one's equipment out of the way of others, observing rules that are formulated for the safety and welfare of all, disregarding skin color, race, religion, and economic status, and respecting varied convictions. Willingness to help others and the observance of rules of etiquette also receive attention. In addition, students and teachers should be thinking of wider applicability of these ideals to life away from school.

Experimental data indicate that such ideals as these cannot be achieved simply as a matter of ordinary procedures. Ideals must be a specific teaching objective (Allport, 1952). One needs to watch a class group for only a short period to realize that ideals are not achieved automatically. Teachers who stress ideals foster such development in pupils. Those who depend upon "catching" ideals are likely to see considerable fumbling. Two aspects of the problem of transfer through ideals need to be emphatically stressed: (1) Ideals are among the more important outcomes of formal teaching; and (2) the outcomes are more likely to be achieved if they are directly and specifically sought.

8. *The role of expectation*   An experiment showing the significance of set, or *Einstellung*, has pertinence for transfer. Six problems to be solved by the formula B minus A minus $2C$ were presented to several subjects. One problem was: Obtain 100 pints of water with three different-sized vessels of $A-21$, $B-127$, and $C-3$ pint capacity. The seventh problem was: Obtain twenty pints with vessels of $A-23$, $B-49$, and $C-3$ pint capacity. Of eleven graduate students and college instructors who tried the problem, none shifted from the B minus A minus $2C$ formula to the simpler one, A minus C (Luchins and Luchins, 1959).

You may simply warn: "Don't be rigid," "Vary your attack," "Look for opportunities for transfer," "Give further examples," and increase the transfer value of what you teach. This preparation, or set, will facilitate transfer, whether by generalization, common components, ideals, processes, or by combinations of all or several of them.

Subject Matter and Transfer   The majority of girls attending high school will become wives and mothers within a period of five years after graduation. Yet curricula give the impression that courses in history or foreign language are more important than a course in marriage and family relationships. Family life is too important to be left to the phenomenon of transfer. The consensus is that an individual's personality and character are largely dependent upon his early home environment; therefore, a healthful family relationship is essential to children's mental health. Yet preparation for family responsibility too frequently fails to find a solid place in the curriculum.

This apparent digression from the subject is to emphasize an important fact about transfer: The greatest gain in any study results from direct emphasis. Family-life education merits direct study. If ideals are important, they should be a direct aim in teaching. The relationship between vocabulary and thinking shows that vocabulary merits direct study—transfer from foreign languages is not sufficient. Emphasis on thinking should not be limited to transfer from mathematics; it should be a direct concern of all teaching. All subjects should be taught so that students learn the art of raising and answering pertinent questions.

Curriculum making is a continuous process. A definitive description of the ideal course of study cannot be given. As times change, so will the basic areas of the curriculum change. But to teach specifically and directly all that the student will eventually have to learn is impossible. If it could be done, the result would be training—leaving no flexibility, no adaptability for novel situations. "Transfer" implies modification and adaptation. For the present, let us be concerned with some illustrations for making the curriculum of maximum usefulness.

Mathematics can and should be taught as a method of thinking. It involves fundamental operations *plus* basic working principles. A student who says, "I added because there were five numbers listed, and you can divide or subtract only where there are two numbers," obviously does not see the problem clearly. Moreover, teachers may use mathematics as an approach to problems that are not ordinarily considered mathematical (Fawcett, 1938). Both thinking and mathematics consist of making assumptions, gathering data, testing the hypothesis, and formulating a conclusion. Mathematics thus provides fertile ground for developing critical thinking, working skills, constructive interests, skill in gathering data, and love of knowledge.

Grammar should be studied from the standpoint of the expression of ideas and the facilitation of communication. Many teachers realize this, but occasionally get lost in the maze of tense, mood, and voice. These are the concomitants of expression and communication; yet all too frequently they have been regarded as the sole basis of English usage and composition. Teachers who view language study as a means for facilitating communication are concerned about transfer *from* expression and communication *to* correct grammatical usage. It is not a matter of choice between grammar and the exchange of ideas, but of the method most likely to motivate the pupil.

Science does teach the need for caution, the importance of suspended judgment, and the necessity for accumulating many data in the solution of a problem *in the area being studied*. But investigations show that the study of science does not improve thinking in general. Obviously, therefore, teachers must stimulate transfer of scientific thinking to areas other than the immediate subject.

Illustrative of the objectives that should be sought in the study of science are those summarized in an investigation for the National Education Association: Teachers should be promoting growth in understanding the generalizations of science; attention should be directed to growth in abilities involved in using the methods of science, which involve—

> . . . perceiving a problem, relating problems to previous experience, formulating hypotheses, testing hypotheses, deriving a conclusion, and applying generalizations . . . one who possesses these abilities would be able to recognize conflicts with previous experience; state

problems in his own words; define the problem; infer; select the most logical guess; differentiate among hypothesis, fact, superstition, and theory; clarify; organize data; devise experiments; establish experimental controls; generalize from specified data; and use generalizations in interpreting new situations.[6]

Finally, science teaching seeks to stimulate growth in scientific attitudes —questioning, seeking reliable information, suspending judgments, and acting on tentative conclusions.

Whatever the subject matter, psychological evidence makes it clear that transfer is a continuing problem for teachers. All teachers must be concerned about methods of teaching and increasing the pupils' confidence, the improvement of thought processes, and the development of socially oriented attitudes and ideals. There is no implication that subject matter is unimportant or even secondary. The implication is that broader educational values must be raised to the level of importance of the subject matter.

Nonspecific Transfer The foregoing discussion has dealt largely with the specific transfer of attitudes, skills, or knowledges. Some other aspects of transfer are of both theoretical and practical interest (White, 1963, p. 217). Transfer can take place between activities that are quite unlike; for instance, there is a short-term facilitation known as "warmup." The teacher, after an invigorating play period, might read a story or show a movie before moving on to having pupils work on arithmetic problems or write a story.

Methods of learning are a second type of nonspecific transfer. Many study techniques are the same for several subjects, but not many students —even college students—outline their responses on a written examination as they would if they were writing a story or theme. Neither do they realize that learning to use carpentry tools is in many ways similar to learning a new language—vocabulary is new, practice is necessary, application is an aid, confidence is necessary. If one has learned to learn, he can apply the knowledge to an English assignment, conducting a meeting, learning a part-time job, or even learning to raise children. Some of the things that should be considered in general methods of learning include making an overview, defining goals precisely, seeking understanding, searching for relationships and implications, attempting to make applications (at least imaginary ones), assuming responsibility for independence and initiative, and planning and organizing efforts. These things can be learned and can be taught—thus facilitating transfer.

Much has been said about reinforcing correct responses, but some

[6] J. Darrell Barnard, *Teaching High School Science*, What Research Says to the Teacher, no. 10, Washington: National Education Association, 1956, p. 9.

studies indicate that learning can be facilitated if pupils also have their errors clearly indicated (Stevenson, Weir, and Zigler, 1959). Logan (1963) has suggested that learning to learn be made more specific by simultaneously emphasizing not only learning the right and the wrong way but also the speed of performance. This has been recognized to some extent in reading (see Chapter 7), typewriting, handwriting, and performance in the laboratory. Much wasted time results from not deliberately teaching for improved speed after the initial need for a careful approach has been passed.

A third type of nonspecific transfer is emotional carry-over, which can be a positive, responsive predisposition or frustrated withdrawal—witness the child who declines to answer the teacher because he is angry with his best friend. Studies of emotional carry-over have been made only on short-term bases; there is the possibility, however, that this kind of transfer is manifest in what is called a "learning block" (White, 1963, p. 218).

Transfer and Out-of-school Life Most investigations of transfer have dealt with the extent to which learning of one subject facilitates the learning of another. More important is the extent to which the study of any subject transfers to life out of school. No doubt, some subjects make a greater contribution to daily living than others. However, carefully selected teaching methods, plus cooperatively determined (involving curriculum experts, teachers, and pupils) specific objectives can increase the amount of transfer to the wider problems of life. Problems that are removed from the immediate environs of the school will naturally arise: How should I get along with my family? How will I use leisure time? How shall I choose a career? How can I improve my personality? More teachers should be concerned with such problems. Implications may be drawn from science, mathematics, social studies, literature, and art for all these problems, and the bearing of these subjects on the life of the individual must be presented as clearly as possible.

Schoolwork need not be motivated only by the practical. Some scholars have presented the thesis that knowledge need not always be pursued with utilitarian values in mind. W. B. Cannon (1940) points out that important discoveries have been made by persons with inquisitive minds who were not looking for practical information but who, nevertheless, perceived important relationships in what they studied. Abraham Flexner, in an article titled "Usefulness of Useless Knowledge" (1939), calls attention to the fact that Einstein, Marconi, Pasteur, Ehrlich, and others were motivated by curiosity. Furthermore, they carried their work forward from a point that had been reached by others who were similarly curious. Future progress, too, will often come as the result of "intellectual adventuring."

If the child or adolescent asks, "What is the use for this or that?" we should try to answer him. On the other hand, there are pupils who are curious—their active mental processes drive them to seek answers *for the sake of obtaining answers*. We can encourage such pupils by permitting them to use the information they have acquired. We can praise their initiative and resourcefulness. For pupils who are less perceptive, teachers are even more responsible for promoting transfer. If a teacher cannot justify teaching a certain subject to his pupils in terms of challenge or usefulness, he ought to give up teaching that subject. It is indeed a poor teacher who cannot find excellent reasons for teaching his subject.

Summary

Transfer of learning is the influence that existing habits, skills, attitudes, or ideals have in retarding or facilitating new learnings. Without transfer, education would be specific, duplicative, and limited. It would have no effect on the expansion and integration of knowledge. The teacher's job in the absence of transfer could be likened to that of an animal trainer. Transfer is the cornerstone on which creative, productive, expanding education is built.

Transfer may be either negative or positive, but instances of the former are few compared with the numerous examples of positive transfer. Mental discipline, which holds that the mind (consisting of faculties) is sharpened or strengthened by vigorous exercise of faculties, should be distinguished from transfer. Mental discipline is an outmoded idea; currently, transfer is explained on the basis of elements or components that are common to two situations, on the existence of generalizations that pervade and influence the new and the old, on the basis of ideals that are inclusive, and on the extent to which an individual's intelligence allows him to perceive the common factors, generalizations, and pervasive ideals.

The theoretical explanations of transfer provide the framework for educational implications and practice. These explanations have been verified in experimental as well as classroom situations. Some of the practical suggestions for improving the amount of positive transfer include the following: Establish clear-cut goals, point out the components (both facts and processes) that are common in various contexts, encourage the understanding of principles, challenge pupils to formulate their own principles (self-discovery), indicate varied applications of common ideals, help pupils develop a set—anticipation—that seeks opportunities for transfer, and encourage the overlearning that makes facts and principles more readily available to new situations.

Individual courses and the curriculum as a whole should be periodically reexamined to see if greater positive transfer to life out of school might be achieved. It must be concluded, however, that it is not the subject that facilitates transfer in the final analysis. It is the teacher's perception of and emphasis on the many avenues of transfer that results in maximum benefit from this pervasive and important phenomenon.

Problems and exercises

1 Why do many schools continue to require the study of Latin, formal grammar, and abstract mathematics, when experimental findings indicate that the supposed disciplinary results do not exist?

2 Suggest a number of specific things that you, as a student of educational psychology, could do to augment the transfer values of the course in educational psychology.

3 What curriculum suggestions do you have that would bring about maximum transfer of learnings?

4 Suggest a number of things that might be done to broaden transfer values from the teaching of reading at the third-grade level.

5 In view of the phenomenon of negative transfer, what precautions should the teacher observe?

6 In terms of your own experience, indicate the operation of transfer. What explanations for the occurrence do you have?

7 What implications for transfer are presented in the statement "Traits of character tend to be specific"?

8 Suggest some ways in which pupils may be encouraged to develop a set that is conducive to transfer.

9 Criticize or defend the statement "All school subjects should be taught with transfer values in mind."

Suggested additional readings

Deese, James: *The Psychology of Learning*, 2d ed., New York: McGraw-Hill Book Company, 1958, pp. 213–235.

The psychological processes involved in transfer are examined by describing experimental investigations. Difficulty, ability, learning techniques, and teaching methods are among the topics discussed.

Kolesnik, Walter B.: *Mental Discipline in Modern Education*, Madison, Wis.: The University of Wisconsin Press, 1958.

In normal operation, making a distinction between transfer and mental discipline is difficult. The modern view is that intellectual development derives not so much from content as from procedure.

Krathwohl, David P.: "The Psychological Bases for Integration," *The Integration of Educational Experiences*, Fifty-seventh Yearbook of the National Society for the Study of Education, Chicago: The University of Chicago Press, 1958, Part III, pp. 43–65.

The guiding principles for facilitating integrative behavior could easily and logically be substituted for the suggestions for facilitating transfer that have been presented in this chapter. Krathwohl's chapter is an excellent example of transfer.

Stephens, J. M.: "Transfer of Learning," *Encyclopedia of Educational Re-*

search, rev. ed., New York: The Macmillan Company, 1960, pp. 1535–1543.

Experiments point the way to improved school practices that will increase the amount and utility of transfer at all levels.

Travers, Robert M. W.: "Transfer of Training," *Essentials of Learning,* New York: The Macmillan Company, 1963, pp. 187–218.

This chapter describes some of the basic research and models that give rise to the explanation of how and under what conditions transfer takes place. Classroom implications are indicated.

Problem Solving and Creativity

Abundant, challenging, and varied experiences must be provided in the classroom. These experiences should be designed to suggest, imply, represent, and resemble rather than duplicate out-of-school situations. Approaches to problems rather than answers to them should be a serious concern of teachers, for life after school will bring problems that have not been anticipated in the best classrooms. If intelligence is to attain its highest potential, it must be used for more than remembering, imitating, and trial-and-error experimenting. If the individual is to realize his capacity for uniqueness, he must be able to create novel responses. If citizens and statesmen are to keep their government dynamic, healthy tradition and custom must be guides rather than rules. If society is to continue to evolve, individuals must be able to adapt to changing conditions. In short, individual and social evolution is dependent upon the ability to think, to reason, and to solve problems.

Teachers in a democratic society should be acutely aware of the nature of problem solving so that they can give effective guidance to pupils in the development of this significant ability (Wolfle, 1962, p. i). In totalitarian societies, it is probably advantageous for pupils to learn by rote answers that have been prepared in advance by "experts." But in our society, the desirable citizen is the one who questions, criticizes, judges, evaluates, investigates present procedures, and suggests means of improvement. This chapter deals with factors that contribute to originality and resourcefulness.

Basic concepts

Thinking Popular usage of the word "thinking" is less discriminating than the usage desirable in the study of educational psychology. The statement "I think I'll take a walk" does not necessarily involve thought processes that will reduce the complexities of a rapidly changing world. The individual could have said, "I'm going for a walk," and the meaning would have been the same. It is true that the individual may mentally "see" himself taking a walk, but no problem is involved. Similarly, one might say, "I cannot think of the title of the book." Again, no problem is to be solved; the individual could have said, "I do not recall the title." The mental process of memory is involved, but there is no novel situation to be resolved. There are, however, popular usages that make thinking synonymous with problem solving, as when a person says, "I'll think your proposition over." He means that he will take some time to weigh, evaluate, and rearrange the elements of the situation in such a manner as to come to a conclusion. This conclusion will enable him to make a choice or a decision. Thinking is the course and train of ideas, the recall and reorganization of facts and theories, that occur when the individual is faced by obstacles or problems. Thinking involves dealing with abstractions, the not yet tangible, and these abstractions are manipulated by means of symbols. Words and numbers, formulas, and diagrams supplemented by words are the symbols. This dealing with the train of ideas, or abstractions, through the use of symbols is the interpretation of "thinking" that is used in this chapter.

Daydreaming Daydreaming is a mental process in which the mind "wanders freely," but is not oriented toward some particular goal. The individual is probably engaged in recalling and imagining, and he may be visualizing situations, but he is not typically conscious of seeking a specifically defined goal. The expression "He is lost in thought" may, of course, mean that he is concentrating deeply upon some problem, but it may simply mean that his "mind" is wandering freely as a result of immediate and objective stimuli. If thinking involves visualization and perception without immediately present stimuli, we say that the individual is engaged in autistic thinking or daydreaming.

Daydreaming as a desirable mode of response should not be summarily dismissed. In his book *The Sleepwalkers,* Koestler (1959) indicates that important discoveries have been made when a person was not "sticking to the subject," when accidental rumination rather than logical thought was the prevailing mental activity. There can be values in sleepwalking in the midst of reality.

Reasoning The word is widely used to describe what many psychologists are referring to when they use the word "thinking." In fact, many psychologists avoid the word "thinking" and use "reasoning" in its place. Reasoning is the process involved in working toward the solution of a problem, the answer to which is not immediately supplied by past experience. Three elements in this process deserve particular consideration. The first element is time. Reasoning involves the *delay* of a response while the reasoner assembles, arranges, and rearranges the information needed for the solution of the problem. The second element is the information itself. Reasoning takes place *only* when the facts pertinent to a solution are known. If a solution is stumbled upon, it is only a trial-and-error answer. The third element is the goal toward which reasoning is directed. These elements can be placed together to form a definition of reasoning: A process of delaying responses until data are arranged into a new combination so that a novel solution to a problem is perceived.

Creativity The man on the street tends to use the word "creativity" in connection with unusual and novel ideas, inventions, constructions, or productions. Some psychologists and educators are less demanding, claiming that creativity is manifested when an individual discovers an idea that is new for him, produces a new word combination, or adapts his behavior to a new setting (Kilpatrick, 1935, p. 4). To be useful, that is, to give the term some power of differentiation—"creativity" should be distinguished from other words, such as "intelligence," "adaptation," and "learning." Thus, the use of "creativity" in connection with the unusual, the "peculiar twist," or the distinctive and novel seems justifiable. High intelligence and creativity are not synonymous because some (perhaps most) bright people tend toward convergence or conformity. The creative person is divergent and adventuresome.

Torrance puts the word and concept on a higher level than the mere contrivance of an individual response by defining creativity as "the process of sensing gaps of disturbing, missing elements; forming ideas of hypotheses concerning them; testing these hypotheses; communicating the results, possibly modifying and retesting the hypotheses." [1] He intends, in this definition, to include adventurous, off-the-beaten-track thinking. Creativity involves a search for new meanings and solutions that combine, invent, and synthesize. It is a restructuring of the perceptual field as the result of sensing some kind of deficiency. An example of this is the case of a boy who was failing in school, withdrawing from athletics, and becoming socially isolated. He literally drew himself back into school activities with his drawing, illustrating poetry, depicting football games, and drawing social scenes (all of which revealed and released his feelings). Finally, he was achieving satisfactorily; previously, most of his teachers had thought him to be "dumb." Another example is the fascinating classroom account by a high school girl of her travels in Sweden—down to the details of temperature, distances walked, people met, communication problems overcome. The author discovered after class was over that this was simply an assigned report in social studies. But it had been handled in a way that was typical for this girl.

Tentative Answers It is said that the completely logical person is not a man of action, a statement based on the assumption that the completely

[1] E. Paul Torrance, *Guiding Creative Talent*, © 1962 by Prentice-Hall, Inc., Englewood Cliffs, N.J. p. 16. By permission.

logical person requires absolute answers to problems before he is willing to act and on the fact that there are no ultimate, unalterable answers. The logical person knows that not all the data are gathered, not all the situations have been defined, and not all the events in an individual's life have been accounted for. Because *all* the data will never be gathered or *all* the alternatives explored, it is necessary to act on tentative conclusions. These tentative conclusions may be regarded as best current guesses, and because they are based on some data, they will be better than stabs in the dark. But experience, evaluation, and changes in accompanying conditions will alter the conclusions, which in turn become a set of improved tentative answers that form the basis for ensuing action. We cannot be practical (in the sense of getting something done) and hold action in abeyance until the answers are complete and indisputably correct.

Reasoning demands that action be checked but not stopped. As individuals trying to achieve our own maximum potential and as teachers trying to help pupils toward better adjustment, we must stress the necessity of learning to act on tentative conclusions. It must be realized that there is a need for balance between what *might* be done about a problem and what *is* done about it. Logical and tentative answers must be put into practice. There may be no ultimate solution, but there is, in all probability, a satisfactory one.

Factors involved in reasoning

Maturation   Different types of problems of different degrees of difficulty may be resolved by the process of reasoning. A young child may assemble jointed sticks to reach an object that is otherwise beyond his reach, but he would find the solution of an algebra problem much too difficult. This difference in ability to solve problems indicates that an important factor in reasoning is maturation. It takes time for the brain and perceptual powers to develop to the point where relationships can be perceived. Moreover, maturation must be accompanied by the accumulation of experience. Here again, we see at work the growth principle— growth is the product of the interaction of the organism with its environment (see Chapter 8).

The part played by maturation in problem solving is of much more than academic interest to teachers. In practice, the situations presented to pupils must be appropriate to their developmental level (Wann, Dorn, and Liddle, 1962, p. 98). Problems that are too difficult will result in blind behavior, retreat, or frustration (Jack, 1934). Blind behavior is illustrated in psychological experiments when a cat in a box slashes about wildly with no semblance of systematic searching or directed effort.

Children show the same reaction when their efforts to open a box are futile, and they tearfully beat the box or the cover. Retreat, or "leaving the field," is illustrated by either actually abandoning the situation or retiring within oneself (as the college student does when he daydreams during an incomprehensible lecture). Pupils in school leave the field by engaging in horseplay when they should be working at their arithmetic or algebra problems. Frustration in children is evidenced by such symptoms as withdrawing, thumb-sucking, and temper tantrums. All warn the teacher that more appropriate challenges should be presented.

Problems appropriate to the pupil's developmental level aid him in acquiring confidence. He grows in the ability to attack more difficult problems and learns the value of a systematic approach to difficulties. The teacher, bearing in mind the importance of problem-solving ability, will (1) show how the problems have some personal meaning, (2) stress the value of *doing* something in addition to knowing something, (3) indicate the relationship of facts to solutions, (4) teach the specific principles involved, and (5) identify the experiences that serve as the basis for those principles (McLendon, 1960, p. 18).

It would be gratifying if we could draw up a list of age-graded maturational tasks that would serve as a guide to teachers in various grades. But research in grade placement, acceleration, and retention in a grade show that maturation is only one factor among many in a pupil's school success. (For example, repeating a grade—thus gaining a year's maturation for the pupil—often appears to result in less progress than would going on to the next grade.) Success is also dependent on experience (see next section) and the teacher's skill in making material meaningful or challenging. Normal three-year-olds have learned to read (Pines, 1963), and elementary pupils have learned algebra; thus no scheme of school organization, however carefully detailed, will provide for the range of differences found at any one school grade or level of maturation (Goodlad, 1962, p. 210).

Experience Maturation and experience are inseparable aspects of problem solving. All reasoning depends on information, as well as on the brain power necessary to utilize that information. People are often considered good thinkers simply because they have experience and information that enable them to deal constructively with a situation. Thus readiness for problem solving is dependent to a very large extent upon a background of experience. The dependence of reasoning on experience suggests four widespread teaching practices that are inimical to reasoning.

1. Rote learning does not foster the development of powers of reasoning; in fact, it makes for negative transfer. Criticism of rote learning

has been made in many connections, but nowhere is the criticism more pertinent than in the context of developing reasoning ability.

In studying how subjects solved a match puzzle (making four squares by moving three of sixteen matches, which originally made five squares), Katona found that knowing the principle involved not only improved immediate results but resulted in still greater improvement after four weeks. He concluded that learning with understanding improves retention and the ability to move forward, or transfer, to another task. Only when the attempt to understand and organize fails is it necessary for the pupil to resort to rote learning (Katona, 1940). The necessity for comprehension is obvious in problem solving, memory, motivation, and transfer; yet many teachers fail to grasp the significance of understanding and are satisfied with verbalization.

If thinking is to take place, the search for information must not be limited by a course of study or by what the teacher deems to be important. The pupil sees learning in a different perspective. The teacher must, therefore, be patient when pupils seem to wander from the subject. Guidance is needed, certainly, but the school must be a laboratory where experiences pertinent to the particular individual are provided. Then education will truly become the reconstruction of experience, which leads to more and effective learning. The role of experience has been summarized in four steps: (1) Children should have continuous experience; (2) experiences should be recorded; (3) experiences should be related through pupil activity; and (4) experiences should be meaningful so that pupils will achieve insight (Blackwood, 1951).

These remarks should not be misinterpreted as a recommendation that facts should be neglected. Data, facts, and knowledge are the tools for and materials of thinking. But repeating the names of the Presidents in order, listing the classifications of insects, or memorizing the theorems in geometry is learning of a limited type. Unless the facts are learned in terms of the individual's own experience, in terms of his understanding of their meaning and importance, in terms of his problems and needs, they are useless in developing his power to analyze, interpret, and synthesize (Tiller, 1962). From the very beginning of the school experience, it is possible to present children with understandable situations about which they are willing and able to learn. Experience, it must be remembered, is a personal affair. Significant problems and significant learning can be stated only in terms of the individual pupil.

2. Another factor inimical to the development of reasoning is the teacher's excessive dependence on imaginary problems. The study of mental discipline and transfer of training indicates that performance of mental exercises is not necessarily carried over to other situations. Emphasis must be on *real* problems that confront the pupil, and stress must be placed on methods of solutions—the sources of information, the classifying of

data, the weighing of relative merits of sources of information. Thus study of any problem should not stop with answers from a textbook; it should include training in the use of encyclopedias and other reference books and emphasize the value of consulting experts. If these methods are stressed, the pupil will be prepared to approach such problems as "How can citizens make their wants known to their elected representatives?" or "How can a hobby be made a source of financial profit?" These problems are quite different from "How many 1-inch cubes will have three red faces, how many will have two red faces, and how many will have one red face if a 3-inch red cube is cut so that there are twenty-seven 1-inch cubes?" The carry-over value of such a problem is negligible. The exercises at the end of the chapters in this book can be artificial if they are answered in terms of "intuitive beliefs." The reader who reflects on his past experiences, consults others about their views, reviews the textbook, and consults supplementary references is forming habits of problem solving that have current and future value.

3. The teacher's desire to answer pupils' questions is another practice that is inimical to encouraging reasoning ability. This tendency is rooted in the psychological orientation of the teacher. If he feels somewhat insecure, he will be afraid that not answering the question will cause the pupil to think less highly of him (Wiggins, 1957, p. 66). A seventh-grade pupil, on the other hand, lost respect for a teacher who told his class that meteorology was the study of meteors. If the teacher is sure of himself or has the requisite knowledge to answer the question, he can with confidence say, "That's a good question for you to study. I'd like to know more about it myself. See what the encyclopedia has to say about it and let me know." Another approach might be to say, "I have some very definite ideas about the problem, but before I tell you what they are I wish you'd formulate an answer—then we'll see how well we agree." Certainly, the teacher is nipping a good educational opportunity in the bud if he answers questions in order to prove himself. Where the teacher has personal knowledge, he might well give answers; but where the question is recognizably part of the field being studied, it is probable that the answer should be withheld.

4. Problems inappropriate to the pupils' level of experience do not stimulate reasoning. The necessity that the teacher observe his pupils to see that problems are meaningful to them has been exceptionally well stated by William James:

> Let us give the name of *hypothesis* to anything that may be proposed to our belief; and just as the electricians speak of live and dead wires, let us speak of any hypothesis as either *live* or *dead*. A live hypothesis is one which appeals as a real possibility to him to whom it is proposed. If I ask you to believe in the Mahdi, the notion makes no electric connection with your nature—it refuses to

scintillate with any credibility at all. As an hypothesis it is completely dead. To an Arab, however (even if he be not one of the Mahdi's followers), the hypothesis is among the mind's possibilities; it is alive. This shows that deadness and liveness in an hypothesis are not intrinsic properties, but relations to the individual thinker. They are measured by his willingness to act.[2]

If the word "problem" is substituted for "hypothesis" in the foregoing passage, the teacher will see that what is a problem to him is not necessarily pertinent for the pupil who has had less or different experience.

Data   Students have objected to examinations in educational psychology that called for stating facts and principles: "You told us that the important thing was to develop the ability to reason." This would be a valid objection if the facts were treated as isolated bits of information or as words to be memorized. But it must be clearly understood that reasoning —in educational psychology and in all other areas—must always depend on facts; the more pertinent the facts, the more direct and incisive the reasoning. A respect for facts is, of course, an important attitude to be developed in school. When pupils get into discussions and arguments, the teacher should ask them to compare the effectiveness of those who marshal the facts and those who make their emphasis simply by means of loudness. Pupils should learn that in evaluating facts, research articles are superior to popular articles; that newspaper accounts are often slanted; and that first-hand accounts are superior to hearsay and rumor. Teachers should commend those who have done research and utilized the findings. When teaching methods provide guidance in the search for facts, suggest syntheses of information, pose new interpretations of material, and provisionally tie factual knowledge into new combinations, a problem-solving attitude is fostered (Thompson, 1959, p. 297). Facts at the recitation level are less useful and less readily remembered.

Scientific investigations—whether in the realm of the natural sciences, education, or psychology—point to the fact that ample data are requisite to problem solving. Scientists emphasize that the solution to problems must necessarily be hidden somewhere in or among the data. If the answer is not discovered, there are only two explanations: (1) The data are as yet insufficient, and (2) the investigator lacks the insight to see the answer. There is no inherent contradiction between learning facts and learning to think.

If we were to differentiate between education and training (and it will be admitted that training has its place), we could safely say that the aim of education is to foster problem-solving ability. This inclusive aim

---

[2] *The Philosophy of William James: Selected from His Chief Works,* New York: Random House, Inc., no date, p. 158. The passage was taken from William James, *The Will to Believe,* 1897.

can only be accomplished if three factors—maturation, personal experience, and the systematic gathering of knowledge—are considered. Only then will pupils gain the preparation to face problems that are not specifically included within the school curriculum, and only then can teachers presume that they have fulfilled their duty in a democratic society.

Steps in problem solving

When one reflects on the many inventions, theories, practices, and situations resulting from reasoning, it is quite obvious that problem solving cannot easily be resolved into a series of orderly steps. Too many factors and processes are involved to permit more than an academic statement. Certain steps will be discussed in this section, but it must be remembered that in a given reasoning process the steps may be rearranged or two or more steps may be taken simultaneously. Nevertheless, it is helpful to understand what the steps are, even though they are taken in reverse or mixed order.

A Felt Need The first step, before the individual projects himself into a problem-solving situation, is a felt need: "The difficulty may be felt with sufficient definiteness as to set the mind at once speculating upon its probable solution, or an undefined uneasiness and shock may come first, leading only later to a definite attempt to find out what is the matter." [3]

Many attempts to teach pupils how to think fail at this initial stage. Problems that pupils do not comprehend and that have no personal meaning are given. Because they do not understand, there can be no felt need. The consequences are superficial performance of the task and dependence upon adult authority for the answer. There is a place for teacher direction and assistance, but the starting point is a problem that pupils can understand and with which they can identify.

Locating or Recognizing a Problem Situation A problem is not a problem because of external conditions alone. The payment of income tax may be a problem for an adult. The payment of the tax may actually in some way interfere with the child's easy adjustment, but is not a problem until recognized as such. A problem, therefore, is an obstacle to adjustment that is recognized by the individual. The more clearly an individual can state the nature of his difficulty, the more likely he is to solve it.

Because problems exist only in terms of the experience of the individual, it can be seen that the teacher's eagerness to *give* answers is inimical to thinking. It is not surprising that pupils in permissive classrooms do more hypothesizing than those who learn to depend on authority (Atkin,

[3] John Dewey, *How We Think,* Boston: D. C. Heath and Company, 1910, p. 72.

1958). The pupil must be allowed to wrestle with situations before he can see the inherent obstacles. If the teacher gives the solution immediately, the time necessary for the student's understanding of the problem is too short. Many authorities complain that teachers are so much concerned with pouring information into students that little time is left for them to ask questions. Teachers are so anxious to provide answers that the pupils' techniques for formulating and asking questions are neglected. Psychologists and teachers who are interested in the future adjustment of pupils as well as in their present behavior must recognize that the questions pupils ask help to develop a lifelong kind of education. Gifted underachievers are too frequently those who resist the conformity demanded by some teachers in "lesson hearing" (Stern, 1962).

The Accumulation of Data   A prime responsibility of teachers is to instill in pupils a respect for factual knowledge and an appetite for its acquisition. The tendency to allow prejudice, tradition, slogans, and clichés to interfere with reasoning processes must be avoided. Reasoning cannot begin with a conviction.

Gathering data to solve a problem is not an easy undertaking. But there is no substitute for this tedious and time-consuming task. In retrospect, much of the time spent will seem to be wasted, because much of the assembled information inevitably turns out to be inappropriate to solving the problem. But it must be repeated that suggestions for the answer will always come out of the data.

Authorities in the field of research state that the "original mind is the informed mind." Competence in research—knowing what is worth investigating, knowing how to select productive methods, and being able to foresee the most likely outcome of study—is the result of being well informed. The accumulation of knowledge in any area contributes to competence.

Although they may recognize the importance of information and its continued acquisition, teachers have apparently grossly neglected the matter of helping pupils record that information. Recognized scholars as a general rule do not depend too heavily on their memories—they "make a note of it."[4] Teachers should begin early to emphasize this important skill. Among the practices involved in gathering and recording data that could be begun as early as the seventh grade and perhaps earlier are the following:

1. Encourage pupils to make a record of sources. Get them to note the writer, the date of the material, and the book or magazine in which the information appeared. Not only will this save time, but it will add impressiveness to their presentation of data.

[4] Francis P. Robinson in *Effective Study*, rev. ed., New York: Harper & Row, Publishers, 1961, p. 34, lists common errors in taking notes and reasons for them that should be helpful to the reader both as a teacher and as a student.

2. Encourage pupils to develop skill in making brief notes. Too much time spent in recording reduces the time available for research. Too many notes discourage the student from using them. Directed practice helps pupils to learn to distinguish significant data.

3. Encourage students to take notes on cards rather than on full sheets of paper. Such notes will require the student to fill in the gaps and to become "active" as he presents his information from his notes.

There is no substitute for gathering data in the problem-solving process, but there are ways of making the laborious process interesting and effective rather than tedious. Habits of orderliness and thoroughness are just as self-perpetuating as habits of sloppiness and superficiality. If the pupil achieves a satisfaction of accomplishment from a thorough job of data gathering, he will be establishing an important aspect of problem-solving skill in his reaction patterns.

Formulating a Hypothesis   A hypothesis is simply a theory or a tentative guess about the probable outcome of a particular situation, and it is based on a certain amount of factual information. As an individual matures and acquires experience that enables him to evaluate his data, his hypothesis will be altered and improved. Thus it can be expected that the typical high school student will have less difficulty in formulating a valid hypothesis than will younger students, but elementary pupils can and do form them (Wann, Dorn, and Liddle, 1962, pp. 102ff).

Whether the hypothesis is stated or brought out by a question such as "What do you think will be the result?" it is up to the teacher to stress the point that the hypothesis is a theory to be accepted or rejected; it is not something that must be supported. This error in reasoning is made by many adults; i.e., they formulate a hypothesis and then seek facts to support it. Pupils should be led to realize that it takes time to formulate a good working hypothesis. This is no less true for elementary pupils who are working on the problem "How playgrounds should be regulated" than it is for high school pupils who are working on the problem "How delinquency can be reduced in our town" or "What is the mathematical formula for timing traffic lights?"

The fact that steps in reasoning do not necessarily follow a sequential order is illustrated in the formulation of the hypothesis. The initial formulation may indicate the need for further data; further data, when gathered, may necessitate a reformulation of the hypothesis. At this step, the biased reasoner will tend to cling to his original theory; the student of superior reasoning ability will keep an open mind, regarding it as tentative, valid in the light of present data, but always subject to alteration. Fortunately, the need for suspended judgment, for revising the hypothesis, can easily be taught both by illustration and by calling attention to its desirability (DeProspo, 1958).

Teachers should encourage pupils to make their own guesses because experience is basic in problem solving. As individuals, students may obtain the facts and look at them with a view to making a hypothesis, and they *may* be able to do so, but group deliberations and decisions have been found to be somewhat more productive of problem-solving skills (Barnlund, 1959). Fifth graders solved more arithmetic problems when working as a group than when working alone (Hudgins, 1960). Thus teaching methods—as well as teacher attitudes toward problems—are of consequence in establishing the conditions that may lead pupils to formulating valid hypotheses.

Testing the Hypothesis Pupils can be asked to try to foresee the consequences of their tentative proposal, or they can be given an opportunity to give it a trial run. If conditions permit, both tests may profitably be made. The ability to foresee outcomes is dependent upon both maturation and experience, but teachers should not wait for maturation, asking themselves, "When is a child old enough to carry on a process of reflective thinking?" Rather, they should ask, "How many opportunities can I give my pupils to anticipate consequences?"

Group discussions, dealing with situations that are real to the pupils can provide the experience that should accompany the process of maturation. Listening, questioning, and commenting are all helpful in forming a hypothesis. By listening the pupil gets ideas to add to his own. Through questioning, he gets information that he thinks is important. In commenting, he rearranges and alters his own ideas. Furthermore, in group discussion the pupil projects himself more firmly into the situation. The child needs to talk about his problems even more than the adult does. In view of these obvious benefits of group work, it seems somewhat odd that it takes so long for teachers to realize that it is so productive (Lorge, 1958). In view of the fact that many problems of citizens must be solved in groups, the motivating factor of social contact, and the advantage of pooled wisdom, the teacher has significant reasons for providing time for group work and group discussion. (See Chapter 17.)

So-called "experimental work" in the high school sciences may or may not teach pupils how to reason. If the problems have meaning for the students, then excellent training is provided. If, on the other hand, the problem is an exercise from a manual, its solution may provide little or no exercise in problem solving. It is necessary for the teacher to stress the probing process, to encourage the pupil to form his own hypotheses and anticipate outcomes. Textbook or manual problems are not necessarily artificial. The point is that the pupil must accept the problem as his own and actively seek the answers, test the hypothesis, and formulate conclusions rather than merely following each of the steps outlined in a manual. Problem solving is an active process and must of necessity involve more than routine, formalized steps.

Testing, whether theoretical or situational, gives additional information or data about the problem. The new information may result in an alteration of the hypothesis. In either case, the various steps in problem solving overlap, repeat, and synchronize.

Making a Generalization   Testing the hypothesis is often the final step in the solution of a problem. However, higher forms of reasoning demand still another step—making a generalization. The generalization is an attempt to give the discoveries that have been made wider application. Attention may be directed to forming a generalization by such questions as "What other situation would this solution seem to fit?" "How could the procedures used for gathering and evaluating data be used in another problem?" or "How can the results of your inquiry be briefly stated?"

This final step is an attempt to consolidate the conclusion in order to conserve the meaning. It is a verbal description of the salient information that has been obtained. The fact that this final step is often neglected is illustrated by the fact that children and adults often attack a problem with no apparent reference to previous problem-solving experiences (Perkins, 1951). Groups in permissive classrooms have been found to be particularly effective in generalizing (Levitt, 1955). The reflection and evaluation involved in generalizing add most to the pupils' abilities to use previous experiences in their attack on ensuing problems.

Teachers have the responsibility for impressing upon students the value of making sound generalizations. One of the defects of much "thinking" is that people jump to conclusions. We see evidence of this all around us: "I once knew a German who was typically egotistic"; "He's a good example of the stubbornness of the Swede"; or "He's a typical only child." Many prejudices have just this basis—jumping to conclusions on the basis of one or two observations that seem to support some popular belief.

None of these steps in problem solving is beyond the level of ability of school pupils. The power to hold an idea in mind long enough to test it and use or discard it is evidenced from the age of two years. By the sixth year, reasoning ability is frequently noticeable. As time, experience, and encouragement play their parts, the ability to reason gains in vigor and quality.

There is no distinctive qualitative difference in problem-solving ability as age increases, but there is steady improvement in the inclination to use it. The teacher's efforts to promote verbal facility, to grant autonomy, to generate interest, and to describe problems in the pupils' terms will contribute to their ability to generalize. No great results should be hoped for. It must be remembered that adults are also naïve and inconsistent when they are dealing with ideas outside the realm of the familiar.

A study of the reaction of several preschool pupils to failure can be interpreted as a situation involving problem solving. These children were asked to do difficult tasks with blocks and puzzles. They were reminded of previous success and shown the significance of former experience to encourage them to continue their efforts. Pupils who received no verbal help with the tasks revealed more immature responses. The experimenter felt that children could profit from encouragement and reminders of previous success in educational situations in general (Keister, 1943, p. 429). Certainly, those who appreciate the significance of success and failure would agree that reminders of past success have merit.

Constructive forward steps in education will be taken when more teachers realize that it is possible to teach children how to reason. Psychological experimentation and observation indicate that reasoning does take place, even among very young people, when they are presented with real problems and when they are given encouragement, time, and guidance in solving them.

An Illustrative Problem   The steps in problem solving in a classroom situation can be illustrated by a case in which the teacher, during the study of a unit on contagious diseases, took advantage of an actual situation in the lives of her pupils. Each of the steps described above was not only apparent but emphasized during the process.

One of the boys in the fifth-grade class had been absent for two or three days. Since he was a leader in both classroom and playground activities, his absence was noteworthy. Pupils asked where he was, but no one knew. One boy stated that he lived not far from the home of the absent boy and would try to find out what had happened. Here was a problem that was felt by the pupils, and guesses about the reasons for his absence were not satisfying. The problem, though vague, was felt, so the teacher (who knew the situation) decided to use the questions as a means of illustrating the approach to problem solving.

The boy who had volunteered to find the reason for his classmate's absence reported that he had gone to the boy's home and was told that his friend had scarlet fever. He learned that the boy would be absent from school for some time. The teacher pointed out that here was the beginning of the process of gathering data and sharpening of the problem. What is scarlet fever? How serious is it? How does it start? Students volunteered answers, but it was felt that better answers could be obtained. Books were used to supply the answers. One pupil was delegated to ask the school nurse several questions. Data were accumulated and the problem became more specific.

On the basis of data accumulated, guesses were made about why one child in school was stricken by scarlet fever and not another. Study and research over a period of several days suggested that perhaps the family's water supply was contaminated; perhaps they did not have window screens; perhaps the boy visited someone who had the illness. These guesses seemed to be within the province of the data gathered; in short, the proposed hypotheses were partially informed guesses.

The hypotheses formulated were tested when the boy recovered and returned to school. He reported that their water came from a well, but that the well was situated a long way from the house or barn. They did have window screens, but the one in his room had a large hole in it. He had not been visiting anyone besides members of the class. Either the well or the screens seemed to be a plausible answer. There was not much chance to test the screen hypothesis further, but more questions were asked about the well. Livestock did sometimes get into the area surrounding the well. It was finally suggested that someone ask the nurse to have the water tested. This was done, and the bacteria count was found to be high. This seemed to be the hypothesis that withstood the test.

The teacher attempted to get the pupils to generalize their experiences in research and problem solving. Among the generalizations formed were the following: One's water supply should be tested periodically; no chances should be taken with broken screens; it is desirable to maintain good health habits so that one is not susceptible to disease; in solving problems, one should go to dependable sources for information; much research is needed to be able to distinguish between seemingly good and really good answers.

These steps are not too difficult for children at the beginning of their school experience. Tenacity such as that revealed by these fifth graders might not be shown by first graders, but they too can feel and study problems. They can gather data. They can make partially informed guesses. They can test the guesses. And they can make limited generalizations. They can evaluate the knowledge and guesses of individual group members. It is well to reiterate that the correct solution of a specific problem (in a classroom situation) is typically no more important than the processes and interests involved.

Creativity

A number of forces have caused creativity to become a concern for many instead of just an interest for psychological researchers. Among these forces might be included foreign threat to American leadership in inventiveness, rapid technological changes that increase the need for further innovation, psychological discoveries of the definitive nature of human differences, and better-prepared and more self-reliant and confident teachers. As knowledge of creativity progresses, it becomes clear that creativity, like personality in general, abounds in intricacies (Wallen,

1964). The concept must of necessity be superficially treated in this context. Some of the salient aspects of creativity and its treatment do, however, emerge clearly.

The Nature and Origin of Creativity First of all, creativity and high intelligence, although positively correlated, are by no means synonymous. Pupils with quite average IQs, because of special interests and certain personality-forming influences, may be quite creative. On the other hand, quite a few youngsters with high intelligence have learned that the way to get along with adults (parents and teachers) is to conform; consequently, if they have a drive toward creativity, they keep a tight rein on it so that it eventually atrophies.

Some believe that the urge to creativity is well-nigh universal; others seem to think that—like musical or artistic aptitude—it is a special aptitude (Torrance, 1962, p. 5; Carpenter, 1962). Whether or not the urge to creativity is universal, it can readily be recognized that forces of conformity, expectation, and conservation of the *status quo* mitigate against the cultivation and flow of the creative impulse. These forces can more readily be understood and constructively dealt with when the divergent nature of creativity is understood.

Creative persons have been found to possess some or several of the following characteristics: (1) They tend to talk fluently and to show richness in the flow of ideas and speed in associating apparently disconnected things and ideas; (2) they are flexible and adaptive in permissive atmospheres and restive under the influence of rigid requirements; (3) they are divergent and inventive, rather than convergent and compliant in their thinking; (4) their good memories and associational thinking cause them to see much that is familiar in the ostensibly new (Guilford, 1962); (5) they tend to reveal humorous and playful attitudes; (6) they have reputations for having silly or wild ideas; and (7) their work is characterized by numerous ideas that are off the beaten track (Torrance, 1961).

It can readily be seen that some of these characteristics would cause many teachers to be uncomfortable. Fortunately, simply recognizing nonconformity (in proper context) as a desirable quality, rather than regarding it as evidence of innate perversity, is the teacher's first step in preserving the source of creativity. All concern does not vanish, because the potentially creative become underachievers (see Appendix) in large numbers, in school. They are the ones who are independent, intellectual, highly verbal ("garrulous," when they irritate others), and sometimes asocial. They do not enjoy keeping in the lesson-reciting, lesson-hearing routines.

Teachers are justifiably gratified by the more conforming pupil, who is sociable, responsible, and persevering, and respectful to authority

(Holland, 1961). There is evidence, however, that creativity and divergent thinking are not "poles apart" from academic achievement and convergent thinking. Both types of thinking require a long immersion in study, both require the accumulation of data, both demand order and organization, and it is hoped, both will result in illumination and inspiration (Murphy, 1956). The major difference between the two types of students, when a difference does exist, is the tendency for the academic performer to reproduce already established conclusions. The creative person, on the other hand, has a drive to go beyond it. He is particularly responsive to an atmosphere in which he is free to, and it is safe to, question. He responds to the opportunity to experiment and adventure (Leese, 1961).

The Process of Creative Thinking Wallas (1926) and Patrick (1955) have identified four steps in the creative process.

1. *Preparation* consists of purposeful study and questioning, experience, and absorption of information that will fill gaps that the creative individual perceives. This is a time-consuming process in which the student steeps himself in the lore of the subject. This involves broad knowledge, because creativity demands new combinations, new relationships, new elaborations, and new implications. The teacher who would encourage creativity can no more depend on inspiration alone than a creative novelist can. He and his pupil must examine purposes, survey available resources, evaluate past experiences, and seek new interpretations. It must be realized that creativity is "ninety-nine per cent perspiration and one per cent inspiration." It is small wonder that a frequently mentioned characteristic of the creative individual is discontent and even unhappiness ("Quotients of Creativity," 1962).

2. *Incubation* in creative thinking is perhaps less susceptible to voluntary control than preparation. The name was probably suggested by the incubation of an egg. Nothing is added to the egg from the outside during this period; it is merely kept warm and "waited upon." In this context, the meaning is that the student is released from the pressure of fact gathering and studying and allowed to wait for the idea to mature. The creative thinker does not completely abandon the idea, but turns it over in his mind leisurely and periodically, but without trying to force the process. Hence the practical implication is to wait, to turn to other things, but not to forget the matter completely. The process of incubation should include (*a*) time for relaxation—release from the tensions of hurry and compulsion, (*b*) time for assimilation of ideas into the thought processes, (*c*) time for the rearrangement of information into various sequences and contingencies, (*d*) time for various ideas to rise to a central place in thought—or to recede to positions of relative significance.

Here is another reason for a variety of class projects and approaches. When a plateau of learning seems to have been reached, it would be well to turn temporarily to other subjects and allow time for incubation. Then, when other events have reduced tension, the teacher can return to the point and hope that illumination will come.

3. *Illumination* is the stage when the hours devoted to study, research, and incubation are rewarded by a clearer conception of the answer to the problem. The school pupil comes to a clear understanding of the situation that was perplexing him. At this time, insight is achieved. The moment at which illumination occurs cannot be stated precisely. But it is certain that preparation and incubation must come first. The only thing that teachers can do about this phase of creativity is to prepare the ground. The teacher should work patiently on the first two steps and then, without letting the problem subject lapse entirely, turn to other things and reduce the pressure to arrive at conclusions. By use of this method, the teacher can logically expect that illumination will occur for many pupils.

4. *Verification,* or *revision,* is akin to generalization in problem solving —after the problem is solved, it is extended to other situations. Verification may be considered to be the process of rethinking to improve the solution. It is the attempt to revise and refine the conclusion. Verification in the classroom consists of putting the brilliant idea into practice—polishing the creative work by critical analysis and further trial and examination. The teacher might ask, "How can we improve our mural?" "What ideas might we add to our proposal for better organization of community recreation?" "Are there any points we have overlooked in the personal health program we have formulated?" or "Does our theory of the causes of crime seem to be sufficiently inclusive?" It is constructive to project the illuminating idea beyond the presently achieved answer. Students should be made to feel that even minute additions to present knowledge are valuable—an attitude that can best be fostered by teachers who do not "know all the answers" and show appreciation for the creative and critical work of their pupils. It is encouraging to a pupil to know that he has solved a problem, but it will also bring him satisfaction to know that the teacher appreciates his achievement. The difference between mediocrity and excellence in creative work is one of degree rather than kind (Patrick, 1935). This also suggests that teachers may reasonably expect all pupils to achieve some success in creative thought and work.

Identifying the Creative Individual Several factors point to the need for better identification of the creative person. The temper of the times is to recognize the importance of the existence and the work of the potentially creative. Different environmental influences may deter or stimulate the manifestation and development of creativity. Hence there has been a recently intensified effort to develop tests of creativity.[5] Among the tests that are currently being used and further tested are the Watson-Glasser Critical Thinking Appraisal, the AC Test of Creative Ability, and the Minnesota Test of Creative Thinking. J. P. Guilford and his associates (1951) have devised and revised a number of such instruments.

Testing for creativity must of necessity involve personality assessment. Although Torrance believes that no satisfactory personality instrument suitable for use in guiding creative development has been developed, he lists a number of already well-known instruments that have proved helpful to teachers and counselors of creative children. They include the Strong Vocational Interest Blank, the Allport-Vernon-Lindsey Study of Values, and the Minnesota Multiphasic Personality Inventory (Torrance, 1962, pp. 67ff). On the Strong test, the creative subject rates high on scales as architect, psychologist, and author-journalist, and low on scales as purchasing agent, office man, or policeman. It appears from such scales that creative persons are interested in meanings and implications but not in details of the practical and concrete. On the Vernon instrument, creative subjects rank high on the theoretical and aesthetic scales. On the Minnesota Multiphasic, creative persons are high on masculinity-femininity scales—having high interest and openness to feelings. These scales are not considered entirely adequate for identifying creativity, and attempts to formulate more precise instruments are in progress.

Not all creative pupils will intrude themselves upon the teacher's attention, but those who do may provide clues as to what to look for in the less intrusive. Included among the items to be observed are the characteristics of the creative listed earlier (see section on The Nature and Origin of Creativity). Children who test the limits of authority should be studied to see if they do so because of emotional instability or because of curiosity. Those who take risks may be potentially creative. Behaviors showing independence may be indicative of creativity. Asking unusual questions is symptomatic of risk taking and curiosity and will be encouraged by teachers who wish to develop creativity. Ziller (1957) has hypothesized that pupils who make early vocational choices—especially those who choose sales work, engineering, education, and business administration—are more adventuresome than those who remain undecided.

The characteristics of creative pupils do not make for comfort on the part of the teacher. Torrance has noted three characteristics that are

[5] J. P. Guilford in "Traits of Creativity," in H. H. Anderson (ed.), *Creativity and Its Cultivation,* New York: Harper & Row, Publishers, 1959, pp. 142–161, has described the problems and approaches involved in constructing instruments that may lead to identifying creative propensities prior to the emergence of the creative product. The description will contribute to a better understanding of some of the difficulties of intelligence testing in general.

outstanding—having silly ideas, nonconformity to standardized dimensions, and being humorous, playful, and relaxed. These, incidentally, play a part in their frequently noted indifferent scholastic achievement.

The three characteristics which emerge strongly would appear to be of considerable importance to teachers and counselors in their efforts to understand and guide the highly creative youngster. In spite of the fact that these children have many excellent ideas, they readily achieve a reputation for having silly, wild, or naughty ideas. It is difficult to determine what effect this derogation of their ideas has on their personality development, as well as upon the future development of their creative talents. The uniqueness of their ideas makes this a really difficult problem, because there are no standards, as in answer books, and manuals. Although their humor and playfulness may win some friends for them, it does not always make them "easier to live with." In fact, it may make their behavior even more unpredictable than otherwise and this probably makes their presence in a group upsetting. Recognizing and understanding these three characteristics are important because each apparently has an important role in making an individual "creative." [6]

Creativity in the Classroom   The essence of creativity is to be unpredictable. It is therefore contradictory to prescribe what can be done to encourage it. There is evidence, however, that creativity appears more frequently in some social and cultural contexts than it does in others. Creativity involves adventuresomeness and risk taking. It may be that repression, discouragement, and derogation will stifle creativity in one person, but similar repression will serve merely to stiffen the spine of another. It may be found, too, that overemphasis on creativity will hamper education for well-rounded development in some pupils (Yamamoto, 1964). The chances do seem to favor taking advantage of research findings. Without prescribing specific procedures, there are indications (seen in earlier sections of this chapter) that some conditions are more salutary for encouraging creativeness than others.

A step in the right direction would be for the teacher to examine his own orientation. Is he sufficiently professionally and emotionally secure to depart from traditional methods and conclusions? Does he teach children or subject matter? Does he seek new methods of presentation? Is he enthusiastic about his pupils and his specialty? Can he regard his own shortcomings with humor? Is he creative enough to add to this list of questions some concerning the self?

Another step would be to see that full advantage is taken of the curriculum. Not only does the creative person reveal his interest and aptitude in a wide variety of fields, but perceiving new interrelationships is

[6] E. Paul Torrance, *Guiding Creative Talent*, © 1962 by Prentice-Hall, Inc., Englewood Cliffs, N.J., p. 81. By permission.

a mark of his creativity. There should be variety for curricular choice and activity. There is a special need for encouragement *and insistence* that the creative child become acquainted with as many disciplines as possible. He should, despite this insistence, have some choice as to how his study may be pursued. While it may be advantageous for many in the class to be exposed to one or two disciplines at a time, it appears that the creative pupil profits from being bombarded with materials from many fields and by many media (Taylor, 1962).

Anderson (1959, p. 237) believes that creativity is characterized by optimum growth in social interaction. Observation of pupil interaction and sociometry will provide clues that allow the teacher to give help in socializing when necessary.

Team teaching, which exposes the pupil to a variety of subjects and their interrelationships and a variety of teachers, is recommended by several authorities (Carpenter, 1962; Mingoia, 1961; Morgan, 1960).

Brainstorming, a technique that consists of having group members suggest ideas as rapidly as possible, prohibiting criticisms, encouraging speaking out, and evaluating at a later session, holds possibilities that have not yet been thoroughly tested (Getzels and Jackson, 1962, p. 124).

Much is summarized about the nature, identification, and encouragement of creativity in the recommendations of Getzels and Jackson. They assert that distinction should be made between:

> . . . intelligence (IQ) and creative thinking
> . . . independence and unruliness and individuality and rebelliousness
> . . . healthy solitude and morbid withdrawal
> . . . tolerance for ambiguity and irresolution and between ability to delay choice and indecisiveness
> . . . remembering and discovering, between information and knowledge, and between the "fact filled quiz kid" and the educated student
> . . . sense perception and intuitive perception
> . . . evaluation and censorship and between judging and forejudging
> . . . organizing the curriculum for information or for knowledge, between organizing it for repetition or discovery, and for organizing it for measuring facts or evaluating wisdom [7]

Summary

Problem-solving ability and creative endeavor stand out as important outcomes of education in a rapidly changing, dynamic society. Both imply the ability to

[7] Adapted from Jacob W. Getzels and Philip W. Jackson, *Creativity and Intelligence,* New York: John Wiley & Sons, Inc., 1962, pp. 124–130.

correlate and integrate facts and to delay, but not indefinitely postpone action.

A factor in reasoning is maturation—the problems tackled by a child are less complicated than problems that could be called "problem solving" in adulthood. Experience is vital, but an explanation of experiences in terms of problem solving enhances the value (for future reference) of experience. A fund of information is essential. Certain educational practices tend to hamper optimum development of problem-solving ability—rate learning, excessive use of imaginary or workbook problems, the teacher's desire to provide answers, and problems inappropriate to the pupil's maturation and experience—and should be looked at critically.

Steps in problem solving have been formally stated but do not necessarily follow in precise order. These steps are having a felt need, recognizing and defining the problem, gathering data, formulating a hypothesis, testing the hypothesis, and—to get maximum benefit—making a generalization.

Creativity is similar in many respects to problem solving, but it goes beyond the data and involves more in the realm of affective response. This is shown in the characteristics of people who are called "creative." They tend to have a rich flow of ideas, are flexible and adaptive, have good memories and associational ability, often have humorous and playful attitudes, and frequently get off the beaten track.

Creativity has been described in terms of four steps: preparation, incubation, illumination, and verification or revision.

Tests have been devised to identify potential for creativity, but there are so many ways and areas in which creativity may function that such instruments must be supplemented with analytical observation.

Although a classroom organized and conducted to foster creativity cannot be prescribed, there are some hints that have proven of value. The teacher must be competent and confident so that he can allow pupils freedom. Variety in the curriculum must be provided. Team teaching is thought to be helpful. Brainstorming has sometimes been productive. But in the final analysis, encouragement of creativity swings back to the personality and resourcefulness of the teacher.

Problems and exercises

1 Why is it so important that people learn to act on tentative conclusions? How would you proceed to put this idea across to pupils?

2 Are pupils confronted by problems of which they are now aware? How can the teacher help pupils become aware of such problems?

3 Prepare a statement that you would present to pupils to explain the importance of a hypothesis and the process of forming it. (Certain class members should prepare such a statement for intermediate school pupils, others for upper-grade pupils, and others for high school students; the statements should be brought to class for criticism and suggestions.)

4 Why is class discussion an advantageous approach to forming generalizations?

5 List five ways in which teachers can encourage pupils to think. Bring the list to class for revision and improvement.

6 Which of the four steps in creative thinking is most clearly distinct from the six steps in problem solving?

7 It has been said that textbooks provide answers and in so doing limit creativity. Does this mean that textbooks should be discarded, or is there some alternative?

8 What are some things that are inimical to creative production? What procedures do you think rate highest priority in fostering creativity?

Suggested additional readings

Dewey, John: *How We Think*, Boston: D. C. Heath and Company, 1910.
This book has withstood the test of time and is still considered to be an excellent presentation of the nature and procedures of problem solving.

Getzels, Jacob W., and Philip W. Jackson: *Creativity and Intelligence*, New York: John Wiley & Sons, Inc., 1962.
The authors describe the varieties of giftedness and creativeness that exist among pupils. They then present a number of contrasts and similarities between the highly intelligent and the highly creative. Case studies are used to sharpen the reader's insight.

Torrance, E. Paul: *Creativity*, What Research Says to the Teacher, no. 28, Washington: National Education Association, 1963.
The definitions, manifestations, assessment, and developmental patterns of creativity are considered. Blocks to and the cultivation of creativity in the school receive major emphasis.

Torrance, E. Paul: *Guiding Creative Youth*, Englewood Cliffs, N.J.: Prentice-Hall, Inc., 1962.
The author's major concern is with the instruments he and others have designed to identify creativeness. Practical applications are emphasized —suggestions are made as to how teachers may discover, maintain, and magnify creativity.

Wann, Kenneth D., Miriam S. Dorn, and Elizabeth A. Liddle: *Fostering Intellectual Development in Young Children*, New York: Bureau of Publications, Teachers College, Columbia University, 1962.
It becomes evident from reading this book that concept development and problem solving are lifelong processes and begin much earlier than was hitherto thought. The authors cite examples of the kinds of problems preschool and kindergarten children work with, and they suggest teaching improvements.

Habit Formation: Application to Study Techniques

5   Among the many purposes of education is improving the life-style of the individual so that he may become more uniquely human (including freedom to choose) and so that he may contribute to the betterment of society. He is better able to achieve such goals if the habits that he inevitably forms are planned rather than fortuitous. We all are, to a marked extent, creatures of habit. It behooves us to understand the nature and role of habits so that we may direct them, instead of allowing them to control us. We speak of habits of study, of emotional control, and habitual attitudes, realizing that these are modes of behavior developed by the individual, habits that either add to or detract from his life-style.

Young people have been advised for decades that they will inevitably become "walking bundles of habits." James (1914, p. 51) has referred to habits as the "flywheels of society." These are sound observations not only for the prospective teacher as a college student but also as admonitions for teachers to give direction to the habits that their pupils are daily forming. The consistency of personality traits is determined by the responses that are built into the organism in the form of habits.

The role of habits

Meaning   Habits are acts or patterns of behavior that have become so easy, through practice, that they occur spontaneously (or automatically) in given situations, without conscious thought or concentration. We usually think of physical habits, but emotional predispositions and stereotyped thinking indicate that there are also emotional and mental habits.

Habits conserve time and energy and thus facilitate adjustment. They also hamper adjustment when they unwittingly narrow the range of deliberate, suited-to-the-occasion behavior.

Habits Make for Economy of Action   If it were not for habits, the day would scarcely be long enough. If every action from the moment of arising, dressing, getting washed, and preparing breakfast had to be consciously planned and separately executed, we would be clumsy, indecisive, and slow. The words we speak are habitually attached to rather definite meanings and objects—habits of word usage thus make communication possible. The mental habits that pupils are forming daily enable them to build on past activities. A steady stream of adjustive actions stems from habits.

Habits May Hamper Adjustment The negative aspect of habits often receives more attention than does the advantageous aspect. Children can and often do form habits of dilatoriness, asperity, carelessness, and procrastination. Unfortunately, the plastic nature of the individual enables him to adjust to these handicapping habits and to live with them. The theory that as growth proceeds, the individual becomes more like himself [1] has its implications for maladaptive habits as well as for habits that make for economy of action. Habits do not occur in isolation; they develop, in hierarchies or families (Maltzman, 1955). That is, several habits are combined to form a complex skill, such as typing or learning to speak a foreign language. Habits tend to be similar, and several habits might be grouped together and termed "laziness" or "industriousness"—a habit pattern or characteristic that might appear in many diverse activities. Because habits do tend to form in groups and to appear in many ways, teachers can hope for *general* improvement of responses. At the same time, the hierarchical nature of habits should cause the teacher to observe conduct while it is still in its more pliable stages.

Habits Play a Paradoxical Role. So-called "good habits" may be carried so far as to become of questionable value. Babies may form such rigid habits about going to bed that any change in the routine will upset them. Schoolchildren may become so habituated to a particular class group that removal from the group becomes a major catastrophe. Reading is, in general, a laudable habit, but some children have developed it to such a degree that it interferes with normal participation in outdoor play activities. There must, in brief, be moderation in the extent to which even "good" habits are maintained. Those in charge of the development of youngsters should see to it that there is enough variation in methods and materials, even within a routine framework, to maintain a fundamental plasticity of adjustment.

Habits should be periodically examined to see whether they continue to be our servants or whether we are becoming their slaves. Education, among other things, has a liberating function (Tiedeman, 1962). We are free—to a large degree—when we know and consider the factors and probable consequences of a choice. Thus the informed and foresighted

---

[1] "Becoming more like himself" implies that behaviors that initially occurred only sporadically become more frequent. Thus an adult's responses tend to be more predictable than those of a child, who is still exploring alternatives.

individual must ask, "Which behavior should I make habitual and which not?" and find his own answer. For teachers to deny the pupil freedom of choice—after providing ample information regarding alternatives—is to ignore a significant aspect of American culture (May, 1963).

Meaning and kinds of habits

A Concept of Habit Habit is one of many names that are given to a not-too-sharply delineated class of learning. The basic feature of the habit is its automatic nature: A particular response has been so frequently and consistently repeated that when the individual is placed in the same or a similar situation, the response is automatically activated. A schoolchild may develop the habit of inattention merely because there is relatively little reason to give attention. He may, on the other hand, consciously set out to establish a response to certain arithmetical combinations so that in similar situations he can respond quickly and accurately. In either case, the factor of automaticity is predominant. Therefore, habit may be defined as a more or less automatic learned response, acquired through repeating that response in an identical or highly similar situation.

Teachers should be careful to give as much emphasis to the situational aspect of habit as to the repetition aspect, because teachers, by their manipulation and alteration of situations, direct the habit formation of pupils. Teachers cannot always force pupils to repeat actions to the point of habit formation, but by recognition and praise, they can reinforce desirable responses that can be consolidated into time-saving habits.

Conditioning and Habits Habit formation is a form of learning; hence, the considerations of Chapter 6, "Factors That Facilitate Learning," are pertinent as we consider the steps in the process. It has been shown that conditioning consists of substituting a new stimulus for a previous one that elicited a given response. Schoolchildren engaged in different activities become conditioned to quieting down when the teacher takes a certain position in front of the room and looks at the pupils expectantly.

The explanation of habit formation by conditioning would be sufficient if the responder were not a living organism—it is of utmost significance for teachers to remember that pupils are not automatons. Thus, one step in habit formation is consideration of motivation. For adequate understanding, the formula $S \to R$ must be changed to $S \to O \to R$.[2] The organism is taken into account by dealing with its goals and motives.

[2] $S \to R$ here refers to the simple combination of a stimulus as it brings forth a definite and dependable response, as might occur when a weight is placed on a balance—the indicator stops at a precise point after moving a certain distance. The $S \to O \to R$ explicitly recognizes the importance of the organism as a changing and responsive factor in a behavioral situation. The O represents the individual as a dynamic, not a

The organism without the habit is different from the organism with the habit. This may be illustrated by $S \rightleftarrows O \rightleftarrows R$; i.e., when an organism has a given habit, it responds to a stimulus differently than when it does not have the habit. Explanations given in arithmetic when the pupils are thoroughly acquainted with number combinations are different from explanations given when they are unfamiliar with such combinations. Instructions to children who have the habit of attending to the instructions of teachers are different from those given to children who have not acquired such habits. The fact that responses are built into the organism means that teachers can foster response differentiation, strengthen responses that have currently low probability of being elicited, and encourage extension of the number of responses that are likely in a given situation (Adkins, 1958).

A living and changing being is involved in the repetition required to establish a habit. Thus although a feature of habit is automaticity, establishing a habit is more than a mechanical process. And habits continuously change; for example, the kind of house that the pupil visualizes when he sees the letter combination *h-o-u-s-e* differs from time to time as he sees different houses, looks at pictures accompanying a story, or draws or paints houses. In addition, individuals who have ostensibly the same habit are different—different organisms; thus two pupils hearing a teacher's statement interpret it differently. Having once responded, the organism is changed and henceforth will see its world in a somewhat different light. The stimulus that is selected from the entire range presented by the world is again dependent upon the changed organism. Thus, a given student may be habitually obedient, but the degree of obedience varies with each of his teachers.

The lack of complete automaticity in habit formation means that the teacher must require more than mere repetition. The multiplication tables should be presented in various ways and used in the solution of many different kinds of problems—e.g., as single entities, in different combinations, in division, and in multiplication. In addition to drill, there must be explanations, discussions, and illustrations. The motivation of the pupil and the timeliness of the problems must also be considered.

Skill habits are only one part of the learning process; there are regular developmental trends in arithmetic, for example, that parallel mental development. Teachers who see to it that each child is prepared for the next step by having completed the preceding steps will have their work facilitated (Morton, 1953, p. 8). Skill in numbers is more than habits of counting, writing numbers, and using numbers in combinations. It also

---

passive, factor in any situation. The organism grows, is responsive to the past as well as to the physical present, and has goals of varied strength that pull him in various directions.

involves knowing what the processes mean and when to use them. We have all met pupils who could count to twenty-five but could not say how many coins have been placed on a table. The story of the boy who wrote "I have gone" on the board a hundred times and then left the note: "Teacher, I have written 'I have gone' a hundred times and I have went home" is not simply a joke. Children do "call words" aloud from a primer without comprehending the story. Algebra problems may be learned without comprehension. Poetry may be memorized without appreciation. It is obvious that repetition, which produces conditioning and habit is only a part of learning.

Permanence of Habits   As needs change, the manner of their reduction must—of necessity—also change (Hunt, 1960). Although habits tend to shape the course of development, change is continuous. Habits persist in similar rather than identical responses—the wrist gets a little lower at the piano keyboard, the pupil slouches more often in his seat, defense mechanisms become more pronounced. We have all had the experience of having someone point out that some error in typing, swimming, or golfing has crept unnoticed into our action pattern.

The ease with which some things are relearned after apparently having been forgotten lends support to the idea that responses are built into the organism, a response is never completely forgotten.

> The organism is different by the new response and all that it brings. Each act of learning adds a certain change and increment to the very structure of the organism itself. Learning thus involves two aspects: one creative, in which a new response is contrived; the other conserving, in which this newly contrived response is added to the very structure of the organism.[3]

Motives and Habits   Initially, habits are developed as a result of motives, but once established, they may become motives, a phenomenon described as "functional autonomy" (Stagner, 1961, p. 336). Although the need which orginally elicited an action has been satisfied, the action itself may become so satisfying that it persists. There is a secondary reward which in turn creates a secondary drive (Zimmerman, 1957). More specifically, the child orginally learned to read because it was expected, his peers were reading, his teacher praised his effort. Satisfying the expectations, keeping pace with his peers, pleasing his teachers were the primary rewards. Once acquired, the skill may become in and of itself a source of stimulation—the rewards are intrinsic within the task. Thus the pupil discovers that he can explore unknown worlds, answer some of the questions he asks, stir up novel issues, foster his own development (he probably would not think in such an academic term), and

[3] William Heard Kilpatrick, *A Reconstructed Theory of the Educative Process*, New York: Teachers College, Columbia University, 1935, p. 4.

encounter excitement—and reading becomes both the motive and reward. Unfortunately, many pupils do not reach this functional autonomy stage in reading. They virtually never read unless it is required—even after they get out of school. Teachers might well consider that facilitating the realization of functional autonomy is as significant as the acquisition of the skill itself. (Other examples of functional autonomy are playing tennis, performing on a musical instrument, knitting, manipulating figures, smoking, and choosing food.)

This functional autonomy is of major importance in explaining the permanence of habits. Teachers who create conditions that make the pupil's schoolwork satisfying, both as an end and as a process, are fostering functional autonomy. Mursell (1952, p. 105) believes that functional autonomy is better achieved through motive satisfaction than simple repetition—an activity, for example, becomes autonomous because the continued pursuit of the activity allows the individual to see more of its value as reducers of need. One of the persistent educational problems we face is making the reasons for schoolwork coincide with the needs of pupils. Although we know some of these pupil motivations—exercise of his *best* capacities, peer approval, unique vocational aims, etc.—the search for better understanding of pupils' needs must continue.

Teachers must frequently listen to the criticism that children are not drilled on the fundamentals. "The children today can't spell or do arithmetic" is a charge the teacher may be called upon to answer (Scott, 1959, pp. 45ff). But we must be careful not to subscribe to the "fallacy of the excluded middle." This is not a case in which opposite poles must be defended. Teachers today do stress drill and habit formation in numbers, spelling, and expression. They do not strive for verbalizations without understanding—as does the mother of the three-year-old who says, "Betty can count to twenty." The fact is that Betty can *name numbers* up to twenty but *cannot count* four coins. Teachers who realize this discrepancy between rote learning (habit) and understanding strive first for understanding. *Then* the alphabet and multiplication tables and algebraic formulas can be memorized—built into habits—for the sake of economy in future effort.

The learner's inner purposes, his motivation, are basic to the formation of advantageous habits. Soldiers and sailors may learn good "housekeeping habits" while they are in service, but unless their need for order and efficiency is perceived and satisfied, those habits will fail to function in civilian life. If the teacher bears in mind the need satisfaction of pupils as he attempts to direct the formation and re-formation of habits, he will be more successful than if he depends on drill and repetition.

Physical Habits The division of habits into physical, mental, or emotional categories is for convenience in discussion. Even skills that seem to be primarily physical have mental and emotional aspects. It is obvious that the lecture method will not suffice in teaching a child to write. But since practice consolidates inefficient movements as well as effective ones, it is important that errors be detected as early as possible and that corrective steps be taken immediately. Some believe that it is often easier to teach "from scratch" than to correct errors after they have been incorporated into the reaction pattern. However, many children do have preschool experiences in writing and bring to the classroom nascent habits of holding the pencil and paper or assuming a certain posture that may interfere with continued smooth progress. While it is not wise to spend a great deal of time on remedial work, it is advisable to make an early diagnosis of errors, correct them, and *practice* the desirable procedures (Freeman, 1954, p. 29).

Other physical habits that may concern teachers have to do with cleanliness, posture, and grooming. Admittedly, these have their emotional components, including attitudes toward self, but they can be approached, in part, from the physical point of view. This includes, as is the case with other physical skills, (1) early detection of errors, (2) instruction in proper techniques (e.g., holding a brush, pencil, or musical instrument), (3) reinforcement of improved responses (by commendation, calling attention to improved production), and (4) giving attention to the matter of the pupil's need reduction. This, in effect, is the procedure used by coaches who permit their players to engage first in the whole game of tennis or basketball and then call attention to inefficient techniques before they become established habits. The player then practices with a specific aspect of the skill in mind—the way the ball is held, the position of the hand at the moment of release, the matter of follow-through. Attention is focused upon the improved ease of execution as well as on the results. These constitute reinforcements, and they are supplemented by words of commendation. Need reduction is served by making the team or beating opponents who had previously been superior.

Mental Habits The facility with which an individual adjusts to environmental factors depends upon his capacity and also upon the consistency with which he uses that capacity. Upon his habits of thinking and of applying himself to the task at hand and his characteristic determination depends his successful adjustment.

> Among the permanent factors [which shape attention] are the individual's *habits of attention and inattention*. He has learned to attend to certain things and to disregard other things. . . . Habits of attention and inattention are established by the child through the influence of older people who point out to him what they regard as worth noticing.[4]

[4] Robert S. Woodworth and Donald G. Marquis, *Psychology*, 5th ed., New York: Holt, Rinehart and Winston, Inc., 1947, p. 406.

Thus in a very real sense, an individual's habits determine the type of person he will be.

Two implications for teachers immediately become apparent. First, it is entirely justifiable to demand attention. If the child were permitted to pay attention only when it suited his fancy, he would have little chance to gain the increased appreciation of values that stems from improved knowledge and nourishes persistent interests. Second, efforts should be made to present the subject clearly and in a variety of ways. Vividness, novelty, and personal significance elicit attention and pave the way to interest development.

One criticism of education and teaching is that pupils are not taught how to think. There are undoubtedly many reasons why they do not, and certainly one of them is that both teachers and pupils are too eager to get answers.

> Human energy is never more extravagantly wasted than in the persistent effort to answer conclusively questions that are vague and meaningless. Probably the most impressive indictment that can be made of our educational system is that it provides the student with answers, but it is poorly designed to provide him with skill in the asking of questions that are effectively directive of inquiry and evaluation. It teaches the student to "make up his mind," ready or not, but it does not teach him how to change it effectively. Any attempt to improve our educational system that does not involve a clear recognition of this defect of it can hardly be expected to lead to substantial reform. In fact, any attempt to reeducate a maladjusted individual that does not leave him with effective techniques of inquiry cannot be trusted to result in substantial and lasting benefits.[5]

A valid starting point for forming the habit of thinking would be to encourage questions. This includes not only the questions asked by the teacher, but also those raised by pupils. Moreover, "sticking to the subject" should not constitute a barrier to the consideration of related topics.

Other kinds of mental habits—order, reading skills, comprehension, mental set—are discussed in the section on Effective Study—an Application of Habit Formation. There the mental, physical, and emotional aspects of habits are illustrated in terms of effective study.

Emotional Habits Attitudes can be used to illustrate a third broad and overlapping class of habits. An attitude may be defined as a predisposition to action. Like other kinds of learning, attitudes are specific to a situation. A child may be tolerant of a newcomer in the group, but intolerant of manifestations of poor sportsmanship. He may be industrious in art activities, but dilatory in academic work. Furthermore, though we have classed attitudes as emotional habits, it must be remembered that attitudes

[5] Wendell Johnson, *People in Quandaries,* New York: Harper & Row, Publishers, 1946, p. 55.

are the result of experience and consequently have intellectual aspects.

Sociologists, psychologists, and criminologists publish ideas and data that agree with the exconvict who asserts that lectures on good citizenship, teaching vocational skills, delegating responsibilities are futile if there is not a change in attitudes, interests, and ideals. It is usually noted that two out of three prisoners return after release, but this also means that one out of three does not return. Like educators, it is this exconvict's contention that individual treatment, with emphasis on constructive attitudes toward self and society, should become the focus of attention (Hollister, 1962). Here again, we see that the individual's feelings are very much a part of the education, or reeducation, milieu.

Although attitudes are specific, they have a tendency to spread. For example, "a person who is insecure *tends* to become more perfectly or consistently insecure; a person who is high in self-esteem *tends* to become more consistently high in self-esteem." [6] Hence, teachers should commend manifestations of desirable attitudes, show how such attitudes can be applied in other situations, and thus encourage their extension. However, a teacher cannot be content with a rational approach to attitudes—direct experience should also be offered. Thus children who manifest racial intolerance should have opportunities to become acquainted with members of various races. When a pupil displays a negative attitude toward reading, it is necessary to provide him with gratifying experiences in the little reading he does. He should be given books of appropriate difficulty and specific interest and the opportunity to retell the story or answer questions about it.

Another important factor in dealing with attitudes is the view that people take toward them. Both teachers and pupils should realize that attitudes change, though frequently the change is almost imperceptible. A study of mathematics and habits of industry has thrown light on the persistence of attitudes. It was found that when students were equated on the basis of "mathematical brightness," the achievement was greater among the more industrious. Moreover, the brighter pupils lost more by indolence than did the less bright. The study concluded that it would be well to advise the mathematics pupil, bright or slow, to avoid forming attitudes that will lead to indolence (Krathwohl, 1949).

Attitudes tend to be contagious; an individual tends to project his own attitudes (Vroom, 1959). Hence, a persisting concern in educational psychology is that of teachers' attitudes. Under the leadership of D. G. Ryans, the American Council on Education conducted an extensive survey of the effect of teachers' behavior and attitudes on pupils. The effectiveness of teachers was judged from principals' reports. The results indicate some goals for teachers to pursue in their own habit formation. Success

[6] A. H. Maslow, *Motivation and Personality*, New York: Harper & Row, Publishers, 1954, p. 43.

in teaching tends to be associated with such things as friendly under-standing, responsibility and businesslike methods, personal stability, courtesy, extroversion, variety of interests, and favorable opinions of pupils (Ryans, 1960).

Numerous research studies point to the vital importance of self-concepts in school achievement and social adjustment of pupils (Gordon and Combs, 1958). These studies consistently indicate that the manner in which an individual habitually perceives himself is a reflection of how others view him, his success in mastering developmental tasks, and his relations with others. Clearly, emotional attitudes are an outcome of one's total interaction with the environment. Teachers play only a part in shaping this environment, but it is an important part. They must visualize the attitudes that are most desirable in the long run and plan approaches for encouraging mental habits that promise the most for the future.

Approaches to habit formation

Formulate Goals   Children in their early years have a tendency to live in and for the present; long-term goals are likely to have little meaning. Goals for youngsters must be immediate and real. As they grow older, long-term goals come to have meaning. Thus occasional reference to the long-term goals of habit formation for youngsters and additional emphasis on them for pupils of greater maturity can develop the tendency to evaluate present activities in terms of later significance.

It is advantageous to discuss with pupils of high school age the nature and formation of habits. Discussions about the significance of goals and the steps in habit formation help them to develop consistent approaches to habit formation. Secondary school teachers report that they have found discussion techniques helpful in determining vocational and life-adjustment goals and in evaluating ethical ideas. Not all pupils will accept the goals, but for at least a few, such discussion is a step forward (Ford, 1962). All pupils should realize that habit formation goes forward by small steps and that improvement in any area is the result of much practice and evaluation.

Begin with Vigor   It is a common practice at the beginning of a new term to spend a few minutes checking enrollment and attendance and then to excuse the class. Such a custom is not in accord with educational psychology. Enrollment and seating details are not the objectives of education, and they should be subordinated to the task at hand, which is to set forth the aims of the schoolwork. Even in a curtailed period (and better to have a full and vigorous one) it is helpful to give the students the idea that vital work is going to take place. The teacher may ask questions relating to the work, discuss some of the objectives and make an assignment (except perhaps in the primary grades). This businesslike approach immediately creates the impression that something significant is going to take place on subsequent days. As James has so fittingly expressed it, "Every smallest stroke of virtue or vice leaves its never-so-little scar" (James, 1939, p. 77). Because the teacher wants to establish habits of industry, application, seriousness, concentration, and attention, it is advisable to begin at once.

The first day is not the only time for the vigorous approach. Every new unit or new objective should be introduced with the reinforcement of enthusiasm. For instance, if the teacher has introduced neatness as an objective, he should insist that pupils immediately practice it. Kindly reprimands and appropriate praise, as reinforcements, give vigor to the new effort. Habits persist because they are reinforced—because they serve a need.

Maintain the Effort with Consistency Unless people make consistent effort, old habits of procrastination, getting by, and hastiness creep back into their behavior. Habit formation, we have seen, involves motivation and repetition. Determining to build new habits is only part of the process. There must be repetition. Thus, in our example of neatness, discussion and illustration must be followed with reminders of the need for consistent effort.

One of the most important factors in a wholesome program of pupil development is consistency. Since many environmental stimulations cannot be easily controlled, it is important that consistency adhere wherever possible (Peck, 1958). Children get a feeling of security from consistent discipline. The inconsistency of teachers or parents in mood, expectations, and limitations of behavior contribute to children's feelings of insecurity. Consistency for the sake of consistency is not recommended, but necessary changes in daily schedules should be countered by consistent teacher behavior.

While considering the role of consistency in habit formation, we should observe that routine must not be carried so far as to result in mere training. It may be that the child can conform to rigid requirements, but perhaps at the cost of failure to develop healthy initiative. Emphasis on habit formation may not be dangerous, but it can be futile. If it is necessary to make a choice, a love of learning is more important than the ability to parrot facts. The goal of understanding meanings should be consistently prominent (Craig, 1957, p. 10). Too much emphasis on learning facts may either (1) push learning beyond maturational levels required for understanding, or (2) lead to neglect of problem-solving, creative, and socializing activities. The teacher's program should aim at enjoyment of learning through understanding, perceiving personal meaning, and meeting the pupils' needs for growth. These broad outlines for consistency do not negate the desirability of variation of materials, methods of approach, or organization of program.

Emphasize the Positive   Much of the effort to alter habits is rendered more difficult because nothing better is substituted. Thus if we are working to reduce vocalization in reading (see section on Improving Reading Habits), it is not sufficient to point out that it is a bad habit. The advice "Try to stop vocalizing" often results in additional confusion. The aim should be to get meaning from the printed material; therefore the emphasis should be on increasing reading speed and improving vocabulary so that the need to vocalize becomes unnecessary.

Instead of shaming pupils to get rid of a habit, teachers should encourage them when they occasionally manifest a better one. An excellent illustration of "accent on the positive" is provided in speech-correction work. The teacher is advised not to call attention to the defect, but to stress the desirable pattern. He is also advised to avoid labeling the child a stutterer but to accept his speech as a natural way for him to express himself. It has often been noted in studies of stutterers that their speech appears to be normal in some situations and for brief periods. These situations occur when the individual gets his mind off his deficiencies and is absorbed in something that he can do and for which he is recognized positively. It is a fundamental tenet of successful work with exceptional children of all types that they be made to feel that they are important and an integral part of the group.

> Although teachers have good intentions, they sometimes fail to teach the child the differences between right and wrong, correct and incorrect. There is too great reliance on words and too little effort to put forth concrete examples, to follow through, and to set consequences. A negative approach emphasizes failure rather than success and thus heightens a child's apprehensions and discouragements.[7]

There are many ways to accent the positive—to reinforce the progress and the occasional, unusual, and commendable actions of pupils. Among these would be granting privileges, keeping charts of progress, having pupils give special reports, displaying a pupil's work, and comments on the report card. These are most helpful in building habits when used in terms of the recognized needs of individual pupils.

Permit No Exceptions   Advising that one permit no exceptions to a proposed plan is actually an additional emphasis on the need for consistent practice. Over half a century ago, William James stated the need for permitting no exceptions emphatically; and contemporary psychologists

[7] Norris G. Haring and E. Lakin Phillips, *Educating Emotionally Disturbed Children,* New York: McGraw-Hill Book Company, 1962, p. 182.

would endorse the advice. "Each lapse is like the letting fall of a ball of string which one is carefully winding up: a single slip undoes more than a great many turns will wind again. Continuity of training is the great means of making the nervous system act infallibly right."[8] The pupil may be trying to establish the habit of pronouncing clearly the final -*ings* of words. If he is encouraged and allowed no exceptions, he begins to form the habit. If he is trying to practice on improved reading ten minutes a day, the successive number of practice sessions is a stimulus, because the reader wants to maintain the record. But if he allows an exception, the next day he is likely to say, "What's the use? I've already broken my record."

This suggestion has its roots in psychological fact. The role of repetition in the process of conditioning is of great importance. The fact that motivation is strengthened by success has been noted in many different situations. Functional autonomy (carrying on an act because the act itself provides the motivation) is more likely to be established by consistently applied effort than by occasional effort. The element of recency—the more recently a stimulus-response has been exercised, the stronger the act becomes—must also be considered important.

Effective study—an application of habit formation

Much of what has been said about habits may be illustrated by showing how these generalizations and principles may be applied to improve study. Most persons use only a fraction of their intellectual potential (Kubie, 1956). On the other hand, experienced teachers are often surprised by the low intelligence test scores of some pupils who have good academic records. A study of 383 Ph.D. holders in biological, physical, and social sciences revealed that 2 per cent of them had IQs of 100 or less in high school, 11 per cent had high school IQs between 101 and 110, and 30 per cent had high school IQs between 111 and 120 (Strauss, 1960). Many factors, particularly motivation and home and school backgrounds, provide partial explanations for this, but certainly one factor is efficiency of study habits.

Define Purposes For either a college student or a schoolteacher, purpose is a first consideration in effective study. The student must define his own purpose by taking a hard look at the future. The teacher who can make clear to pupils the importance of what they are doing—largely in terms of their present needs—is taking the first step toward improved study. It should be remembered that habits persist (become functionally

[8] William James, "The Laws of Habit," *Talks to Teachers on Psychology*, New York: Holt, Rinehart and Winston, Inc., 1899, p. 69.

autonomous) only when they serve a need[9] and disappear when no need or purpose is satisfied. When pupils can see that application to study gets recognition, increases their power, takes them toward their immediate or long-term goals, study becomes important enough to warrant the expenditure of time and energy.

> We may teach with machines, with television, with teams of pre-professionals, para-professionals and post-professionals, with overhead projectors and underhand methods, scientifically or artistically, and logically or illogically, but our efforts may all seem a little foolish to our critics and more ridiculous to our captive subjects if what we teach and what we reward, immediately or in Heaven, is something that makes little difference in the youth's struggles to attain self-regard and to attain acceptance from those who count in his world.[10]

Develop Interests Much of what is heard from the man on the street leads one to believe that interests are inherent—that one just has, or does not have, interest in certain things. The truth is that interests develop from knowledge, experience, success, and the exercise of talents. Interests cannot be given; they must be created. Even interests that stem from association with an admired person are the result of a particular kind of experience. As a teacher, you can help pupils develop and maintain interests that contribute to effective study in a number of ways.

1. Relate the new to what is already known. When new topics are introduced, show how they are related to previous reading and discussions. Pupils can be asked to point out the relationships of the new to the old. School subjects should be related to one another (Goodlad, 1958, pp. 180ff). The use of review periods serves not only to consolidate learning, but also to show relationships and foster interest.

2. Make knowledge as personal as possible. Try to show how pursuit of a subject can serve the pupil's needs—how science contributes to health, living conveniences, transportation, manufacturing automobiles, etc., or how social studies are concerned with the things that are related to what parents read in the newspapers and discuss at the table—or better yet, what the youngsters are seeing on television,

3. See that information is acquired. Because interests are developed rather than inherent, the student must take the first step by acquiring the habits of paying attention and doing assignments. Once this is accom-

---

[9] Allport suggests that "functional autonomy" be used to represent the portion of life that is oriented toward the future. The term is particularly pertinent here, as we consider that purposes are the pull of the future. See Gordon W. Allport, "Psychological Models for Guidance," *Harvard Educational Review*, 32: 373–381, 1963.

[10] Joseph Leese, "Highlights on Research on Teaching and Learning," *High School Journal*, 45: 320, 1962.

plished, attention—and interest—on subsequent occasions comes easily. It is the continued demand for attention when the pupil sees no personal relationship and makes no progress that must be questioned, but the occasional attention that precedes the first step can reasonably be demanded.

4. Arrange for success. Tasks scaled to the ability of pupils and to their past performances makes the distribution of the experience of success equitable. Expectation that all pupils in a class will perform at one level has long been a valid criticism of much classroom teaching. Rates at which pupils progress vary, and there should be some provision for individual deviations from the core curriculum (Capehart, 1958, pp. 204ff).

5. Use instructional materials and resources. Motion pictures, slides, transparencies, models, murals, displays, dramatic productions, relics, and realia can provide a sense of reality and a here-and-now flavor to subjects. They are an effective—and economical—means of introducing abstract subjects. Visits to institutions, factories, farms, dairies, sewage-disposal plants, museums, and laboratories capitalize on the real and concrete. These interest-evoking approaches should, however, be means to the end of getting the pupil to become personally responsible for his further pursuit of the subject.

6. Encourage participation in school activities. Some pupils, particularly high school pupils, do not develop an interest in schoolwork because they never become an integral part of the total school program (Havighurst and others, 1962, p. 62). In view of the many activities which characterize the modern school—athletics, orchestras, singing groups, publications, dramatics, science and literary clubs, and student government—the question is largely one of helping the pupil find where he can best fit and checking to see that no one is bypassed. Attention should be given to the costs, which some pupils find prohibitive.

7. Encourage use of what is learned. One often hears the complaint "We didn't even discuss the reading assignment," or "The exam didn't cover the outside readings." A pupil's apparent short attention span is actually a manifestation of his disinterest in learning things for which he can see no use, and it is relative to adult-imposed activities. We all have noted the satisfaction that pupils get from trying to use their first few lessons in French or Latin. More ways should be found—recitation, demonstrations, imaginative dramatic productions, role playing—to permit pupils to use what they learn.

Recitation (meaning to re-cite, not just to repeat) is one of the effective ways to use material. It should be recited in new contexts, in several illustrations; it should be restated in wholes, in response to staccato questions, in oral and in written form. If the material is worth learning in the first place, it is worth consolidating. True recitation uses the law of exercise, it stimulates thinking, it indicates gaps in knowledge, it provides clues to errors, and it provides exercise in the transfer of learning.

Develop the Mental Set for Study   Mental set is a predisposition to act in a certain way—it can be a temporary or a persisting condition. Mental set for study would include not only interest, but also the inclination to do something about the particular project now. The conditions that make for interest development and the emotional atmosphere of the school or home contribute to mental set, but choice—understanding, use of what is learned, and progress enter here—is also an important aspect of mental set. It helps to say, "I will." The advice to start vigorously is justified in terms of mental set. Favorable mental set is encouraged if pupils have materials at hand, adhere to a schedule, perceive clear-cut goals, do the lessons for themselves rather than "for the teacher," and know what to look for. Pupils remember best the things that they intend to remember (Ausubel, Schpoont, and Cukier, 1957). The physical conditions of the classroom condition mental set, but positive mental set makes it probable that negative physical conditions can be ignored. Pupils cannot always have ideal light, quiet, and comfortable room temperature. Attempts should be made to teach the important lesson that attitudes toward work and the ability to do it are more important than the physical working conditions.

Students should be encouraged to develop the habit of concentration. Purpose, interest, and background affect the ability to concentrate but so does habit. Some pupils learn to concentrate in the library despite the traffic and at home despite television and noisy children in adjacent rooms; others use these as excuses for not concentrating. Rapid reading demands more concentration (see section on Improving Reading Habits) than does slow and leisurely reading; it should be encouraged by and practiced under the direction of instructors who themselves have learned this skill. Skills of concentration are acquired rather than inherited. Robinson, summarizing many years of research at Ohio State University, suggests five factors that foster habits of concentration: (1) work-study skills, including positive attitude, preliminary surveys of work, asking questions on headings, alternation of activities; (2) planning time and settling down to work promptly; (3) improving the conditions for work; (4) analyzing the reasons for pursuing the study (motivation); and (5) keeping a chart of progress (Robinson, 1961, pp. 68–100).

Make a Time Schedule   Successful persons, whether in adult life or in school, work by a time schedule. The schedule is not always written out, but their time is planned. Incentive is added if it is written. In the elementary grades, where school periods are scheduled by administrative policy, a student's schedule is less important than it is in high school when he has free periods and must plan for supplementary study. Schedules help to improve the use of time but they do not work automatically—they must be made to work. It is easier to make them work if certain factors are considered in the plan: (1) Include all required activities (classes, regular appointments); (2) allow time for meals, sleep, personal duties; (3) indicate study periods, showing precise times and places—regularity of place contributes to favorable mental set as habits form; (4) allow for "free study" periods to complete work not finished during regular study periods or to spend in recreational reading; (5) allow time for fun and recreation. Some schedules are self-defeating because they are too firmly devoted to work. It is better to have a less stern schedule that can be made to work than to have one so tight that it produces frustration.

Making the schedule work should involve the steps in habit formation indicated above: the definition of purposes, a vigorous start, permitting no early exceptions, and maintaining effort. Schedules tend to improve study habits because they reduce feelings of guilt about not studying enough; little time is lost in shifting from one activity to another; and they make settling down less difficult (Robinson, 1961, p. 73).

Improve Reading Habits Despite electronic gadgets and teaching aids, books remain the major tool for learning. Some authorities are recommending that 60 per cent of the space in school libraries should be occupied by study carrels (*Shape of Education*, 1964, p. 20). Because of the importance of reading, one must question the cliché "Practice makes perfect." Practice does not necessarily mean improvement—one "perfects" what he practices. If a student has faulty reading habits, practice consolidates them. Research has shown that college students read little, if any, better than high school students; reading skills appear to level off at the point where formal instruction in reading typically ceases. Both groups read about 180 to 230 words per minute of narrative or descriptive material. Excellent readers may read four times as fast and comprehend and retain the material. Good readers average 500 to 750 words a minute. But *without practice devoted explicitly to improve speed*, there is little change from the 200 word-per-minute rate through the high school and college years.

Contrary to what might be thought, the older student can improve more rapidly than the younger one. This is because reading is, in part, a matter of bringing meaning to the printed page, and the more mature student has the broader background of experience with which to make the words meaningful. Also contrary to what is often thought, slow reading does not improve understanding. Concentration is required for rapid reading—the mind cannot take little side trips, as it can in slow reading; in addition, groups of words come together in closer time context and thus yield more meaning. The slow reader is a "word" reader—the fast reader is an "idea" reader.

Before considering the steps involved in teaching pupils to read more rapidly, it should be noted that there should be different rates. Poetry should not be read rapidly. Directions for assembling a complicated piece of laboratory equipment, for example, should not be read at top speed. There are times when it is advisable to go off on a mental side trip to contemplate the meaning and implications of a particular passage. But by and large, most of the reading that pupils do can be done more rapidly and more effectively. The following suggestions for improving speed are most pertinent for work with upper-grade and high school pupils:

1. Practice on easy, interesting material. Changing any habit—even handicapping ones—causes discomfort, so instead of practicing on school assignments, use novels and interesting articles, treatments of special hobbies. Discouragement with the feelings attendant on changing habits is less likely to occur if there is no responsibility for the material on an examination.

2. Practice *regularly* for short periods. A few minutes a day (the author has advised two periods of ten minutes daily in his reading-improvement groups) is better than an hour or two on weekends. Besides, much of the pupil's reading is in short periods rather than long sessions, so the short periods have an element of reality.

3. Read with the specific objective of improved speed. Permit the pupils to read for five or ten minutes and have each one check where he is when time is called. Count the words. Have them mark off 100 more words in the same book and tell them to try to reach the mark in the same amount of time they took to read the first passage. This should then be done repeatedly in daily exercise of about ten minutes.[11]

4. Read for idea at all times. Not only after each reading period of ten minutes, but after reading almost anything worth reading, the next minute or two should be devoted to reflecting on what has just been read. Practice reading for the main ideas. This process of reflection is one of the more effective ways to become active, rather than merely passive or accepting, in the reading process.

5. Encourage the building of vocabulary. Building vocabularly is important in itself because words are the means by which ideas are

[11] The author has conducted reading groups in terms of the steps outlined here and has in a period of seven to ten weeks seen an *average* doubling of initial rates—with no loss in comprehension—for all those pupils who could report that they practiced daily. Many have tripled their rates—going from an initial rate of 250 to 800 words or more per minute. Test questions are asked in the group sessions after each short reading period, and the students are asked to reflect on every passage they read during their independent practice sessions.

understood, retained, and expressed. The better the vocabulary, the more precise and concise is self-expression and the more accurate an understanding of others—either in reading or listening. In reading, the more strange words encountered, the more frequently the rhythmic eye movements that are essential to good reading are interrupted. Listing new words on cards or in a notebook *and* reviewing them periodically are habits well worth encouraging.

6. Keep a record of progress. Keeping a chart such as the one in Figure 7 is an incentive to regular practice, and it provides an immediate knowledge of progress, which tends to sustain interest. A student who reported that she had tried several times to improve her reading speed without perceptible results doubled her rate under weekly supervision, but she attributed much of her success to the necessity of marking the chart and the knowledge that she was progressing.

Some of the literature on developmental reading asks the reader to cease making regressive eye movements, to stop making vocalizations, to try to reduce the number of fixations per line, and to practice not fixating at the extreme ends of lines of print. Absence of vocalizations and regressive eyes movements (see Glossary) and few fixations per line are characteristic of good readers. The author feels, however, that these are symptoms (not causes) of effective reading. They will disappear with improved skill. Conscious attention to them distracts the student and impairs his concentration. In a developmental program, the reader has enough to do with pushing himself for speed and attempting to remember accurately what he reads. In most cases, fixations, regressions, and vocal-

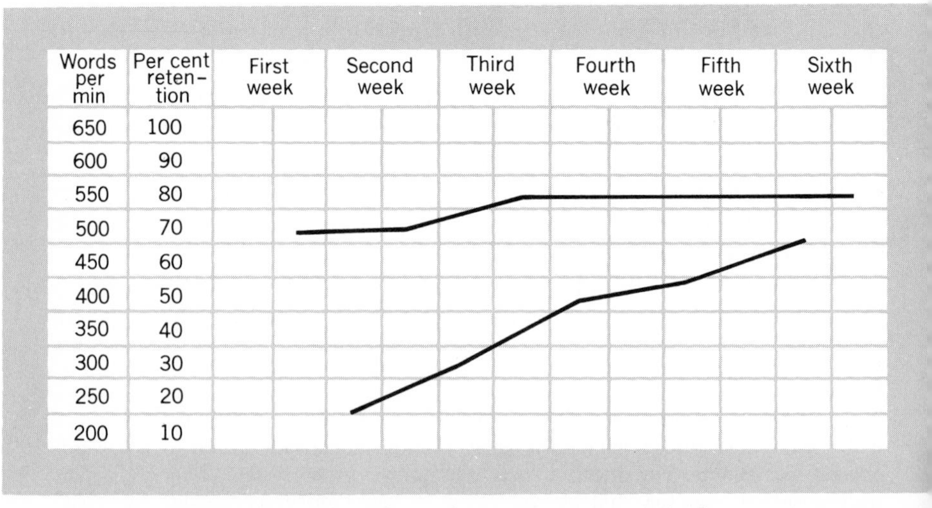

Words per min	Per cent retention	First week	Second week	Third week	Fourth week	Fifth week	Sixth week
650	100						
600	90						
550	80						
500	70						
450	60						
400	50						
350	40						
300	30						
250	20						
200	10						

FIGURE 7. *Developmental reading—chart of progress. (Words per minute can be entered to suit the individual rate on initial testing.)*

izations take care of themselves when improved speed and comprehension are achieved.

Machines that cause a shutter to descend at varying speeds down the pages, progressively covering lines of print, have been used to increase reading rates. These are good motivating devices—keeping the reader under pressure to read more rapidly. However, marking off more words each week can also keep one reading under pressure. Marvel (1959) found that determination (verbal set) to read faster resulted in greater gains in rate and retention than did work with a tachistoscope (see Glossary). The machines demonstrate that reading habits can be changed, but so does the reading chart. Machines tend to limit the variety of material that will be practiced. Pupils can use a variety of materials for practice between the weekly checkups without the machine; however, the checkup should be on the same sort of material so that weekly comparisons will be valid. Ultimately one will have to read without a machine, so it seems that the expense is hardly warranted.

Develop Personal Involvement in Study The steps outlined for developing interest are also ways of becoming more personally involved in study, and there are also techniques for doing this in daily study habits. Robinson (1961, pp. 29–30) has epitomized some of this involvement in the SQ3R formula. In addition to personal involvement, other psychological principles are inherent in the method. The steps, with the representative psychological factors included in parentheses, are shown in the following passage. It should be noted that "involvement" might have been mentioned as a psychological factor at points other than the one indicated:

The SQ3R Method of Study-reading and Partial List of Psychological Factors

Survey Glance over the headings in the chapter to see the major points that will be developed. Read the summary.
(Mental set conditions learning; a view of the whole improves perception.)

Question Turn the first heading into a question. Use conscious effort to formulate a question for which an answer must be found. (Active involvement improves learning; purposeful effort is more economical than random effort.)

Read Read to find the answer to your question.
(Behavior is goal-seeking in nature; understanding of purpose improves learning.)

Recite Look away from your book and briefly recite the answer to your question. Jot down cues in outline form. Question, read, and recite for each section.

(Active recall is at a higher learning level than is recognition; learning should be active rather than passive.)

Review   Look over your notes to get a bird's-eye view of the points and their relationships. Check your memory by reciting subpoints. (Repetition strengthens mental connections; meaningful learning is more efficient than is rote learning; mastery retards forgetting.)

Results of the SQ3R method should be (1) faster reading, (2) location of important points, (3) better retention of key points, and (4) an outline for later review.

Personal involvement can also be increased by careful note taking. The author favors taking notes after reading a whole section. This prevents interruption of the rhythm of good reading and also provides perspective on what is worth recording. Notes should be brief. Light check marks may be used to locate important passages and to indicate words that should be added to the vocabulary list. Students should be advised to take permanent notes (in ink and on cards or notebook paper); some able students recopy their notes for an additional review.

Personal involvement may be increased by preparation for participation and actual participation in recitations and discussions. Special reports and demonstrations are effective and have long been used as a way of increasing personal involvement. Conversely, the lecture method is increasingly questioned, even at the college level. However, personal involvement is an individual matter, and while some students gain more from small group activity, others do profit from lectures (Beach, 1960). Clearly, teachers must continue to seek information about their pupils and to study their individual reaction patterns to see how each one's involvement may be increased. One way is the use of a study-habits checklist or a problems checklist (Frankel, 1960). Observation and checklists will again illustrate the fact, too easily overlooked, that a behavior (study habit) is comprised of many contributing, precipitating, incidental, and tangential conditions. A prescription—a cureall, a system—for study will not work effectively for all pupils.

Encourage the Search for Meaning and Relationships   Education has often been criticized because it involves too much learning of inert, unrelated knowledge (Dressel, 1958, pp. 3ff). Teachers can counter this criticism and help their pupils develop better study habits if they encourage the search for relationships. They can indicate the relationships that exist between ideas, subject-matter areas, school, and life, and they can also ask and encourage pupils to do this independently. Bright students often find these relationships without help, but most need some help and encouragement. The search for meaning and relationships is another way for a pupil to become active rather than passive in his study habits. Review periods are excellent times to give pupils exercise in the

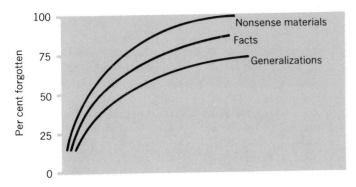

FIGURE 8. *Curves of forgetting. The shape of the curve in relation to elapsed time must be considered representative. Variations in thoroughness of learning, completeness of understanding, personal need, and the like, would make substantial differences in the shape of the curve.*

habit of searching for relationships. When they can discover such relationships, they have much less need for the artificial rewards of grades (Bruner, 1961), which too often become the pallid reasons for studying. The importance of meaning and relationships in learning and study is indicated in Figure 8, which is representative of many studies of retention and forgetting.

The search for meanings can be intensified by other factors that have been recommended for the study program; e.g., the habit of actively building vocabulary, taking notes *and reviewing* them, the preliminary scanning of material, and the immediate reflection on what has been read. In addition, practice should be given in studying the charts, diagrams, and tables that often are included in texts. Too often these are skipped; but quite typically the author has included them in this book because they condense and summarize what it would take many words to explain.

Summary

Much of what is learned in school and in daily life becomes consolidated in the organism in the form of habits. Depending on their nature, these habits make for economy of effort or hamper future adjustment. It is traditional to think of habits as being rigid—almost mechanical—responses, but they do in fact change little by little as their need-serving purposes change. Habits may themselves, through functional autonomy, become motives. Habits have physical, mental, and emotional components—all of which are involved in an understanding of their nature.

To form helpful habits or to break harmful ones, certain approaches can be used to advantage. The conscious formulation of a goal, beginning with vigor, consistently maintaining effort, placing emphasis on positive aspects of a habit system, and permitting no exceptions (especially in early stages of the program) are helpful.

Habit formation was illustrated in terms of developing effective study techniques. Good study habits include the *development* of interests. This can be accomplished by seeking relationships of the new with what is already known, by making knowledge personal, by acquiring information, by arranging for some degree of success, by using illustrative materials, by encouraging wider participation in school activities, and by using what is learned. Mental set is important in getting at and sticking to work. Set is conditioned by previous experiences and immediate physical and psychological conditions, but freedom of choice must also be taken into account. The economical use of time can be enhanced by planning and following an hourly time schedule. Reading habits can be markedly improved by consistent and purposeful effort. Checking both rate and comprehension is essential to improved reading habits. The active search for meaning and relationships constitute not just techniques but also motivation for improved study habits.

Problems and exercises

1 Make a close check of the things you do through habit during a typical day. List twelve that you consider most important (both negative and positive) to see which might be worth modifying.

2 How do you account for the lack of follow-through on some of the behaviors you have in the past resolved to make habitual?

3 What are the psychological explanations for emphasizing the positive as the teacher tries to help pupils form new habits; e.g., neatness and system in written reports and notebooks?

4 What are some ways in which teachers might help pupils develop an interest in arithmetic? In grammar or science?

5 Talk with someone who reads in excess of 700 words per minute to discover some of the specific problems he encountered as he developed such a rate.

6 For a period of three weeks read some light and interesting material to see how much speed you can gain with two 10-minute periods *every* day.

7 Why would a student who achieves a speed of 550 words a minute at the end of five weeks of practice be back a year later to, say, 375 words per minute?

8 Talk with five high school pupils to see if and why they use (or do not use) a time schedule. How valid do you think their explanations are?

9 How would you explain the SQ3R method of study to high school freshmen?

Suggested additional readings

Dewey, John: *Human Nature and Conduct,* New York: Vintage Books, Random House, Inc., 1922, pp. 14–42.

In these two chapters, the author describes how habits function in social relations and discusses the nature and meaning of will. He shows that character is a matter of habits and indicates that a habit does not of necessity involve repetition.

James, William: "The Laws of Habit," *Talks to Teachers on Psychology,* New York: Holt, Rinehart and Winston, Inc., 1899 (ed., 1939), pp. 64–78.

This chapter presents positive suggestions for forming and breaking habits and illustrates how these suggestions may be applied. Even though written more than half a century ago, the author's remarks are highly pertinent today.

Robinson, Francis P.: *Effective Study,* rev. ed., New York: Harper & Row, Publishers, 1961.

The author's findings during more than twenty years of research and experimentation in methods of study are presented in terms of the SQ3R method. The book contains suggestions for improved study and some exercises in their implementation.

Spache, George D., and Paul C. Berg: *The Art of Efficient Reading,* New York: The Macmillan Company, 1955.

This work is representative of many books that deal with instructions for reading more efficiently. Various types of reading matter are used for illustrative exercises.

Woodley, Colin E.: *How to Study and Prepare for Exams,* New York: New American Library of World Literature, Inc., 1961.

The title of this paperback may be inappropriate because it seems to indicate that the purpose of study is to pass examinations. Nevertheless, the suggestions on reading, time scheduling, note taking, and reviewing are pertinent in a more general way for both high school and college students.

Factors That Facilitate Learning

6 A person always takes what he perceives to be the shortest route to a goal. For countless generations, people have sought easier ways to do things. This is fortunate for education, the more fortunate because it does not have to be taught. It is wise to seek easier ways to do and to learn. But all methods now known require *some* effort. This chapter describes means of facilitating learning, but even the most effective require individual activity and responsibility.

Many factors that affect learning are discussed in detail elsewhere in this book, e.g., readiness, mental set, teacher personality, motivation, and mental health. Here we are concerned with a few important and readily applicable factors that do not have prominence elsewhere.

Improving learning techniques

The most effective way to learn about factors that facilitate learning is to apply them to your own study techniques. You may already use some of the techniques to be discussed; others may be developed to improve your efficiency.

The Value and Implications of Meaning The significance of learning goals and the individual's acceptance of them (goals must have personal meaning) have been discussed elsewhere. Once the goals are accepted the meaning of studies may be enlarged. One way, of course, is to take the daily small steps of studying and experiencing that lead to the development of meaning. A second way to enhance meaning is to take a broad view of the course, unit, and individual assignment—to anticipate what is coming, to reflect on the ramifications and relationships of the various topics and subdivisions. Students are advised to preview —to anticipate—when reading a book (Bennett, 1957, p. 65), but few can assert that they do it. Yet this activity could yield the gestalt that enhances meaning—the chance to see the whole picture, pick out the figures, and relegate the incidental and peripheral to the "ground." A third way to enhance meaning is to

120

approach the subject indirectly—almost incidentally—reading and experiencing beyond the textbook and assignments. This has been referred to as "free reading" in the chapter on study habits—the material may be essays, related texts, biographies, novels, or articles that relate in a general way to the topic at hand. Many of the titles in the Suggested Additional Readings sections of this text are of this type. As in the case of travel, social contacts, and other wide experiences, related reading is an effective way to build meaning—especially if a conscious search is made.

As a teacher, you need only to translate the foregoing into methods of helping pupils perceive meaning.

Intent to Learn Learning takes place most readily when a student not only understands and accepts a goal, but also becomes active in its pursuit. Moreover, a student learns what he intends to learn. Let us say that the topic at hand is employment of young people. One of you may decide that the crux of the matter is educational preparation: After investigation, that one will be able to report, "Ten per cent of those with less than high school education are unemployed, five per cent of those who have been graduated from high school are unemployed, while two per cent of those with some college are unemployed" (*Manpower Challenge*, 1960, p. 17). A classmate, however, may feel that the key issue is the distribution of jobs. His studies and learning will certainly concern the distribution of the labor force among professional, business and managerial, service, skilled, labor, agricultural, domestic, or unskilled types of employment.

It is a matter of common observation, supported by experimental evidence, that a genuine intent to learn is an aid to rapid and permanent learning. When pupils know what is expected of them, when goals are definite, when a personal goal is involved, or when results are apparent, learning is facilitated, effort is more intensive and better organized, understanding is enhanced, and attention is focused on the task at hand.

What a pupil intends to learn is influenced by his level of aspiration. Experimental evidence indicates that a student's level of aspiration changes in accordance with his degree of success and tends to be somewhat higher than his present level of accomplishment (see section on Rivalry and Cooperation and Chapter 11, section on Level of Aspiration). However, the goal of an individual pupil must be in accord with his ability. The intent to learn can be intensified when well-selected tasks lead to the success that keeps aspiration at an appropriate level. That is, the slow learner should have an aim slightly higher than his present level of achievement; the aim of the rapid learner should be considerably higher. The latter should not be satisfied with "getting by"—as many are. By referring to data from ability tests, examination of past records, evaluation of current interests, the teacher should be able to scale the daily tasks and thus guide students in developing appropriate aspirations.

The degree of intent to learn is indicated by certain psychological concepts. In addition to the intentional learnings just discussed, there are "concomitant learnings"—learnings acquired without deliberate effort or conscious intent. What a pupil learns about the use of periodical guides, government reports, pamphlet files, and the like, as he searches for information relating to employment might be considered concomitant learnings for example. With a shift in emphasis on the part of the teacher and pupil, these skills could become an aspect of intentional learning.

Many concomitant learnings should not be left to chance. Attitudes toward school, predisposition toward democratic responsibility, and attitudes toward oneself might very well be brought into the focus of intentional learnings. Teachers should seek to evaluate current concomitants to see if they are worthy of more deliberate focus. The whole area of concomitant learning becomes more important as the responsibilities of the school increase. When it was deemed sufficient that the school teach its students to read, write, and compute, the concomitants were not considered important. But as it was recognized that ideals and attitudes could be taught and that attitude formation could not be avoided simply by "sticking to the subject," study of the nature of concomitant learning became more important.

Teachers owe it to their students to bring such general subjects to their attention. They owe it to their students to let them know how they stand on most issues—though they *should not impose their own views*. There is no need to view discussions that lead to an appraisal of values, attitudes, and ideals as tangential. They are part and parcel of the educative process. Attitudes will be formed by evasion as surely as by planned discussion.

It is especially important that the school experiences be pleasant so that pupils will develop favorable attitudes toward study and the continuation of learning. Teachers have neither the wisdom nor the time to teach all the things that students will need to know in their lifetimes. But salutary contacts with teachers and the opportunity to deal with meaningful situations will serve to make continued learning attractive. There are few concomitants of learning that are of greater importance than the development of a love for learning.

Distributed Effort Spacing efforts in intentional learning is economical. Experiment after experiment demonstrates that more is learned when the periods of study are spaced rather than massed (Knapp, Dixon, and Lazier, 1958; Oseas and Underwood, 1952). This is especially true of textbook learning as contrasted to, say, learning a foreign culture "on the spot." An hour every other day spent on the study of educational psychology for ten weeks will result in more thorough and permanent learning than will the same number of hours concentrated in the final three days of the term. One-half hour a day for two weeks will result in more progress in learning to play a musical instrument than seven hours of practice in one day. There are several explanations for the effectiveness of spaced practice or distributed effort.

1. Attention fluctuates. It is easier to stick to the job at hand for short periods than for long periods. Long periods of study do not necessarily mean long periods of concentration.

2. Jost's law states that in the case of associations of equal strength but different recency, further practice strengthens the older rather than the newer association. Thus going back to a subject studied a week ago is better than restudying that subject immediately.

3. Incorrect associations are forgotten more quickly than correct ones. Hence, spaced practice, as contrasted to the immediate repetition of an error, tends to allow the incorrect response to be recognized and dropped.

4. There is a tendency on the part of the organism to resist early repetition of an act (Hilgard, 1962, p. 298). Resistance is built up as effort continues. Hence, the attempt to perform the same act repeatedly within a short space opposes a natural tendency. The organism requires rest.

Some precautions should be taken in spaced activity. Too rapid a succession of events may be harmful. If a new activity intervenes too promptly, consolidation of learning will be less likely. Therefore, study periods should be short enough to avoid fatigue and long enough to allow an idea to jell.

Massed practice may have advantages. If the material to be learned is easy, there is no point to distributed effort. In problem solving, it is often advantageous to stick to the subject for as long as possible; however, an interval of rest might allow the relaxation that permits a certain factor to fall readily into place (Stagner and Karwoski, 1952, p. 261). If motivation is high, massed practice can pay dividends—language camps for wartime interpreters used long, concentrated days of drill and practice to good effect. A lawyer may advantageously use massed effort when he is cramming on a case in which remembering details over a period of months is unimportant.

The question is often raised: How short or how long should study or practice periods be? To a certain extent, the answer depends on the individual, the conditions, and the material. Obviously, if periods are too short, so much time is spent in getting started—time is required for warming up—that comparatively little time remains for the actual task. Also, the more mature the individual, the more capable he is of prolonged work. A concert pianist would be unlikely to allow himself only fifteen-minute practice periods. For schoolwork in the elementary grades, fifteen- or twenty-minute periods are found to be advantageous. College students can profit from one-hour periods devoted to one type of activity. High school pupils are found to profit from periods somewhere between these two extremes.

Providing for distributed effort The traditional division of the school day into periods makes distributed effort feasible. However, the idea of distributed effort is continuation of effort on the same task and in the same direction in successive periods—the teacher should show how the lesson for today builds upon yesterday's lesson. In memorization, the teacher should point out the importance of distributed effort giving pupils practice in applying the principle by spending a few minutes each day in recitation.

Since fluctuation of interest is considered one justification for distributed effort, it is wise to plan for variety in individual lessons. For example, instead of having the class do algebra problems from the book for the entire period, the teacher might spend only a part of the time working problems, devote some time to reviewing general principles or rules, give part of the time to applications to problems taken from daily experiences, and review problems that were studied a week or two weeks ago for a part of the period.

Distributed effort is particularly advantageous in learning routine skills, such as typing and shorthand. Teachers should provide for drill, it is true, but the practice periods should be short enough to encourage sustained effort. The criticism that massed practice causes boredom and that boredom causes needless errors is good reason to conscientiously plan for distributed effort. Teachers can help pupils capitalize on the economy of distributed effort by giving tests periodically rather than relying on a midterm or final test that will prompt pupils to cram.

Overlearning If learning is defined as the ability to perform an act, repeat a list of words, or recite a verse once, then overlearning can be defined as continued practice after a criterion level has been achieved. Experimental results show that overlearning results in more accurate retention over a longer period of time than practice that ceases at the point of initial learning (Holland and Porter, 1960). If multiplication tables can be learned from twenty repetitions, thirty repetitions make it more likely that the learner will be able to repeat the tables after a week without practice.

The advantageousness of overlearning depends on the thoroughness of the initial learning. The skills of swimming or skating are not readily forgotten because practice usually continues after acquisition of the skill. In academic subjects, overlearning gives the law of exercise an opportunity to operate during the extended practice period.

The gain from overlearning decreases as additional practice continues: 100 to 200 per cent overlearning is better than 50 per cent overlearning, but the additional gain is not proportional to the extended effort (Krueger, 1929). It is therefore recommended that overlearning be confined to from half to double the number of repetitions required for original learning. However, it is worth noting that overlearning need not consist of mere rote repetition. Overlearning can also be effected by reviewing materials just read (but not complete rereading), reciting to oneself, placing the material in a new context, or reading similar materials in another text.

Encouraging the practice of overlearning All pupils from the intermediate grades up should understand the principle of overlearning and take responsibility for applying it. In the primary grades, overlearning is employed through drill, repetition, and review. In the upper grades, too little attention is paid to overlearning. As soon as pupils are given assignments that are to be prepared ahead of time, they should be encouraged to review immediately the work they have just completed. Teachers can stress overlearning by presenting material in a new context, using illustrations, making applications, holding class discussions, and encouraging pupils to bring materials previously studied to bear upon current projects.

Whole Learning and Part Learning When a student sets out to memorize a long poem or prose passage by reading and rereading the entire selection until it is memorized, he is employing the whole-learning method. If he learns the passage verse by verse or paragraph by paragraph, repeating each one until it is memorized, he is using the part-learning method. In general, memorizing is facilitated by the whole method.

Let us assume that a pupil is trying to learn four stanzas of four lines each. If the part method is used, the end of line four is most closely associated with the beginning of line one, and the fourth line of verse two is most closely associated with the first line of verse two, etc. Thus he must learn the parts *plus* the connections—the process adds up to a greater total than when he is learning by the whole method. Perhaps you may recall a time when, in attempting to recite a poem, you finished the second verse and started immediately to repeat it instead of going on to the third verse. If the whole method is used, the end of the first verse is properly associated with the first line of the second verse.

Actually, the problem is probably best solved not by a choice of one method or the other, but by a combination of the two. The teacher may start by helping the student gain insight into the meaning of the entire selection or task (Katona, 1942). As the whole is attacked, some phrases will be found to be more difficult than others. These may be learned as parts, then each part put into its total context. Progress may seem to be slower, but actual experimentation indicates a saving in total time. Circumstances that determine the choice of method are as follows:

1. The whole method is more advantageous with meaningful material. Understanding of the entire unit favors the use of the whole method.

2. The more intelligent the pupil, the greater the likelihood that he

will profit from the whole method. Slow learners tend to make better progress with the part method—actually, for them the *understandable* whole unit is smaller.

3. The method is dependent to an extent upon the size of the unit to be mastered (Hovland, 1951). For example, a student would not be likely to set out to memorize an entire book by the whole method.

Experimental studies of the relative advantages of whole and part methods point to some tentative conclusions. In the later stages of learning, a pupil may profit from the part method—for example, he might devote special attention to certain verses in a poem. While meaningful material lends itself better to the whole method, parts may also be meaningful. As the material seems to become more logical and better organized, the whole method should be favored. Actually, the cases are so varied that no firm or conclusive generalization should be made (Deese, 1958, p. 203).

Capitalizing on whole and part learnings If we accept the thesis that understanding is primary in learning, then the merit of whole learning must be stressed. If comprehension is a primary consideration, part learning, or the fragmental approach, is subject to criticism. Teachers should try to give their pupils some preliminary comprehension of an entire unit. They may describe the scope of problems to be studied, indicate some of the difficulties to be encountered, and preview the material. The author encourages his students in educational psychology to read completely through some text in educational psychology within the first two weeks of the course. This rapid overview helps students to anticipate problems, grasp relationships, and perceive goals. It should be noted that this approach makes use of spaced practice: McGuigan suggests that this might largely explain the superiority of the whole approach (1960).

Obviously, it is not possible to comprehend a whole course on the first day. A student could no more understand the whole of arithmetic than he could sit down and play "America" on a clarinet the first time he took the instrument in his hands. But the role and function of arithmetic should be explained in the clearest possible terms, and the end objective should be at least vaguely understood.

Devices for presenting the whole are motion pictures, illustrative stories, broad outlines of the areas to be covered, and a general preview of the material. At the end of the unit, the teacher can tie all material together through a review or summary. An approach to studying the whole is to use all academic subject-matter divisions to solve problems. This plan is implemented by the use of units, problems, and projects. Criticism that pupils are in danger of missing some important fundamentals is sometimes made of this approach. Planning by the teacher (e.g., the use of a checklist of essential items) can avert this danger; at the same time, he can see that subject matter is presented in terms of the natural inter-relationships that will characterize its later use.

One practical matter that relates to the whole-part procedure is school organization. Schools dominated by the subject-matter viewpoint are likely to have one period devoted to language, one to arithmetic, one to spelling, etc. This breaks the day into too many short periods. High school is dominated by schedule to an even greater extent than the elementary school, but the growing popularity of the "double period" indicates resistance to this type of program. Larger units of time allow for field trips, excursions to museums, and viewing and discussion of motion pictures and make the whole approach possible. The core-curriculum approach goes a step further, grouping together the learning experiences that are designed to help pupils live in a democratic society. Evaluative studies indicate a slight but consistent superiority of the core-curriculum approach over subject organization in terms of students' knowledge, critical thinking, work habits, and social skills (Capehart, 1958).

Knowledge of Progress Effective learning can be stimulated by capitalizing on knowledge of progress. The learner profits from feedback, recognition, or response, which tacitly or verbally says "Right" or "Wrong." The need for some such response, e.g., the infant's need for response or recognition from his mother, is often included in the category of basic human needs. School pupils, too, need response or feedback. This can be given in several ways; one important way is to inform them about their progress.

Knowledge of progress enables a student to check on the results of his efforts and makes it possible for him to identify errors and successes. Too often we have practiced the wrong (or at least awkward) effort and then had the double duty of unlearning the erroneous as well as learning the correct. An example may be found in target shooting, where it is helpful to know where each shot was placed so that correction can be made for each person's average error (Goldstein and Rittenhouse, 1954). Some of the effectiveness of programmed learning (see Chapter 18) is dependent on the immediate knowledge of results. Such knowledge is an important source of motivation as well as information. For example, we generally like to take the vocabulary or information tests that are published in magazines and newspapers, but dislike them in many other situations. Part of this reaction is due to the immediacy of information about how well we did.

Scores on achievement examinations, graphs showing spelling scores, a checklist of books read, a chart showing samples of handwriting, a list of topics studied in history or geography—all make it possible for the teacher to capitalize on the value of knowledge of progress.

If two equal groups of pupils are given a learning task and the teaching methods are the same except that one group is informed of progress and the other is not, the informed group accomplishes more. Thus an incentive to continued learning is knowledge of gains. For example, two equated groups of fourth graders worked twenty periods on arithmetic —the total time being the same for both groups. Members of one group kept charts of individual and group progress. The other group worked without records or knowledge of results. The informed group improved 12 per cent more than the uninformed group (Panlasigui and Knight, 1930).

There are three reasons why knowledge of progress is such an effective technique. First, it tends to make the goals more concrete. You can test this in developing your own vocabulary. If you simply study words in a haphazard fashion, the chances are that as time goes on you will devote less and less attention to such study. If, on the other hand, you keep a word list or a set of vocabulary cards, the growing list and the knowledge that you have mastered some of them will be a strong incentive to continued effort. Second, interest tends to wane during periods of study: Checking on progress or receiving the teacher's reports of progress breaks the periods of study, and as variety is introduced into the learning exercise, interest is sustained more readily. Third, knowledge of results helps to capitalize on the law of increasing energy, which states that the closer one gets to his goal, the greater the effort he puts forth (Wheeler, 1940, p. 139). You have all experienced or witnessed the feverish activity that characterizes the end of the term. It is usually easier to write the last five pages of a term report than the first two. As the goal comes nearer, more energy seems to be available. Knowledge of results has the effect of introducing intermediate, short-term goals in addition to the ultimate and final goal—thus providing a more frequent resurgence of energy (Loree and Koch, 1960).

According to research workers, knowledge of results leads to improved performance because (1) such knowledge tends to encourage repetition of successful actions, (2) it helps the performer correct or improve unsuccessful actions, and (3) it gives one an incentive to do an accurate performance, while lack of such knowledge removes the incentive. Classroom teachers who habitually inform their students about results can confirm these statements. These conclusions are confirmed in studies dealing with teaching machines. As is shown in Chapter 18, "Programmed Learning and Auto-instruction," a very basic feature of teaching programs is knowledge of correct responses. This immediate feedback provides much of the motivational power that gives psychological support to programmed learning.[1] In one type of program (linear), the material is so constructed that few errors occur, but the student knows how accurately he is responding almost sentence by sentence. In another type of program (branching), an error of a specific type leads the student immediately to the kind of material that will correct the wrong impression (Crowder, 1963).

In the absence of programmed learning, teachers can make use of knowledge of progress. A word of approval or a hand on the shoulder as the student composes his theme, does his arithmetic, or colors his picture is much more of an incentive than most teachers realize. Comments written on papers—preferably without the abstraction of a grade —provide the needed feedback. The teacher cannot be excused for failing to return to pupils papers that he has required them to submit. Individual and class progress charts can be used much more widely. Progress charts need not have the same effect upon pupils as status charts. If the teacher interprets progress in terms of growth "from where you were to where you are," the pupil can more easily bear the disappointment of not being at the head of the class. Group evaluation discussions can provide some realistic and immediate feedback.

Recitation   The word means telling again, repeating, or rehearsing particulars, and it commonly refers to an audible process, but the meaning need not be so restricted. Recitation can also be subvocal. If a student restates to himself what he has just read in a chapter, he is employing self-recitation. Both vocal and subvocal recitation have been found to be helpful in retaining material (Peterson, 1944) for a number of reasons:

1. The learner makes use of the cues for remembering that he will employ at a later time.

2. He discovers immediately the most difficult portions of the lesson and applies his time and effort accordingly.

3. He is immediately aware of the degree of success being achieved; hence there is immediate motivation.

4. He is employing the principle of exercise: he is using the material before a time lapse causes forgetting.

5. Either in or out of school, he will use the material in some kind of recitation; therefore, he is learning the material as it will be used.

6. Recitation provides some of the feedback that enables the teacher to know whether or not the class is understanding him (Cronbach, 1963, p. 397).

Too much emphasis cannot be placed on the importance of activity in

[1] Consider the feedback in learning to pronounce a word. The young child is corrected when he says, "Muvva," the adult's pronunciation becomes the learning stimulus, and the new attempt (hopefully) is approved. Feedback is also supplied by knowledge that a response is correct or incorrect.

the learning process. Speed, precision, and permanance of learning are enhanced in proportion to the amount of activity involved in the process. Therefore, the learning task must challenge the individual's interest and elicit his cooperation. Reading, listening, and seeing are all helpful forms of action; but recitation is more direct and overt.

Recitation can and should mean more than simple restatement. It should mean placing the material in a different setting, applying it in a new situation, viewing it in another perspective. Thus as a student recites a history or psychology lesson, he should plan to make applications of the lesson, attempting to see the material in relation to contemporary and personal problems. The study exercises placed at the end of the chapters in many textbooks may require additional time, but in terms of total learning achievement, the amount of time required is small in comparison to the proven advantage in learning. The real question is not whether a student has time to recite but whether he can afford *not to take the time* needed for it.

The wise use of recitation   Recitation is widely used in schools and therefore should be examined psychologically. It has been seen that children learn what they do. Too often recitation consists of giving back isolated and comparatively meaningless facts that the pupil has gleaned from a book. Memorization may be a form of learning if *changed* response is all that is implied by the term "learning"; memorization is not necessarily learning if "learning" implies *improved* response. Yet teachers have been known to criticize a pupil's recitation because it was not in accord with the words printed in the book. For example, a pupil responded to the teacher's question "What is the flying time from Seattle to Alaska?" with the answer "From two to ten hours." The teacher marked his answer incorrect because the text said it was five hours; he made no inquiry about the answer, although it may have been correct, depending upon whether the flight was from Seattle to Anchorage, to Nome, or to Point Barrow, and whether the flight was by jet plane or by bush hopping.

Recitation should mean the *reuse* of information in new contexts. Teachers who use the discussion or conversational method as a means of developing a topic that has been studied are employing recitation in its most profitable form. Problem solving tends to minimize the acquisition of facts for the sake of answering the teacher's questions and to emphasize the functional use of knowledge. Some of the advantages of such an approach include the following:

1. Material is used in a manner similar to that in which it will be used at a later time.

2. The method stresses pupil activity at the level of interpretation rather than rote repetition.

3. The method tends to encourage pupil initiative and resourcefulness.

4. Training in expressing personal ideas is provided.

5. The method helps pupils avoid an attitude of blind acceptance of the printed word.

If recitation is to have these advantages, much depends on the teacher. The work must be planned with a degree of flexibility that will allow pupils to exercise some freedom. Teacher guidance must be exercised so that discussion will constantly be directed to the problem at hand, but pupils should be led to participate in planning the discussion. Care must be taken to see that all members of the group are given an opportunity to participate; otherwise aggressive pupils may monopolize the discussion.

One of the greatest handicaps to realizing the full potential of the recitation procedures recommended here is what might be called the "teacher's complex." This refers to an attitude on the part of the teacher that the question has not really been answered unless it has been answered in terms that he has had in mind. This does not mean that the teacher should not be well informed; rather, it is a matter of keeping pupils from developing the feeling that there is little use in answering questions because the final wording will have to come from the teacher.

Active recall   This form of recitation places personal responsibility on the learner, requiring him to remember or reconstruct the material without cues.[2] If you were to attempt to remember the material in this chapter by referring to paragraph headings, you would be using recitation but not active recall. If, however, you tried to remember the material with the book closed, recalling as many of the paragraph headings as possible without the use of clues, you would be using active recall. Matching and multiple-response questions are known as "recognition" items; they are easier than "completion" questions, which demand active recall.

Experimental studies reveal that learning of both nonsense and meaningful materials increases in proportion to the amount of active recall used in the learning process. The reasons are obvious. Active recall allows the student to detect errors and to determine where the difficult portions are. It gives practice in using the material. It gives the learner an opportunity to project himself into the situation as learning proceeds. Active recall is a challenge to thoroughness in learning, and thoroughness is an important factor in retention (Muehl, 1959).

A student's approach to study is different when he intends to utilize active recall. He notes headings, emphases, and illustrative materials. The inevitable consequence is effective learning. If, on the other hand, he reads materials merely to get to the end of the chapter or assignment, a belated attempt to recall is of little avail. In short, habitual active recall

[2] In some situations it is wise to take advantage of cues; see section on The Use of Learning "Crutches."

reinforces the intent to learn. The mediocrity of many high school and college students can be attributed at least partially to their habitual neglect of active recall (Rubenstein and Aborn, 1954).

Implications of active recall   Pupils should be encouraged to be vigorous in the learning process. The entire emphasis of active recall is making learning more than a passive process. Pupils should be encouraged to recall the information just read. They should be asked to apply what they have previously learned to some current problem. "What have we studied that is similar to this?" "How does this relate to our lesson of last week?" "What previous data have we encountered on this topic?" Such questions from the teacher encourage active recall. Pupils should realize that the few extra minutes involved will mean more permanent learning. You can make use of active recall if, when you finish this chapter, you close the book and for a few minutes think back over the chapter. Try to recall headings, arguments, justifying points, *and* apply your own challenges.

Applying What Is Learned   A good deal of the criticism of so-called "traditional education" stems from the apparently slight attention devoted to making applications. In traditional education, according to its critics, "Facts are isolated. Materials are far removed from the experience of the pupils. Learning consists of acquiring and giving back the conclusions stated in a textbook." These criticisms need not and should not be valid. The value of making applications can be firmly rooted in an individual teacher's educational philosophy (Bond and Kegler, 1961), regardless of his training or the school in which he teaches. Some of the psychological justifications for a studied attempt to make applications in the classroom are:

1. Making applications gives the learner something to which to tie his information. The principle of learning by association is thereby utilized.

2. Directed learning is purportedly designed to solve problems. Hence, making applications encourages the use of learning—information is made functional.

3. If applications are demanded, teaching must attach the new to the old—the pupil's background of experience is called upon.

4. Man is a goal-seeking organism, and making use of knowledge provides a purpose for learning—it yields reinforcement.

Classroom implications of applying what is learned   Studies of recall in learning show that a greater amount is remembered when application is involved. English teachers may encourage writing sentences and themes that call for the application of rules of grammar. Teachers of mathematics should attempt to show how rules and theorems are used in the solution of problems. Teachers of science might show how facts are applied in laboratories and industry. Unfortunately, application is neglected in many instances. Too often, for example, social studies teachers confine their teaching to the materials in the text; some even regard students' questions as impertinent. Obviously, it would be helpful to study civics by dealing with problems currently being faced by the community in which the pupils reside. Problems of delinquency and indigency might well be studied by analyzing social and economic conditions in the area. After the rules or principles of a subject are applied, additional problems should be presented to give more practice in making applications.

The criticism of artificial learning has been made so frequently that teachers are becoming well aware of the necessity for encouraging students to make applications. However, they must study their pupils' needs. Students are encouraged to make applications when school work meets their needs. Problems are problems when pupils accept them as such (Dewey, 1933, p. 15)—not otherwise. Participation in school government, programs of foreign exchange students, work experience education, or community projects are ways of helping students recognize the value of and need for the application of knowledge.

The Use of Learning "Crutches" The merits of applying knowledge should not be supported so enthusiastically that you repudiate learning crutches; i.e., counting by using fingers or citing a rule for spelling (*i* before *e* except after *c*). Such crutches are sometimes criticized because they might become habitual. Experimental investigations, however, indicate that students tend to eliminate the longer, ultimately inefficient patterns in favor of shorter, easier performances (Thorndike, 1931, p. 14). For example, Brownell and Moser showed that children typically abandon the crutch of writing down the numbers remaining in an arithmetic problem such as the following:

$$\begin{array}{r} 61 \\ 722 \\ -683 \\ \hline \end{array}$$

The results of fifteen days of practice, a delayed test after thirty days, and a retest after the fiftieth day are shown in Figure 9.

Teaching implications of crutches Crutches may facilitate learning by simplifying the initial learning task. They tend to be abandoned when learning has been consolidated. However, insecure pupils may continue to use them when they are no longer essential. Then it is helpful for the teacher to point out that the crutch is no longer needed (e.g., vocalizing in silent reading) and encourage the pupil to abandon its use.

Activity—A Requirement for Learning Distributed effort, overlearning, memorization, active recall, and making applications stress the importance

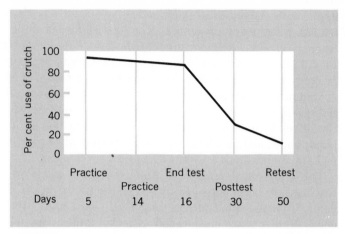

FIGURE 9. *Change in dependence on crutches in borrowing in subtraction problems.*
SOURCE: W. A. Brownell and H. E. Moser, Duke University Research Studies in Education, no. 8, Durham, N.C.: Duke University Press, 1949.

of activity. Two points warrant further discussion. First, there are varying degrees of activity. Listening to a lecture is an activity, but listening, reciting, and discussing involve more activity. Second, activity does not necessarily involve muscular movement. One can be mentally active as well. Listening may be a passive process, or it may involve acceptance or repudiation of the idea presented—even though the individual does not vocalize his reaction (Smith and Hudgins, 1964, p. 204).

Learning proceeds in even the poorest school. The pupil learns something—if it is just the habit of sitting, standing, or marching at a given signal. Quite obviously, some activities are more educational than others: When meaning, purpose, self-identity, usefulness, and significance are a part of learning activities, we shall have schools that contribute maximally to the overall object of education, i.e., more harmonious adjustment to the many problems an individual faces (Espenschade, 1963, pp. 3ff).

Insight (the perception of relationships) and understanding (the comprehension of application, meaning, pertinency) are important aspects of such learning processes as the foregoing. For instance, many children of preschool age have learned to count to ten or twenty without comprehension. The counting is a mere verbalization—not a means of evaluating quantity. When meaning is lacking, learning is superficial. Distributed effort is less effective when understanding is lacking; e.g., when fifth graders memorize a section of *Paradise Lost*. The advantages of overlearning are quickly lost if there is no comprehension of what is learned or opportunity to use it actively. There is a twofold advantage in learning that is accompanied by understanding and insight: (1) Such learning takes place more rapidly than it would through the processes of trial and error; and (2) it is likely to be permanent because insight brings comprehension of relationships.

The learner can develop insight in several ways. First, he must get the objective clearly in mind by asking himself, "What am I trying to accomplish?" "What is the value of this material?" "What is the nature of the information?" "How can the knowledge or skill be used?" "Is the material similar to anything I have experienced before?" "What would be an advantageous method of attack?" Laboratory exercises and demonstrations can do much to add reality to these questions. Fourth graders were able to study gear ratio, principles of force (frame design), chemistry, acceleration, and material (oil, rubber, steel) because a bicycle was upended on a table in the classroom (Hone, 1962).

Second, the learner should preview the material. Pupils should be encouraged to glance over the paragraph headings before thoroughly studying a chapter or to look over a task in its entirety before attempting to accomplish it. For example, if you were working a wire puzzle, it might pay to look it over and try to formulate an approach rather than to begin immediately to manipulate the object. The author knows a mine mechanic who, when sent to do a repair job, habitually sits and looks at the machine to be repaired for a few minutes. He asks a few questions of the operator before beginning the job of disassembling. He has the reputation of doing the jobs more rapidly and thoroughly than mechanics who begin their work immediately.

Third, the learner should be sure that antecedent elements or fundamentals have been mastered. A student cannot translate Latin passages without a Latin vocabulary. He cannot solve an algebra problem without a knowledge of arithmetical combinations, nor can he master history or psychology without the ability to read. Preliminary learning activity leads to insight and, in turn, insight is conducive to retention.

Another extremely important factor in achieving insight is intelligence. Because the individual learner is able to do little about his intelligence, it is important for both the teacher and the student to realize when a task is so difficult that its pursuit is relatively fruitless. Here, of course, is the basis for the frequently reiterated statement that schoolwork must be appropriate to the developmental level of the individual (Crandall, 1963, p. 439).

Implementing the need for activity in effective learning Being "active in the learning process" means that the child should be involved. Pupil activity may be stimulated in a variety of ways, such as participation in curriculum planning and discussions and conversations. The experience unit (see Chapter 14, section on Experience as a Learning Avenue) is increasingly being used to add meaningfulness and activity to learning. Whether the teacher adopts the unit or the subject-matter approach, he can expand pupil activity through field trips, excursions, and visits to courts and legislative bodies or businesses and industries. One high school class vitalized its study of government by placing the teacher's name on the primary ballot for mayor and campaigning for him. They succeeded in getting him into the final election, and although another candidate won the election, the teacher candidate received more votes than the incumbent mayor, who was running for reelection. Said the teacher, "Both the students and I learned a lot about politics in a democracy." There can be no doubt that this participation in affairs of the city was a genuinely educative experience.

Projects that involve construction (playgrounds, recreation centers, and parks) have been developed to make pupils more active. Some subjects, such as science and art, readily lend themselves to pupil activity. Many teachers correlate activities with strictly academic subjects to increase pupil activity, which suggests that pupil activity may be largely a matter of teacher initiative and ingenuity. (As noted earlier, activity need not be of the gross motor variety.) Getting pupils to take a stand on some issue is being used as an invigorating approach to pupil involvement in social studies; e.g., "Government deficits foster inflation" or "Movies should not be limited in any way" (Metcalf, 1962; Remmers and Franklin, 1962).

Improving learning conditions

If the factors that facilitate learning are to be maximally effective, it is largely up to teachers to set the stage for their implementation. The following suggestions are based on some of our knowledge of learning principles and procedures.

Aids to Learning One of the ways to make learning concrete and meaningful is through audio-visual or instructional aids. Motion pictures, filmstrips, slides, radio, phonograph records, globes, maps, diagrams, experimental apparatus, demonstration materials, pictures, and models and slides give additional meaning to verbal descriptions. The advocates of such materials stress the word "aids." They do not recommend that such materials become the sole means of instruction, but that they be used as supplementary devices.

There is a belief that some individuals are eye-minded, some auditory-minded, and some verbal-minded. It is doubtful that people can be so sharply classified. It is agreed, however, that the more sensory avenues utilized in learning, the more effective learning will be. The fact that curricular materials are being presented vividly in many ways—motion pictures, television, closed-circuit television, language laboratories, programmed learning—may be attributed in part to recognition of varying abilities to comprehend the abstract as contrasted to the concrete (Harcleroad, 1962).

Because of their variety and vividness, instructional aids speed and strengthen learning. The development of language in children shows why learning aids are so valuable. Words are only conventionalized symbols. It takes time, experience, and contact with both words and objects to establish the relationships between individual words and their referents (Chase, 1957, p. 174). But if direct contact had to be made with everything, the learning process would be discouragingly slow. Instructional aids provide substitutes for objects and situations that cannot be supplied in the classroom.

Max Wingo, in summarizing some of psychology's implications for elementary education, states that all academic skills involve both the symbolic and the abstract. Arithmetic especially involves "highly conceptual material." The schoolchild must proceed from concrete experience to the abstractions of arithmetic and language, and the way is prepared by meaningful learning. Teachers must provide a variety of experiences that permit the children to use the skills and knowledge they have acquired. Using the skill extends and strengthens it in preparation for next steps. Audio-visual aids to instruction provide opportunities to extend experiences. Hoping for circumstances that will clarify meanings is not enough; they must be planned as carefully as is the teaching of the abstract and the symbolic (Wingo, 1950, pp. 291ff).

The value of learning aids is indicated by the enthusiasm with which youngsters greet the announcement of a movie or demonstration. They willingly assume a great deal of responsibility for booking the movie, setting up the apparatus, and running the machine. The author was impressed with the interest of a class of eighth graders as they studied an advanced physiology text before and after watching a classmate cut up the lungs of a cow. The "carver" had bicycled for miles the previous Saturday to get the lungs from a slaughterhouse and had made a detailed study in preparation for the demonstration.

Teaching aids, or audio-visual aids, are a means of increasing the meaningfulness of schoolwork. But they are only aids and should not be so enthusiastically used that effort is not called for, overlearning is neglected, or socialized recitation is scorned. When motion pictures are shown in connection with particular classwork, but without discussion of their meaning and relationship to other phases of study, there is little value for students, for example.

Only faint glimmerings of the potential of teaching aids have been evident up to this point. Successful experiences with teaching machines have been reported (see Chapter 18); in addition closed-circuit television, telemated lectures, electronic learning laboratories, and extended out-of-school experiences add to the possibilities of meeting more pupils "where they are" (Wisconsin Improvement Program, 1959–1961, 1962).

The Role of Success Experimentation with both animal and human subjects shows that successful performances tend to become consolidated and unsuccessful performances tend to be eliminated (Whiting, 1962). The fact that some behavior is not successful in the eyes of an adult does not mean that the child's action has failed. Youngsters who indulge in temper tantrums may not get their way about food choices, playthings, and freedom, but the tantrums are successful in that they call attention to the children's wants. When tantrums are completely ignored by patient and consistent parents, the undesirable behavior is eliminated. When excuses are not honored by teachers, pupils cease to give them. The explanation for the role of success in consolidating learning is based on the law of effect—responses that lead to a state of satisfaction tend to be strengthened.

Evidence of the role of success is widely prevalent. Pupils who enjoy a degree of success in school (1) learn school subjects and (2) learn to like school. Pupils who do not have the experience of success learn to dislike school and obviously do not learn the lessons that are presumably taught. The implications are clear: Teachers *must* provide every child with an opportunity to do work of which he is capable (McCandless, 1957).

The desire for achievement is frequently listed as one of the fundamental characteristics of human beings. Success adds to the zest for living. However, teachers must not think that the notion of what constitutes success is the same for everyone. Getting high grades or getting along with the teacher is regarded as "failure" frequently enough so that it is more than an exception to the rule. Certainly, the concept of success varies considerably from one social class to another (Terrell, Durkin, and Wiesley, 1959). Instead of looking for some new teaching technique or for some new incentive, teachers may find it profitable to search for an understanding of what constitutes success in the eyes of the individual pupil.

Praise and Reproof One way to give information about progress toward goals is to utilize praise and reproof. Both are found to be more stimulating to learning than withholding all comment. In experiments, regardless of the actual merit of work, groups have been consistently praised, reproved, and ignored. The praised groups made better average scores than the reproved groups, and the reproved groups made better average scores than did the ignored groups.

In this connection, there are sex differences. Boys are much more frequently (three times as often) blamed or criticized than girls (Meyer and Thompson, 1956). This may be quite normal in our society, in which boys are expected to be aggressive, noisy, and buoyant, and girls are taught the kinds of behavior that find approval in school. However, to handicap boys for manifesting behavior that is socially sanctioned by using practices that are inimical to learning is a matter worth the teacher's serious attention.

The impact of praise or reproof depends partly on the pupil. Timid, insecure pupils with limited ability are likely to be crushed by blame or criticism. The confident, able student will not long be awed by criticism—in fact, it may spur him on to greater effort. Pleasant consequences seem unimportant to students who like the task and have a strong desire for self-respect (Frederiksen and Gilbert, 1960). With due consideration for the limitations of personality inventories, it has been found that students who make high scores on introversion are constructively affected by praise, while the extroverts responded constructively to blame (Thompson and Hunnicutt, 1944). Thus it is evident that teachers must be attentive to the responses of individuals and groups so that the use of praise and reproof may be adapted to the current situation.

Rivalry and Cooperation Learning is always personal; nevertheless, some general tendencies can be noted. Learning often proceeds more satisfactorily in a group situation than on an individual basis. Both group rivalry and cooperation frequently stimulate rapid learning. Thus, the modern school, which emphasizes a socialized setting for instructional activities, is capitalizing on proven psychological phenomena.

The effect of rivalry was tested in an experiment involving fourth and fifth graders who were solving addition problems. Rivalry was stimulated between groups equated on the basis of ability, sex, and age by placing scores on the board and calling out the names of the members of the winning group. Over a period of a week, the experimental groups showed marked superiority over the control groups, who were taught in the ordinary manner. In the experimental groups, the effect of rivalry was greater for younger pupils and those who were lowest on the intellectual scale (Hurlock, 1927). This study, often cited in educational psychology, deserves careful examination. We need to know how much of the result is due to the Hawthorne effect (see Glossary) (Roethlisberger, 1941). We need to know what effect there was on pupils who were not successful competitors and what the impact would have been over a period of time. These considerations are important because competitive incentives are so much a part of many school practices.

Rivalry or competition on an individual basis is also found to be a positive factor in learning. But care must be taken by the teacher to avoid arousing jealousy, envy, or animosity, which are inimical to mental health. Furthermore, the contest must be held in some activity in which there is the likelihood, or at least the possibility, of winning. Thus many questions remain unanswered. What effect does rivalry have upon the chronic loser? We know that the loser tends to "leave the field"—he is tardy, becomes a dropout, is psychologically "absent," and tends to lower his level of aspiration. In short, focusing on the top performance damages the self-respect of the mediocre and low-level performer (Elsbree, 1941). In a nation whose goal is the development of the talents of all pupils, competition must be seriously questioned both psychologically and philosophically. In competition, the goal often becomes a matter of beating the other person rather than focusing on a level of performance—doing the task well. Competition may divert talents, encourage aggression, and lead to the development of false values (Combs, 1957). The competitive marking system, as a major school practice, should be scrutinized in the light of psychology (Smith and Hudgins, 1964, p. 252).

Competition with one's former record—rivalry with oneself—possesses some of the advantages of interpersonal competition and avoids some of the dangers. There is a greater likelihood that goals will be within the reach of the individual; thus frustration, defeat, and the lowering of level of aspiration are avoided. Teachers should encourage pupils to compete with their own records. The attempt to do just a little better and to grow a little beyond the present point of development is a practicable method of capitalizing on the motivating power of competition.

As is the case with competition, cooperative activity capitalizes on the human desire for recognition and is an even more satisfactory way of securing approval. Social approval can be won by service and concern for the interests of others. Of course, some individuals are more responsive to the cooperative approach than others. But it is entirely within the realm of probability that the lack of a cooperative attitude is due to the experiences of the individual, including school experiences. Social psychologists point out that in some societies the entire culture fosters cooperativeness, solicitousness, gentleness, and unaggressiveness (Mead, 1930).

It may be noted in our own culture that children's and adolescents' play groups and gangs· display conflict, competition, and cooperation. One seems to be about as "natural" as another. This should be realized by the teacher because of the widespread misconception that competition is the typical, normal motivating factor among humans. This realization could well be the start of more constructive growth through group activity. Skinner (1945) has suggested that by "multiple schedules of reinforcement"—immediate reinforcement of small or approximate successes—cooperation can be learned as readily as any other behaviors. This notion has been supported by a study of pupils who were promised a group reward and not only performed successfully, but worked more cohesively, made more positive suggestions to each other, and were less antagonistic then when rewards were individual (Grossack, 1954).

It has been indicated that the problem is not one of choice between cooperation and competition. So-called "cooperative" games may generate considerable competition. The important factors are the kind of social situation, the kind of personalities being dealt with, and cultural expectancy (Stendler, Damrin, and Haines, 1951). It appears that the teacher can find no ready-made answer; it is necessary to study individual pupils and their influence on one another. The established classroom atmosphere is another factor. In short, the teacher is largely responsible for creating the framework in which either competition or cooperation can be effective.

School situations characterized by cooperation may contribute to learning without running the danger of stimulating envy, jealousy, or animosity. Conditions that encourage the constructive use of cooperation include the following:

1. Relatively small groups of four or five students rather than large groups

2. Teachers who are themselves cooperative and democratic and thus able to encourage the use of similar techniques by their pupils

3. Relative homogeneity within the group and similarity in size, age, and ability rather than marked disparity between pupils

4. Variety and abundance of equipment, which eliminate the possibility that many may desire the same tool or device at one time and thus tend to maintain a cooperative attitude

5. Ample play and work space, which tends to avert personality clashes and stimulation of competitive attitudes

Guidance Certainly there can be no doubt that guidance straightens and clarifies the pathways of learning. But it is possible that too much dependence is placed on the role of guiding learning activities. A summary of experimental data on the role of guidance concludes that mere guidance is not enough. Animals guided by hand through a maze did not learn to run through it. Self-initiated activities and dependence upon the slow processes of individual intellectual growth are essential features of learning through guidance (Whitla, 1962). Hence, when the father or teacher does the algebra problem there is no assurance that the pupil learns algebra. Guidance may be a useful *supplement* to goal-directed pupil activity.

Effective guidance of learning activities is essentially a process of preventing or correcting errors and encouraging actions that are most likely to lead to success. Some authorities advocate allowing the learner to experiment before introducing suggestions. Others recommend coaching the learner before permitting any attempt at performance. These authorities feel that it is easy to learn incorrect methods and that "unlearning" must then be added to the learning process. However, consensus favors allowing learners to experience and experiment first. The advocates of this approach assert that initial guidance tends to make the learning piecemeal rather than integrated.

Suggestions about learning concepts are almost the same. It is recommended that guidance be kept at a minimum in the early stages of learning, though it is necessary to give enough initial instruction so that the nature of the task is understood. For example, when pupils are learning to multiply, the general concept of multiplication should be presented and suggestions made about the placement of figures. Then problems with which the pupils may deal are presented. Guidance is offered when it is needed, but not necessarily whenever it is requested. Too many teachers explain by doing the problem. The pupil thinks he understands until he is left to his own devices. An essential feature of good learning is a chance to do, to experiment, to try, to experience individually. Care must be taken that guidance remains guidance. This is exactly the point that personnel workers and guidance experts emphasize—that the individual must, in the final analysis, be allowed to make his own decision (Tiedeman and Field, 1962).

Effective guidance is largely dependent upon motivation. The college student may believe what he is told about effective methods of study, but lack the drive to practice what he hears. Children may be impressed by the harmful effects of germs, yet find it inconvenient to wash before every meal. There must be balance between guidance sufficient to stimulate activity and the withdrawal of guidance before the pupil loses initiative or, worse yet, becomes dependent. It is at the point of withdrawal of guidance that many parents err in dealing with their adolescent sons and daughters.

Summary

This chapter is concerned with factors that facilitate learning but do not receive particular emphasis in other chapters.

Many things can be learned by rote or imitation, but both acquisition and retention are facilitated by the understanding of meanings. Making an overview and seeking a perspective usually aid the development of meaning. Daily study, taking small steps, and the active search for relationships outside the specific field of study are helpful in developing meanings.

Experiments indicate and experience confirms that distributed, spaced effort pays bigger learning dividends in terms of total time than does massed effort. There are occasions when concentrated effort is advisable. For the most part, however, distributed effort is recommended for more durable learning, for difficult subjects, where interest may lag, and where incorrect impressions should be corrected.

Overlearning—the continuation of practice after achieving a criterion level—is recommended for things to be memorized and for perceptual motor skills. Even when things are learned on a higher level (e.g., in terms of interrelated meanings), overlearning in the form of review, recitation, summarization, and specific attempts at consolidation is recommended.

Knowledge of progress—given by brief comments, by a nod, a hand on the shoulder, as well as grades—provides both incentive and direction for the learning processes.

The attempt to use active recall—trying to remember without cues or clues —calls for more personal involvement than does a cued response. Both types of recall should be employed by the learner: active recall first, then cued recall.

In order to give meaning, to intensify the intent to learn, to justify over-learning, and to implement knowledge of progress, pupils should have the opportunity to apply what they learn.

The use of learning crutches cannot be condemned because they lead to inefficient habits. Studies indicate that learners tend, without direction, to eliminate the crutches as skill and knowledge improve. In instances where this elimination does not occur, the teacher should encourage and guide the pupil in the abandonment of the crutch.

Learning conditions can be improved by recognizing and implementing the foregoing recommendations. In addition, audio-visual aids to learning, seeing to it that *all* pupils achieve some degree of success, the judicious and appropriate use of praise and reproof, emphasis on surpassing one's own record, emphasis on cooperative activity, and the parsimonious use of guidance—all facilitate learning.

Problems and exercises

1 Make a list of twenty words that are new to you. At one sitting, learn ten of the definitions, noting the exact time it takes to thoroughly learn the entire list. Divide the time by 5 and study the other ten in five daily periods of that shorter length. Which process do you feel resulted in better learning?

2 For a week try the experiment of reciting to yourself the materials you have studied *before* attending class. Does it make any difference in what you get out of class?

3 For each of the factors that facilitate learning, suggest some classroom implications in addition to those cited in the text. Which of the factors are employed in this exercise?

4 What are some ways in which you might apply overlearning to your present academic activities?

5 Discuss with a classmate profitable and unwise ways in which teaching aids have been used in the classes you are now taking. Do you feel that valuable opportunities have been bypassed?

6 Draw up a chart of progress for some class you are now taking—or one that you will probably teach. Present it to some of your classmates for suggestions.

7 Cite some instances in which you have observed both praise and reproof being used constructively in the classroom.

8 Make a list of school practices that tend to encourage an unwholesome type of student competition. Could these be eliminated by better teacher guidance?

9 Does the statement "Guidance is seeing through Johnny so Johnny can see himself through" have any implications for classroom practices?

10 Which of the principles in this chapter do you feel is of least importance? Of most importance? Does your answer agree with that of your classmates?

Suggested additional readings

Bernard, Harold W.: "Teaching Methods and Mental Health Practices," *Mental Hygiene for Classroom Teachers*, 2d ed., New York: McGraw-Hill Book Company, 1961, pp. 236–257.
This chapter deals with the roles of interest, pupil purposing, and human resources in the school. The considerations point the way to securing better results in the teaching-learning situation.

Clymer, Theodore, and Nolan C. Kearney: "Curricular Provisions for Individual Differences," *Individualizing Instruction*, Sixty-first Yearbook of the National Society for the Study of Education, Chicago: The University of Chicago Press, 1962, Part I, pp. 265–282.
Factors that facilitate learning include materials centers, time blocks, small classes, scheduling, grouping, and audio-visual aids; but the ultimate results depend on the teacher's use of these resources.

Dubridge, Lee A.: "Educational and Social Consequences," in John T. Dunlap (ed.), *Automation and Social Change*, Englewood Cliffs, N.J.: Prentice-Hall, Inc., 1962, pp. 26–42.
This chapter places the problem of facilitating school learnings squarely in the context of current problems of the technological world in which we live. The practical implications are generalized, due to space limitations.

Melton, A. W.: "The Science of Learning and the Technology of Educational Methods," *Harvard Educational Review*, 29: 96–106, 1959.
The author contends that our scientific knowledge of learning is far from complete (we have only islands of knowledge), that we need to know more, and that we need to develop a science-based management of learning in children.

Rethlingshafer, Dorothy: *Motivation as Related to Personality*, New York: McGraw-Hill Book Company, 1963, pp. 318–340.
The author discusses conditioning, rewards and punishment, and information about progress in the light of experimental evidence and relates these to the facilitation of learning.

Language Development

7

Studies attribute man's superiority to other animals mainly to his brain, his ability to use his thumb and fingers in opposition, and his capacity for language. There is no need to minimize the importance of a complexly organized brain or to underrate the importance of thumb-finger opposition. But as a matter of practical concern to the student of educational psychology, little can be done about the brain or, aside from practice, about thumb-finger opposition. A great deal can be done to facilitate growth in language and communication.

Gestures and grimaces are used in communication and are, strictly speaking, a part of language (Goffman, 1959), but words and their combinations are its major features. Language allows man to take into account the past and to anticipate the future. It is through language—through the development of abstractions—that the thoughts and discoveries of previous generations are combined with those of the present generation. It is through language that the discoveries of the present are shared. It is through language that the divergent views of men are correlated and combined. It is through language that we as teachers do our work. Personality itself is dependent upon and revealed through language. An individual's mental health is partially dependent on the description of his feelings and others' understanding of them (Johnson, 1946, pp. 91ff). In short, language is at the core of most, if not all, of man's adjustment and the concerns of educational psychology.

The importance of language

Vocabulary and Intelligence   Much study and research has been devoted to the problem of measuring intelligence. Weighing the brain, examining the depth and number of convolutions of the cortex, analysis of the nature and frequency of electrical impulses have not been particularly fruitful so far as measurement is concerned. Thus far, the most satisfactory approach to mental measurement is the intelligence test. And a prominent feature of most intelligence tests is a substantial section on vocabulary. Individual tests, such as the Stanford-Binet and the Wechsler-Bellevue, contain sections in which the vocabulary of the subject is sampled. Group tests, such as the California Test of Mental Maturity and the Kuhlmann-Anderson, have sections in which success depends upon comprehending word meaning. Word association tests have been used to assess creative talent with promising, though not conclusive or exclusive, results (Taylor, 1961, pp. 62ff). This emphasis on vocabulary as a means of intellectual assessment is not surprising when we consider that comprehension of the environment and the ability to manipulate it as well as to function within it are largely dependent upon words (Fischer, 1964).

It would be distinctly erroneous to assume a one-to-one relationship between intelligence and success or between vocabulary and intelligence. Abstract capacity, motivation, experience, and opportunity must all be taken into account in success and functional intelligence. Nevertheless, superior vocabulary is a prominent characteristic of successful persons. Major business executives rank high in vocabulary (*Mental Efficiency Clinic Bulletin*, no. 1). Whether vocabulary is cause or result of high intelligence, the fact remains that it can be improved by specific and directed practice, drill, review, and intentional usage. Drill should be meaningful—words should be taught in combinations and relationships. Manuals designed to help the high school pupil prepare for and succeed in college place considerable emphasis on vocabulary (Brownstein and Wiener, 1958, pp. 14ff).

A study of the relationships between vocabulary, intelligence, and scholastic achievement of college freshmen indicated that the best *single* indicator of potential scholarship is vocabulary. In this study, the correlation between grade-point average and psychological rating was .46 ± .046, while the correlation between vocabulary score and grade-point average was .53 ± .042. That intelligence test scores and vocabulary are related, but not equivalent, measures is indicated by the correlation of .64 ± .034 between these two measures (Bernard, 1940). If these two scores were measures of the same thing, then the coefficient would have been close to 1. It seems perfectly possible to increase the student's scholastic potential, if not his intelligence, by emphasizing vocabulary development. Even in mathematics, where one might not expect to find such a relationship, research studies have indicated that better-than-average vocabulary in pupils with a mental age of fourteen years was associated with better success in algebra. The differences in accomplishment (involving substitution, graphs, equations, exponents, etc.) of pupils equated on the basis of mental age was significantly greater for those with the better vocabularies. Words sharpen discriminative powers, have a positive influence on transfer, become drives to conduct, make for economy in adaptation to current and future situations (Dollard and Miller, 1950, pp. 101–106).

Another possible indication of the relationship of language to intelligence may be seen in studies of deaf children. Typically, the hard-of-hearing and the deaf make somewhat lower scores than children with normal hearing. Further, the greater the extent of hearing loss, the lower the subject scores on typical intelligence tests. Efforts are constantly being made to devise tests for the deaf that will depend less on language factors, but results to date have not been particularly encouraging (Dicarlo, 1959). Blind or visually handicapped children are less likely to have significantly lower intelligence test scores than the deaf. It appears to be possible that by limiting communication deafness simultaneously limits the optimum development of intelligence as it is currently measured. It must be remembered that the differences indicated are group differences. It would be erroneous to believe that *because* a child is blind or deaf he must of necessity be lower in intelligence than a child who has no sensory handicap.

As a rule, bright children learn to talk sooner than children of average intelligence and, age for age, have larger vocabularies. In fact, one of the first indications of unusual intelligence is the early development of speech (Terman, 1925, p. 21). However, delayed speech development is not a sure indication of slow mental development.

Adjustment and Language   Language plays a major role in the individual's adjustment to his environment. Many of the difficulties in which we all find ourselves may be traced to the inability to make wishes and demands clear to others. This type of difficulty is faced by adults as well as children, as is indicated in the following:

> A practicing psychiatrist, Dr. Coyne Campbell, speaking in 1941 before the Central States Speech Association meeting in Oklahoma City, expressed it (the role of language in adjustment) so pointedly and so simply that it will serve our purpose well to recall his main statements. What Dr. Campbell said, in effect, was that the patients who were brought to him because they had been judged to be seriously maladjusted or even "insane" showed one chief symptom: *They were unable to tell him clearly what was the matter.* They simply could not put into words the difficulties with which they were beset. Surely no one who has made it his business to help people in trouble has failed to observe their relative inarticulateness.[1]

A large part of problem solving consists of defining the problem, and words and combinations of words are necessary to describe a situation

[1] Wendell Johnson, *People in Quandaries,* New York: Harper & Row, Publishers, 1946, p. 15.

to ourselves as well as to others. Words enable us to think about objects and situations when they are not immediately before us. Studies of memory show that verbalized events, ideas, and principles are relatively easy to remember; thus language helps us to assemble materials in such a way that they can be used. Language facilitates generalization and permits us some independence from the present by letting us look into the future and recall the past. Our dependence on language shows vividly when we are strangers in a foreign land who want to know how to get to a certain theater or find a clean, reasonably priced hotel.

To a marked extent, thinking is a process of talking to oneself. During this process there is a delay between stimulus and response, while we discriminate between objects and situations that are recalled or anticipated in terms of names and descriptions previously learned (Lazarus, 1961, p. 87). Language with both its cognitive and conative aspects forms the very pattern of our lives.

> Our reaction patterns—our semantic habits, as we may call them—are the internal and most important residue of whatever years of education or miseducation we may have received from our parents' conduct toward us in childhood as well as their teachings, from the formal education we may have had, from all the sermons and lectures we have listened to, from the radio programs and the movies and television shows we have experienced, from all the books and newspapers and comic strips we have read, from the conversations we have had with friends and associates, and from all our experiences. If as a result of all these influences that make us what we are, our semantic habits are reasonably similar to those of most people around us, we are regarded as "well-adjusted," or "normal," and perhaps "dull." If our semantic habits are noticeably different from those of others, we are regarded as "individualistic" or "original," or, if the differences are disapproved of or viewed with alarm, as "screwball" or "crazy." [2]

Communication and Language   The most obvious importance of language, of course, resides in its use as a conventionalized system of social communication. Social organization is formed through communication, and its stability depends on facility in communication. To human beings, words are more than symbols—they are ideas and bonds of relationship. Language not only provides a vehicle for communication, but it aids in the acquisition and preservation of new ideas. Through usage and custom words came to mean precise and specific things. At home, in school, at play, and at work, communication is an integral part of the situation. Many of the arguments in which we find ourselves involved are the

[2] S. I. Hayakawa, "How Words Change Our Lives," in Richard Thruelsen and John Kobler (eds.), *Adventures of the Mind*, First Series, New York: Alfred A. Knopf, Inc., 1959, p. 238.

result of "foggy" communication. Often the argument is resolved by discovering that "we were talking about the same thing all the time."

It is possible that the whole course of our present world may have been changed by the misunderstanding of one word. In 1945, when the Japanese answered the Potsdam terms for surrender, they used the word "*mokusatsu,*" which was translated to mean "to ignore." The meaning intended by the Emperor, the Foreign Minister, and the Cabinet members was "to withhold comment while taking time to consider." This error is thought to have resulted in the use of the atomic bomb and the invasion of Manchuria by the Russians (Coughlin, 1953).

The importance of clear communication is to some extent illustrated by the fact that nations speaking the same language characteristically find themselves in accord, while those speaking different tongues view each other with suspicion. This is reflected in the preamble to the Constitution of the United Nations Educational, Scientific and Cultural Organization (UNESCO), which reads, in part:

> For these reasons the States parties to this Constitution, believing in full and equal opportunities for education for all in the unrestricted pursuit of objective truth and in the free exchange of ideas and knowledge, are agreed and determined to develop and to increase the means of communication between their peoples and to employ these means for the purposes of mutual understanding and a truer and more perfect knowledge of each other's lives.

The National Defense Education Act of 1958 places language activities high on its list of priorities in providing institutes, scholarships, and fellowships designed to improve communication between *all* people. Hundreds of high school students, through the efforts of parents and the American Field Service, are being sent to foreign nations for summer, semester, and year-long study to improve the communication suggested in the UNESCO preamble.

Teachers would be more effective if they would conscientiously work to make communication clearer and more facile. In fact, teaching would be simplified by the realization that some of the difficulty of getting across subject matter lies in clumsy communication. Teachers at all levels will do their pupils a great service by (1) stressing vocabulary development in general, (2) providing exercises leading to verbal facility, (3) encouraging the learning of the important key words in specialized fields of knowledge, and (4) by setting a good example of pronunciation, precision in word selection, and enthusiasm for linguistic development.

Earl J. McGrath, former U.S. Commissioner of Education (1953), pointed out a new responsibility of the elementary school in teaching foreign languages. Whether we wish it or not, United States citizens are in a position of responsibility. American citizens who speak other languages with facility are needed. McGrath does not defend foreign language study on the basis of mental discipline or increased facility in English: he believes it is required for the sake of communication and understanding. Along with many scholars, he stresses the impossibility of appreciating a nation's culture without a knowledge of its language. Achieving insight into other cultures through familiarity with the associations and stereotypes of words and phrases is considered not only the most advanced stage of language learning, but also the primary purpose of language study (Lambert, 1956).

Whether McGrath was highly instrumental in stimulating interest or simply perceived the growing and insistent need, the fact remains that in the five years following 1950 the number of elementary pupils studying foreign languages increased fortyfold—from 5,000 in 1950 to over 271,000 in the fall of 1955 (Birkmaier, 1958), and the number of students enrolled has increased four times more since 1955 (Hechinger, 1963). Growth in this field, among other things, implements the recommendations of those who have studied the problems of gifted children and feel that language study is one way to take care of their need for intellectual challenge. Also, there is apparently recognition of the facts that growth takes place most rapidly in the early years and that those who learn another language when they are young speak with less difficulty and accent than those who learn at a more advanced age.

Research has not clearly indicated that one method of teaching foreign language is clearly superior to another (Mueller and Borglum, 1956). However, many hypotheses are holding, if not gaining strength. One is that audio-visual techniques are not an adjunct to foreign language teaching but an essential part of the program. Since not all pupils should be studying the same things at the same rate, foreign language study is not recommended for all; however, estimates of the number of pupils who can profit from it run as high as 85 per cent (Kaulfers, 1956).

The emphasis is increasingly on study of a nation's culture and intercultural understanding as well as reading and speaking the language (Birkmaier, 1958). This trend is in accord with the psychological principle that an economical way of learning is by integrating activities and understanding meaningful relationships. Language study is justified on the basis of developing cooperative relationships between people, not in terms of economic or political advantage or discipline of the mind. This accords with the principle that education is the development of the whole person —in his emotional, moral, and social functioning as well as in his intellectual behavior. Support for the validity of this view is found in a study dealing with the relationship of bilingualism to prejudice: Strong racial prejudice was shown to accompany slight knowledge; but Spanish subjects who had either no knowledge or a great deal of knowledge of

Anglo culture had little bias, that is, both high and low bilingual scores were associated with low-racial-attitude scores (Johnson, 1951).

Conant has indicated that one important reason for offering foreign language study is that young people should have an opportunity to find out whether they have a talent for language. If the talent is undetected, it will never be developed. Further, if students have experience with a foreign language before encountering stereotyped evaluations of the merit and difficulty of a second language (Conant, 1959, p. 71), resistance to language study never develops. This view accords with the educational orientation of developing the unique talents of individuals instead of focusing so largely on seeking mediocrity for all.

The concentrated study of foreign language is not recommended for all pupils. For many such study might be confusing and interfere with wholesome personality development. Carrow (1957) compared monolingual and bilingual third graders and found that the monolingual pupils excelled significantly in oral reading, hearing, and speaking vocabulary and in comprehension of oral reading. They had no advantage in silent reading comprehension, spelling, or verbal output. The relative ease with which some children learn an additional language is not sufficient justification for introducing it into the program of all pupils. For most, efficiency in the mother tongue should remain the matter of primary concern (Bongers, 1953).

How language develops

Language Development in Infants Language begins with the so-called "birth cry," before there is any conscious thought of communication. Development continues with the cooings and babblings of infants in their first half year of life. Here is an excellent illustration of the fact that development begins with the organism. The infant may make single-letter sounds, like *mm, d, oo,* or *ah,* and these quickly become two-letter sounds like *ba, wa,* or *do.* These babblings are repeated throughout approximately the first year.

The next (overlapping) step in development is acquiring passive language—understanding words but not being able to use them. This occurs during the latter part of the first year and the early part of the second year. The baby shows by actions that he knows what "water," "dog," "milk," and "bath" mean, but he is unable to say the words. This understanding is the result of conditioning—hearing the word repeatedly in conjunction with the presence of the object.

The passive language stage is quickly followed by the development of active vocabulary. Out of the infant babblings come such sounds as *da, ma, wa,* and *poo,* which are interpreted by fond adults as "Daddy," "Mamma," "water," and "spoon." The praise received, the satisfaction felt, and the objectives gained strengthen the association for the child, and he too makes the functional connection. He then uses the word to get what he wants. If the words he invents are understood, he may not readily put aside the incorrect pattern of speech. The comparative development of speech in children who have different family groupings indicates how important reinforcement and understanding are in communication. Twins, who are with each other more than with adults and older children, develop comparatively slowly. Children with siblings do not develop so rapidly as only children, whose major communication must of necessity be with adults (Anastasi, 1958, pp. 289ff).

As the child gains ability to make sounds at will, imitation begins to function. If pressure is avoided and patience is exercised by the instructor, the child responds to instruction and will try repeatedly to imitate the sounds the instructor makes. The fact that imitation plays a large part in language development is illustrated by the existence of dialects, brogues, and accents. It is interesting to see teachers of deaf, hard-of-hearing, and speech-defective children capitalize on the willingness of pupils to imitate. Because imitation is so important in language development it is difficult to overemphasize the importance of having models who know grammar, who enunciate clearly, and who have a command of words sufficient to encourage vocabulary growth.

> Many of the more obvious misconceptions involve misinterpretation or lack of understanding of words and phrases. Thus a child was overheard giving this version of the pledge of allegiance to the flag: " I pledge a legion to the flag of the Republic of Richard Sands; one nation and a vegetable with liberty and justice to all." Another sang: "Long train run over us" ("Long to reign over us"); and another patriotically intoned: "I love thy rots and chills" ("rocks and rills"). After a moment's hesitation on a line in "The Night before Christmas," a child came forth with: "I rushed to the window and vomited (threw up) the sash." One youngster for several years patriotically sang, "The grandpas we watched were so gallantly screaming." [3]

Such errors occur not only with primary pupils; the slips that occur in recitations and discussions and the boners on examinations constantly remind teachers that older pupils also need help in understanding.

As the child moves from passive and experimental to active speech, shame and ridicule should be avoided. Motivation and contacts with ideas, concepts, and people are all part of the developmental pattern. Gains in vocabulary can safely be attributed to the number of times

[3] Arthur T. Jersild, *Child Psychology,* 5th ed., Englewood Cliffs, N.J.: Prentice-Hall, Inc., 1960, p. 366.

a pupil sees or hears the words in meaningful contexts (Eichholz and Barbe, 1961).

Improvement of Oral Communication Skills Language skills vary greatly among children who are first entering school. Unless these differences are taken into account, there will be a tendency to shame the ones of lesser ability. Implied comparisons, such as "Notice how well Mary expresses herself," indicate that the speaker is failing to take individual differences into account. The result will be discouragement on the part of some pupils and unwarranted self-satisfaction among others.

Personality should also be considered. What appears to be a difference in intellectual development may actually be the difference between shyness and aggressiveness. The shy pupil should be encouraged and praised for what he does say. He should be shown that he is accepted by the group and helped to build self-confidence through the acquisition of skills. The child with aggressive tendencies should probably not be discouraged unless he becomes socially offensive. His tendency to interrupt and monopolize class time may be redirected. Studies of children who stutter and stammer show that emotional problems, not physiological and mental disabilities are most frequently the causes of the defect (Knott and others, 1959). In fact, classroom teachers can give substantial aid to stutterers simply by giving attention to emotional factors to the extent that would be desirable if there were no defect. Specifically, shaming should be avoided, sarcasm must be eliminated, pressure should be shunned, and attention should be directed to desirable speech patterns rather than imperfections.

Experience is necessary in language development. The outmoded concept that children should be seen and not heard must be completely cast aside. Children need a great deal of opportunity to talk, as well as something to talk about. Opportunity to recite is a step in the right direction. Having children tell the class what happened over the weekend gives desirable exercise. Field trips, class projects, and motion pictures give common experiences that provide topics for discussion. The recent classroom development of using small committees and work groups is particularly encouraging from the standpoint of exercise in oral communication.[4]

Oral communication should also be emphasized in the upper grades and high school. Although criticism should be kept to a minimum, attention should be directed to word usage, acceptable grammatical form, and syntax. Leaving oral communication to the speech and English teachers is not enough. Effective communication is so important that every teacher needs to lend his support to language development. All teachers can contribute to the requisite psychological reinforcement.

[4] It is recommended that the technique of sociometry be used as a guide in order to form the most effective groups (see Chap. 12).

Development of Reading Skills Reading has been defined as getting meaning from the printed page and as bringing meaning to it. Both concepts have important developmental aspects. Words are conventionalized symbols; they have definite connotations that must be learned if the reader is to perceive the author's meaning. In addition, words inevitably remind the reader of certain ideas he has gained from experience. Thus the word "mother" may remind one reader of a source of affection and protection and another of a whining and sometimes cruel critic. A dog may be a faithful pal or a snarling beast. A plant is a thing of beauty to one and a place where daddy helps produce automobiles to another. Just as the child brings his moods from home to the school, so does he bring his own meanings to the symbols on the printed page.

The need to accumulate such meanings is one reason why reading cannot profitably begin before the child attains the mental age of 6½ years. This does not mean that teachers must passively wait for mental development to take place. Actually, there are prereading experiences that will hasten reading readiness. Storytelling, conversations among children, question-and-answer sessions, and meaningful experiences all assist in developing reading readiness.

Additional readiness factors are normal sensory acuity (eyes and ears), physical health (muscle tone and vigor), perceptual development (discrimination between words and figures), conceptual development (awareness of meanings), motivation, emotional stability, and social adjustment (Harris, 1961, pp. 20–22). The teacher's minimum responsibility is awareness of these factors. Other responsibilities include physical comfort (proper seats and lighting) and stimulation of growth (provision of developmental experiences).

Many types of readiness are involved in reading (Marksheffel, 1961). The modern first-grade teacher recognizes these by starting with experience charts. The teacher prints on a large piece of paper for all to see reports on experiences that the pupils have had together and now want to see as reading material. Next, pupils are provided with preprimers, primers, and first readers. One pupil may be ready to read a preprimer, but not a first reader; nor does such difference in readiness cease at the first grade, though it is perhaps of greatest importance at that level. Adults may stop reading a certain article because it has no interest or significance for them even though they can interpret the symbols. But the situation in school is quite different; students may not stop when the material lacks interest. Increasingly as they go through the upper grades and high school, they are given reading assignments without prior preparation in the form of preview of introductory discussion—assignments for which they may not be ready. Then their indifference is criticized. Pooley asserts that the importance of discussion preparatory to reading cannot be overstressed (1961, p. 46). Being ready involves, in addition to the ability to see the significance of content, preparation for the difficulty of the material. Difficulty of material is referred to as "readability," and it is an evaluation of length and complexity of sentences, difficulty of vocabulary, and organizational sequence as well as interest appeal (Faison, 1951).

There is much criticism to the effect that children today are not reading so well as children of yesteryear. It is alleged that the neglect of phonics has resulted in a nation of poor readers and indifferent spellers. Psychologically, these accusations are of interest primarily from the standpoint of the motives of the accuser (Do his wife and mother reject him?), the climate that elicits the criticism (Do parents read and endorse the accusations because of jealousy of their children's status?), and the impact on children (What is the value of condemnation as a motivator?). The facts are that more children are reading better today than ever before (Gates, 1962). Phonetics are taught by trained teachers in appropriate time sequences and for specific purposes. Children can and do use the phonetic symbols as printed on the flyleaves of dictionaries. Phonics are used *after* diagnosis for remedial work (Filbin, 1959).

The "logical" approach to reading—building from letters, syllables, and individual words—for beginning readers is questioned because many English words are not pronounced phonetically, e.g., "slough," "sough," "though," "tough." Scholarly investigations indicate that there are good readers (and poor ones) who have been taught by the whole-word-and-meaning approach *and* by the phonetic approach (Witty and Sizemore, 1955). Phonics have a place in developmental reading programs (for teaching word attack), but timing and individual differences must be considered. Currently, teachers favor the "psychological" approach, in which learning is attacked in terms of the learner's needs and interests; his current achievement status, his background of experience, his overall development, and the personal meaning that reading selections have for him all receive emphasis on the basis of experimental evidence.

An illustration is afforded by a glance at a first-grade reading lesson. The youngsters had taken a trip to the school heating plant; afterward, they asked the teacher to write on the experience chart an account of what they had observed. Words such as "furnace," "ventilator," and "radiator" occurred in the story. During recess, the author asked some of the children what the words were, and they were able to read them without difficulty. It seems that first graders often have less difficulty in distinguishing between words like "Christmas" and "ventilator" than they do with "house" and "horse," or "saw" and "was," when the stories in which the latter occur are not intimately related to their experience. In a good reading situation, there is likely to be a variety of books in order to meet the interests and abilities of various pupils rather than one basic text.

Throughout the program, the attempt is made to capitalize on the motivational power of success.

There is at present a tendency to consider reading as one aspect of a comprehensive language-arts program. There is constant emphasis upon the importance of meaningful reading, which includes understanding, evaluation, and interpretation. In school, as in life outside of school, the important feature of reading is the individual's reaction: Understanding words is only a first step; an individual's ability to select, interpret, and apply facts according to his purpose in reading is a skill that needs to be continuously exercised at all levels of his education and in his vocation. "The accountant, the salesman, the merchant, the skilled and semiskilled workers, all interested in self-improvement, should all be afforded the opportunity of securing up to date knowledge and skills." [5] To prepare for pupils' continuing self-improvement, the complete school reading program must include (1) experience dealing with vocabulary and concept development, (2) continuing instruction in silent reading (see Chapter 5), (3) emphasis on comprehension and interpretation, (4) instruction in adapting the rate of reading to the purpose of the reader and the nature of the material, and (5) practice in the skill and habit of critical reading (DeBoer and Whipple, 1961, pp. 65–72).

Many teachers feel that interest in reading and in continued independent reading is more important than a skill that is acquired at the expense of enjoying reading. Justification for this view is found in the fact that many adolescents and adults do little reading other than comics and picture magazines after their formal schooling has ended. Because it is not possible to teach young people all they need to know before they leave school, it is important to give them a chance to develop skill and interest in reading that will open the way to continued learning. Meaning, interest, and directed and continuous growth deserve attention. They are as important in developing reading skills as they are in other aspects of development such as personality, vocational skills, or functional citizenship.

Reading Interests of Children   Many of the needs of children—to satisfy curiosity, to become independent, to gain power over things—suggest that they want to know about things and people. Age seems to influence a child's succession of interests in animals, nature, and people, but, of course, there are other influences. Experience, success, contagiousness of others' interests must also be taken into account. Hence, the rough guides that can be derived from research on children's interests must be regarded as just what they are—rough guides. Teachers should seek to know the interests of individual pupils.

[5] John F. Kennedy, *Program for Education*, 88th Cong., H.R. Doc. 54, Jan. 29, 1963, p. 12.

An effective criterion for young people's books is that good children's books also appeal to adults (LaRiviere, 1963). The author observed this to be true in a seventh-grade class taught by a teacher who consistently makes reading interesting to most of her pupils. Occasionally she reads aloud from books she selects or which pupils bring to her. On this occasion she was reading from a Newberry Award book,[6] De Angeli's *The Door in the Wall* (1949). The pupils groaned when it was time to stop, and the author got hold of a copy of the book so he could finish it—later purchasing a copy of his own.

Studies have been made of the reading interests of children of various ages, and books that tend to correspond with these interests have been listed in various publications.[7] Librarians will give recommendations on the latest publications, which have been evaluated by experts in terms of difficulty, interest level, and suitability for various purposes such as social development, scientific knowledge, vocational exploration, and even bibliotherapy.

The teacher's interest and enthusiasm is of utmost importance. Being able to recommend a book that is similar to one to which the pupil has just responded with more than his usual enthusiasm provides an incentive. Being able to point out some of the features of a book that are especially worth noting (motivation, personality traits, scientific facts, etc.) helps the pupil realize that he is making progress. Being able to relate books to particular pupils and their interests reveals the knowledge of individuals that promotes feelings of worth.

Development of Listening Skills   Listening is a principal source of learning throughout life. Much that the young child brings to school in the form of facts, beliefs, and attitudes he has acquired through listening. With maturity, more refined and sophisticated listening skills are required (Pooley, 1961, p. 46). Yet the acquiring of listening skills is largely left to incidental and fortuitous learning.

The need for developing listening skill may in part be illustrated by personal reflection—you probably have often found yourself taking a speaker's first few words and going off on your own train of thoughts, or you have finished (not always accurately) the sentences of a slow

[6] The Newberry Award book is selected annually by a committee from the American Library Association for the most "distinguished literature" for children. Also of interest may be the Caldecott Medal book, an annual selection of the best picture book. The reader will find these regularly announced in the *Saturday Review* and *Publishers' Weekly* as well as being mentioned occasionally in other journals.

[7] May Hill Arbuthnot, *Children and Books*, rev. ed., Chicago: Scott, Foresman and Company, 1957. Annis Duff, *Longer Flight*, New York: The Viking Press, Inc., 1955. Alfred Stefferud (ed.), *The Wonderful World of Books*, New York: New American Library of World Literature, Inc., 1952. Staff of Intergroup Education in Cooperating Schools, *Reading Ladders for Human Relations*, rev. and enlarged ed., Washington: American Council on Education, 1948.

speaker. Mental wandering, erroneous anticipating, and casual listening indicate the need for giving attention to the listening process. The possibilities that inhere in directed practice are suggested by the development of hearing acuity and listening accuracy on the part of the blind person. Determined individuals learn to walk confidently without dog or cane by depending on echoes from nearby objects. They report that after losing their sight as students, they developed vastly greater ability to listen carefully and remember what they said.

Providing a good model to listen to is a first consideration. A teacher who pronounces each word without running two or more words together and pronounces each "ing" ending completely assists this aspect of communication. Good models are provided by the tapes and records in language laboratories, though unfortunately, these are usually supplied only in foreign tongues. Reading good literature aloud provides an opportunity to practice listening skills and at the same time may provide incentive for independent reading. Checking up frequently on what has just been said or read motivates discerning listening (Stephens, 1951, p. 331). Brief oral reports on carefully selected books about which the reporters are enthusiastic provide others with exercise in listening and may possibly arouse their interest in further reading. Drill, often referred to disparagingly, has a definite place in economy of learning. Listening drills that demand accurate interpretation and attention to details have their place in both elementary and secondary instructional programs.

Development of Writing Skills   From the professor who allegedly must "write or perish" to the person who has only to write an occasional letter to a loved one, written communication has significance. For the professor and the occasional letter writer, the first item of significance is to have something to say. Unfortunately, not enough teachers seem to realize this important fact as far as pupils are concerned. The consequence is that much of the emphasis in teaching written communication is on legibility, form, paragraph unity, choice of words, rather than on the message—the pupil's purpose for writing. The appearance, the style, and the spelling overshadow the matter of communication. As a writer, the pupil is so concerned with form, style, and spelling that he avoids writing as much as possible because of the long association with criticism. The teacher's orientation of "Now I have to spend three hours *correcting* papers" is ultimately reflected in the pupils' reluctance to submit themes, stories, and reports and in their procrastination about writing a letter. If the creative idea were primary, both teacher and pupil might find greater enjoyment in writing.

For the average youngster, handwriting may begin before school entrance. The child's motivation probably stems from his awareness that he can create something (scribbles) on a piece of paper and from his desire to imitate. We wonder why this eagerness to place marks on a piece of paper is so often extinguished and conclude that the criticism, the imposition of adult standards, and the failure to perceive personal purpose in the activity must be blamed.

No method of handwriting instruction has yet been proven definitely better than another. This probably is due to the different muscle development, the different capacities for coordination, and the handwriting models of each individual. Similarly with cursive or manuscript style; the advantages of the one are balanced by compensating advantages of the other—legibility and similarity to print favoring manuscript, and speed favoring cursive (Burrows, 1959, p. 26). It appears that the important considerations are to provide suitable models, to allow for individual differences, to emphasize the values of writing (let students perceive their increasing power over time and distance), and to provide encouragement.

Research reveals guidelines for applying psychological principles to teaching handwriting. Individuals must be permitted to develop their unique styles rather than being held to a standard. Imitation is a better source of motivation than threat and coercion. Relaxation is essential to coordination—of muscles and mind and milieu. This can be promoted by the classroom atmosphere of acceptance, guidance in holding the pencil and placing the paper, fit of desk, and correct posture. Avoid long practice (drill) periods; instead, use incidental instruction to encourage spacing and care in forming letters (including some attention to uniformity of size), keep a record of progress, and use constructive criticism, coupled with praise (Freeman, 1954).

Motivation to write, as a means of communication, can be begun in the primary grades, where pupils are encouraged to dictate their stories to the teacher.[8] The teacher then presents the material on an experience chart so the "dictator" can see his message in action and all may gain practice in reading. The important thing is that pupils have the feeling that their messages are being communicated. Similar motivation can be arranged in the later grades when pupils' stories and themes (not just the *best* ones) are tacked to the bulletin board or bound in a class magazine. The teacher may ask the young author to read or to permit the reading of his story in class. Some polishing of form, some attention to spelling, some effort at improved clarity is in order if the message remains the primary focus.

Certain time-sanctioned procedures that have *not* stood up to the testing of research also need to be mentioned. Among these are encouraging children to plan stories before they write, checking the mechanics as they write, experimenting with words for the sake of

[8] Practical suggestions for motivating pupils to write freely and creatively are contained in the chapter on writing in Natalie Robinson Cole, *The Arts in the Classroom*, New York: The John Day Company, Inc., 1940.

using "colorful" or "different" ones, studying vocabulary lists, writing for school newspapers, and requiring self-evaluation of writing. These procedures have been found wanting both by research and by informal approval of some sensitive teachers. Examination of these techniques in relation to basic motive and need as well as satisfaction derived therefrom reveals the infringement upon personality. Writing to use certain words required by someone else is directly contrary to the nature of communication, which is a matter of ideas first and foremost. Words are the means to an end, not goals in themselves.[9]

At the high school level, the "message" may remain uppermost if students write about the things that take place in clubs or on the athletic field, about visitors with special messages and routine class procedures—things that are real in their lives. The writing should be the students' own, not the edited product of the teacher. School newspapers and magazines may be helpful if the goal is to provide satisfaction to the young writers rather than to gain prestige for the school. Mechanics should be a concomitant of the message transmittal, not the first order of concern. Style and clarity can be accomplished by the pupil's reading his material aloud and by the teacher's editing *with* the pupil.

None of the foregoing statements implies that there is no place in the school for grammar, provided it is taught in meaningful and functional situations. Keeping in mind the primary function of composition, which is improved communication, the teacher should point out persistent errors in a kindly and encouraging manner. He may list the rules of grammar that should be taught and check them off as they are dealt with in connection with student writings. The grammatical rule is dramatized by calling it forth from the examples provided in the pupils' work (Wolfe, 1958, p. 195). It may be necessary to deal with gerunds several times, while one or two discussions of the agreement between subject and verb will suffice. The emphasis should be upon clarity of expression and pupil satisfaction, rather than on the elimination of error as an end in itself. When pupils see, hear, and use acceptable forms of expression, correct expression is on the way to becoming habitual (Heffernan, 1951, p. 93). Without an idea to express, the rules of syntax will be relatively meaningless. Those who are most prolific in the use of language are said to be those who have the most ideas to express. However, opportunity for free expression may very well stimulate ideas.

Interest in written communication can be stimulated and maintained by the following:

Pupils must have leads in the selection of topics.

Variations in style should be encouraged rather than criticized.

[9] Alvina T. Burrows, *Teaching Composition*, Washington: National Education Association, 1959, p. 22.

Criticism of grammar and spelling should be held to a minimum and kept as impersonal as possible.

Both the initial teaching and review of important concepts should occur as the occasion arises from pupils' work.

All teachers should be partners in teaching written communication; it is not the sole responsibility of the English teacher.

The major function of written communication is to convey thought and meaning; and class exercises should exemplify that recognition.

Successful performance should be acknowledged.

Summary

One of man's most distinctive characteristics is his ability to use language. It permits him to behave more intelligently by tying together the past, present, and future. It captures concepts which are useful in solving problems.

A major function of language is to facilitate communication between one's immediate and international neighbors. The study of foreign language not only provides the basis for more extensive communication and for cultural broadening but also gives able students a source of curricular enrichment. Such study gives many others the assurance that they can learn a second language when it is needed later.

Learning oral language depends on good models, having something to communicate, and emphasis on the positive. Reading skills should receive attention continuously throughout the elementary and high school years. Instruction must go beyond "word calling" and have personal meaning in the life and experience of the pupil. Vocabulary development, instruction in silent reading, comprehension and interpretation, practice in varying speeds, and critical reading all deserve attention in the balanced program of reading instruction designed to promote pupil self-realization.

Listening skills, because so much of what we know comes from hearing, should be specifically taught and practiced. Currently this is left largely to incidental learning.

Written communication is the highest level of language development but there has been extensive failure to teach it effectively. Too much emphasis on the mechanics of writing has obscured the basic purpose of communication. Form, style, grammar, organization are important, but should, for purposes of motivation, be concomitants (but not incidentals) of the message transmittal function. Encouragement of writing, with emphasis on the presentation of ideas, is a responsibility of all teachers at all levels.

Problems and exercises

1 Argue for or against the proposition that it is possible to increase one's intelligence by thoroughly studying and increasing vocabulary.

2 What important bearing does Dr. Campbell's statement that the mentally ill are unable to tell what is the matter have upon psychotherapeutic techniques?

3 Arrange for a panel discussion or debate on the subject, "Foreign language in the elementary curriculum."

4 Make a list of specific activities and teacher emphases which would enhance language development in the elementary grades. Would the same list be pertinent in high school?

5 Expand the explanation given in the text for stating that reading is a matter of *bringing* meaning to the printed page.

6 Observe the teaching of reading in the fourth grade at three different times (and places) and make a list of what you regard as the strengths and weaknesses of the program. Deal with both materials and methods.

7 Talk with some pupils in high school about their "free" reading habits. What are some of the factors that characterize those who read the most?

8 Describe some exercises you might use in the subject you teach to improve listening skills.

9 Get hold of three or four papers written by high school pupils. Do you feel that these reflect major concern with mechanics or with the communication of ideas?

10 Reflect on your own attitude toward writing. What are some of the background experiences which might account for this attitude?

Suggested additional readings

Brooks, Nelson: *Language and Language Learning: Theory and Practice*, New York: Harcourt, Brace & World, Inc., 1960. 238 pp.
It is probable that those preparing to be teachers of a second language have been or will be advised to read this book. It discusses justification, psychological aspects, program, language laboratory, and other methods, materials, etc. The emphasis is on cultural communication.

Hechinger, Fred M.: "Foreign Language Stages a Comeback," *Saturday Review*, 44 (7); 64–66, 1963.
This is a pertinent discussion of the importance, techniques, and extent of foreign language teaching in the schools. The focal importance of the teacher is emphasized.

Heffernan, Helen (ed.): "Experiences Designed to Encourage Language Expression," *Guiding the Young Child*, Boston: D. C. Heath and Company, 1951, pp. 93–113.
Through case examples, this chapter describes what can be done to help children in language development. The importance of experience and consistent example is stressed. Some views on bilingualism are included.

Herrick, Virgil E.: "Basal Instructional Materials in Reading," *Development in and through Reading*, Sixtieth Yearbook of the National Society for the Study of Education, Chicago: The University of Chicago Press, 1961, part I, pp. 165–188.

This chapter describes basal reading materials in terms of continuity of development; a section that cites available materials is included. The task of the teacher is defined by areas needing attention (scope, sequence, and organization).

Irrig, Madeline: "Developing Character through Reading," *Wilson Library Bulletin,* 33: 571–573, 1959.

Titles of specific books that will appeal to preadolescents and adolescents and bear upon the development of particular aspects of personality, such as habit formation, emotional stability, morality, and aspirations, are given.

Growth and Its Relationships to Learning and Teaching

8

As a student today and as a teacher tomorrow, you will find few problems as basic, as pervasive, and as recurrent as that of dealing with growth. Your task as a teacher will be to stimulate and direct pupils' growth in physique, mentality, emotional control, and social personality.

The study of growth is important for many reasons. It is widely recognized that good instructional practices must be based upon the growth, or readiness (see Glossary), of the pupil. Since human beings have little, if any, predetermined conduct—we call it "instinct"—they must "grow" into the kinds of behavior that will facilitate adjustment. *We must learn to work in accord with natural growth principles, rather than in opposition to them.* Education itself is both a product and a process of growth. Education and full living for each of us is a growth process.

It is the task of applied educational psychology to point out ways in which growth can be facilitated by discovering, describing, and creating the conditions that are favorable to growth. Thus the study of growth is not only basic to the study of learning and teaching—it *is* that study.

The nature of growth

Basic Concepts Understanding the relationships of growth and learning can be facilitated by indicating the nuances of difference between some closely related terms. "Growth" may be thought of narrowly as sheer increase in size, but in educational and psychological literature the term includes also maturation, development, and learning. "Maturation" refers to the process of coming to maturity or reaching stages of development. The infant matures in the process of becoming an adult, and the term is thus an overall concept; but parts of the organism also mature. For example, the nerves, without perceptible increase in size, change in the process of myelinization and, without exercise or experience, become more efficient in message transmission. Maturation is a biological—as contrasted to a psychological, or learning—

164

phenomenon. "Development" refers to progressive changes in the organism and embraces not only physical change (e.g., altered body proportions), but also change in function (e.g., strength and coordination). "Learning" is the aspect of development that connotes the modification of behavior (usually we think of improvement) that results from practice and experience.

The relationships of all these concepts are clear as the child learns to read. A certain level of growth is requisite so that he will have achieved eye coordination and the ability to concentrate. He must have experienced widely enough so that words mean something to him. This is the groundwork (readiness) for further development in intellectual and social performance. All facets of the human organism and personality are involved in these unceasing and permeating phenomena. In this chapter some of the phases of growth will be examined, and generalizations about this fundamental process will be formulated.

Growth—A Creative Process Inasmuch as growth involves organization and reorganization, it is a creative process. Every act of an organism alters its possible and probable future behavior. A baby's first steps represent progress toward his ultimate ability to run. Each word he says is progress toward his ability to converse. As the individual adds strength and organization to his activities and is guided toward constructive behavior, his potentiality for full, happy, and harmonious living increases.

Growth is a creative process in that the individual chooses the aspects of the environment to which he responds. For example, as you read the morning newspaper, you—your intelligence, your previous experiences, your mood—create your own response. If you all read the same news item, some of you will be discouraged, others will be challenged, and still others will find nothing of importance. Newspapers and books are more than words placed in a certain order. For the reader, a book includes the meaning which he brings to the printed page.

Growth can be slow and tortuous. Its course can be a wandering path. Nevertheless, it is inevitable. If growth is to be made maximally creative, it must be directed. "Certainly those who have faith in intelligence will believe that our prospect of getting satisfactory results will be greater if we know what we are about when we undertake this very important task of directing the experiencing of the young." [1] Teachers who understand the nature of growth, including its creative aspects, will be better able to encourage optimum development in their pupils.

The Nature of Personality Development Children are born with varying potentialities for developing social personalities. Mental and physical predispositions prompt the child to be optimistic and cheerful or pessimistic and doleful, lethargic and stoical or active and responsive—some authori-

[1] John L. Childs, *Education and Morals*, New York: Appleton-Century-Crofts, Inc., 1950, pp. 11–12.

ties even postulate personality types around body structure (Sheldon and others, 1954). A person's rate of learning, his endocrine balance, his bodily strength, and his stature all contribute to the effect he produces on others. These personal attributes are quickly and continuously modified by his experiences. The whole family climate and relationships with siblings and parents help to determine, within the limits set by heredity, the manifestation of his personality. Many errors in interpreting personality could be avoided if parents and teachers realized that the development of personality, like other phases of psychological growth, is the result of multiple causation (Stagner, 1961, p. 18).

Four major factors influence the growing individual's characteristics and behavior. *Biological factors,* such as genetic structure, physical build and appearance, and rate of maturation, all bear on how the individual acts and how others perceive him. The human influences on him and the way others perceive him are determined by his *cultural milieu.* The way he is raised—the values, ideals, and goals he is taught—has a strong impact on his personality. His *personal history,* his experiences with things and people, also influences his personality development. Finally, there is the *specific situation,* as contrasted to the general or typical environment, that shapes his immediate response and must be taken into account in personality development (Mussen, 1963, p. 57).

Biological factors are important in setting limits and may determine whether an individual becomes a star athlete or an honors scholar, but his values and motivations (culture and personal history) are always interacting influences. Because the culture is such an important factor in personality development, cultural influences are discussed in detail later; the fact that an individual's socioeconomic status profoundly affects his social and educational behavior, for example, is illustrated (see Chapter 16).

Success in any line of activity depends to a large extent upon a person's ability to get along with others, which means development of the ability to adapt his behavior to various situations and people. The important and complicated lesson of social adaptation can best be learned in the school, where contacts are wider and more impersonal than they are in the home. Moreover, some control can be exercised in choosing the experiences that the child will have.

Principles of growth

The foregoing generalizations about the nature of growth form the basis for a more detailed examination of its processes. The following principles are applicable to mental, physical, and personality growth and development.

Growth Is a Function of the Interaction of the Organism and Environment A long-time concern of biologists, psychologists, and educators has been the relative influence of heredity and environment. Some believed heredity to be the important factor; others considered the environment predominant. The question is of fundamental importance to the teacher. If heredity is believed to be the important factor, then it is logical to wait and see what nature has given to the individual. His traits, according to the extreme proponents of this view, would be the result of the maturation of latent hereditary characteristics. This, in the author's view, is an unproductive and pessimistic orientation.

Most authorities today would be counted as interactionists. They believe that heredity provides the potential, which is acted upon by a dynamic environment. Therefore, an attempt should be made to provide for each child a stimulating environment. If 90 per cent of the personality is due to environment, so much the better. If 50 per cent of the mature personality may be attributed to the environment, there is much with which to work. Even if only 10 per cent is due to environment, it is still the only factor that can be influenced by educators.

Heredity can never be sharply differentiated from environment; the two operate concurrently and cooperatively. For example, after a time, transplanted cells become an integral part of the area to which they are transplanted (Sperry, 1959). A skin cell transplanted to the spinal cord becomes not skin but a part of the spinal cord. Apparently, the development of a cell is determined both by heredity and environment. It is impossible to believe that the single cell, which is at first the fertilized ovum and later the entire organism, will grow without being influenced by both its prenatal and postnatal environment. It would be best to regard heredity as providing potential for development, setting the bounds beyond which environmental stimulation cannot cause the individual to develop (see Figure 10, page 168, and Figure 18, page 305).

Certainly, some characteristics seem to be predominantly a matter of heredity—color of hair, facial features, and stature—though stature, within limits, is subject to environmental influences. Orientals reared on the West Coast of the United States are, on the average, slightly heavier and taller than their brothers who were raised in their native lands, though their facial characteristics are still dissimilar to those of Occidentals. On the other hand, language, specific interests, and social behavior seem to be determined by environmental influences. A Japanese born and raised in the American culture speaks and behaves as do his fellow Americans. He has no oddities of pronunciation or accent. Such observations verify the generalization that growth is the product of the interaction of the organism with its environment.

The nature-nurture, or heredity-environment, controversy has perhaps nowhere become more lively than in the study of intelligence. Not long

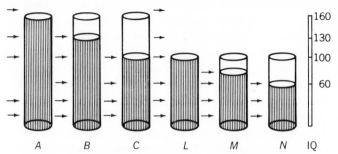

FIGURE 10.   Schematic representation of interaction of heredity and environment in intellectual development. Let the cylinders represent hereditary potential for development of intelligence (IQ) and the arrows represent the stimulating value of the environment. The three left-hand figures show a potential for 160 IQ, but B and C, with less stimulating environments, develop only part of the potential. L has less potential than A, B, and C have; but in terms of the potential, the environment is sufficiently stimulating to promote maximum growth. N has the potential for average development (about IQ 100), but the poor environment results in a low development of test intelligence. C develops average intelligence, but in terms of the potential, shows low realization. Figures A and L show full realization of potential, due to appropriately stimulating environments; B and M show high realization of potential; and C and N show low realization as a result of poor or frustrating environment. The arrows above figure L represent the notion that stimulation cannot affect growth beyond the hereditary potential.

ago, the theory that the IQ was constant (that is, that the rate of mental development for a given person was constant) was rarely questioned. Recent experimental evidence points to the conclusion that under certain conditions there is a possibility that the IQ may be markedly changed by environmental and personality factors (Sontag, Baker, and Nelson, 1958).

There is hesitancy to accept the view that IQ can be uniformly raised for groups of individuals by providing a stimulating environment; testing instruments and techniques currently in use are too inadequate to prove that actual changes are extensive (Ewers, 1956). But there are hereditary limitations to the changes that a salutary environment can produce. The environment determines, to a marked extent, the degree to which innate potentialities are realized and the way in which they are utilized (Bronfenbrenner, 1963, p. 532). The more stimulating the environment, short of pressure, the greater will be the realization of the child's capacity. The stimulation value of the environment is not absolute. For one person, an environment may be stimulating; for another, it may be boring, and for still another, it may be overwhelming. *Stimulation is a matter of what an individual can stand in terms of his present status and capacity* (M. C. Jones, 1957).

There is increasing evidence that we have but small conception of what the upper limits of intelligence might be. Better birth conditions, more immediate and intimate mothering, reduction of emotional stress in the home, the development of stronger self-concepts, better teachers, and more appropriate teaching techniques all might contribute not only to the more rapid acquisition of knowledge, but also to the development of vastly increased *potential* for learning and adaptation.

Encouraging discoveries about the educability of slow-learning children indicate the importance of the human and physical environment (Kephart, 1960). Teachers would be well advised to cast their lot with the environmentalists, if a choice must be made. Certainly, there is evidence that growth in intelligence, as in other areas of personality, may be retarded or accelerated by environmental factors. The process is one of interaction. It is a matter of the individual's choice (interaction) of those aspects of the total surrounding stimuli (the environment) to which he (the organism) will respond. The teacher who accepts this view will be inclined to study the pupil to determine his present status, how it was achieved, and how to provide him with situations that will be personally stimulating and of maximum benefit.

Educational implications of heredity-environment interaction The teacher has two guides in deciding what kind of school environment will be most effective for individual pupils. One is data derived from intelligence tests (which assess potential and accumulated experience), achievement batteries, interest inventories, diagnostic schedules, and readiness scales. If such data are wisely used, the teacher improves his chance of *starting with the student where he is.* It is disappointing to see how often test results are simply filed away in a cumulative folder and extracted only during teacher-parent conferences. In many schools, however, teachers plan individual programs, and one child is given a reading readiness program while some of his classmates are tackling the first reading books; others, who have learned to read before coming to school, may be reading independently for fun or information or pursuing some other project. Test results may mean that a freshman is offered the choice between general mathematics or algebra. A high score on English tests is less likely to mean that a student can be excused from the prescribed curriculum, but fortunately, the trend toward differentiated independent work seems to be accelerating.

The other guide is observation. Teachers know that routine school pursuits are not stimulating to a particular child when they observe that he is inattentive or idle, teases his classmates, or devotes his time to activities not in the schedule. Teachers have challenged such pupils by giving them appropriate work to do, by assigning them special reports, and by encouraging them to undertake leadership responsibilities.

Pupils whose test data place them in lower categories are often irritable, excessively quiet, or easily discouraged. They may refuse to do the work placed before them and are frequently inattentive and idle. Teachers must learn to experiment boldly and repeatedly until a feasible approach is found. Giving the pupil an easier book to read, praising him for less-than-average accomplishment, delegating to him some simple responsibility (even though he seems not to have earned it), and making sure that tasks are understood are techniques whose results can readily be observed. One teacher gave a large, over-age, and slow-learning bully self-confidence by making him responsible for playground materials. It was up to him to see that everyone had a chance with bats and balls. He earned status by taking particular care of the smaller pupils.

The principle that growth is a product of the interaction of the organism with its environment obviously indicates that each child should be helped to achieve the greatest possible realization of his abilities, short of frustration. Some should be praised for less than the average amount of work; others should be stimulated to read more, write more, and do more difficult problems than other class members. Each pupil needs the experience of success. But unless tasks of varying degrees of difficulty are devised, the inevitable result is continuing easy success for some and repeated frustration and failure for others. Each child needs direction— to be steered into areas where he can have the degree of success that will merit commendation. He needs to experiment; to participate in field trips and visit museums, industrial plants, and the like; to report on independent travels; and to read and ask questions. All pupils need to learn to be good followers, and many of them need experience as leaders in appropriate undertakings. *It is in adapting learning experiences to the needs of individual pupils that a teacher capitalizes on the interaction between heredity and school environment.*

Growth Proceeds More Rapidly in the Early Years   In a brief period of nine months, from the time of the fertilization of the ovum, the human organism develops from an almost weightless cell to a body weighing about 7 or 8 pounds—increasing in weight 500 million times. In fact, by the end of the embryonic period (the end of the tenth week after fertilization) there has been an increase in mass of some 2 million per cent. Just as remarkable is the growth in terms of differentiation. Body parts have become 95 per cent differentiated (legs, arms, eyes, ears, etc.) by the end of the embryonic period. The neural system and the brain have already grown rapidly, and at the time of birth, the brain will contain 95 per cent of the number of cells it will ever have. Body proportions change markedly during the prenatal period. Thus prenatal growth is characterized by vast increase in size, gross changes in proportion, and increased differentiation of body parts. "A waggish mathematician has figured out that if the organism were to continue to double itself in size at the embryonic rate, it would be as large as the whole solar system by the age of twenty-one years. It is just as well that this tremendous rush of growth soon begins to slow down." [2]

Although growth does slow down in the postnatal period, it continues at an amazing pace. The neonate's most striking characteristic is his utter helplessness—a characteristic that marks him as a human being. In the first year, the infant is expected to triple his birth weight. By his second birthday, he is approximately half as tall as he will be as an adult. Just as noticeable as his growth in size is his growth in independence.

Psychological growth during the preschool period (roughly from ages two to five years) continues apace. There is a remarkable improvement in coordination, perception, differentiation of behavior, and acquisition of skills. Growth in these characteristics is so rapid during this period that even the comparatively uninitiated person can tell the difference between a 2- and a 2½-year-old child, whereas it would be exceedingly difficult to perceive a difference of six months between persons in their twenties. The preschool child learns to feed himself, he develops regular patterns of sleep and can put himself to bed, he learns to dress himself (though buttons, hooks, and zippers may cause some difficulty), and he acquires control over the processes of elimination. Language development continues for years, but the preschool child can make himself understood and can control others through language. He is rapidly acquiring the ability to get along with his brothers and sisters and other children in the community. He is learning to get along with adults, though frequently they thwart his desire for independence. He gains some understanding of time and numbers. His fundamental personality traits (cheerfulness, friendliness, volubility, perseverance, etc.) are becoming crystallized. All these developments take place in the short period of four years.

Grade-school children continue to grow rapidly, and the most noticeable growth is in further development of skills. A new and complicated skill, reading—a fundamental tool in our civilization—is acquired. Personality traits are further consolidated. Skills in social adaptation are improved.

Growth takes place more rapidly in the early years, but it is important to realize that growth continues throughout life. While it is probable that broad patterns of personality are established before school age, *the manifestation of personality traits is subject to modification during the*

[2] Florence L. Goodenough and Leona E. Tyler, *Developmental Psychology*, 3d ed., New York: Appleton-Century-Crofts, Inc., 1959, p. 67.

entire life span (Stevenson, 1953). Intelligence, in terms of modifiability, plasticity, and retentiveness of the brain, may have reached its maximum development during the first twenty-five years, but the use to which that intelligence is put is a matter of personal concern for those who have reached maturity, middle age, and old age. The fact that early growth is rapid must be viewed realistically, but not necessarily pessimistically.

The educational significance of early rapid growth Various authorities state that it is in the first five, six, or eight years that the broad fundamental patterns of behavior are developed. This does *not* mean that the personality is irrevocably set. The idea that responses are solidified in these early years and that little change will take place thereafter is erroneous. It is important to recognize the tendency and to make the early school years as enjoyable and productive as possible. It may very well be that in the first school years, much of a person's love for continuing learning will or will not be generated.

Increasing recognition of the school's responsibility for emotional adjustment and social development of its pupils is evident (*Basic Approaches to Mental Health in the Schools*, 1961). Adequately trained teachers are first concerned with their pupils' habits of adjustment and then with the acquisition of academic skills. They recognize that some children cannot or will not learn until destructive emotions have been reduced and that others will learn more efficiently when their social and emotional needs are well on the way to being met. They feel that the interests, ambitions, attitudes, and ideals that the child is formulating are as important as his academic learning. For such sensitive teaching, well-qualified and highly trained teachers are sorely needed (Herge, 1958). Such teachers appreciate and accept their responsibility for making the child's early formal learning experiences enjoyable.

The rapid growth rate of children should be recognized, but not forced. Thus, for example, the wisdom of beginning school at an early age is questioned by some authorities. On the other hand some maintain that, because of the rapidity of early growth, social experiences on a wider scale than that provided in the home should be begun at the age of three or four years. Others believe that the child should stay in the home longer in order to develop feelings of security and of being loved. A generalization does not suffice. Individual differences must be recognized. Wide experience would probably be fruitful if teachers were careful not to try to make the immature child fit a pattern of behavior more appropriate to a child who had matured more rapidly. *Opportunity without rigid prescription is the recommendation that accords with this principle of growth.*

Rapid early growth also necessitates concern for the child's health during the early school years. Although children seem to be ceaselessly active, they tire easily because of the immaturity of body tissues and because rapid growth demands large expenditure of energy. Fatigue may result in loss of appetite, low resistance to disease, restlessness and irritability, listlessness, and inattentiveness, and it contributes to slowness and perhaps difficulty in learning. The child suffering from fatigue comes to believe he cannot learn so well as others, and his reputation is that of a slow learner. One should expect and perhaps encourage frequent absences for minor illnesess during this period of rapid growth. Tired children find it difficult to cooperate, their initiative is frequently low, and their attention span is comparatively short (Bernard, 1961, pp. 28–34). For these reasons, the child must have balanced programs of rest and activity both in the home and at school.

Teachers sometimes feel that their efforts are fruitless because so much has taken place in a child's life before he enters the classroom, and because his attitudes toward learning seem to be thoroughly set. However, even if the rate of growth is slowing by the time the child enters school, there is a steadily increasing ability (not capacity) to learn as age increases. The curved lines *A-B* in Figure 11 represent the rate of mental development. The stippled area plus the cross-hatched area represent the background for learning possessed by a nine-year-old.

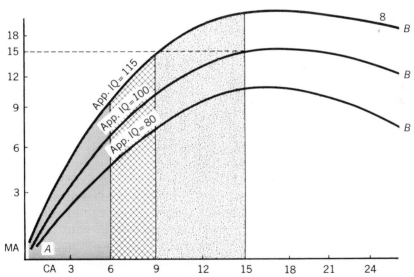

FIGURE 11. *Intelligence and the ability to learn change as the individual grows. The altitudes of the curves represent speed and retentivity of learning (capacity) of three individuals. Shaded areas represent chronological age on one axis, mental age on the other. Thus the curve's altitude reveals the individual's operational ability to learn. A forty-year-old person may be less agile in intelligence than a twenty-year-old, but his greater accumulation of experience represents a functional advantage in learning.*

It is fallacious to believe that capacity for learning is dependent solely upon the altitude of the curve; even when the curve declines, as it is purported to do after the age of twenty-two to twenty-five years, there remains an enormous capacity to learn that is based on native ability *plus* accumulated experience. Early learning is important, but it is rarely too late for the normal individual to learn, and the importance of experience is often underestimated. An adult may well feel sympathy for the child who is faced with many problems that must be attacked with a relatively meager background of experience (Frank, 1952, p. 18).

The Stage of Maturation Influences the Result of Training Before training, instruction, and teaching can be productive, appropriate inner growth must take place; the muscles, nerves, and brain must have developed to a proper degree. Some parents are eager for their child to walk so that they can boast to relatives and friends. They hold the child upright, they place his feet for him, they hold attractive toys before him, and presently he walks. It is not likely that their efforts speeded his walking; it is likely that he has had the strength to walk for some time and merely needed the neural maturation that would enable him to maintain balance and achieve coordination. Studies of preschool children indicate that the most mature acquired skills in buttoning, cutting with scissors, and climbing more easily than the less mature. In the latter part of one experiment, children made relatively more progress than at the beginning because they were then more mature (Hilgard, 1932). The importance of maturation has also been noted in toilet training. Parents who wait until the baby has developed sufficiently discover that the child acquires the ability to keep clean and dry almost overnight. This does not mean that maturation determines teaching entirely and that we just wait for it to occur—Bruner (1963, p. 47), for example, asserts that almost any subject, in some form, might possibly be taught to any child.

The role of maturation is well illustrated in the development of reading skills. Experiments, observations, and measurements have established the fact that trying to teach a child to read before he has reached a given degree of maturity is relatively fruitless. Among the characteristics that indicate readiness to read are a mental age of about 6½ years, adequate visual power, adequate hearing, emotional control consistent with first-grade level, the desire to read, and a background of experience (Blair and Jones, 1960). Even though a child is seven years old, if he has not achieved the appropriate mental age for reading, he is likely to have so much difficulty that he will develop negative attitudes toward reading. If he is far below the necessary mental age, he may not learn to read at all; certainly, his progress will be slow and faltering. On the other hand, if he has reached the requisite minimum mental age and has developed the other characteristics required for reading readiness, his progress is likely to be rapid and gratifying.

Educational implications of readiness The outcome of training is partially dependent upon maturation. E. L. Thorndike, in discussing the "law of readiness," stated:

(1) that when a conduction unit is ready to conduct, conduction by it is satisfying, nothing being done to alter its action; (2) that for a conduction unit ready to conduct not to conduct is annoying, and provokes whatever responses nature provides in connection with that particular annoying lack; (3) that when a conduction unit unready for conduction is forced to conduct, conduction by it is annoying.[3]

This law is all too frequently ignored in the actual teaching-learning situation. Perhaps because of required or traditional curriculums, teachers try to teach reading, arithmetic, algebra, and social abstractions when the child reaches the prescribed chronological age. The consequence is that much teaching is done at or near the frustration level of some pupils.

Recognition of the necessity for maturation has been given in the primary grades in the form of reading-readiness programs. Readiness is achieved by allowing time for the maturation of mental abilities and for stimulating it through experience. A readiness program must generate interest, stimulate eagerness, and cultivate desire. Field trips, visual aids, storytelling (by both teacher and pupils), listening games, and experience charts (records made by the teacher of events that the children relate) are used in readiness programs. Vision, hearing, and general health are given attention. Thus an effective readiness program allows for intrinsic growth and, through meaningful experiences, develops conceptual background.

It should not be inferred that readiness to learn occurs at a precise point on a scale. A mental age of 6½ years is not the only requisite. It might be better to think of several types of reading readiness—a time to begin reading, a time to read about things the pupil has not himself experienced, a time to evaluate what is read, a time to appreciate the chronology of history, a time to draw inferences, and the like (Gates, 1953). It takes time and experience, not merely a mental age of 6½ years, for full comprehension. This leads to the further conclusion that readiness for one teacher's method of teaching may not be readiness for another teacher's method.

Unless psychological maturation and its educational parallel, readiness, are recognized and applied, the inevitable result will be frustration for

[3] E. L. Thorndike, *Educational Psychology: Briefer Course*, New York: Teachers College, Columbia University, 1914, p. 55.

the pupil. "The child's learning must be well within the range of his emotional, social, and physical *readiness*, and not just at the extreme point of his endurance. Learnings which do take place under the latter conditions are usually so suffused with negative attitudes that the learning is emotionally crippling to the learner." [4]

The principle of multiple causation must be recognized in assessing the interaction of maturation and the results of instruction. For years, it was thought that the formal study of arithmetic should be delayed until about the third grade. But the competency with which some first graders use arithmetic clearly indicates that readiness is related to methods of instruction. When problems come from the pupils' lives, when understanding takes precedence over rote learning, and when the relationships of processes are made clear, pupils can master number concepts and processes that were formerly considered too difficult for them (Buswell, 1960). At the University of Illinois, investigations into arithmetic teaching have shown that the act of pupil discovery is important; sixth graders in a Harvard experiment learned geography better when they themselves developed theories about the location of cities; recent studies reaffirm the value of knowing principles and weaving facts into them; and intellectual excitement is more likely if it is worth the individual's knowing—useful beyond the learner's immediate need (Bruner, 1963, pp. 21–31). Thus the way learning is structured shapes the phenomenon of readiness. The teacher cannot evade his own responsibility by citing the child's immaturity.

The foregoing does not mean that readiness can be ignored. Children must progress through certain developmental stages before they can be expected to participate successfully in number work. A child is not yet ready to do real addition if he counts objects to get a sum. If he must add in order to find the product of two numbers, he is not ready for multiplication. For teachers, this suggests that *if the child cannot meet the traditional standards, the standards and methods should be altered to correspond to the developmental stage of the pupil* (Ilg, 1951).

Similar needs for readiness have been discovered in relation to handwriting. Some researchers find a marked relationship between maturity and handwriting, while others find it to be of little significance (Harris, 1960). Reversal (writing *d* for *b* or *p* for *g*, or writing *s* backward) can be expected of children of five or six, and the teacher should avoid making an issue of such errors (Ames, 1951). Manuscript writing does appear to be appropriate for the developmental stage of primary youngsters, and because, in learning to read, he learns the manuscript letters, it is doubtful that he should be subjected to possible confusion by the early

[4] *Fostering Mental Health in Our Schools*, 1950, Yearbook of the Association for Supervision and Curriculum Development, Washington: National Education Association, 1950, p. 4.

introduction of cursive style. The transition to cursive writing should probably be delayed until the age of eight or nine years. Actually, there is some doubt that cursive writing is fundamentally speedier or otherwise more advantageous than manuscript writing at any age (Hildreth, 1945).

Maturation probably plays a less important part in learning as the individual approaches his adult level of intelligence. However, an example of the role of maturation in later learning can be seen in the study of algebra. Experiments indicate that among high school students of equivalent IQs there are fewer failures in algebra when it is studied in the junior year than in the traditional freshman year. But the principle of multiple causation and recent successes in teaching both algebra and geometry to selected upper-grade pupils suggest that factors other than maturation be studied. Selection on the basis of ability—special tests for mathematics capacity, for example—has proved to be wise, but *pupils who are selected on one measure show almost as much variation in other respects as do unselected groups of pupils* (Cronbach, 1963, p. 253). Thus in addition to special selection on the basis of ability, for example, attention must also be given to students' understanding of meanings, causal relationships, vocabulary, and the basic processes, as well as to their individual differences in maturity (Gibb, Mayer, and Treuenfels, 1960).

Much has been written to the effect that school tasks must challenge the pupil. Hence, there may be such a thing as overreadiness—having passed beyond the time to "strike when the iron is hot." [5] Our society is geared to learning certain things at certain times. Retarded readers in the intermediate grades often complain that the materials provided them are too babyish, for example. And the same may be said of emotional learnings. Williams claims that if normal heterosexual attitudes are not learned during adolescence, technical intervention (psychological or psychiatric aid) will be required to achieve them later (1930, p. 113). Older persons who are determined to get a college education are often able to deal with their overreadiness successfully; however, such strong motivation is relatively infrequent. The learning of school subjects is a developmental task, and our culture demands that these tasks be learned at or about a certain time—failure to do so increases the likelihood of encountering difficulty. Effective teachers must be concerned "teachable moment."
about the timing of their efforts: Havighurst (1953, p. 5) refers to the

Patterns of Behavior Appear in an Orderly Growth Sequence   Growth is not random and haphazard, but a regular step-by-step process. Any skill, trait, or knowledge must have its proper antecedents; in turn, it

[5] See item 2 in the quotation from E. L. Thorndike, section on Educational Implications of Readiness.

forms the foundation for the next level of growth. The baby creeps before he crawls and crawls before he walks, and the growing child walks before he runs and runs before he dances. He babbles before he says words, says single words before he constructs sentences, communicates orally before he writes, and writes simply before he composes learned dissertations.

The regular and sequential appearance of behavior patterns makes it possible to judge the maturity of a given individual. Not all persons of the same chronological age have matured at the same rate: Some are at one level in the general sequence of behavior patterns, while others may be markedly lower or higher on the developmental scale. Edgar A. Doll has devised a scale for evaluating the social maturity of an individual—an example of growth sequences.[6] Representative items in the scale are:

TABLE 1

Behavior item	Age, years
Grasps objects within reach	0–1
Drinks from cup or glass unassisted	1–2
Puts on coat or dress unassisted	2–3
Buttons coat or dress	3–4
Goes about neighborhood unattended	4–5
Prints simple words	5–6
Uses table knife for spreading	6–7
Tells time to quarter of an hour	7–8
Reads on own initiative	8–9
Makes minor purchases	9–10
Makes telephone calls	10–11
Is left to care for self or others	11–12
Performs responsible routine chores	12–15
Follows current events	15–18
Has a job or continues schooling	18–20
Uses money providently	20–25
Promotes civic progress	25–+

Source: Edgar A. Doll, *The Vineland Social Maturity Scale,* Vineland, N.J.: The Training School, 1936.

The complete scale has several items for each year, and the composite score is indicative of a given level of maturity. Some persons, for ex-

[6] A manual of instructions and explanations of theory and use of the scale is Edgar A. Doll, *Measurement of Social Competence,* Philadelphia: Educational Test Bureau, 1953. This manual makes the scale a more usable tool for teachers who wish to understand their pupils better.

ample, make telephone calls before they make minor purchases, but nevertheless, the general sequence tends to hold true.

This regular sequential appearance of behavior patterns is the basis for constructing intelligence tests. The Stanford revision of the Binet-Simon Scale, which has been the standard reference for many intelligence tests for some years, uses certain developmental items to determine the mental development of an individual. *Some* of the items and the years in which they are usually accomplished are cited below:

TABLE 2

Item	Year	Month
Identifies body parts: hair, mouth, ear, nose, hands, eye	2	
Names objects: chair, automobile, box, key, fork	2	6
Compares size of balls	3	
Sorts black and white buttons	3	6
Names opposites: "Brother is a boy, sister is a. . . ."	4	
Identifies use of materials: "What is a house made of?"	4	6
Forms triangle from square piece of paper	5	
Tells what part of a picture is missing	6	
Points out similarities: wood and coal, etc.	7	
Remembers details from a story	8	
Copies design from memory	9	
Repeats six digits	10	
Repeats sentence from memory (15–16 words)	11	
Understands abstract words: pity, curiosity, etc.	12	
Unscrambles a sentence	13	
Solves oral problem of determined difficulty	14	
Differentiates abstractions: laziness and idleness	Average adult	
Repeats six digits in reverse of order presented	Superior adult I	
Explains meaning of proverbs	Superior adult II	
Repeats thought of orally presented passage	Superior adult III	

Source: Lewis M. Terman and Maud A. Merrill, *Stanford-Binet Intelligence Scale: Manual for Third Revision, Form L-M,* Boston: Houghton Mifflin Company, 1960, *passim.* Used by permission.

In this scale, there are six items for each half-year through age four; beginning with the fifth year, there are six items for each full year, and the individual taking the test is credited with two months' mental age for each item successfully accomplished. Frequently, the subject fails all the items for a given year and accomplishes one item among those for the next year. But in spite of such variations, behavior development is generally sequential.

Educational implications of sequential growth School curricula should be and, to a large extent, are based upon the characteristic pupil-development patterns. It is recognized, for instance, that appropriate activities for children in the primary grades should utilize the large muscles of the body because children are not ready for fine coordination. Large blocks, crates, oversize crayons, and large pieces of heavy paper are replacing the cutting, weaving, and writing activities of an earlier day. The short attention span characteristic of six- and seven-year-olds demands frequent variation of activities. Children in the intermediate grades are gradually expanding their interests, their writing is improving rapidly, and most of them are capable of mastering some number concepts. Differences between individual children are becoming more pronounced, and the variety of interests and abilities must be recognized if some pupils are not to be frustrated. Children in the upper grades are expanding their horizons in many ways, especially in social activities. They are interested in people and imitate others with sincerity and persistence. Their attention span is longer, and they will like and profit from drill, though they may still have difficulty in working abstract problems. Boys are interested in demonstrating their muscular strength, and both boys and girls are interested in personal appearance.

The adolescent years see merely an expansion and intensification of the growth trends that have previously been noted. There is an increased interest in sex. The expanding social horizon of adolescents makes adaptation to their peers more important than their relations to adults. Teachers and parents would do well to recognize this factor and use less pressure in trying to persuade them to conform to adult standards of dress and behavior. Girls spend much time shopping, fixing their hair, and in other ways attempting to establish themselves in their feminine roles. Such interests are recognized in some schools, where classes in charm or personality development are included in homemaking courses; but all too frequently these natural evidences of development are ignored or even discouraged. For instance, as adolescents grope from dependence on parents to independence in their own lives, they encounter various stages. These typically include crushes (strong liking for an older person), "life-long" pals of the same sex (but the friendships do not last), puppy love (admiration, perhaps secret, for another of the other sex the same age), and finally, mature love (though love for one of the other sex in middle-class culture will normally be experienced four or five times prior to marriage). Adults should recognize these stages and lend encouragement and assistance to the adolescent growing through the experience. It is necessary that growing individuals go through all the stages of development; otherwise, according to some psychiatrists, their growth to genuine maturity will be hazardous (Farnham, 1952, p. 114). Forcing the issue by giving dancing lessons or requiring prematurely adult dress and grooming for high school students or opposing the adolescent modes is to ignore the naturalness of these sequences.

At Glencoe, Illinois, teen-agers were helped to perceive stages of development by observing younger groups—kindergarten, primary, and intermediate pupils—and then discussing the typical and atypical behavior they saw. After having supplementary skits, films, and discussion panels, the youngsters came to a better understanding—as revealed by their discussions and behavior—of the meaning and implications of maturity (Kaiser and Timmer, 1964).

Sequential social development can be recognized in class units, projects, or subjects that start with pupils' experience and proceed to the general and abstract. Thus in a class in government, the teacher might start with local government and the way it affects young people, with visits to community political divisions, or even with problems of class or schoolwide government. Study of state and national government may be undertaken after matters that most intimately concern the student have been discussed. Learning that is abstract and remote from the student's experience is likely to result in mere verbalization, devoid of real understanding and manifested by parroting of statements made in a book.

Mead asserts that persistent emotions of the adolescent are carried over from childhood as "unfinished business." Often the adolescent has not had the freedom to develop the strength necessary to assume the new and heavy responsibilities placed upon him. His inconsistency is simply probing for answers. His interest in sex and sex play, far from being abnormal, is a search for reassurance that he is growing and developing normally. His occasional rebellion against parents is an attempt to grow in independence. He needs the help and counsel of teachers who do not punish and browbeat, but listen attentively. He needs developmental sequences in the form of part-time work, summer institutes, travel, and group work with his peers, which will foster emotional growth and provide a meaning for and direction to life (Mead, 1960).

Each Individual Has His Own Rate of Growth Some children grow rapidly, and some grow slowly. Some reach maturity at an early age, and some never become "adults" in the broad sense of the word. It is as if some traveled by ox cart and some by jet plane. Some achieve prominence in their teens, others in their twenties, and a few achieve prominence after they have become sexagenarians.

The fact that different parts of the organism grow at different rates complicates evaluation of growth rates. A child has many ages: a chronological age, a mental age, an educational age, a grip age, a carpal age, a dental age, a social age, and an organismic age—to mention only a few of the discrete phases of growth that have been measured at the present time. A given child will show much variation in these ages, and the older he is, the greater the variation. Moreover, growth in some one area may proceed unevenly. That is, though a child has learned to feed himself, to tie his shoes, or to say "Please," he may not give consistent evidence of it.

Individual growth rates tend to remain constant A child who is tall for his age at two years will *probably* be tall as an adult. A child who has an IQ of 80 at four years will be *likely* to have an IQ within 5 or 10 points of 80 when he is fifteen, and one who has an IQ of 120 will *tend* to maintain that IQ in later years. When growth curves of several children for any one trait are superimposed, they tend to follow the same general pattern, and there is little crossing of the curves of different individuals (see Figure 12).

The concave curve A in the figure represents growth taking place at an increasing rate. The straight line B represents growth taking place at

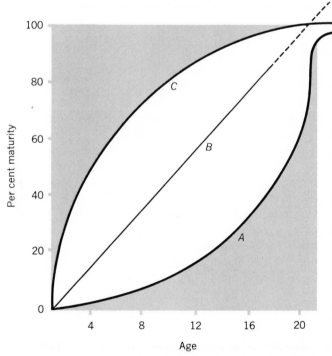

FIGURE 12. *Some representative growth curves. A, growth of sex organs and sex function (slow initial growth); B, growth in chronological age (uniform rate throughout); C, growth of head, body, or height (rapid initial growth).*

the same rate each year. The convex curve *C* represents growth taking place at a decreasing rate.

Educational implications of individual growth rates The problem of dealing with individual differences is one of the most pervasive with which the school has to deal. Books on psychology and education constantly reiterate the importance of realizing that children grow at different rates and consequently differ markedly in personality and physical and mental development. Some of these differences result from different socioeconomic backgrounds and are evident in pupils' reaction patterns—differences in family behavior habits, diet, cultural opportunities, ideals, attitudes, and adjustive actions. Other differences are still more obvious—differences in energy output, learning ability, interests, background information, body build, height and weight, resistance to disease, temperaments, and physical attractiveness.

Dropouts may be accounted for, in part, by the school's failure to solve the problem of dealing with individual differences. Emotional disturbances at home, lack of family tradition of education, need for income, lack of skill in making peer relationships are other reasons. But certainly there has been failure to reach the goal of providing "each child with the type of training and education best suited to him as an individual and to his expected needs as an adult." [7] Tapfer has shown how paying attention to individual growth rates can help reduce the number of dropouts. He identified forty high school boys in their junior year who, on the basis of criteria established through study of the previous year's junior dropouts, had high potential for dropping out. Half of them were given weekly sessions in individual counseling and had program adaptations, while the remainder continued as usual. At the end of the year, 79 per cent of the "counseled-adapted" group were still in school, while 43 per cent of the control group had left (Tapfer, 1962). The experiment emphasized a well-recognized fact: Not all can run the same course at a prescribed rate of speed. The bright students mark time or become bored, while the slow ones are frustrated by tasks that are too difficult and stop trying or drop out.

The teacher who is interested in improving instruction must often chart the course. Each teacher can provide a *variety* of activities in a given class or grade. Often he is able to select reading materials at several grade levels, schedule arithmetic classes of varied difficulty and types, and scale requirements for groupings of pupils of somewhat similar interests and mental development. Teaching machines and programmed studies are being used to provide some of this needed individuality (Trenholme, 1962).

An eighth-grade teacher conducted a project centering on social organization in Mexico and included various activities. This variety per-

[7] "High School Drop-outs," *NEA Research Bulletin*, 38 (1): 14, 1960.

mitted scaling work to individual growth rates. Each activity involved one or more students, and only the results of work were brought to the attention of the class as a whole. Some students made contacts with a visiting Mexican lecturer by telephone, visited and made a report on Mexican art in the local museum, studied the menu of a Mexican restaurant, borrowed native costumes from Mexican neighbors, and made musical instruments from gourds. Others drew and painted pictures and a mural, ordered books on the topic from the central library, and read and made reports on material ranging from first-grade books to the *Encyclopedia Britannica.* The culminating activity was a Mexican festival in costume to which parents were invited. It involved committee work, the allocation of individual responsibilities, manual labor, art work, reading, computation, and social and business contacts. The result was meaningful learning scaled to ability. Only two pupils failed to participate readily or wholeheartedly, and they were recent additions to the class.

Ability to predict individual rates and patterns of growth—mental physical, and social—is helpful in establishing educational objectives, and it helps teachers to avoid expecting too much of some and too little of others, thus reducing the possibility of frustration. Vocational, academic, and avocational suggestions of guidance programs are based on the relative constancy of individual growth rates and patterns. In general, the dull tend to remain dull, and giftedness shows itself relatively early. Delinquency has its warning signs in predelinquent behavior (evidence of social and personal maladjustment). The bright second grader has a better chance of election to Phi Beta Kappa than a pupil who spends two years in second grade. But these are tendencies; marked environmental changes may effect a change in growth rate. Further, an individual may be a "late maturer."

Growth Is Continuous and Gradual—It Is Not Saltatory This is the most encouraging of the growth principles, but it can also be a most discouraging one. Intellectual and educational growth take time, effort, and money, and no magical transformations of personality or intellect can be expected.

A fallacy is involved in the use of the words "stages" and "levels" in discussing growth. If we were to visualize growth as taking place on an inclined plane rather than in sharply demarcated stages or levels, we would describe the process more accurately. Childish conduct develops gradually from infancy; adolescent conduct is the result of continuous growth from childhood. It is impossible to draw a sharp line of distinction between the levels; there are clear differences between the mid-points of the various levels, but the borderlines are vague. It is sounder to think in terms of expansion and emergence of traits and abilities than in terms of sudden transformations and distinct levels.

Competence in problem solving—like physical growth and social development—is the result of continuous development. Experiments show that children of preschool age are capable of solving problems that require insight. As the child grows, his competence increases largely because of maturation (Wohlwill, 1960), although child psychologists and educators emphasize the importance of giving him experiences that will expand his conceptual range (Hunt, 1961).

Educational implications of the continuity and gradualness of growth
It would clearly be an overstatement to assert that any particular principle has *the* most important implication for education. But certainly the principle of continuous, gradual growth is worthy of constant attention at all educational levels. Hurry, impatience, and prodding are not in accord with this principle. Educational achievement, vocational prominence, artistic accomplishment, or mere competence in daily living is not achieved suddenly, but is the result of numerous successive steps.

Teachers must know that they cannot expect sudden transformations of personality in their pupils. At the same time, they can be assured that the expenditure of effort and the passage of time will inevitably show results. If it were possible to see, on the same day, a pupil as he is on the first day of the term and as he is at the end of the term, the gain would be apparent. Equivalent tests (see Glossary) given at the beginning and at the end of the term serve somewhat the same purpose.

Students need the help of teachers to understand that by enlarging knowledge and establishing daily habits, they lay the foundations for later competence. Their haste to leave school, to take a job, to become famous, and to establish families must not interfere with their taking advantage of continued, directed, and purposeful steps. Many persons are in such a hurry to achieve fame and accumulate fortunes that they fail to achieve the balanced living that is conducive to sound mental health. Yet steady growth is what makes us most acceptable to others and provides the deepest inner satisfactions.

Growth Is a Matter of Both Differentiation and Integration Prenatal physical growth provides an excellent illustration of differentiation. During the initial days of development (known as the period of the ovum), the baby to be is merely a rounded mass of cells. During the following period, up to about nine weeks (period of the embryo), the body parts are clearly distinguishable, or differentiated. During the next phase (fetal period), growth is largely concerned with increase in size of already differentiated parts. Shortly after birth, some teeth have become differentiated; as age increases, certain tissues become more clearly distinguished as bone.[8] The wristbones of a five-month-old child are

[8] The change of cartilaginous tissue to bone, which is revealed by X-ray, is used as an index of skeletal age.

much farther apart than those of a five-year-old child, and those of a five-year-old are farther apart than those of a sixteen-year-old. Differentiation is also seen in physical action. A six-month-old baby grasps a small object with a sweeping motion of the entire hand. Soon after his first birthday, the child is able to pick the object up by his thumb and forefinger.

The increasing accuracy of perception is also a function of the differentiation processes. At first, the infant responds to all persons as if they were his mother, then males and children are eliminated, and still later only a specific woman is seen as his mother. Language development during the life span involves differentiation. At first, the child refers to all toy animals as "doggie" or "kitty," then toy ducks and bears are eliminated from the dog concept. The word "dog" is later attached to live dogs. As perception is further differentiated, dogs are seen more precisely. Dalmatians, Airedales, pointers, and Pekingese are recognized as specific kinds of dogs. Growth in vocabulary is but one illustration of differentiation.

The development of skills, concepts, and knowledge is similarly a matter of differentiation and specificity. Complex responses, such as catching a baseball, are not built from the separate acts of reaching, grasping, and decreasing muscular tension. The total act is involved at the beginning; only later are the parts of the act analyzed. Pupils learn school subjects in a similar manner. Writing the story or telling about an incident should take precedence over diction, pronunciation, sentence structure, spelling, and capitalization (Millard, 1958, p. 193). These details are important, but they come as the result of the integrated (albeit not always beautifully integrated) effort.

Integration takes place concurrently with differentiation. Integration is coordinated, harmonious, and efficient behavior. The skilled athlete in action provides an example of integration, revealing its emotional, mental, and physical aspects. He is excited, or at least sufficiently concerned to do his best; he has planned a procedure that, he thinks, will obtain the best results; and he wastes no energy. The phenomenon can readily be seen by comparing an eighth-grade second baseman with a big-league ball player. The eighth grader is tense, he runs hard, he plunges for an easy bounder, he throws with a mighty effort—into the ground or over the first baseman's head. The big-leaguer smacks his glove and relaxes in position. A sizzling liner over the pitcher's head hits in front of second base and bounces over the base. Somehow, the second baseman is there at precisely the right moment. He dips his glove and, all in the same series of movements, turns, steps, throws, and the runner is out. Integration means that all parts are working harmoniously and efficiently toward a planned and specific objective.

Integration is also well illustrated in speech. The baby has difficulty saying a single word—he purses his lips, opens his mouth wide, sticks his tongue out—and perhaps says something understandable. Increasing integration over the years may result in his becoming a skilled actor or speaker, whose words are accompanied by integrated inflection, gestures, and facial expressions.

Personality integration, the harmonious and effective working together of abilities, energies, aspirations, and motives, is frequently mentioned by psychologists and educators as a concern for all. Actually, conflicts between abilities, desires, and social demands are normal, and inconsistency of behavior is normal. The fact remains, however, that the tendency toward integration is a fundamental aspect of growth.[9] It is a driving force toward a goal that is never completely achieved. From the educator's standpoint, it might be advantageous to think of integrating as a process rather than integration as an achievable goal or a characteristic of completed growth.

Educational implications of learning as differentiation and integration The roles of differentiation and integration can be illustrated in language development. Communication is such an important aspect of total living that precise and selective use of words (differentiation) should be emphasized by every teacher. The differences between "cat" and "dog" and "boy" and "girl" are problems for preschool children. The differences between "surprise" and "astonish," "infer" and "imply," and "healthy" and "healthful" are problems for high school and college students, in whom the process of differentiation is still incomplete. Integration is involved in combining words into incisive and economical sentences; in addition, the inflections, pauses, and combinations of sentences that make meaning most clear and forceful must be used.

The breakdown of schoolwork into subjects facilitates differentiation. However, curriculum makers warn that this breakdown may go so far that the student fails to see the interrelations between subjects and life itself. Differentiation should not be fostered at the expense of integration.

Integration is the process of synthesizing the various aspects of physical, environmental, and personality attributes and of becoming a functioning part of social groups. There are several ways of capitalizing on this process in teaching-learning situations. One way to achieve integration in education is to emphasize the relationships that exist between various school subjects.

Teachers may show that data from other subject areas can be used in solving current problems. For example, he can approach subject matter with "Last week we discussed . . ." or "That should remind you of. . . ."

[9] Arthur W. Combs and Donald Snygg, in *Individual Behavior*, rev. ed., New York: Harper & Row, Publishers, 1959, p. 46, assert that the great driving force in life is the need for ever more adequate ability to cope with life—a concept that appears to be very close to integration.

Integration may also be facilitated by using problems and projects as points of departure rather than ends in themselves Still another way to achieve integration is to organize the subject matter so that the larger aspects of the topic stand out clearly and the details are presented in terms of the larger whole.

Personality integration is of special importance, and the teacher must watch for evidences of lack of integration, such as (1) inconsistency between professed knowledge and action; (2) failure to apply knowledge in creative responses; (3) acceptance of facts, but failure to apply them; (4) lack of readiness to revise hypotheses, opinions, and beliefs; (5) statements made without corroborative evidence; and (6) condemnation of others for doing what the individual does himself (Megroth, 1949). Seeing the lack of integration is, of course, only a first step. The next task is to diagnose the difficulty and take remedial action.

The development of socially integrated people, able and interested in cooperating in the improvement of society, has been a goal of our educational system during our entire national history. The school, where experiences can be selected and guided, provides time and place to develop such individuals. Because one of the major problems of the nation and the world is understanding, the study of semantics, or the meanings of language, is an important facet of education. The practical implications are obvious. Students at all levels must be given many opportunities to exchange opinions through conversation, discussion, and debate—recitation and listening to a teacher are not enough. Problem and project methods must be utilized, and students must be given an opportunity to become increasingly self-directive. Working cooperatively on common problems in the school also will accomplish at least a degree of the desired integration.

Certainly the above suggestions do not exhaust the school's possibilities for encouraging differentiation and integration. Both processes should be a concern of the entire school organization, affecting the staff's teaching philosophy, the curricular orientation, and the attitude toward pupils.

Correlation, Rather Than Compensation, of Traits Is the General Rule

"Unto every one that hath shall be given" is nowhere more clearly shown than in the field of psychology. Despite what we might wish to be the case, and contrary to what is sometimes believed, deficiency in one aspect of the organism or personality is not compensated for by giftedness or strength in another. Although the relationship is not sufficiently uniform to warrant prediction in individual cases, there is evidence revealing a low but positive correspondence among the traits or abilities possessed by any one person. Slightly more often than not the child who has a high IQ will have greater physical strength, more skill in physical activities, fewer sensory handicaps, be taller, heavier, more resistant to disease, better looking, and more socially adaptable than his peer of the same age whose IQ is markedly lower (French, 1959, p. 37). Such remarks as "beautiful but dumb" and "strong back, weak mind" are based on either ignorance or generalization from insufficient data.

Correlation holds for both personality assets and liabilities. Just as the gifted child has fewer sensory defects than do other children, so does the handicapped child often have multiple handicaps (Katz, 1955). Crippling is often accompanied by visual and auditory handicaps. Endocrine dysfunction often accompanies and may cause low vitality or low mentality. Recent research has, however, strongly indicated that personality defects that seem to accompany handicap may be a function of treatment and perception, rather than being the normal concomitant of handicap (Lange, 1959).

There is ample evidence that many teachers think in terms of compensation rather than correlation. Such teachers hasten to recommend shopwork or physical education classes for the pupil who has difficulty in academic work. The pupil who is slow in academic work *may* do well in the shop, but rarely because he has outstanding talent for manual work. His good work is due to the extra time he spends on it.

These remarks do not hold for another kind of compensation. A person may compensate for a shortcoming by spending more time in developing that area or by abandoning his ambitions in one area and substituting others. But there is nothing innate or intrinsic in such compensation; it is the exception rather than the rule. For every Edison or Roosevelt, there are hundreds of individuals with similar handicaps whose accomplishments are inferior or mediocre. A person does not necessarily have great drive or a high level of aspiration *because* he has a handicap.

The principle of correlation can be observed in a visit to any school. The child who is best in arithmetic is frequently near the top in spelling, is popular with his classmates, and plays vigorously and well. The one who is slow in arithmetic is likely to be slow in social adaptation, to experience difficulty in reading and social studies, and to have symptoms of maladjustment. It might be desirable to have things otherwise, but the fact remains that there is a tendency "for the rich to become richer and for the poor to become poorer."

Educational implications of the correlation of traits The practical import of the principle that there tends to be correlation, rather than compensation, of traits has to do with understanding, teaching methods, and curriculum. Teachers should avoid the temptation to steer a child into physical activities, construction exercises, or repetitive art productions *because* he is slow in academic pursuits. The time has arrived when we should emphasize the "slow" in "slow learners," rather than thinking of them as nonlearners. Their scholastic program should be designed to meet their level—it should not be neglected or eliminated.

Of course, many children have special talents. Alert teachers seek to capitalize on these by providing a variety of activities—costuming, construction, stage management, ticket taking, as well as acting are parts of the whole in a dramatic production. While it is likely that traits and abilities will be positively correlated, there is some possibility that a slow learner may have special talents—leadership qualities, athletic prowess,[10] or skills as magicians or singers. Pupils with artistic talent do sometimes experience difficulty in the traditional subjects. When these talents are noted, they can be used to build ego strength that prompts the individual to try for goals at more difficult levels.

The teacher's attitude toward his pupils is an all-important factor in their development. Teachers sometimes make the mistake of assuming that the larger children in the class are older than their peers and consequently less intelligent. Actually, the intellectually accelerated student is sometimes the largest but, being young, may lack background experience. Conversely, a child who is small for his age seems uncommonly bright. The result is that children often develop unwarranted feelings of inferiority or superiority that could be avoided if the teacher took more care in evaluating his pupils.

Summary

The processes of growth have direct and important implications for teaching and learning. Whether the immediate concern is mental, emotional, or physical growth, these processes operate in orderly, predictable ways. Knowledge of them can help the teacher do his work more effectively.

Growth results from the interaction of the organism with its environment. Hence, it is a function of the individual's perception of himself and his milieu, as well as being a function of congenital equipment and external surroundings. Teachers can alter perceptions and the nature of the school environment to fit the current status of the individual.

Growth takes place most rapidly in the early years, so primary teachers have much impact on establishing attitudes toward continued learning as well as the tools for learning. It is important not to place sole emphasis on the words "early years" because the words "growth takes place" are also part of the principle—in short, later years must not be discounted.

The effect of training is dependent on the stage of maturation; that is, learning takes place most rapidly when the individual is "ready" for it. Readiness, however, can be fostered by appropriate experiences in number concepts, social contacts, and acquaintance with the physical world.

[10] Contrary to popular belief, it is a mistake to think that athletes are necessarily poor students. Studies indicate that athletes have, on the average, higher intelligence than their nonathletic classmates. When their time is not taken by training and practice for athletic contests, their marks are slightly superior to those who are regularly nonparticipants.

Patterns of behavior appear in an orderly sequence and thus enable teachers to predict, from present status, what the individual will probably be like later in terms of intellectual ability, social adaptability, and in personality and character.

Each individual has his own growth rate, or pattern, which means that education will be most effective when differences between pupils are given functional recognition.

Growth is a matter of both differentiation and integration. Teachers should point out significant differences in the concepts they teach and show how these are related in the *total* pattern of living. Applications, examples, illustrations, and emphasis on problem solving capitalize on this principle.

Correlation rather than compensation is the general rule for the distribution of traits and abilities. Hence, teachers can expect much from able pupils in many areas of functioning, but must scale down most expectations for the less able. Exceptions will occur so teachers should be alert to the existence of unique abilities in all pupils and provide opportunities for their exercise when found.

Problems and exercises

1 Observe an eight-year-old and tell how his growth can be considered a creative process.

2 Cite some examples in which the environment seems to have been more important than hereditary factors in shaping an individual's life. Cite some in which heredity seems to be dominant.

3 What is your reaction to the thesis that older persons can learn better than young persons when rates of intellectual growth (IQ) are the same?

4 Do you think there might be a "social readiness" that is similar to "reading readiness"?

5 If a child has not reached the maturity necessary for beginning reading successfully, should he be kept out of school for another year?

6 As an element in sequential growth, what are some behaviors you might expect of adolescents that are not clearly apparent in young children (intermediate grades)?

7 Devise your own list of implications for teaching based on the fact that growth is continuous and gradual.

8 Describe how differentiation and integration are involved in the study of sociology. Do the same for the study of a foreign language.

9 Cite some examples that indicate that teachers do or do not recognize the principle of the correlation of traits.

Suggested additional readings

Bernard, Harold W.: *Human Development in Western Culture*, Boston, Mass.: Allyn and Bacon, Inc., 1962, pp. 54–85.
Using much the same set of concepts that appears in this book, the author

provides further illustrations and data on the basic principles of growth.

Eaton, Joseph W.: "Adolescence in a Communal Society," *Mental Hygiene,* 48: 66–74, 1964.
This account of adolescent strivings toward maturity in Hutterite communities of the Dakotas, Montana, and parts of Canada shows how intimately psychological growth processes are related to one's culture.

Goodenough, Florence L., and Leona E. Tyler: *Developmental Psychology,* 3d ed., New York: Appleton-Century-Crofts, Inc., 1959, pp. 115–125.
The course of development is epitomized, using the concepts of homeostasis, motivation, and learning as the basic processes that explain the gradual changes of behavior and feelings of individuals.

Harris, Dale B., (ed.): *The Concept of Development,* Minneapolis: The University of Minnesota Press, 1957.
Various authorities from the biological and social sciences examine the concept of development and suggest implications for teachers, parents, and society in general.

Martin, William E., and Celia B. Stendler, *Child Behavior and Development,* rev. ed., New York: Harcourt, Brace & World, Inc., 1959, pp. 95–126.
In this chapter, the authors deal with developmental direction, maturation, the effects of practice, and the concept of developmental spiral. Personality and physical growth are used as illustrations.

Mussen, Paul H., *The Psychological Development of the Child,* Englewood Cliffs, N.J.: Prentice-Hall, Inc., 1963.
This paperback succinctly presents a synthesis of contemporary research on principles of development. Separate chapters deal with biological, cognitive, personality, and social development.

The Nature and Measurement
of Individual Differences

You will soon be faced
by a class of students. Whether that class is composed of first
graders, fifth graders, or high school seniors, the pupils will by
no means be alike. If there are thirty pupils in the class, there
are many more than thirty problems to solve if you wish to be
effective. Your words of advice will be attentively listened to by
some; others may not even know you are speaking. Some will
quickly and eagerly do the tasks you assign, others will do them
reluctantly and laboriously, still others will be so preoccupied
with extraschool events or so low in ability that they will neglect
academic tasks completely. Classification of these pupils into
interest or ability groups will reduce the range of differences and
make teaching somewhat easier. But it is safe to predict that your
success will largely depend on your understanding of their differences and your resourcefulness in capitalizing on them. Specialization characterizes our society: thus the school's encouragement of diversified interests and cultivation of students of varied
ability levels may be a significant contribution (Shane, 1962).
Your recognition of pupils' individual differences will also make
a sound contribution to their mental health and their effectiveness.

Some basic considerations

The Normal Curve of Distribution   This curve is a graphic representation of the similarity and differences found when a large
group is measured for any one trait, such as height, weight, intelligence, knowledge, interest, or friendliness. Figure 14 shows five
different measurements. Item 1, intelligence, shows that the IQs
of the great majority of children range between 90 and 110. The
flatter curve shows a greater overall range in IQ, from 60 to 140,
with fewer falling between the points of major cluster (90 to 110).
Item 2 shows the range and cluster of a specific trait of personality. Data for such evaluations may come from a combination
of pupils' ratings of their peers, teacher judgments, and personality inventories. Item 3 is indicative of differences in knowledge
that will characterize any group. In a typical fifth grade, reading

FIGURE 13. *Instructional devices are now available that make it possible to do more about individual differences than just talk about them.*

ability will cluster about fifth-grade level, some pupils will read only at the second-grade level, and a few will easily read materials ordinarily considered to be of high school level. Similar differences would be found in language usage, vocabulary, arithmetic, social studies, or spelling. Even if the group were a so-called "homogeneous group" (members selected on the basis of similar IQ, similar physical and social maturity, and similar academic achievements, etc.) there would still be marked differences, though the range would be less on the areas that had been used in selection, and the point of major cluster would be higher. Items 4 and 5 show differences in ages among children with fourteen teeth and the weight of several girls at age nine. Each of the items should be considered as unrelated to the others.

Some of you have as much knowledge about educational psychology now as others will have at the end of the term—in spite of the fact that you are all in one class and that a process of selection has been going on since the beginning of your school careers. All this indicates the futility of attempting to teach all pupils as though they were "average." While well over one-half of a typical fifth-grade class (see Figure 14) reads at just about fifth-grade level, another curve drawn to plot interest and competence in other subjects would probably assume a much different shape. The most important practical problems that you will meet in the classroom—maintaining steady progress in learning, discipline, motivation —hinge upon an operational knowledge of individual differences.

The Fallacy of Distinct Types   There are fat people, and there are thin ones. There are people at the top and at the bottom of a group with respect to a particular characteristic. Some people are introverts more of the time than they are extroverts; some people are bright in most things, and others are rather consistently dull. But the notion that these extremes of distribution constitute sharply demarcated types has been repeatedly refuted by scientific investigation. There are not just two types of students in an educational psychology class or just three types of pupils in a fifth-grade class. Yet the terms "fifth graders," "good readers," "cooperative pupils," and "ten-year-olds" are used as if there were clearly defined types. In a recently published book, we learn that seven-year-olds "are sensitive to the feelings of those about them and desire approval." The interests of boys and girls are growing apart. They are full of energy but tire easily; they think in concrete terms; they are highly competitive; and they enjoy songs, nature stories, and movies.

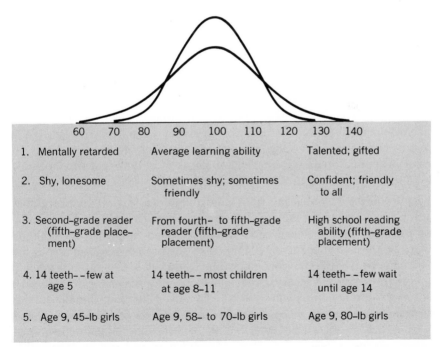

	60	70	80	90	100	110	120	130	140
1.	Mentally retarded			Average learning ability			Talented; gifted		
2.	Shy, lonesome			Sometimes shy; sometimes friendly			Confident; friendly to all		
3.	Second-grade reader (fifth-grade placement)			From fourth- to fifth-grade reader (fifth-grade placement)			High school reading ability (fifth-grade placement)		
4.	14 teeth--few at age 5			14 teeth-- most children at age 8–11			14 teeth- -few wait until age 14		
5.	Age 9, 45-lb girls			Age 9, 58- to 70-lb girls			Age 9, 80-lb girls		

FIGURE 14.   *Normal curve of distribution. The curve will be higher for groups in which some selection has been made—flatter when individuals in the group are unselected.*

They are beginning to understand time and money. Such information about seven-year-olds may be helpful to teachers if it is understood that many of these things can be safely said of five-year-olds. *Some* of these characteristics will not appear until age nine in *some* individuals. In short, defining by characteristics must not blind teachers and parents to the fact that there are individual differences. Types exist only as *hypothetical* averages (fifth graders) or as *extremes* of a continuous distribution (fat and lean).

> This proclivity of man to classify anything and everything on the the basis of hard and fast lines of demarcation has met with considerable objection from both statistical and psychological angles. While it is a well-known truism that men differ among themselves in a great many respects, it is obvious upon critical reflection that unless we insist upon comparing the relatively few extreme cases usually available, they do not necessarily differ in the clear-cut type sense.[1]

Subdividing the school population on the basis of known characteristics of the group, the typical interests of pupils of a given age, or the rates of learning, which are probably in terms of rates of mental development, can help teachers hit closer to the developmental needs of pupils (Wilhelms, 1962). But a great deal of instructional effort will be futile unless the teacher appreciates the fact that there are pupils at the extreme ends of the curve. He must also realize that those in the center of the curve on one measurement may be at the extreme ends by another kind of measurement. For example, pupils from lower socioeconomic groups who are high on the intelligence curve do not rank as high in achievement as middle-class pupils. Immigrants do not immediately internalize the achievement motivation that is characteristic of our culture (Rosen, 1959), yet the uninformed teacher, acting on superficial indications, tends to treat all pupils of similar intellectual status as if they had similar motivations.

The Value of Differences   Individual differences are of immeasurable value to society, even though they are a constant challenge to teachers. In primitive groups, when each family provided its own food, built its own shelter, and made its own clothes, it was probably advantageous for everyone to possess the same skills and knowledge. But in our complex and highly integrated society, specialization and uniqueness are necessary for our continued existence. One man makes his contribution to the welfare of society as a whole by becoming a scientist (and in a specialized area). Another makes his contribution by becoming a philosopher. Another becomes a teacher, another a homemaker, and still another a dis-

[1] Louis P. Thorpe, *Psychological Foundations of Personality*, New York: McGraw-Hill Book Company, 1938, p. 314.

tributor of goods. The contributing citizen and educated person must be a high-grade specialist who has a sound general education (Drucker, 1959, p. 140).

Individual differences also are of value to the individual himself. While a person may not have even average finger dexterity, he may be a gifted teacher for example. Another may be gifted in mathematics and gain satisfaction for himself through recognition of his talent and achievements. This, of course, does not mean that any individual will always be able to do the things he is most able to do, nor does it mean that pupils in school should do only the things that they like to do. In the world of work, the individual will frequently have to do the kind of work that society needs to have done (Bernard, 1962, p. 286); only a fortunate few may be able to make their choices on the basis of interest and aptitude. But recognition of individual differences in school provides the ego support that makes an individual capable of yielding readily and graciously to demand.

School personnel must recognize their responsibility for developing differences if unique talents are to be developed and if pupils are to develop the ego strength essential to adaptability. Thus the orientation point in democratic education should be the uniqueness of each child (Schreiber, 1963). While mass education has merits in disseminating knowledge, education that really recognizes the individual holds forth the promise of self-realization for pupils and improvement for society. Suppes (1964) regards individual differences as being the principle of learning which is as yet unaccepted in day-to-day classroom practice.

Measurement of individual differences

Limits of Measurement Human traits are so complex, so interrelated, that precise measurement is difficult—if not impossible—for most of them. Devices are available to measure height, weight, blood pressure, white corpuscles, albumin, bone ossification, and the like. But no tool is available to measure intelligence, drive, honesty, social adjustment, etc., with like precision. Data obtained from tests yield valuable approximations of traits, abilities, and qualities, but it is important to remember that intelligence, personality, and social maturity are so complex that single measures are subject to much doubt (Thompson, 1962, p. 42). Despite their limitations, psychological tests yield much valuable information from which inferences may be made. Teachers should regard intelligence tests, personality inventories, and rating scales as instruments that provide valuable data for evaluation—rather than exact measures. It is unlikely that we will ever have a device for measuring "innate" intelligence, because human traits always develop in the context of diverse and changing environments (Hodgkinson, 1962, p. 91).

A test is a sample—a sample of blood, a sample of behavior, or a sample of a total situation. Several samples enable the investigator to make a more accurate guess about the total than if he had to operate completely in the dark. For example, a diamond drill is bored into a mountain from different positions and at different angles. This enables the engineer to determine the length, breadth, and depth of an ore-bearing fault. The assayer then analyzes different sections of the core taken by the diamond drill and determines the richness of the ore in terms of the amount of worthless rock, copper, silver, and lead for each section of the core. But the final judgment about the amount and quality of the ore can only be determined by driving a tunnel, taking out the ore, and having it milled. Do the mine owners or stockholders get rich? It depends on the efficiency of the mining, the market value of the ore at the time it is shipped, the distance and availability of transportation, and the honesty of the book-keeper. Tests (samples) have played a part in the solution of a problem. They have reduced the possibility of error, but they have not covered the entire situation.

Psychological testing is somewhat similar. Samples of intelligent behavior are taken by testing the individual's ability to comprehend and handle numbers, to perceive and interpret symbols, to understand words, to solve problems. Informed estimates are made by psychometrists about the total area of intelligence and the potential for cultivating special skills. Developing the individual (driving the tunnel) is the responsibility of teachers, who seek to perform their work with the least waste. Predictions can be made about the ultimate adjustment of the individual, but the environment (market conditions) that greets him at the time of graduation will influence the subsequent course of his life. Tests have played a part, but they provide only the basis for more accurate predictions. Tests provide clues for making more accurate estimations, they assist the teacher in answering specific questions about particular pupils. In the final analysis, tests must be interpreted in terms of corroborative evidence, other teachers' reports, the pupil's past record and your own observation and judgment of the pupil (Rothney, Danielson, and Heimann, 1959, p. 22).

Concepts Involved in Testing   In today's culture, tests are important in the lives of individuals. In order that they be as accurate as possible, certain criteria have been evolved for judging them.

1. A test should be standardized (see Glossary).[2] If a test is to be of maximum usefulness, it should be applicable to more than a small group. Standardization involves several considerations. There should be set pro-

[2] Teacher-made tests, of value for use in local situations and specific learning situations, need not meet this criterion. They should, however, approach satisfaction of the remaining criteria.

cedures for giving the examination. Directions must be carefully and uniformly worded, and exact timing must be observed. Children from one region or locality should not be favored or discriminated against. Hence, when the test is being developed, it should be given to children in various localities to see whether there are regional differences that must be taken into account. The norms (or standards—from whence comes the name) are often stated in terms of pupils' age, sex, socioeconomic condition, or grade achievement (Baron and Bernard, 1958, pp. 44ff). When the test has been administered experimentally to hundreds of subjects in various localities, a given score is often expressed in terms of IQ, mental age, grade equivalent, or percentile rank (see Glossary).

2. A test should be objective. The personal biases of the examiner should be reduced to a minimum. The feelings, hopes, likes, and dislikes of the person administering and scoring the test should be largely eliminated. "Objectivity" implies that a given answer is either right or wrong. There should be wide agreement on the correct answers and upon the meaning of those answers. Objectivity is easier to maintain in group testing than in individual testing. Hence, individual tests must be administered *only by specially trained technicians.* However, in the hands of a trained worker, the individual test is superior because it allows for interpretation of intention, motivation, and application and thus yields data beyond the test score alone.

3. The test should be easy to administer. The teacher should be able to administer the test with the facilities that are ordinarily available in the classroom. The directions should be understandable and easily followed by the examinee. Inability to comprehend the directions may prevent a subject from doing a task which he has the ability to do. Simplicity of scoring and interpretation also come under the heading of ease of administration.

4. A test should be valid. The items in the test should actually sample what the test is designed to measure. An achievement test that requires a great deal of reading during the examination may be invalid because the score depends more on reading ability than on knowledge of the subject matter. The author once administered a standardized arithmetic test in which much reading was involved. The test was invalid because poor readers could not read and work all the problems in the time allowed.

The test should agree with other measures. This quite frequently involves computing correlations (see Appendix) between test scores and other *quantitatively* expressed measures. Classroom grades may be correlated with intelligence tests to see that the measures of achievement accord with the measure of intellect. The judgments of experts, expressed on a numerical scale, may be used to compute the validity coefficient of intelligence tests. When teachers select tests, they should see whether the publishers are proud enough of their statistical validity to publish the results.

5. A test should sample widely. No matter what the test is designed to measure, questions should be varied. In arithmetic tests, the problems should embrace all the processes. In reading tests, poetry, directions, stories, and technical passages should be included. In intelligence tests, numbers, vocabulary, problems, abstract materials, and memory should be included. One of the major objections to theme-type tests, which are often used in classrooms, is that the sampling is too limited. For instance, one pupil might know twenty incidents in American history but not know one of two called for on a two-question test; another might know only the one incident out of a possible twenty, but get as high a score on the two-item test as the pupil who knew much more. It is safe to say that the more widely the various items in a test explore knowledge and experience, the better the basis for estimating the quality or area being evaluated.

6. A test should be reliable. The reliable test can be depended upon to yield like results under similar conditions. A test is reliable when the results of one administration agree with the results of another administration to a like group, or when two administrations of equivalent forms of the test give the same general results for the same person. Reliability thus indicates accuracy and consistency of measurement; it is determined by experimentation and experience.

It is extremely difficult to construct a reliable test. In consequence, tests very rarely have "equivalent forms" that are actually of the same degree of difficulty. For example, two teachers were using form A and form B of a given reading test. Each gave one form of the test at the beginning of the term and the other form at the end of the year. The one who gave form B first found that her pupils made a very gratifying gain. The other, who used form A first, found that the class average was practically the same at the end of the year as it was at the beginning. In fact, some pupils had apparently retrogressed in reading skill. Such an event would, of course, indicate that the test lacks reliability.

A test may be reliable without being valid. The arithmetic test referred to above, which contained much reading, gave consistent measurements. Successive administration of equivalent forms to the same individual yielded scores that were much alike. Yet it did not measure ability in arithmetic and therefore was not valid. On the other hand, if a test is to be valid, it must also be reliable.

7. A test should be economical. Economy involves both time and money. Simple equipment, a relatively limited number of carefully selected items that obtain wide sampling, and ease of scoring are essential.

But an inexpensive test that is easily administered may contribute so little to understanding and guidance that any cost is excessive. Moreover, the tests must be valid and reliable, or the price tag will have little meaning. Teachers should seek the advice of experts, study published reviews of tests, and examine test manuals when selecting tests.[3] The seven criteria listed above may be used as a basis for making a choice.

The Measurement of Intelligence As is the case with other kinds of psychological and educational measurement, intelligence is measured indirectly by means of what the individual knows and does. In short, intelligence is inferred from samples of various kinds of behavior.

The units for evaluating intelligence are the mental age obtained by testing and the intelligence quotient. Typically, the mental age (see Glossary) of the subject is divided by his chronological age and multiplied by 100 to give the IQ. When the child's mental age is the same as his chronological age, he has an IQ of 100 and is considered "average." Actually, it is worth noting that "average" in intelligence is a *band*, not a point; i.e., average IQ varies from 85 to 115, or from 90 to 110. (Some authorities make the average band wider than others do.) Growth in mental age, as in other aspects of growth, tends to slow down as maturity is approached. When children reach about sixteen years, it is helpful to replace the IQ connotation with measures of their relative standing within a group, such as decile or percentile ratings (see Glossary).

It is apparent that the mental-age unit is not an equal distance between levels of difficulty of performance, as are inches on a yardstick; i.e., the difference between an MA of one year and an MA of two years is not the same as the difference between an MA of fourteen years and one of fifteen years. The unit for each year is determined by studying a large number of individuals of various chronological ages. Tasks that are performed by the majority of three-, seven-, or fourteen-year-olds are, on the basis of this *average* performance, assigned a mental age value of three, seven, or fourteen years. This may be clarified by citing some of the typical tasks at various age levels that are used in the third revision of the Stanford-Binet tests of intelligence.

Year III-6 months
    Compares size of balls
    Assembles "patience pictures"
    Discriminates animal pictures
    Identifies objects or names action shown in pictures

[3] The *Mental Measurements Yearbook*, published periodically by the Rutgers University Press and more recently by the Gryphon Press, Highland Park, N.J., should be consulted by teachers and by others responsible for selecting tests. Tests of many types are described and critically reviewed in terms of the claims made for them, their limitations, and their justifiable usage.

Sorts black and white buttons
Comprehends and answers simple questions
(The subject is given one month's MA credit for each correct response as identified in the manual.)
Year VII
Identifies absurdities in pictures
Describes similarities (wood, coal, etc.)
Copies a diamond
Solves a social problem
Recognizes appropriate opposites
Repeats five digits
(The subject is given two months' MA credit for each correct response at years V and above.)
Year XIV
Scores seventeen on Stanford-Binet vocabulary list
Formulates principles from observed occurrence
Solves verbal problem
Solves a problem requiring ingenuity—getting one pint of water with three-pint and eight-pint measures
Retains directional orientation as turns are described
Tells how things usually thought of as opposites can be considered alike—winter, summer.[4]

Other test items have similar mental age values. If the sum of these values equals the chronological age of the subject being tested, the resulting IQ is approximately 100. But if a seven-year-old answers all the items on the Year VI level, two on the Year VII level and, in addition, two items on the Year VIII level, two on the Year IX level, one on the Year X level, and one on the XI level, but misses all on the next level, his total mental age is ninety-two months (two months' credit for each answer at these levels).

TABLE 3

Number of items	MA equivalent, months
Up to 6-year level, all	72
Seven-year level, 4	8
Eight-year level, 2	4
Nine-year level, 2	4
Ten-year level, 1	2
Eleven-year level, 1	2
Total	92

[4] Lewis M. Terman and Maud A. Merrill, *Stanford-Binet Intelligence Scale, Manual for Third Revision, Form L–M*, Boston: Houghton Mifflin Company, 1960.

Ninety-two months, or seven years and eight months, is found on the tables in the manual and for age seven years yields a "deviation IQ" of 109.[5] If a subject were not to answer the number of items that is average for his chronological age, his IQ would be less than 100.

The above examples are based on what is known as an individual test —one tester for one examinee. Not all schools can afford the cost of such accurate and detailed testing, so group tests are more frequently given. These group tests are also known as pencil-and-paper tests—each subject is presented with a test booklet in which he records his answers in writing. He answers as many of the questions as he can in the time allowed, and his score is simply the total value of his responses, which can be translated into a mental-age unit. This, in ratio to his age in chronological years, yields the IQ.

Authors of tests attempt to make various tests yield equivalent values. But there is usually some variation from test to test, depending on what the particular authors believe to be the most important components of intelligence. Moreover, as has previously been indicated, a subject will earn somewhat variant scores on equivalent forms of tests bearing the same title because he may feel better on one day than another or because his emotions (poise or motivation) are different. This indicates the fallacy of saying that a child has an IQ of precisely 92, 107, or 132. Tests are so variable that they should be identified by name. Thus, instead of saying, "Bill has an IQ of 98," it would be more indicative of the teacher's knowledge of the nature and purpose of the test if he were to say, "Bill has an IQ of about 100 on the Blank Test." (Incidentally, it is erroneous to speak of an IQ test; it is an "intelligence test.")

At the high school and college levels, students' mental ages are increasing less rapidly than their chronological ages. Corrections must then be made to compute the IQ by using a denominator that is less than the actual life age. Thus, it is more informative to speak of a percentile rank than to use the term "IQ." The percentile rank indicates a person's relative position in a theoretical group of 100. If his rank is 35th percentile, his score exceeded those of 35 per cent of the group. The highest percentile rank would be indicated by 99—the subject exceeded the score of 99 out of 100 other subjects on the measure concerned. Assume that a test containing 100 items was given to 100 subjects. The top score was 75, the lowest score was 25, and 12 students in the middle of the distribution received a score of 52 (44 students received more than 52, and 44 received less than 52). The student receiving 75 would have a percentile

---

[5] A measure of intelligence based on the extent to which an individual's score deviates from a score that is normal for the subject's chronological age. In the above example, the IQ based on the formula $MA/CA \times 100$ would be 110. (The difference of one IQ point is well within allowable limits of accuracy.)

score of 99, the one receiving 25 would have a percentile score of 1, and the middle 12 students would be in the 50th percentile.

The IQ can be translated into percentile rank, which indicates the pupil's comparative standing in the class. Thus, on one widely used group intelligence test, sample IQs and their meaning in percentiles are as follows:

TABLE 4

Score	IQ (at age 12)	Percentile
5	82	6
17	94	30
29	106	70
35	112	84
44	121	96
56	140	99

An individual scoring over 140 IQ on this test would still be ranked in the 99th percentile, and theoretically no pupil would exceed him in a group of 100. In general, an IQ of 140 would occur only once in 200 to 250 cases, depending on the test used.

Evaluation of Personality The measurement of personality is under much the same handicap as measurement in intelligence testing. There is no way to measure it directly—it must be inferred from verbal or overt behavior. Among the techniques for evaluating personality are (1) rating scales, (2) attitude scales, (3) interest inventories, (4) adjustment inventories, (5) projective techniques, and (6) observations. Each of these approaches gives a picture of the individual and—if the teacher observes the inherent limitations of each method—provides a more objective view than could be achieved by personal observation alone.

Much research is being devoted to personality assessment, but success to date has been limited. Such instruments must be used with great caution. Any important conclusions drawn about an individual from such tests should be accepted only when confirmed by repeated observations, diagnostic interviews, or other complementary data.

1. A rating scale asks others to evaluate the person being studied. A pupil may be asked to indicate the five individuals with whom he would most like to work, to play, to talk, etc., in the order of his choice. Or five names may be given, and the respondent is asked to relist them in the order of his preference. Two features of the rating scale are significant: (*a*) There must be a rather intimate acquaintance between the rater and the subject, and (*b*) the technique is obviously subjective in

nature—in fact, the result may indicate as much about the rater as about the subject. Subjectivity cannot, however, be summarily cast aside because part of our definition of personality (see Glossary) concerns the impact that a person and his behavior have on others.

2. An attitude scale asks the subject to tell how he feels about certain propositions or situations. The scale may be based on from two to five degrees of attitude: simply "like" or "dislike"; or "like very much," "like mildly," "no feeling," "dislike mildly," or "dislike intensely." Attitudes regarding peer relationships, family life, school responsibilities, community activities, racial questions, or religious attitudes may be investigated. The value of such a scale is limited, because the subject may tend to give answers that he feels will please the teacher. The scale is artificial in that some of the situations may not have been encountered by the subject, and while he may answer the questions honestly, his conduct in the actual situation may vary from his answer. However, if the limitations are kept in mind, the attitude inventory may be helpful when considered with other data.

3. The interest inventory is an approach to discovering a pupil's interests. Interest inventories are widely used in occupational counseling —the inventory is not a measure of ability, but indicates whether or not the pupil's interests are similar to those of people who are satisfied in various occupations. They can also be used to guide the selection of study units, extra reading, hobby development, and special reports. An additional point worth considering is whether schoolwork should follow a pupil's presently indicated interests or whether he should be motivated by the "stick behind," as Huxley put it (1956), to develop other interests.

4. The adjustment inventory consists of questions that delve into the emotional, social, and school life of the individual. The questions often concern health routines and personal habits. The following questions are representative of those found on adjustment inventories:

> Are your eyes very sensitive to light?
> Did you ever have a strong desire to run away from home?
> Do you sometimes feel that your parents are disappointed in you?
> Has either of your parents frequently criticized you unjustly?
> In school is it difficult for you to give an oral report before the class?
> Do you sometimes envy the happiness that others seem to enjoy?
> Do you frequently have spells of dizziness?
> Do you get angry easily?
> Do you ever cross the street to avoid meeting somebody?
> Was your father what you would consider your ideal of manhood?
> Does criticism disturb you greatly?
> Does it upset you considerably to have a teacher call on you unexpectedly?

Do you worry too long over humiliating experiences?
Do ideas often run through your head so that you cannot sleep? [6]

Clues to pupils' behaviors in various areas (home, school, community, health, etc.) may be supplied by instruments, and they should be supplemented by interviews and observation. A general comparative picture of one pupil can be gained, but probably the inventory's greatest value is the possibility of using the subject's atypical answers as *the starting point for an interview*. The greatest benefit is derived from the inventory when the causes of shyness, antagonism toward parents, frequent headaches, vague worries, etc., are discovered. Sometimes the teacher can be helpful in bringing about a change in regime or attitude that will help the pupil improve his adjustment.

5. Projective techniques include a wide variety of approaches to the study of personality. By the projective technique (see Glossary), the respondent adds structure to an unstructured situation. Persons giving "average" responses are adjudged normal, while those giving unique reports are considered deviants from the normal. Study of both typical and atypical responses given by an individual permits an expert to get a view of the "private life" of the subject.

Play techniques are used in a similar manner. A child is given some toys —what he does with them and what he makes them do enable the analyst to see motivations, interests, and biases that the child would be unable to verbalize. The play situation is undirected (unstructured)—what the child does with the toys is the structure, which he contributes to the situation. Likewise, the ending that a child gives to an incomplete story or the meaning that he attaches to a picture provides clues to his personality orientation.

These techniques are valuable in the hands of an expert, but the teacher can also use the principles to advantage. Observing the way a child plays spontaneously, the recurrent themes expressed in his paintings and drawings, and the kinds of stories he writes give the teacher valuable clues to his problems of adjustment. However, it cannot be too strongly emphasized that direct interpretation is only for the expert. The teacher should use what he sees as clues for further investigation. He should seek to corroborate what *might be* with evidence gleaned from other sources —inventories, other teachers' reports, and other children's reports.

6. Teacher observation is an important aspect of evaluating pupil personality—it is the most continuously employed evaluation technique. Observation, to be most reliable, should be supplemented by formal instruments, such as sociometry, anecdotal records, the behavioral journal, and teacher-made and standardized tests. But the informal day-to-day glimpses

[6] Hugh M. Bell, *The Adjustment Inventory: Student Form*, Stanford, Calif: Stanford University Press, 1934.

of pupils in action should not be discounted as a significant source of data, and the teacher who looks for repetitive patterns in individual pupils as they attack tasks alone and as they work and play in groups will sharpen his observational powers. Asking why a pupil behaves as he does aids in maintaining objectivity, and examining his own reaction to behavior should become a habitual part of the teacher's observation. Because most psychological tests—especially personality tests—are fallible, the teacher should question their data when they conflict with his own observation and experience. There should be balance between holding rigidly to conclusions based on observation and too ready acceptance of clues from formal instruments.

Measurement of Achievement   Most valuable for the classroom teacher, the achievement test measures status in terms of subject matter—reading, arithmetic, language, algebra, history, science, etc. Such tests, adequately standardized, objective, reliable, and valid, enable us to assert that pupils in the third grade vary from first grade to eighth grade in reading ability, for example. When the teacher has an objective means for evaluating differences such as this, he sees the futility of teaching as though all pupils were alike.

Achievement tests are frequently designed to indicate status in one subject. Others, known as achievement batteries, are divided into parts that yield separate scores in such subjects as language, reading, arithmetic, spelling, science, and social studies. The raw scores are easily translated into meaningful data—grade norms, age norms, or percentile ranks for various ages and grades. In turn these data can be used as a guide in selecting appropriately graded reading material, planning individual assignments, and placing pupils in proper grades or on "tracks" (see Glossary) appropriate to their developmental rates.[7] This information may also be helpful in the diagnosis of specific difficulties; e.g., poor work in arithmetic may be a reflection of the fact that a pupil has difficulty in reading.

One of the best uses to which teachers can put these instruments is to give one form of the test at the beginning of the term and an equivalent form at the end of the term. This procedure has two very significant advantages: (1) The teacher can see the progress a given pupil has made, even if he is below class average on both tests, and thus the test prevents

---

[7] Note that the sentence says "as a guide in. . . ." A beginning eighth grader whose average achievement score was seventh grade would not appropriately be placed in a slow track if illness or several changes of school had kept him from school for prolonged periods the previous year. It is common practice not to place in the fourth grade a large, socially mature but slow-learning youngster who chronologically belongs in the fifth grade; rather, appropriate learning tasks can probably best be assigned on an individual or small-group basis within the fifth-grade setting.

uncalled-for discouragement on the teacher's part; and (2) both the superior and the slow pupil can profit from seeing objective evidence of their own growth. The superior pupil will probably feel encouraged only when he has maintained his relative advantage: The slow pupil can see that, in terms of where he was at the beginning of the year, he *is* growing, even though slowly.

If standardized tests are to have maximum value, they must be administered and scored strictly in accordance with the directions provided in the instruction manual. Since they are standardized on the basis of the procedures indicated in the directions, any deviation will warp the results, and an erroneous "measurement" will result. Some teachers have "shaved the time" on the first administration and allowed a minute or two extra on the second, or they follow advice on the first test and give no help, but ignore the directions and give a little help on the second. Such procedures, of course, merely result in wasted time and effort. At best, tests are only approximations. Any procedure that distorts the results invalidate the data that are obtained.

Aptitude and Diagnostic Tests An aptitude test is designed to estimate probable future performance. An intelligence test might justifiably be considered an aptitude test—one that indicates an important part of capacity to perform in many areas. There are, in fact, intelligence tests called Differential Aptitude Tests, The General Aptitude Test Battery, and The Factored Aptitude Tests, and there are others with similar names.[8]

An aptitude test may also be considered a prognostic test—it attempts to predict the future performance of the individual in a specific area. Thus there are reading-readiness tests that predict the probable course of the pupil's acquisition of reading skills. There are musical ability, or aptitude, tests that predict the individual's probable success in singing or playing some musical instrument. Aptitude tests have also been formulated to predict success in mechanical pursuits, foreign languages, and various branches of mathematics. Test results may be used to section classes into ability groups or to determine whether the probability of failure is so great that the student should be advised to take other subjects.

There are loose-leaf publications, known as "college profiles," or "freshman profiles," that indicate the probability of a student's success in college in terms of the typical entrance examination scores made by college freshmen at given colleges in previous years. Subject selection, college selection, or classification into groups is safe when the scores of the subject are extremely high or low. But individual differences vary on a continuous scale and are of degree rather than of kind. Hence, difficulty

[8] See *The Use of Multifactor Tests in Guidance*, Washington: American Personnel and Guidance Association, no date. (A reprint series from *Personnel and Guidance Journal*.)

is encountered with pupils on the borderline between superiority and normality and normality and inferiority—in such cases, other factors should be considered—past performance, application and tenacity, and expressed desire of the pupil. If the case is still doubtful, there remains the pragmatic test, namely, a "trial run" in the area concerned.

Diagnostic tests further illustrate the range and variety of differences in the classroom. A diagnostic test deals with specific subdivisions of a subject and consequently suggests some specific remedial procedures for the teacher. (Actually, no test is diagnostic or remedial—the teacher makes the diagnosis and prescribes the remedial work on the basis of all data, including test data, available.) A diagnostic test in arithmetic may indicate that a particular number combination is giving difficulty (for example, a persistent answer that $8 \times 7 = 54$) or that a particular process (addition, subtraction, multiplication) is inadequately understood. A diagnostic test in reading may indicate the need for vocabulary drill, the need for attention to details, or failure to comprehend meaning. But the teacher himself makes the particular diagnosis on the basis of evidence.

Both aptitude tests and diagnostic tests illustrate the desirability and advantage of specificity in testing. Knowledge of human differences becomes more helpful as it becomes more precise. As test users, teachers need to understand that ability tests are not tests of potential. Because ability tests depend on inferences from accomplishment, the person who has lacked opportunity to fulfill potential will appear to have less potential than he actually has.

> Human resources are not merely found and preserved (as are natural resources)—they are created. To a still unappreciated degree, intellectual potential can be created and stimulated, rather than merely unearthed and discovered. The socio-educational process does not merely utilize and exercise talent; it also plants and fosters talent. Our mass-testing programs are not now used in conjunction with social-regenerative efforts, but they could be redesigned for such use.[9]

Use and misuse of measurement

The Improvement of Instruction   The all-inclusive aim of psychological measurement in the school is to understand pupils better and to improve instruction. These aims are reflected in the following list of values of testing:

1. Tests help in evaluating progress toward goals. By giving tests at the beginning and end of the term, the teacher has an objective aid in

[9] Joshua A. Fishman and Paul I. Clifford, "What Can Mass-testing Programs Do for—and—to the Pursuit of Excellence in American Education?" *Harvard Educational Review,* 34: 68, 1964.

evaluating pupil growth in specific areas. After determining the probable reasons for success or failure with given pupils, the teacher can then formulate new procedures for the coming year.

2. Tests may show where emphasis has been placed. Achievement and diagnostic tests can show the teacher whether or not balance has been maintained in the instructional program. For instance, they may show that insufficient attention has been devoted to vocabulary or use of reference materials in the reading program. They may show that problem solving has been emphasized to the exclusion of drill on fundamentals of multiplication, division, etc., in the arithmetic program.

3. Tests can help to determine effective methods. By comparing the progress of two groups that are approximately equal in mental age, chronological age, grade level, etc., through initial and end-of-the-term tests, the comparative values of two teaching methods can be evaluated.

4. Tests can help to motivate pupils. While high test scores are not the sole aim of education, such scores can provide a source of motivation. As we have seen, knowledge of progress is an effective means of motivation both for individual pupils and for an entire class.

5. Tests can help to maintain standards. By referring to the norms accompanying the test, the teacher can decide whether or not his class is *approximating* the results that are ordinarily expected of groups similar to his own.

6. Tests give training in thinking and using language. In taking a test, the pupil has an opportunity to use what he knows in a different context from that which occurs in daily classwork or in his out-of-school life. The more such opportunities are provided, the more firmly consolidated learning will be. Although many tests call only for recitation of facts, many others call for the use of facts in solving problems.

7. Tests can be used in pupil guidance. The data supplied by tests can be effectively used to *help* pupils select future courses. The data may also be used to *help* the pupil select the curriculum—vocational or academic—from which he will probably profit the most. Of course, such a choice is not automatic—interests, school background, socioeconomic status and the probable future of the chosen occupation should also be considered (Rothney, Danielson, and Heimann, 1959, p. 22).

8. Tests are a valuable part of pupil records. Test data are widely understood; and when they are entered in a pupil's permanent record, they enable subsequent teachers to understand him. There are two precautions: The name of the test, the form used, and the date of administration should be entered along with the results; and the teacher should use such data as *background information*, not as a measure of status.

9. Tests can be used by supervisors to help teachers. The supervisor who appreciates the values and limitations of tests can use the data to suggest changes and improvement in teaching procedures. However, if

tests are used as the sole criterion for evaluating teacher effectiveness, they are being grossly misused. The general atmosphere of the school, the composition of the particular class, and the materials and resources available to the teacher are other factors that should be taken into consideration. The test data should serve only as *supplementary* evidence.

Precautions for Using Tests   The value of tests in determining individual differences will be greatly enhanced if the user is fully aware of the things that tests do *not* do. It cannot be stated too emphatically that present psychological and educational tests do not measure with the accuracy of a yardstick or a laboratory balance. Psychological tests yield only approximations, estimations, and indications, which are extremely valuable if used with due regard to the limitations.

Tests do not measure motivation. An intelligence test does not indicate the determination of a pupil to use effectively the intelligence that is indicated on the test (L. M. Miller, 1961, p. 2). A reading readiness test does not measure the willingness of a child to keep trying to master reading skills. A reading achievement test does not measure the quality of books that pupils voluntarily select for leisure-time reading.

Tests do not provide answers. High blood pressure, rapid pulse, and high temperature do not reveal the patient's illness, but they do help the doctor make a diagnosis. Scores on a variety of tests do not tell the teacher how to bring about better adjustment on the part of the pupil, but they help him to determine the area of need.

Tests do not provide a valid basis for assigning marks. Even though the progress indicated by initial and end-of-term tests is used in grading, home background, illnesses, absences, and distracting (and sometimes valuable) interests must also be considered if evaluation is to take individual differences into account.

It is obvious that educational tests are not either-or matters. The wise teacher will accept them for what they are worth, not as perfect instruments. The warning in the old cliché "The clumsy carpenter blames his tools," should be heeded by the teacher. He must use testing tools skillfully rather than expect the tests to do the work. This skill is not a native endowment; it comes from study and practice. The imperfections inherent in educational and psychological tests impose serious obligations upon those who use them, because in using them, they are dealing with human lives.

Summary

As teachers we are frequently disturbed and sometimes bewildered by the range of differences we perceive in a class of fifth-grade geometry or English composition pupils. It is somewhat comforting to plot these differences on a normal curve and see that few students are at the extreme ends of the distribution and that most are sufficiently alike so that some effective communication in groups is possible. Measurements of individual differences serve, however, to warn that grouping on one measure does not serve as an index of homogeneity in another measure. Further, the distribution of differences provides warning against classification of individuals into "type" categorizations—third graders, athletes, scholars, adolescents—with meaningful accuracy. Fortunately, the philosophy of American public education emphasizes the value of human differences and adjures the teacher to capitalize upon them.

Much research work has, and is, being devoted to the more accurate assessment of differences. Many valuable instruments have been devised, such as intelligence, achievement, aptitude, and diagnostic tests. These, when used with due precautions for their inherent limitations, provide valuable clues to the understanding of individual pupils and, consequently, for the improvement of instruction. In order to be of greatest value, standardized tests should satisfy such criteria as objectivity, ease of administration, validity, reliability, breadth of sampling, and economy.

Tests should be viewed as clues, samples, and indications rather than precise measurements of traits and potentials. Tests should serve as supplementary data to the teacher's observations. As such, the teacher's judgment and evaluation should be a large factor in the assessment of differences. In the final analysis, it is the teacher's skill in understanding and dealing with differences that provides the basic strength of formal education.

Problems and exercises

1 Try to obtain from one of your college instructors or some teacher you know the raw scores obtained from the administration of a standardized test or an objective test containing about 100 items. Draw a curve of distribution for the scores by placing each score on a horizontal line and using the number of pupils earning each score as the altitude for each score column. Draw a line joining the tops of the columns. Does the line resemble the normal curve of distribution? How would you explain the shape of the curve?

2 Would the plotting of weight or of knowledge of items on a 200-item test of American history be the more likely to approximate a normal distribution curve for an eighth-grade class?

3 Are individual differences becoming more or less valuable today than was the case 100 years ago?

4 Explain in your own words the meaning of the terms "standardized," "validity," "reliability," "objectivity," and "adequate sampling."

5 When a child has lived in a poor environment and has not had a chance to learn the facts involved in a standardized intelligence test, would you say he is any less intelligent than another child of his age who has had the chance to learn these facts?

6 Cite a number of reasons for the skepticism that some persons have about the value of personality inventories.

7 What classroom uses would you suggest for a personality inventory? For an interest inventory?

8 Get several of your classmates to draw their conception of such abstractions as happiness, sadness, liberty, and selfishness. Is there any similarity in the drawings? Get the individuals to tell why they drew what they did.

9 Suggest several uses to which an achievement battery might be put at the eighth-grade level. At the high school level.

10 Consult Oscar K. Buros (ed.), *Mental Measurements Yearbook* (the latest edition available) and make a list of aptitude and/or diagnostic tests that could be useful at the school level for which you are preparing to teach.

Suggested additional readings

Anastasi, Anne: *Differential Psychology*, 3d ed., New York: The Macmillan Company, 1958, pp. 23–56.
Through text and by diagram, this chapter explains the meaning and interpretation of the distribution curves which graphically present information on human variability.

Baron, Denis, and Harold W. Bernard: *Evaluation Techniques for Classroom Teachers*, New York: McGraw-Hill Book Company, 1958, pp. 44–86.
These chapters define and illustrate some of the basic concepts used in making the results of tests of maximum value to classroom teachers.

Goldman, L.: *Using Tests in Counseling*, New York: Appleton-Century-Crofts, Inc., 1961.
This book, which won an award from the American Personnel and Guidance Association in 1962, presents practical and understandable explanations of the use of psychological and educational tests.

Pinneau, Samuel R.: *Changes in Intelligence Quotient*, Boston: Houghton Mifflin Company, 1961.
The author describes research studies on the changing IQ with both conceptual and statistical interpretations. Among other things, the use and value of the deviation IQ is considered.

Review of Educational Research, vol. 32, no. 1, *Educational and Psychological Testing*, February, 1962. 114 pp.
The nine chapters in this volume epitomize some of the recent significant research on various aspects of measurement: development of achievement and aptitude tests, personality tests, and the use of tests in research.

The Nature and Nurture of Intelligence

10

Earlier chapters have emphasized that man's capacity to use language facilitates his adaptation to and progress in the world. So do his ability to use tools (facilitated by thumb-finger opposition), to remember, to make analogies, to discern relationships, to think abstractly. His ability to grow, through both direct and indirect experience, is likewise part of his intelligence—his potential for solving problems.

While no problem is finally solved, the basic problem of education is without doubt a matter of directing intelligence to the understanding and control of perplexing situations. There are some who say that emotional control and direction are the big tasks of education, yet analysis seems to indicate that if emotion is to be wisely controlled, it must be through directing intelligence. The recent momentum of technological advance has emphasized the need for capitalizing on man's intellectual potential. From 1960 to 1970 the number of occupations classed as professional will increase 43 per cent (Bienstock, 1964). It is calculated that by 1975, twice as many scientists and engineers will be needed as are annually being prepared (Impellizzeri, 1961). Developing the intellectual potential that is available is rightly considered a crucial problem of national survival. For such reason, few problems are more important for teachers than to understand the nature and nurture of intelligence.

The concept of intelligence

Definitions of Intelligence　L. M. Terman states that intelligence is the ability to do abstract thinking.[1] That is, through the manipulation of symbols (largely words), the intelligent person is able to think about and deal with things and ideas without the material presence of them. Intelligence is thus the ability to per-

---

[1] Most of the widely used intelligence tests (both individual and group) resemble to a greater or lesser degree the Stanford revision (Terman's work) of the Binet-Simon tests. Many of the norms established for other tests are compared with the norms for the Stanford test.

ceive relationships and to solve problems. Intelligence in action involves direction, adaptation, and self-criticism in mental adaptation (Terman, 1960, p. 6).

E. L. Thorndike (1927, p. 22) states that intelligence is the ability to make good responses and is demonstrated by the capacity to deal effectively with novel situations. Just as there are different kinds of situations, there are also different patterns of intelligence—abstract, mechanical, or social. For example, the skilled leader of people may be quite inept in mechanical matters, such as the repair of his automobile; the skilled mathematician may evidence bewilderment when faced by the ramifications of man's behavior in political groups.

George D. Stoddard (1941) suggests that intelligence is the ability to understand problems that are characterized by (1) difficulty, (2) complexity, (3) abstractness, (4) economy, (5) adaptiveness to a goal, (6) social value, and (7) the emergence of originals.

David Wechsler, who has developed widely used individual intelligence tests for both children and adults, defines intelligence as "the aggregate or global capacity of the individual to act purposefully, to think rationally and to deal effectively with his environment." [2]

Other authorities have postulated definitions of intelligence, and the definitions have much in common. They may be summarized by stating that *intelligence is the ability to make facile and appropriate adjustments to the various facets of one's total environment.*

It has been stated, somewhat facetiously, that intelligence is what is measured by intelligence tests. The statement is not completely absurd. Each designer of an intelligence test has started with a concept of what intelligence is and has formulated problems and questions that probe into the facets of the governing concept. Test makers have from the beginning sought to correlate and corroborate what they found in the tests with life situations. Intelligence test ratings do often correlate positively, and sometimes highly, with demonstrated ability to do a job, to do academic work, and to solve problems and with the judgment of experts who have observed the behavior of the testees. Intelligence test items are not merely arbitrary questions but representative samples designed to test the individual's total performance.

The Function of Intelligence When discussing intelligence, it is extremely difficult to distinguish what it is from how it functions. It will be noted that all the definitions of intelligence given above directly state or imply the matter of adjustment. In this connection, one further concept may be given: Intelligence is a congeries of abilities to learn in varied

[2] David Wechsler, *Measurement of Adult Intelligence*, 3d ed., Baltimore: The Williams & Wilkins Company, 1944, p. 3.

situations, to understand and collate broad, subtle, and abstract facts with speed and accuracy, to focus mental processes on problems, and to display flexibility and ingenuity in the search for solutions.

Correlates of intelligence

Age The ability to adjust to one's environment increases as the individual grows older. Infants have less capacity for adjustment than do six-year-olds, and six-year-olds have less adjustive ability than do normal twenty-year-olds. The relationship of age to intelligence may occasionally present a problem for teachers. The youngster with the highest IQ in the class may not always be the most intelligent. A child who is two years older chronologically than a child whose IQ is points higher might actually be more intelligent in terms of adjustive ability (mental age). Teachers must be careful to note the age of children with respect to their intellectual development, particularly in the primary grades. A difference of a few months in chronological or mental age will be much less discernible in the secondary school. For example, a parent asked a first-grade teacher how her young son was getting along in school. The teacher said, "Just fine," and mentioned some of the good habits and attitudes he had developed, but she placed little stress on his reading progress. However, his reading was what concerned the mother. "He did not get as good a grade as his brother did in the first grade." The teacher knew the answer: "But there's a year's difference in their ages. Your older boy was born in January and could not enter school until he was almost seven. Your younger boy was born in December and entered school before his sixth birthday."

Theoretically, it appears that intellectual growth ceases at the age of twenty or twenty-five years. Growth is more rapid and continues for a longer time for more intelligent persons, while the person of less intelligence grows more slowly and ceases to grow at an earlier age. However, the important consideration again is the definition of intelligence. Is intelligence largely a matter of learning ability as such, or of learning ability with respect to *new* things? It is conceivable that a person of eighteen may be better able to learn something that is *entirely new* because of greater mental retentivity and adaptability. But the more experienced the individual, the rarer are his chances of encountering something entirely new. Past experience in seeing relationships, discovering meanings, and perceiving implications is a factor in learning that is no less important than mental retentivity and adaptability. The fifteen-year-old has a limited background of experience to which he can attach new meanings. The twenty-five-year-old with approximately the same IQ has almost half again as much experience. Thus, just as the child of two will learn less than a child of six with the same IQ, the person of thirty or forty years will learn more readily than the fifteen-year-old. The older person, despite somewhat lessened powers in terms of mental adaptability, can still learn. The factors of motivation and time must also be considered. The child of school age is urged by teachers and parents to use his learning powers. A great deal of his time is devoted exclusively and intensively to learning. The older person has less time to give to learning because of family and occupational demands. The records of military personnel who have taken advantage of educational assistance by Federal or state government after completing service give support to the idea that age increases learning efficiency. In one study, students who were older by four to six years than the typical college student made better records than younger students when both groups were comparable in terms of intelligence test scores and high school records (Tead, 1947).

Reports on the study of the processes of aging have, in the past decade, begun to compete in volume with studies in child development. Several points that are important to teachers have emerged from such studies. (1) Doubt is beginning to arise that there is necessarily a psychological involution that parallels or is concomitant to degeneration of biological function (Gerard, 1959, p. 264). (2) There is a growing belief that lack of motivation is as important a factor in low intelligence test scores of older persons as is the phenomenon of actual mental decline (Kuhlen, 1959, p. 852). (3) Many studies are in agreement with Jones's findings that intellectual decline with aging is not general; i.e., there is a steady growth in vocabulary subtests, a constancy in arithmetic tests, and a decline in subtests involving performance (Jones, 1959, p. 700). (4) Many authorities believe that the mind atrophies more through disuse than as an inevitable function of growing older (Donahue, 1957, p. 59).

Kaplan (1952) supports the foregoing in a summary of research which points out that there is a loss of reaction but an increase in dependability of judgment. There is a loss in sensory acuity but an increased proficiency in tasks demanding accuracy. Older professors are not uniformly inferior to younger professors in learning. Older persons often test lower on certain subtests of intelligence tests, but higher in vocabulary, opposites, and disarranged sentences. He concludes that when a mental function is used, it does not atrophy. There is a strong temptation to say that intelligence is a matter of habit to some degree. Age is not merely a state of mind. It is a condition to which one must adjust. But the fact remains that older people can learn. Often they are superior to younger persons because of their habits and background. One cannot safely make inclusive generalizations about the relationship of age to intelligence.

The implications of this discussion are twofold. First, all teachers have the professional opportunity and obligation of infusing into their pupils a desire for learning that will last a lifetime—of helping pupils build the habit of continuous learning. Second, there is the personal challenge of nurturing one's own habit of continuous learning so that his later years can be productively satisfying—and so that his rate of decline (if inevitable) can be retarded.

Heredity The parents of gifted children are generally superior in intelligence. The parents of slow learners are generally below average in intelligence. One study shows that almost one-third (31.4 per cent) of a group of gifted children came from families of professional people despite the fact that the professional group constituted only 2.9 per cent of the population studied (Terman, 1925, p. 64). Another study found that 48 per cent of a group of eminent men were the sons of eminent fathers (Carroll, 1940, p. 28). The chances of a person's having a father who is listed in *Who's Who* is about 1 in 2,000, yet of 578 children who were tested and found gifted, 3 had fathers who were so listed. Other studies give similar indications that mental and personality defects as well as giftedness tend to run in families; but while the role of inheritance is recognized, it is necessary to recognize that environment must also be taken into account (Goodenough and Tyler, 1959, p. 60).

The principle of heredity is further complicated by Galton's principle of heredity regression; that is, a given child theoretically receives only one-half of his heredity from his immediate parents, one-fourth from his grandparents, one-eighth from his great-grandparents, etc. Sooner or later the ancestry of gifted children and those less richly endowed in intelligence becomes common stock. The principle of hereditary regression suggests to teachers that they cannot be sure that children of intelligent parents will be similarly intelligent—or that dull parents will have children who are equally dull. In fact, the chances are against that occurrence. Children tend to regress toward the *average*. Children whose parents have a midparent IQ of 135 will *tend* to have a somewhat lower IQ—between 100 and 135. Children whose parents have a midparent IQ of 64 will tend to have a somewhat higher IQ—between 64 and 100. However, in terms of probability, there is a greater chance for the more gifted parents to have a child with an IQ of 150 than for parents with a midparent IQ of 64 to have such a child.

The major conclusion to be drawn from heredity as a correlate of intelligence is that we avoid, to the best of our ability, permitting potential at any level to suffer underdevelopment. That we are not succeeding is attested to by data on school dropouts and what is known as "underachievement."

A study of 4,900 "bright" high school students recently conducted in New York City (the Talent Preservation Project) reports that 54 per cent of the boys and 33 per cent of the girls had scholastic averages which, halfway through high school, were already so low that their admission to college was in doubt. These students represented the high-ability populations of their classes in 39 academic high schools; and of the 4,900 only 20 per cent were able to complete the first three terms of senior high schools without faltering at some point and getting grades below 85. Obviously, the percentages reported by these studies are not what is significant; what is important is that they all support the impressions of teachers, that, for one reason or another, a large proportion of capable students are not doing work commensurate with their capacities.[3]

Environment Investigations have long pointed to the thesis that *individuals evidently develop only the portion of their potential that is required by their environment*. Many children living in areas of low cultural status are average in intelligence at the younger ages (indicating average potential), but as they grow older they have lower IQs in proportion to their ages. In studying canal-boat children in England, Gordon found that younger children had higher IQs than older youngsters; children under six years of age averaged about 90, while their older brothers and sisters averaged about 70 (H. Gordon, 1923).

A study of isolated mountain children led to the same conclusion. Intelligence tests were given to children from four communities—all of which were isolated, but each was characterized by a different degree of isolation. Communities in which the family stock was much the same—English and Scotch-Irish—were selected. The IQs of six- to eight-year-old children were much the same in the different areas, but the greater the isolation, the lower the IQs at ages above eight. The lower IQs of the older children were also related to the amount of schooling. The children of the community that had sixty-six months of school in the twelve preceding years had higher IQs than the children of the community that had thirty months of school in the same period. It was concluded that children develop only as the environment demands. The isolated environment is enough to stimulate a child up to four or five years; as he grows older, more stimulation is required to encourage continued growth of intelligence (Sherman and Key, 1932). Many questions about the study are worth considering: Did brighter people leave the community? Were the same children used on repeated tests? Are standard intelligence tests fair to mountain children?[4] These are questions worth answering.

[3] Irene H. Impellizzeri, "Nature and Scope of the Problem," in Leonard M. Miller (ed.), *Guidance for the Underachiever with Superior Ability*, U.S. Office of Education Bulletin 1961, no. 25, 1961.

[4] Allison Davis and Kenneth Eells have designed the Davis-Eells Games, a test of intelligence or problem-solving ability that is purported to reduce the handicap of cultural poverty. The items used are of a kind and variety that children from all socioeconomic classes will have equal opportunity to know. The vocabulary and grammatical construction do not favor any population group. It is free from reading

But whatever the answers, we cannot afford to take chances with children by withholding from them the best cultural environment possible.

There appears to be a need for early and continued stimulation if one is to realize his potential. It has been noted that children who score high on initial tests show less improvement on subsequent tests than do those who score lower on initial tests. This suggests that typically the bright child has been stimulated to achieve more of his potential and has less room for improvement. Conversely, the slower child has achieved less of his potential and has room for improvement. Thus, he responds more readily to what for him is a markedly more stimulating environment. Children from orphanages sometimes improve their test ratings after being placed in good foster homes. But the fact remains that foster children more closely resemble their true parents in intelligence than they do their foster parents (Honzik, 1957)—there are limits to what environment can do.

A number of environmental factors that appear to be conducive to optimum intellectual development can be inferred from various studies. (1) Parents who take an interest in children and who have both the time and inclination to talk to them and answer their questions have a higher proportion of children who score high on tests and do well in school. (2) The same factors of love, acceptance, and consistency of treatment that are conducive to mental health appear to have a salutary effect on intellectual development. Here we can go back to Maslow's theory that higher needs (self-actualization) become predominant only after the lower (physiological and safety) needs are well on the way to being met (see Chapter 4). (3) Parents who encourage emotional dependence in their children appear to retard their mental development (Sontag, Baker, and Nelson, 1958). Aggressiveness, self-initiation, and competitiveness are personality attributes that accompany intellectual growth. (4) If we can take language development and reading skill as evidence of intellectual development (and both are prominent in tests of intelligence), then homes in which there are books to read and an adult example of interest in reading are positive influences. (5) The studies by Gordon and Sherman suggest that communities and homes in which there is contact with the mainstream of life are helpful. Contacts that can be made through travel—visits to museums, zoos, libraries, concerts, theaters, parks—are an intellectual stimulant (Hillson, 1961, p. 5). (6) Most studies of socioeconomic class point to the conclusion that those from the higher classes tend to make better scores on intelligence tests than those from the lower classes (Pinneau and Jones, 1958).

requirements (Davis & Eells, 1963, pp. iv, v). Some who have reviewed the test are not convinced that the tests are actually "culture-fair." Others feel that even if a distinction could be made, the differences discovered would not be helpful because adaptations still have to be made to the wider culture.

However, *many* of the higher scores of lower-socioeconomic-class pupils overlap the scores of higher-socioeconomic-class pupils when the scores are plotted on separate distribution curves.

Sex There are differences between males and females in specific aspects of intelligence, but it is pointless to speak of superiority or inferiority of one sex or the other (Anastasi, 1958, p. 497). On the average, males demonstrate *slight* superiority over females in general reasoning, arithmetic reasoning, ability to detect similarities, and certain aspects of general information. They tend to excel girls in speed and coordination of large body movements, spatial perception, and mechanical aptitude. Boys seem to have a stronger motivation for achievement (Walter and Marzolf, 1951). On the average, females have *slight* superiority in memory, language usage, manual dexterity, numerical computation, and perceptual speed. It is commonly thought that girls develop facility in language usage at an earlier age than do boys. However, it has been shown that boys are not inferior to girls in learning to read *after* auto-instructional devices have provided them with frequent and equal opportunities to respond (McNeil, 1964). Boys show greater variability than girls in the range of intelligence; that is, more boys than girls are defective in intelligence, but also more boys than girls are markedly superior.

Some persons have gone so far as to recommend that boys start school at a later age than girls because of their lesser facility in language usage and reading. Such broad recommendations blithely disregard individual differences within a sex, different subabilities in intelligence, cultural expectations, and varied motivation. Any differences in intelligence between boys and girls are so slight as to have no significance for educational procedures. Moreover, apparent differences may be due as much to cultural differences—the role assigned to the sexes by society—as they are to innate factors. The significant conclusion to be drawn is that *differences between the sexes are smaller and much less significant than the differences within the sex.* Even though girls *generally* are more verbal than boys, and boys are *generally* more mathematically apt, there are enough boys who are superior to girls linguistically and enough girls who are superior to boys mathematically so that no *general* curricular provisions should be made on the basis of sex. No assumptions regarding intellectual differences between boys and girls can be safely formulated. It is absurd to think that girls should start school a year earlier than boys. It may be very wise to start one particular girl to school a year later than other girls—or boys.

Race Widespread notions about differences in intelligence between races are also based on tenuous assumptions. Research studies reach the same conclusion—*differences between the races in matters of intelligence* *are much less significant than the differences within the race.* Differences in intelligence, character, social skill, artistic temperament that are attributed to race are inevitably explicable on the basis of genetic potential—quite apart from race—and experience. Those who subscribe to such beliefs have limited experience, are generalizing from insufficient experience, or are the victims of selective perception. A most cogent statement in this whole matter has been formulated by Paul A. Witty: "Let us therefore abandon a superstitious anachronism which leads us to stigmatize various racial groups and to condemn them to meagre educational experience and opportunity." [5]

It is true that many studies show that when a group of Negroes, Indians, or Mexicans is given an intelligence test, the average score may be somewhat lower (5 to 10 IQ points) than the average of a group of white children. Such data, acquired in the earlier days of mental testing, have been taken at face value. It is presently considered necessary not only to interpret test data in terms of many concomitant variables (motivation, opportunity, prejudiced perception, social-class expectations), but also to realize that tests do not have universal validity when used with groups other than the standardizing population (see Glossary) (Angelino and Shedd, 1955). For educational purposes, race differences are negligible if all the groups being studied have the same cultural and educational environment. Generalizations about groups do not hold for individuals. Therefore, teachers must be just as aware of the potentialities that reside within individual members of a minority group as they are of the potentialities of children of majority groups.

Emotional Factors The dean of a certain school of education told of an experience he had had with aptitude tests. A man who wanted to study for his doctor's degree took the prescribed qualification tests. His score on the mental ability test disqualified him. He went to another school with an equally good academic program where different criteria of admission were used. The student obtained his degree with honors and later became one of the outstanding men in his field. The dean of the school which had disqualified him said, "I am sure that the test gave a good indication of his ability but there is one thing it did not show—his determination and drive to use what he had to good effect." This assertion indicates that "test intelligence" and the ability to use what one has are positively correlated, but not perfectly.

It is common for teachers to become well acquainted with a given pupil, judge him to be average, superior, or dull on the basis of his work, and then discover that the recorded intelligence score of the pupil is at wide variance with their otherwise *justified* judgment. They note

[5] Paul A. Witty, in Charles E. Skinner (ed.), *Educational Psychology*, Englewood Cliffs, N.J.: Prentice-Hall, Inc., 1936, p. 463. Used by permission.

frequently that the child with an IQ of 100 is accomplishing just as much as is one with an IQ of 120, despite the fact that the latter is living up to reasonable expectation.

These statements are not based on chance observations—though such evidence is not necessarily without weight. Experimental studies show that when babies in orphanages are cuddled, talked to, and cared for individually, they respond by being more active and alert, talking more—or trying to talk more—and playing more constructively. Children attending preschool have made gains in intelligence test ratings during the year, and some of these gains are attributed to the fact that they have become better adjusted to the new situation and have established rapport with the examiner (Olson, 1959, p. 112). For this reason, intelligence tests are not administered during the opening days of school, but only after the children have become somewhat adjusted to the situation in which they find themselves.

For teachers, the importance of the reciprocal role of intelligence and emotion lies mainly in helping the pupil make effective use of what he has. Fear generated in the classroom by threatening punishment and failure must be avoided. Interpersonal dislike and even hatred among students must be avoided by shunning autocratic and highly competitive situations. Anger and frustration should be reduced by seeing to it that the tasks assigned are appropriate to each child's ability. Constructive emotions must be employed by seeing that each pupil gets some satisfaction from achievement. Cooperative activities should be encouraged so that friendliness and sympathy will be generated. Pupils should see clearly the goals toward which they are working and should be helped to realize that the goals have personal pertinence. Democratic methods should be employed so that each child has a feeling of personal worth. Provisions for individual differences are inherent in all these suggestions. Differentiated assignments enhance feelings of security, provide the thrill of accomplishment, and make the pupil feel that both his limitations and his abilities are recognized by others.

Health and Physique Studies have previously been cited which show that gifted children are, on the average, taller, heavier, have fewer sensory defects, and a lower incidence of illness than those with lower intelligence. Obviously, when one is in good health, he tends to have greater drive to participate vigorously in difficult situations. Perhaps teachers can do little about the child's health, but that little may be the weight that tips the balance in favor of a higher operative intelligence.

There is some evidence that diet plays a part in the growth and development of intelligence. In one instance, forty-one children who were diagnosed as suffering from malnutrition were matched with a group of control children and fed a more nutritional diet for a year and a half to two years. The experimental children averaged a gain of 10 IQ points, with the greatest gains accruing to the children below four years of age. The control children did not gain (Poull, 1938). Gains ranging from slight to marked have been noted after providing additional amounts of thiamine in children's diets. Even if the early gain is only slight, it is felt that the cumulative gains over a period of years may mean the difference between superiority and mediocrity (Harrell, 1946). Two groups of children, one high and the other low in blood plasma ascorbic acid concentration, were given a supplement of orange juice over a period of time. The group that was high in ascorbic acid had higher IQs to begin with, but the other group (lower in both ascorbic acid and IQ) gained in IQ. It was concluded that changes in ascorbic acid concentration were closely paralleled by changes in average IQ (Kubala and Katz, 1960). Numerous studies attest to the value of adequate amounts of milk in increasing children's height and weight. Of particular interest to teachers are data indicating that giving children milk in addition to the usual allowances has the effect not only of improving general health but also of increasing mental alertness.

It should be noted in such studies as these that changes will occur only when the subject has a dietary deficiency that is remedied by the special diet. Additional thiamine, ascorbic acid, or milk will not aid the child who already has an adequate diet. It follows that not all the teacher's problems will be solved by improved diets. But increased learning ability comes from many small improvements. For example, primary school children have small stomachs and high demands for food to support both rapid growth and high activity and thus need frequent meals; the practice of giving a morning snack may be a small step toward improving their school performance.

The responsibility of the school for the pupil's diet has been only sporadically recognized. There is a more widespread recognition of responsibility for health factors in the matter of sensory acuity. When a child is cut off from intimate contact with his environment by a visual or auditory handicap, his intellectual development suffers. Defective vision or hearing is an insufficient basis upon which to judge that a given child will have less than average intelligence. But when hundreds of children with such defects are considered, a tendency is noted for those with sensory defects to have slightly lower than average intelligence in proportion to the seriousness of the defect. A child who does not see and hear clearly has a poorer operational environment than the child who has normal sensory acuity.

There is, of course, the possibility that the hearing defect or visual handicap cannot be corrected. In such cases, it is desirable that the regular program of work be adapted to the child. Recognition of the importance of such procedures is growing, but at the present time it is estimated that only about 10 per cent of the pupils in need of special work programs are receiving them.[6]

One implication of the foregoing data is that teachers should be aware of the importance of health factors and sensory defects if they are to help each child achieve optimum mental development. They should read the reports of periodic physical examinations and be alert to the symptoms of fatigue and sensory handicap. Symptoms such as restlessness, drowsiness, inattentiveness, frequent illnesses, unexplained nosebleed, decreasing accomplishment in school, pallor, and pains in muscles and joints should serve as signals to the teacher that the child needs medical help.

The IQ: constant or variable?

The "Constant IQ" Theory   A rather sharp controversy developed in the middle 1930s between adherents to the theory of the "constant IQ" and proponents of the "wandering IQ" theory. Support for the constant IQ hypothesis is received from the typical data secured from intelligence testing. By and large, repeated tests of the same individual over a period of time indicate that mental growth is fairly constant, thus the same IQ is indicated by repeated measurements. This may be seen from the graphic representation shown in Figure 15. Repeated testing will usually not yield *exactly* the same IQ score for a given pupil but will show slight fluctuations, i.e., within a range of about 10 points. Thus, a child with an IQ of 95 on one test is considered to have a constant IQ if scores on other tests are 90, 93, and 101.

Such variations as these have been noted since the formulation of the first intelligence test and have been attributed to the limitations of the testing instrument, to the testee's lack of understanding of previously given tests, or to varying degrees of motivation. Fluctuations were not considered to be indicative of a real change in mental ability.

The Changing IQ   Adherents to the changing IQ thesis point to the steady accumulation of data which indicate that changes are typical rather than exceptional. A study by Sontag, Baker, and Nelson, in which it was found that 62 per cent of their subjects changed more than 15 IQ points in either direction during the years three to ten, is quite representative (1958). The fact of change as far as test results are concerned is indisputable; whether the altered score is indicative of changed ability to adjust to one's environment is the basic issue. Implicit in much of the recent literature is the conclusion that changes greater than 5 to 10

---

[6] It is recommended that teachers become acquainted with this area by taking courses in the education of exceptional children or by reading books on the subject.

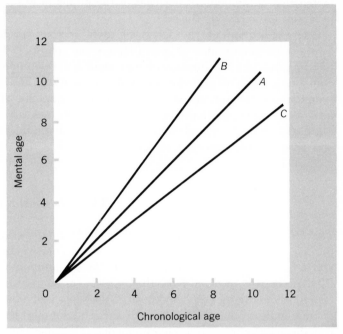

FIGURE 15. *Schematic portrayal of constant IQ. Subject A grows at the rate of two years mentally for each two years of chronological age. According to the formula MA/CA × 100 = IQ, his IQ is 100 at two, four, six, etc., years. Subject B grows at the rate of twelve months mentally for each chronological period of nine months (four years mentally in three calendar years, etc.) and, according to the formula, has an IQ of 133 at any given age. Subject C grows at the rate of nine months mentally for each calendar year (three years' mental growth on his fourth birthday) and has an IQ of 75.*

points are indicative of changed rates of intellectual growth and ability to adjust.

One pioneer study on the changing IQ concerned identical twins reared apart. Since identical twins have the same hereditary potential, any differences in ultimate ability may be presumed to be due to environmental differences. In the study of nineteen pairs of twins, it was found that in about half the pairs there was little difference in IQ after a period of years (one pair separated at the age of three was tested at the age of fifty-nine). This was not surprising because the quality of their environments was deemed quite similar by the five judges. In eight cases, the IQ varied by 10 to 24 points. In five of these cases—those who showed the greatest difference in IQ—there was a difference in schooling of four to fourteen years. The estimated educational advantage of the environment was rated much higher for the twin with the higher IQ, and the social advantages were superior, though not consistently so (there were a few cases in which the social rating was higher with no superiority in IQ). The greatest difference was 24 IQ points. The twin with the superior rating had been graduated from college and had become a teacher, while her twin had only two years of regular schooling. In the five cases in which differences in schooling were four to fourteen years, the IQ differences were 7, 12, 19, and 24 points (Newman, Freeman, and Holzinger, 1937).

IQ changes in children attending preschool were studied at the University of Iowa Child Welfare Research Station. In one study it was found that children attending the preschool made gains in accordance with length of time and regularity of attendance on the average. Gains up to 40 IQ points were recorded in some instances. Children who attended preschool for three years made an average gain of 10.5 points. Children who originally tested average made greater gains than those who originally tested superior—a gain of 18.9 for average children attending over three years, and a gain for superior children of 11.5 points (Wellman, 1940, pp. 377ff). For several reasons (lack of similarity between tests for various ages, rapid growth, conditioning circumstances at the time of testing, motivation of the test subject), one should not rely too heavily on these early changes. It is generally recognized that early childhood tests are not sufficiently reliable for long-term predictions of later intellectual status (Bayley, 1958).

Studies of the changing IQ have been critically examined by various authorities, and doubts have been raised as to whether or not the results are genuinely encouraging. There are questions about the statistical treatment of data, possible bias of examiners who may be hoping for favorable results, the effects of practice on the pupils who take the tests, and the shortcomings in the tests themselves (McNemar, 1940). A few of the questions have been answered, some of the data reanalyzed, and the conclusions have generally been confirmed (Wellman and Pegram, 1944). Continuing studies have yielded similar encouraging results—Levinson, for example, found an 11.8-point gain for boys over a two-year period on the Wechsler Intelligence Scale for Children.[7] However, it is probably well not to become too enthusiastic about the results. For instance, articles on mental deficiency have been written for popular magazines and have raised hopes that resulted in cruel disappointment for parents of retarded children. There are children whose potential is

---

[7] A gain of 11.8 points for an individual would not be surprising; for a group, where scores are changing both up and down, it is more significant. See B. M. Levinson, "Subcultural Values and I.Q. Stability," *Journal of Genetic Psychology*, 98: 68–82, 1961.

such that any additional stimulation beyond what they receive in a relatively easy environment will only produce frustration. A good working hypothesis is that appropriately stimulating environments do in some cases have the effect of raising test intelligence. But intelligence tests do not invariably tell how bright or capable of learning an individual is; we know only that he has at least as much intellectual potential as the test indicates (barring errors in administration and interpretation), but how much more he has is in many—perhaps most—cases still an unknown.

Factors associated with changing IQ There are several important conclusions to be drawn from changing IQ studies. One is that the changes in environment that accompany upward shift in test scores should take place early in life (Macfarlane, 1953). This accords with conclusions about other aspects of child development: The habits of response and the attitudes toward self progressively become more stable, thus the earlier attempts to affect them are made, the more effective those attempts will be. However, the meaning of "early" is changing from the preschool period to a later time. Bradway and others have found IQ to rise most perceptibly in the early adolescent period, for example. They conclude (as have others) that intelligence does not stop growing at the age of sixteen (Bradway, Thompson, and Cravens, 1958).

Another conclusion.is that the change in environment must be rather large. Most children do not experience a shift from cultural impoverishment to a culturally enriched milieu. This fact, indeed, probably explains why IQs do not change significantly and consistently more than they do. If a child has an intellectually stimulating home when he is ten years old, it is quite likely that he had similar stimulation at the age of one or two. Moreover, relatively few children are provided with the stimulating environments provided in the experimental situations in which the largest changes have been noted.

It is easy to think of a stimulating environment as one in which there is an opportunity for free and varied play; one in which there are books, records, and musical instruments to attract the child's interests; and one in which adults are responsive to children and are themselves vocal, interested in a variety of pursuits, and seeking self-improvement. Emotional dependence on parents is inimical to optimum mental development (Sontag, Baker, and Nelson, 1958). Children who are competitive, curious, and highest in need achievement more frequentlly make upward movement on tests than do those who are lower on these variables (Kagan, Sontag, Baker, and Nelson, 1958).

Data from changing IQ studies provide an optimistic outlook. The conclusions support Kubie, who, after describing man's intellectual potential, states, "This gives us some hint of the immeasurable creative potential which lies hidden in the mind of every man, waiting for us to learn how to unleash it. And my point is that there are signs that we stand on the frontiers of this exciting new existence." [8]

Adaptations to intellectual differences

The Challenge of Differences The student of educational psychology may be able to recite proven facts about differences in intelligence— how many pupils cluster about the average, what the range of differences is, and how many pupils are at the extremes of the distribution. The books tell us that intelligence is a matter of degree. The difference between a pupil with an IQ of 130 and a pupil with one of 70 is a matter of degree. But all this information remains theoretical until the beginning teacher sees these differences in the classroom and begins to appreciate their significance.

The differences between Johnny with his IQ of 130 and Tommy with his IQ of 70 seem to be much more than a matter of degree. Johnny quickly covers the material that is assigned and asks penetrating questions about what he has read. These questions suggest to the teacher that he find extra reading and research that will be of interest to Johnny. Johnny shortly comes back with suggestions of his own for additional research, which the teacher readily endorses. The teacher's job here is to provide encouragement and to suggest directions for independent research and experiment. Tommy, on the other hand, after repeated explanation, varied approaches, and concrete explanations comes up with absurd answers. Tommy is a well-behaved, likable boy, but he just does not seem to understand geometry. Explanation, drill, and demonstration seem to have no effect. Finally, while he is studying parallel chords intersecting a circle, Tommy is asked why angle A is equal to angle B. He replies, "The square on the hypotenuse of a right-angle triangle is equal to the sum of the squares on the other two sides." This gives rather clear evidence that the subject is over Tommy's head, so the teacher tells him to "study" *National Geographic* when he comes to the geometry class and he will receive a passing grade. This is not a good solution, but when special classes are not available, it is better than humiliating Tommy with both daily frustration and final failure.

Your study of intelligence will have little meaning unless it suggests techniques for dealing with the differences that you will inevitably encounter in your teaching career. We can admit that the aims of education are the same for every individual: health, command of the fundamental processes of living, worthwhile personal relationships, vocational efficiency, civic participation, beneficial use of leisure time, character, and so on.

[8] Lawrence S. Kubie, "Hidden Brain Power," *Saturday Review*, 39: 26, Oct. 13, 1956.

But the approach to these aims must of necessity be varied. An IQ may be regarded as a symptom; diagnosis must deal with explanations of *why* a test score is what it is (Levinson, 1964).

Characteristics of the Slow Learner There may be slow learners whose IQs are in the normal range (90–110) but most of them will be found in the IQ categories below 90. In actual practice, teachers may find that it is necessary to deal with pupils who will profit little from typical academic pursuits. The lower the IQ of the child, the less likely it is that he will attend school, and the more likely it is that he will be treated by other agencies. "Trainable" mentally retarded children have IQs between 30 and 50, and the aim is to help them become capable of self-care and socialization. In general, children with IQs between 50 and 75 are regarded as "educable," but it is difficult to keep them in school and interested unless special classes are organized for them. It is also desirable that their teachers be specially trained to provide suitable material and appropriate timing and, consequently, motivation. Interest in slow learners [9] has increased significantly in recent years; one important discovery has been that such pupils are much more capable of learning—at their pace—than was formerly thought to be the case (Pines, 1963). Moreover, it has been found that in the upper range of the educable, regular school attendance not only produced improved behavior, but tended to help the pupils make greater gains in mental age than did the lower IQ groups and those who stayed at home (Hottel, 1958).

Mental test results indicating below-average intelligence is the characteristic most readily discernible in slow learners. It is necessary to give an individual test to obtain reasonably reliable results, because physical handicap and emotion problems may mask average intelligence in some slow learners (Kirk and Johnson, 1951, p. 39). Slow learners are notable, of course, for their comparative retardation in academic achievement; hence, achievement tests should supplement the data from mental tests. The slow learner needs about three times as many experiences to consolidate learning as does the normal and bright pupil. Even with extra time and repetitions, the slow learner often reaches the ceiling of his ability and fails to learn what is expected of his peers in the same class-

[9] The term "slow learner" is not altogether satisfactory. It is used to avoid the stigma of "mental retardation" or "mentally deficient." The slow learner not only has a slower rate of learning, but also is qualitatively different. He comprehends and remembers somewhat less and is less perceptive of relations and contrasts than is the normal pupil. IQ does not tell the entire story, but we generally speak of mental retardation below IQ 75, while the slow learner has an IQ from 75 to 85 or 90. The important thing is to avoid placing the slow learner in competition with peers who are average and above and will, by their consistently superior academic performance, cause the less apt pupil to withdraw—physically or psychologically. Special curricular provisions must be made to suit the nature and speed of the slow learner's abilities.

room. Recent research, however, is undermining many past beliefs about the futility of teaching the mentally retarded. The fact is that they do learn in accordance with their mental age. It takes more time, more repetition, and special educational provisions—but they can learn and can become assets rather than liabilities in society(Dunn, 1963, pp. 82ff).

Slowness in academic accomplishment is typically paralleled by slowness in social maturation. The Vineland Social Maturity Test was originally devised by Edgar A. Doll for youngsters in homes for the mentally retarded, and is widely used for validation of the impressions that experienced teachers form. It should be expected that social adjustment will be difficult, and the consequence of frequent and repeated failure is individuals who are insecure, reticent, and recessive. Rejection by peers seems to be based on social ineptness rather than on scholastic deficiency (R. V. Miller, 1956).

Suggestions for dealing with slow learners The following observations will serve to show how knowledge of the psychology of individual differences and the nature of intelligence may be applied to the classroom situation. They will also serve to illustrate the futility of directing teaching at a hypothetical average pupil.

1. The slow learner will be more strongly motivated by praise than by criticism.

2. Examples, experiences, demonstrations, and illustrations serve to make learnings concrete.

3. Repetition of facts in different contexts and drill on fundamentals (such as numbers and English usage) will be helpful.

4. Emphasis should be placed on the development of traits of punctuality, neatness, health, etc., with specific suggestions for practical applications.

5. Slow developmental rates require patience on the part of the teacher.

6. Specific direction and prescription are desirable and gratifying.

7. Reading and number work should emphasize everyday situations, such as reading signs and directions, making change. Illustrations should be simple and specific.

8. Abilities in various areas—music, manual arts, arithmetic, reading—will vary widely, and an attempt must be made to capitalize on pupils' strengths whenever possible.

9. Promotion must of necessity be largely dependent on social and chronological age. Grading must be based on personality growth rather than on academic achievement.

10. Immediate rewards, short-term goals, praise, and encouragement are effective motivators. The slow learner appreciates being told what to do.

11. Schoolwork should be closely related to the simple occupations slow learners will probably have as adults.

12. Slow learners need more, rather than less, schooling than average and superior children. The adolescent years may be profitably devoted to continued schooling.

Characteristics of the Rapid Learner Several words are used to designate students who are in the upper section of a normal curve of distribution in adaptability. "Gifted" is a frequent designation, with IQ scores being one of the important criteria of identification. Authorities vary somewhat with regard to their ideas of what this score should be—130, 135, and 140 have all been recommended. All authorities do agree that whatever the score, other criteria (past performance, motivation, special abilities) should be used in conjunction with the scores. One difficulty with the word "gifted" is that it is sometimes used to indicate special talents—leadership, musical talent, artistic talent—and the importance of the IQ is lessened as an identifying characteristic. "Genius" was used occasionally, but the term has been dropped in professional literature for the most part. "Genius" refers to ability *plus* achievement and is therefore rather meaningless for pupil populations—though the term continues to be used by the general public. "Talent" is sometimes used synonymously with "gifted," but talents do sometimes exist without exceptionally high IQ (Angelino, 1960, p. 90). "Creative" is another word that appears to be used by some as an alternate for "gifted." But again, "creative" has special usage and can more advantageously be used to designate that special element, i.e., that combination of emotional factors which contributes to inventiveness, personal openness, and curiosity that fosters new combinations of ideas. Many rapid learners do not have this characteristic. For the classroom teacher, interest probably focuses on the fact of rapid learning. This usually depends to a considerable extent on high IQ, but on occasion also includes creativity and the exercise of special talents. With this introduction, we can list a number of the characteristics of the rapid learner that have significant implications for the teacher.

Rapid learners find schoolwork rather easy—about half the students in *Terman's Genetic Studies of Genius* (1925) could read before they entered school.

Rapid learners frequently are among the youngest in their class. They may have skipped a grade or they may not have been retained in a grade despite missing considerable time because of illness or moving.

The rapid learner tends to excel in all his school subjects, though rapid learners are not a homogeneous group; the range of their differences in any one area or subject is almost as large as the range for unselected pupils (Cronbach, 1954, p. 230).

Rapid learners typically have a wide range of interests. Further, these interests tend to be somewhat mature; rapid learners lost interest in the games played by their agemates at an earlier time.

Rapid learners, as a group, are superior in character and personality traits according to tests and the judgment of observers. The idea that they are queer or asocial is distinctly erroneous, according to numerous researches (Lewis, 1943).

Dealing with rapid learners in the school   A basic problem of educational psychology must always be that of recognizing and making adaptations for individual differences. Nevertheless, some generalizations about groups of individuals will be pertinent. The following points should be considered as being indicative rather than uniformly applicable to all superior children.

1. Blame and censure will be more effective with the gifted child than with the slow learner—though this should not be interpreted as a blanket recommendation.

2. Verbal descriptions and generalizations can serve to abbreviate and consolidate learnings.

3. Repetition is boring, yet many teachers make the mistake of giving these pupils more problems rather than more difficult ones or problems with ramifications. Study beyond that required of the average or slow learner is stimulating and gratifying to the gifted child.

4. Character traits are important and will be developed through challenge, meaning, and elaboration of school tasks.

5. An abundant supply of books, laboratory equipment, and illustrative material must be provided. From these, the bright child may select and utilize such materials as are in accord with his personal aims.

6. Reading should expand, clarify, and enrich daily experiences. Numbers can be used as tools for thinking and for consolidating generalizations.

7. Abilities are more evenly distributed among gifted children than among slow learners. For gifted children, emphasis should be placed on well-rounded development and the expansion of interests rather than on existing interests to the exclusion of diversification.

8. Acceleration (skipping of grades) is recommended up to two years,[10] *provided* the child is mature enough for the social and interest level of students in the grade to which he is promoted. Grading can be rigidly based on academic performance and on expectation.

9. Typically, the gifted child has much drive and originality. Permissiveness and challenge are more effective than prescription of work.

[10] This is an impressionistic conclusion not shared by this author. Research data provide little evidence that acceleration beyond two years is handicapping. It has yet to be proven that acceleration cannot exceed two years. See Dan C. Shannon, "What Research Says about Acceleration," *Phi Delta Kappan*, 39: 70–72, 1957.

10. Schoolwork can profitably be of traditional academic nature, designed to give a liberal background for later professional preparation.

Projects and experiments designed to recognize individual differences, especially to meet the needs of the gifted, have been going on for some time. Since 1900, Cleveland has had what are now called "major work classes" for able elementary pupils. The range of differences in both the regular and special classes is thus reduced. In classes for the gifted, enrichment rather than acceleration is the emphasis; pupils delve more deeply into subject matter, often the same subject matter that is taught in regular classes. In addition to content, the program aims to develop alertness, initiative, creativity, critical thinking, ability to plan and judge, to share and work cooperatively, and to exercise leadership (Barbe and Norris, 1954). It is felt that the advantages outweigh any disadvantages, and the major work classes continue. In some places, whole schools are devoted to the needs of the gifted. Hunter College in New York, which maintains a demonstration school, is an example. The special schools most frequently heard about are those in New York City, which maintains the High School of Music and Art, the High School of Performing Arts, and the High School of Science. These names do not imply specialization to the neglect of a rounded education—each maintains a curriculum that satisfies general educational aims in addition to the professed specialty (Dunn, 1963, pp. 216–219).

Summary

Universally acceptable definitions of intelligence are difficult to formulate, but there is little argument as to the personal and cultural desirability of possessing and developing it. Intelligence grows at various rates throughout the first two decades of life (perhaps longer). Heredity plays a major role in one's ultimate intellectual status, but environmental factors are inextricably woven into intellectual behavior. Moreover, it is the environment—no matter how small or large a function it has—that can be manipulated after birth. There are some subtle differences in the mental abilities of boys and girls, but whether these are constitutional or cultural is yet to be determined.

During the first thirty years of the existence of the concept of the IQ it was thought that rates of mental growth were inherent and characteristically steady. For the last thirty years, it has been realized that growth rates are a function of the interaction of hereditary potential *and* environment. Cultural deprivation and emotional disturbance are inimical to optimum mental development. Good health, proper diet, rich intellectual opportunity, and environments that produce emotional stability, independence, and self-confidence are productive of optimum developmental rates.

Schools and teachers can capitalize on knowledge of the nature and nurture of intelligence when appropriate provisions for differences in presently indicated levels of intellectual functioning are recognized. Slow learners need protection from the humiliation of competing against those who are markedly superior. They need repeated, concrete, specific, and simple experiences in order to realize their limited potential. Rapid learners need fewer repetitious experiences. They need the challenge of attacking the ramifications of knowledge; they can generalize and profit from abstractions. They especially need a balance between prescription and wise teacher direction. All kinds of learners need the challenge of learning environments that allow for the development of self-confidence, which stems from approval, acceptance, and the experience of success.

Problems and exercises

1 What are the practical implications of a definition of intelligence? What definition of intelligence do you think most appropriate for teachers?

2 Do you think that intelligence tests that provide subtests of the different components of intelligence are superior to those yielding a "global" score?

3 Have you seen any evidence among acquaintances that points to the effectiveness of environment in stimulating or limiting mental development?

4 Has your school experience given you any reason to believe that some teachers think there is a difference between boys and girls in the rates of mental development?

5 Discuss with some teacher you know the subject of emotional factors in intellectual development and report your findings in class.

6 Would differentiated instruction for slow learners and bright children be undemocratic?

7 Would you give the top grade in the class to a bright child who was at the top of his class in arithmetic but had not applied himself diligently to his work? Explain your answer.

Suggested additional readings

Drews, Elizabeth M.: "The Schools: Climate Affects Fallout," in Daniel Schreiber (ed.), *Guidance and the School Dropout,* Washington: National Education Association, 1964, pp. 24–37.
  The author indicates that children can learn much better than they have been given credit for when teachers' methods and attitudes provide a climate favorable to learning.
Dunn, Lloyd M. (ed.): *Exceptional Children in the Schools,* New York: Holt, Rinehart and Winston, Inc., 1963.
  This book deals with the definition, description, and educational provisions for many kinds of exceptional children—speech defective, deaf and hard of hearing, blind and partially sighted. The classroom teacher may be particularly interested in the chapters on the mentally retarded and the gifted.
Goldstein, Herbert: *The Educable Mentally Retarded Child in the Elementary*

School, What Research Says to the Teacher, no. 25, Washington: National Education Association, 1962.

The author describes the difficulty of precisely defining the educable mentally retarded child and suggests means of identification. School programs suited to slow learners are described.

Shertzer, Bruce (ed.): *Working with Superior Students,* Chicago: Science Research Associates, Inc., 1960.

This book, prepared under the auspices of the North Central Association of Colleges and Secondary Schools, is the result of "A project designed to identify superior and talented high school students, to provide guidance services for them, and to motivate them to make appropriate educational and occupational choices."

Thompson, George G.: *Child Psychology,* 2d ed., Boston: Houghton Mifflin Company, 1962, pp. 393–449.

This is a scholarly and readable summary of research in the nature, measurement, and development of intelligence. The author has the courage of his convictions, which he states frankly.

Motivation of Learning

11

A persistent problem of education is motivation. For centuries it was widely, but not universally, believed that whippings or canings were effective means of motivation. Aldous Huxley has stated that, whether by carrot in front or stick behind, the important thing is to induce children to make some slight intellectual effort toward learning (1956). The question of how to induce children to learn is not easily answered. The cliché "You can lead a horse to water, but you can't make him drink" is readily appreciated by parents who have tried to make a baby eat something he did not want and by teachers who have tried to elicit pupil effort. Teachers can expose a pupil to knowledge, but he does not necessarily partake thereof —at least he does not necessarily learn what the teacher desires to teach. Learning does take place even in the worst of schools, however, since development of attitudes about school and its personnel and pursuits cannot be stopped. The practical problem in motivation is to find approaches that will make the child more eager for the kinds of learning that the school endorses.

The basic role of motivation

The Place of Motivation in Education Since teaching is "the direction of learning," we must know something about how learning activities can best be initiated and sustained. Educational philosophers have for centuries been concerned about the objectives and content of education. Historically, it seems that motivation has been taken for granted. In a society that seeks to educate *all* its children, the art of directing and controlling motivation is of major importance. It is not enough to know about the abilities, interests, and characteristics of pupils. An inert organism—one without tensions or goals—has no response and will give none until tensions are generated and goals established. Moreover, in the school these goals must be such that they can be translated into the planned activities of the school. Thus motivation assumes the starting role, a role that is to obtain initial attention.

The causes that underlie behavior are always multiple and   **237** *complex rather than single and simple.* There are no nostrums, panaceas, or formulas that the teacher can use in reaching all pupils. The problems of motivation cannot be disposed of in a chapter. Actually, the chapters on intelligence, social class, characteristics of pupils, growth, and learning all contain considerations that have implications for motivation as related to classroom activities. This chapter is merely an introduction to the subject as a whole.

Motivation and the Teacher   The success of a teacher is to a very large extent dependent upon his ability to motivate pupils effectively. As a successful engineer of learning activities, he must plan strategies and tactics, assemble materials, guide pupils' assumption of responsibilities, and oversee activities to the end of arousing pupils and encouraging them to maintain effective pursuit of the learning goals. Often pupils enter the school with certain goals (perhaps somewhat vague ones) in mind, and little arousal is required. Others are reluctant, resistant, or less perceptive and require more assistance. It is highly probable that if a teacher does not know the basic factors involved in motivation, pursuit of learning goals will not be maintained with vigor, as it must be, for motivation is more than an explosion, such as the explosion of powder in a cartridge; it is also a propelling force, like gasoline in an automobile.

There is another reason, perhaps a more important one, for a careful study of motivation. The truly educated person is one who continues to study after his formal schooling has been completed. If a course is really successful, the student continues to study the subject after he has received his final grade. Teachers who "motivate" by means of demands and threats may get a degree of conformity that is temporarily satisfactory. An example is the literature teacher who assigned thirty pages a day in a book on contemporary American literature and then gave daily tests. The test consisted of citing one line; for this line, the student was to supply the name of the poem or story, author, period, and message carried by the piece as a whole. The students were motivated to do the reading; but even some of the successful students vowed never to read "literature" again.

Another teacher of literature worked with individuals in interpreting stories and poems. All pupils were given a chance to participate. Much time was devoted to relating the characters and incidents of literature to the problems and events in the pupils' own lives. Some discussion was held with individuals or small groups who had been previously guided into reading selections that accorded with their interests and would encourage further reading.

It is safe to assume that if the students in the two groups were of equal ability, more from the latter group developed a continuing interest in literature.

The Meaning of Motivation Motivation is the stimulation of action toward a particular objective where previously there was little or no attraction toward that goal. It is the process of arousing, maintaining, and controlling interest. If we truly understand motivation, we know why a pupil makes one choice and not another. Boys often prefer playing football to solving problems in arithmetic. Girls frequently engage in gossip with greater enthusiasm than they display in searching for data on the Mayan empire. But while these statements are generally true, they are not true in many specific cases. There are boys who prefer to work problems in arithmetic, and there are girls who enjoy reading history. The search for the reasons behind the individual's choices is the study of motivation.

Adults assume that the lessons taught in school should take at least temporary precedence over some of the activities that attract youngsters outside school. However, *the individual always takes what he perceives to be the shortest route to the goal* (Wheeler, 1940, p. 38), and pupils frequently do not see school tasks as the best way to independence, productivity, adulthood—or whatever they may consider desirable development. The basic task for the teacher then becomes learning how to stimulate pupils to choose topics, activities, and goals that have long-term significance as well as immediate appeal. At this point practical means of developing motivation may sometimes fail, and techniques that stress an immediately desirable choice may interfere with equally desirable but remote choices. For example, a pupil may be motivated to memorize a long list of Latin words by being given an A by the teacher and a dollar for the A by his father. But the emphasis on the A and on the dollar tends to obscure the long-term value of his study. This was well expressed by F. E. Bolton over three decades ago.

> On graduation from high school, what a boy loves is vastly more important than what he knows. What companions does he choose? What books does he read voluntarily? What ideals does he harbor? These are the really significant characteristics which will determine his life's career. Does he chum with wholesome pals, does he read choice literature, does he enjoy good lectures, does he participate in harmless recreation, does he take an interest in civic welfare? Or, does he seek vile companions who tell smutty stories and enter into questionable escapades, does he read trashy and indecent magazines and books, does he sneer at the church, the school, good books and all serious activities?
>
> His attitude toward society and its problems, his attitude toward religion and morals, his attitude toward duties and obligations are vastly more important than the few items of intellectual knowledge he has gained. His spontaneous likes and dislikes, his loves and his

hates, his longings and aversions will really determine what manner of man he shall be.[1]

All the choices and attitudes cited in this quotation are related to motivation. Those having the greatest long-term significance are the ones that go beyond gaining attention or getting the student to complete his lesson. The long-range values reside in pursuits that contribute to his being a better person in five or ten years and activate his continued pursuit of knowledge. The teacher's contribution will be greatest when his aims and methods for teaching (and motivation) accord with basic facts concerning growth and personality.

Practical Approaches to Motivation Many books and pamphlets approach motivation on the "how-to" basis, listing a number of techniques that will obtain the immediate result desired. Thus, first graders are encouraged to learn to read and to continue to read by the use of praise. The teacher encourages the third grader to learn to spell by pinning his better papers on the bulletin board. He motivates the fifth grader to study history by planning and producing a dramatic program. He encourages the eighth grader to study civics by taking the entire class for a day's visit to the city hall. High school pupils are stimulated in their efforts to write by working on the school paper. Other high school youngsters work their heads off to get on the honor roll. These practices have worked and deserve the attention of the prospective teacher. However, it is more practical to know *why* praise stimulates effort, *why* symbols, honor rolls, and activities are effective motivators—when the "why" is understood, greater versatility in teachers is probable.

All behavior is caused, and understanding pupils entails comprehending the causes. The author, visiting a fifth-grade class, sat near a pupil who was the teacher's "boy with problems," as it was later discovered. During class activities, the boy kept saying to himself, "What'll I do? If I go I'll have to buy a present. I'll miss the next *Wagon Train* show on TV, but maybe that won't matter." These remarks were occasioned by his reading an invitation to a birthday party. He was rocking back and forth in his chair, kicking the desk in front. There was real danger of his falling backward on a pupil who was working at a floor-level bookshelf. The teacher finally took hold of his chair and asked him to help a slow-learning girl with her arithmetic. He protested audibly and was then told to get busy on his own work. The incident illustrates the necessity for understanding causes. The boy's problem needed to be understood, and the teacher was working on it. She already had much useful information (one of the major factors was parental pressure on him to be the best pupil in the class); but she also had the problem of imme-

[1] F. E. Bolton, *Adolescent Education,* New York: The Macmillan Company, 1931, p. 175. Used by permission.

diately stopping his disturbance of other children and classroom routines. Two motivational implications are clear: We can motivate children by the application of tested techniques, but those techniques will be more appropriately used when we understand the theory of the cause of individual behavior.

The theory is that successful motivation in the schools should stem from meeting the fundamental needs of children. When specific motivators fail (such as getting good grades, helping others, or recognition), then the teacher must ask, "What fundamental need has been neglected or temporarily satiated?" When it is recognized that theory provides guidelines and suggests solutions, techniques for motivation can be adapted to particular individuals and to the specific times and conditions inherent in the immediate situation.

A youngster is not "instinctively" desirous of displeasing adults. He simply takes what he perceives to be the shortest route to his goal. He does not displease adults when the activities most attractive to him are the ones that adults believe to be worthy. If we can understand what makes some activities more attractive than others, we will know better how to make school tasks more attractive in terms of the pupils' perceptions. An inclusive approach to this understanding is the study of basic needs.

Basic needs of children

Some Concepts of Needs   The discussion of motivation through an analysis of needs is a theoretical approach. It is difficult to state basic needs to the satisfaction of all concerned, and various authorities have conceptualized them in somewhat different terms. The basic idea is that unfulfilled needs result in maladjustment, but there are exceptions—one child who apparently is not loved deeply by his parents may be well adjusted, but another upon whom love has apparently been lavished may be poorly adjusted, for example. However, the exceptions are understandable *when other and all needs are considered.* The statements of needs become a basis for improved understanding of children and adolescents. The following list presents varied basic human drives or needs as noted by various authors:

Thomas [2]

New experiences	*Response*
Security	*Recognition*

Symonds [3]

Be with others	*Gain attention*

[2] W. I. Thomas, *The Unadjusted Girl*, Boston: Little, Brown and Company, 1923.
[3] P. M. Symonds, "Human Drives," *Journal of Educational Psychology*, 25: 694, 1934.

Symonds (cont.)

For approval
Be a cause
Mastery
Maintain self

Security
Affection
Curiosity

Maslow [4]

Physiological
Safety
Belongingness or love

Esteem
Need for self-actualization
Aesthetic needs

Carroll [5]

Physical security
Emotional security

Mastery
Status

Leuba [6]

Physical: food, water, elimination of waste, protection, muscular activity, optional stimulation

Acquired: gregariousness, attention, approval, please others.

It is apparent that there is considerable duplication in the lists and that the longer lists break down items in the shorter lists. It is not so apparent where basic needs, in the sense of being essential to life, begin to merge into needs that are learned or acquired from the customs and culture of the environment in which the individual develops. Leuba (1961, p. 453) makes the important point that the persons and situations connected with the satisfaction of biological needs are highly influential in the development of acquired needs. We must realize that one's early life and his school experiences shape his needs and motivations.

Another list of basic needs, derived from experimental studies and clinical experience, has been postulated by Maslow (1954, pp. 80ff). He admits certain instances of lack of continuity, but states that when needs are satisfied at one level, a next higher order of needs becomes prepotent. Thus the satisfying (not necessarily 100 per cent) of low-level needs predisposes the individual to seek goals at a higher and more productive level. Maslow is skeptical about drawing conclusions for human behavior from animal studies because of the neglect of purpose and proposes the following as characteristically human needs:

1. *Physiological needs* These needs are usually not powerful in well-

[4] A. H. Maslow, *Motivation and Personality*, New York: Harper & Row, Publishers, 1954.

[5] Herbert A. Carroll, *Mental Health in Modern Education*, Fifty-fourth Yearbook of the National Society for the Study of Education, Chicago: The University of Chicago Press, 1955, part II, pp. 61–70.

[6] Clarence J. Leuba, *Man: A General Psychology*, New York: Holt, Rinehart and Winston, Inc., 1961, pp. 66, 453ff.

fed, adequately housed, Americans. They are emergency needs that occur rather rarely but are likely to be prepotent when present. The needs are for food, water, oxygen, sleep, activity, sex, and sensory satisfaction.

2. *Safety needs* The individual seeks safety. Neglected children appear to be dominated by safety-seeking behavior if their physiological needs are satisfied. Children prefer care during illness, routines, dependable parents, and an orderly world because of the need for safety. They need the feeling of security that comes from structure, discipline, and consistency. Permissiveness *within limits* rather than unrestricted freedom is needed by children so that they can perceive their world as being organized rather than unstructured.

3. *Belongingness and love needs* When physiological and safety needs are fairly well met, the need to give and receive love emerges as the next order of priority. Hunger for affectionate relations is, when unsatisfied, a basic factor in psychopathology.

4. *Esteem needs* All people need a "stable, firmly based high evaluation of themselves" (Maslow, 1954, p. 90). This entails a self-respect and esteem from others that is rooted in achievement relative to capacity. The need is satisfied by (*a*) confidence and independence and (*b*) recognition, attention, and appreciation from others.

5. *The need for self-actualization* This means that what a person can be, he must be—his potentialities tend to be actualized. Before this level is reached, the other needs must be satisfied; when achieved, the result is a healthy individual who reaches the full realization of his potential.

6. *The aesthetic needs* This level of needs was proposed after Maslow's earlier postulations (1943); it appears only in some mature individuals, but is frequently seen in healthy children. It is the craving some people have for beauty, order, symmetry, and completion.

School personnel should seek to organize their work so that some opportunity is given to each pupil to satisfy his basic personality needs. Teachers will be more effective as they work in accordance with, rather than in opposition to, fundamental needs—whether basic or derived. How this may be accomplished is suggested in the following sections.

Physiological Needs Teachers have not always been concerned about the bodily needs of children, but this recognition is increasing in classes for handicapped children as well as in classes for normal children. It is realized that *the determiners of behavior are always multiple, and intellectual activities are conditioned by bodily processes and attendant feelings and emotions.*

> Everything one does involves body functioning, so the condition of the body and the state of its physiological processes have a part in determining how one feels. A child's mood and feelings will al-

ways depend, in part, upon factors such as the following: whether
he is hungry or full; whether his body nourishment is adequate,
inadequate, or inappropriate; whether he is tired or fresh; whether
he has free energy to spend and is not permitted to do so, or whether
the situation demands more energy than he has; whether he has a
headache, a cold, indigestion, or some acute or chronic infection
somewhere in his body; whether his sense organs are functioning
effectively, or whether he strains to see or hear; whether his body
is growing at the same rate as the other children and whether it has
reached the same maturity level or is conspicuously different in size
or shape or has obvious defects; whether his skills in using his body
surpass or fall short of those of the children with whom he is compared or compares himself; whether his hair, facial features, general
appearance, and grooming are attractive to others, repellent to others,
nondescript, or conspicuously different.[7]

Paul J., whose family was in difficult financial circumstances, was causing some trouble in the sixth grade. He was only a fair reader, and his
arithmetic was poorer than aptitude tests predicted. He displayed a
resentment toward the teacher and had a few physical clashes with classmates. His work was sporadic, and in general he manifested an "I-don't-
care" attitude. Praise, bestowal of responsibilities, careful selection of
books, and individual attention did not change the situation. One day
the teacher noticed that he squinted and twisted his head when looking
at the chalkboard. The teacher began to suspect poor vision and later
noticed other symptoms. A visual examination confirmed the suspicion.
With his astigmatism, Paul probably saw only a blur from the back of
the room, the ophthalmologist reported. Paul's behavior changed markedly when the Lions Club obtained glasses for him.

Teachers of children with sensory handicaps stress the importance of
giving their pupils as close a contact with their environment as possible.
The first step in their education is to identify their visual or auditory
defect and then to reduce that difficulty to a minimum. Teachers in
regular classrooms must also realize that their work will go more smoothly
when children's physiological needs are being met. Often children are
not dressed warmly enough for comfort. Others may not have had an
adequate breakfast. The beauty of *Thanatopsis* will probably not compete
with physical discomfort as a "motivator."

Proper room temperature, circulation of fresh air, and adequate lighting are important. If the need for glasses can make one child difficult in
school, it is obvious that glare or dingy lighting will have a negative
effect upon several children. The teacher is also responsible for alter-
nating periods of active and sedentary work. Many schools do not have
regular recess periods in the elementary grades; instead, the teacher

[7] Daniel A. Prescott, *The Child in the Educative Process*, New York: McGraw-Hill
Book Company, 1957, pp. 399–400.

watches for signs of restlessness after a period of quiet work and when they appear announces a play period.

It is pertinent to add that many of these responsibilities can be turned over to pupils. One pupil can be responsible for seeing that windows are opened after a play period and that the room is warm during quiet periods. Another can see that shades are properly drawn. A "captain of recess" can be named to see that rubbers and coats are worn outside. The pupils will profit by sharing responsibility, and the teacher's burden will be lighter. It is the teacher's responsibility, however, to check periodically to be sure that chairs, desks, and tables are the proper size. This is particularly important in the lower and upper grades, when pupils are growing rapidly. "The mind can absorb no more than the seat can endure."

Classroom furniture should be arranged primarily on the basis of physiological need. If stationary seats must be used, they should be placed in a corner or at one side of the room in order to leave a large open area where freedom of movement is possible. This also leaves room for construction of models and replicas or a stage for an illustrative drama—both of which are motivational techniques that recognize the physiological need for activity.

Matt B. regularly fell asleep in class, and the teacher finally became impatient and told him to stay awake or stay away. It appeared that Matt was not greatly motivated in the direction of ancient history. The teacher later discovered that Matt was greatly motivated, but that physiological needs took priority. Matt's father did not approve of education and told his son that going to school would not excuse him from farm chores—nor would there be any money for "fancy clothes." Matt got up at 5 A.M. to do his chores and after school held two jobs, firing a bakery furnace and acting as bellboy at a small hotel until midnight. The next time this teacher had a sleepy student, he first sought for understanding—and in the next case it was an underactive thyroid gland. *Physiological needs must be met or on the way to being met before the next higher order of motivators become predominant.*

Safety Needs The educational implications of safety needs are fairly clear. *Pupils need and appreciate routine and regularity.* This was demonstrated to the author, visiting a seventh grade, by a girl who asked for attention and stated with concern, "We did not put arithmetic on the board today." Each morning, the teacher listed the day's activities on the board. This day, because they were to watch a television broadcast of the President's Inaugural Address, there just was not time enough to schedule all subjects even in shortened periods. No doubt, students who had stronger feelings of security would welcome a change in schedule, but for some, adhering to a schedule was important. This can be noted particularly among some handicapped pupils and slow learners who, the teacher fully realizes, can depart from schedule only at the cost of upsetting some of them.

Safety needs also tend to be filled when the teacher's behavior is consistent. Whether his tone is optimistic and cheerful or stern and demanding, the students can work more effectively if they can depend upon his mood. It has also been noted in experimental and classroom situations that pupils generally are better motivated when expectations and assignments are clear (Sears and Hilgard, 1964). Consistency is helpful, especially to the pupil who tends to be insecure. Written work to be handed in should not be demanded on one day if excuses are to be honored at another time. Similarly, grading should not be based partially on conduct and attitude at one time if it is to be based entirely on achievement on other occasions. When a test is announced, it should be given on schedule. Surprise tests are of doubtful motivating value if the policy of surprise tests has not been discussed and established. It follows that assignments made on a punitive basis are more likely to harm class morale than to be effective motivators—except for the few pupils who are highly curious or fact-oriented.

Solution of the problem of discipline is partially based on safety needs and partially on other needs. As Maslow indicates, children need discipline *within limits.* Choosing the more advantageous behaviors is too much of a burden for the immature, inexperienced individual, and firm direction and policies are appreciated. *Children need discipline in order to perceive an orderly, organized world.* When discipline is weak, the child, the teacher, and society are in danger (Hymes, 1955, p. 3). Observance of group welfare, conformity to legal requirements, respect for authority and learning, and temporarily setting aside one's own immediate wishes are lessons that must be learned if one is to feel safe in society (G. D. Stephens, 1958). Rules and regulations, like routines, help to provide an aura of safety.

It must be remembered that the ultimate goal of discipline is to help the individual become independent, self-directing, and able to function in democratic society. This imples that discipline must be reasonable and cooperative rather than arbitrary and autocratic. Such discipline should be characterized by four basic considerations: It should (1) recognize the inherent rights and dignity of the individual, (2) be based on the humanitarian ideals of freedom, justice, and equality, (3) aim at self-direction and self-discipline rather than unquestioning obedience, and (4) entail a clear understanding of the goals at which discipline is directed (Sheviakov and Redl, 1956, p. 7). Such discipline, which tends to satisfy safety needs, promotes motivation, which can then stem from higher-level goals.

Belongingness and Love Needs Art K. had again fought with a classmate. The fourth-grade teacher had pleaded with him not to pick on others. She had punished him and had sent him to the principal. But there were still periodic fights. Praising him on days when there were no fisticuffs was no solution. But the remark "Art, some of the big boys in the upper grades are picking on our boys. You are a big, strong fighter and you can protect the little boys" worked. Art was big and strong. He was big because, as a slow learner, he was behind a grade. The cause and the remedy for his difficulties could be stated in terms of belongingness needs. He wanted to have a significant role in the group, but his inability to do effective schoolwork denied him the feeling of belonging. Fighting had been his attempt to win a place.

Babies, children, and adults need affection. The words "a warm, responsive personality" are encountered frequently in psychological literature. They describe any person, pupil or teacher, who feels secure and can radiate security in establishing contact with others. Characteristically, one who has not had the opportunity to give and to receive affection presents a hostile front. He is often defensive and, being afraid, assumes the attitude of not caring or of not wanting affection. The situation is aggravated because the pupil's need for affection causes him to act in such a way that it is difficult for others to be affectionate. *When one is most unlovable, he is most in need of love.* There are many such emotionally wounded children in school. Motivation can be provided by sensitive teachers who have their own feelings under control. The teacher must be genuine when he says to the child, "I like you," and he must show it in actions. Well-integrated teachers are effective with all types of pupils. Weakly integrated teachers are ineffective with all but the "strivers" (Sears and Hilgard, 1964). This is but another indication of the fact that when the child's need for affection has been at least partially supplied, it is more likely that he can be motivated by the traditional approaches.

One of the frequent concomitants of underachievement (see Glossary), which is an aspect of motivation, is the pupil's frequent change of residence—perhaps safety needs seem threatened. However, if the home is secure, change of residence is of little consequence (Schorr, 1958). When the home is not stable, the child encounters school difficulties. For a period of time, such youngsters do not *belong* in the new social group, and special efforts must be exerted to make them feel welcome. Teachers have approached the problem in three ways, by (1) using group and individual counseling to encourage pupils to make their classmates feel at home, (2) designating duties and responsibilities in such a way that *all pupils* become functioning members of the group, and (3) grouping pupils sociometrically (see Glossary, page 487) so that there is mutual attraction and support—pupils must feel that others like them and they must be free from fear of not being accepted.

Belongingness is sought in the primary grades by having teachers "pass along" with pupils; i.e., one teacher stays with a class through both the first and second grades. It is thought that the less frequently the young pupil has to adjust to key adults, the greater the likelihood that the school will resemble the familar home situation.

The relationship of belongingness and motivation is probably best shown in studies of school dropouts. For a long time dropping out of school was thought to be a function of intelligence or the lack of it, but it becomes increasingly clear that ability to do schoolwork is not of first importance (Bristow, 1964). Much more significant is the fact that dropouts have not become an integral part of the school. They have not participated in school activities—parties, sports, club activities, band, orchestra, choruses, or held office (Tapfer, 1962). There is no open sesame for this phase of motivation. Some teachers will merely question, others will advise, some will use a variety of attacks. Siggins asserts that some of the teacher factors that make pupils want to learn are almost indescribable (1961). It does seem clear that *when pupils feel that they are part of the group, desirable and purposeful learning activities are facilitated.*

Esteem Needs   Teachers frequently voice an effective motivational principle, "*Find something the pupil can do—something that makes him feel important.*" One evidence of inadequate motivation is dropping out of school, and a lack of status looms large in explaining dropouts. Major characteristics of dropouts are shunning extracurricular activities, which causes difficulty in maintaining status, and lack of esteem of teachers and peers ("High School Dropouts," 1960). The teacher's effectiveness in motivation can be increased by (1) recognizing the importance of status and (2) realizing that children of different socioeconomic backgrounds achieve status in different ways.

Fundamentally, the need for status is the same everywhere. Each human being wants to be recognized as a worthy person in the group in which he lives. If he cannot get approval, he may have to be satisfied with forcing recognition. Though the need for status is the same everywhere, the way in which it is achieved is not. Males of the Arapesh tribe in New Guinea achieve status by developing what we would call femininity, while the Mundugumors, also in New Guinea, place a high value on fighting, conflict, and ruthlessness (Mead, 1939).

The teacher will be well advised to recognize that there are differences in the ways of achieving status in our own society. Children from the lower class achieve status by being pugnacious and aggressive. Children from the middle classes achieve status by being well behaved: Parents praise them for avoiding battle. The lower-class boy who earns status with the teacher by avoiding battle loses prestige in the eyes of his playmates for being a softy. But the middle-class boy, by the same behavior, is successful. An emphasis on grades and marks will be a source of strong motivation to the middle-class child, whose parents believe in the monetary and cultural value of an education. Grades are often less important to the lower-class child, whose parents feel they are getting along pretty well with limited education. In order to motivate these lower-class children, the teacher should recognize their view of life; they have a relatively high reality orientation that makes the practical and immediate of value. Deferring gratification to earn diplomas and degrees is less important than learning something that will get the individual a job and give him independence. Thus the abstract curriculum (college preparatory) is less appealing than the vocational and commercial curriculum (Havighurst and Neugarten, 1962, p. 240).

A practical problem that illustrates the role of esteem and motivation may be found in many schools in states where the laws specify compulsory school attendance until age eighteen. Some teachers and administrators want the age minimum reduced because many of these unmotivated youths are troublesome, but the fault is not entirely that of the eighteen-year-olds. Since their grade-school days, teachers have probably tried to motivate them with the threat of poor grades or the promise of good ones. When this motivation proved relatively meaningless, teachers became disgusted with the stubbornness of pupils who would not learn despite ability and incentives: In consequence, these pupils felt that school had nothing for them. But another generation of eighteen-year-olds under another teacher orientation could be different. Today teachers should recognize that there are different ways of achieving status; consequently, there are different methods for using status as a motivator.

The study of class structure will not give the teacher much that is necessary to understanding the different paths by which a student seeks status. Praise, whether deserved or not, may work well with one who is little recognized at home; to another, even well-deserved praise may be meaningless. It has been found, for instance, that some children do things for which they know they will be punished simply because they get recognition; the child's level of aspiration conditions his response to esteem.

Physiological, safety, belongingness, and esteem needs should not be too sharply differentiated. The child whose uncorrected vision prevents his taking part in ball games is denied satisfaction of both physical and social needs, and his emotional turmoil may keep him from being motivated to work hard on arithmetic, algebra, or literature. The girl who is concerned about protruding or missing teeth has a physical difficulty that has its greatest impact in terms of esteem and belongingness needs.

Self-actualization Needs   After other needs have been met, the baby trying to walk, the youngster learning to read, the adolescent trying to throw a football, and the girl seeking approval of adults all show the drive for self-actualization. Because "one must be what he can be" (Maslow, 1954, p. 91), the pupil with athletic ability will train and drill; the pupil with musical talent will practice eagerly; the pupil with mathematical aptitude will work assigned *and* unassigned problems; the pupil with linguistic ability will study without being forced. It should be noted, however, that self-actualization need not entail unusual talent. A run-of-the-mill athlete, a thorough workman, and a good mother may be self-actualizing when they are sufficiently motivated to do their best. At the highest level, self-actualizers are those rare creative individuals who are more frequently found among the intellectually gifted. Most persons are satisfied with lower-order motivations (Chaplin and Krawiec, 1960, p. 348).

Individual differences are, of course, important in the approaches to self-actualization. Much, perhaps all, of what was said in Chapter 9 on individual differences has direct bearing on self-actualization. Varied curricula, provisions of choices in student activities, plans for independent study, and availability of guidance and counseling workers all have a place in providing opportunities for and challenges to self-actualization. Students should be given information derived from tests and observations about their abilities and aptitudes. *Then they should be able to choose the type of knowledge or skills desired, with flexibility as to the time they will devote to developing that knowledge or skill* (Wrenn, 1962, p. 87). The lock-step formula of education (annual promotions and uniform curricula), which is so strongly condemned by philosophers and educators, can also be criticized by psychologists.

The urge for self-actualization becomes prepotent after other more basic needs have been satisfied, at least in part. In addition, there must have been some success in achieving goals that are real and important to the individual. There must have been parent, peer, and teacher approval of behavior and accomplishments. There must have been considerable evidence of faith in the individual so that he can feel free to act on his own and assume responsibility.

Examination of a case in which a young man seemed to approach self-actualization will be informative. Craig appeared at the counseling center where the author supervised counselor trainees. He wanted suggestions for a college where he could combine the study of mathematics and science with the opportunity for participation in college symphonic music. The counselor asked what his father, a teacher, thought about college choice, and Craig said, "We just talk about it, but my dad rarely expresses opinions on my major decisions. He will refuse permission for me to go out if I've been on the go too much. But choosing a college is my job. That's why I come to you—I will not feel any guilt, or whatever you might call it, if I go counter to anything you might advise." During the course of the conversation, the boy indicated that he had applied for an American Field Service Scholarship. He had not yet told his parents about this application.

It was later learned that Craig did go to Germany for part of his senior year. While in Germany, he was elected president of his class (he returned before his term of office started). Besides participating in school politics, he was active in musical activities and publications and maintained his honor roll status.

Much later, the author talked with the parents about Craig and discovered the following: They planned not to make decisions for him. He readily got the clarinet and saxophone he decided he wanted, and he used them effectively. The parents regularly attended the school activities in which he engaged when they were open to the public. It was also learned that the summer before Craig went to Germany, he conducted his own symphony orchestra composed of about twenty classmates and chosen instrumentalists from other high schools. Playing was the sole objective. The following summer, he led a group of eight students who met weekly to give, listen to, and react to book reviews. Craig had the nerve to apply at only one college (Harvard)—he was selected and made the Dean's list his first semester.

Let us look at a case where self-actualization was defeated: Alfred was first called to the author's attention by a college admissions officer who wanted to know whether the boy could be accepted as a risk or a challenge. Alfred's reports showed that he had made a fair record in high school but had flunked out of two Western colleges and one in the East. His aptitude tests were encouraging. A call to his former high school principal offered a clue to his ineptitude. The mother was a constant source of irritation to his high school teachers. She selected Alfred's courses, she determined the amount of homework he was to do, she approved or disapproved (generally disapproved) his choice of girl friends, and she selected his school activity program. She had frequent conferences with college professors and deans about how Alfred could be helped. This had involved two plane trips in one semester for conferences in the East. The case was a challenge. The admissions officer made an appointment with the boy, who came with his mother. An interview was held with the mother alone; at this time she was told, "Perhaps something can be done. But Alfred must make up his mind for himself. He must freely choose to make this fourth try at college. If he does not so choose, it will be best to forget it. The courses, the hours of study, the activities he pursues must be his own choices." It was not a conference; it was brutally frank advice, and the mother was told, "It is your fault." The mother verbally agreed, but as she departed she said, "Well, I'll talk with him and see if I can't get him to settle down." The boy at this time had no chance to achieve self-actualization—perhaps if and when he got the chance, it would be too late.

Youngsters from the very beginning of their school experiences should make some of their own choices. It should be realized that self-chosen pursuits are more powerful motivators than those imposed or selected by the teacher. One experimenter intentionally interrupted children when they had partly finished a drawing. She found that, while the pupils were disturbed by arbitrary interruptions at any time, they were more disturbed and more determined to go ahead with what they were doing when they were drawing what they had chosen than when they had been told what to draw (Olson, 1959, p. 318).

As the child makes thrusts for self-actualization, he must learn through consistent discipline and kindly direction the boundaries of his activities and the penalties for exceeding them. It must be realized that motivation is an individual matter—each child has, by his experiences, become more acutely aware of some aspects of his environment than of others. This means that *a numberless variety of experiences must be provided in the school if an appeal is to be made to individuals.*

Fundamental needs are the basis for motivation. This has been at least partially validated by experimental evidence, clinical experience, and observation, which indicates five basic drives: physiological needs, safety needs, belongingness needs, esteem needs, and the need for self-actualization. Some of the practical and time-honored approaches to motivation will now be examined to see whether they accord with theory. If they do, the teacher will have a test of the validity of current practices as well as a directional beacon for his own innovations.

Motivational techniques in terms of needs theory

Some Basic Considerations   Theoretically, if an individual had no needs, he would come to a complete state of rest. He would have reached a state of homeostasis. No such state is known to exist for human beings. Maslow's theory avoids this issue by suggesting that need satisfaction at one level merely makes need pursuit at a higher level more attractive and possible. It seems that humans are by nature perverse—as soon as current wants are satisfied, a new order of wants emerges. It should also be reiterated that needs do not have to be completely satisfied before others appear. The practical aim for educators is to approach the satisfaction of needs or to ensure that needs are on the way to being satisfied. If the child feels that progress is not being made toward need satisfaction, he will fight or flee, either psychologically (symbolically) or actually. He will either manifest overt, objectionable, and disconcerting symptoms or withdraw. If progress is being made toward need satisfaction, he will be motivated to exert goal-seeking effort.

The study of comparative culture and individual differences makes it easy to understand why there are so many successful motivational techniques. Some will be more successful because they are in closer accord with natural growth tendencies; others will be successful because they accord with needs that have emerged as a result of acculturation. Some techniques will fail because they are at an inappropriate level in terms of an individual's experience.

Rewards Rewards may be either symbolic (gold stars, medals, or honor rolls), material (a piece of candy, a sum of money, or the right to participate in student activities or to hold office), or psychological (knowledge of progress, recognition of adequacy or growth toward adequacy). Rewards, by ensuring safety, indicating esteem, and leading to belongingness, have their place in motivating the pupil in his *initial* contacts with an area of knowledge. Because contact is required to build an interest in an activity, idea, or person, rewards are commendable in the role of making introductions. Some psychologists and educators frown on rewards because they too frequently become ends in themselves. The father of an able high school mathematics student suggested that his son study a college text along with the high school text and got the retort "Well, Dad, you can't do any better than an A." Bruner (1961) has argued against external rewards because they encourage conformity and rote behavior and discourage autonomous action. If there is no motivation for continued activity after the reward has been won, we are stopping short of motivation for self-actualization. Scholars are concerned about this when they speak of extrinsic and intrinsic motivation. Extrinsic motivation arises from factors outside the individual, whereas intrinsic motivation relates to the general personality of the individual and his identification (see Glossary) with an activity (Di Vesta, 1961). It is possible that extrinsic rewards (high marks, parental approbation, helping the class or school gain a good reputation) may lead to intrinsic motivation. That is, the knowledge gained may become of interest (intrinsic) to the individual, and further knowledge may be pursued after the extrinsic motivators have waned or ceased to exist. We hope that this generation of functional autonomy will occur routinely, but too often effort ceases as soon as the possibility of the extrinsic reward disappears.

Rewards for learning should be such that, after serving in introductory roles, they lead students to learning activities outside the classroom. The teacher must be careful to emphasize to the pupil his newly gained competence, his increased knowledge, and his improved social skills and status. The pupil's real reward for reading is the contact with reality through written words. His reward for improved mathematical skills is his increased power over a technical environment. The reward of saying "I can do it" is more important than the symbolic status of a good grade or a certificate of completion.

Grades and Marks When grades are based on interpersonal comparisons of academic achievement, some pupils will inevitably earn a "respectable" grade too easily and develop habits of superficiality, conformity, and dilatoriness; others will develop feelings of inferiority and discouragement toward their schoolwork. When there is no acceptable escape from failure, there may be serious effects on the pupil's personality ("Pupil Failure and Nonpromotion," 1959). If, however, grades are based on the ability of pupils and if pupils' backgrounds are considered, they can be highly useful in informing the pupil of his progress; in this case, the grade is much less likely to become the primary objective of learning. The need for belongingness, esteem, and self-actualization demands that each child be judged in terms of what he is and what he can become.

> Recognition of the limitations of marks may suggest some of the things that classroom teachers can do even when required to prepare school marks for the office file. First, define very clearly what each mark means in terms of pupil *development*, using descriptions of activities other than, or at least in addition to, mere repetition of memorized material. Classroom teachers may enlist the aid of pupils and parents in defining the kind of development that is expected. Then pupil growth in those activities can be observed from landmarks estimated at the beginning of the period of instruction. We should always be mindful, while doing so, that growth rates vary from pupil to pupil.[8]

School activities and evaluative techniques should lead to goals that students are aware of and wish to attain.

Success The drive for skill, competence, and success motivates the continuation of activity, and there is wisdom in the cliché "Nothing succeeds like success." Explanations for the motivational character of these learned drives include conditioning, tension reduction as the result of goal achievement, and the power of verbal stimuli to evoke muscular and emotional response (M. Brown, 1961, pp. 138ff). *Schoolwork must be sufficiently varied so that every pupil has a chance to succeed at his level.* The youngster who has learned that he is unable to get the highest grades may think of himself as being unsuccessful when he gets a C—especially if his parents and teachers concur. Success may come through a variety of experiences—not just the academic—if the pupil and key adults set a high value on them. Providing these varied opportunities for success thus accords with the needs for esteem, belonging, and for a degree of self-actualization. Success tends to build self-confidence (Rhine, 1957), while failure impairs efficiency; furthermore, failure often leads

[8] John W. M. Rothney, *Evaluating and Reporting Pupil Progress*, What Research Says to the Teacher, no. 7, Washington: National Education Association, 1955, p. 9.

pupils to set unrealistic goals, while success tends to encourage realistic goals.

Consideration of success needs has bearing on the matter of school dropouts, which has become a national concern. This concern is not because so few pupils remain in school; the fact is that a greater portion of pupils of all ages are in school than ever before. The problem is that the number of alternative routes or places for today's youth have been so rapidly and markedly diminished. There is no simple solution to such complex problems as dropouts, but curriculum changes, such as special classes, remedial work, and language development, and the prevalence of middle-class values all suggest that the pupil needs success if he is to stay in school (Bristow, 1964). The pupil needs the success of being part of the school, i.e., being in school activities. He needs the success of human acceptance, and he needs to have nonpromotion and failure eliminated as a means of curriculum adjustment. He needs the success of passing grades, which can be awarded only when the learning material is appropriate to his background and ability.

The surge of popularity of programmed learning (see Chapter 18) is due—to a remarkable extent—to the confirmation of success, which is called "reinforcement."

Praise   Praise that is deserved is an incentive to effort at all life stages after the individual has acquired the ability to use language. It is not necessary that one practice deception in its use. The ability to praise is largely a matter of a personal orientation that causes one to see others clearly and to understand them. As soon as the teacher is able to perceive —in addition to academic achievement—humor, leadership, curiosity, in-dependence, artistic aptitudes, a ready smile, the ability to "bounce back," and other valuable human traits, he can begin to answer the needs for esteem, belongingness, and self-actualization. Some teachers chron-ically find occasions for criticism, while others take such joy in contacts with pupils that praise is almost second nature. Thus it is not surprising to find that the effectiveness of praise depends upon the person giving it (Schmidt, 1941). Intermittent comments are as effective as those given for every pupil action (Mech, Hurst, Auble, and Fattu, 1953). Teachers should note the effect of praise and blame on individual pupils. Some can be commended for relatively minor accomplishments because of their limited ability, while others will be motivated only by praise for genuinely noteworthy accomplishments related to their high ability. It should be noted that praise (or approval) can be indicated nonverbally—a nod, a smile, placing one's hand on the pupil's shoulders, or merely stopping long enough to take a good look at what is being done.

Blame or Reproof   Experimental evidence indicates that blame or reproof is a positive incentive in some cases. It is best to use it sparingly and when it is deserved, which involves knowing the individual upon whom it is used. Blame, when used on retiring students, appears to reinforce existing feelings of inadequacy and therefore dampens motivation. Extroverts, on the other hand, accomplish less when praised than when they are blamed. A possible explanation is that the self-actualizing person is less motivated by acceptance and esteem needs and more by what appears to be a genuine assessment of his progress toward self-fulfillment.

The successful use of praise or blame depends upon the student and his needs and prior experiences. The implication for teachers is that they should watch the effects of praise or blame on the individual student, the frequency with which each can be used, and their own feelings when each type of verbal reinforcement (see Glossary) is employed. It should be noted, in concluding the discussion of verbal reinforcement, that being ignored provides less motivation than either praise or blame. The need for recognition is active in most pupils.

Competition and Cooperation Rivalry is a potent incentive under certain conditions but can be destructive under others. It is not stimulating to either the winner or the loser to compete out of his class. Competitors should have some chance of winning; *competition should involve a degree of equality among contestants.* In athletics, this means leagues comprised of schools of the same size, varsity against varsity, class teams against class teams, and the like. Academically, when there is no ability grouping, the mental lightweights must compete against the mental heavyweights—in which case, it is difficult for either to achieve esteem and belongingness needs. Even when there is some equality of competitors, teachers should stress friendly rivalry rather than rivalry that breeds interpersonal antagonism. There are three kinds of effective rivalry:

1. Interpersonal competition among peers often encourages spirited rivalry.

2. Group competition where each member can make a contribution and is involved in the group's success is a strong motivator.

3. Competition with oneself, with one's previous record, can be effective and is highly recommended by mental hygienists.

The needs for self-actualization, for approval, for belongingness, and for safety indicate that cooperation, at least as a learned response, is as strong an incentive as is competition.[9] There are many who believe that society is "fiercely competitive" and that children must learn to compete

[9] Robert Ardrey, in *African Genesis,* New York: Atheneum Publishers, 1961, develops the thesis that a strong drive (instinct) is competition for territory. The drive exists among insects, fish, birds, and mammals, and is often more powerful than the sex drive.

ruthlessly in order to survive. Others point out that no society can afford indiscriminate competition because cooperation is the main function of society (Combs, 1959, p. 327).

The choice between cooperation and competition is largely a matter of the philosophical orientation of the teacher. Experiments show that individual achievement, as judged by the passing of tests, is fostered by both techniques. Competition provides excellent opportunities for learning to adjust to social realities (Symonds, 1951). Cooperation, involving skills from many pupils, should probably be emphasized more frequently, because the outcomes of such activity are more closely in accord with the stated purposes of education.

Knowledge of Progress   It has previously been stated that pupils should know the goals for which they are striving. It is desirable that pupils formulate their own goals, but if the goals are stated by curriculum committees, they should be accepted as personal goals by the learners. A corollary to the value of clear goals is that *pupils' knowledge of their progress is an extremely effective form of motivation.* In one experiment, fifth- and eighth-grade students who corrected their own papers and made charts of progress and were thus immediately informed of results showed marked and continued superiority over those who did not share in this activity (F. Brown, 1932). When students were given periodic opportunities for evaluating their work, they made higher test scores than those who did not follow this procedure (Duel, 1958).

A revealing incident regarding knowledge of progress concerns the work of a teacher who enjoyed a sound reputation in the community. She had been hired as a replacement for another teacher who, in the principal's estimate, was excellent—the pupils did well on standardized tests, behaved well, and seemed to enjoy school. But parents complained that the pupils were not learning. The replacement teacher seemed no more effective than the former, but parents were enthusiastic. Asked what the key to her success was, she answered, "I wonder if it is because the last few minutes each day I ask the pupils to discuss what we have learned today."

Among the advantages of machine teaching and programmed learning (see Chapter 18) is the pupil's immediate notification of success or failure (Holland and Skinner, 1961, p. 61). Other ways in which teachers may keep pupils informed of progress are praise or reproof and comments about specific ways to improve performance. Teacher-pupil conferences have been found to be particularly effective, especially at the upper-grade and secondary levels. Charts of progress can be used in many subjects. Workbooks, if not used too steadily and as busy work, tend to keep the student informed of his progress. Such techniques are advantageous because the time intervals between evaluations are short and tend to stress continuous evaluation rather than an end-of-term grade. In terms of basic needs, knowledge of progress capitalizes upon status, esteem, and self-actualization.

Novelty The drive toward self-actualization leads pupils to relish the new and the different. Their need for safety causes them to appreciate routine and regularity. Hence, novelty must be introduced in the context of the familiar. The motivation derived from visiting an industrial plant will be greater if the pupils are subject to familiar rules of order and courtesy or if the visit is made in company with their classmates and regular teacher—variety is the spice of life if the variety is not presented in a completely unfamiliar context. This may be observed when the teacher points out the relationship between the new and the already known, uses familiar procedures, and himself shows enthusiasm for the expansion of knowledge into new areas. Many previously indifferent pupils have been spurred to activity when the teacher's says, "I don't know the answer and we should know. Kathy, will you look it up for us, please?" Interest is often sustained or revived by variation in the teacher's technique. Incidentally, novelty may explain many instances in which an experimental technique seems superior to the older method—the variety, rather than the technique, is the motivator of extra effort.

Appropriate Tasks for Level of Aspiration The term "level of aspiration" refers to the degree of difficulty of a task or goal that the individual will accept and strive for. It is closely related to the concept an individual has about himself and his powers. The level of difficulty accepted is not only a motivating factor, but a result of preceding motivation (see Figure 16). That is, a child will attempt to dress himself if he has experienced some success and approbation from previous efforts at self-help. A pupil will attempt to make a report in social studies if he has been successful in previous participation and has developed some familiarity with reference materials. A freshman will attack algebra with confidence if he has found arithmetic within his grasp and has used it to solve problems. The teacher is largely responsible for designing the level of difficulty, but only the pupil can determine his level of aspiration. In Figure 16, if the pupil shown in *c* were to accept the task indicated, his level of aspiration would be inappropriate to his potential. If the child in *b* were to accept the task, his level of aspiration would only serve to intensify feelings of discouragement and defeat when the inevitable failure occurred. The importance of having the teacher find tasks of an appropriate level of difficulty has been demonstrated experimentally (Wenar, 1953).

There are four ways in which teachers can implement the principle that *goals should be attainable and pupils should feel that they are able to achieve them:*

1. Test data help the teacher to form a valid estimate of the pupil's potential and the appropriate goals.

2. The pupil's behavior provides clues: If the goal is too high, he will be tense or show withdrawal tendencies; if the goal is appropriate, he will proceed cheerfully and confidently to the job at hand.

3. A study of the child's past record (report cards and cumulative folders) provides information that helps the teacher to synchronize ability and aspiration.

4. The pupil should be allowed to voice his feelings about the appropriateness of the tasks.

Pupils should not work constantly at or near frustration levels, nor should they be allowed to get by simply because they reach age-grade standards. A succession of developmental lessons that will stimulate each child to work close to his *presently indicated* level of ability should be planned. A diversity of abilities and interests, rather than an attempt to make champions in arithmetic, language, drawing, tennis, or basketball because unusual capacity has been indicated, should be the aim. Teachers should make special efforts to prevent above-average and gifted chil-

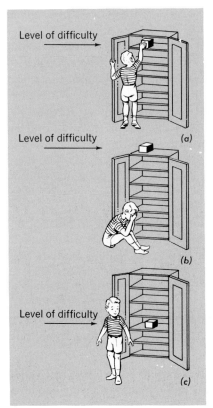

FIGURE 16. *Level of aspiration.*
(*a*) *By stretching slightly, the pupil can perform the task and accepts the challenge presented.*
(*b*) *The task is too difficult in terms of the ability of the child. There is no challenge. Forcing or pressure will cause him to leave the field by running away or by showing such traits as sullenness, anger, and disobedience.*
(*c*) *The task is too easy. The child responds by becoming bored or transferring attention to other pursuits. If he is forced to work at this level, he will do so with superficiality, boredom, and feelings of compulsion.*

dren from being satisfied with mediocrity. Appropriate praise, personally significant goals, the equitable distribution of success, and teacher-pupil evaluations can help in the establishment of appropriate levels of aspiration and urge pupils toward self-actualization.

The challenge of developmental tasks

The Concept of Developmental Tasks Prescott (1938), Frank (1952), and others (National Society for the Study of Education, 1953) who have called attention to basic needs have fanned into flame a revolutionary idea: *Effective educational programs are those that meet the needs of children and youth.* The idea that pupils should learn what adults consider necessary is giving way to the concept of needs, which makes the child the center of educational effort. This does not mean that the teacher should jump to meet the immediate whims and fancies of pupils. It means that pupil growth requires the satisfaction of basic needs just as plants require air, water, light, and balanced food to grow in a healthy manner.

Robert J. Havighurst (1953), working with the University of Chicago Committee on Human Development, is among those who have given impetus to another stimulating idea, that of "developmental tasks." Developmental tasks have their roots partly in basic and learned needs and partly in the demands of culture. The concept checks the tendency to study the individual apart from his environment and takes functional cognizance of the fact that one must live in a social world. A developmental task is a responsibility imposed by society and by growth phenomena and progressively demands more of the person. Instead of saying "Life is just one darn thing after another," it would be more accurate to say "Life is just one developmental task after another." That is, more and different things are required of a child than of a baby, more of an adolescent than of a child—even in one's declining years, new developmental tasks must be faced.

Developmental tasks are obligations that arise during a broadly defined period of life. The successful performance of these tasks leads to happiness and subsequent successful achievement; failure leads to personal unhappiness and disapproval by society, as well as to difficulty with later tasks. This concept has an advantage over the needs concept in several ways. It indicates the age at which particular demands become most insistent, and it draws attention to the requirements of society. It recognizes the individual's need for freedom and, at the same time, calls attention to the restraints of society.

Developmental Tasks as Motivation It is easy to conceive of motivation as something that propels or pushes an individual in a given direction.

But motivation may also be thought of as something that pulls a person toward a particular goal. Just as a plant growing in a partially darkened room will send its shoots toward the sources of light, so is the human drawn toward a particular objective or activity. This is not a new point of view. It has been referred to in this book in the references to purposeful and purposive behavior (see Glossary). The individual is striving toward something. It has been referred to elsewhere by the term "hormic" and "teleological" (Chaplin and Krawiec, 1960, p. 326). "Hormic" (from the Greek word *horme*) means purposive, and "teleological" means being directed toward an end. Hence, developmental tasks have rather clear motivational aspects. They have to do with the drives that are rooted in the individual's growing mind and body and with his adjustment to the demands of culture.

It is sometimes difficult to maintain respect for individual differences when one is oriented toward basic needs. It may appear that the motive of needs is common to all, but actually we know that not everyone is attracted to the same goal. Again, the concept of developmental tasks helps to maintain perspective. For example, in the materials below, it appears that developmental tasks differ somewhat in the various social classes of the overall American culture. Children from the extreme upper and extreme lower classes are not uniformly attracted to the same goals or moved by the same incentives as children from the middle class. The readiness of a pupil to undertake his next developmental tasks depends upon his previous experiences, including his social contacts; thus motivation will be easier for the teacher if he takes note of differences in native endowment, personal experience, and cultural pressures. In fact, education as a whole—not only motivation—is largely a matter of educational sequence (Klausmeier, 1953, p. 86), and desirably this sequence should be related to the sequence of developmental tasks.

Developmental Tasks of School Pupils　The completion of developmental tasks may be thought of as forward thrusts in growth. As each task is completed, the person may coast along rather easily on a plateau until his growth brings him to the next rise (or task) in his development (Havighurst, 1952, p. 120). In general it can be said that *the problem of motivation is simplified when the methods and approaches of the teacher accord with the biological, psychological, and cultural bases of the tasks.* The brief analysis of seven tasks of childhood and nine of adolescence, presented below, point out some of the educational implications.[10]

[10] For important details and additional significant educational implications, see Robert J. Havighurst, *Developmental Tasks and Education,* New York: Longmans, Green & Co., Inc., 1952. Data for this presentation used with permission of the publisher.

Developmental Tasks of Middle Childhood (about 6 to 12 years)

Learning Physical Skills for Games

Biological basis: Growth of bone and muscle and development of coordination.

Psychological basis: Sanction of peer group, which is becoming important.

Cultural basis: More is expected of boys than of girls from all social classes.

Curricular import: Ability grouping should help those having difficulty.

Building Wholesome Attitudes toward Self

Biological basis: Strength and physical appearance and glands condition the individual's acceptance by self and others.

Psychological basis: Approval by agemates largely depends on abilities.

Cultural basis: There is some variance between classes regarding habits of cleanliness and sexual experimentation and curiosity.

Curricular import: Teachers can aid by sociometric groupings and by health habits are part of the educational task.

Learning to Get Along with Peers

Biological basis: The development of physical skills and acceptable physique are fundamental to good relations with peers.

Psychological basis: Growth moves the child away from the family into the world of his peers.

Cultural basis: Lower-class children have somewhat more freedom than the middle-class children, who have greater parental control.

Curricular import: Teachers can aid by sociometric groupings and by knowing the functions and power of the peer group.

Learning an Appropriate Sex Role

Biological basis: There is little sex difference in the early part of middle childhood, but the later part shows clear distinctions.

Psychological basis: Parents, other key adults, and siblings have taught boys to behave as boys and girls to behave as girls. Parental identification is an important conditioning factor.

Cultural basis: A fighter is admired in lower social classes but the middle-class boy is expected to fight only in self-defense.

Curricular import: The school's function is mainly remedial, but it would help to have a greater proportion of male models (men teachers) in the early grades.

Learning to Read, Write, and Calculate

Biological basis: Growth processes provide a readiness (see Glossary) for these learning experiences.

Psychological basis: The peak of development in these skills is reached at about twelve or thirteen years of age.

Cultural basis: The middle-class parent demands a higher degree of development than the lower-class parent, but technological change is demanding a higher level of skills from all.

Curricular import: All kinds of motivational and teaching techniques must be used to bring more pupils closer to realization of their capacities.

Developing Concepts Necessary for Everyday Living

Biological basis: Mental maturation is necessary to comprehend abstractions.

Psychological basis: Concepts develop from earlier concrete experiences.

Cultural basis: Common concepts are space, high, fast—concepts having varied meanings for social classes are nurse, park, travel.

Curricular import: Concrete experiences can be provided by field trips to museums and industries, attendance at concerts, laboratory demonstrations, and exhibits.

Developing a Scale of Values

Biological basis: The assimilation and accommodation involved in a rational scale of values requires mental maturity (Piaget, 1952).

Psychological basis: Identification with parents is basic to the development of conscience (the warning voice of parents).

Cultural basis: There are great differences in the "rules" (morality) for various social classes.

Curricular import: The school assists in this task by direct teaching of morality, punishment and reward, the teacher's example, and providing opportunity for peer group experiences.

Developmental Tasks of Adolescence (about 12 to 18 Years)

Accepting Physique and Sex Role

Biological basis: Pubertal changes involving endocrines, sex organs, and sex characteristics set the task.

Psychological basis: A concern about normality and marked changes in interests and activities occur.

Cultural basis: Attitudes toward females vary with the current mode and social-class orientation of the individual.

Curricular import: Biology and health classes should emphasize the wide range of normality. Peer groups should provide practice in democratic processes.

New Relations with Peers of Both Sexes—Learning to Become Men and Women

Biological basis: The approach of sexual maturity sets the task.

Psychological basis: The individual actively tries to outgrow his parents, and group approval becomes of dominating importance.

Cultural basis: Attitudes toward sex experimentation and age of marriage vary widely between social classes.

Curricular import: The normality of sexual development can be taught in hygiene classes; student activities can provide contacts between the sexes; dancing and art classes can teach an appreciation of the human body.

Developing Emotional Independence from Parents

Biological basis: Growth in physical size, mental development, educational progress, and sexual maturity all contribute to this need.

Psychological basis: Adolescents experience ambivalance; they are torn between the desire to depend on and be independent of parents.

Cultural basis: The task is more difficult in middle classes than in upper and lower classes because of the desire for upward mobility in middle classes.

Curricular import: Parents as well as adolescents need instruction and counseling for the task. Teachers play a key role as adults who recognize the approaching adulthood of young people.

Achieving Assurance of Economic Independence

Biological basis: Havighurst claims no biological basis for this need, but the author believes it has a basis similar to that of the need for emotional independence.

Psychological basis: This is found in the desire to grow up, the symbol of which is the earning of income.

Cultural basis: The task is rather easily accomplished in lower classes, but the period of dependence is prolonged in the upper and middle classes.

Curricular import: Increased importance of general education in the technological world of today makes it incumbent upon the school to stress the value of the educative process and to make it attractive. Adolescents must be prepared for increasingly long periods of dependence.

Selecting and Preparing for an Occupation

Biological basis: The achievement of adult size and strength in the latter part of the period prepares the individual for the task.

Psychological basis: Social expectations and the adolescent's interests predispose him to occupational study and planning.

Cultural basis: The working role is *most* important in American society. The choice of a career is difficult in the upper and middle classes, but simply getting a job suffices in the lower class.

Curricular import: The school should (1) take responsibility for vocational guidance, (2) provide general education in a vocational setting, and (3) set higher academic standards for those choosing professions.

Developing Skills and Concepts for Civic Competence
Biological basis: The adult size of the brain and maturity of the nervous system provide the basis for this task.
Psychological basis: Individual differences pave the way for many approaches to civic contribution.
Cultural basis: Social expectations are strong in the upper and middle classes, but there is little pressure in the lower class.
Curricular import: Citizenship experiences can be provided through student activities, and the curriculum should include social studies, history, and contemporary problems.

Desiring and Achieving Socially Responsible Behavior
Biological basis: None—the basis is provided by the influence of society.
Psychological basis: The process of living binds the individual to his social group.
Cultural basis: There is much pressure for conformity from the upper and middle class but less from the lower.
Curricular import: The study of the nature and needs of the local community, the literature of the region and the nations, and the observance of traditional ceremonies all contribute to achievement of the task.

Preparing for Marriage and for Family Life
Biological basis: Sexual maturation provides the physical basis for the task.
Psychological basis: Attitudes toward marriage are greatly influenced by family experiences.
Cultural basis: The stability of marriage is conditioned by social class, with upper and middle classes having more stable, and lower classes marrying early and establishing unstable, unions.
Curricular import: Instruction, often avoided in the secondary school, should be provided on sex, courtship problems, and experiences with young children. Home-management problems should be introduced.

Building Values and Ethics Harmonious with Science
Biological basis: None.
Psychological basis: The more intelligent individuals have greater drive

to accomplish this task. It is conditioned by many, perhaps most, of life's experiences.

Cultural basis: Each society and each class is unique. In America the upper and middle classes accept scientific evidence, and the lower classes tend to ignore it.

Curricular import: The school should help to inculcate democratic values, provide practice in their use, and bring them into accord with contemporary scientific knowledge of man and his world.

The meaning and nurture of interest

The Nature of Interest Interest may be defined as the focusing of the sense organs on or giving attention to some person, activity, situation, or object. It may be a temporary or permanent feeling in which a preference is present. It is an outcome of experience—not a gift—and is at one time both result and cause of motivation. Too many teachers look only for the presence or absence of interest and condemn the student whose interest is low or lacking. When teachers recognize that interest stems from personally challenging tasks and some degree of success in their pursuit, they will assume some responsibility for its creation and development. Strong interest creates a drive that will lead to organization of efforts in the consistent seeking of a goal. The strength of such drive is partly dependent upon endocrine functioning, physical stamina, and endurance, but it is also dependent on experiences that have resulted in some need satisfaction. Teachers should also remember that interest is conditioned by groups, such as the family and peers, in which the pupil functions away from school (Carsley, 1957).

When teachers "make a subject interesting," they present the action or study in terms of the pupils' personal orientation (needs). A seventh-grade teacher working on a unit on China illustrates the sequences. She brought to class a record of Chinese music, some trinkets, a jewel, a brass bell, some lanterns, and a silk robe. After her oral presentation, the pupils were allowed to look at and handle the materials. Many questions were asked, some of which were answered by other pupils and some by the teacher with "We'll see." Pupils told about Chinese objects they had at home—some had been sent or brought back by older siblings or relatives who had traveled overseas. Plans for developing the unit were discussed (personal involvement), and various projects were suggested. Some of the projects would require considerable reading and research. The difficult projects held the possibility of high grades and were to be presented before the class as a whole. Not all the pupils undertook to do the more difficult tasks. Some were quite content to work on foil facsimiles of jewel boxes. Others made lanterns. The more ambitious pupils read encyclopedias and advanced reference books in preparing reports on the economic and social conditions of coastal China. All the students participated in some way in the final project, which consisted of a Chinese dinner to which parents and friends were invited and at which the local Chinese consul was the speaker. Any observer would have been struck by the sincerity and application of all the pupils. Reference materials for the unit ranged from books that could be read by average second graders to books that would have been respectable sources for a college student. On three visits, the author noticed one boy copying a wall chart. According to the teacher, the boy had still not learned to read, but found satisfaction in his responsibility for copying a sign that was to be placed over one of the displays at the dinner.

The Influence of Goals Without goals, man can and often does wander aimlessly in life. Many diversions and temporarily attractive activities interfere with self-actualization. Because goals give direction to action, they must be of genuine concern to educational psychology. Pupils' perceptions and acceptance of goals are thus central problems in education.

> In the course of an individual's growth and development and as a product of his experience with the world around him, certain aspects of the perceptual field become more or less clearly differentiated from the remainder of the field because they satisfy need. These differentiations are called goals. Thus, certain objects, feelings, or events become differentiated as more or less related to the satisfaction of the basic need for a more adequate self. The newborn infant has few if any goals beyond the extremely undifferentiated one of maintaining organization. In time, however, with the differentiation of certain objects, persons, and sounds, which accompany the satisfaction of his basic need, his goals become more clearly defined. In time, the goals differentiated by a particular individual may become permanent and characteristic parts of his personality.[11]

Much of the teacher's effectiveness depends on his own perception of educational goals and his ability to clarify them for pupils. *There should be less emphasis on the child's pleasing the teacher and more on the formulation of goals that accord with the child's needs* (Swenson, 1950, p. 257). This involves knowing the characteristics of pupils, their interests, their understandings, and their basic drives.

The need for status and esteem suggests another effective approach to motivation in goal setting—enlisting pupil participation. This does not mean that pupils will state the objectives of learning; but it does mean that they are going to *help* state them. Pupil discussion will help clarify goals because they are then stated in terms understandable to pupils.

[11] Arthur W. Combs and Donald Snygg, *Individual Behavior*, rev. ed., New York: Harper & Row, Publishers, 1959, p. 102.

Giving attention to individual differences implies that there should be a wide variety of goals rather than the single goal of subject-matter mastery. Goals increase the probability that one will navigate rather than drift. Goals influence the degree to which one will pursue individual aims and values and the extent to which he will be responsive to group needs and wishes. Goals help in evaluating the relative importance or unimportance of alternative activities. They lend power to ongoing activities. But the goals must be clear to be most effective. Teacher-pupil planning is relatively ineffective if the plans are filed away only to be brought out when the supervisor visits. *There must be periodic reexamination of the extent to which goals are being realized and plans for the next steps toward their achievement.* Should any teacher feel that this is a time-consuming process, let him answer the question; How much time is wasted in trying to force pupils to reach teacher goals that are neither understood nor accepted? (See the example of Timothy, Chapter 1.) Establishing and keeping in mind a number of goals is not easy, but neither is growing to effective maturity a simple accomplishment.

Individual Differences   The important subject of individual differences is dealt with elsewhere in our study. Basic needs are common to all pupils; however, there are differences in their intensity, due to degrees of prior satisfaction. The degree of satisfaction depends on varied experiences and varied capacities. Needs differ in their intensity at different ages; they also vary with the cultural conditioning of the child (see Chapter 16). The same observations are pertinent when motivation is viewed from the viewpoint of developmental tasks.

If the teacher understands differences between pupils, uses materials that are appropriate to these differences, and permits each child some freedom for growth toward his unique self-actualization, he is providing the basis for immediate and effective motivation (B. F. Brown, 1963). More important still, he will be providing the kind of motivation that leads the pupil repeatedly to the fountain of knowledge.

Summary

It is generally believed that man has potentials far greater than he has realized. The explanation for this lack of realization is inadequate motivation—one of the most pervasive challenges that teachers face. Motivation can be improved by devising educational processes that will aid in the fulfillment of basic and acquired needs. Many lists of needs have been formulated, and most lists include such things as physiological satisfaction, security, achievement, recognition or status, the need to love and be loved, and mastery or self-actualization.

A helpful concept of needs has been devised by Maslow, who postulates a sequential hierarchy of needs. As low-order needs approach fulfillment, a higher order of needs assumes priority. From low to high, these needs are physiological, safety, belongingness and love, esteem, and the need for self-actualization. They all suggest procedures that teachers may employ.

The use of rewards, incentives, praise, censure, competition, and cooperation can be made more effective in motivation if they are thought of in terms of the needs being satisfied—or blocked. As teachers come to know pupils and their special needs, they can be instrumental in establishing appropriate levels of aspiration.

The concept of developmental tasks also has practical implications for motivation in school. These tasks are aspects of development successively faced by individuals as they live and grow. The tasks have their roots in physical growth, psychological development, and cultural conditioning; thus in a very real sense, they consider the child as a whole. There are many ways in which teachers can aid, through what they are and how they teach, in children's task achievement.

The individual is not endowed with interests; they develop as the result of contact, familiarity, personal challenge, and the experience of success. The teacher can implement the growth of interest by being enthusiastic, clarifying goals, and giving attention to individual differences. To the extent that teachers are successful in stimulating the development of interest, they assist pupils in becoming self-actualizing.

Problems and exercises

1 What are some physiological needs with which teachers might occasionally be concerned?

2 In groups of two or three, discuss ways in which self-actualizing needs might be met by teachers themselves.

3 What are some implications of the statement "A teacher cannot make a subject interesting?"

4 Do you think that a formal statement of goals should be written on the board? Or would it be more pertinent to make a record of them for each child?

5 Does the assertion that the key to motivation lies in attention to individual differences mean that no generalization can be safely made about motivation? Give illustrations to support your answer.

6 What are some of the ways in which pupils view grades and marks? Take a sample of views from your own class group.

7 What are some of the advantages of viewing motivation in the light of developmental tasks?

8 How might the teacher aid adolescents to achieve the task of becoming emotionally independent of parents?

9 Account for the development of one of your strong interests and suggest some implications your case might have for teachers.

Suggested additional readings

Brown, Judson S.: *The Motivation of Behavior,* New York: McGraw-Hill Book Company, 1961, pp. 138–193.
Modern man, with small likelihood of suffering from hunger, thirst, or prolonged pain, finds that most of his motivation springs from learning and acculturation. In this chapter, "Learned Responses as Sources of Drive," the author deals with fear, anxiety, goals, verbal stimuli, and conditioning as motivators.

DeHaan, Robert F., and Jack Kough: *Helping Children with Special Needs,* Chicago: Science Research Associates, Inc., 1956.
There are editions of this booklet for both elementary and secondary teachers. Not only are the special needs of handicapped pupils discussed, but there are sections on procedures to be used with varied and specific talents.

Eiserer, Paul E., and Stephen M. Corey: "How Youth Learn to Meet Their Needs," *Adapting the Secondary-school Program to the Needs of Youth,* Fifty-second Yearbook of the National Society for the Study of Education, Chicago: The University of Chicago Press, 1953, part I, pp. 44–61.
Problems of motivation, learning, and appropriate behavior are discussed from the standpoint of how pupils view them. Many practical suggestions are given.

Havighurst, Robert J.: *Development Tasks and Education,* 2d. ed., New York: Longmans, Green & Co., Inc., 1952.
This book deals with some little-recognized factors in learning, especially the impact of social classes. Biological factors are given unusual recognition. Implications for education are challengingly presented.

Maslow, A. H.: *Motivation and Personality,* New York: Harper & Row, Publishers, 1954, pp. 63–122.
In the three chapters indicated, the author presents propositions that he feels must be incorporated into motivation theory, describes the needs that are back of motivation, and shows how need gratification leads to learning, health, and personality integration.

Rethlingshafer, Dorothy: *Motivation as Related to Personality,* New York: McGraw-Hill Book Company, 1963, pp. 318–340.
The chapter "Motivation and Learning" presents some of the experimental bases for effecting motivation in the schools.

Emotional Aspects of Education

12

It seems highly probable that the teacher's and pupils' ability to understand, control, and direct emotions would be the single most productive factor in vastly improving learning efficiency. The anonymous individual who said that "the intellect is a mere speck afloat upon a sea of feeling" was a wise psychologist. As teachers, we should realize that much, perhaps most, human behavior is instigated and sustained by emotion. We should like to believe that man's action is directed by thought processes—that his behavior is rational. But an examination of the evidence leads inevitably to the conclusion that emotion is a dominating factor. Kubie presents an intriguing challenge in asserting that man's brain is far more capable of solving problems than we can yet imagine. The reason why we have not made better use of latent capacity, why we use only a small fraction of our potential, is that "almost from birth we are continuously blocked by conflict among internal factions" (Kubie, 1956).

The teacher who recognizes the partnership of emotion and reason has taken a large step toward accomplishing the basic objectives of education. Such a teacher will consciously aim at greater emotional maturity for schoolchildren at all levels (Patterson, 1952). Briefly stated, this maturity will consist of (1) inhibition of emotions that deter development, (2) cultivation of higher tolerance for disagreeable circumstance and conflict, and (3) enhancement of the emotions that facilitate social and intellectual efficiency.

The nature of emotion

The Meaning of Emotion   Some psychologists would like to get rid of the word "emotion," believing that it is vague and relatively meaningless—as is the word "instinct"—in that it covers a multitude and variety of conditions. Specifically, "emotion" may mean the upset conditions of hate or fear in which physiological functioning prepares for fight or flight. These emotions may lead to harm or destruction of self or others. On the other hand, "emo-

271

tion" may mean the positive conditions of love and ambition. Physiological functioning in these emotions leads to a feeling of euphoria, which in turn may lead to the improved welfare of self and others. "Emotion" may mean a rather transitory state, such as brief attention, or an enduring interest that drives an individual toward a difficult goal. It may mean a relatively mild feeling, such as friendliness toward a peer; an intense feeling, such as a paralyzing fear during a flood or bombing; or even the chronic anxiety produced by threat of school failure.

Emotion is more than overt activity, though it is largely upon overt activities that evaluations of emotion are based. The important factor is the inner feeling that stimulates a certain activity or creates a predisposition to engage in the activity. There is a frequently cited, though oversimplified, definition: Emotion is a feeling state (affective experience) accompanying an upset condition of the organism: It is a stirred-up state of the mental and physical aspects of the individual.

To the teacher, this means that pupils should be helped to control emotions that are detrimental to progress and enhance emotions that are constructive. Teachers are important members of the "health professions" that seek to develop high-level "wellness." The common aim of teachers, physicians, and those in the mental health professions is more than bringing about a freedom from illness; it is to promote ways of living that will maximize the chances for the individual to achieve his potential (Kaufmann, 1963). To fulfill this dynamic function, the teacher must know how emotions affect the lives and learning of pupils so that he may more steadily help them to move forward to higher levels of functioning.

Physiological Aspects of Emotion   W. B. Cannon (1929) has formulated what is sometimes known as the emergency theory of emotions. He theorized that emotion has certain physiological aspects which prepare the individual to meet an emergency. These physiological responses include the release of adrenin, or adrenalin (a hormone secreted by the adrenal glands), into the blood stream. This causes an increased rate in heartbeat, raises the blood pressure, causes more rapid respiration and constriction of the blood vessels on the surface of the body, makes possible the more rapid coagulation of blood if there is a cut or wound. The flow of digestive juices is inhibited. These reactions prepare one for fight or flight to cope with the emergency.

These physiological changes do not cause the emotion—though they are a part of the emotion. Researchers have injected adrenin into the blood stream of experimental subjects and reported that some subjects experienced a variety of emotions, others felt no emotion at all, while the remainder said they felt that they were about to have an emotional experience (Cantril, 1932). Thus it becomes evident that a situation is necessary to precipitate the emotion.

It is believed that these physiological responses were a great advantage to man at some time in his history. They prepared him for vigorous action, thus aiding his survival. But it is doubtful that these responses are such an advantage to man in civilized society. In fact, in view of the restrictions placed by society and culture on the actions that might result from these responses, such emotions are unhealthful. For instance, when one becomes angry and cannot burn up the extra energy made available to him because present-day custom does not permit getting rid of emotions through violent conflict, a kind of poison is created in his system. Hence, physical and mental health hazards are involved in repressing emotional reactions.

It is obvious that emotional states cannot be ignored. Emotions are conditioning the pupil's responses, whether we wish it or not. We must act upon the knowledge that fear and anger are handicaps to effective learning. Thus we see the physiological justification for avoiding anger-producing shaming and sarcasm. Fear of crucial examinations or punishment should be replaced by more positive means of motivation. Anxiety about status generated by discrimination or by failure to live up to expectations may compound learning problems.

The daily practitioner of educational psychology will seek to understand the nature and extent of the emotions that the child brings to school from outside sources. This will involve a knowledge of home and community relations. If the pupil is worried about family problems, his emotional state will inhibit learning; he may appear to be mentally slow or seem to lack motivation to do the work of which he is capable (Haring and Phillips, 1962, p. 68). The teacher may be helpful by showing the pupil another way of looking at the problems or handicaps. He may arrange a conference with parents to explain the emotional burdens placed on the child.

In the past, emphasis in the school has been placed on acquiring knowledge and skill. At present, attention is given to the development of the "whole child." This does not mean that a choice need be made between knowledge and the child; it is a matter of recognizing that learning proceeds more effectively when pupils are not emotionally disturbed. Guidance in personality adjustment is an integral part of instruction. Research shows that emphasis on meeting the emotional needs of pupils improves their learning (Christensen, 1960). Among pupils who have minor personality disturbances, it has been found that the amount of reading gain was proportional to the gain achieved in emotional adjustment (Bills, 1950).

The Piling Up of Stimuli Stimuli that produce emotion have a cumulative effect. The barking of a dog may not bother us at first, but as the barking continues, we become increasingly irritated. The ebullient energy of children may be gratifying to the teacher early in the day, but the energetic child may be a source of irritation in the afternoon. Similarly, children may be only slightly bothered at first by the insistence of the teacher that they accomplish more in reading, arithmetic, or algebra, but as the pressure continues, their resentment and hostility mount. Pupils may at first be able to cope with the strident demands of an autocratic teacher, but they often find it increasingly difficult to contain their emotion as the demands continue. In counseling sessions when the pupil recalls all the unpleasant things in school, at home, or with peers, this piling up is called the "accumulation of negative experiences."

The film *The Other Fellow's Feelings* [1] shows this cumulative effect in the classroom. An adolescent girl dropped a bottle of perfume. A boy held his nose and then decided to have some fun by calling the girl "Stinky." For a period of time, both in and out of school, the boy held his nose or repeated the appellation. The teacher noted a falling off in the girl's work, but an interview with her did not disclose the difficulty. Finally, the girl broke out in tears while trying to recite in class. Minor disturbing influences finally assumed major proportions.

Two suggestions for the teacher can be made. First, minor irritations can be detected by "feedback." This may be accomplished by periodic questionnaires that allow students to check the things they like or dislike about a class or teacher. Typically, these are anonymous. This will not work in the primary grades, but intermediate- and upper-grade pupils make surprisingly incisive evaluations. Brief diaries submitted periodically may focus upon feelings aroused in class activities. Oral gripe sessions may pinpoint some irritations if the teacher can avoid becoming defensive or punitive because of pupils' frankness. Steps may then be taken to remove or reduce the sources of irritation. Second, teachers may help pupils take a different attitude toward the disturbing influences through group discussions and individual conferences. School practices that deserve consideration in this connection include overemphasis on grades, competition that involves unequally matched contestants, class sessions requiring pupils to sit still for prolonged periods, class sessions in which there is distracting noise or inadequate lighting, and demand for immediate and strict obedience.

There is also a positive side to cumulative effect of emotional stimuli. Small daily satisfactions that derive from accomplishment may serve to establish enduring interests. Much of the success of programmed learning, in which the pupil gets "reward" for correct answers on brief bits of material, is attributed to this piling up of small satisfactions (Suppes, 1964). The assurance that one is accepted by the group can fortify him for meeting instances in which he encounters hostility. Daily acts of kindness on the part of the teacher will help pupils to accept firm handling of undesirable behavior. Moreover, emotional maturity will be

[1] *The Other Fellow's Feelings,* Young America Films, Inc. (10 minutes, black and white, sound).

achieved through this slow piling up of mild and pleasant emotions. Emotional immaturity indicates that disintegrative emotions have accumulated too rapidly for the individual to absorb.

The Genesis of Disruptive Emotions Not all disruptive emotions and their causes can be discussed here. Some of the more obvious ones are dealt with, but they are indicative rather than inclusive.

Teachers need to appreciate the influence of physical condition upon emotions. Some children are inadequately fed before coming to school and are disposed to temper tantrums. Others may be irritable because of a headache that results from defective and uncorrected vision, and irritability may also be a symptom of an illness such as mumps. Children are likely to become angry when they are tired, ill, sleepy, or hungry (Jersild, 1960, p. 290); thus it would be well for teachers to make a special effort to remain calm just before lunchtime and just before the close of the school day.

Pupils may be irritable because of tension between their parents. Their uncertainty at home may make them less confident at school, with the result that they are less competent than they might be otherwise. An autocratic father or mother may have made difficult demands at home. The tension is released by a tirade against a classmate who the child knows will not fight back. Perhaps he has found that he can vent hostility upon the teacher. The good teacher is aware of these factors in the development of disruptive emotions, and instead of demanding the respect that is "due his position," he begins to wonder what is behind the pupil's hair-trigger emotions.

There is the possibility that susceptibility to disruptive emotions is due to innate differences. The delicate child may have more difficulty in achieving emotional control than those who are physically robust. Children with a sensory defect or glandular imbalance may have a lower tolerance for upsetting stimuli than normal children. Whatever the reasons, it must be realized that each child has his own unique threshold for dealing with problems (Lynn, 1960).

School conditions may be factors in the genesis of disruptive emotions. Children who are enrolling in a particular school for the first time are under emotional strain. The frequent rigidity of curricular demands are mentioned in educational and psychological literature. The practice of threatening school failure is gradually disappearing as a result of experimental findings of mental hygiene and psychology ("Ten Criticisms of Public Education," 1957, p. 152).

The Genesis of Constructive Emotions Interest, affection, friendliness, respect for individuality, and humor bring about constructive emotions. The emotional atmosphere of the home and the school is important. Bodily predisposition to experience enjoyment comes through proper diet, sleep in adequate amounts, balance between rest and exercise, and the correction of sensory difficulties. The school experiences of the pupil should be gratifying. He should receive understanding and help in his peer relationships. Some attention should be given to special interests that have become or are becoming a part of his personality.

Dealing with some disruptive emotions

Although it is not possible to distinguish sharply between salutary and upsetting emotions on the basis of the physiological processes involved, there is a difference in their effect. Fear produces the same endocrine effects as love; but extreme fear inhibits action, interferes with digestion, and makes the person feel ill, while love stimulates activity, aids digestion, and produces a feeling of well-being. Hence, the aim in dealing with upsetting emotions is to reduce or eliminate them. The aim in dealing with constructive emotions is to enhance their effect.

Anxiety It is probable that the negative, handicapping emotion most often present in the classroom is extreme anxiety. However, there is no clear-cut evidence that all degrees or forms of anxiety should be eliminated, even if it were possible to do so. The problem is to achieve some balance between anxieties that have positive motivational value and anxieties that render the individual incapable or less capable of achieving somewhat in accord with his indicated potentials.

Just as the practical implications of anxiety are equivocal, so too is the meaning of the word. One cannot be sure just where anxiety becomes fear or where productive anxiety intensifies to become stultification. One cannot be sure whether "anxiety" means a chronic and generalized condition or a specific and temporary emotion. The effect of anxiety in different individuals is similarly uncertain.

As used here, anxiety refers to a painful unrest of the mind involving apprehension or foreboding in relation to what is impending or anticipated. Anxiety is the response to a subjective danger, while fear is a response to objective danger (Jersild, 1960, p. 270). This differentiation is related to the idea that anxiety is produced by a threat to the ego, by something that is perceived as limiting one's self-realization (Goldstein, 1952). Finally, anxiety is a response (fearful in nature) that is out of proportion to reality. Thus one pupil may become handicappingly anxious about a given test when others realize that the result will constitute only a part of the final evaluation; e.g., most colleges will make exceptions to a "cutting score" on achievement or aptitude test batteries.

Several theories are designed to explain the arousal of anxiety. Freud (1936) suggests that anxiety is generated if the child, who is dependent on his parents for care and protection, is separated from them, if they are separated from each other, or if they quarrel or fight, which seems to him to presage separation. Anxiety also may arise when the child's need for instinctual gratification conflicts with environmental demands (cultural expectations), according to Freud. Chronic anxiety, according to Horney (1945), stems from an environment that is inconsistent, unjust, or harsh—one in which there is a limitation of opportunity to grow in self-reliance. Any of three "strategies" may be used as a defense. One may move *with* people by being meek and self-effacing, he may move *against* people by being aggressive and competitive, or he may move *away* from others by becoming withdrawn or aloof. These behaviors, of course, often compound his problems of adjustment. Sullivan (1948) believed that anxiety has its roots in the interpersonal relations of parents and child. Anxious and self-rejecting parents are likely to cause the child, through empathy and imitation, to develop similar characteristics. Such parents have low opinions of themselves and doubt their ability to succeed in any situation, especially a new one. Their child tends to develop such self-doubt. Self-rejecting parents are so dissatisfied with themselves, and thus with their lot, that they preach dissatisfaction with the world. They may attempt to compensate for their own inadequacies by insisting on greater accomplishment from their child than can objectively be expected, and thus goals for the child are always so much higher than his present achievement that he develops anxiety about his performance and potential.

O. H. Mowrer (1960) stresses the idea of a distinction between overt, instrumental responses that help the individual control his environment and emotional responses that cause him to expect or prepare for response. Anxiety is included in the latter group, since the anxious individual is alerted and sensitive to stimulations. *Mild anxiety thus facilitates the acquisition of new responses, but intense anxiety narrows the perceptual field and impairs constructive responses.*

It is apparent from the foregoing that the causes of anxiety are general. Anxiety is an individual response and does not necessarily follow from a specific kind of situation; for example, frequently only one of two siblings who receive much the same parental treatment will become ridden by anxiety. Anxiety is an inevitable aspect of living when one must adjust to social expectations. In mild forms, anxiety is an aid; in severe forms it is a handicap to adjustment. The handicapping forms can to some extent be reduced or avoided by consistent rules, clear-cut but kindly authority, and interpersonal relations in which emotional conflict is minimal.

Anxiety in the classroom Mild anxiety functions in a positive manner for some learning, but severe and very low anxiety seem to retard learning. Reed (1960) found that studies of the relationships between anxiety and competent schoolwork reveal that "middle" anxiety is more favorable than extremely low or extremely high anxiety. This is not a consistent finding because apparently there are age differences, sex differences, and individual perceptual differences that condition the existence and impact of anxiety (Di Vesta, 1961).

Although anxiety typically refers to a chronic characteristic, motivation from anxiety can be modified by control of situational factors. Reassuring instructions improved the performance of high-anxious pupils, but seemed to impair performance of low-anxious pupils in a complex learning task (Sarason, 1958). This suggests that the teacher observe and learn how individuals respond to given instructional methods. However, some general guides are available. Because anxiety consists of apprehension about the future, it follows that in learning new and difficult material stress-producing methods should be avoided. On the other hand, there is greater likelihood that stress will have value in the familiar and less difficult situations (Castaneda, Palermo, and McCandless, 1956).

Anxiety may stem from sources beyond the school. English children showed higher test anxiety than equivalent groups of American children. This is attributed to the greater importance of examinations in tracking or streaming (see Appendix) in England (Sarnoff, 1958). The cultural origins of anxiety are also shown in the Yearbook of the Association for Supervision and Curriculum Development, *Growing Up in an Anxious Age* (1952).

As an important interpreter of the culture, the teacher needs to set a good example by being aware of and controlling apprehensions of his own that have dubious bases. Further, group counseling shows that it is possible to reduce anxieties through discussion (see Chapter 15). Anxiety about examinations might be allayed by giving them frequently enough and assigning them a proper place in the total evaluation scheme so that no one examination becomes crucial. In fact, examinations can be used as a learning device if the papers are returned immediately and the answers discussed, and the same examination may be given again after the questions and answers have been explained. These steps, plus not permitting too much to hang on one score, can help to overcome "test neuroses." Guidance in developing study skills, as well as social and personal guidance, can enhance an individual's confidence that he can meet the problems of life as they are encountered. Certainly, the acquisition of knowledge and its by-product of building ego concept will be helpful in keeping anxiety at a productive level.

To the extent that anxiety is a generalized trait, confidence in one area gives the individual a sense of self-sufficiency that will spread to other activities. A pupil's success on the playground will help him show confidence in the classroom. His ability to roller skate will encourage him to learn to ride a bicycle. One teacher had noted that an academically inept sixth grader did not show hesitancy about reciting. One day he asked the boy how it happened that he had so much assurance in class. The boy's answer was "I know that I'm not very good in arithmetic and language, but I can always win the other kids' marbles."

Tactics that reduce self-confidence, such as shaming, ridiculing, or ignoring, should be avoided not only for the reduction of nonproductive anxiety but for mental health in general.

Fear   One of the most common disruptive emotions is fear—the tendency to run away from or avoid certain situations. It is closely related to anxiety but is more intense and specific. There is less likelihood that the individual can live successfully with fear than with anxiety. Hence the teacher should be alert to the manifestation of fear—fear of certain classmates, of examinations, of the teacher himself. Many fears are irrational, but—as in the case of anxiety—they cannot be explained away. Ignoring fear, ridiculing the pupil for being afraid, and forcing him into the fear-producing situation (swimming or reciting before an audience) will do more harm than good (Jersild, 1960, p. 282). The confidence and support of the teacher, the development of skills, and the enhancement of feelings of worth are all small steps in the right direction. The positive steps are finding the cause of the fear, setting a good example in the presence of the feared situation, providing some enjoyable accompaniments parallel to the fear-inducing situation (emphasize the personal or class achievement of a public recitation), praising the willingness to try despite fear, and providing practice of skills (pretending) designed to cope with the fear.

The major distinction between anxiety and fear is that the former is general and is related to a subjective danger. Fear is a response to an objective situation and is specific. The antidotes are quite similar in both cases, and the suggestions for diminishing anxiety are pertinent for the control of fear. For example, techniques employed to enhance ego concepts will diminish both fear and anxiety.

Aggression   Another emotional response that is almost as common as anxiety in the classroom is aggression. Typically, aggressive or hostile behavior is the result of frustration; thus teachers will profit from knowing the psychological origins of frustration and something about how to avoid it.

Frustration results from the thwarting of a motive—the more or less complete blocking of activity directed toward a goal. It is related to conflict (a normal clash between incompatible aims or desires) but, as the term is used here, frustration stems from opposition of impulses more formidable than is the case in normal, surmountable, on-going conflict; it is the underlying threat of frustration that makes conflict stressful (Coleman, 1960, p. 152). The reaction to frustration varies: In some cases the individual retreats, withdraws, ceases to struggle; in other cases, he attacks people or things about him. The problem presented to teachers is twofold—to reduce the chronic conflict situations that can be influenced, or to aid the pupil in finding healthful ways of expressing aggression.

Aggressiveness may be perceived in attacks on persons (especially children so small that the aggressor is "safe") and property, swearing, talking back to teachers, asking persistent bothersome questions, blaming others for difficulties. We should also recognize displaced aggression—venting hostility on objects or persons other than the cause of the frustration; destruction of school property is the obvious example. Just as little is resolved by an angry parent's spanking his child, so too is little accomplished by the teacher's taking direct action. The immediate situation may be controlled, but the underlying feeling, which may not be an outcome of the immediate situation, remains to break out at another time or place.

A school situation contributing to the origin of aggression is maintenance of grading standards that place unrealistic demands for achievement on pupils with less-than-average intelligence—competition (for grades) between those who are unequal. Also, many pupils become aggressive when their home backgrounds are such that the school's social demands (courtesies, dress, behaviors) conflict with what they have previously learned.[2] Certainly we cannot ignore the patterns of parental behavior and the treatment of children (regardless of social class) as one of the sources of aggression that the pupil carries into the classroom. One of the common responses to a punitive, aggressive parent, especially the mother, is aggression expressed in delinquency (Young, 1956). Teachers can bring their own frustrations—from marital discord, thwarted ambitions, indebtedness, and illness—into the classroom and be guilty of aggression toward pupils. Some teachers—like people in general—express their aggressions readily, while others have learned to control its manifestations. Some have learned to displace aggressive tendencies in hobbies or leisure-time pursuits. The point is that teachers themselves should not be overlooked as a factor in the aggression of pupils. Finally, we should not minimize the fact that, despite the expressed ideal to the contrary, discrimination against various ethnic groups is all too common; it tends to arouse feelings of hostility and aggression and at the same time makes the victim feel guilty and unworthy.

That aggression may be reduced by removal of its causes is implied in the description of the causes; let us turn now to constructive ways in which aggression may be expressed. Play therapy has been employed to

[2] See Chap. 16 for a description of differences between various social classes in attitudes toward school attendance, school marks, sex experimentation, observance of the law, age of marriage, age of beginning work, etc.

relieve aggressions of seriously disturbed children. In such therapy they may throw, step on, smash, squeeze, and twist toys and dolls. There is no "Tsk, tsk. Nice children don't do such things." It is realized that such aggressive responses and releases precede more constructive behavior. Play therapy is not a classroom technique, but substitutes are available. Children can be encouraged to express their hostilities in themes and stories of violence. One seventh-grade boy was preoccupied with drawing scenes of death and destruction—shooting, knifing, bombing, and car and train wrecks. The teacher masked her concern with the persistence of this theme, and toward the end of the school year, the pupil changed rather abruptly. The pictures of violence became less frequent and greatly subdued. He worked much harder on school tasks. It was fortunate that the teacher had recognized the need for him to work off hostilities before emphasizing academic tasks.

Much can be accomplished in a counseling situation. Some teachers take time after school to let the aggressive child talk out his difficulties. It should be understood that the purpose is to let the pupil vent his feelings. The pupil will stop telling how he perceived the provocation or will cease describing his feelings if teachers say, "You shouldn't feel that way," "He didn't mean to hurt you," or "Here's a better way of handling the situation." Help can be given in the *ventilation process* by really listening—trying to understand instead of getting a word in. Ask a brief question to clarify the point, look at the pupil, say "I see." Much aggression will be sidetracked if he comes to know that someone cares, will listen, and is trying to understand. In dealing with aggression and with symptoms of other problems, the teacher should admit that some cases are puzzling and seek the counsel of other teachers, counselors, and supervisors and administrators (Rubinfeld, 1962). To try to conceal one's own bafflement is to run the risk of precipitating his own aggression toward the pupil.

Group counseling provides an avenue for the release of aggression. Six underachieving high school boys were being observed by counselor trainees. They were in their fifth session when one lad became particularly obnoxious—he interrupted others, snorted at the observations of the counselor, made sarcastic and belittling remarks to the other boys, and criticized teachers. Two trainees later remarked that they would have "straightened him out." The counselor, however, ignored the disrupter. At the close of the session he asked for a summary. Two or three boys said, "Let Steve do it." At the next session, Steve was a much more constructive participant. We cannot be sure just what the dynamics of the situation were. It can be guessed that Steve had worked off some of his hostilities and that his peers controlled him much better than an authority person could have. This appears likely because it is adult authority against which adolescents often rebel.

Athletic participation, especially in contact sports such as football, wrestling, and boxing, is regarded as an acceptable avenue for working off aggressions. For this reason, strong emphasis upon varsity teams at the cost of extensive, inclusive, intramural programs is questioned from the standpoint of sound psychology. The emphasis on intramural programs and the classification of competitors by size and age is much better. In this situation, those who are failing (one symptom of emotional difficulty) are still given the opportunity to displace their aggressions.

Other aspects of the curriculum may be employed to displace aggressions. As suggested above, art classes and art activities can provide the opportunity for release through painting and drawing. The stories and themes written in English classes can serve the double purpose of learning self-expression and providing for the verbal release of aggression. Pounding and molding clay or whittling and carving wood—both calling for muscular energy—can be used in much the same manner as play therapy. Some feel that reading provides a release for many emotions, including aggression (Hutt and Gibby, 1957, p. 416).

Prejudice Substantial numbers of pupils in our schools are Negroes, Mexicans, Puerto Ricans, or Jews, and there is no denying that they are frequently the recipients of prejudicial treatment not only by other pupils but also by teachers. Factors outside the school may originate or encourage the attitudes underlying such treatment. For example, for the past decade newspapers have headlined various incidents that have attended attempts at integration of Negroes in the schools; it is not a problem that can be resolved within the school alone, but progress can be and is being made. But even pupils who have had favorable experiences with a minority group may still develop anti-Negro or anti-Mexican bias because to do otherwise would be to risk ostracism by the dominant group (Sarnoff and Katz, 1954). Unfortunately, the issue is complicated by the fact that the person who is the subject of biased views tends to become defensive. He takes umbrage easily, perceives slighting intent in the teacher's innocuous remarks. His apprehensiveness leads him to read into the teacher's routine behaviors an element of threat and damage to self-esteem. Thus a gap begun by factors outside the school is widened by subjective factors.

Constructive approaches, but not final solutions, to the reduction of prejudice can be made in the schools. Obviously, the salient factor is the teacher's attitude. It has been found that one person who is supportive can be of substantial value in reducing anxieties and feelings of inadequacy (Juul, 1961). In dealing with children, references to national, racial, or religious background should be avoided. Heaton suggests that school entertainments should not include an all-Negro chorus. There is some danger that asking Orientals or Mexicans to put on dances wearing their native costumes may engender negative feelings. Dramatic productions in which stereotypes are portrayed or in which dialects are used have been protested by adult organizations (Heaton, 1952, p. 21). Gradually, to be sure, a permissive atmosphere can be created that will allow for the free expression of feelings. Feelings are contagious, so a first step is for the teacher to examine his own prejudices *and* control them. Pupils can be led to discuss how they might feel if others made fun of them or called them names. Such discussion lets pupils know that others too can hurt, feel angry, or be afraid—the humanness of everyone is emphasized. Group discussions dealing directly with real problems that arise in the school should be a part of the program of studies.

Lewin advises that there is no use ignoring the fact that a child belongs to a minority group. In fact, those who later have the most difficulty are frequently the ones who experienced the least prejudice in childhood. They should be forewarned that they will later encounter *some* (they also run the danger of forming stereotypes) persons who will reveal prejudice. They should be instructed that membership in two or more groups is natural and normal; and that they can and must function in several groups. It is not a matter of being neither one thing nor another but a problem of how to behave in various groups (Lewin, 1948, pp. 169–185).

The impact of prejudice on the part of the giver, as contrasted to the recipient, deserves consideration. In class discussions, it will be well to consider that the prejudiced person hurts others as well as himself. His perspective is limited, his thinking is restricted by preconceived notions, his logic is destroyed by jumping to conclusions. It is also worth bringing out that often the prejudiced person is fundamentally weak and trying to disguise his weakness by scapegoating. Emphasis should be on the attempt to build his own ego strength by emphasizing positive personality attributes.

Because goals are more readily achieved when they are clearly defined, it is obvious that the teacher should not leave to chance the basic attitudes that are being formed and re-formed. Along with the conception that the school is concerned with the whole child must go the responsibility for conscious attention to attitudes (Bullock, 1962).

Anger The procedures involved in teaching the control of anger are quite similar to those suggested for dealing with aggression. The example set by others is important. The development of skills that will lead to fewer thwarting circumstances and experiences that aid in understanding people and things will reduce occasions for anger. The Biblical admonition that "a soft answer turneth away wrath: but grievous words stir up anger" is psychologically sound—meeting anger with anger tends to build up the emotion. Trying to reason with an angry person is difficult because neither party can stay reasonable for long, so ideas, suggestions, and admonitions about controlling temper should be brought out after the storm has passed. Yet all too frequently, the angry individual is dealt with immediately; He is banished from the room, sent to the principal's office, or otherwise punished at once. This does not mean that pupils should rule the roost, but the teacher's insistence on reasonable conformity can take place after a time for cooling off (Prescott, 1957, p. 75).

Values of Disturbing Emotions It is generally desirable to reduce upsetting emotions. However, dogmatic judgment about them is complicated by the fact that some positive values may accrue from anxiety, anger, and prejudice. Fear has the value of helping to keep individuals out of danger. Anxiety about examinations may cause the pupil to apply himself more assiduously to his work.

Certain kinds of anger may be advantageous. Anger with oneself for doing less than he is capable, anger about unjust situations, and anger with obviously unfair individuals may serve to motivate an otherwise complacent person. The values of aggression depend in part on where it is directed. It is pertinent to suggest that the treatment of anger in the classroom should avoid involving a conflict of wills between teacher and pupil.

Prejudice may also be justified. Defined as a strong dislike for unjust behaviors, prejudice might well be encouraged in the upper grades and in high school. Dislike for war, for inequitable opportunity, for unfair treatment based on skin color or national origins, or for international unselfishness may serve to motivate individuals to become a counteracting influence. This kind of prejudice is, however, directed against practices rather than persons. It is impersonal rather than personal. It is general rather than specific, and it is directed rather than uncontrolled.

Dealing with the constructive emotions

The problem of dealing with the constructive emotions is not substantially different from that of eliminating or reducing the strong negative emotions. What is done to reduce anxiety and aggression will also enhance such emotions as sympathy and affection. The positive approach to emotional control will be studied in this section by dealing with affection, sympathy, pleasure, and humor.

Affection For educational purposes, "affection" may be defined as a mild emotion characterized by a feeling of fondness, tenderness, or attachment to others. Affection is an important factor in daily living.

The role of affection in the school is twofold. One aspect is the affection of the teacher for pupils. Studies of best-liked teachers show that pupils respond favorably to qualities that underlie affection, such as sympathy, kindliness, patience, courtesy, and interest in others (Gowan, 1957). On the negative side, it has been shown that delinquency can be traced, in part, to lack of affection or a feeling of the individual that others have no affection for him (Kvaraceus, 1958). Affection, as an element in the atmosphere of the classroom, must not be forced, because children are quick to detect sham. Genuine affection arises from a sincere interest in children and a knowledge of their abilities, problems, and limitations.

The other aspect is the growth of affection in children. The example set by the teacher is important. Not only must the teacher use patience in dealing with pupils, he must also notice and praise its manifestation in his pupils. Many primary teachers have found that keeping small pets in the classroom can be a means of encouraging gentleness in children. A few words of counsel can help pupils transfer this conduct to human relationships. Group work, committees, group discussions, and classroom projects are all means of providing opportunities for children to develop the familiarity and understanding that leads to affection.

In work designed to encourage affection, it will be well to capitalize on the revelations of sociometric grouping. This technique can be used to help a social isolate become better oriented or to increase the productiveness or motivation of individuals. The technique can also be used to develop affection. The starting point is for the teacher to ask, "With whom would you like to work in preparing a panel discussion?" or "Which pupil would you like best as a substitute?" or "By whom would you like to sit?" (See Figure 17.)

Because affection must be built upon existing foundations, certain principles should be observed in sociometric grouping. However, they should be applied in accordance with the particular conditions.

1. Mutual choices should be placed together.

2. Isolates (unchosen or rarely chosen pupils) should be given their first choice.

3. A minimum number of isolates should be placed in a group.

4. Stars (much chosen pupils) need not be given any of their choices (though no effort should be made to avoid giving them one of their choices). Their position as stars is probably indicative of their ability to adjust to many different personalities.

5. Natural groupings should be maintained to as great an extent as possible. (Thus, in Figure 17, 2, 3, 5, and 7 would form a group; however, since 2 and 7 are both stars, it might be well to make each the nucleus of a different group.)

6. The more difficult it is to follow the foregoing principles, the smaller the groups formed should be.

It should be noted that groups should be re-formed from time to time for various purposes. If a different question were used as the basis for the

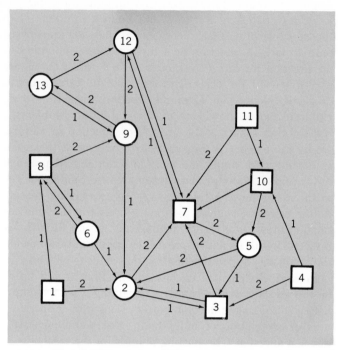

FIGURE 17. *Sociogram in which squares represent boys and circles represent girls. The number by the line indicates first or second choice. Numbers 7 and 2 are "stars," or much-chosen individuals. Numbers 1, 4, 11 are isolates—not having been chosen by anyone so far as the particular question was concerned. Numbers 2 and 3, 12 and 7, 13 and 9, and 6 and 8 are mutual choices.*

sociogram, different formation would undoubtedly result. Moreover, as pupils extend their intimate knowledge of one another, they will tend to make different choices.[3]

Sympathy Sympathy is the emotional source of the ability to put oneself in another's place and share his satisfactions and disappointments. It is a quality basic to good human relations and to personal welfare. Psychiatrists and psychologists state that one of the important steps in treating many kinds of mental disorder is to get an individual "outside himself." Some emotional illness is primarily due to the fact that a person is "all wrapped up" in his own problems, difficulties, and desires. In such

[3] A detailed explanation of underlying principles and suggestions for various uses of sociometry is briefly and clearly given in Helen Hall Jennings, *Sociometry in Group Relations*, 2d ed., Washington: American Council on Education, 1958.

cases, the person is encouraged to develop interests that concern the welfare of others and to stimulate effort for the good of his fellows.

An effective starting point in developing sympathy is to stress the practice of courtesy. By encouraging pupils to act courteously, there is the possibility of stimulating in them the feeling of sympathy. If they lend a guiding hand to the blind, assist the crippled, and make allowances for the slow learner, it is more probable they will *feel* sympathy.

Peer groups provide a setting in which sympathy and other positively oriented attitudes are developed. Adolescents value traits that promote facile group functioning (Feinberg, Smith, and Schmidt, 1958). This is also true of younger children, but their attitudes are developing, and aggressiveness—the traditional trait of boys—is more likely to be tolerated than it will be at a later age (Marshall, 1961). Another approach to the development of sympathy is to seek human understanding. Scholars working in the area of racial understanding point out that much intolerance is attributable to ignorance. When one becomes acquainted with those of another race, instead of depending on clichés and the opinions of prejudiced people, he tends to become tolerant. The study of children of other lands in grade school and social living and sociology in high school has the same effect. The teacher should state specifically that one aim in such study is the development of sympathy.

The teacher also should have a genuine feeling of sympathy. The teacher's development of sympathy will follow the same course as that of the pupils: (1) treating children courteously, (2) knowing something of their individual problems and potentialities, and (3) attempting to place himself in the position of the pupil.

Pleasure A state or feeling of gratification or satisfaction may be considered a definition of the term "pleasure." The pleasure may be very mild, as the enjoyment of rest after activity, or it may be intense, as the stimulation one feels upon hearing a masterful artist sing. Pleasures derive mainly from two sources: (1) the satisfaction of basic needs, and (2) the exercise of one's capacities. Children enjoy running, jumping, and romping because of their capacity for physical activity. By and large, competent pianists or golfers find pleasure in the exercise of their skills. These sources of pleasure suggest rather obvious techniques by which teachers can help pupils derive pleasure from their educational pursuits.

Schoolchildren will achieve pleasure from their school activities if those activities are designed to satisfy such basic needs as security, accomplishment, adventure, belonging, and physical satisfaction. The relationship of need satisfaction to pleasure further emphasizes the child's need to be accepted for what he is by both pupils and teacher. The necessity for designing schoolwork appropriate to individual capacity is especially apparent in the need for accomplishment.

The exercise of one's capacities as a step toward the achievement of pleasure indicates two school responsibilities. One is to provide a variety of work. This means exacting academic requirements for some; recognition of athletic prowess for others; the opportunity to participate in musical productions for others; and leadership challenges, manual arts, and homemaking for still others. The second responsibility is to encourage the development of skills. It is the developed and exercised capacity that gives satisfaction. One who has a capacity for playing a good game of tennis but who has never held a racket in his hand has no opportunity to achieve pleasure from tennis. The same principle applies to skills in arithmetic, writing, and science. Research studies have repeatedly indicated the value of social skills as a source of satisfaction for children of all ages (Goertzen, 1959).

Humor A sense of humor adds greatly to the enjoyment one derives from life. Opportunities to exercise a sense of humor should be consciously sought in the classroom. This requires more than a good-humored teacher; it involves the need for insight into the cause of humor. In the primary grades, humor is occasioned by what seems to the adult crude showing off and perceiving the unexpected. Young children find humor in surprise, defeated expectation, relief from strain, and sudden feelings of superiority or embarrassment (Jersild, 1960, p. 251). Thus, first graders think that making faces is extremely funny or find the spilling of paint or a box of crayons quite humorous. An adult's stumbling or falling is very funny. Teachers should recognize that what an adult would often consider as a cruel sense of humor is simply a developmental stage in children.

At a somewhat later stage, children find humor in incongruities. Pupils in the intermediate and upper grades find humor in crude (to the adult) play on words or in practical jokes, and these forms of humor may be found at the high school level. Another stage of development is represented by an increase in amusement at jokes about sex (probably arising from embarrassment) that are perhaps only partially understood. These developmental stages prepare for the basic element of adult humor—the occurrence of the unexpected in the place of an event for which set has been established.

An understanding of the developmental stages of humor will help the teacher in encouraging the exercise of humor in the classroom. He should make an effort to laugh with students rather than at them. Teachers are known to use sarcastic witticisms that are anything but humorous to the pupils. Since laughter fosters a healthy functioning of the body and increases the enjoyment of living, there should be an attempt to make schools less solemn than they often are. This is accomplished by relaxed and confident teachers.

Projective techniques and emotional release

The Definition and Purpose of Projective Techniques A projective technique is a means by which a more or less neutral situation is given meaning by the individual responding to it. By supplying meaning or form to the "unstructured" setting, one *projects* his own feelings or perceptions into the stimulus situation. This may be clarified by describing the pioneer technique—the Rorschach blots. These symmetrical blots of ink might have been made by dropping ink on a piece of paper and folding the paper to produce two symmetrical halves. The subject is then asked to tell what he sees in the blot—just as we use our imaginations to see various animals, objects, and characters in clouds. The individual "puts himself into" the blot to give meaning to what is in reality meaningless, and thus what one sees is a revelation of himself (Rorschach, 1932). Murray's Thematic Apperception Test consists of a series of pictures about which the subject is asked to tell a story. Because the picture might tell any number of stories, what he does tell is a revelation or projection of the individual (Murray, 1938). Such techniques, in the hands of properly trained persons, are used to supply clues to better understanding of the thoughts and emotions of individual subjects.

Projective techniques can also be used as a means of emotional release, and it is felt that one experiences catharsis from some kinds of projective techniques. A child who senses that it is wrong to repudiate a parent (for either a felt or a justifiable reason) may be unwilling to kick or curse that parent. However, under the guidance and encouragement of a therapist, he will play with dolls in such a manner that the doll child injures the doll parent. It has been experimentally confirmed that such play enables many children who are experiencing difficulties to exercise their negative feelings more wholesomely.[4]

Play therapy, Rorschach blots, and the Thematic Apperception Test are not classroom techniques and should not be used by untrained teachers. However, modification of projective techniques are quite feasible. Some pupils find release in creative writing. Upper-grade-school and secondary school pupils release their feelings and perhaps get a better perspective of their problems through writing that places the author in the role of a hero (Schukart, 1950). It seems obvious that the junior high school boy who wrote the following poem gained both understanding and release from his composition.

> *Pretty Anna May Malone*
> *Had a heart as hard as stone;*

[4] See Clark E. Moustakas, *Children in Play Therapy*, New York: McGraw-Hill Book Company, 1953, for detailed explanation of the advantages, limitations, and uses of the technique.

Every year since she was eight
She has been my best playmate.

I half loved that Irish kid
'Till she said just what she did,
Said for me her love was through
'Cause she'd heard I'm half a Jew.

She doesn't need to feel high-toned
'Cause her dad kissed the blarney stone.
I don't think I know it all
'Cause my dad had a wailing wall.

Time will show you, Anna May,
The big mistake you made today.
It's the truth I'm half a Jew
But that's the half that cared for you.

Finger and brush painting, crayon and pencil drawing, and clay model-ing have also been used as projective techniques for both emotional release and—if cautiously and tentatively interpreted by the teacher—im-proved understanding.

Using Projective Techniques in the Classroom An understanding of the purposes of projective methods and a partial use of the principles involved will help teachers resolve some of the difficult problems of emotional adjustment (Fisher and Cleveland, 1958, p. 77). The underlying concep-tion of projective techniques suggests that the manner in which an indi-vidual does his work, the manner in which he meets and deals with his peers, as well as the way he paints and plays in experimental situations, reveal his inner self. (Incidentally, this has a rather revealing implication for the teacher: The way in which he describes the personality of his pupils is indicative of his own personality traits.)

Awareness of behavior as a symptom will help teachers see the futility of trying to alter established modes of pupil conduct without first deter-mining the causes. This conduct may be undesirable, such as imperti-nence, disobedience, showing off, or bullying. Or the conduct may be apparently desirable, such as overconscientiousness in work, excessive neatness, excessive quietness, or quick subservience to the will and re-quests of others. When the teacher takes the view that such behavior is symptomatic, he will have taken a large step toward constructive assist-ance. He can help pupils get therapeutic release from play activities if he guards against showing shock. When a child builds something in clay and seems to take delight in destroying what he has created, the teacher should avoid saying, "Why, Bill, that's an awful thing to do!" It will do boys no great harm to make dire threats about murder and mayhem when they are playing Dick Tracy and gangsters. It is a part of the wisdom of the organism to attempt to effect an equilibrium in the face of a disturbing influence. Spontaneous play of children tends to follow this procedure if there is not too much adult domination and moralizing. One of the important elements of projective techniques is permissiveness, a technique that has been used successfully as an approach to remedial reading (Dahlberg, Roswell, and Chall, 1952).

There are opportunities to approximate projective methods in formal curricular pursuits. Art, language study, literature, physical education, and practical arts may provide the pupil who has problems with an opportunity for release. Teachers should encourage spontaneous creation in writing and drawing. Giving advice on the proper techniques for handling materials does not violate this principle of freedom.

Several aspects of the curriculum require rather rigid conformity. Words must be spelled in a certain manner, and the solution of algebra and arithmetic problems is rather stereotyped. The names of objects and persons must be pronounced in certain ways. Without questioning the great advantages of conformity, we can say that these situations sometimes produce stress in some children (Burrows, 1959, p. 29). Some of the stress may be avoided by permitting freedom where conformity is relatively unimportant. Art, music, and dancing have for ages been avenues for emotional expression and for building interpersonal unity. However, even such avenues for expression as these may become stilted and formal if the emphasis is on the outcome rather than on the process.

It is clear that teachers should permit and encourage all creative variations that do not actually interfere with accomplishment. The value of creative expression emphasizes the importance of recognizing the emotional elements involved in most schoolwork. Projective techniques may be utilized in many areas to release disturbing emotions in routine activities. A manual-arts teacher, concerned because his shop was becoming the "dumping ground" for pupils who were unable to adjust satisfactorily to academic work, decided to see what he could do to help pupils. Instead of emphasizing craftsmanship, he encouraged boys to do what they wished in the shop. He discovered that it was possible to help many boys merely by providing an opportunity for creativity and accomplishment. He also found that in the atmosphere of freedom, the boys slowly began to reveal to him some of their felt difficulties. Learning these difficulties made it possible for him to give constructive advice and to devise additional opportunities for release.

Teachers of English have found that they can help pupils put up with some of the negative conditions in which they find themselves by encouraging them to write themes on "My Pet Peeve," "My Favorite Sport," or "My Ideal Teacher." Poems that express secret feelings are often given to teachers who have the confidence of their pupils with the request that they should not be shown or read to other people. The important things for the teacher to remember in utilizing projective techniques are to (1) avoid moralizing about the activity, (2) permit and encourage the feeling of freedom, (3) seek to develop a high degree of rapport with the student, (4) accept the child and his activities as objectively as possible, (5) provide as great a variety of free and creative activities as is feasible, and (6) remember that constructive emotional development is at least as important as academic accomplishment.

Emotional maturity

The Relative Nature of Maturity Although the word "mature" means ripeness, or full development, the psychological meaning is more flexible. Obviously, a child is immature as far as physical development is concerned. He may be mature in the sense that he has reached the development typical for his age. A four-year-old who has a temper tantrum only once every three or four weeks may be considered mature. A six-year-old who dawdles on Saturdays is mature. An adolescent who quickly recovers from a broken heart is mature for his age and is developing toward conduct which will be mature when adulthood is reached. It appears, therefore, that maturity is not an absolute—it is a process.

Emotional maturity is the process of acting one's age. The teacher should not expect children to reach a stability of interest beyond their years. He should not expect the adolescent boy consistently to be a gentleman. He should not consider it odd that freshman girls develop a crush on him. He will consider it normal for a senior girl to be "madly in love" once, twice, or thrice. Self-acceptance is an important aspect of emotional maturity (Wenkart, 1955), and it must be preceded by acceptance from others; to push pupils through developmental stages too rapidly is to imply dissatisfaction with them. Teachers should realize that what sometimes appears to be objectionable behavior is in reality a developmental stage *and* a valuable experience.

Some Criteria of Emotional Maturity Man's capacity for development and adaptation to changing conditions is probably his outstanding characteristic. Today's children continue to prove the validity of belief in man's adaptability. Children are bombarded with information, and they absorb it with astonishing ease. Even preschool youngsters, perhaps largely because of television, but also because of radio broadcasts and parental conversations, know something about atomic energy, rockets, cataclysmic events across the world, racial minorities, and social struggles on other continents (Wann, Dorn, and Liddle, 1962, p. 6). This information and the wide variety of their daily experiences contribute to both emotional turmoil and rapid emotional maturing (C. Lewis, 1946). The provision of guidance can enhance the speed and direction of their development. The problem for parents and educators is to establish goals of emotional maturity and work for their achievement. A suggested list of criteria, or goals, follows:

1. *Inhibition of direct expression of negative emotions*   This does not mean that feelings of anger or fear should or could be suppressed. It does mean that direct attack and flight should take place less often. The school can help by providing substitute activities that permit the release of tensions.

2. *Cultivation of positive, upbuilding emotions*   Emotional maturity is not so much eliminating disruptive emotions as it is providing commendable substitutes. This can be fostered by experiences of success—in social contacts, in physical activities, subject-matter mastery, and the development of skills.

3. *Development of higher tolerance for disagreeable circumstances*   This, too, is the result of successful experience, which provides compensations for the inevitable failures and the disagreeable experiences.

4. *Increasing satisfaction from socially approved responses*   Growth from the natural egocentricity of childhood to the sociocentric ideal of adulthood is the result of personal success, plus close association with individuals who are trusting and trustworthy.

5. *Increasing independence of action*   Socially oriented independence is the result of guided experience that provides degrees of freedom commensurate with the ability to exercise judgment.

6. *Ability to make a choice and not brood about other choices*   This is probably best accomplished by permitting children to make choices when the stakes are not great. Heavy responsibility placed on youth may be a contributing factor to chronic worry.

7. *Freedom from unreasonable fear*   Concern and forethought should not be confused with fear. The experience of success and contact with confident adults foster this goal.

8. *Understanding and action in accord with limitations*   No one can be the top man in everything. Acceptance of limitations may be fostered by widening the range of activities that are functionally recognized and praised in the school.

9. *Awareness of the ability and achievement of others*   Stress on group accomplishment can be a powerful source of motivation as well as a source of gratification.

10. *Ability to err without feeling disgraced*   This will be fostered by parents and teachers who realize that errors are educative.

11. *Ability to carry victory and prestige with grace*   This will grow from the equitable distribution of the experiences of success and failure. Stress on cooperative activities and team and school victories will be steps in the right direction.

12. *Ability to bounce back from disappointing experiences* Experience is the great teacher. But the experience must be scaled to the developmental level.

13. *Ability to delay the gratification of impulses* This is one of the distinct differences in pupils from the lower social classes, who present many problems in school, and those of higher socioeconomic origins. Many adults fail to achieve this goal.

14. *The enjoyment of daily living* The opportunity to engage in challenging but achievable tasks is the major contributing factor. The exercise of mental, physical, emotional, and spiritual aspects of the human personality are the avenues to the enjoyment of living.

Many scales have been devised to evaluate emotional maturity, using such criteria as those listed above, but there is much doubt concerning their validity and reliability. Consequently, they should be interpreted and used with genuine caution. Some of the scales are designed for self-rating and can serve to provide guidance for the individual. One such scale is the California Test of Personality, which contains twelve subdivisions. The test is available in five levels, from kindergarten to adult ages. Indicative of the questions asked (together with the subdivision concerned) are the following:

1A. *Self-reliance*
> 9 Is it hard for you to admit when you are wrong?

1B. *Sense of Personal Worth*
> 23 Do people seem to think well of your family's social standing?

1C. *Sense of Personal Freedom*
> 41 Do you feel that you are bossed around too much by your folks?

1D. *Feeling of Belonging*
> 57 Do you have enough friends to make you feel good?

1E. *Withdrawing Tendencies*
> 70 Are you sorry that you are continually growing older?

1F. *Nervous Symptoms*
> 83 Are you more restless than most people?

2A. *Social Standards*
> 102 Should a person be courteous to disagreeable people?

2B. *Social Skills*
> 115 Do you find that it causes you trouble when you help others?

2C. *Anti-social Tendencies*
> 131 Do you often have to fight or quarrel in order to get your rights?

2D. *Family Relations*
> 146 Do you usually like to be somewhere else than at home?

2E. *School Relations*
> 157 Does it seem to you that many of your teachers are nervous?

2F. *Community Relations*
   173 Do you live in a rather uninteresting neighborhood? [5]

Probably the best use of such scales is in teacher-pupil conferences and as the basis for group discussions. Drawing conclusions from the comparative scores is hazardous because phases of development for various individuals are difficult to standardize (Stolz, 1958). However, the maturity levels suggested by the criteria listed above and by maturity rating scales are achievable to some degree. Julian Huxley proposes that the next steps in man's evolution will not be biological, but states that there are infinite potentialities for increasing psychosocial understanding (1953, pp. 160–166). Emotional control would be basic in such a development, and helping pupils achieve emotional maturity gives the teacher a chance to participate in the challenge of the future.

Summary

Emotions include drives that lead to accomplishment and self-realization as well as drives that limit and cripple one's potentialities. The teacher is inescapably concerned with enhancing the constructive emotions and reducing or sidetracking destructive ones. Because emotions have a cumulative effect (build-up), even the mild ones must be considered.

Anxiety, it has been found, has both favorable and unfavorable effects on learning. Low or mild anxiety seems to prompt and promote the learning of academic and social skills. High anxiety causes the individual to retreat or become so defensive that he is unable to marshal his resources for positive learning. A good adult example, suitable tasks, social skills, and self-respect are among the factors that keep anxiety within suitable bounds.

Aggression arises from blocked motives and may be directed against self or others or both. Because aggression sometimes stems from out-of-school situations, the problem is to provide suitable outlets: Vigorous play, athletic competition, art activities, and free writing may release tensions.

Affection, sympathy, pleasure, and humor are, like the negative emotions, influenced by adult example, peer relations, self-concepts, and background, as well as by the immediate school situation. Group discussions of all emotions—their values, dangers, and control—have been found to be beneficial.

Projective techniques are not classroom devices, but the ideas underlying them can be employed, i.e., freedom of expression, release of emotions, better understanding of surface behavior by others, and respect for individuality.

Emotional maturity is relative to age. Expecting too much of young children places burdens on them and deprives them of going through normal develop-

[5] Ernest W. Tiegs, Willis W. Clark, and Louis P. Thorpe, *California Test of Personality*, 1953 rev., California Test Bureau, Monterey, Calif. By permission California Test Bureau, Monterey, Calif.

mental stages naturally. There are means for children and adults to check their own maturing processes and consider their emotional behavior objectively.

Problems and exercises

1 Describe some situation in which the contributing (background) factors have appeared to be more significant than the precipitating factor.

2 Observe a class of primary youngsters and note any behaviors or attitudes that might be interpreted as anxiety. What do you think might have been done to relieve the anxiety? Do the same for a high school class.

3 Explain the dynamics of the advice that evidences of aggression should not be dealt with by an angry teacher.

4 How would you explain the fact that aggression in the classroom is evidenced more frequently by lower-socioeconomic-class pupils? What are some weaknesses of this contention?

5 No matter what level of pupils you intend to teach, propose a plan for the reduction of prejudice.

6 Formulate a rationale for the development of affection and sympathy through the use of sociometry.

7 How does the use of basic ideas underlying projective techniques fall short in achieving emotional maturity?

8 How does emotional maturity for a seven-year-old child differ from that for a junior high school pupil?

9 Describe some evidences of emotional immaturity in an adult you have observed. What earlier experiences might have changed his pattern of responses?

Suggested additional readings

Coleman, James C.: *Personality Dynamics and Effective Behavior,* Chicago: Scott, Foresman and Company, 1960, pp. 318–345.

This chapter on "emotional competence" analyzes the components of emotions, suggests ways of strengthening constructive emotions, and discusses the problems of balance in dealing with fear, anxiety, and hostility.

Grimes, Jesse W., and Wesley Allinsmith: "Compulsivity, Anxiety, and School Achievement," *Merrill-Palmer Quarterly,* 7: 247–271, 1961.

The authors emphasize the value of studying individual pupils in terms of their motivations in order to hypothesize as to the teaching approaches that will be most effective. One method for all will be ineffective.

Haring, Norris G., and E. Lakin Phillips: *Educating Emotionally Disturbed Children,* New York: McGraw-Hill Book Company, 1962.

Parents are involved in a structured program—one with specific limits and requirements—that is designed to introduce order into the lives of confused youngsters. The focal role of the teacher is emphasized.

Hymes, James L., Jr.: *Behavior and Misbehavior,* Englewood Cliffs, N.J.: Prentice-Hall, Inc., 1955.

This short book stresses the fact that misbehavior is an attempt to bring about a resolution of stress. Different children have varied goals, and these must be recognized in correcting misbehavior and in promoting adjustive behavior.

Peller, Lili E.: "The School's Role in Promoting Sublimation," *The Psychoanalytic Study of the Child,* II, 437–449, 1956.

Using Freudian psychology as a point of departure, the author questions the advisability of either strictness or permissiveness. Rather the emphasis is on opportunities for catharsis which promote ego development.

Personality and Its Development

13

In everyday usage, "personality" refers to "IT"—the impression one makes on others. As a psychological term, "personality" is a much more complex concept, and there is not complete agreement as to what is basic, what is acquired, and why personality develops as it does. The term is inclusive; every chapter of this book is immediately or ultimately concerned with some significant phase of personality. However, basic educational considerations can more easily be comprehended by specific references to the more salient features of personality.

The meaning of personality

Definition Personality is the total configuration of individual characteristics and modes of behavior that shape one's adjustments to his environment, especially traits that influence his getting along with others and himself (Hilgard, 1962, p. 447). Physique, temperament, skills, interests, fears, hopes, likes and dislikes, looks, feelings, habits, and knowledge are included. Personality embraces what one is, what he can be, and what he hopes to be. Because personality includes one's adjustment to others, it also includes the reactions of others. These considerations subject personality to growth influences—hereditary potential, environmental factors, and personal reaction are involved, along with processes of differentiation and integration. In none of us is personality static. It is notably responsive to the total culture—to peer contacts, teacher behavior, and other factors of classroom climate, among other things.

The above concept indicates that when a teacher describes the personality of a pupil or a fellow teacher, he is to some extent describing himself. He is portraying himself through his own reaction about as accurately as he is portraying the personality of his subject (see Chapter 21). Thus our evaluation of a teacher who characterizes Johnny as an ignorant, dirty, disobedient boy would be quite different from our evaluation of a teacher who describes the same pupil as a slow learner who is handicapped by an impoverished cultural background. The well-grounded teacher will seek to *evaluate the social aspect of personality in terms of causative and contributing influences rather than in terms of personal reaction.* Teachers should bear in mind that personality is a composite unit consisting of mental, emotional, physical, physiological, social, and perceptual factors.

Aspects of Personality Because of the complexity of personality, we must content ourselves with indicating the general factors that contribute to shaping it; but we must remember that in individual cases one factor may outweigh the others.

1. *Inherited factors* Recent years have seen a shift in the perception of the role of inheritance. Formerly, interest was focused on which traits were inherited and which seemed to be most responsive to environmental influences. Today the conclusion is that *genetic factors produce dispositions or potentials for development rather than directly producing either bodily or behavioral traits* (Lazarus, 1961, p. 229). It is still believed that heredity sets limits beyond which the individual may not develop, no matter how salutary his environment. It is to be hoped that teachers will realize the existence of these limits and cease giving pupils the mistaken notion that they can be or do anything they wish if they just work hard enough. Belief in this erroneous idea is manifest in our application of age-grade standards, when we fail or shame pupils because they do not grow and learn at a prescribed rate. The result is a great deal of unnecessary discouragement and frustration.

Recognition of inherited limits need not lead to resignation to the *status quo* in development. The truth is that we do not know—nor is there any way of knowing—what those limits are. For example, an intelligence test does not measure inherited potential; it merely indicates the present degree of development of that potential. If we accept the idea of limits, then we shall be on the watch for indications that the pupil is being pushed and prompted beyond his potential (Dunn, 1963, p. 96). These indications may reveal themselves in various ways: sleepiness, nail biting, inattentiveness, frequent throat clearing, restlessness, or outbursts of anger.

The role of heredity in aspects of development is variable. It seems smaller in intellectual development than in physical characteristics, which are least responsive to environmental variables. Social personality (barring clinical types of defectiveness) is less limited by heredity than either physique or intelligence and appears to be most responsive to environmental variables. It is comparatively easy to see hereditary limits in the size of children. It is less easy to perceive them in terms of ultimate intellectual development; indeed, what often appears to be relatively superior intelligence is merely the possession of much and accurate information of a simple sort. It is comparatively difficult to perceive or determine experimentally how heredity has influenced social personality.

The interaction between heredity and environment is clearly illustrated by the view that is currently taken of the famous study of the Jukes family made in 1874 (Dugdale, 1877). Of 1,200 descendants from a given marriage (exact information was available for 709), most were criminals, paupers, and dependents. The large majority also revealed low physical standards. At first this degeneracy was attributed to heredity, but it is now considered important that these people, besides having poor heredity, lived in a poor cultural environment. A similar study of the descendants of Martin Kallikak (a fictitious name), a Revolutionary soldier who had children by a feeble-minded barmaid, was also believed to indicate the role of heredity. Of 480 descendants, 143 were feeble-minded, and many were sexually immoral, intemperate, delinquent, or criminal. It is today deemed important that the role of environment be considered along with the role played by heredity.

Studies of gifted individuals follow much the same line. The descendants of Jonathan Edwards and Sarah Pierpont were, over a period of 200 years, college presidents, professors, authors, lawyers, judges, and statesmen to a greater extent than could be attributed to chance (Carroll, 1940, p. 27). In addition to heredity, these individuals had the advantages of stable homes, financial security, and superior educational opportunities.

Many desirable and undesirable qualities of personality can be attributed largely to glandular balance, which may be considered an aspect of heredity. The glands of internal secretion, the endocrines, such as the thyroid, pituitary, pancreas, gonads, and adrenals, influence personality traits to a marked degree. Each of these glands pours secretions known as hormones directly into the blood stream. Unless these secretions are available in delicately balanced proportions, the whole system is affected, and marked deviations in appearance, growth processes, emotional control, intelligence, and behavior may result (Shaffer and Shoben, 1956, p. 374).

Knowledge of the function of the endocrine glands is far from complete, but the use of such information as we have has resulted in momentous transformations of personality. Glandular therapy is, of course, a medical problem. The teacher's role is to recognize that glands play an important part in pupil behavior and to be slow in condemning or categorizing deviants.

A teacher would not be likely to label a child "lazy" if he were aware of the medical diagnosis of hypoactive thyroid. One teacher, typically tolerant of questionable pupil behavior, nevertheless was somewhat insulted by a high school girl's regularly sleeping or dozing in class. One day the girl, perhaps noticing the irritation, said to her, "You may have noted my sleepiness. I have a hypoactive thyroid. I'm taking thyroxin and I'm really much better than I used to be." A hyperactive thyroid may result in quite different problems. The pupil may fidget, seem unable to stay in his place, or insistently demand attention by raising his hand to recite. His overactivity can be better tolerated when one appreciates that the glands are exercising some control of personality manifestations. Hyperthyroidism is rare before the age of ten, but it occurs most frequently after that, especially among girls, and is accompanied by instability, moodiness, restlessness, and excessive activity (Newman, 1955, pp. 391ff).

Some endocrine imbalances involve changes in blood sugar and blood calcium. Children who have this problem are often negativistic, inattentive, lacking in initiative, and antisocial, and have physical symptoms as well. Other endocrine glandular imbalances have less readily identifiable influences on behavior. The gonads, pituitary, pancreas, and adrenals are known to have certain effects on growth, but the psychological impact is variable; i.e., the same defect may cause one child to be meek and retiring but render another aggressive. "All geneticists are agreed that what is inherited by organisms from their forebears is a range of capacities to respond to a range of environments." [1] Determining factors in the response may be age of onset of an imbalance, plus the type of treatment at home and school. Because individuals suffering from glandular imbalance are more vulnerable than others to stress of any kind (Gleghorn, 1953), teachers play a real part in determining the responses that youngsters make to their handicaps.

In many cases, glandular influences are simply particular kinds of inherited influences. In other instances, they may be due to congenital or environmental factors. *Glands, like heredity, provide a potential for reaction—what that reaction will be depends partially on how the child is treated in school.*

2. *Physique and personality* A problem that interested students of personality even before psychology was recognized as a scientific study is the relationship between physical build and personality. E. Kretschmer postulated the theory that the thickset, round person (pyknic body type) is gay, good-humored, and happy. The lean, underdeveloped person (asthenic body type) is polite, sensitive, and cold. The athletic, strong, well- and symmetrically-developed individual has a personality midway between those of the pyknic and asthenic types. Still another body type, the dysplastic, fits none of the foregoing categories because of asymmetrical development, i.e., thickset upper body and either lean and slight or muscular lower body. He is a mixed type. Research supports this body-type theory to a limited extent, but objections are made to it because it tends to place human beings in fixed categories and ignores the molding influence of environment.

Physique is, no doubt, related to personality but not so consistently as to allow definite personality predictions for individuals. Endocrine dis-

[1] Roger J. Williams, "Chemistry Makes the Man," *Saturday Review*, 40 (14): 44, 1957.

turbances do manifest themselves in physique and social behavior, as is demonstrated in mongoloids and cretins. There may be other relationships. The fat boy may be good-humored because he cannot fight—not because he is fat. The perception of one's own physique must not be discounted.

William H. Sheldon has postulated three major body builds—the endomorph (the obese person with abdominal predominance), the ectomorph (the lean, delicate individual with large surface in relation to weight), and the mesomorph (the athletic type with a predominance of bone and muscle). Briefly, the personality typical of the extremes of each of these types is described as follows:

a. The endomorph is inclined to physical gratification, is a pleasure lover, and enjoys association with others.

b. The ectomorph is self-sufficient, enjoys intellectual pursuits, and has a sensitive nature.

c. The mesomorph enjoys physical exertion, is energetic, and loves competition.

An interesting feature of Sheldon's theory is that he provides for continuous variation in type rather than postulating a trimodal distribution of body types and personality. A given individual is considered to have one or more characteristics of each type; for example, an extreme endomorph is a 7–1–1, a 1 being assigned for minimum mesomorphic and ectomorphic qualities, and a 7 for maximum endomorphic features. An extreme mesomorph would be a 1–7–1, and an extreme ectomorph a 1–1–7. The total is not always 9; a person might be a 2–7–1, a 3–4–3, or some other index combination of less than extreme proportion or a rather balanced distribution of morphological measurements (Sheldon and Stevens, 1942).

An apparent defect in the theory is that each of us has seen heavy-set people (endomorphs) who are scholarly and introverted, thin persons (ectomorphs) who are lively and active, and bony, muscular individuals (mesomorphs) who are passive and phlegmatic. An unanswered question is whether or not the development of a personality at variance with bodily predisposition has not been purchased at the cost of stability and sound integration.

In summary, the many unanswered questions about the relationship between body build and personality make it imperative that *teachers should take care not to categorize pupils on the basis of superficial observation of their physical characteristics.*

3. *Environment and personality* In addition to heredity, glandular balance, and body build, the environment helps determine personality development. Modern advances in medicine and hygiene have influenced personality by making the physiological and safety needs less demanding and thus releasing man to seek the higher-level needs of love and self-

actualization. Governmental, community, and religious institutions as well as local customs and mores play dynamic roles in forming personality. From the standpoint of the teacher, the more insistent influences are probably the pupil's home, his socioeconomic status, and the community's educational institutions.

Environment may counteract much of heredity's influence. One study shows that, depending on the environment, children may either be like their parents or develop diametrically opposed characteristics (Crandall, 1963, p. 427). For instance, children reared in homes where parents are exceedingly dominating tend either to be excessively submissive or to develop patterns of behavior quite like those of their parents. This finding is in accord with the widespread belief of child specialists and psychologists that the home is of prime importance in shaping the personality characteristics of children. If a favorable home environment for the child cannot be achieved, then the duty of the school is to compensate for deficiencies in love, security, acceptance, or tolerance.

Teachers must overcome the misconception that there is an average or typical home. The varied socioeconomic conditions that prevail in any community make for vastly different social goals, ideals, and attitudes (Miller and Swanson, 1958). There are, for instance, different vocational goals and different attitudes toward education; some parents do not consider a college education for their children, while others tacitly assume that college is an integral part of their lives. There are different attitudes toward such problems as drinking, morality, religion, and racial relations. Teachers of civics, sociology, and history can quickly discern differences in political attitudes; some pupils will stoutly defend paternalism in government, while others will as vehemently support free enterprise.

By the time the student enters high school, his social class has gone a long way in determining the "path of life" he will choose. The school provides a common educational background and some common experiences. But the social lines of the community shape what the particular child *chooses* to learn. A teacher can present the same material to all pupils, but the pupils will not learn the same things. What one learns is not determined solely by his status in society, but it is certainly influenced by that status (Anderson, 1961).

When cultural conditions seem to limit the likelihood of an individual's developing his latent talents, there are ways to interrupt the perpetuation of those limitations. Some individuals who get a glimpse of a better life can generate the initiative to overcome environmental handicaps. Teachers can, through personal creativeness, provide the hope and stimulation for pupils to rise above the restrictions of their social status. This has been demonstrated in several of our major cities. Daniel Schreiber (1960) talked with defeatist parents in New York City, encouraging them to work for better things for their children. He held high goals before pupils and encouraged them to believe that they could achieve them (see below, "higher horizons"). In a slum area of Los Angeles, Isaac H. McClelland tirelessly prodded pupils to use their minds—praising their successes and shaming their failures. Pupils who had previously never dreamed of going to college found that they could get in and stay there until graduation ("Wasted Talent," 1960). Both these teachers and Clifford J. Campbell, of Chicago's Dunbar Trade School (Rummell, 1948), emphasized what many psychologists have been saying: *we really do not know how much the mind can achieve until consistent effort is made to develop its potential.*

The power of teachers to change the course of life for pupils is not a recent discovery. Teachers have been known to improve nutritional standards in their communities, to persuade citizens to beautify homes and yards, and to encourage sanitation projects. But the school influence does not stop at change in the physical environment—personality may also be changed. An example is a study made at Locust Point, a section of Baltimore, Maryland. In 1914, a survey there found that 166 out of 1,502 schoolchildren were so subnormal and poorly adjusted that only discouraging prophecies about their futures seemed to be realistic. It was expected that these pupils would in large numbers become delinquent, alcoholic, feeble-minded, or dependent. But steps were taken to avoid these results. A school plant was erected that was to serve as the social, educational, and recreational center of the community. Curricular modifications were made to fit the needs and developmental status of the children. Teachers were carefully selected to provide kindly and realistic education. The follow-up study, made seventeen years later, showed highly encouraging results. Of the 166 pupils in the original survey, data were secured on 122. Three-fourths of that number were entirely self-supporting and adequately adjusted. The incidence of illegitimacy, prostitution, delinquency, and dependency was less than might have been expected during the Depression.

It is possible that the original prognosis for Locust Point was incorrect —some of the children might have made satisfactory adjustments as they matured. But it would certainly seem that the enlarged school program had helped, and the data point to the influence of educational philosophy and teacher personality. The director of the study, Dr. Ruth Fairbank, gave the teachers most of the credit for the transformation of personalities.

> Here, again, we find the effect of contacts in those early years with teachers who were not convictionless, but aggressively determined not to lose an opportunity to inculcate good old-fashioned morality, embodying principles of decency and respect for individual personality and clean-mindedness. The most striking result of this survey is to be found in the lasting impression made on these people in childhood by one of the teachers who came in closest contact with

them. Science has no tests to evaluate the influence of personality, but the tests of life on growth and development tell the story.[2]

While recognizing the roles of heredity, physique, glandular function, and social status in the formation of personality, the role of the school and the teachers must also be acknowledged.

4. *Personal response* Two individuals perceive the same stimuli in different ways; they react to the same handicaps or opportunities in different manners. The concept of personal response has been incorporated into the so-called "triangle of life" (see Figure 18).

It would be easy and logical to argue that the three-sided theory of personality is in reality only two things; that is, one's response is an outcome of one's potential as acted upon by environment. The fact remains that even if this be correct, responses do differ. *Heredity and environment are welded together as interdependent influences by the way one reacts to what he is and has.* This has been demonstrated in the Fels Research Institute in investigations of IQ changes. Boys and girls tested annually for four years between the ages of four and twelve were grouped into the 25 per cent who gained most in IQ (upper quartile of changes) and the 25 per cent whose IQ changed least (lower quartile). Those who gained were found to be aggressive, independent, and competitive. Being overly dependent was found to be detrimental to optimal intellectual development (Sontag, Baker, and Nelson, 1958). Apparently, the children who seek need satisfaction through aggressive, competitive

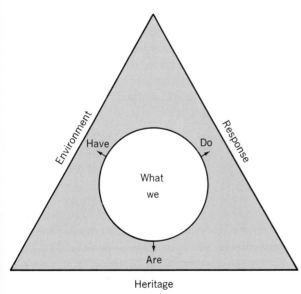

FIGURE 18. *The triangle of life. The circle represents the individual whose course of development is influenced by what he has (his environment), what he is (his inherited potential), and what he does (his response to his environment and potentiality.)*
SOURCE: *H. E. Walter, Genetics, 2d ed. New York: The Macmillan Company, 1938, p. 280. Courtesy, Estate of H. E. Walter.*

[2] Ruth E. Fairbank, "The Subnormal Child—Seventeen Years After," *Mental Hygiene,* 17: 207, April, 1933.

behavior are laying the foundation for superior achievement—or making use of their potential.

Whether the IQ changes created the aggressiveness or the aggressiveness created the IQ changes we do not know. It does seem certain that given kinds of atmospheres stimulate predictable kinds of behavior. Moreover, we must be sure to avoid ascribing a one-to-one relationship to aggressiveness and IQ. Other factors (potential, opportunity, perception of one's world) must also be considered in intellectual growth. The practical import for teachers is that the following can be recommended as means of fostering improved individual responses:

Faith in the ability of pupils to accomplish can be shown by establishing high, but realistic, expectations.

Freedom to experiment, to find out for himself, and to make mistakes should prevail over the pupil's anxiety to provide the correct answers to problems immediately.

Situations can be devised so that competition occurs between peers— where *all* pupils have a chance for victory.

Counseling and individual conferences should encourage pupils to make maximum use of what they have and to view discouraging environmental conditions as a challenge to growth.

Assessment of personality

Because personality is such a complex entity and because it is responsive to environmental, hereditary, and perceptual factors, its assessment is extremely difficult. Actually, everything that one does is indicative of his personality; thus any formal evaluation is limited to the range of response allowed by the particular instrument or technique being used. Even more than is the case with intelligence tests, methods of personality evaluation are only partial and incomplete—they should be used tentatively and with caution.

Personality Inventories Intelligence and achievement tests must be included in gaining understanding of pupils. Though the areas probed by such tests are certainly aspects of personality, they are dealt with elsewhere in this volume; here we consider only tests that are called "personality inventories."

Our very great need to understand individuals has led to much experimentation on means of standardizing measurement of personality. To date, the degree of success is quite disappointing to those who desire easy and accurate evaluation. Some authors assert that most personality tests—and there are scores of them—lack comprehensiveness and validity and have only limited value for special purposes (Baughman and Welsh, 1962). Others assert that it is psychometric innocence, naïveté, mistaken faith in statistical measures, and a desire to keep up with others that lead to the use and popularity of personality inventories (Rothney, Danielson, and Heimann, 1959, p. 283). The author believes that it is our great need to understand better the pupil's personality that leads us to grasp at the supposed values of instruments purporting to do the job.

There are several reasons why the use of a static instrument cannot capture the essence of an individual's dynamic pattern of behavior, mood, and temperament. There are different kinds of personality shown in the home, at school, and at play and work; and one's answer to items would depend upon how he interpreted the question to which he is responding. In addition, we learn early in life that many of our ideas, aspirations, and fantasies are strictly private, and often hide them even from ourselves; it sometimes takes years of therapeutic treatment for us to begin to get an honest portrayal of them. Moreover, the instruments are subject to faking. Rapport with the examiner is vital. If one has little confidence in him or wonders how the test might be used, he is likely to ask, "What business is it of his?" One's mood varies from day to day. A happy or unhappy experience a short time before taking the inventory might color many of an individual's responses and lead to an atypical final score. At least in some instances, unjustified claims in inventory manuals have been made, and the person who is not thoroughly acquainted with the limitations of all test procedures might well arrive at mistaken conclusions.

Some authorities believe that personality inventories may provide limited means of evaluating self-perceptions—an important concept in motivation and learning. If the inventory is used carefully and if results are corroborated by other data, this is a valid contention. However, these instruments should be used as leads or indications, rather than as means for providing conclusions. Classroom teachers might well turn to other techniques for personality appraisal.

Projective Techniques Projective techniques are plans for having the subject put structure into an unstructured situation. An example is the Rorschach tests; ink blots of various design and sometimes color are shown to the subject, who tells what he sees in them (Rorschach, 1937). Another example is the Murray Thematic Apperception Test (TAT); a number of drawings are presented to the subject, who is asked to tell what is portrayed (Morgan and Murray, 1935). Because the blots and pictures may be considered to have various meanings, what the subject reports seeing in them is considered to be a portrayal (projection) of himself. These and similar instruments, such as doll play, when used by well-qualified psychiatrists and psychologists, provide valuable clues for understanding motives and behaviors of individuals. Because of the need for combining results with other pertinent data and the need for caution in interpretation, the teacher's use of them should probably be limited to the conclusions that the qualified examiner discloses in consultation.

Rating Scales Because the data are obviously tentative and pertinent to limited situations, self-rating scales, such as the Sarbin Adjective Check List (1955), Problem Check List, and the Schrammel-Garbutt Personal Adjustment Scale, can be helpful to the classroom teacher. If the teacher remembers that the results may not be an accurate picture of the personality *as perceived by others*, the view the individual takes of himself may be helpful. For example clues may be afforded that the individual is hesitant, lacking justified self-confidence, and may need a little more support and encouragement than most of his peers.

The Sarbin Adjective Check List consists of 200 adjectives, such as "stable," "optimistic," "intelligent," "relaxed," "ambitious," "easygoing," and the like. The respondent checks words that he believes characterize himself. In a study of underachievement, while results were not entirely consistent, male underachievers tended to have negative feelings about themselves, and female underachievers were ambivalent, viewing themselves negatively in some ways and positively in others. It is clear, however, that there is—on the whole—a difference between the ways underachievers and those who achieve in accord with their indicated capacities feel about themselves (Shaw, Edson, and Bell, 1960).

A particularly interesting rating scale is the "Guess Who" scale, which has peers rate each other. They are asked to guess who talks a lot, laughs rarely, waits for others to speak, is friendly, etc. The scale has particular value in that the teacher will often see that he perceives a certain pupil in a way that is quite different from the ways in which the pupil's peers perceive him. It is helpful, too, to get some tentative insight into what impression a pupil is making on others. Sometimes a few words of advice or some role playing (assuming either imaginatively or overtly the part or function of another) about skin color, linguistic accents, or manner of dress will relieve what could otherwise be a distressing situation for one or many pupils. Scales are thus a means of increasing the sharpness of the teacher's perception of pupil personality.

The teacher can form a tentative opinion as to whether a pupil is justified in having the view of himself that is indicated, or whether the view of others is warranted. If the views do not seem to be justified, pointing out contrary evidence over a period of time may help to change opinions. If the views do seem to be justified, the teacher can help the students concerned to develop skills, knowledges, and habits that warrant an upward revision of self-concepts and views of others.

Sociometry Sociometry is a readily available technique for evaluating social personality. Discussion is omitted here because the details are cited in Chapter 12.

Observation of Pupils This is the most readily available means of understanding pupils, and it should be a studied approach. One danger is that the overactive and sometimes obstreperous child will be noticed and the meek and quiet one overlooked. There is also a danger that the unusual activity rather than the typical, routine, characteristic behavior will be noticed, or on the other hand, the teacher may be so used to routine behavior that only transitory notice is given to the unusual act or accomplishment. But despite the difficulty in gaining knowledge of pupils, such knowledge is important, for it has been found that teachers, lacking such knowledge, have tended to fall back on subject matter, social and educational tradition, and routine teaching methods. As a result, they have been more dominating and directive than they have been facilitative and creative (Anderson, Brewer, and Reid, 1946).

One way to come to know the pupils and to counteract the tendency to teach by routine and prescription is to make use of anecdotal records. These are brief, periodic, descriptions of typical pupil behaviors.[3] Prescott, who has worked for several years in helping teachers develop techniques for better pupil understanding, lists the characteristics of a good anecdote as follows:

1. It gives the date, the place, and the situation in which the action occurred. We call this the setting.

2. It describes the actions of the child, the reactions of the other people involved, and the response of the child to these reactions.

3. It quotes what is said to the child and by the child during the action.

4. It supplies "mood cues"—postures, gestures, voice qualities, and facial expressions that give cues to how the child felt. It does not provide interpretations of his feelings, but only the cues by which a reader may judge what they were.

5. The description is extensive enough to cover the episode. The action or conversation is not left incomplete and unfinished but is followed through to the point where a little vignette of a behavioral moment in the life of the child is supplied.[4]

An example of an anecdote that meets the foregoing criteria gives us a glimpse of Jane:

February 8, 8:50 A.M.—Florence came to school today. She asked to move her seat next to Edith. I allowed her to do so. Jane also moved hers, so that a group of four was formed: Edith, Doris, Florence, and Jane. 12:30 P.M.—I was on the playground today. I allowed the children who had been ill with colds or who weren't wearing proper clothing to stay inside. These included Edith, Florence, and Jane. (Setting) I hadn't been out there too long when Florence came

---

[3] "A Manual for the Behavior Journal" describes values and methods; it may be found in Willard C. Olson, *Child Development*, 2d ed., Boston: D. C. Heath and Company, 1959, pp. 467–473.
[4] Daniel A. Prescott, *The Child in the Educative Process*, New York: McGraw-Hill Book Company, 1957, pp. 153–154.

out crying. She said that Jane had pushed her seat away from Florence. I went over to her and put my hand on her shoulder. She shrugged it off (mood cue) and started yelling (mood cue), "I don't care, she told lies about me." I said, "Jane, please come into the hall with me." She ran out of the room ahead of me into the cellarway and hid her face against the wall. I said to her, "Suppose you tell me your side of the story, Jane." No answer. "Are you annoyed because Florence played with Edith?" Jane started to cry and said, "I asked Florence to help me and she wouldn't do it. Then she said I was laughing in the hall, and I wasn't. She wouldn't answer me when I talked to her, so I pulled her hair." I said, "Florence has to have other friends, too, and she won't like you any better if you do things like that. The best thing to do is to wait quietly. She will come back to you. The two of you have been friends all year. It would be a shame to break up that friendship now." She stopped crying and asked me to send Florence out. I did, and as we came down the hall Jane met us and said, "I'm sorry I pulled your hair, Florence." She took Florence's hand. Florence said, "That's all right Jane. Let's go wash your face." [5]

Preparing good anecdotes on a number of pupils is admittedly a time-consuming project, but it will pay dividends in terms of time saved from disciplinary actions and wasted teaching effort. The resulting improved understanding will pay its greatest dividend in the satisfaction the teacher has from seeing optimum development in more of his pupils.

The school and pupil personality

Next to early home influences, the school is probably the most powerful factor in shaping the development of personality. It is here that the growing student learns to react in wide social context, to develop his constitutional potential, and to control and direct his basic temperament. If the personality lessons we learn are to be most beneficial in pushing the student toward the pursuit of higher-level needs, *he must not only be understood as an individual, but his environment must be such as to foster the desired kinds of behavior,* and at least something is known of the nature of such salutary environments. Whether or not the aims of school are stated in terms of academic knowledge of behavioral patterns, personality is being changed as the aims are achieved. Too often, emphasis has been primarily on the correction of deficiencies. While such correction is necessary, the more recent emphasis on self-realization, the expansion of the positive, is commendable. Working to change personality may be pursued (1) by alteration of specific aspects of the environment or (2) by giving attention to the total school atmosphere.

[5] *Ibid.*, pp. 156–157.

Experimental Modification of Personality An example of altering specifics is provided in the experiments of Lois Jack, who recognized in child behavior the trait of ascendance, a "pecking order." Children were brought in pairs into a play situation that consisted of a limited number of sand toys. Ascendant behavior was judged from (1) verbally demanding materials, (2) forcefully trying to get toys, (3) obtaining materials, (4) snatching materials, (5) directing the other child's play, (6) securing compliance of the other child, (7) ordering the other child about, and (8) providing the pattern that the other child imitated. The more submissive children were given special training in using the toys competently in order to build up their confidence. As they gained in competence and self-confidence they became more ascendant in comparable experimental situations (Jack, 1934).

This experiment was repeated by D. V. Mummery (1947), who verified the earlier conclusion that self-confidence underlies manifestation of the trait of ascendance. In this study, a "wholesome degree" of ascendance was emphasized; that is, the child was not encouraged to be aggressive or dominant, but the experiment was planned to discourage submission.

The teacher who wants to build a child's confidence may do so by helping him build a skill. If the pupil develops feelings of inferiority because of academic difficulties, he should be given a chance to demonstrate the skills he has. Thus, one poor student who declared he hated schoolwork asserted one day that he could write a better song than the one the class was singing. His teacher encouraged him to try it. He did, and the song was good. It was sung by his classmates, and thenceforth he took a more confident and aggressive part in classwork. Similar results were obtained by a teacher who gave a high school boy responsibility for arranging stage lighting—his success flowed over into interest and competence in literature. A girl's poems were read in class and published in the school paper—prior to the teacher's discovery of them, the poems had been hidden. Recognition helped the girl gain confidence, which showed in improved work in mathematics. A junior high school girl gained skill in square dancing. The principal took her dance group to other schools for demonstration, and the girl became perceptibly more outgoing personally and more productive academically. Developed skills give a person confidence, and that confidence may permeate behavior patterns beyond the area involving the specific skills. These experiences and experiments underline the advisability of looking for opportunities to give each child a feeling of competence, success, and worth.

The Effect of the Total School Atmosphere An example of giving attention to the total school atmosphere is afforded in the higher-horizons program spearheaded by Daniel Schreiber (1960). The setting was in

New York City's Manhattanville Junior High School 43. The objective was to discover, identify, and stimulate academically able students in a culturally disadvantaged group. Steps in the total process included (1) identifying "college-able" students through tests, teachers' ratings, and counseling interviews, (2) stimulating them to think of college by pointing to examples of persons with similar backgrounds who made good (thus emphasizing that avenues are open), (3) creating college aspirations by taking them to research centers, libraries, professional schools, and hospitals and by seeking scholarship support, (4) educating the community and parents to accept the worthwhileness of college by personal interviews (parents were found to be not so uncooperative as busy making a living), (5) educating the faculty through in-service training programs, teacher conferences, and having teachers accompany pupils on planned trips, (6) guiding pupils and parents in individual and group conferences, some of which took place before or after regular school hours, thus requiring an extended school day, (7) providing remedial work to bring pupils to and beyond grade level, and (8) raising the cultural level of pupils by taking them to concerts, operas, theaters, and local college campuses and by securing books for them at wholesale prices.

The results of the higher-horizons program are encouraging. Eighty per cent of the pupils planned to finish high school, and three-fourths felt that their ambitions had been raised. The year before the project was started, 42 per cent of the pupils were graduated from high school, whereas 80 per cent were still in the project after three years, and others had transferred to other curricula and schools. Students made an average gain of 4 points on the Otis Mental Ability Test.[6] Some pupils from the project became delinquent, but the incidence of delinquency from Manhattanville Junior High School was smaller than that from other comparable schools, and did not show the increase that was being noticed city-wide.

The Teacher's Impact on Pupil Personality   The school's most important influence on pupils is provided by the teacher. He sets the tone of the classroom and establishes the mood of the group. He is the authority figure providing the direction for behavior. If well liked, he is a model and is consciously imitated; if he is disliked, pupils may still unconsciously absorb his manners and attitudes. Buhler reports that a dominating teacher may force an already shy child into further withdrawal. A teacher with social-class prejudice may generate negative attitudes toward learning on the part of those children. Teachers who have colorless, drab personalities may cause pupils to be restive and inattentive (Buhler, 1952, p. 162ff).

---

[6] A gain of four points would be insignificant for an individual but such a gain for a group (where losses also occur, as the result of test variability) may be regarded as indicative of real gain.

The result of much research on the effect of teachers on pupil personality has been summarized as follows:

> It would appear that personally maladjusted teachers may or may not affect the personal and social adjustment of their pupils in an adverse way, depending upon the type of overt behavior through which the teacher resolves her psychological frustrations. The maladjusted teacher who makes her adjustments through *impunitive* (glossing over difficulties) and *intropunitive* (self-blaming) patterns of behavior may be extremely unhappy herself, but have essentially no negative influence on her pupils' growth and adjustment. However, there is a high probability that the maladjusted teacher who employs *extrapunitive* (blaming others) patterns of behavior to reduce her psychological tensions will have an undesirable effect on the psychological growth and adjustment of her pupils. The children in her classroom will probably suffer intense frustration and pain as she vents her aggressive tendencies through sarcasm, threats, inconsistent episodes of anger, and corporal punishment. . . . There seems to be little excuse in a democratic society for *forcing* children to suffer the taunts and gibes of a bitter teacher. This bleak picture of certain teacher-pupil relationships is only partially mitigated by the remarkable resiliency with which children respond to social pressures from all adults.[7]

Curriculum and Personality The curriculum must be appropriate for the child for him to approach his potential. For example, the parents of a feeble-minded girl dreaded having her placed in a special class for mentally retarded children. They felt that she needed the stimulation of brighter children. They had scolded her and tried to shame her to become more like her normal older sister. After repeated conferences with the psychologist and the psychiatrist, they allowed her to be placed in the class for children with retarded mental development. The parents learned that children with less intelligence than their daughter knew more than she because the instruction and curriculum were appropriate and the children could compete on their own level (Kammett, 1951).

Hoyt (1964) has reported studies on the nonacademically oriented student indicating that those who appear to be academically inept may give quite another account of themselves when the primary curricular emphasis is on work skills. Kupferman and Ulmer (1964) have also achieved gratifying results with eight-to-twelve-year-old boys who have a handicraft program in an industrially oriented school setting. Discipline problems diminished, schoolwork improved, goals were clarified, and boys stuck to projects they would previously have abandoned.

The curriculum is also influential in the motivation of unusually able

[7] George G. Thompson, *Child Psychology: Growth Trends in Psychological Adjustment*, 2d ed., Boston: Houghton Mifflin Company, 1962, p. 670.

students. At the present time, about 40 per cent of students who are in the upper third in intellectual ability do not enter college (Wolfle, 1960). Many factors contribute to this loss of talent—family educational tradition, socioeconomic-class identification, financial resources, local availability of educational opportunity, personality adjustment patterns, and health— but appropriate, challenging curriculum must also be included.

> Recognizing that the child often does not need drill to learn, he (the teacher) allows the child to discover new relationships, to experiment and explore. He accepts the child as a partner in the exciting search for knowledge. Independent study, creative experiences in science, mathematics, art, and music, and wide contact with the minds of others through books and class visitors are all essential aspects of a challenging program which can stretch the mind and the imagination of the child.[8]

Special classes, independent study, advanced sections of regular classes, individual instruction, research projects, and revised systems of evaluation are used at both the elementary and secondary, but particularly at the secondary, level to assist in providing appropriate challenge to able students. Whether we consider the slow learner or the gifted pupil, an important principle is that *education must provide the opportunity for success that derives from exerting one's best efforts.*

Teaching Methods and Personality Competitive attitudes are fostered by many aspects of our society, including the highly competitive structure of school life. For competition to make optimum contributions to personality, it must be adroitly handled by teachers. Adversaries of approximately equal ability or status should be matched; competition in which success or failure is inevitable for one of the opponents is not highly beneficial to either the winner or the loser. The easy winner has no challenge to exertion, and the inevitable loser must protect himself by withdrawal or adjust by lowering his self-esteem. Competition should also be geared to the age of the pupil. Cooperation is a more mature level of behavior than competition, but children seem to prefer the competitive situation (Stendler, Damrin, and Haines, 1951). It appears that cooperative abilities must be carefully nurtured in a society that regards it as desirable.

The late Kurt Lewin and his associates have shown how methods of dealing with children can be arranged to produce predictable kinds of behavior. Groups of ten-year-old boys, equated as far as possible, were subjected to autocratic, democratic, and laissez-faire leaders. In the authoritarian climate, policy was determined by the leader, steps were dictated one at a time, the leader designated working groups and tasks,

---

[8] Anna R. Meeks, in Leonard M. Miller (ed.), *Guidance for the Underachiever with Superior Ability*, Washington: U.S. Office of Education, 1961, p. 38.

and praise and criticism were of a personal nature. In the democratic climate, politics were matters of group decisions, goals were discussed and the leader suggested alternatives, members were free to work with whom they wished, division of tasks was left to the group, and the leader praised or criticized impersonally. In the laissez-faire group, there was complete freedom for group or personal decision without leader intervention, the leader said he would help if asked but took no other part—tasks and groupings were determined without the leader's participation. Comments on the work being done were infrequent. After six weeks it was noted that aggressive actions per meeting were thirty-eight for the laissez-faire group, thirty for the autocratic group, and twenty for the democratic group. Some of the boys in the autocratic group were apathetic, and others stopped coming. Boys were asked to evaluate the work and declared that they did not like the autocratic group—*but* they directed their hostility to other boys. Boys in the laissez-faire group felt they needed more direction and help. They appreciated and liked the democratic leader. Scapegoats were created in the autocratic group, and the products of their labors were ultimately used as weapons of warfare. When the leaders left the room, the autocratic group quickly deteriorated; in the democratic group, there was little difference in the work atmosphere (Lewin, Lippitt, and White, 1939). Repetitions of the experiment in which leaders switched roles indicated that the results were an outcome of the behaviors rather than the personalities of the leaders.

If children are to develop the quality of independence, which is valued so highly in our society, they must be given freedom to think, choose, and act on their own, but this must not be confused with lack of direction by the teacher. Democracy also demands the ability to delegate responsibility and the development of specialties. In their training and experience, teachers have specialized in order to give responsible direction, and they should not neglect to use their wisdom for the benefit of the pupils. However, as pupils grow and gain experience and knowledge, they should be allowed more freedom in self-direction.

Another aspect of democracy that has great value for wholesome personality development is the concept of the intrinsic worth of the individual. To the extent that the teacher actively recognizes the worth of each child, he will be enhancing the pupil's feeling of personal significance and security. Among other things, this means that a pupil should be commended for the effort he exerts and for the quality of work that is proportionate to his present ability. To say to Sue, "See how neat and well behaved Sally is," is more likely to foster feelings of personal insignificance or resentment toward the teacher or Sally than it is to provide Sue with an incentive for improvement. Giving appropriate praise, taking time to listen to pupils, and showing interest in their comments and activities are classroom essentials.

Being a democratic citizen implies that each individual has a part to play that is significant to others. The belief that there should be no social isolates is based on psychological fact as well as on cultural mores: Human beings develop by virtue of association with others (Goodson, 1960, p. 12). The use of sociograms (see section on Dealing with the Constructive Emotions, Chapter 12) is one technique by which teachers may perceive the lonely one and find clues for encouraging activities that will involve all pupils. Encouraging children to work in groups and providing them with opportunities to do so gains support from experimental findings. Much schoolwork can be better oriented and better motivated if greater emphasis is placed on group accomplishment than upon competitive systems of grading that reward only individual achievement (Hudgins, 1960).

The Teacher's View of Personality Problems A big step forward in helping pupils build more healthy personalities will be taken when all teachers understand so-called "problem" behavior. E. K. Wickman (1928), in a still widely quoted study, showed that teachers were more likely to consider whispering, inattentiveness, carelessness in work, tattling, and disorderliness as serious problems and less likely to be concerned about shyness, withdrawal, and daydreaming. Psychiatrists, on the other hand, were inclined to take another view. They considered that the more serious problems were shyness, withdrawal, and daydreaming. Follow-up studies indicate that in recent years teachers have come to see more clearly the serious implications of such behavior (Hunter, 1957), though there is still much room for improvement. The contemporary view is that isolated behavior, whether it be shyness or bullying, should not be considered too seriously and that the child should be viewed in his total behavior system. Any one trait may be of considerable importance, but its significance cannot be determined in isolation. The frequency of manifestation and the combination of one trait and others to form a disturbed pattern of behavior are important. It is the child, not the trait, that should be watched (D. James, 1950).

Teachers are in a better position to help personality development when they recognize what is important and significant and what might better be overlooked. They need to know that the child who reveals several atypical behaviors and does so consistently is more in need of attention than one who makes a gross, but rare, misstep. Moreover, they must realize that the behavior is a symptom of difficulty and look for the sources. Again, appropriate help can best be given when the teacher knows something of the biological, medical, social, and educational history of the child (Trillingham, 1962, p. 245). Knowledge of these factors will often lead to the identification of basic needs that are not being satisfied; once the needs are recognized, means of satisfying them become evident.

Summary

Concepts concerning personality pervade the whole field of educational psychology. Teachers have the task of providing the best context possible for the development of hereditary potential. Fortunately, more can be done to alter personality in general than presently seems possible in intellectual and physical characteristics. Many factors contribute to atmospheres favorable for personality development: Prominent among them are faith in the ability of people to change for the better; providing freedom for development of unique interest and abilities; seeing that pupils have the chance for success, which leads to strong ego-concepts; and individual assistance in overcoming handicaps and in using strengths wisely.

The best help can be given when one's pupils are understood. Approaches such as personality inventories, projective techniques, and rating scales aid understanding, but the most reliable and readily available method for teachers is controlled observation. The time invested in recording observations pays dividends in terms of improved help for children.

Experiments show that personality responds to specific environmental changes. Developing skills, fulfillment of needs, and effective key adults in the child's life are particularly productive of personality change. Whole school environments have been altered with encouraging changes in goal orientation on the part of pupils. The teachers can be either a positive or a negative force. The kind of curriculum, the teaching methods employed, and the view that teachers take of pupils are of great importance. Both research and practice show that personality can be modified so that desirable personal and social goals may be achieved.

Problems and exercises

1 In what way does the description of another's personality tend to reveal the personality of the person doing the describing?

2 What are some of the reasons why a pupil might be recalcitrant and pugnacious in school? What implications do these reasons have for teachers?

3 Do you believe that body build plays a significant role in personality orientation? Cite reasons for your answer.

4 What are some of the attitudes and behaviors of teachers who have the most beneficial effect on pupil personalities?

5 What experience with personality inventories have you had that leads to a favorable or skeptical view of their use by teachers?

6 Visit some elementary or secondary school, follow a particular pupil for a day, and make a "behavior journal" that reveals his personality. Read it in class and have your fellow students evaluate it.

7 What do you think are the major obstacles to using such techniques as those employed in the higher-horizons project on a larger scale?

8 How might teachers go about changing their own personalities? (Several inferences may be drawn from various discussions in the chapter.)

9 What are some curricular changes that you think would make a better setting for favorable development of pupil personality?

Suggested additional readings

Borrowman, Merle L.: "Traditional Values and the Sharing of American Education," *Social Forces Influencing American Education,* Sixtieth Yearbook of the National Society for the Study of Education, Chicago: University of Chicago Press, 1961, part II, pp. 144–170.

All chapters add to an understanding of personality in our culture. The chapter indicated discusses regional and historical concepts of certain of our values and ideals.

Hall, Edward T.: *The Silent Language,* Garden City, N.Y.: Doubleday & Company, Inc., 1959.

This fascinating short book shows how deeply specific cultures affect individual personalities. Reading the book helps to provide understanding of how highly modifiable the human personality is.

Hodgkinson, Harold L.: *Education in Social and Cultural Perspectives,* Englewood Cliffs, N.J.: Prentice-Hall, Inc., 1962, pp. 208–237.

The author gives some indication of the complexity of forces that produce personality. He suggests some knowledge that should be developed if we are to understand why individuals behave as they do.

Kvaraceus, William C.: *Delinquent Behavior: I, Culture and the Individual,* Washington: National Education Association, 1959, pp. 24–61.

Although this book is written with a view to understanding the delinquent personality, the pages indicated reveal some of the facts, myths, and processes that are pertinent to all personality development.

Rethlingshafer, Dorothy: *Motivation as Related to Personality,* New York: McGraw-Hill Book Company, 1963.

Specific factors that influence personality orientation and that the individual brings to the learning situation are discussed in this chapter.

Thompson, George D.: *Child Psychology,* 2d ed., Boston: Houghton Mifflin Company, 1962, pp. 560–618.

Some of the material deals with preschool age, but much attention is given to school practices and experiments that will facilitate good personality development.

The Child as a Learner

14

The twentieth century has been called the century of the child because so much has been learned of their nature and development that the lot of children has been greatly improved. It is known that children are marvelously tough, pliable, teachable. The variety of child-rearing practices around the world shows this. While many practices reveal accumulated wisdom, others are of dubious value. Some dubious practices—whip the reluctant learner, keep the inattentive after school, discipline the child's mind with difficult subjects —are yielding to research findings. Some of the recent insights will be examined in this chapter, and some of the accumulated wisdom of the ages will be emphasized for its pertinence to teaching.

Elementary teachers, the teachers of children, have a role of considerable importance. It is they who determine, to a marked degree, whether pupils will enjoy and anticipate learning or whether they will dislike and avoid formal learning in the future. To the extent that teachers understand and work in accord with the nature of children, they will promote a basic enjoyment of learning. All that has previously been said about learning processes, transfer, motivation, emotions, and intellectual growth may also facilitate the child's enjoyment of learning. What will later be said of mental health, language development, and culture has similar pertinence. The goal here is to stress certain psychological facts about children that have not been stressed in other contexts.

Development is continuous, and no learning processes are unique in children (White, 1963, p. 196), but some of the social pressures, needs, and abilities of children are different enough from those of adolescents to warrant attention.

Some psychological characteristics of children

Children Are Interested in Process One practical difficulty facing teachers is this: Young persons do not have the maturity and experience to enable them wholeheartedly to accept the purposes formulated by adults. Adults do not always seem to understand that children are not simply miniature adults. If a child were asked and could comprehend the question "Why do you do that?" he might reply, "It's fun to do it." His orientation is weighted toward the action, not toward the results—particularly the long-range results—of the behavior. This can be illustrated in the actions of a very young child—age eighteen months to two years. He drops a spoon, and his mother picks it up, saying, "Don't do that again." But he does drop the spoon again. He has simply discovered that spoon dropping is fun and that it is a way to play with his mother.

Children of school age will ask innumerable questions. The parents and teacher, having read books on child psychology, patiently answer the questions in terms the child can understand, and he does understand. Presently, the child's lack of experience shows itself when he runs out of questions. He then repeats the same questions, which are again answered, and finally the adult says, "I answered that. You tell me." And the child can give the answer. He enjoys and is interested in the process of talking —*his* goal is the activity of talking. This is not to deny that many questions are asked for information; but information seeking does not explain the repetitive question. Similarly, children run, shout, tussle, paint, and perhaps even read because of the joy they receive from the particular activity. They derive pleasure from sensory experience. They relish movement, pressure, taste, sound, and odor. They repeat experiences that yield

FIGURE 19. *Children often learn more effectively when they can be physically active in their learning projects.*

SOURCE: *Courtesy of Department of Instructional Materials, Portland, Ore., Public Schools.*

these sensory gratifications and seek new sources of stimulation (Stone and Church, 1957, p. 150). Information getting is only part of the child's goal.

The implications of the child's interest in process are obvious for the primary teacher. Pupils are interested in learning. The joyful news "I can read!" is an indication of their interest in performance. Children do not need to be stimulated by gold stars or A's and S's as symbols of their progress. The development of adequacy is the child's underlying purpose (Combs and Snygg, 1959, p. 45), but the meaning of "adequacy" changes as he grows older and develops in many ways. Culture in the form of traditional academic standards soon makes its impression, as fourth graders reveal when they report to their parents, "I got an A in arithmetic" or "I got 100 in spelling." The child apparently begins to think that mere improvement over yesterday's status is of little concern to the adult.

The child's interest in process can be used by the teacher if he makes the shift from process to product slowly and progressively. As children grow, they do become interested in results, but one must be careful not to ask young children too frequently, "Why are you doing that?" "What is it you are painting?" "Where are you going?" The time will come when the baby will use blocks to make forts or castles, not simply pile them up and knock them down. Similarly, if we do not get too anxious about reading, the time may come when children will read because it is fun to find answers, not because they can or are expected to. It is advisable to capitalize on the child's natural inclination for activity and delay the emphasis on symbols as goals, because both school and life demand the continued process of adjusting. It is worth noting that feelings of success occur during the process of achieving and disappear after attainment (Barker, 1942). Hence, the least teachers can do is to manifest interest in what is going on instead of stressing the end product exclusively.

"Activity" need not mean physical activity at any level of education. But in the early elementary grades, activity should frequently involve muscular and bodily movement. In the early grades, children must have a chance to touch, manipulate, act, play, imitate, and move about freely. But it is a mistake to believe that children are always on the move, that they are never still—there are many times when they sit quietly and pensively. Curricula and teaching methods must allow for and capitalize upon children's basic predisposition to alternate between rest and activity.

Children Need Immediate Goals   As pupils grow older, more distant goals (products) become increasingly important. However, before long-term goals become operative, immediate goals must be postulated and stressed. To the young pupil, "this afternoon" and "tomorrow" are more important than "next week" and the "end of the term." For example, primary teachers have noted that if several weeks are devoted to preparing a Christmas program, interest wanes before the actual performance. Consequently, they stress "finishing the decorations today, sending the invitations this afternoon, and completing the costumes tomorrow."

Immediate goals should also characterize teaching objectives. The need for immediate goals is explained by the young pupil's short attention span and his lack of an accurate concept of time. He will try and often can pay attention for twenty or thirty minutes, but he is likely to develop unnecessary tensions. The teacher should be on the alert for evidences of fatigue, such as restlessness and wandering attention, and shift to another activity as soon as practicable. The duration of the attention span varies greatly with age and still more with the importance of the task. A nine-year-old may spend all morning with his mechanical building set, but find twenty minutes' drill in arithmetic boring beyond endurance.

Every teacher has the responsibility of telling his pupils what they will get out of the subject he teaches—purposeful activity is preferable to purposive activity in the classroom. Although the pupil's ability to comprehend the significance of the future will grow steadily from the first grade, the elementary teacher should study the reactions of pupils to see how effective reference to the future is.

A feeling of success or failure need not stem from an absolute standard of performance. What is success for one person may be failure for another (Terrell, Durkin, and Wiesley, 1959). However, experiments show that appropriateness of a child's goals depends on the kind of experiences he has had and his self-concept. Successful pupils (ones who achieve in accord with their indicated abilities) tend to have aspirations that are in line with their previous performance (Worell, 1959). If pupils frequently fail (receive disapproval from teachers or feel they could have done better), they lose self-esteem and tend to set levels of aspiration that are below their indicated ability (Davids and White, 1958). Pupils in the latter group may hope for too much—they are visionary dreamers, perhaps hoping to receive approbation for high ambition—or they may simply cease trying. Thus it is clear that the feeling of success, which mental hygienists deem to be so important, depends to a large extent upon the teacher's recognition of individual differences, and offering the child opportunity to participate in tasks he considers important. As he matures, these tasks may become more abstract in meaning and remote in time.

The old idea that a child would rather have a quarter today than a dollar tomorrow has psychological validity. It is a mark of maturity to look toward the future in evaluating the present. Teachers should not only give attention to immediate goals for children, but gradually begin to show them that remote considerations should also receive attention.

Children Need Routines Consistent routines will give the child feelings of security and comfort (Maslow, 1954, p. 86). This does not mean that a questionable method should be adhered to simply for the sake of consistency. There are many valid reasons for interrupting a routine. But teachers should see to it that a guiding sequence of activities and a somewhat uniform method of treatment are complemented by variety and contrast.

The desire for routine is manifested at a very early age. When a baby is put to bed, he must have his drink, throw a kiss to all the members of the family, hear a story, say his prayers, and have a certain toy. If the routine is completed, he will go to sleep immediately and quietly. But if the routine is upset, there is likely to be a somewhat stormy period of protest. Children in school show the same desire for routine. They miss the spelling period if it does not take place at the usual time. They show a preference for the game they have played on previous days.

The desire for routine also shows itself in reactions to the environment. Abrupt changes often cause emotional disturbances, and migratory family habits are recognized as factors contributing to problem behavior. To the extent consistent with progressive goals of education, teachers should provide for schedules and uniformity in methods and approaches. Conflicting values in the home and the school cause other difficulties in adjustment. Children with problems are frequently those who have discovered that the procedures and aims of the teachers do not parallel those of their parents at home (Kvaraceus, 1959, p. 101). The teacher can avoid some of this type of conflict by learning something about the home and guarding against condemning words or actions.

As far as possible, *the teacher should be consistent in his moods, routines, and disciplinary attitudes and approaches.* Several factors support the desirability of consistency:

1. Consistency tends to reduce anxiety. Some anxiety, especially that connected with the realization of goals, facilitates learning; but too much anxiety and anxiety that is not goal-connected are incompatible with efficient learning (Wiener, 1959).

2. Consistency of approval for some acts and disapproval for others gives the pupil a clear-cut goal. Children do need and seek the approval of others, including teachers.

3. When habits that are to be cognitively based are strengthened by knowledge of how to react (having a consistent model), their information is facilitated (Baldwin, 1955, p. 454).

While consistency is only one of the elements that make up a good classroom situation, it is highly desirable. The practical implications are many. Teachers should not allow pupils to interrupt each other on one day and condemn such behavior the next day. Questions should not be received courteously from some and be regarded as impertinent from others. Horseplay should not be accepted on one occasion and criticized on another. Teachers should strive daily to avoid sarcasm, shaming, and ridicule. Courteousness on the part of both pupils and teacher should be a consistent factor if the goal is building strong ego concepts in all pupils.

Play Is Important Business Mental hygienists encourage all persons to round out their lives by regularly participating in some form of recreation or play, and child psychologists stress play as the important business of a child. In the child's eyes play is a natural and significant activity: From the adult standpoint it is important because it promotes efficient learning. It gives the child an opportunity to come in close contact with his environment. It builds muscle and fosters physical endurance and provides an opportunity to practice the physical skills of balance, timing, and co-ordination. It provides for the acquisition and exercise of social skills—cooperation, conversation, mutual respect, friendliness, and courtesy. It provides emotional satisfaction in that it fills the need for companionship, achievement, recognition, and freedom. Play is also helpful in releasing negative emotions, such as fear and anger—thus providing for emotional catharsis (Jersild, 1960, p. 242).

Helpful insights have been derived from experiments in which children regressed to infantile patterns of behavior when their play activities were frustrated. They were first permitted to play freely in a room with rather limited materials. Next, the toys were placed with many others in another part of the room, and each child was allowed to play there long enough to become thoroughly interested (that is, to form a goal). Then the first toys were picked up and placed back in their original place; the child was led back to the limited materials, and a wire screen was lowered, blocking the child off from the more attractive play situation. Regression was shown by relative lack of constructiveness in play, decreased freedom of movement, decreased verbal activity, decreased happiness, and increased restlessness and aggressiveness, shown by hitting, kicking, destroying (Barker, 1941).

This experiment suggests that the child takes his play seriously because his goals come from play. If adults are to be instrumental in building healthy ego concepts, they must avoid belittling the child by making disparaging remarks about the silliness or futility of play. Further, just as an adult dislikes interruptions when he is engrossed in work, the child reacts strongly to interruptions of his play activities. Teachers should look at the educational potentials of play and seek to enhance them by encouragement, by occasional participation, by providing variety, and by supplying appropriate materials.

Capitalizing on the importance of play in the classroom is by no means a matter of watering down the curriculum. Rather, encouraging play—

a great deal of it—recognizes a basic psychological characteristic of childhood (the thrust for social and physical competence). There is good reason to agree with the child-guidance experts when they say that depriving children of sufficient opportunity to play may impose handicaps that they may never completely overcome. This is seen in adults who, as children, were kept too busy at schoolwork or had no companions "fit to play with" and who now lack social graces or facility in basic physical skills or who are so serious about their profession or occupation that they have no time for recreation.

There is great possibility of utilizing play as a source of motivation for effective learning. Playing store or playing at being mayor calls for application of knowledge. Making a game of spelling or arithmetic in no way diminishes the need for accuracy or for exact knowledge. In one of the most interesting class sessions the author has observed, two girls in a high school social studies class recounted a make-believe journey they had taken to Bolivia. Their account of a descent from high altitudes via narrow-gauge railroads, their experiences in the market, and their observation of schools and artisans at work revealed a background of patient and detailed research.

Whether or not play can always be used as an approach to learning, certain elements—fun, freedom, and friendliness—that are associated with play should be used in effective teaching. A courteous, relaxed, active classroom atmosphere certainly does not connote drudgery and compulsion. The more closely teachers can make their schoolwork resemble play, the greater the likelihood that work will become a vital, welcome activity.

One further advantage of play activities in the classroom is that teachers can observe and better understand pupils as they express themselves in nonverbal language. Dominant personality trends may be noted in members of the group—the child who characteristically stands doubtfully on the fringe; the one who frequently shoves, bumps, hits, and snatches; the one who subtly manipulates others; the one who confidently provides the ideas and assigns the roles; the one who talks much and does little.

> For children, play may be conceptualized as the "royal road" to thought processes, for although children during the period we are discussing have not yet learned consciously to inhibit their thoughts, they are less able to communicate them to us directly through their verbalizations. During play, we may observe at first hand, if we observe carefully, both the conscious and unconscious thinking processes and thought products which would otherwise be more likely to escape our attention. Moreover, play reflects much more than some aspects of the child's personality; it also reflects some aspects of the child's culture.[1]

[1] Max L. Hutt and Robert G. Gibby, *The Child*, p. 190, Copyright 1959, by Allyn and Bacon, Inc., Boston. Reprinted by permission of the publisher.

Observation is only the beginning of a much more challenging task. The wise teacher does not simply step in to force participation, to curb the garrulous, to put down aggression, or to slow the manipulator and idea man. Rather, *he seeks to understand the motivations and basic needs* being revealed to see if there are more constructive ways in which the needs may be met. Some basic personality trends probably should be encouraged; others need to be redirected. There are no panaceas, no blanket prescriptions. The teacher needs ingenuity and creativeness, and his first step is seeing what takes place during play.

Children Need Acceptance and Approval Many aspects of schooling must be carefully examined in the light of children's need for acceptance and approval. Among them are age-grade standards and the school's orientation to middle-class culture.

The need to master subject matter has led to rather rigid standards that cause some children who fail to meet them on schedule, to feel unworthy or incompetent ("Ten Criticisms of Public Education," p. 143), and their reaction is to strike back. *Children defend themselves by behaviors that disrupt school routines and threaten the teacher's prestige.* Yet it is these pupils (but not their behaviors) who are most in need of understanding and acceptance and approval. The teacher's tone of voice, his willingness to give assistance, his deemphasis on grades, and his emphasis on individual progress can reduce the likelihood of the child's feeling unaccepted.

Many children, approximately half of them, come from the lower social classes. Not only do they have the task of learning subject matter, but their load is doubled by having to adapt to a new culture—the middle-class culture of the school. Disapproval of lack of cleanliness, outspoken language, disdain for school—all of which are more frequently met in lower-class pupils than among those of the middle class—is not easy to express without permitting a pupil to infer disapproval for himself. It is accomplished by teachers who can give appropriate words of praise, "How clean your hands are today," "You said that quite correctly," "This is much better than yesterday's paper." Approval can be expressed by a brief hug or a pat on the shoulder when a child is told to keep clean or to stop using certain words or when he says "I hate school."

Acceptance is difficult when a child is chronically aggressive, disobedient, or impudent. Circumstances must dictate the advisability of condemning the behavior and accepting the child or accepting both behavior and child. Much depends on the teacher's attitude toward himself and his role as teacher. If he can see that the behavior is more than just a challenge to his prestige and authority, he can accept more. If he is insecure, his defenses must be put into action—ordering "Stop," banishing the child, or sending him to the office. It will be very helpful if he can realize that behavior is caused, and misbehavior is also caused. Misbehavior is the child's way of saying, "I'm hurt," "I need help," "The pressure is too great" (Hymes, 1955, pp. 84ff). *Showing acceptance and approval is facilitated by knowledge of the child's abilities and backgrounds —to know is to understand.* We would all readily stop to bandage the crushed finger, but first aid for the crushed spirit, which shows no bright flow of blood, is less readily proffered. It is also helpful to know that the hurt or the need for help or the pressure underlying misbehavior often comes from outside the school.

Child Behavior Reflects Parental Handling A child brings his family to school. His self-confidence, his willingness to converse with others, and his interest in school tasks all more or less directly reflect the way he has been treated at home (Hoffman and Lippitt, 1960). Many of his attitudes —toward work, toward discipline, toward honesty, and toward cooperation—have had their genesis in what he has heard and experienced in his family group. Even a boy's scholastic aptitudes, numerous studies indicate, are related to the pattern of relationships he has had with his father (Carlsmith, 1964).

Parents want to be assured that their children are progressing just as rapidly and performing just as well as others in the class. Despite individual differences, teachers at times try to secure this end in an attempt to please themselves and the parents. As one teacher said, "Of course I urged and encouraged constantly—aided and abetted by parents who urged, threatened, and no doubt bribed. Small wonder that the reading did not improve. I took away the third-grade readers and, from the discards in the basement, dug up some old primers and first readers. The children in the slow group could read these, and our reading class became the happy experience it should always have been. My pupils were pleased with their success and enjoyed the stories. I am a happier teacher, too."

The obstacle to using differentiated methods and materials seems to be a lack of courage on the part of administrators and teachers. As one teacher vehemently put it, "Teachers and administrators are afraid to tell a parent that his son or daughter cannot compete with other individuals in the class. Subterfuge, underhandedness, and subtle segregation all combine to make one realize that when a teacher or administrator yaps about treating each child as an individual, they are really mouthing 'flapdoodles.' They are giving lip service to something they don't really mean." Certainly, it is true that the most frequent response from teachers who are advised to use differentiated instruction and goals is, "The parents will object to having their children treated differently." This is not uniformly true. Parents are concerned with the welfare of their children, and when the case is clearly and fairly presented, most of them will agree to the teacher's plan (D'Evelyn, 1957, pp. 17ff).

The following passage illustrates how the open and honest approach can help both parents and the child:

> After about a month the parents began to see that, whether or not Edith's retardation was real or due to emotional causes, she would nevertheless benefit from placement in a class where there was a differentiated program planned to meet her needs and where the teacher, because of the lower register, could give her more individual attention. They began to realize that the increased sense of failure she experienced in the fourth grade increased her emotional problems. With the school's cooperation, the social worker and the parents sat in the "CRMD" ("Children with Retarded Mental Development") class for a few sessions. Both parents were impressed with the enthusiasm of the children and their active participation in the lessons. Mrs. A. was somewhat concerned, however, over what she considered the lack of quiet and order in the room. Mr. A. commented on how much the children knew and was surprised to learn that Edith, who knew far less, had a higher I. Q. than many of them. . . .
> The child was finally in a situation where she could participate and compete at her own level.[2]

Frankness in dealing with parents is dictated by the fact that a child's psychological orientation is largely determined by parental attitudes and treatment. For the maximum welfare of the child, the teacher must present the facts and then hope that the parents will be convinced. Certainly, the possibility of encountering parental objection does not warrant ignoring the problem and thereby reducing the child's chances to develop to his greatest potential.

Another way in which the child brings his family to school is in his worry about family welfare. Illness at home, family quarrels, or financial problems may make it difficult for the child to concentrate on school activities. The teacher can become aware of such problems by talking with the pupil, visiting his home, or reading the reports of other teachers who do so.

These generalizations are just as pertinent for the high school teachers as they are for the grade school teachers. The high school youngster may be under pressure at home to accomplish or may have family troubles that hamper his progress at school. His attitude toward school is a reflection of family orientation.

Psychological factors in teaching approaches

Teacher-Pupil Relationships as a Psychological Factor in Learning   Salient factors in teacher-pupil relationships include the following:

[2] Pauling H. Kammet, "Parents' Attitudes toward 'Special Classes' for Mentally Retarded Children," *Understanding the Child*, 20: 114–115, 1951.

1. *Acceptance* Acceptance begins with a teacher who has faith in himself and his professional competence. It also involves a functional recognition (the recognition shows in practice) of the pupil's mental, emotional, social, and physical limitations. Acceptance also means that the teacher has patience with the slow process of growth. The child is the focus of acceptance—this need not imply the acceptance of deviant behaviors.

2. *Security* A feeling of being liked and accepted is partly responsible for the child's sense of security. But feelings of security are also dependent upon the child's knowing what he can do and accomplish. Therefore, it is incumbent upon the teacher to see that tasks are scaled to the level of the child's ability and that every child has some experience of success. Feelings of security will be enhanced when classroom duties are so distributed that all may feel that they are contributors.

3. *Yielding to differences* Balance should be struck between authoritarianism and lack of direction. The child's tendency to shyness should not be met with firm determination to make him participate and be congenial. One child's belief that it is all right to help another should not be branded as cheating, nor should another child's refusal to help others be viewed as selfish. There are children in the normal range who play at the expense of schoolwork, and there are also those who do their schoolwork at the expense of play. Each should be permitted to approach his learning tasks as he desires until his action interferes with others or until his own future adjustment is threatened.

4. *Democratic procedures* Democracy implies mutual respect, cooperative planning, and shared responsibility and power. The voice of the pupils should be considered in formulating aims and in planning activities. "The basic method of democracy is the functioning of group intelligence, the ability and disposition of a social group to come to agreement on common goals and to direct effective action toward attaining those goals. The intelligent group, as does the intelligent individual, determines purposes and pursues them through *thinking*." [3]

5. *Friendliness* The word comes close to epitomizing the foregoing factors. Teacher-pupil relationships cannot be of the most salutary kind unless the teacher genuinely likes the pupils. To this end, the teacher can do two things: One is to become so familiar with the characteristics of children that he knows what can be expected of them; the other is to become acquainted with each child as an individual, with his abilities, his interests, his neighborhood, his home background, and his record of past performance. The teacher can show friendliness by being consistently courteous, taking time to listen, and avoiding situations that undermine a healthy self-concept.

[3] Howard Lane and Mary Beauchamp, *Understanding Human Development*, Englewood Cliffs, N.J.: Prentice-Hall, Inc., 1959, p. 101.

The importance of teacher-pupil relations becomes clear if we recall our own early school experiences. One is suddenly thrust into the strange world of school with a surrogate parent in charge. He must learn to sit still for what seems to him long periods of time. He must learn to suppress the desire to speak until it is proper to do so. He must adapt his physical needs to a new schedule. He must no longer kick and scream when he does not get his way. And in all this, the strange adult moves with absolute authority and omniscience. In such a world, a kind word, a pat on the head, a friendly smile, or an expression of praise makes a tremendous difference—to upper-grade and high school pupils as well as the primary pupil.

The Teacher's View of Deviant Behavior The teacher should always remember that all behavior is caused and try to understand the causes. Unfortunately, many teachers either do not see the implications of the fact that behavior is caused or find it inconvenient to apply their knowledge to exigencies of the moment. For example, if a recalcitrant child disturbs the teacher's equilibrium by challenging authority, the teacher can scarcely take time to search for causes when the symptom is being so obviously flaunted before the eyes of twenty or thirty other pupils.

Yet there is another view of the picture. The child is misbehaving, but not because of a desire to create a disturbance or because he is innately ornery. His behavior is a nonverbal way of saying that something is bothering him. Unless something is done to remove or mitigate the fundamental cause, correction of the symptom is temporary at best. Suppressing a child's desire to talk loudly, at length, and frequently may only result in his destroying property or picking on other children. Similarly, insisting that the excessively quiet child recite more often and join in group activities may only force him to retreat further from the group. Permanent improvement in his behavior and attitude will result only from improving his self-confidence and helping him become aware that he has something to contribute. As we have seen in many different contexts, this is a matter of giving him experience and training in play, work, and social intercourse.

Misbehaving children are frequently children who fundamentally dislike themselves—a reflection of the low opinion that others have of them. They misbehave to confirm the low evaluation of others and because they are convinced that they deserve the punishment or blame which results from their misbehavior. Getting at the roots of this type of misbehavior would mean helping the child to build a different concept of himself. The teacher could point out the things (however few they might be) that are likable, the skills that are commendable, the achievement that others do appreciate and make these the focus of attention instead of confirming the child's sense of unworthiness. Some will say, "But this is unrealistic," but let them consider what methods can and do work. The answer is that thus far we have found nothing else (punishment, incarceration, failing grades, retention in a grade) that will work. Getting the pupil to like and value himself does help; it is true mental hygiene—effective and durable.

Contrasting viewpoints on what constitutes problem behavior might well be studied. Teachers typically view such behavior as disobedience, fighting, profanity, and masturbation as evidences of maladjustment; they are relatively unconcerned about shyness, fearfulness, dreaminess—in fact, it is rather comfortable to have quiet, obedient children in class, and they are often regarded as model pupils. On the other hand, child specialists, psychologists and psychiatrists, are deeply concerned about shy, recessive behavior and are less disturbed by aggressive manifestations. No doubt the teacher has some justification for his view—aggressive behavior does upset classroom routine. But to the psychologist, the withdrawn child has been defeated in his battle for recognition and security —he has quit struggling. The modern teacher must realize that such a child also has real problems. Shyness may have back of it such handicapping feelings as guilt, overdependency, and a sense of inferiority or rejection—all of which intensify the problems of adjustment if no antidote is provided (Lindgren, 1959, pp. 136ff). In addition, shyness and withdrawal tend to keep the child from gaining the experience and knowledge that would improve self-confidence and enhance the probability of future success (Lazarus, 1961, p. 322).

It is worth noting that when teachers become aware of pupils' problems and seek to find solutions, scholastic work improves. In one study of fourth- to sixth-grade children teachers used the Wishing Well Test and the Ohio Social Acceptance Scale to locate pupils' needs. Concurrently, they took a child development course that emphasized the nature and satisfaction of needs. Children who had learning difficulties were placed in equated (mental test data) control and experimental classes. The control classes were taught by teachers who did not take the course and who did not know the real nature of the attempt to meet children's needs; the experimental classes were taught by teachers who were involved in the study. Using achievement test data, the above adjustment scales, and teachers' estimates, it was concluded that the project resulted in improved learning, better personal adjustment, and greater social acceptability, not only for the few pupils who had received special consideration but for the entire membership of the experimental classes (Burrell, 1951).

Experience as a Learning Avenue   All learning is experience, and for the young child that experience should be overt. There are at least three sound reasons for this assertion: (1) As discussed earlier, the child is interested in process; (2) he is not used to sitting for long periods and has a strong drive toward physical activity, and too much sedentary work bores him; (3) his experience is still too limited to allow him to derive much meaning from verbal abstractions.

These factors provide the base for such teaching procedures as the experience chart in reading and the experience unit in other studies. The experience chart is simply a book that the teacher writes for the pupils—large enough for all to see clearly. The teacher records what the youngsters tell him in their own words—what they have seen, felt, and done. Thus they may tell what they saw on a walk through a park or along the streets. Their experience chart may describe their visit to the school boiler room or the part they played in a fire drill.

Another approach to vitalizing instruction in terms of the real and meaningful experience of the child is the experience unit. This is a series of lessons centered about some integral part of the pupils' lives.

> An experience unit is a cluster of educative experiences, organized through pupil-teacher planning, placed within the functioning framework of the developing child in his social and physical environment in terms of the needs and purposes of the child and his society, and utilizing, to as great a degree as possible, the useful resources to be found in the material and cultural environment, to the end that the democratically determined purposes of the schools may be achieved.[4]

Except for a general outline and description of resources available, the experience unit is not planned in detail in writing. It develops as the teacher leads his pupils through progressive learning experiences. Because the unit develops from life experiences, the so-called "vicarious," or indirect, experiences are not ruled out. Much time would be required for direct experience, and the school day is not long enough to provide many opportunities for first-hand contact. Hence, audio aids should be used as supplements—recordings, radio programs, and brief talks that are related to what the pupils have directly experienced are invaluable in expanding their world. Visual aids, such as motion pictures, filmstrips, models, replicas, and samples can be used to supplement personal adventures and observations. Transition from the specific and the concrete to the general and the abstract should be gradual. If the teacher attempts to make this important transition too suddenly, enduring antagonisms toward school activities may be engendered.

Research shows that experience is an important factor in readiness for learning (Frandsen, 1961, p. 94). The child who has a home in which there are many books and magazines is better prepared for learning to read than the one who lacks such resources. The youngster who has worked with his father's tools has an advantage in the wood or the metal

[4] Robert H. Beck, Walter W. Cook, and Nolan C. Kearney, *Curriculum in the Modern Elementary School*, rev. ed., Englewood Cliffs, N.J.: Prentice-Hall, Inc., 1960, p. 204.

shop. The pupil who has traveled extensively has an advantage in geography and social studies over the one who has not ranged so widely. Sometimes the school staff makes an extra effort to expand the experience of pupils by providing contacts outside the school; this was done on a large scale and with gratifying results in the higher-horizons program in New York City (1961).

Pupil Participation in Planning   There are several good reasons for encouraging pupil participation in planning. Pupil planning makes behavior more purposeful. It capitalizes upon the need for personal involvement in learning and the learning process. It gives the child a chance to satisfy his need for independence and his curiosity. It provides him with valuable experience in social intercourse. Moreover, it tends to prevent unrealistic and meaningless programs, since the children will suggest problems and propose solutions that are related to their current interests and experiences.

Pupil participation does not mean that school activities are determined by the fortuitous interests of children. There is still a place for the teacher's guidance and counsel. However, the pupil should have an increasingly large part in planning as he grows mentally and socially, because experience adds to his effectiveness in participation.

The late Kurt Lewin (1939) conducted a series of experiments which suggest that democratic procedures can improve the teacher's effectiveness. Kelley has described a vocational school in which there was a disproportionate number of academic and social misfits; student participation in government was tried in this school, and the results far exceeded both hopes and expectations. Destruction of school property and open conflicts with teachers were reduced. Attendance improved, and dropouts diminished. Both curricular and extracurricular activities functioned more smoothly than was the case when the school was run by adults alone (Kelley, 1962, pp. 83–85).

Too often we tend to think that opportunities for self-direction and participation in student government should be reserved for the more mature students. The author observed student participation in a third grade, where the day's concern was for a boy whose noon movie ticket had been confiscated by upper-class monitors because he was misbehaving. The third graders were discussing what should be done by their class representative in the next council meeting. Some felt that since the ticket had been paid for, it should not be taken away. Others felt that the upper-class monitors should have referred the case to the principal. Some stated that a warning should be sufficient. The boy himself said that he had been warned earlier, but he believed that one or two days away from the movie would be enough. The meeting closed. It was decided to let the matter drop, when a little girl said, with a lisp, "Well, when he goes to a movie and goofs off, it's like he was taking a lot of kids' tickets away from them when they can enjoy the movie."

Democratic practice probably should not be justified in terms of the teacher's advantage. Because democracy depends on participation of the individual in the solution of common problems, it should be a function of the school to provide such experience. Modern schools have accepted this responsibility and encourage youngsters to participate in degrees appropriate to their social and intellectual maturity.

Experiments do not prove that acquisition of subject matter is any greater with pupil-planned programs that with set curricula. In fact, it is recognized that the method is slow. For example, fewer arithmetic problems are solved, though accuracy is improved, when pupil planning and cooperative work are involved (Klugman, 1944). Less material is covered in the social studies, though it is more thoroughly understood. But if the "whole" child is taken into consideration, it can be seen that his participation in social situations is as important as his academic learning.

Teacher-Pupil Evaluation   There has long been dissatisfaction with the process of grading pupils simply on the basis of subject-matter achievement, because educational objectives include much more than factual knowledge. One approach to the improvement of evaluation is to make it a cooperative, cumulative, and continuous process (Rothney, 1955, p. 3). The shift from grading to cooperative evaluation is another form of the emphasis on pupil experience and pupil planning and capitalizes on the same psychological factors. It is an attempt to help the pupil perceive his goals more clearly, to stress his personal growth rather than his competitive status, to make his purposes specific and tangible, and to encourage his growth toward greater independence. Like pupil planning, teacher-pupil evaluation can be instituted by degrees as pupils gain in experience.

Such evaluations can serve to make the pupil's academic learning more meaningful. When he keeps his own scores on spelling tests and arithmetic exercises, he begins to see that the scores have a personal reference. Graphs of progress drawn by the pupil will motivate him, as well as providing a concrete basis for measuring his growth.

Perhaps one of the greatest values of pupil participation in evaluation lies in its influence in improving rapport between home and school. If pupils evaluate themselves in terms of cooperatively determined objectives, they are not going to go home and report, "Oh, we just played today" or be so likely to criticize the teacher for being unfair. They will know what their "play" was for and be able to report their activities in terms of educational objectives that parents will understand.

Ability Grouping   Until recent years, there were many and heated arguments regarding the merits of ability grouping. Today it is a commonly accepted practice for grades as a whole and for working groups within a grade (*Wisconsin Improvement Program,* 1962). Grouping by ability provides a means of adapting instruction to meet the needs of more individuals than does grouping by age or grade placement alone. The special class, a form of ability grouping, for slow learners or accelerated learners is now regarded as sound educational practice. Ability grouping means placing pupils in working groups that are selected so that the range of differences within a class is reduced to some extent. The factors used in ability grouping are by no means uniform, but they may include IQ, social maturity, physical development, past school record, and achievement test data. Teachers' judgments should always be used with such data, and transfer of individuals between groups should be possible. Grouping or tracks do not entirely solve the problems of meeting individual differences, but the possibility of adapting instruction to differences is improved by the reduction in the range of differences. It is recognized that slow learners need more repetition, more frequent concrete illustrations, and a slower pace than do other pupils. Rapid learners need less repetition and drill, can grasp abstractions, and are eager to move rapidly to new challenges. The effects of ability grouping are readily seen in discussion: In heterogeneous groups, a few individuals are likely to dominate; in ability groups, discussion includes more pupils because fewer feel they can dominate, and no one feels that he need be timorous in making comments.

Conant, while admitting that ability grouping is highly controversial, recommends that it be used for required courses and that the very slow learners have special teachers. He endorses ability grouping for each class, not across-the-board grouping, which tends to segregate the bright, average, and slow for all activities (Conant, 1959, p. 49). Leadership, artistic ability, athletic skill, and musical talent are not necessarily distributed among the pupils who have mathematical aptitude or reading skills, and the groups will and should be different for mathematics, football, chorus, and class officials. Anderson, in a review of the use of grouping, reports that permanence in grouping was typical a few years ago, but that today there are few schools in which there is not considerable relocation and shifting of students within classes throughout the school year (Anderson, 1962, p. 264). This shifting and the differing composition of each class group is what distinguishes ability grouping, as the term is used here, from segregation of pupils. In the latter case, the differential distribution of separate abilities is ignored; a group is formed and stays the same for the entire program of school activities.

Some people feel that ability grouping is undemocratic, while others say that it is democratic because it provides the best chance for each to develop his potential. Some state that slow learners get inspiration from bright pupils, while others believe that slow learners are unjustifiably discouraged by brilliant classmates. The basic goal for teachers is to treat pupils alike in areas where they are alike, but to treat them differently in the areas where they are different, whether there is ability grouping or not (Olson, 1959, p. 275). Perhaps the reason why experiments on grouping have shown equivocal results in terms of academic learning is that teachers have been led to believe that grouping is something more than just an approach to meeting differences. Ability grouping is an expedient, but it makes finding the time to work with individuals possible. Of course, good jobs of teaching have been done by teachers in one-room schools consisting of eight grades. However, this does not prove that even better jobs cannot be done with less wide-range groups. In the final analysis, the most effective teaching will result from knowing individual children, as well as children in general, and applying that knowledge.

Summary

Much progress has been made in understanding the nature of children, but erroneous notions and practices have a disconcerting persistence. Teachers should know that children, in contrast to adults, are generally more interested in processes than in ultimate results. They tend to be more interested in the immediate, concrete, and personal than in the remote, abstract, and impersonal. Despite a cult of freedom for children there is sound evidence that children want and need guidance, order, routine, and consistency. The repetition of behavior inherent in these needs is basic to habit formation. Play is important business for the child. Involving, as it does, process, concreteness, immediacy, and individuality, play is a significant learning arena. Play has additional importance to teachers when they learn to interpret the personality orientations that play activities reveal. Everyone needs acceptance and approval, but children, who are forming their self-concepts, particularly need acceptance and approval. Teachers can be more accepting when they reflect on the fact that child behavior reflects parental handling. If they could see the child at home, they probably would often wonder why he was not much more difficult.

Teachers can reveal their knowledge of children as learners by accepting them, building their security through appropriate tasks, recognizing differences, using democratic procedures, and being friendly, and realizing that deviant behavior is a symptom of lack of need satisfaction. Children learn through experience; as they mature, experience can become increasingly vicarious, or indirect. A valuable experience is participation in educational planning and in student government. In both areas, adults are pleasantly surprised to see how able even the very young are in such activity. Evaluation that fosters growth rather than identifying status is an emerging emphasis in children's education. Ability grouping, which reduces the range of differences in class groups, is an increasingly popular process for recognizing the variable nature of children.

Problems and exercises

1 Does the assertion that children are interested in process deny that their behavior is goal seeking in nature? Explain.

2 What evidence have you seen that supports or denies the contention that children appreciate routines?

3 Observe a group of first graders playing spontaneously. List both the social skills and information that you believe they can or do learn.

4 Reflect upon your own past experience and evaluate the statement that children bring their families to school.

5 Draw up a checklist of items to help a teacher and his pupils direct attention to the physical condition of their classroom.

6 What are the practical implications of the statement that teachers should give more attention to recessive traits in pupils?

7 Try to find a classroom in which teacher-pupil planning is practiced, observe a class session, and report the specific events which transpire.

8 Have four class members stage a debate on a topic related to ability grouping that has been formulated by the entire class.

9 Will ability grouping generate feelings of either superiority or inferiority that will nullify the advantages of reducing the range of differences?

Suggested additional readings

Baughman, E. Earl, and George S. Welsh: *Personality: A Behavioral Science,* Englewood Cliffs, N.J.: Prentice-Hall, Inc., 1962, pp. 225–256.
Factors outside the home that shape children's personalities—such as schools, social class, teacher's personality, peer groups, and mass communication media—are discussed.

Bernard, Harold W.: *Human Development in Western Culture,* Boston: Allyn and Bacon, Inc., 1962, pp. 180–222.
These two chapters deal with the needs, patterns of development, and developmental tasks of both early and middle childhood. The nature of developmental tasks is related to Western culture.

D'Evelyn, Katherine E.: *Meeting Children's Emotional Needs,* Englewood Cliffs, N.J.: Prentice-Hall, Inc., 1957.
This small book deals with the needs of children, shows how need deprivation results in aggression, dishonesty, shyness, school failure, and the like. Practical suggestions for achieving understanding and dealing with such behavior are offered.

Gordon, Ira J.: *Children's Views of Themselves,* Washington: Association for Childhood Education International, 1959.
This booklet describes the effect that children's views of themselves have on their actions and aspirations. The source of self-concepts and ways in which adults can help build wholesome ones are indicated, but not prescribed.

Prescott, Daniel A.: *The Child in the Educative Process,* New York: McGraw-Hill Book Company, 1957, pp. 99–150.

Details are cited as to how test data, anecdotal reports, play activities, pupils' compositions, and teacher-pupil evaluations are used as clues to the better understanding of children.

Stevenson, Harold W., assisted by Jerome Kagan and Charles Spiker (eds): *Child Psychology,* Sixty-second Yearbook of the National Society for the Study of Education, Chicago: The University of Chicago Press, part I, 1963.

This book, which shows a marked shift in emphasis in the past decade, describes the short-term, intensive study of particular variables of child behavior. Biological and sociological as well as psychological factors are considered.

The Adolescent as a Learner

As the branch of knowledge that deals with improving the effectiveness of learning, educational psychology must be concerned with many problems. Contemporary developments in learning theory are tending away from single and simple explanations; e.g., stimulus-response (S → R) or stimulus action on organism leads to response (S → O → R). Instead, there is increasing attention to larger situational and peripheral contributing factors. As students of educational psychology, you are concerned with the teacher's knowledge of subject matter and teaching techniques and also with his personality, interests, and values. Similarly, you are concerned not only with the intelligence of students, but with their emotions, their social milieu, their aspirations.

The learning of adolescents in our culture is conditioned by their intelligence and their interests. This fact has long been recognized. Recent advances indicate that we can know more about the *shaping* of this intelligence and the *forming* of these interests if we study the source of the adolescent's emotions, his social orientations, and his unique aspirations. His social class origins provide part of this knowledge. The total culture, particularly in Western society, provides additional clues as to why adolescents behave as they do—including their response as learners in school. This chapter will deal particularly with the problem of a better understanding of the American adolescent. Recent research findings will be discussed, and ways of capitalizing on this information will be suggested.

The meaning of adolescence

A Definition of Adolescence The basic meaning of the term "adolescence" is simply growth toward maturity. It is the period between the onset of puberty and maturity—*roughly* ages fourteen to twenty-five years for males and about twelve to twenty-one years for females. Many books on education and psychology embellish the definition by referring to it as a period of stress and strain, a time of rapid growth and perplexity, or a period during which the individual is neither one thing nor another. There is enough truth in these concepts to make them helpful in gaining an understanding of adolescents. Lewin (1939) was one of the first to state these conditions by referring to the adolescent in the sociological term "marginal man." He refers to the adolescent's uncertainty and his exploratory behavior as a search for status, belongingness, and identification in a cognitively unstructured life space. More specifically, the adolescent is not a child, but neither is he accepted as an adult; he has previously known his body, but new sensations, urges, and potentialities arise and make strange and uncertain an area that was previously familiar; he tends to be oversensitive (as are other minority groups) because his role is not clearly defined; he encounters conflicting values and expectations that further complicate his dealing with his emerging role. The adolescent is an individual undergoing a special set of developmental tasks.

Precise knowledge about adolescence is needed by all teachers. The primary teacher needs such knowledge to help pupils develop the attitudes and skills that will prepare them for this phase of growth. The upper elementary teacher needs the information because some of his pupils are entering this phase of development. The high school teacher needs the knowledge so that he can work with, rather than against, the basic phenomena of adolescence.

Adolescents—Not a Unique Breed One major reason why adolescents are misunderstood stems from the belief that they are a unique breed. Some writers would have us think that they are totally unlike children and totally unlike adults. Objective psychology, however, continues to stress that growth is continuous and gradual. An individual does not suddenly become a different person because the sex organs mature, because the hairline on the forehead alters, because hair grows in the pubic area and under the arms, because the angular lines of the girl change gradually to curves, or because the boy's voice changes. It would be well for all teachers to keep in mind the statement: You are today becoming what tomorrow you will be.

It is also necessary to recognize that while adolescents are not unique as adolescents, they are unique as individuals. But this uniqueness is also characteristic of children and adults. Adolescents in the same family are different in size, intelligence, interests, and social personalities. Twins are different despite the identity or similarity of their inherited potential. Adolescents from different social classes differ in their attitudes and ideals. Young people from rural districts differ perceptibly from their urban peers. In short, some of the uniqueness of adolescents lies in their individuality rather than in their adolescence.

Basic Needs of Adolescents Like children and adults, adolescents need to love and be loved, to have new experiences, to achieve recognition, to be independent, and to satisfy physical needs for warmth and food. However, some of these needs may be intensified or may take a different direction during adolescence. The adolescent's search for new experiences will take him beyond the school and the neighborhood that were his world as a child. He still needs recognition by parents and teachers, but recognition by his peers now becomes a much more dominating influence. As his body grows to adult size and proportion, he asserts his need to be independent more aggressively. This latter need is the cause of some difficulty with *some* adolescents. Parents, who live with the young person continuously, may fail to see this insistent need and consciously or unconsciously hinder its development.

Horrocks (1962, p. 516), after reviewing the nature of needs and the methods of discovering and classifying them, reports results of a study of 654 adolescents and their most consistent needs. It was found that they need (1) to conform to the approved behavior, values, and standards expressed by parents, teacher, and peers, whom they consider important; (2) to receive affection that is sincere and uniqualified; and (3) most importantly, they need to "work hard, endeavor, and attain worthy goals." It should be noted that the intensity of these needs varies somewhat with the stage of adolescence, that boys have somewhat more difficulty in fulfilling them than do girls, and that these needs are, in part, an outcome of experience and learning and thus a function of the cultural milieu.

Adolescence is a period during which already established growth trends continue. It is a period during which basic needs are fundamentally the same but vary in intensity as a result of broadened life experiences and altered influences. Adults can best help adolescents by understanding the sources of their perplexities. Specifically, adults can help meet needs by talking (not preaching) with them about behavior and its long-term consequences, giving them affection that stems from understanding, and helping them establish vocational goals and find part-time jobs. The developmental task of achieving assurance of economic independence is highly significant in a society which prizes one's productivity (Bernard, 1962, p. 272).

Popular half-truths about adolescents

Many of the current ideas about the nature of adolescence stem from theories that have now been disproved. Some of these theories will be examined in this section.

Pubertal Changes Explain Adolescence It has been thought that the onset of puberty marked a unique period in the life of the individual. Current emphases tend to discredit this theory. Actually, fewer changes take place during adolescence than during an equal number of years beginning with birth. There is little or no psychology that is limited to adolescence; the "psychology of adolescence" simply consists of phenomena that can be studied with profit when we are dealing with young people. Kuhlen (1952, p. 1) states that adolescence has been highly over-dramatized: It is not typically a time of unusual stress that arises from physical growth processes; it is simply a time when certain developmental problems are confronted. Jessie Bernard (1961) asserts that teen-age culture is a product of the affluence of our society—the characteristics once typical of college age youth are becoming those of high school age. In addition, the phenomenon of social class must be considered in interpreting the behaviors of adolescents. Thus adolescence must be considered in the context of the developmental trends begun in childhood, and it must be studied in terms of maturation and culture.

Adolescents Are Awkward It is difficult to determine the origin of this popular misconception. Perhaps it arose from the fact that some adolescents are as large as adults, and because of their size observers expect them to be as graceful and well coordinated as the adult. Generally, they are not so well coordinated as adults. But they are better coordinated than younger persons. Your own observation will confirm this statement. Adolescents are less stiff when dancing than their younger schoolmates or siblings, they skate better, they play games with more skill, they fall less frequently. Thus there is little reason to think of this period as the "awkward age." One of the few experimental studies on this matter showed no evidence that awkwardness is caused by rapid growth (Dimock, 1935). Later studies have tended to confirm the conclusion that coordination, like other aspects of growth, follows an orderly progression (Goratos, 1959). Such lack of coordination as does exist is, in some measure, due to the misconception rather than to innate growth factors or tendencies; that is, the adolescent is *made* awkward by misinformed individuals who allude to "typical awkwardness" when a young person stumbles. Such comments make the adolescent self-conscious and likely to appear more awkward than he really is. "That is, an adolescent does not behave in any given way *because he is an adolescent.* He is an adolescent because his behavior takes on characteristics which are conveniently described as adolescent." [1] In short, stereotyped beliefs do not enhance our understanding of adolescents.

It has been observed that movement and posture are clues to one's personality trends. Feelings of inferiority or inadequacy may be reflected in stooped posture or slouching movement or in a cocky, swaggering attitude. A healthy, well-adjusted individual often has poise, good posture, and graceful, coordinated movement (Millard, 1958, p. 87). There is some

---

[1] John E. Horrocks, *The Psychology of Adolescence,* 2d ed., Boston: Houghton Mifflin Company, 1962, p. 356.

specificity in motor skills, i.e., superiority in some, mediocrity or inferiority in others, rather than a general status. But it should be noted that there is a relationship (either cause or result) between personal adjustment measures and measures of physical growth and skills (H. E. Jones, 1949, p. 152).

Teachers will do a service to adolescents if they display confidence in youth and avoid disparaging remarks. They should help to provide them with occasions when they can practice physical skills. Opportunities should be provided for success, which will generate feelings of confidence. Competition between or comparison of unequals is clearly harmful (Horrocks, 1962, p. 416). Emphasis must be placed on the growth and progress of youth, not upon their lacks, as is so often the case. For example, we incline to concentrate on the distressing rise in delinquency, quite forgetting that there is a heartening rise in college attendance— 35 per cent of college age youth are today going to college in contrast to less than 5 per cent before World War I (Bennett, 1964).

Adolescents Are Inept Socially No doubt there are adolescents who are lacking in the social skills considered desirable by adults. Much of this ineptness is, however, the result of inexperience and self-consciousness. The educational significance is obvious: Adult standards must not be used for judgment; opportunities for social experience must be provided; patience with the slowness of growth must be exercised; optimism, based on the continuousness of growth, should prevail.

There is evidence in the behavior of today's youth that a positive approach bears fruit. When they are given the opportunity to express themselves in class, they develop the skill to express themselves in public. One adult observer came from a city council meeting on the civil rights of Negroes (a problem being studied in the school) and remarked, "I was amazed at the ability of high school youngsters to get up and straightforwardly express a fair and sensible point of view. When I was in school, neither my classmates nor I would have thought of such a thing."

Adolescents Are Cantankerous and Negativistic To a certain extent these characteristics are the result of commendable aims on the part of youth. When adolescents are given freedom by parents and teachers to exercise their need for independence, they often cease to be resistant and negativistic. Negativistic traits are a healthy indication that the individual wants to become self-directing. However, negativism does not always prevail, and the degree of rebellion varies from one individual to another. "Research findings disagree with the popular stereotype of rebellious adolescent behavior." [2] The problems involved in the matter of independence

[2] Robert C. Bealer and Fern K. Willits, "Rural Youth: A Case Study in the Rebelliousness of Adolescents," *Annals of the American Academy of Political and Social Science,* 338: 63–69, 1961.

and self-direction are difficult for both the adolescent and his parents. The adolescent justifiably feels that with increasing age and experience he should be allowed more freedom of choice in activities. He wants to choose his clothes and his friends and regulate his schedule. The parent feels justified in thinking that as long as he is providing food, shelter, and an allowance, he has a right to regulate the young person's life. Teachers can help simply by showing the parents and the young person that there is a dilemma. It is by no means a one-sided problem.

Some of the adolescent's negativism stems from the fact that he is seeking his purpose in life. This too is a commendable goal. Throughout Western culture, many of the problems of adolescents arise primarily from the uncertainty of adults regarding the role that should be given to youth. Their uncertainty leaves young people confused and ambivalent about their own present status. Hence, adolescent struggles are at once "a hopeful and disturbing condition" (Mays, 1961). And at school, many adolescents are unable to accept the goals for the future that formal education sets for them because of their social backgrounds or physical or mental limitations. They are anxious to achieve independence from adult influence, but they are uncertain. Their negativism is a symptom of their own uncertainty.

Teachers are in a good position to help solve this problem. They should attempt to show the adolescent that his parents are genuinely interested in his welfare. This can be accomplished through counseling procedures and through encouraging adolescents to discuss their problems with parents among themselves. Teachers can also help the parents see more clearly the causes of what they view as objectionable behavior. Teachers can, better than parents, persistently indicate that a period of long dependency and prolonged education is a worthwhile investment for adolescents, parents, and society as a whole.

Of course, a large majority of adolescents do not develop the trait of consistent negativism. Teachers and parents should look for healthy growth patterns and consider these just as characteristic as those which tend to arouse antagonism. This "looking-for-the-positive" orientation is valid for two reasons: The first is that by and large we tend to see what we look for; the second is that adolescents—like others—tend to do what is expected of them.

Adolescents Are Growing Rapidly   In terms of the current use of the word "adolescence," the period is one of decreasing, rather than rapidly increasing, growth rates. There is a period of rapid growth *just before* adolescence (preadolescence), at about ages nine to fourteen (experienced by boys a year or two later than by girls), which is characterized as a "growth spurt" (Stuart, 1958, p. 90). It should be noted that growth in this period is not nearly so great as growth during the prenatal period, nor is it so great proportionally as it is during the first year after birth. Whereas an individual's height has been increasing at, let us say, about 3 inches per year, during the preadolescent growth spurt height increases only 4 or 5 inches. Similarly, weight has been increasing rather steadily at about 5 pounds per year after age two, but typically the growth spurt results in an increase of only 6 or 7 pounds annually.

The current growth status of the preadolescent and adolescent is more important to teachers than is the rate of growth. One individual may be only about two-thirds as tall as the tallest, and others are in between, and their weights are proportional (Bernard, 1957, p. 37). Two significant points may be noted. One is that the differences cannot be accounted for by a one- or two-year growth spurt; the differences have been increasing over a number of years. The other is that the problems of adjustment for the individual, if any, stem from the perception of differences in gross size rather than from a period of accelerated growth.

The differences between individuals and the average difference between boys and girls present problems. In junior high school, boys are not quite so ready as girls for dating, dancing, and mixed parties. How to arrange suitable heterosexual experiences becomes a problem for adolescents, parents, and teachers. The difference in individual patterns sometimes creates problems when boys and girls perceive themselves to be out of step with their peers. Feelings of inferiority or oddity hamper their free movement in social experiences and adjustments (Frazier and Lisonbee, 1950). While these difficulties create temporary problems, they appear to have little permanent effect in terms of adult adjustment (M. C. Jones, 1957). Teachers should, however, realize the acuteness of feelings of differences and help by doing things that build stronger ego concepts.

Adolescents Are Bothered by Sex Maturation Parents of today's teenagers report that they had little or no instruction and consequently tended to worry about certain aspects of their development, particularly if it was very different from that of their peers. Maturation did bother many adolescents. Boys worried about nocturnal emissions and experimental manipulation of the sex organs. Girls were embarrassed by the development of their breasts and the fact that their clothes revealed their changing outline, and many were frightened by their first menstruation. These reactions generally occur when adolescents are unprepared for the manifestations of maturation. Today's more informed adolescents are concerned about sex, but their concerns are about its social rather than its physical aspects (Harris, 1959). There may be many aspects to this difference in approach. For example, boys and girls today seem to adults to be in too much hurry to grow up, and the steadily lowering age of marriage and the disquieting number of high school marriages contributes to that viewpoint. The increasingly high rate of illegitimate births

(Gies, 1962) is an additional concern and certainly offers no consolation to those concerned with our present methods of dealing with sex maturation.

When teachers and parents have given adolescents objective instruction about the meaning and onset of puberty, its outward manifestations will cause less perplexity. They will regard the changes as indications that they are coming into their own as men and women. They are proud of their emergence from childhood. The fact that many uninformed boys and girls ultimately developed into normal adults should not constitute an endorsement for failing to instruct today. The focal factor in good adjustment is love and acceptance by one's family. This is the primary means of sound sex education. Having confidential talks, questions freely answered, and sex education is simply a bonus in a salutary situation.

The adolescent's behavioral responses to puberty are environmentally induced. Teachers can contribute to a sound environment by studying and evaluating their own response to sex, their discussion of sex, and their sexual behavior; and then (if they are emotionally secure) be members of the group whose specific job it is to provide sex education. Many case studies illustrate the fact that what occurs in childhood is of importance during adolescence. It is the consensus of those who have worked with adolescents charged with sex delinquency that lack of early preparation is a contributing factor (Hull and Cummings, 1953). For example, if a child's questions about sex are answered frankly and freely, he will be well prepared to accept the changes of puberty. If, on the other hand, adults are reluctant to answer such questions, he is likely to develop an abnormal curiosity about what seems to be so secret. Parents have frequently been surprised to find how nonchalantly a youngster accepts information that is emotionally very difficult for them to impart.

Parents and teachers should make it clear that sex is (1) a drive to action and accomplishment—in dress, companionship, work, in general—not just to sexual gratification; (2) a social urge that attracts men and women and boys and girls; (3) an emotion that involves other emotions, i.e., love, understanding, mutual interests, and loyalty; and (4) a cultural as well as an individual matter. Failure to recognize these aspects is likely to cause unnecessary disillusionment and frustration when the adolescent makes errors.

Traditionally, schools have been concerned with academic and vocational goals to the neglect of problems of personal adjustment. This neglect is being remedied in some schools where specific courses in sex education (more frequently called "social hygiene," "personal problems," or "human relations") are being devised and implemented. LaBrant suggests that there be an assigned—not an incidental—place for discussing sex, dating, petting, individual differences, and variations in patterns of growth rates (LaBrant, 1955, pp. 230, 134). Courtship, marriage, and relationships with parents are frequently recommended aspects of such courses (*The Adolescent in Your Family,* 1954, pp. 65–72). Such courses, plus teachers who can and will deal frankly with incidental questions, can help make the adolescent's attitude toward sex one of healthy concern rather than one of perplexity and embarrassment. We should learn to deal with sex in its larger cultural frame rather than setting it apart as an isolated phenomenon. Such an approach will do much to improve the psychological climate in which realistic learnings of all kinds can best develop.

Some facts about adolescents

Growth Progresses Steadily Changes in the nature of growth occur not only in childhood and adolescence but in maturity and the later years. Some aspects of growth are *predominant* in some periods, but basic needs remain fundamentally the same. Frank states that each individual must pass through life along the same broad highway, but that each does so at his own rate. There is an orderliness and regularity in human individuals (Frank, 1951, p. 67). Each period in the individual's life is an outcome of what has previously occurred and a preparation for what will happen next. The whole span of life is important. It is foolish to state that any specific period is the most important period. Every period is important, as is evidenced by man's lifelong struggle to improve himself and his environment.

There are no cataclysmic changes in a person's development, despite periodic changes in growth rates, as may be noted in delinquent behavior. Before the adolescent engages in sex delinquency, stealing, destruction of property or violent crimes, there are danger signals. For example, the youth typically becomes surly at home and in school, defies conventions, and in other ways indicates that he is becoming maladjusted. Those who understand the symptoms that precede the breaking point can be of great help. It is believed that many shocking crimes might be avoided if attention were devoted to the fulfillment of needs or to the treatment of personality when these first symptoms of dangerous tensions occur. Teachers are in a strategic position to aid in the prevention of trouble (Kvaraceus, 1959, p. 122). But it is not easy unless the teacher himself is emotionally mature. Predelinquent behavior often takes the form of disliking school, teachers, and principal—it is not confined to academic difficulty. It has been said that when a child is most unlovable, he is most in need of love. The statement presents a challenge to the teacher of adolescents as much as it does to teachers of younger children.

It might be well to consider that not only do schools have difficulty in preventing delinquent behavior, they may sometimes actually contribute to it. In a study of 761 delinquents, it was found that forty times as many boys and seventy-five times as many girls repeated three or more school terms, in comparison with members of the control group. It was also found that the school might be not only contributing to but precipitating delinquency because delinquency rates decreased when school was not in session (Kvaraceus, 1944).

Delinquency is here cited merely as an example of the continuity of development. Commendable patterns of adolescent behavior show similar sequential development.

Adolescents Are a Minority Group Youth's minority position is one of the factors that may be said to *cause* adolescence. The cultural role of the adolescent is more important in explaining his psychological character-istics than is his physical growth. Minority groups are usually viewed with cynical, critical eyes—and adolescents do not escape being a scape-goat minority (Kelley, 1962, p. 20).

In 1800 in the United States, life expectancy at birth was a little over thirty-five years. At present, it is about seventy years for white persons.[3] This means that the proportion of adults to young people is becoming greater. Whereas in 1800 over one-half (58 per cent) of the population was under twenty years of age, today only one-third is in the under-twenty age bracket. Forecasts by the Metropolitan Life Insurance Company indi-cate that by the year 2000 only 25 per cent of the population will be under twenty. The minority position of adolescents is becoming more acute with the passing years. When adolescents made up a large part of the population, they necessarily assumed places of importance. They were given jobs outside the home and assigned responsibilities in the home. In the days when many parents died at the age of thirty, forty, or fifty, it was necessary for adolescents to assume responsibilities at an early age. But today, when parents are able to support their children for longer periods, the period of dependence is often prolonged. Labor re-quirements are currently such that the largest group of unemployed is the fourteen- to twenty-four-year age group (Baer, 1961). The minority position is one of social and economic importance as well as one of statistics.

The adolescent, as a member of a minority group, is subject to pres-sures. He feels that he does not belong, that he is different, and that others view him with suspicion and hostility. These characteristics are found in all minority groups who suffer from unenlightened treatment. The minority position of adolescents makes their struggle for recognition more difficult. There are laws which prevent adolescents from taking jobs, establishing their own families, and taking responsibility for their own

[3] Life expectancy at birth for white females is seventy-three years; for white males, sixty-seven years. See "Longevity Changes Little in Recent Years," *Statistical Bulletin, Metropolitan Life Insurance Company*, 39: 1, June, 1958.

actions. These laws and customs undoubtedly have advantages for youth. But it is necessary to realize that many of the difficulties of this age stem from culturally imposed conditions.

Adolescence Is a Cultural Phenomenon In her studies of culture in Samoa and New Guinea, Margaret Mead has brought to our attention the fact that puberty is not necessarily accompanied by the problems that typically characterize adolescence in our country. In those societies, pubertal ceremonies result in the child's formally taking the step from childhood to adulthood. Little stress and strain devolves on the individual as he assumes a mature role in society (Mead, 1939). But the situation is different in our society. The period of dependence is prolonged by extended compulsory education and by child labor laws (Goldberg, 1964). Industrialization in our society has resulted in strong competition, except during periods of war, in the labor market. Laborers protect themselves from the competition of youth by supporting extended compulsory education and sponsoring child labor laws. The shift in the adolescent's share of the total population structure alters his role. Rapid technological and ideological change creates a gap between the generations larger than that existing in less rapidly changing societies. Women's predominance in child rearing virtually excludes men's participation, and although this is unchosen and undesirable, it is a factor in adolescent behavior. The uncertainty of military service and the threat of annihilation are among the factors that make the adolescent's world unprecedentedly complex. Finally, the uncertainty of adults themselves and the conflict between professed ideals and daily living disturb adolescents.[4] All these factors complicate and intensify the adolescent's transition to adulthood.

Steps toward solving these problems and turning the conditions to advantage can be accomplished by recognizing adolescents' needs in our culture. More effort must be directed to devising curricula and methods that suit various objectives. For adolescents who will continue academic work in college, the traditional approach in secondary education will continue to be suitable. But the objectives of education must be accepted *by youth*. Each adolescent must perceive that methods and curricula meet *his* needs. Vocational emphases are of value, but such problems as consumer education, preparation for marriage, functional citizenship, the maintenance of health, and the use of leisure time should also receive concerted attention (*Adapting the Secondary-school Program to the Needs of Youth*, 1953). One widely accepted view of youth's dilemma and approaches to its solution is presented in "The Ten Imperative Needs of Youth."

1. All youth need to develop salable skills and those understandings and attitudes that make the worker an intelligent and productive

---

[4] These receive more extended treatment in Harold W. Bernard, *Human Development in Western Culture*, Boston: Allyn and Bacon, Inc., 1962, pp. 255–259.

participant in economic life. To this end, most youth need supervised work experience as well as education in the skills and knowledge of their occupation.

2. All youth need to develop and maintain good health and physical fitness and mental health.

3. All youth need to understand the rights and duties of the citizen of a democratic society, and to be diligent and competent in the performance of their obligations as members of the community and citizens of the state and nation, and to have an understanding of the nations and peoples of the world.

4. All youth need to understand the significance of the family for the individual and society and the conditions conducive to successful family life.

5. All youth need to know how to purchase and use goods and services intelligently, understanding both the values received by the consumer and the economic consequences of their acts.

6. All youth need to understand the methods of science, the influence of science on human life, and the main scientific facts concerning the nature of the world and of man.

7. All youth need opportunities to develop their capacities to appreciate beauty in literature, art, music, and nature.

8. All youth need to be able to use their leisure time well and to budget it wisely, balancing activities that yield satisfactions to the individual with those that are socially useful.

9. All youth need to develop respect for other persons, to grow in their insight into ethical values and principles, to be able to live and work cooperatively with others, and to grow in the moral and spiritual values of life.

10. All youth need to grow in their ability to think rationally, to express their thoughts clearly, and to read and listen with understanding.[5]

If the thesis is accepted that adolescence is, in part, a cultural phenomenon, then it is obvious that the school alone cannot solve the problem. However, the school can enlist the aid and support of other community organizations. Business and industry can and, in some communities does, help to solve the problems of youth by cooperating in school work-study projects. These projects permit coordination of the pupil's work in school with on-the-job training experiences (Greenleaf, 1955, p. 98). Citizens' advisory councils have been formed to study ways of meeting the needs of youth in community and leisure-time activities. Youth councils in which youth are encouraged to find the answers to their own problems have been found effective. Park bureaus, city planning commissions, juvenile correctional authorities, and public health departments all have a part to

[5] National Association of Secondary-school Principals, *Planning for American Youth*, rev. ed., Washington: National Education Association, 1951, p. 9.

play that should be correlated with the work of the school. Many communities have comprehensive programs of this type in operation.

The school is in an advantageous position to coordinate the resources of the community. It is present in every community. It has the largest resources in staff, equipment, and property of any agency. Through the pupils, it has a close and useful contact with parents. But in view of the rapidly expanding enrollments and the shortage of teachers and buildings ("Teacher Supply and Demand in Public Schools," 1962), immediate action is needed if schools are to enlarge their role. However, the time is right for schools to go beyond the traditional bounds of subject-matter instruction and begin to meet the needs of youth.

Teachers will probably have to supply the initial leadership for this forward step. By virtue of their education, they can learn about the psychological factors in adolescence that are of maximum importance, and they have an even better chance than parents to discover the environmental problems that disturb adolescents. Basically, as previously emphasized, the needs of adolescents are the same as those of other age groups. Teachers must learn how to work in harmony with these needs *through the existing culture*.

Some educational implications of adolescence

Youth Needs a Purpose   It has been shown that competition on the labor market, sentiment against early marriage, and extended education have served to prolong the period between the achievement of physical maturity and the achievement of functional maturity. Much of the feeling of uselessness that adolescents sometimes develop can be avoided if they can be given responsibilities which they feel are important. This was clearly demonstrated during World War II, when youth had a job to do. They became important in the eyes of the adults of the nation. But the fact of most significance was that they recognized their importance. They efficiently took up the tasks assigned them. Many of them grumbled about the interruption of their educational plans or their plans to go to work or to get married. But few of them were so dissatisfied that they failed to perform the functions that were assigned to them. The number who caused difficulty in the armed services was substantially smaller than the number who, in what is called "ordinary times," become delinquent.[6] Of course, war is no solution to the problems of youth, nor

[6] There was an increase in reported delinquency during the war years, but this was due to increased attention devoted to delinquency and the increased perplexity of those youth who were left behind. A great proportion of delinquency was found among those who were less than sixteen years old—below age for military service.

is military service the only way to use their abilities. The point is that when youth is given a purpose, some of its perplexity disappears (Dansereau, 1961).

Some of this purpose can be supplied by the school. Revisions of the curriculum that recognize varying backgrounds, abilities, and ambitions of youth will be a step forward. Leisure-time pursuits, boy-girl relationships, family life, relationships with adults, community services, part-time employment, and consumer economics are other problems of basic importance. Genuine participation in student government, a place on scheduling and curriculum committees may be, in part, a way to give youth a feeling of significance. School-sponsored community clean-ups and area redevelopment have been successfully used in some systems.

Youth's need for purpose can also be fulfilled by other agencies. Parents must come to recognize the necessity for a progressive unloosening of the apron strings. Business and industry must come to realize that their participation in work-study programs is an economic advantage as well as a social service. The Peace Corps can provide for a few the responsibility of an adult and socially contributing role. It can give physical release to those who feel confined by the lack of opportunity in their own community. Churches can institute programs that will be of aid in the daily life and problems of youth. And in all of this, *the participation and counsel of youth themselves should be enlisted.*

There is evidence in the high divorce rates of early marriages, the rise of illegitimacy, the unemployment rates of young workers, and the low occupational level of early school-leavers that emancipation can come too early—especially in our complex society. All the psychology of learning points to man's responsiveness to his milieu. The adolescent can and, to a remarkable degree, does respond constructively to the pressures that surround him. In the right atmosphere, there is no reason why education cannot be prolonged (as it is now in the upper and middle classes), why marriage cannot be delayed (as it is now in Ireland), or why the young person must begin work at an early age (witness the progressively shorter work week with no decrease in production). But youth need to know why life is so different for them than for their parents, why education is important, and why leisure needs to be planned. Moreover, they need the opportunity to discuss it, debate it, and challenge the ideas rather than to be arbitrarily told. Youth can be helped to take advantage of delayed emancipation when they and those in the helping professions understand and deal with the dynamics of the situation.

Talcott Parsons (1964) has emphasized that youth in a rapidly changing society have a difficult time stabilizing their values. There is bound to be some discontent and much search for far higher attainments. He feels, however, that they are doing a commendable job of adjustment and that they do work in the mainstream of current American values. He reports that youth are eager to learn and are ready to accept responsibility. This view—realistic and optimistic—is one which teachers might well adopt as they evaluate and work with adolescents. Many youth programs have failed before they began because they were planned and organized by "experts" and imposed upon youth. Autonomy is as important to adolescents as it is to adults. In the educational field, guidance programs, curriculum revisions, and improved grading techniques have failed not because they were faulty, but because they were imposed.

A first step in developing the capacity for self-direction is to provide youth opportunity to discuss their problems. The formation of youth forums is an example of such methods. The YMCA, the YWCA, and other youth organizations have been active in this field. Some communities have encouraged adolescents to plan and build their own youth facilities. In these communities, youth quickly gained respect for property rights. Churches that enlist the participation of youngsters in choirs, fund raising, and other programs geared to their needs find youth becoming more reverent. Stores in which friendliness is shown and in which service is characteristically informal have no difficulty with their youthful customers. The school could profit from these experiences by seeking opportunities for its students to exercise self-direction.

It must be realized that ability in self-direction will grow with practice and that youth's decisions will not always accord with the adult view (Kelley, 1962, pp. 136–140). As adults, we need to recall that we too, in our adolescent years, were viewed with some distrust and disdain by our elders and that we too found ourselves at odds with some of the requirements imposed upon us. Specific issues and disagreements should not be considered alone; we should examine the basic orientations and needs. Teachers and parents need to realize the pervasiveness of the antithesis of self-direction—authoritarianism—in our society and seek its reduction. The probability is that youth are much more capable of self-direction than some parents and teachers think.

Youth Needs the Help of Understanding Adults   Growth is characterized by both progressions and regressions. An ability that is manifested on one day seems often to have disappeared by the following day. The young person will staunchly defend his right to make his own decisions at one moment and request advice and counsel at the next. "Please give me credit for knowing when to come in at night" is soon followed by "Do you think I should wear a white or a colored shirt?" Wise parents have learned to be patient with this apparent inconsistency.[7] Teachers

[7] Highly recommended for additional reading as a description of young people's inconsistency is an article by John Levy and Ruth Munroe, "The Adolescent and His Happy Family," in Jerome M. Seidman (ed.), *The Adolescent*, rev. ed., New York: Holt, Rinehart and Winston, Inc., 1960, pp. 385–393.

will more readily avoid dogmatism and authoritarianism when they realize that the inconsistency of youth is a normal aspect of maturing.

One of the persistent and highly admirable needs of young people is to outgrow adult domination, particularly parental domination. Since the other adult with whom he is best acquainted is his teacher, he turns to the teacher in the attempt to free himself from parental domination. Should the teacher assume a substitute-parent role (by being dogmatic and authoritarian) and thereby fail the youth, the young person has no adult to whom he can turn in his need for mature counsel. If, on the other hand, the teacher will listen, talk with the youth, and act as a coworker, the youth will consider the adult view of problems.[8]

Youth Needs to Know That They Are Like Others As the world of the adolescent grows beyond the immediate family to include other persons, his need to identify himself with and be like his peers increases (Seidler and Ravitz, 1955). But different rates of growth and varied inherent potentials result in an increasing differentiation of individuals. Body builds differ, puberty begins at various ages, differences in family and cultural backgrounds become increasingly apparent, and different interests develop. Therefore, since the youth desires to be like his peers, uncertainty about himself grows.

The counsel of adults can be of some help. But probably the young person's greatest help in accepting individual differences will come from discussions with other adolescents. One youth bemoans the fact that he has moles on his face, that he has bowlegs, or that he is short or tall. Another reveals his unhappiness about his unsightly acne, his inability to buy clothes similar to those of others, his difficulties with his parents, and his dissatisfaction with school. As these problems are discussed, each comes to realize that his feeling of difference is shared by others of his age group—even though the feelings are generated by different problems. Slavson calls the process of coming to realize that one is not so different from others "universalization." It evolves particularly in guidance groups where, through listening to the problems and feelings described by others, one's own tension and feelings of guilt are reduced and thus one is able to build a stronger ego concept.

> The discovery that one is not alone in an undesirable trait or in failure allays guilt and bolsters self-esteem. Failure, even if it is not consciously admitted or verbalized, leads to self-devaluation and feelings of unworthiness. On the other hand, the discovery that others,

[8] It is worthwhile for the teacher to ascertain the adolescent's attitude toward his parents before calling for parental assistance. In some cases, a great deal can be gained by avoiding contact with parents. This idea runs counter to the advice most frequently given, but it does work in many instances. The youth and the teacher can work out approaches to difficult problems; but when the parent is called in, some youth feel that the teacher is in league against them with their parents.

too, are subject to similar inadequacies and errors and are comrades in distress decreases onus and stigma, setting one up in a better light. Universalization is inherent in guidance groups with all the salutary results of relaxing the individual and thus making him accessible to learning and evolving new patterns of behavior.[9]

The School and Social Pressures Increasingly, the literature on adolescence recognizes that the adolescent is much concerned about *his* conception of the group's desires. Teachers should help him avoid the error of accepting the opinion of an aggressive or vociferous minority by encouraging frank discussion. Moreover, all adults must recognize the importance of the adolescent's dressing like his peers, having similar freedom, acting in the current mode, and being with the gang. These things do not take place readily in an authoritarian atmosphere. Self-direction, self-maintenance, respect for peers and group interaction are essential parts of a salutary developmental climate (Glanz, 1962, p. 234).

Behavior patterns and ideals differ in various social classes. Teachers must realize that it is not an inborn tendency that makes the adolescent question or even spurn their counsel. When he disagrees, it simply indicates that his background has been pointing in another direction. He may not see the value of continued education. His concept of what is moral or immoral, ethical or unethical, may differ from that of the teacher. Good rapport with adolescents is partially contingent upon our recognizing and respecting these differences.

The teacher who desires to influence the conduct of the adolescent must exemplify the behavior, attitudes, and ideals that he would have the young person emulate. There is no choice in this matter. Whether we wish it or not, our conduct does influence that of the adolescent. One of the most difficult problems we have to face in this area is that all too frequently the adolescent has not had an adult who helped him to establish a high goal.

Summary

Learning takes place in a total context of past and future, home, community, world events, and the school. Teachers can provide the best climate for learning when they know the forces that shape the behavior of their pupils. Intelligence, health, bodily vigor, incentives, and motivation all play a part. An important part of the total context is the phase of development through which the learner is passing. One of these phases is adolescence—a phenomenon produced and complicated by physical, mental, and emotional development taking place in a variety of cultural settings.

Certain half-truths hamper our understanding of adolescents. Among these

[9] S. R. Slavson, *Child-centered Group Guidance of Parents,* New York: International Universities Press, Inc., 1958, pp. 287–288.

are the beliefs that pubertal changes account for much of adolescent behavior, that adolescents are awkward, inept socially, growing unusually rapidly, and bothered by sex maturation.

The foregoing partial truths border on what actually is the situation. Adolescents, despite a deceleration of physical growth, are growing steadily. They are a minority group, and the usual suspicions about minorities contribute to their being misunderstood. To a remarkable extent, adolescent behavior is shaped by cultural factors—and teachers should know about these salient, contributory cultural features.

Teachers share heavily in the responsibility of helping youth find a purpose in life, for seeing that they have some freedom in self-direction, for seeking to understand them as individuals and a group. Adolescents, through group discussions, should come to know that their problems are much like those of their peers. As rapid social and technological changes increase the gap between generations, the importance of peer culture is increased, and the need for adult understanding remains a continuous challenge.

Problems and exercises

1 Are stress and strain an inevitable aspect of adolescence, or the experience of only certain adolescents? To the extent that stress is present, is it greater or less than it is in previous or subsequent periods of life?

2 Are there any aspects of growth, any special needs, or any temporary problems that are unique to adolescence?

3 Defend or attack the thesis that adolescent awkwardness is in part caused by the accusation that they are awkward.

4 What do you think Mays means by the statement that adolescent struggles are at once "a hopeful and disturbing condition"?

5 What do you think would be a constructive approach to sex education? Consider both content and method.

6 For each of the half-truths mentioned in the chapter, describe how acceptance of it as truth might hamper adolescent development.

7 What are some specific problems connected with the adolescent's membership in a minority group?

8 Describe how each of the factors mentioned in the first paragraph of the section on Adolescence Is a Cultural Phenomenon influences the status of adolescents.

9 What are some existing school practices that deny or provide opportunities for self-direction?

10 What are some things on the role of the school that you would add to the section on The School and Social Pressures?

Suggested additional readings

Bernard, Harold W.: *Adolescent Development in American Culture*, New York: Harcourt, Brace & World, Inc., 1957.

The adolescent's developmental tasks, such as peer relations, emancipation from parents, educational and occupational adjustment, marriage, etc., are discussed in the light of our current social milieu.

Bernard, Jessie (ed.): "Teen-age Culture," *Annals of the American Academy of Political and Social Science*, 338: 1–138, November, 1961.

This issue contains articles on teen-age culture as it is seen in various parts of the world. Athletics, moral codes, work, delinquency, and teenagers in minority groups are dealt with in separate articles.

Coleman, James S.: *The Adolescent Society*, New York: The Free Press of Glencoe, 1961.

Adolescents in northern Illinois supplied the answers to questions regarding values, interests, and activities of teen-agers. The author points to the ever-widening gulf between the adult's and the adolescent's world as a major challenge.

Kelley, Earl C.: *In Defense of Youth*, Englewood Cliffs, N.J.: Prentice-Hall, Inc., 1962.

The author describes the problems, rationale, and results of giving young people recognition, responsibility, and individuality of purpose in a vocational high school *during the Depression years*, 1932–1938. This paperback book is highly recommended for its realistic and optimistic tone.

Wrenn, C. Gilbert: *The Counselor in a Changing World*, Washington: American Personnel and Guidance Association, 1962.

Although written for counselors, the descriptions and challenges presented in terms of changing American culture are equally pertinent for teachers as they work with adolescents in today's schools.

Cultural Influences—
The Role of the Social Setting

16

Educational psychology, like the school itself, is responsive to new demands and new insights. A shift in emphasis is taking place in educational psychology from study of the individual as a physical and physiological organism to study of his functioning as a social creature. While physical factors are still considered, the pervasiveness of cultural factors is being more clearly recognized. This is not so much a new emphasis as it is a matter of a more explicit and more definitive delineation. The principle that growth is a product of many interacting forces is recognized. Despite tests of ability, achievement records, and daily observation in the school, a teacher cannot understand his pupils unless he knows something about their life outside of school—the patterns of their home life, neighborhoods, and socioeconomic class. These are powerful factors in shaping the pupil's thinking, habits, and actions (Havighurst, 1962, p. 223).

It is easy for teachers to assume that the cultural background of their students is about the same as their own. Furthermore, cultural influences are hard to understand because of our tendency to think of America as a land of rather homogeneous people with common traits and attitudes. Actually, it might be more fruitful to think of the *differences* that exist between a group of pupils in one area and those of another. The motivation, discipline, and teaching problems of a teacher in Brooklyn are considerably different from those facing the teacher in Montana. Attitudes encountered in pupils in Georgia may contrast sharply with those held by pupils in upstate New York. Moreover, within these contrasting communities are large differences in socioeconomic status. These contrasts are just as important in learning and behavior as are body chemistry and inherited potential.

It is impossible within the limitations of this chapter to discuss in detail the effect of differential cultural impact. Entire books have been written about communities and the contrasts within them.[1]

[1] See Suggested Additional Readings at the end of this chapter. A suggested assignment is reading and reporting on some of these books, with attention given to the psychological and educational import of the materials.

It is hoped that the limited discussion here will help make teachers aware of the danger of thinking in terms of "typical" pupils and encourage them to make a careful study of the community in which they live and teach.

Contrasts between communities

Children in Greenwich Village   In a study contrasting two communities, Claudia Lewis noted some twenty years ago that it would be a mistake to think of a typical family or a typical child in Greenwich Village (in New York City), but says that if the families and the children were averaged, certain trends would be evident.

> Their families scarcely could be called a homogeneous group in any simple racial, religious, or cultural sense. If there are any brothers or sisters in the family, it is seldom more than one. Frequently both parents are engaged in professional work as a matter of choice—statistics for one recent year showed that 69 per cent of the mothers worked outside of the home—making it necessary to turn the children over to maids in the after-school hours. Family incomes, ranging from $3,500 to $6,000, are usually adequate to provide for good health, though living quarters in Village apartments are anything but spacious.
>
> A few of the children are adopted, and a few come from homes where parents are separated or have remarried, but actual count shows that the percentage of such children is probably smaller than commonly supposed—only about 12 per cent on the average.
>
> In short, then, these are the children of a professional group living in Greenwich Village, and the fact that they are enrolled in the Harriet Johnson Nursery School usually indicates an intelligent and devoted interest in their development on the part of their parents.[2]

As far as the teacher is concerned, the importance of the family and its way of living lies in the effects on the children. Hence we turn to a word picture of the children who attend the Harriet Johnson Nursery School.

> Can we sum up in a sentence what we mean by "the children in the Harriet Johnson Nursery School"?
>
> Perhaps first of all we think of them as beautifully robust, healthy children with sturdy bodies. Almost simultaneously we think of them as very vocal children. They talk clearly, constantly, copiously, with a facility and pace that is paralleled only by their muscular activity in general. Harriet Johnson children seem never still for long. They must be running, rushing, hopping, jumping, twisting, turning, most of the time. . . . Indeed, the very troubles that arise among the

[2] Claudia Lewis, *Children of the Cumberland,* New York: Columbia University Press, 1946, p. 6.

children are hardly to be separated from the idea of social activity and the working out of social techniques through this activity. Nor can they be separated from the picture of intensity with which these children approach every part of their world. They are intense in their play, their anger, their enthusiasms.

That these are gifted children of a high level of intelligence is evident even without the IQ scores to corroborate the fact. Their awareness is keen, their curiosity in the world about them eager and strong. . . .

Needless to say, teaching such children is something of a strenuous adventure in ingenuity and patience, a vigorous exercise in skill of understanding, in ability to turn what might be chaos into something more calm. The rebels must be helped through their rebellion. Destructiveness, when it goes out of healthy bounds, must be channeled into constructiveness through the vital and interesting play opportunities, materials, and ideas presented to the children, as well as through the warm, solid, bolstering relation of friendliness and understanding that is established with them.[3]

Regardless of the locale, it is necessary for the teacher to exercise patience and ingenuity. Children from any neighborhood feel the spirit of rebellion—though they may characteristically manifest it in varying ways. Understanding and simple friendliness are characteristics we should like to see in all classrooms. *But* the exercise of patience, ingenuity, friendliness, and understanding differ with the community. This may be seen by considering Claudia Lewis's experiences in another community.

Children in the Summerville Nursery Miss Lewis spent 2½ years teaching in a nursery school for mountain children in Tennessee. Here, too, there were marked differences between children, but there were also characteristics that set them off from other groups with which she had worked. The mountain children were shy and quiet. Their response to teacher suggestions was slow, though they seemed to be happy and interested in what the teacher was doing. Screaming and shouting occurred with less frequency and intensity than had been noted in the Greenwich Village school. Temper tantrums were infrequent. There was considerably less speech facility. Their play was repetitive and relatively unimaginative. Interpersonal aggression was infrequent, and direct attacks upon the teacher were extremely rare (only two or three such occurrences in the time she was with them). Stanford-Binet scores were markedly low on the sections dealing with language usage. The pupils were interested in art activities, such as painting, drawing, and modeling, but the products were crude. Despite such differences and the fact that the health of these mountain children was not robust—running noses and open mouths suggested bad tonsils, and sores and rashes were common—she noted

[3] *Ibid.*, pp. 22–23.

that these children passed through the same developmental stages as the Greenwich Village children.

Some of the differences may appear to be a matter of degree. The mountain children probably have less physical energy than the Harriet Johnson children—a fact which may to a large measure explain their comparative inactivity, comparative peacefulness. Likewise, IQ scores of the two groups would seem to indicate, on the surface at least, that there is a considerably lower level of intelligence among the mountain children—though this is dangerous ground to tread on. We have no way of knowing what would happen to the IQ of a mountain child who grew up in the stimulating environment pressing upon the New York child at every turn.

We have seen that Cumberland mountain children can develop some of the same kind of creative originality that distinguishes the Harriet Johnson children so markedly. Even Cumberland mountain children, so shy in the beginning, can become very noisy, can giggle now and then over "dirty" words, can boast toughly of their powers to kill and shoot, can sometimes fight and hit each other for what they want, can gang up against certain of their peers, can rebel on occasion.

And here we come to the outstanding difference between the two groups. "Rebel on occasion," I say. But why does the occasion arise so seldom among the mountain children, and why, when it does arise, are the manifestations of rebellion so mild in character? Why doesn't J. W. [a Cumberland boy] ever hit the teacher and call her Dope, and fling himself on the floor in a tantrum? Likewise, why are his conflicts with the other children, and indeed all of his aggressive expressions, colored with less emotional intensity than David's [a Greenwich Village boy]? And why, whether or not it has any connection with his aggressiveness, is his creative output also lacking in what we might call the "intensity" that characterizes Stephen's?

Here we see that we cannot meaningfully describe such differences as a matter of "degree." The factors responsible for them are imbedded in the particular kind of home and community conditions, standards, patterns, under which the children grow up.[4]

Summerville is a region that can no longer support its population. Sixty per cent of the inhabitants are on relief. Mortgages cover more than half the property. There is no electricity and no plumbing, and some houses have no outhouses. The homes are small—simple shacks surrounded by bare ground trampled by chickens, dogs, pigs, and children. The parents look older than their chronological age. Like the children, the parents differ widely one from another. Some are neat, healthy, and cheerful, while others are patently discouraged, stooped, and sad in speech and action. But they are all kind to their children. They spend much of their

[4] *Ibid.,* pp. 52–53.

time with their offspring—in fact, all of it—since the younger generation is not shooed out of the house. The whole family goes to bed and arises at the same time.

We could say that the placidity of the Summerville children seems to derive from a culture markedly different from that of Greenwich Village. Youngsters have the same schedule as adults (they are even allowed to attend dances late at night). There is no special food or diet for babies—they eat what and when they want. There is no hurry about toilet training or weaning. The whole family takes turns rocking and playing with the baby. One father carried his one-year-old son on his shoulders for 2 miles while rounding up his cows just because he wanted the baby with him. Both the mother and the father spend much time at home, and the result seems to be less conflict in parental authority. There is a large yard to play in, and beyond that the whole mountainside. A child does not have to stay in bed when he is ill if he does not want to—or go to school if he would rather not. Children are taught that stealing is wrong. Sex is not explained to them; in fact, an attempt is made to hide from them the origin of babies. Respect for elders and for religion is consciously inculcated.

Contrasts in Personality Miss Lewis does not conclude that children are better off in one community than in another. But her presentation does suggest the question: Does the high development of intelligence, persistence, and creativity demand conflict, thwarting, and strong stimulation? There is not sufficient evidence at the present time to indicate the answer. But the import for teachers is clear. Not only do children differ one from the other in any given community, but the problems that the teacher will face vary from one locality to another. Generalizations about children must be interpreted in the light of community influences.

It is not enough for teachers to study about children from books. They must, if they are to have the understanding that will be most helpful, know something of the way life is lived in the community where they teach. This knowledge cannot be gathered from academic study alone. It must be the result of the teacher's continuing study of the community in which he lives and teaches. This study should include the places where people live, including the size and number of rooms per person, the size and condition of yards, space between homes, play space and play facilities, cleanliness of the neighborhood, the books and magazines in the home, the distance of residences from business or industrial establishments, and the appearance of adults who are on the streets of the area. Such data will provide a basis for understanding the really important psychological factors involved in adjustment. Psychological criteria would include the attitude of parents toward, and relationships with, children. The attitude of the parents toward neighbors, the law, social conventions, and education should also be considered. The employment status and prospects of the father and perhaps of the mother might well have an important bearing. It has also been said that pupils in the school behave differently because homes differ in warmth and indulgence or rejection, acceptance or criticalness and punitiveness; in being democratic or autocratic; and in degree of child freedom (Baldwin, Kalhorn, and Breese, 1945). These are not community or social class characteristics, but noting these factors and the existing contrasts should increase tolerance for the lower-class youngster, who at present carries (projects) his neighborhood discouragment to the school.

Contrasts within communities

The Meaning of Social Class   It is difficult in our democratically oriented United States to accept the notion of social classes. Ideas of equality, justice, fraternity, and freedom and opportunity to develop one's potentials are deeply ingrained—a function of our culture. But the facts that have been derived from numerous and continuing community case studies show that privilege for some and deprivation (of needs and opportunities) for others is a result of socioeconomic status (Havighurst and others, 1962, p. 12).

The criteria by which social class is determined, or approximated, include amount of education, occupation, amount of income, source of income (wages, salaries, rents, or royalties), place of residence (high on the hill, suburban, or "across the tracks"), kind of residence, *and* behavior. Behavior, including dress, is perhaps one of the more obvious criteria of social class. Social class influences the language and grammar one uses, the interests he has, the regard and relationships he has with his immediate and remote associates, his hopes and aspirations, and his regard for social amenities.

Social class is somewhat more palatable when we consider the phenomenon of mobility. Social class lines are neither rigid nor impenetrable, and there is much shifting (studies indicate 25 to 50 per cent) of individual status during a lifetime. It is possible, by developing special talent (art, music, athletic), to rise to a higher class. Education is a means (not always readily available) by which one may rise on the social scale. One may marry into a higher or lower social group, but most practice the proper behaviors of that class before being accepted. It should also be made clear that social class, like IQ,[5] is a continuous distribution; and

[5] High and low IQs are found in all social classes, although not in the same proportions. It is felt by some that part of the differences that do exist is a function of the instruments used for testing. See Kenneth Eells, "Some Implications for School Practices of the Chicago Studies of Cultural Bias in Intelligence Tests," *Harvard Educational Review*, 23: 284–297, 1953.

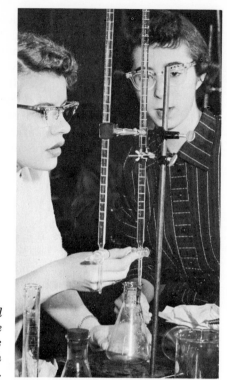

FIGURE 20. *Pupils will want to learn what "the culture" suggests as being most worth learning.*

many individuals are on the borderlines of categories. Individuals and families may possess about as many criteria of, let us say, the lower middle class as of the upper lower class; at the same time, they may possess a characteristic of the upper middle class.

There are different categorizations of social class. Some authors make five groupings, a few make reference to three or four, and some designate six groups. In some communities, a three- or four-group system fits the situation quite well because of the virtual absence of people at either the high or low end. American *culture* is predominantly middle class, but our *population* is largely lower class (see Table 5.)

Class Structure in American Culture The foregoing generalizations may be brought into focus by an examination of how they operate within a community. The following paragraphs describe class characteristics, giving special emphasis to schoolchildren.

The highest social class, class I, is based on the combination of economic, legal (inheritance), and family factors. One must be born into this class, which comprises less than 3 per cent of the total population. There is a great deal of emphasis on "good blood." Families are small—usually consisting of the parents and one or two children—and divorce is firmly

TABLE 5

Designation	Class	Percentage distribution [*]
I	Upper-upper ⎱ Lower-upper ⎰	1–3
II	Upper-middle	7–12
III	Lower-middle	20–35
IV	Upper-lower	25–40
V	Lower-lower	15–25

[*] Percentages are variable because one community, a medium-sized university town, for example, may have a larger proportion of upper-middle class persons than a larger manufacturing city. *Source:* Robert J. Havighurst and Bernice L. Neugarten, *Society and Education,* 2d ed., Boston, Mass.: Allyn and Bacon, Inc., 1962, p. 21.

condemned. Family income may be very high, but the average is somewhat less than in class II. Sources of income are rents, royalties, and dividends from stock rather than salaries. There are two or three cars in the family—expensive cars are common—and the older children have their own late-model sport cars and convertibles. Extensive ownership entails heavy taxes, so there is a desire for low assessments and tax rates, which is fulfilled through control of political organizations. (A sorely needed high school building was kept from becoming a reality through the efforts of this class.) (Hollingshead, 1949, p. 89.) Leisure is dignified. Office girls do the work in the business establishments, and maids, housekeepers, and gardeners free class I adults for travel, shooting, fishing, and country club activities. Most of the middle-aged persons have attended college, though there is a smaller proportion of college graduates among the older persons. The majority of young persons attend college, but are likely to be in liberal arts rather than in the professions (Davis, 1953). Fewer class I than class II students complete college. All class I families belong to a church, and those churches are largely supported by them. However, attendance is infrequent and irregular. Proper clothes—exclusive tailor-made models—are vital, as is proper stationery. There is an emphasis on maintaining position. High personal morality is prevalent, especially among the older citizens, but incidents of gambling and drunkenness do not result in arrests. Because this is a relatively small group and because children are sent to exclusive private schools, public school teachers do not see pupils from this class.

Those in class II have achieved their positions by virtue of their own efforts or have inherited their place from their parents. They attempt to identify themselves with class I, but advancement is difficult (Warner, 1953, p. 56). Both the men and the women are extremely active in civic affairs because their positions depend on *current* wealth and leadership. Class II people live in the best residential communities, and virtually all own their homes. Law, medicine, dentistry, and engineering, privately owned businesses, and salaried positions provide the means by which this group attains top rank in income. Some help is available in the home to free the wife for her community obligations. Marriages are stable, and there are typically two or three children in the family. *Education is vital.* The class as a whole is better educated than is class I. The occupational aim of boys is business or a profession. Girls are educated for a "desirable" marriage, though there is no attempt to "get rid of them." Most families belong to a church, and attendance and leadership are concomitants of their membership. Travel is limited, but the great majority belong to the country club. Their seriousness toward education and their sophistication make the children much appreciated by teachers.

Class III members are much aware of class lines. They see class I as superior, but class II as much like themselves. They look down upon class IV, but do not scorn its members. They believe class IV persons simply do not have quite the ability to do better, but they attribute their own inferiority to the efforts of class I and II to hold them down (K. B. Mayer, 1955, p. 64). Income is from wages and salaries, and 20 to 30 per cent of the wives work as teachers, bookkeepers, seamstresses, and secretaries. According to Hollingshead (1949, p. 97), these families come closest to fitting the popular-magazine stereotype of the typical American. They strive to live in the best residential districts, and many of them have succeeded; most of them live in desirable districts; and two-thirds are homeowners. Despite overlapping, lines indicating the status of residents can be drawn on a city map (Havighurst and others, 1962, p. 8). Church attendance is higher, on the average, than it is in any other class. Marriages are contracted at somewhat younger ages than in class II, and the number of children per family is higher. Marriages are stable, and wives are faithful, but a few husbands stray. Relatively few fathers have been graduated from college, and only a few mothers hold a college degree. They are typical joiners of clubs, lodges, and societies. A few belong to the country club. Their social activities are reported in the newspapers. The striving for upward mobility in this class is perhaps somewhat more apparent than it is in other classes (Hollingshead, 1949, p. 102).

Class IV members are cognizant of their inferior status. They resent the attitudes of the upper classes and avoid contact with the class below. They are regarded as poor but honest—hardworking persons who never seem to get ahead financially. There is little chance for saving, though about half of them are buying a home. Dependence on relief is common during hard times and not unknown at other times. Families are unstable, with one-third of them being broken by separation, divorce, or death. Young people marry at an earlier age than those from the classes above, and the average number of children per family is higher. A third of the mothers work at nonprestige jobs outside the home and, in addition, bear heavy household burdens. The women are not joiners of civic and community organizations. The educational achievement of parents is below the national average, and the example set for children, though perhaps not verbalized, is to leave school as soon as possible. Church is either enthusiastically accepted or vehemently shunned.[6] Leisure time is consumed by radio, movies, and television, with little reading of books and magazines and newspapers, other than the local ones. There seems to be an attempt on the part of men to get away from the tired, irritable, and frustrated wife, whose task is somewhat too difficult for her (Hollingshead, 1949, p. 110).

Class V is regarded as the scum of society by the other groups—delinquent, immoral, slovenly, lazy, and cantankerous. The members themselves are passive. Their past efforts have been to no avail, and they see little prospect for betterment. These are the people in whom there has been developed little capacity for delayed gratification of impulses. This is seen in their early marriages, high rate of illegitimacy, early school leaving, and frequent job changes. Clothes, furniture, and food are not begged for, but members of this class know how to make their needs known in an effective manner. Rummage sales are an important source of clothes. Bank credit is unknown, and the loan companies are very careful about making loans to class V members. Many are employed irregularly and are undependable workers because they will leave a job readily and without notice. They are excluded from the better residential districts and live in undesirable areas. Their homes are run-down boxlike affairs with coal or wood stoves and worn-out furniture, and their closets consist of nails in the wall. Their homes are near the railroad tracks or the swampy river bank—not on the bluffs. Because parents, relatives, and children live in two or three rooms, privacy is almost unknown. Divorce, separation, and desertion are frequent, and over half the homes are "broken." The marital pattern has been referred to as "serial monogamy" or "tandem marriages." The author knows of a case in which three brothers attending a school located near the paint and ladder factories each had a different surname. Few of the parents have been graduated from elementary school. Religious ties are weak. There is virtually no membership in organizations. Leisure activities consist of gambling, gossip, attendance at cheap theaters, and drinking—none of which is pursued by the family as a unit. These people are well known to the police, sheriff, judge, and social worker.

School-age Children in the Socioeconomic Structure It is in the young people that teachers observe the phenomenon of social class providing

---

[6] While some churches have a cross section of social membership, others cater to a limited range of social status (Havighurst and others, 1962, p. 15).

privilege and opportunity for some and denial and deprivation for others. Dodson (1963) refers to the condition of those in the lower social class as "slum shocked"—apathetic, suspicious, and listless. Teachers seeking to understand their pupils are inevitably faced with the necessity of trying to perceive motivations in terms of the family and community forces that shape those motivations.

1. *School life*   The various high school curricula—college preparatory, general, and commercial—have definite prestige values and are chosen accordingly. Although the college preparatory course is chosen by most pupils from classes I and II, the range of choice in the other four classes is greater. The proportion of those from classes IV and V who choose the college course is small (less than 10 per cent), as is the proportion from classes I and II who choose the commercial. The fact that courses are chosen with less adherence to class bias than is shown in some other aspects of life reveals mobility in action. Kahl (1953) gives credit to early parental pressure and early school success for the occasional high educational ambitions on the part of lower-class boys. Herriott (1963) attributes the high educational ambitions of those who choose to attend college despite low income and low status and the repudiation of college by high-ability upper-class youth to (1) the assessment of self in comparison to others, and (2) the level of expectations that the individual perceives important people in his life (parents, teachers, friends) have for him. These self and other evaluations are important variables in the relationship of class and school attendance. These considerations are especially important for the teacher, who wants to see that latent talent is developed, regardless of its socioeconomic origin.

The experience of educational discouragement and disenchantment for lower-class pupils begins with the marks they receive. Many studies (Hollingshead, 1949, p. 175; Wilson, 1959; Sexton, 1961, p. 82) show that grades are distributed according to class lines—the great preponderance of A and B grades goes to the "uppers," and the great preponderance of C and D grades goes to the "lowers." The distribution does not accord with either tested intelligence or scores on achievement tests. There are many understandable reasons for this. Lower-class children do not verbally endorse education, and their behavior in school is more often of the nonappreciated variety than is the case among those from the "better homes." Upper-class pupils are more likely to have the travel, trips, and cultural experiences that give them the background to understand the things that are dealt with in textbooks. It is natural for teachers to see pupils most like themselves in a favorable light and to want to help them. Lower-class pupils are likely to carry into the school their parents' attitude that struggle against the odds (including the "haves") is somewhat fruitless. Hollingshead found that, despite the better grades of the upper-class pupils, parent-teacher conferences concerned grades. On the other hand, despite lower marks of lower-class pupils, the conferences with parents concerned disciplinary matters.

Boys in all classes participate in sports in about equal proportions. Other than this, the lower-class pupils are likely not to be a very significant part of school life. The fact must be faced that pupils from the lower class have twice the adjustment problem of other children when they go to school. The school is a middle-class institution in terms of behavior, values, and language. *Not only must the lower-class pupil adjust to curricular demands, but he must also adjust to a different kind of culture.* Some youngsters are kept out of school affairs on the basis of costs—uniforms, musical instruments, club dues, and even the cost of books—while others are functionally excluded because of their behavior. Lower-class pupils are made to realize that they come from the wrong side of the tracks (Havighurst and others, 1962, p. 72). One girl, asked if she cared for the school dances, replied that she did not even know they were held (Havighurst and others, 1962, p. 62). Hollingshead found that participation in school affairs was 100 per cent in class I, but less than 25 per cent in class V. Many youngsters from class V are very much aware of the fact that their peers look down upon them and feel that there is very little in the school for them.

2. *Cliques and dates* The formation of cliques of two to twelve pupils definitely follows class lines. The belief that pupil groups, at least in high school, are formed on the basis of age, intelligence, and interest is not supported. Should two girls from different classes become friendly, it is not uncommon for the other clique members to show their disapproval; and unless the friend is dropped, the girl will be dropped from her own clique. Over half the cliques for both boys and girls are composed of members of a single class. About one-third of the cliques cross one class line, and 4 per cent cross two class lines. Three-fourths of "best friends" are within the same class. One's reputation is largely a matter of the clique with which one associates.

Dates also follow class lines. The majority of dates are within one class, but may spread to four classes. For example, class IV dates include those from all other classes, but the dates with class I are only 3 or 4 per cent, and with class V, only 6 or 7 per cent. Clearly all other classes tend to avoid class V. Out-of-school dates are more frequent among class IV and V boys and girls, and the boys find dating difficult because of the lack of money.

The sex taboo operates for all classes, but it is violated more frequently by girls and boys from classes IV and V. Hollingshead cautions against generalizations regarding sex behavior because of community mores requiring reticence in asking questions regarding this aspect of behavior, but says, "No case was found in which the boy [admitting sex relations] belonged to a lower class than the girl. Clearly in this small sample there was a strong tendency for young Elmtown males to exploit lower-class females sexually. . . . Irrespective of the number of cases, the available figures throw a narrow beam of light on the question of whom young males in our society seek out for sex thrills" (Hollingshead, 1949, p. 240). The problem of cliques and dating leads Hollingshead to conclude that the behavior of adolescents clearly reflects the adult class structure.

3. *Attitudes toward religion* Young people adopt the religion and acquire the attitudes of their parents in much the same way that they take on other behavior and attitudes. Devout parents raise devout children. The lower the class level, the greater the percentage of nonaffiliation with any church. The higher the social class, the greater the number of youth organizations within the church specifically designed to meet the needs of youth. However, these needs are social rather than religious. Membership in church-affiliated youth groups follows the same pattern of exclusion and inclusion that characterizes cliques and dominates dating patterns. Some ministers and some churches frown upon motion pictures, dancing, and card playing, but this disapproval has little effect upon the young people; they go the way dictated by the standards of their class, and if they are detected, they are likely to withdraw from active participation in the church group.

One element in this picture is of particular interest to young teachers because they may possibly encounter similar situations: Some ministers find that working with young people in the lower classes is an unrewarding activity, and beginning teachers in large cities are often assigned to the most difficult schools, which enroll primarily lower-class pupils— it is a victory to be assigned elsewhere. Even teachers with the service point of view find their efforts yielding small dividends. The pupils, for a multiplicity of reasons—family orientation toward education, family instability, illness, peer attitudes, impoverished living, discrimination— respond with apathy, sullenness, and mistrust (Dodson, 1963).

4. *Work experiences* A part-time job is part of the culture for pupils of the middle class and below. Moreover, these part-time jobs and the jobs taken after leaving school compare roughly with their parents' jobs, at least on the hierarchical level. Those who go to work early are likely to become skeptical about the relationship of education and job performance. This is in accord with the world of reality, if the thesis proposed by Schill (1963) is correct; i.e., education must be in line with the kind of work one performs or is likely to perform if it is to serve its maximum mobility function. When and if youth of the higher classes take jobs, they do so as clerks in the better stores or as office workers for professional people. Parents of those in the higher classes make the contacts for their children, while the lower-class youth have to get their own jobs. Clerking or office work is high on the prestige scale; paper routes and

baby-sitting are intermediate; and waiting table (except in high-class restaurants), washing dishes, and refuse hauling are low in the hierarchy.

The myth that every boy may become a millionaire or President or can climb the economic and social ladder to occupational prestige is discredited as studies of the impact of socioeconomic status on youth continue. This is reflected rather clearly by the fact that occupational aims tend to accord rather well with the promise that class structure holds for youth in the various social classes. Except for the few from the lower classes who go to college, prediction of work success can be made on the basis of such factors from childhood as intelligence, social status, personality adjustment, and family stability (Havighurst and others, 1962, p. 137). Work-study programs, which have been tried in all too few cities, are proving to be helpful in pupil motivation, reality testing, and pupil understanding of the importance of educational underpinnings (Sexton, 1961, p. 209).

The problem of work and education is becoming highly critical, as 26 million youth enter the work force in the 1960–1970 decade. In addition to the fact that the war babies are becoming adults, unskilled jobs are becoming obsolescent due to automation and mechanization (*Challenge of Jobless Youth*, 1963, p. 3); the demand for educational psychology as applied to motivation of lower-class pupils has taken on emergency proportions. Never has the demand for recognition of the need for continuous learning been so insistent as now, when rapid change makes retraining and reeducation a normal aspect of living.

5. *Recreation and pleasure* Presumably the cultural and recreational facilities of a community are open to all social classes, but the facilities do not reach all young people equally. The library, for instance, may be much used by some, and others hardly know of its existence. Large-city museums, theaters, and orchestras may exert an influence on a small number of youngsters, but special efforts must be made to bring these to the awareness of others, much less make them a factor in their lives (Schreiber, 1960). Commercialized recreation—roller-skating rinks, amusement parks, and bowling alleys—exercise a major influence on working-class families but are viewed with suspicion by middle-class youth, who tend to avoid them. This group has youth centers or teen centers available, and these have some supervision from church or adult service agencies (Havighurst and Neugarten, 1962, p. 197). Such organizations as Boy Scouts and Camp Fire Girls are middle-class agencies, and virtually no lower-class children belong. Movies are attended by all classes with some differences in size of cities, in choice of theaters, and in rates of attendance, which increase with higher social status. Private dancing parties are held for children of the middle and higher classes, while young people of the lower class attend public dances—if they attend dances at all.

Drinking is indulged in by some youth of all classes; unpleasant incidents are hushed up for those in the higher classes, and the process of scapegoating is in evidence when those of the lower classes are involved. Hollingshead (1949, p. 320) found drinking a difficult subject on which to get evidence—as was the case with sexual experimentation. Young people of all classes resort to the conspiracy of silence when adults attempt to discuss these topics.

Reading is not a popular pastime, and nonreaders tend to look down on those who have reading interests. The magazines commonly read by young people are the slicks. The reading of books by children of the upper classes is largely to supplement schoolwork. A few girls from the lower class use it as an escape mechanism. Those who do read for recreation are more likely to be middle- and lower-upper-class girls. Not only does the example of parents influence reading patterns, but the content of books is not meaningful to those in the lower class. Books, especially textbooks, do not base content on the whole range of social experience. The experiences of the lower-class children are excluded (Burton, 1953).

6. *The school's holding power*   Much of the impact of class structure is indicated and revealed as a symptom by the school's holding power or lack of it. Prior beliefs that dropouts result from the desire to get a job, desire to get married, dislike for teachers, lack of ability to do schoolwork, and inappropriateness of the curriculum are shown to be excuses for what is more basically a function of socioeconomic status. Going to work at an early age and getting married at an early age are social class characteristics of the lower half of the population. They are manifestations of the need for immediate gratification—an understandable result of the marginal living, the constant frustration, and the chronic disappointment that are normal in these classes.

The belief that intelligence determines the length of one's stay in school does not hold up. Upper- and upper-middle-class children in the lower quartiles of intelligence stay in school, while those of the lower classes tend to show high dropout rates. There is little difference in the intelligence ratings of lower-class boys who drop out and those who stay in school (Havighurst and Neugarten, 1962, p. 233). Girls stay in school or drop out somewhat more in relation to intelligence than boys; boys are more likely to stay in or drop out in relation to their position on the social status scale.

The tendency to leave school early begins to manifest itself in elementary school and gains increasing momentum by age sixteen. Girls stay in school somewhat longer than boys do. By age seventeen, almost half of class VI boys and girls have dropped out, while the percentage is negligible for class I (see Figure 21). Davie (1953) found that by the time youth were of college age, class I individuals were almost five times over-represented in the quota-fulfillment rate in terms of their number in the

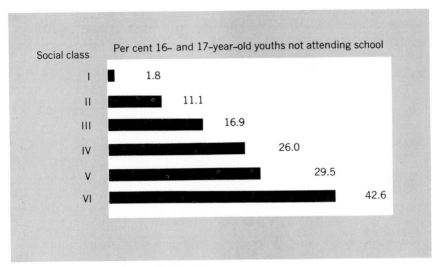

FIGURE 21.   *Social class and school dropouts.*
SOURCE: *Adapted from Charles M. Allen, Combating the Dropout Problem, Chicago: Science Research Associates, Inc., 1956, p. 11.*

total population, while class VI individuals were virtually unrepresented in the liberal arts college category.[7]

School withdrawals follow the family pattern—the number of years children attend school tends to be only a little higher than that established by their parents. Dropouts have significantly lower scholarship and attendance records than do those who remain in school. Scholarship and attendance seem, however, to be more a manifestation of orientation toward the value of an education, level of aspiration, degree of participation in school activities, and whether or not the individual finds an adult in school with whom he can identify (Herriott, 1963) than it does a manifestation of intelligence. Thus dropouts are associated with economic pressures, peer relationships, appropriateness of curriculum, participation in school life, and treatment by the teacher—in short, a function of social class. The financial strain of buying books and clothes that make the pupil comfortable, having money for dates, dues, and admissions, as well as the necessity for helping out at home are all difficult problems for class IV and V youngsters. Children's teasing is often referred to by the school-leavers. They feel the pain of being isolated from student groups

[7] Where a quota-fulfillment rate of 100 would indicate attendance in proportion to a class's numbers in the total population, class I had an index of 494, and class VI had an index of 18 in the liberal arts college category. Class I had a quota-fulfillment index of 6 in the nonattendant category, while class VI had a quota-fulfillment index of 151—about 50 per cent overrepresented in this category.

and activities. The sentiment is often expressed by teachers that withdrawal is good riddance—get rid of the "bad apples." Add to all these factors the difference in value systems of teachers and these pupils and there is little difficulty in comprehending, at an intellectual level, the psychology of motivation that is operative.

Social Class in the Total Culture   Most of the studies referred to above have been sponsored by The University of Chicago Committee on Human Development. That privilege or deprivation is determined by social class membership is a belief currently noted in many publications. One such publication, of particular interest because it represents the work of a large committee and many authors, is that of the Association for Supervision and Curriculum Development of the National Education Association. In this publication, it is brought to the attention of the reader that children from some classes find the culture of the school at considerable variance with their out-of-school culture. "As they find their own backgrounds disapproved and themselves cut off from participation, children from ethnic and economic sub-groups have two strikes against them in learning new ways to get along in the school and in the larger society." [8]

The problem of social class cannot be overlooked on the grounds that it concerns only a few children. It is estimated that about two-thirds of all American children come from native American stock below the middle class or from racial and ethnic minority groups—Negro, Indian, Mexican, Oriental, and Puerto Rican.

A major shortcoming of the concept of social class is that it does not fully explain the value orientations of school pupils (Hodgkinson, 1962, p. 28). Values derive largely from parents; in turn, parents have origins in and values stemming from social class. Both parents and pupils, however, have simultaneous relationships in various groups—two or more social classes, various churches, political groups, and the like. These are not clearly differentiated as criteria of social class any more than amount of education is a decisive clue to social class status. It is not to be expected, therefore, that certain values are perfectly correlated with social status; but in the final analysis, it is the value orientation of the pupil that so largely concerns the teacher, i.e., explains the behavior of the pupil. Kluckhohn (1953, pp. 343–357) has summarized the central values in American society in five basic questions with three categories of answers:

What are man's innate predispositions?

Evil	Neither good nor bad	Good

What is man's relationship to nature?

Subjugated	Man in nature	Master

[8] Elizabeth Hall Brady, "Children Bring Their Families to School," in *Fostering Mental Health in Our Schools,* 1950 Yearbook of the Association for Supervision and Curriculum Development, Washington: National Education Association, 1950, p. 30.

What is the significant time orientation?

Past   Present   Future

What is the valued personality type?

Being   Being-in-becoming   Doing

What is the dominant relationship of man to others?

Lineal (age and   Collateral (individual in family)   Individualistic
heredity)

American values are predominantly in the third category of answers, but the other values do exist. These value orientations are very valuable in *predicting* differential behavior in the school. They might arise from racial or ethnic origins, from rural or urban residence, or from atypical interpersonal relationships; but the most helpful explanation is social class membership.

In view of current data concerning the influx of youth into adulthood and the shrinking market for unskilled workers [9] it becomes urgent for teachers at all levels to seek to encourage values that will keep young people in school: In school, they may gradually learn that man may choose his place in society—as opposed to the defeatism of the lower class; that the future has significance for all; that the individual is valued because he can do those things (work with his head) currently demanded by society. More young people must develop value orientations that will place and keep them in the main current of American life. The old nostrums of teaching a trade and of teaching a skill will no longer provide even a palliative. Teachers have the task of teaching the alienated 35 to 45 per cent of the population that a much greater percentage of them can achieve in the academic situation and thus be better prepared for the uncertainty and the changes of the future.

Teachers in the social setting

The Socioeconomic Status of Teachers   If we are to realize educational objectives, particularly the objective of maximum self-realization,[10] it is

---

[9] The number of young people reaching age eighteen jumped a full million from 1964 to 1965. It will go from 2.2 million in 1950 to 3.8 million in 1970. In addition, the manual jobs will decrease during the years 1950 to 1970 from 39 to 34 per cent of all jobs, though the actual number of jobs will increase; in farm employment, however, there will be a decrease in both number and percentage. These data indicate that the problem of the school dropout—the one who has not accepted at least middle-class values—will be increasingly alienated from the mainstream of society. Herbert Bienstock, "Realities of the Job Market," in Daniel Schreiber (ed.), *Guidance and the School Dropout*, Washington: National Education Association, 1964, pp. 84–108.

[10] Self-realization, as one of the objectives of education, pertains to one's desire for learning; for speaking, reading, and writing his language; for having skills in computing, listening, and observing, protecting and improving health, pursuing recreational, intellectual, and aesthetic interests and activities; and for giving responsible

necessary that teachers understand the implications of their own class origins. It is too easy to think that one's own family and educational experiences are typical. If there is truly to be understanding and empathic treatment of *all* children, teachers must realize that there are psychological factors barring the way to an objective view of pupils and their behaviors.

The great majority of teachers belong to the middle class.[11] Some start in the middle class and stay there; a very few start in the middle class and move upward; and some start from the lower class and move upward successfully. It can be seen from the data presented earlier that the last group have a struggle to (1) overcome the barriers of peer and teacher attitudes, and (2) resist the tendency to place them in terminal high school curricula. To stay in college, they must have learned middle-class values to some extent. When they become teachers, it is only natural that they should reflect middle-class ideology and attitudes. Consciously or unconsciously, they seek to maintain or consolidate their status. Some teachers are helpful to pupils from the lower classes. A principal stated that "teachers who were raised in the middle class tend to offer much help to lower class youngsters. Teachers who came from the lower class steer clear of implicating themselves" (M. Bassett, 1962). How teachers react to pupils who are or might be engaged in upward mobility depends as much on personality orientation as it does on the teacher's own class origins. Some teachers recognize the struggle and are very strict and demanding because they want pupils to develop the attitudes and skills that will facilitate the climb. Others treat children protectively because they do not want to add disadvantages and deprivations to what the children already experienced at home (Wattenberg, 1957).

The Viewpoint of the Teacher Even after a teacher has come to realize that class structure places limitations upon the opportunity of all pupils to develop their potential, his problems have not ended. Attempts to improve the viewpoints of children from the lower classes, to accept them in spite of their behavior and attitudes, and to view them objectively despite soiled clothing, body odors, and dirty faces and hands are not always rewarding. A considerable degree of hostility is expressed toward

direction to one's life—including the development of one's potentialities. See Educational Policies Commission: *The Purposes of Education in American Democracy,* Washington: National Education Association, 1938, pp. 47–108.

[11] In 1957, 12 per cent of teachers came from professional and semiprofessional families, and although the unskilled labor group constitutes about one-third of the total population, only about 7 per cent of teachers came from this group. See "The Status of the American Public-school Teacher," *NEA Research Bulletin,* 35 (1): 9, 1957. W. Lloyd Warner, in *American Life: Dream and Reality,* Chicago: The University of Chicago Press, 1953, pp. 176–180, states that 90 per cent or more of our teachers are from the middle class.

the middle class (teachers included) by some members of the lower class who have not been successful in school (Havighurst, 1961, p. 127). There is also the possibility that some in the middle class will look askance upon the teacher's efforts. There may be a tendency to avoid association with the teacher who seems to be giving insufficient attention to the upper-middle-class pupil. Thus the teacher will find his own security threatened. In addition, the protective shell of the lower classes is likely to cause pupils and parents to resent the well-meaning advances of the teachers. The teacher, on inviting the parent for an evaluative conference, may be greeted with "What trouble has Johnny been getting into now?" This is an attitude developed from the past, when the teacher only came around to make a complaint. Finally the pressure exerted to make the teacher conform to the mores of the community is well known. These mores include looking down upon and discriminating against those who, it is felt, have "bad blood." Community pressure is the more urgent because of recent concern that teachers should become a part of community life. Here again, identification with the more unfortunate in the community incurs the possibility of increasing social distance between the teacher and those of his own class.

There are, of course, many reasons why one enters teaching; as one of the "helping professions," teaching tends to attract those who are inclined to be sympathetic, tolerant, and understanding and to adopt the ideal of social equality. It seems probable that, once having recognized the existence of the problem, teachers are likely to take firm action in helping the less fortunate. Continued professional study, particularly of psychology, cultural anthropology, and sociology will aid in broader orientation. There must be an attempt in teacher-education programs to help teachers develop an objective orientation.

Implications of Cultural Influences for the Teacher   There is no easy solution for the many social and educational problems posed by the existence of social classes and by their impact on the living and value systems of individuals (K. B. Mayer, 1955, p. 1). It is likely that each teacher will have to work out his own approaches in light of the local situation. The author feels that it will be somewhat easier to avoid discrimination when one is forewarned of the problem. It may be that a successful approach will be found among the following suggestions.

1. It may be necessary to adopt broader educational goals. The academic approach has limited appeal (Burton, 1953). For those who are contemplating college, the academic approach may be sufficiently stimulating. For those who cannot reasonably hope to attend college, craftwork, shopwork, and emphasis upon daily problems of living (e.g., marriage and the family) and social understanding may be more realistic. Nor would those who continue their educations suffer from such an emphasis.

2. Learning processes should embrace various approaches rather than

depending solely upon reading and listening. Audio-visual aids, excursions, utilization of resource persons, displays, and laboratory experiences tend to broaden understanding of one's culture, foster recognition of individual merit, and encourage the youngster to stay in school (Schreiber, 1960).

3. Teachers should participate more widely in the life of the community. This will make them conscious of differences in the community and will also make it possible for them to use the life of the various social classes as the basis for group discussion and examples. Davis (1955, pp. 241ff) insists that we cannot generalize about children; but that generalizations about children of a particular class tend to be more accurate than those concerning children of all classes. Hence teachers who do not understand lower-class children find it difficult, if not impossible, to motivate the great masses of these children in school. More than any one other factor, this explains the phenomenon of school dropouts.

4. Because frustration often leads to aggression, the youngsters in the lower classes need opportunities to get rid of their tensions. They particularly need the satisfaction that comes from successful group participation and the assurance of being wanted and considered valuable despite their limited background. Techniques for releasing tension, such as psychodrama, sociodrama, expression through art, spontaneous play, athletics, and music, should be more widely utilized.

5. Less attention should be given to group tests of intelligence, for they weigh the verbal factor too heavily. Some persons have recommended that points be added to the scores of youngsters from the lower socioeconomic levels in recognition of their relatively poor environments. Others have recommended that tests be discarded until they can be made to account for differing opportunity. Perhaps it would be wiser to use tests with due regard to their limitations and as supplements to other sources of information about pupils (Eells, 1951).

All these points may be summarized by saying that a wide variety of incentives should be used so that the school has wider appeal. In short, the whole problem means putting into action the theory that individual differences should be recognized in effective educational programs. Education should enable every individual to make his unique contribution to truly democratic living.

Summary

If teachers are really going to understand learners in the classroom, they must know something about the molding forces of culture—especially the impact of socioeconomic class in the formation of attitudes, habits, and levels of aspiration. Children differ in eagerness and aptitude for learning pursuits not only when communities are compared, but when children from various social strata in a community are studied.

Much as we dislike the notion of social class in democratically oriented America, the fact is that membership in a given social class provides privilege for some and imposes deprivation for others. The gap between privilege and deprivation cannot be eliminated, but it can be narrowed by educational provisions and practices. Fortunately, mobility is not only possible but highly probable for many. In the process of facilitating mobility, more of the human potential of our nation will be effectively utilized.

About half our population belongs in the two lower classes. The pupils who drop out of school or remain in school without personal involvement come primarily from these two classes. The facts belie the belief that these phenomena can be explained on the basis of ability. Lower-class pupils absorb from parents a skepticism about education that imposes the double problem of adjusting to another culture and adjusting to the curriculum among other things. Fortunately, the involvement of an interested adult (the teacher) can be a powerful help. Involvement in school activities might well become a problem for discussion by pupils of all social classes and vigorous leadership by teachers. The problem is intensified by the rapidly increasing need for extended and continuing education in our mechanized and automated economy.

Teachers must examine their own biases and orientations with regard to social class and its impact on the educability of youth. Although teachers are predominantly middle class or upwardly mobile from the lower class, their experiences are not necessarily typical. They must have encountered some key adult who encouraged them to develop their talents. Instead of repudiating their past, they might well consider becoming the key adult in the lives of the many who need support as pupils seek to develop their potential and overcome the burden of their current milieu.

Problems and exercises

1 How would you explain the fact that relatively little space is devoted to a discussion of social classes in education and psychology texts?

2 If the choice were presented, would you prefer to raise your children in the Cumberland or in Greenwich Village?

3 To what extent would you agree that rapid mental development is purchased at the price of emotional stability?

4 Have you had experiences in your own home town that give evidence of class lines and distinctions?

5 Take a series of walks through various parts of a medium-sized city to see what evidences of social class are observable in the various districts.

6 Ask some pupils in the upper grades or high school to trace on a city map the area with which they are familiar. Study this in relation to the description they write of how they spent the last two weekends.

7 Evaluate the statement: There is a danger present for society as a whole in the fact that class I people are not reproducing themselves.

8 Since the sex taboo operates for all classes, how would you explain the fact that the taboo is more frequently violated by persons in the lower classes?

9 Do you think work-study programs (permitting students to work part time under school supervision and for school credit) would tend to make the holding power of the school stronger for lower-class pupils?

10 What specific steps could and should the staff members of an elementary and a high school take to mitigate some of the impact of social class on pupils?

Suggested additional readings

Barrett-Lennard, G. T.: "Significant Aspects of a Helping Relationship," *Mental Hygiene*, 47: 223–227, 1963.

The teacher, as a member of one of the helping professions, will find here some positive suggestions for facilitating the growth of others—especially those handicapped by low socioeconomic status.

Havighurst, Robert J., P. H. Bowman, G. P. Liddle, C. V. Mathews, and James V. Pierce: *Growing Up in River City*, New York: John Wiley & Sons, Inc., 1962.

This book is a report on social class as a basic and determining characteristic in the lives of boys and girls. A longitudinal approach is used to determine how children in the sixth grade will do in the later years of high school and in adult life.

Harvard Educational Review, vol. 23, nos. 3, 4, *Social Class Structure and American Education*, 1953. (Special issues.)

Various authors—Burton, Davie, Kahl, Loeb, and others—deal with different phases of social class and the implications for school workers. Each issue concludes with a critique and a bibliography.

Herriott, Robert E.: "Some Social Determinants of Educational Aspiration," *Harvard Educational Review*, 33: 155–177, 1963.

The author suggests that staying in school or level of achievement is not simply a function of social class. There are intervening variables in (1) how one sees himself in comparison to a reference group, and (2) how one perceives the expectations that important people have for him.

Mayer, Kurt B.: *Class and Society*, Garden City, N.Y.: Doubleday & Company, Inc., 1955. (Paperback.)

This book deals with social class from a sociological rather than from an educational viewpoint. The distribution of life's chances in terms of social class and the impact of class on personality are among the issues considered.

Sexton, Patricia Cayo: *Education and Income*, New York: The Viking Press, Inc., 1961.

The author presents the thesis that the American goal of education for all has been rejected and that the public school fails to facilitate social mobility—that, in fact, the school is an agency of social and economic discrimination.

Group Processes in the Classroom

Much of the literature on education emphasizes the need and desirability of individual development, individual treatment, and understanding the pupil as an individual. With no thought of challenging such emphases, it is doubtful that we should really want to go back to the good old days, when one learned to be a lawyer by reading with a local judge. Most of us would prefer to have a doctor who has studied under several specialists, who has engaged in seminars, and who has observed and discussed the work of many surgeons rather than one who has simply gone the rounds with an older physician. Apprenticeship has its advantages, but apprenticeship is looked upon as being most advantageous when supplemented by other educational approaches.

Emphasis on the individual has its justifiable and firm place in our educational scheme. Group processes also have a place in educational practice—a place recognized in fact, but less in theory. Group processes are just as much in need of being understood as individual pupils are in need of understanding. In spite of the fact that we have dreamed of individualizing instruction, the reality is that teachers are group workers. Their class is a group, and the small sections formed in terms of ability, academic status, or interest are groups. The morale of the teaching corps, the spirit of the school, the community's view of the school are all aspects of group processes. Indeed, the American ideal of mass education demands a sharp focus on group behavior.

The fact is that group behavior has always been a concern of education. Recently, this concern has been intruding more obviously in discussions of education. As the work of sociologists, social psychologists, and cultural anthropologists reveals more insights into group processes, more implications for the field of educational psychology will be perceived. This chapter brings to focus some of the phenomena of group behavior that can be used advantageously by the classroom teacher.

Need for the group emphasis

The Concept of Groups   Strictly speaking, groups are more than collections of things or individuals. A group is a number of individuals bound together by some common factor or factors—age, interests, purposes, or abilities. It is a number of objects (rocks, reptiles, trees) or individuals capable of being regarded as a collective unit because of identifiable common characteristics. Psychologically, a human group is a configuration of persons perceived and functioning as a whole or gestalt. Members of a group perceive themselves to be alike in significant ways; through social interaction, they depend on other group members to play specific roles in their common pursuits (Lambert and Lambert, 1964, p. 87).

Group concepts have long been an emphasis in educational literature, as is evidenced by such well-known terms as "play groups," "ability groups," "control and experimental groups," "normative groups," "peer groups," "cultural groups," "minority groups," "in-groups," "out-groups," "marginal groups," "face-to-face groups," "secondary groups," and the like (Good, 1959, p. 255).

It is not enough to know that groups exist and function in educational settings. The problem for students of educational psychology is to understand how, why, and under what conditions the functioning of groups can become more productive. This subject is known as "group dynamics," and it involves a number of considerations relating to the interactive psychological relationships by which group members share feelings, aspirations, and ideas and thus achieve some common perceptions and community of action. Such interactive relationships derive in part from the broader culture, but also in part from the immediate and spontaneous mood of the group.

Additional light will be thrown on many complex and perplexing educational problems—discipline, mental health, achievement motivation, staying in (or dropping out of) school—as further understanding of group dynamics is developed. Some of this knowledge is now available to teachers.

The Need for Understanding Groups   The aims of education, as formulated by the Educational Policies Commission of the National Education Association, have been reduced to four (each containing several subdivisions): (1) self-realization, (2) human relationships, (3) economic efficiency, and (4) civic responsibility (Educational Policies Commission, 1938). Clearly the last three have considerable reference to group processes. No matter what line of work one follows, his success is conditioned to a considerable extent by his ability to get along with others. It has frequently been stated that teachers who fail do so because of ineptness in human relations or lack of skill in group functioning, not because of lack of knowledge of subject matter. Because man is a social creature, even the objective of self-realization is at many points dependent upon the functioning of such groups as the family, peer group, socioeconomic class, and various school and class groups.

The need for studying group dynamics is made clear when we list the many group roles that an individual must play. His behavior in the family is different from that displayed in the classroom. One's reactions at a basketball game are different from reactions in church or at a concert. Individual roles differ in terms of the composition of the group, as in the above examples. Roles differ in terms of the function of the group; e.g., the same boys behave differently—are different individuals—in the science laboratory and on a street corner watching the girls go by.

Another group situation that parents and teachers are aware of has to do with peer relationships. In the adolescent and preadolescent years, as youngsters are trying to outgrow dependence on parents, they have deep feelings about the vital necessity of peer approval. They feel that they cannot belong to the group unless they wear the right clothes, share the approved goals, talk the same slang. Conflict with parents and emotional conflict within themselves arise when clothes, goals, and language are disapproved by parents.

Some years ago, Prescott expressed, with gratifying clarity, the need for understanding group behavior as it relates to classroom functioning. After some brief remarks about the influence of weather and climate on reactions, he says:

> There is another sort of weather to which all human beings are exposed. It is the moods of their fellow men, with whom they work and play and live. Different people tend to create different climates of feeling among their associates; and different groupings of people show prevailing moods as different as the weather of the arctic and the torrid zones. Some groups swelter at their tasks in the heavy, humid oppressiveness of obligatory functioning, like a sea-level metropolis in midsummer. Others buoyantly undertake common responsibilities with the light, stimulating freshness of the autumn in high altitude dryness. The whole odor of life is sweet or sour, fragrant or foul, tangy or stifling, according to the moods we inhale from those around us. . . .
>
> The question must be raised, then, whether the emotional climate common in the school classrooms of the country is a wholesome climate or not. Is this climate a joyous, buoyant one appropriate to our usual picture of childhood as "happy"? Or is it dull, uninteresting, monotonous, and heavy? Or is it full of tensions, bickerings, repressions, and feelings of failure? Does the child unconsciously absorb the feeling of certainty that he has a significant role in the world and is a valuable person? Or does he get the sense that life is a jungle battle with no holds barred and his own lot a sorry one?

Does the child feel that people are "with him" and that as a part of a larger whole he and mankind are moving toward brighter days? Or is he led to feel that other persons are essentially his antagonists, or at best the setters of unimportant and distasteful tasks? [1]

The foregoing illustrates the enormous impact of groups on behavior. Groups (family, social class, school) do much to supply the social factors in motivation. Anthropologists indicate that man is humanized by his membership in a group, and teachers, despite clichés about "individual development," work primarily with groups. Yet the topic of groups rarely merits distinctive treatment in educational psychology texts. Some justification for this may reside in the assertion that educational psychology gains much of its material from other divisions of psychology (Warburton, 1962, p. 371). Another justification for the separate treatment of group processes resides in practicability; rarely can one so readily see the truth of the gestalt orientation that the whole is greater than the sum of its parts. Teachers are frequently puzzled by the fact that they have excellent rapport with a class one year and the next year have a series of disturbing crises with an apparently similar group. Psychologists have recently discovered that sometimes group therapy is more effective than individual therapy (see section on Counseling under "Groups in Action" below).

Factors in group dynamics

There are, of course, many factors that make groups work effectively and many that are detrimental to their functioning. The factors listed below are indicative and representative. In an area that has only recently come to be studied analytically, it is highly probable that new insights will be numerous.

Individual Goals and Group Goals Whether or not goals have been formulated consciously, all groups have them. Individuals voluntarily join groups because personal goals can be satisfied in the group; often many in the group are seeking the same personal goals. In addition, the group may adopt group goals that are not part of the individuals' initial interest. For example, three young adults may join a charitable group to acquire congenial companions, a fourth may join to be seen in the right places and enhance his prestige as a lawyer. All may join in providing clothing and shelter for itinerant workers and their children.

Before a child enters a classroom group, goals have been formulated by curriculum design. Some individuals may not accept the goals that have served in previous years. Those who do not accept will exclude themselves from the group, be excluded from it, or seek to destroy it.

[1] Daniel A. Prescott, "Emotional Weather," *Educational Record,* 20: 96–97, 1939.

This is what occurs in the cases of problem children, dropouts, and children who are expelled from school. Correctives and punishment have been applied in such cases; but if teachers perceived these behaviors as group phenomena, different approaches might be tried. For example goals might be modified so that more pupils would accept them; attempts might be made to get pupils to perceive existing goals as having personal meaning; and both approaches could be discussed by the group.

Another approach is for the group to have its goals in addition to the goals of individuals, e.g., preparing for a visit-to-Germany evening in which pictures, art objects, relics, music, costumes, and language will be presented to friends and parents as part of the work in advanced German. Group goals could include preparing posters for a dance, contributing to the March of Dimes, earning a high scholastic reputation for one's school. Wishing to remain a member of the group, an individual works toward these goals (speaking German, making a poster) not because of his personal acceptance of the goals, but because he wants to remain a member of the group. His need to be a member transcends the learning goal at least temporarily, and gives the teacher time to deal with task motivation. This emphasis was a powerful factor in the success of a school in an underprivileged area in which the staff gave attention to making the school a youth center, with youth participating in planning and policy making (Kelley, 1962, pp. 33–37). Learning as a goal is not forgotten. Learning is simply made to parallel the emphasis on the school as a group that can and must serve many needs of young people.

Participation One of the obstacles to participation in classroom groups is the fact that membership is mandatory. Pupils cannot select those with whom they are supposed to communicate. Often the result is that they are more concerned about the social relationships than about the learning to be achieved or the problems to be solved. Classroom groups are in this way almost unique.

> Not only is *what* shall be done a "given" but *who* shall do it is also a given. Both the goal and the participants are *mandatory*. The answer obtained from certain parents as to why they send their children to school is that "You can get sent up the river if you don't." And the answer obtained from certain children to to why they attend class is that "You can get sent up the river if you don't." The school and the classroom are perhaps the extreme instances in the United States of group participation required by society entirely apart from any ascertained volition of the participants themselves.[2]

[2] Jacob W. Getzels and Herbert A. Thelen, "The Classroom Group as a Unique Social System," *The Dynamics of Instructional Groups,* Fifty-ninth Yearbook of the National Society for the Study of Education, Chicago: The University of Chicago Press, 1960, part II, p. 55.

Most other groups (military organizations and offenders assigned to traffic school excepted) are voluntary—if not in terms of membership, at least in terms of stated purposes. Sociometry can provide useful clues in forming school groups in which interaction may take place easily despite the mandatory character of the school situation. Because of the halo effect, limited personal experiences, and rapidly changing social customs, few teachers have the ability to make accurate judgments regarding the generally respected peers, the cliques, and the likes and dislikes of the students. In the earlier years, boys choose boys and girls choose girls as associates; but this changes gradually in the intermediate grades, and choices follow community patterns. It is then that racial, religious, and socioeconomic factors enter into the formation of subgroups. It has also been found that similar personality traits tend to be factors in group solidarity.

Thus in forming groups, teachers should counteract the compulsory aspects of membership by seating students who like one another together, by choosing for small groups students who express mutual (or at least one-way) attraction. Sex (depending on age) and perceived interest, similarity of traits, similarity of background, and comparable levels of intellectual functioning should be considered. How much weight to be given these factors varies with the nature of the task. It has been found that task-oriented study groups result in greater behavior and personality change than do discussion groups. Friendship, cooperativeness, and general adjustment is greater in task-oriented than in role-playing or discussion groups (Mann and Mann, 1959). It may be hypothesized that absorption of a new group member is more readily achieved if the introduction is to a group tackling a problem rather than a discussion group.

The experience of success or failure conditions the group's acceptance of new members. With a background of failure, the group is more likely to view a newcomer as a resource person who can aid in getting the correct answer or in suggesting a more profitable approach. With a background of success, the group is more inclined to view the newcomer as an unwelcome source of disruption and to rate him lower than the failure group does (Ziller and Behringer, 1960).

Cohesiveness When a group is bound together tightly by common and cooperatively determined goals, when the backgrounds of members are similar, and when the group remains intact despite changing conditions, it is said to be cohesive. One advantage of a cohesive group is that it is more capable of maintaining forward movement in spite of frustrations (French, 1944). Another advantage is that a cohesive group has greater power to command conformity than one that is less firmly knit (Coch and French, 1948): Unhappy or discontented pupils are not allowed to set the overall tone of the group. This explains, in part, why teachers find some classes easier to work with than others. One teacher reported to the author that changes in schedule were disturbing, content of the course was criticized, and assignments were resisted in one group, but a second group took all these matters in stride. The difference, in retrospect, seemed to be that in the first case the group broke apart; the critics were ignored or bypassed by the forward-moving pupils, who simply would not be bothered by the unrest and withdrew from the informal gatherings of the larger group. In the second and more cohesive group, the eager students were concerned about others, discussed their views, explained the discrepancies in the program, and analyzed the motives of the teacher.

Group cohesiveness is dependent also upon the effectiveness of subunit communication. Thus, it is to be expected that sociometric groupings (see Chapter 12) increase group solidarity and productiveness—the members feels comfortable with one another. Another factor is the size of the group—it must be large enough to present diversity of views and small enough to allow for the participation of all members (Thibault and others, 1960). Precisely how many constitute an effective communication group has not been determined because size must be considered in relation to purpose, individual roles, leadership, and in particular, the sensitiveness of the teacher in diagnosing group action.

Goals are a factor in cohesiveness, but it is not clear which precedes the other. It would seem that commonly accepted goals contribute to cohesiveness, but cohesiveness makes more probable the acceptance of group goals (Zander and others, 1960). Starting at the goal-establishing end, self-determined rather than imposed goals are superior for establishing group unity. In the learning of motor tasks (e.g., writing and laboratory skills), those who participated in discussion about the necessity or desirability of change and the nature of the skills sought learned much more and more rapidly than those who were simply told what to do. Moreover, there was less aggression and less interpersonal resentment in the discussion-oriented groups (Zander, 1950).

There may be circumstances under which group unity is not highly desirable. It has been found, for example, that open groups, in which there is changing membership, are more creative than closed groups, in which new members are not accepted after original formation of the group. Following failure, an open group perceives a greater probability of attainment than does a closed group. Following success, the closed group is more likely to perceive the probability of future success (Ziller and others, 1962). Rather than drawing conclusions as to possible action based on such experimental results, the teacher should infer clues to be used in the analysis of what is happening in his own class groups.

Competition There is widespread belief in American culture that the spirit of interpersonal competition should be inculcated into children so that they can meet the exigencies of a competitive life. One hears also that much in American culture demands an ability to cooperate. An overemphasis on competition inhibits effective group action, but there is also the danger that too much group endeavor may inhibit individual initiative. The dilemma should be viewed in terms of broad and varied educational goals. Cooperative effort becomes difficult when group members are competing for their individual goals; there is a disruption of coordinated efforts, of friendliness, and of pride in the group and an inhibition of the ready exchange of ideas. The competitive grading system, which is currently widely used, is an example of the creation of mutually exclusive goals that disrupt class harmony (Deutsch, 1949). Actually, the evidence that individual pursuit of even strictly academic goals is superior to group pursuit is equivocal. Add the desirability of learning to work with others in various pursuits, and the weight shifts to the desirability of coordinated group action.

Democratic Procedures The essence of successful group action is a democratic orientation—shared opinions, designated responsibilities, respect for the individual specialist, the reign of group intelligence. We see too much evidence about us that the democratic orientation has not been thoroughly assimilated. One of the more dramatic evidences was the susceptibility of American soldiers to brainwashing in the Korean conflict. It has been reported that American prisoners of war could easily be set against one another and made to submit meekly to propaganda by removing their leader whom they seemed unable to replace. In contrast, Turkish prisoners of war remained intact as a group; when their leader was taken away, he was simply replaced by another who was respected by the group and who became the authority. Mayer (1956) attributes much of the weakness of American prisoners to the failure of American teachers to teach a clear and pointed concept of democracy.

Aspects of democratic processes appear at many points in the discussion of group processes. The group determination of goals is an example. The assuming of responsibility in a task-oriented group is another. The desirability of having the teacher act as a group member instead of the voice of authority or a trainer appears frequently in discussions concerning the success and value of group approaches. It is not surprising that Trow and others designate the teacher's role as "democratic strategist" as one of the three important group roles, along with instructional and therapist roles (Trow, Zander, Morse, and Jenkins, 1950).

Knowledge of Group Dynamics There are several reasons why knowledge of group behavior may be helpful to teachers *and* pupils. For example, the phenomenon of "behavioral contagion," the spontaneous imitation of behavior initiated by one person, calls for an analysis of interpersonal influences. The fact that deviation from group norms contributes to the exclusion of the offender or the disintegration of the group indicates the desirability of having pupils examine the dynamics of group processes. When individuals vary in their needs for achievement or for belonging, the solidarity of the group is threatened. For such reasons, the group should at times focus very specifically upon what is going on, what roles are being played by various members, and how functioning can be improved. The successful group leader will on occasion ask very personal questions such as "How do you feel about that statement?" "Does it seem that Terry is trying to avoid discussion of the central issue?" "You seem restless today—is there some special reason for it?" These questions direct attention to processes rather than the direct solution of the problem. The teacher's knowledge of group dynamics should be shared with pupils. Such sharing makes it appear that the teacher is one of the group and enhances communality of purpose; it also increases the possibility of successfully transferring group functioning to other situations.

Need Satisfaction Group action, whether for remediation of emotional problems, prevention of maladjustment, or development of an individual, is dependent for success on the existence of common needs. This conclusion, derived from therapeutic experience, has direct implications for personal-development groups.

A basic assumption is that one voluntarily joins a group (school groups are not likely to be voluntary) because he feels that in some way joining will satisfy a need. If one is drafted instead of joining voluntarily, he fails to become an integral part of the group until he perceives that the group as constituted can fill either a developmental or deprivation need for him (Jensen, 1960, p. 83). Friendships that provide a supportive atmosphere are essential to need satisfaction; they must exist within the group or be developed. If showing off or other means of getting attention become prominent, it is an indication that those concerned do not perceive the manner in which the group may satisfy their needs. On the other hand, when participants give help, comment favorably on contributions of others, joke and otherwise show satisfaction, or agree and understand, they lend solidarity to the group and also indicate that needs are being met (Bales and Strodtbeck, 1960, p. 625).

It has been found that comparable age and similarity of intelligence and interests tend to weld groups together. Students, as growing and untested persons, need social approval and the feeling that they can make a contribution to the group. Anything that threatens the prestige they may already have earned will cause them to withdraw from the group or to attempt to destroy or cripple the group itself. Thus the extent to which students reward or coerce one another becomes a prominent factor in the success or failure of the group (Zander and Cohen, 1955).

Role of the Teacher as Classroom Leader   There can be no doubt that the teacher is, in the final analysis, the official leader of the classroom group, but his role will be challenged on occasion.

> This is not to say, of course, that the authority of the teacher must be exercised in an authoritarian manner or that there are not *informal* lines of authority among the pupils themselves. Indeed, even formally, authority can in fact be delegated for certain functions to the pupils, and frequently is. But such delegation cannot occur without the teacher's permission, given explicitly or implicitly. If one thinks of authority, control, and leadership in political terms, it is clear that the classroom group, at least in its formal aspects, is about as far from democracy as one can get. Not only do the students have no control over the selection of their leader, they normally also have no recourse from his leadership, no influence on his method of leadership beyond that granted by him, and no power over the tenure of his leadership. There are very few working groups in our society in which these essentially despotic conditions are legitimately so much the rule.[3]

Other Group Roles   Studies of the impact of the teacher on pupils frequently place emphasis on personality attributes. In some pioneering experiments on groups, however, Lewin and his students showed that leaders could assume various roles—autocratic, democratic, or laissez-faire—and produce predictable results (Lewin, Lippitt, and White, 1939). Subsequent investigations have shown that teachers can get results by centralizing authority within themselves or by increasing the independence of students (decentralizing authority) and the social access of members. This can be accomplished if the teacher talks less and provides more time for and attention to students' comments and questions. By spreading verbal participation and using students' ideas, whether they are pertinent or off the subject, he increases the leadership and prestige of students. This necessitates the differentiation of assignments to accord with ability. It also involves time for student-teacher planning, which clarifies goals and makes them more personal for the pupils. Group action is facilitated when teachers use indirect rather than direct influences. Some of these influences have been presented as contrasts by Flanders (see Table 6).

These two columns do not necessarily mean a choice between good and bad, salutary and injurious. Group action has its advantages, but so do strong leadership and informed authority. Teacher-directed learning, with a high degree of frequency, is economical of time when pupil motivation

[3] *Ibid.*, p. 56.

TABLE 6

Indirect influence	*Direct influence*
Accepts, clarifies and supports the ideas of students	Presents lectures about the idea or area of knowledge
Praises and encourages	Gives directions and orders
Stimulates participation by asking questions	Criticizes or disparages pupil contributions in hopes of change
Asks questions designed to give orientation	Justifies his own position or ideas

Source: Ned A. Flanders, "Diagnosing and Utilizing Social Structures in Classroom Learning," *The Dynamics of Instructional Groups,* Fifty-ninth Yearbook of the National Society for the Study of Education, Chicago: The University of Chicago Press, 1960, part III, p. 204.

is strong. Group action can often bolster weak motivation. The fact that the immature pupil—often the adolescent—wants and needs the structure that teacher control provides has been mentioned in Chapter 15.

Roles in Teacher-centered and Reality-centered Classrooms Groups in school have distinctive characteristics because of the personalities and motivations of pupils and teachers and the influences stemming from the organization and operation of the group as such. Improved results may be obtained from group interaction when the roles of all are identified and an effort is made to see that all necessary roles are filled.

A teacher-centered classroom is one in which the teacher makes the major decisions about content, activities to be pursued, and the individual roles to be performed. He acts as the judge for punishment and rewards and is responsible for the morale of the group. Some pupils are quite content with such an organization. They willingly play the "faithful servant" role and not only try to conform to the teacher's wish, but cultivate his approval and try to anticipate his desires. Other students, however, object to this role; they not only resent the servant role, but try to cut the faithful servants down to size. In effect, they become rivals—they are like children who have older, prettier, or more talented siblings. Still another role in the teacher-centered classroom is that of the rebel who expresses resentment in various ways. Rebels may subject the conformists to scapegoating, criticize the assignments, incite other students to resist the teacher, or question the statements and ideas of the teacher beyond reason.

The reality-centered classroom is characterized by student participation in decisions concerning content, method, and role assignments. Students set the standards of behavior and help to enforce them. The teacher does not abdicate his authority role, but neither does he act as dictator. He points out limits, explaining their justification. He expects pupils to act within the limits and encourages response and productivity. There are more roles in the reality-centered classroom than in the teacher-centered context. These roles are of two major types—the task roles and the group-building and group-maintaining roles.

Roles of Pupils The particular roles played in a group vary according to the task and its stage of development. Benne (1954) has listed the task roles in a problem setting. In the *initiating* role, someone suggests what to do, what to discuss, or what method to use. Data are required to solve a problem, and two roles are significant—the *information-seeking* and the *information-giving* roles. It is interesting for teachers to observe the consistency with which these roles are characteristically assumed by certain pupils. There is a *clarification* role, which is filled by those who restate, cite examples, ask questions, and suggest implications. Finally, it is necessary to collate the various ideas, so a *summarizing* role has its place in effective group action. The teacher should point out the necessity of filling these roles and assist students in assuming them (C. W. Taylor, 1961).

Groups, to be effective, must be sustained; threats to solidarity must be eliminated, and communication must be kept open by people who play the *building* and *maintaining* roles. When problems are difficult and failure is imminent, someone must fill an *encouraging* role, giving praise, summarizing progress, and specifying individual contributions: This is not an easy role because progress can be inhibited if praise is not merited, if contributions are not really significant, and if individuals do not actually deserve commendation. Ideas sometimes clash, and someone to play a *harmonizing* role is needed to minimize differences, indicate that each has some points, and recall how much there is in common. Keeping the channels of communication open is a constant challenge, and it may mean asking for opinions from those who have previously been silent, limiting the time for each person's comments, and maintaining order so that everyone has a chance to participate: Benne (1954) calls this the *gate-keeping* role. *Standard setting* is still another role; it becomes operative when there is verbal or tacit agreement that action should be by consensus or by majority rule. The standards agreed upon are not always desirable, as is the case when only students from a given social class are listened to or when there is exclusion of some pupils because of language accent, skin color, or religious affiliation.

A number of negative roles may be perceived in group functioning; you have probably seen these roles played in your own group experiences. The roles are self-explanatory, but counteracting them requires rather intimate knowledge of individual motivation. Among the negative roles are *aggressor, blocker, recognition seeker, playboy* or *show-off, dominator, individual-help seeker* (as contrasted to those oriented to solution of the group problem), and *special-interest pleader* (Trow, 1960, p. 34). Still another role is that of the *indifferent acquiescer*, who is not sufficiently involved to make a contribution and thus does not facilitate forward progress. It might well be noted that sometimes the one whom we may designate as "playboy" uses humor not to impede progress—though this is the immediate impression—but because he himself feels or perceives in others a mounting tension that, if unrelieved, will ultimately retard forward movement.

Groups in action

Discussion Techniques   There are no sure-fire techniques for generating effective discussion, but some maneuvers may be productive. As indicated above, groups imply some community of purpose; hence class involvement is facilitated when pupils feel that the group is theirs, and they are more likely to feel this when they have been allowed to make some suggestions and decisions. When difficulties arise, it is well to stop to analyze the nature of the obstacle. It is better to deal initially with problems that are somewhat neutral in tone—study habits, best-liked subjects, future occupations—and leave until later topics such as school cliques, racial prejudices, disliked grading systems (Caldwell, 1960, p. 46).

The physical arrangements are significant. Discussion demands freedom of communication, which is facilitated by face-to-face arrangements among other things. Circles, semicircles, or rectangles with the teacher sitting with the group makes communication easier because (1) the consent of the teacher is not deemed vital, and (2) participants can watch to see when others have finished or still have a point to make.

In sophisticated discussion groups, it may be noted that leadership often shifts from one person to another. Certainly the teacher should attempt to shift the leadership to one or more students. This may be facilitated by first discussing the roles to be filled—leader, evaluator, etc. (see section above on Group Roles of Pupils)—and asking how these roles might become functional in the present group. Benne (1954) has suggested that knowledge of group dynamics should not be restricted to the teacher; pupils should know the required roles, observe them in operation, evaluate their functioning in the current group, and assume responsibility for filling them. This procedure has the double advantage of making group members aware of their individual roles and facilitating group action.

Buzz sessions have been used with varying results. They are formed by breaking up a large group into small discussion groups of five or six persons. Each may discuss the same topic or be assigned a subtopic related to the major concern of the large group. Usually the "buzz" lasts only five to fifteen minutes; after this time, a selected member of the group reports to the larger group. Not all buzz groups are successful. There must be a clearly understood purpose, and a leader, a recorder, and an evaluator may need to be designated. When a group bogs down, someone must redistribute membership so that an effective leader can initiate action.

Brainstorming has been used in business and in colleges. It merits consideration, at least at the high school level, for appropriate problems, i.e., those that are personal and about which group members have some information. Essential elements in brainstorming are preparation; stimulation of sensitivity to the problem; encouraging all to participate and listening to all ideas, even the most absurd ones; prohibition of *all* criticism during the session (it should follow in another session); recording all ideas; and presentation of findings (Wetzler, 1962). The productiveness of brainstorming is such that the method merits much more trial and experimentation. To date, experimental groups have been markedly more creative (when rated by trained evaluators) in terms of number and quality of ideas than control groups (Meadow, Parnes, and Reese, 1959).

One of the obstacles to genuine discussion groups is the teacher's difficulty in shifting from the ordinary classroom approach in which he is the authority to an approach that permits others to feel that their voice is of consequence. This may be accomplished by reflecting or mirroring— itself a somewhat difficult technique. Mirroring consists of refraining from giving answers or evaluation and, instead, restating or rephrasing in slightly different words the ideas expressed by pupils (Caldwell, 1960, p. 48). Thus when a pupil asserts that he thinks he got an undeservedly low grade, the teacher might say, "Paul believes that the grading system needs some improvement." Betty states that she studied hard for the role of a certain character in a class play, but Sue got the part; the teacher may respond, "Is Betty suggesting that the designation of cast members be approached more democratically?" Mirroring is typically needed only at the beginning of group discussion; as the teacher retires from the leadership role, such reflection becomes less important.

Silence can be helpful in improving pupil contributions. Silence can be used to increase the anxiety of pupils (or teachers), and someone hastens to fill the gap. If the silence is uncomfortable and too prolonged, it may inhibit participation. But a silence in which group members are given time to weigh and assimilate ideas is worth cultivating.

The fact that some discussion groups have been successful means that some of the foregoing factors have been operative—whether consciously or inadvertently applied. Because so many experiments show that opinion changes are greater in discussion groups than in ordinary instructional groups, because pupils need to exercise skills in human relations, and because we hope that ultimately students will become self-sufficient, there is sound reason for teachers' persistence in making increasing use of discussion (Pennington, Haravey, and Bass, 1958). Whether or not group discussion methods are superior to other methods for acquiring information, there is considerable evidence that group methods promote problem-solving skills, consolidate learning, and encourage freedom of thought and a spirit of inquiry.

Counseling   A considerable amount of concern and controversy has arisen in some circles about teachers or school counselors becoming therapists. The concern stems from a fear of doing the student harm or "pushing him over the brink," but the author knows of no studies that document this possibility. In any case, the teacher is already involved by the mere presence of an emotionally disturbed pupil and ignoring him has greater potential than talking with him for pushing him beyond the tolerance level. Some are not so concerned about the teacher's attempting to aid the disturbed child. Proff (1962) states that there is evidence that giving the disturbed pupil almost any kind of attention may be helpful. Psychiatrists at the University of Oregon Medical School in Portland are actively seeking to give help to teachers in doing a better job in a situation that is well-nigh unavoidable anyway. There are not sufficient psychiatrists and consulting psychologists to serve all who need help. Better work can be done with referred cases if teachers can supply information; and during periods of delay prior to help by highly trained professionals and after release during readjustment periods, teachers can give substantial help to the mentally ill pupil (Saslow, 1963; Butler, 1962). Arbuckle (1962) contends that it is necessary to work with *all* pupils who are still in school. Whether the process is considered therapy or counseling makes no difference. The fact remains that education must be concerned with all phases of development—intellectual, social, and emotional. The helping function of school workers, especially counselors, demands that they do on occasion become involved in therapy.

The author suggests that teachers stop trying to avoid participation in "therapy." Rather, they should seek to learn more about the methods available and use them more effectively. One of these methods is group discussion of personal problems.

Initially, group therapy was used in order to save time and reach more people with the personnel available. It was soon discovered that forward movement was often more rapid in some kinds of problems and for some kinds of people through group therapy than through individual therapy. Several explanations for this have been advanced. One is that the individual is helped by discovering that others suffer from situations similar to his own, which he had hitherto thought to be unique (Slavson, 1958, p. 287). Advice and suggestions coming from one's peers are sometimes more acceptable or seem more practical than those coming from experts. Apparently, the individual thinks that peers have had actual experience, whereas the expert, with his textbook knowledge, does not *really* understand. One sometimes feels freer to talk candidly with peers than with the professional, who, he fears, might make judgments; thus catharsis (see Appendix) is more readily achieved through discussion with peers. Counselees may feel threatened by the individual approach, whereas in groups they feel the protection of others who are somewhat like themselves (Froelich, 1958). Group counseling provides a somewhat better setting for practicing changed orientation and behavior than does the individual counseling setting (D. H. Jenkins, 1949).

Group counseling was used as an initial contact with counseling for a group of graduate students. They observed participants who came to the counseling center once a week. In one case, there were four boys and four girls from two high schools; all were referred because the school counselor had data showing that the pupils worked consistently below indicated capacity.

The first session consisted of introductions and speculations by the students as to why they had been sent to the center and what might be accomplished. The counselor did not ask, "Are we on the track?" "Shall we get busy?" but looked at the pupil when he was discussing what might be or was likely to become pertinent and looked away when the pupil took too much time on topics that appeared to have no relevance.

During seemingly casual conversation, words such as "brother," "sister," "mother," "teacher," "principal," "dating," and "school subjects" occurred. Context and degree of intensity with which the words were uttered led the counselor to say, "Tell me more," or "What about your sister (teacher, mother)?" There is enough in common in an area such as underachievement so that a topic on which there is real feeling (e.g., high-achieving older siblings, parental criticism) is readily and widely discussed. When it comes to a solution, questions such as "What part do you play?" "How can the situation be improved?" soon begin to confront an individual with his own individual responsibility (Fullmer and Bernard, 1964, pp. 183ff).

There was a series of eight sessions. As has been the case in comparable sessions reported in the literature, there were no sharp increases in achievement scores or grades. But subjects reported feeling better about themselves and others, and observers felt that improvement in conduct of the young persons in the group was great enough to be clearly perceptible.

Summary

A teacher's effectiveness is, to a large extent, dependent upon his ability to work effectively with groups. The learning climate of the school is dependent on the congeniality and orientation of the classroom group to a marked degree. Unfortunately, the dynamics of groups has not been a typical or even frequent emphasis in educational psychology or teaching methods.

The effectiveness of groups can be enhanced by a clear delineation of group goals, which are not always synonymous with individual goals. Class groups are not initially voluntary, but the negative aspects of compulsory membership can be offset by applied sociometry, by clarifying purposes, and by recognizing individual needs. Cohesiveness is strengthened by communication, by balance between success and challenge, by using democratic procedures, and by knowing group dynamics and explaining them to pupils.

Successful group dynamics stem from filling such roles as leadership (whether democratic or authoritarian); pupil involvement in class activities, including both goal determination and method of approach; and capitalizing on knowledge of group roles. Pupils may take various roles, such as initiating, information giving, information seeking, clarifying, and summarizing in problem-oriented groups. Roles that appear in both problem-oriented and social groups are building, maintaining, encouraging, harmonizing, gate-keeping, and standard setting. There are also a number of negative group roles; they have been identified as aggressor, blocker, recognition seeker, playboy, dominator, individual-help seeker, and indifferent acquiescer.

Seeing to it that the group-building roles are filled can facilitate both group discussion and group therapy. Group therapy, perhaps called by a different name, can be made to function in the classroom when problems of a personal nature—study, social relations, teacher-pupil relationships—are made the business of the class.

Problems and exercises

1 Is there much or little group interaction in your educational psychology class? How would you explain the situation with regard to its group solidarity?

2 Describe two or three occasions in which you have perceived effective group action that apparently stemmed from clarity, importance, or immediacy of goals.

3 To what extent and in what manner does the amount of participation of an individual affect his group involvement?

4 Are there any situations where authoritarian leadership might add to group cohesiveness?

5 How might you go about explaining group dynamics to a seventh-grade class? To some juniors in high school?

6 What do you perceive as the distinction between teacher-centered and pupil-centered classes?

7 Attend some group meeting other than your present class and report back the extent to which various roles were clearly evidenced.

8 In the activity involved in the preceding problem, did you see any blockers, playboys, or indifferent acquiescers?

9 Contrast an effective and ineffective discussion group. How would you account for the difference?

Suggested additional readings

Bonner, H.: *Group Dynamics: Principles and Applications,* New York: The Ronald Press Company, 1959.

Chapter 8, "Group Dynamics in Education," indicates that there are both advantages and disadvantages in group processes as a teaching approach. Some students react favorably and others negatively to group methods.

Caldwell, Edson: *Group Techniques for the Classroom Teacher,* Chicago: Science Research Associates, Inc., 1960.

The primary focus in this booklet is upon interpersonal relations and individual feelings. Those who criticize the teacher as a therapist will probably not react favorably to the principles (pages 22 to 25) or to the problems mentioned.

Fullmer, D. W., and H. W. Bernard: *Counseling: Content and Process,* Chicago: Science Research Associates, Inc., 1964, pp. 183–206.

A detailed analysis of the processes involved in personality change as facilitated by group counseling is presented. A paradigm of development as seen in groups is shown.

Grambs, Jean D.: *Understanding Intergroup Relations,* What Research Says to the Teacher, no. 21, Washington: National Education Association, 1960.

This booklet discusses the problems of nationality, race, and religion as they affect group solidarity in the classroom. Approaches to the resolution of conflict in the classroom are suggested.

Henry, Nelson B. (ed.): *The Dynamics of Instructional Groups,* Fifty-ninth Yearbook of the National Society for the Study of Education, Chicago: The University of Chicago Press, 1960, part II.

Three chapters are devoted to the meaning and importance of groups, five chapters deal with the unique features of the classroom as a social-psychological group, and five are concerned with the analysis and handling of groups to make them more effective.

Lippitt, Ronald, and Ralph K. White: *Autocracy and Democracy: An Experimental Inquiry,* New York: Harper & Row, Publishers, 1960, pp. 61–88.

The chapter deals with the experimental methods and findings used in assessing the results of consciously planned and executed types (democratic or autocratic) of leadership.

Programmed Learning and Auto-instruction

Programmed learning and auto-instruction are new applications of principles of learning in the sense of the recency of their widespread use and public recognition. Actually, neither principles nor methods are new because they have been used experimentally for a number of years. The cogency and value of the experiments with machine teaching are only now coming to be realized.

Auto-instruction is of interest for several reasons. There is the possibility of making revolutionary strides in the speed and accuracy of common learning tasks. There is the possibility of achieving better pupil motivation, which will contribute to the reduction of dropout figures, increase levels of average educational achievement, and promote the improved development of individual talents. There is the possibility of increasing the scope of pupil skills. Some of these possibilities are in the conjectural stage, some in the experimental stage, and some have been at least partially realized in present practice.

Of particular interest to the student of educational psychology is the fact that programmed learning and auto-instruction afford excellent and clear examples of certain principles of learning. These principles function in other contexts, but they are particularly appropriate here.

Definition of terms

Auto-instruction   As the name implies, some kind of mechanical presentation of learning materials is involved in auto-instruction. Audio-visual aids in the form of sound films and slide projections have long been used, but they were not called "auto-instruction" because the teacher was present to introduce the material, lead discussion, and formulate conclusions and summaries. Moreover, the use of these devices was incidental to the conventional modes of instruction. If the student were to start the machine without the teacher's assistance, review material, and test himself at the end of the instructional unit, one could call the process "auto-instruction" or "machine teaching." Machine teaching includes language laboratories in which the student plays a record or tape recording of a foreign language and attempts to learn the vocabulary, speech structure, pronunciation, and accent of the language concerned.

Another early application of auto-instruction was involved in developmental reading programs. The objective was to improve one's speed of reading with a concurrent improvement in comprehension or, at least, no loss in comprehension. This machine teaching was highly successful when properly used, i.e., with regularity, appropriate and varied material, and continual attention to comprehension. It continues to be a part of the curriculum of some high schools and colleges. Special courses are sometimes given to businessmen, public officials, military leaders, and the like. A doubling of reading rates, with no loss of comprehension per unit of reading, in a period of eight to ten weeks is typical. The machines are simple. A book is placed in a frame in such a position that a curtain, like a miniature old-fashioned window blind, descends down the page, progressively covering more lines of print. The speed of the curtain's descent can be electrically controlled or regulated by graduated spring tension. The speed is scaled on a words-per-minute basis. The reader is being gently and constantly urged to improve his speed. Each pupil sets the machine at a few words beyond his present rate. On the completion of the reading selection, he counts the words, divides by the number of minutes the selection took, and records his rate. Next he takes a test on the reading selection to determine his comprehension. Keeping a record of rate and comprehension provides an incentive to increase the rate and improve or maintain comprehension. This is done by maintaining focus on comprehension (clear-cut goal) and by providing reinforcement in the form of immediate knowledge of results.

The more recently developed auto-instructional plans are somewhat more elaborate. One machine, the Auto Tutor Mark II, resembles a television set on which frames of an instructional program are presented. The frame may contain 200 or 300 words; they are followed by multiple-choice questions. Correct answers are obtained by pressing a button. If the student's answer is correct, a frame of new material appears, and the process is repeated. If the answer is incorrect, the next frame suggests the possible error and tells the student to press a button for another try. This machine was designed by Norman A. Crowder, who believes in feeding information in relatively large blocks (Deterline, 1962, p. 40).

The machine devised by B. F. Skinner feeds information in smaller units. The psychological justification for the smaller unit is that the human organism is rewarded (reinforced) by small, simple, and regular gains in performance (Holland and Skinner, 1961, p. vi). Moreover, Skinner contends that errors should be corrected immediately; otherwise, the wrong response has a greater chance to be retained. Ideally, the program should be so constructed that errors occur rarely, if at all. Another justification for small units employing fill-in questions is that responsibility is placed on the learner for supplying the answer; in contrast, the student merely has to choose (at the recognition level) from among the alternatives presented by the machine in the multiple-choice items.

Programmed Learning The term refers to the arrangement of instructional material in progressive sequences. In one kind of program, each sentence builds on the previous one. This may be clarified by reproducing a portion of *The Analysis of Behavior,* an introductory psychology text. The first sequence appears originally on page 1; the next following sequence shown here appears on page 2, etc.

		page 1
Stimulus (*tap on the knee*) 1-7	Technically speaking, reflex involves an eliciting stimulus in a process called elicitation. A stimulus _____ a response.	1-8
elicits 1-8	To avoid unwanted nuances of meaning in popular words, we do not say that a stimulus "triggers," "stimulates," or "causes" a response, but that it _____ a response. page 2	1-9
elicits 1-9	In a reflex, the stimulus and the elicited response occur in a given temporal order; first the (1) _____, then the (2) _____. page 3	1-10
(1) *stimulus* (2) *response* 1-10	A kick of the leg is _____ by a tap on the patellar tendon. page 4	1-11
elicited 1-11	The time which elapses between the onset of the stimulus and the onset of the response is called the *latency.* Thus the time between tap and kick is the _____ of the knee-jerk reflex. page 5	1-12
latency 1-12	The weakest stimulus sufficient to elicit a response marks the *threshold* of the reflex. A tap on the knee will not elicit a kick if it is below the _____. page 6	1-13

		page 7
threshold	If you blink when something brushes your eye,	
1-13	the _____ is a response.	1-14
		page 8
blink	A puff of air striking the eye will elicit a blink only if the force exerted by the air exceeds the	
1-14	_____ value.	To p. 1 1-15
		page 1
threshold	The fraction of a second which elapses between "brushing the eye" and "blink" is the _____	
1-15	of the reflex.	1-16
		page 2
latency	In the patellar-tendon reflex, a forceful tap elicits a strong kick; a tap barely above the threshold elicits a weak kick. Magnitude of responses thus depends on the intensity of the	
1-16	_____.	1-17
		page 3
stimulus (tap)	The magnitude of a response corresponds to (is a function of) the _____ of the stimu-	
1-17	lus which elicits it.[1]	1-18

Note that the answer to an item appears on the next page This occurs for this program for seven panels of items and responses, when the full set is completed on page 8. After reading page 8, one returns to page 1. The entire set was designed for use in a teaching machine, but it can be used as a programmed textbook, as here. Holland and Skinner point out that it is essential to write the answers before turning the page to check for the correct response. In short, one must commit himself, or he tends to be satisfied with vague and poorly formulated guesses.

The word "program" refers to the instructional material devised for the machine or contained within the programmed textbook. It consists of carefully selected subject matter (stimuli) to which the learner makes frequent responses. Typically, the program begins with something familiar to the student and leads him by small steps to increasingly difficult and less well-known material (Henry, 1961). The steps are small because it is essential that successful performance, as a factor in motivation, be

[1] James G. Holland and B. F. Skinner, *The Analysis of Behavior*, New York: McGraw-Hill Book Company, 1961, pp. 1ff.

virtually ensured. The learning sequences or programs may be contained in memory drums, disks, slides, tape recordings, or programmed books.

Linear programs The example provided is a linear program. The student is presented with small steps, and he must respond to each consecutive step. Moreover, the steps that must be taken are the same for all students. This is considered to be an advantage by some because the small sequential steps reduce the probability of making errors, and people learn best when mistakes are held to a minimum (Klaw, 1962).

Branching programs The contrast to a linear program is a branching program. Multiple-choice questions and larger units of instruction are involved in branching programs. If the student makes a correct choice, he proceeds normally. If he makes an error, he is shifted from the main line of progress onto a branch where he gets additional instruction, and the specific error is clarified. Still another wrong response directs him to further supplementary material in which that specific error is clarified. If the student gives a series of correct responses, he may be directed to skip a number of frames so that the material to be studied will be somewhat more difficult and challenging.

The following examples illustrate a branching program as devised by Norman A. Crowder:

Lesson 1   The Power of Numbers

A modern electronic computer performs complicated mathematical calculations in a matter of seconds. Inside the computer, electrical impulses are translated into a number system which differs considerably from the one commonly used in pencil-and-paper mathematics.

To understand how a computer uses its unique system of numbers to perform such amazing feats, we will have to spend some time dissecting and examining more closely the number system we already know.

Our familiar number system uses ten different numbers: 0, 1, 2, 3, 4, 5, 6, 7, 8, and 9. Each single numeral is called a digit. Because the system uses ten different numerals or digits it is called the *decimal* system (Latin *decem* = ten). The arithmetic we learned in school is decimal arithmetic.

We are so familiar with the decimal system and decimal arithmetic that the decimal system may seem to us the "natural" system. Actually it is only one of many systems of writing numbers.

Now here is a question on the material you have just read. Select what you believe to be the correct answer and turn to the page number indicated to the right of the answer you choose.

Would you say that the two numbers 492 and .29 are both written in the decimal system?

Answer

Both 492 and .29 are written in the decimal system. page 4

Only .29 is written in the decimal system. page 8 [2]

If the student says 492 and .29 are written in the decimal system, he turns to page 4, which tells him:

Your Answer: Both 492 and .29 are written in the decimal system.

You are correct. The word "decimal" refers simply to the fact that our common number system uses only ten different numerals, or digits. With these ten single digits (0, 1, 2 . . . 9), we can count up to 9. Beyond 9 we must use combinations of these numerals, such as 1 and 0 for ten (10), and 1 and 1 for eleven (11), etc.

Do you know, or have you ever heard of, a number system for representing quantities other than our familiar 10-digit decimal system?

Answer

Yes. page 14.

No. page XIV.

I'm not sure. page 1111 [3]

If the student's answer is "Only .29 is written in the decimal system," he then goes to page 8, where he gets some "remedial" information:

Your Answer: Only .29 is written in the decimal system.

Well, let's see.

You once learned that

$$.29 \ = \ ^{29}\!/_{100}$$

and

$$.4 \ = \ ^{4}\!/_{10}$$

and

$$.333 = \ ^{333}\!/_{1000}$$

Fractional quantities such as .29, .4, and .333, written with the aid of the "decimal" point, are called "decimal" fractions. You probably were thinking about this use of the word "decimal" when you decided that the decimal fraction .29 is written in the decimal system and the whole number 492 is not.

The fact that no decimal point is shown does not exclude the number 492 from the decimal system. The word "decimal" means "ten." The decimal system is a number system which uses ten different digits. Both whole and fractional numbers may be written with decimal system digits.

The number 492 and the number .29 are both written in the deci-

---

[2] From *The Arithmetic of Computers* by Norman A. Crowder and Grace C. Martin. Copyright © 1960 by U.S. Industries, Inc. (Tutor text). Reprinted by permission of Doubleday & Company, Inc. P. 1.

[3] *Ibid.*, p. 4.

mal system because they both use the decimal system digits—which are 0, 1, 2, 3, 4, 5, 6, 7, 8 and 9.

Please return to Page 1 and choose another answer.[4]

Branching appears to have the advantage of making the instruction somewhat more individualized than is the case in linear programs. The better student is rewarded (reinforced) by being directed to skip a number of panels, and the one who has made errors is provided with material that will supplement and improve his next choices. The linear program is also called a "single-track program," while the branching program is called "multiple track" (Cook, 1961).

Scrambled text A scrambled text is one in which a branching program is carried. The material is presented in a sequential, but flexible form. The student, instead of studying pages in consecutive order, is directed to additional review or explanatory material, depending upon the nature of the answers he has chosen at given points in the program (Crowder, 1963).

Hawthorne Effect One concern of those attempting to evaluate the merits of auto-instruction is whether the effectiveness of learning programs is due to the programs or the fact that they are experimental. The Hawthorne Works of the Western Electric Company demonstrated that workers' feeling that management was taking a personal interest in them resulted in improved production, apparently regardless of what was done (Drever, 1952, p. 115). Thus increasing lighting would improve production, another increase would have the same result, and another change would still improve output, even though lighting were decreased.

Educators are concerned about the Hawthorne effect because, in the past, educational innovations have typically resulted in improved learning. This may have been due not so much to the new method or material but to its newness and possibly to the teacher's and pupils' enthusiasm for the variation. Thus the impact of auto-instruction must be evaluated in terms of continuation of improved results after the novelty has worn off.

Psychological factors in machine teaching

Established principles of learning receive their validation from the results obtained by the learner. The statement of a principle does not justify a teaching method; but if a method shows positive results, we can then say that the validity of the principle has again been supported. Several principles find support in the use of machine teaching (Hilgard, 1961).

Learning Is an Individual Process Exposed to what is ostensibly the same situation, pupils do not learn the same things or at the same rate.

[4] *Ibid.*, p. 8.

Backgrounds for perception differ, interest is focused on various items and concepts, data are grasped with different speeds and in different degrees of comprehensiveness. When a teacher stands before a group of thirty pupils, some pace must be set. Some assumption as to the present state of knowledge and interest must be made, and a guess must be formulated as to whether progress will be slow, average, or rapid. Programmed learning makes it possible for the pupil to begin at an appropriate point and to proceed at his own unique pace. Teachers have sought to avoid the fallacy of teaching thirty pupils the same thing by having them work in small groups or by devising individual projects. Auto-instruction makes furthering this individualized emphasis more feasible. The self-pacing aspect of programmed learning partially resolves the problem of rapid and slow learners, for whom adaptation to the average pace is inappropriate.

Learning Is an Active Process We learn by doing. We learn what we do. These statements have been made so often that it is easy to dismiss their cogency, but they remain as significant aspects of learning. Action need not be overt. It can and does include thinking, feeling, and accepting or rejecting. It is possible for a pupil to be present physically but far removed mentally in an ordinary classroom situation. It is less probable with programmed learning, although the pupil "turned loose" with a programmed text and not required to write his answers may react somewhat passively and superficially. It is still less probable with a machine; the pupil must be active and attentive or he cannot respond

FIGURE 22. *Automated instruction adds variety to learning pursuits and adds to creative possibilities for the teacher.*

correctly and move to the next frame. Linear programs in particular demand constant attention to the task at hand. It is probable that the key to success in much programmed learning resides in the fact that it involves the individual so actively in the learning process.

Knowledge of Results Facilitates Learning   Experiments as well as classroom practice have indicated that *immediate knowledge* of results provides helpful incentives to learning; in fact, this immediate knowledge of results is one of the strongest psychological principles favoring programmed learning. In general, teachers have sought to capitalize on this principle by making comments on a pupil's work in progress and on work that has been completed. Graphic representations of daily or weekly scores on various tests keep the student cognizant of progress. Diaries have been helpful when they emphasize "what I have learned today." Gold stars, grades, and honor rolls are thought to represent a form of knowledge of results that is an incentive to some pupils. When comparative grades are used, some pupils get low grades and earn no stars; despite the fact that this constitutes knowledge of results (or status), results are not uniformly gratifying. In programmed learning, on the other hand, knowledge of results—specific knowledge of correct response and of errors within the program—is particularly effective because it is immediate and because it is personal. The negative interpersonal comparison factor is not prominent; individual progress is tangible.

The Understanding of Relationships Aids in the Acquisition of Knowledge   Ideas and facts are best understood and remembered if they are related to the immediate and familiar—the new is better understood when it is related to that which is already known. Gestalt psychology stresses this unity and relatedness in many of its formulations of principles (Wheeler, 1940, pp. 270–274). Programmed learning is characterized by continuity between ideas; each sentence logically leads to the next fact, which in turn prepares for the following one. "The program builder cannot be as arbitrary about content as the ordinary laboratory student of learning; the programer has to make one step fit the next and provide the hint or cue for the next." [5]

Learning Is Facilitated When Study Occurs at Spaced Intervals   Again, the plan of the programmer is to keep presenting new, related, and progressive material. A new concept may be given, mentioned again in the next frame, then three or four frames later, and then with diminishing frequency as the idea is incorporated into the total body of knowledge. This orderly, spaced use of new knowledge (vocabulary, for example) is used in writing beginning-reading textbooks and in algebra and geometry textbooks, but the idea tends to be ignored in most other subject-matter

[5] Ernest R. Hilgard, "What Support from the Psychology of Learning?" *NEA Journal*, 50 (8): 20, November, 1961.

contexts. The programmer, however, keeps this in mind because he must provide clues and indicate relationships so that learning may take place the first time through.

Anxiety Detracts from Optimum Learning   It has long been accepted that fear of the birch rod, the anxiety produced by low grades, and the threat of failing to pass to the next grade do not produce good learning situations. Pupils tend to avoid the tension-producing situations by truancy and dropping out of school, and they have frequently done so. There is yet no proof that programmed learning will prevent this avoidance behavior, but it should be reduced. In programmed learning, one knows he can learn, and that knowledge is immediately confirmed. Again, we are reminded of the importance of Skinner's observation that the human is reinforced by any simple gain in competence (Klaw, 1962, p. 20).

Reinforcement Increases the Probability of the Repetition of a Response   This idea is implicit in the principles that have been mentioned. The precursor to the principle of reinforcement is Thorndike's law of effect: "When a modifiable connection between a situation and a response is made and is accompanied or followed by a satisfying state of affairs, that connection's strength is increased. When made and accompanied or followed by an annoying state of affairs, its strength is decreased." [6] Reinforcement is the occurrence of an event that increases the probability that the same response will recur in the presence of the same stimulus (Deterline, 1962, p. 27). In laboratory animals, the reinforcement may be food, water, release from confinement or absence of mild electric shock. In human subjects and in programmed learning, the reinforcement is achieving the goal of a correct response, the reward of a new frame, and the challenge of a new problem. One must pay attention to what he is reading or his very next response may go awry. Thus attention and careful work are frequently and periodically rewarded.

Lack of reinforcement leads to extinction of a response. If a response is not in some way rewarded, there is a tendency to try other kinds of responses that will be reinforced. This explains, in part, why learnings are not more consistently consolidated in the classroom. The teacher's commendation, the earning of a grade, and the immediate presentation of new material after a correct response are not so frequently and not so immediately given as in the case of programmed instruction.

Generalization Consolidates Learning   This is one theoretical explanation for the phenomenon of transfer of learning (Scholckow and Judd, 1908). Generalization is one of the steps involved in problem solving. It has repeatedly been emphasized that when a pupil studies for and

[6] E. L. Thorndike, *The Psychology of Learning*, New York: Teachers College, Columbia University, 1913, p. 4.

formulates a generalization, he retains the material better than if he were to aim at mere reproduction (rote memory) or the discovery of isolated facts. Thus we rely heavily on generalization to aid in the eventual application of school learnings to out-of-school life situations.

Generalization occurs to some extent with every reinforcement; i.e., a response tends to recur not only on the presentation of the same stimulus but on the presentation of similar stimuli (Deterline, 1962, p. 31). Moreover, in much programmed material, the design points toward the forming of generalized concepts or principles.

Unanswered Questions   There are still several questions related to the effectiveness of machine teaching and its implications.

Will teachers, gaining time by freedom from drill and from rewording and repeating the textbook, meet the challenge to study and promote better social processes? When freed from correcting compositions and scoring tests, will they be sufficiently challenged to extend their own knowledge so that they can lead different pupils through the first few steps of pursuing creative insights?

Will pupils become better readers as the result of working with programmed materials? Or will the saccadic nature of reading panels interfere with the rhythm that is characteristic of rapid and efficient reading? Will pupils tend to "program" the ordinary book, i.e., proceed by small steps, ask and answer questions on the material, pay close attention, and review what they have read? Will they come to feel that finishing the program is the end of their educational journey rather than the beginning of the foundation for developing individual distinctiveness?

Are there printed instructional materials that should not be programmed? Plays, novels, and poetry should probably not be included, but how is balance to be achieved? Physics and mathematics have, for example, proved to be highly appropriate for programmed learning, while certain other subjects have not (Deterline, 1962, p. 73). Besides determining which subjects can most feasibly be programmed, it seems probable that research will provide new insights into how to deal most effectively with nonprogrammed instructional materials.

How do students react to programmed learning, and how important is their reaction? This double question has been investigated many times, and the answers are not yet clear-cut. Much depends on specific factors, such as preparatory set, method of presentation, type of program, and usefulness (or meaning) to the student. The linear program appears to appeal to some pupils, and the scrambled-text format evokes favorable response from others. The amount learned does not have a consistent effect on pupils' attitudes (Eigen, 1963). Novelty, the teacher's own attitude toward programming, and the accuracy, thoroughness, and appeal of the program are factors that must be critically evaluated during the time of first implementation and trial.

Unanswered questions should not prevent the use of programmed instruction. Even if the ultimate destiny of programming is similar to that of extreme progressive education, it can at least be said that the teacher's study and experimentation will involve him more actively in the teaching process. Involvement is what we desire in the student's learning.

The role of the teacher

The term "machine" appears to be somewhat unfortunate. A frequent criticism of mass instruction has been that it is rote or mechanical. There is apprehension that the machine will produce "robot" humans, who have been conditioned to make uniform responses. A number of proponents of teaching machines suggest that some are apprehensive lest the machine stultify the emergence of creativity. Further, these proponents suggest that some fear that the live teacher will be displaced by an impersonal machine—technological unemployment will spread to the teaching profession. These apprehensions could simply be dismissed by asserting that while there is some slight justification for them, fears probably should be allayed.

Auto-instruction and Creativity It is true that the response to a panel of programmed material has been predetermined. So have responses to teacher-presented material been predetermined. There is no acceptable alternative to the response of 9 for the stimulus 3×3. Regardless of logic or system, there is a difference in the pronunciation of words that are much alike in spelling—"slough," "tough," "bough," "though," etc. One must respond to these stimuli in an automatic manner, but having learned the responses, he can go on to be creative.

Take My Word for It

I must confess it puzzles me
A little word like rough
Must always be pronounced by rhyme
With cuff and muff and fluff.

And yet there is another sound;
When one speaks of a cough,
Why must forsooth, it ever rhyme
With off and doff and toff?

Another funny thing to me,
If I bog in a slough,
I tell the tale to listening ears,
And rhyme the word with goo.

James Stevens

It may be that machine teaching is more creative than much human teaching that occurs in the classroom, especially the lecture type. In teaching mathematics, for instance, the teacher writes an example on the chalkboard, explains the steps, executes the process, and points to the answer. In order to capitalize on pupil participation, he may select a student to do these things. If the student can already do the example, one may question whether he is either learning or being creative. The other students are reacting in various ways. Some have completed the problem. Some have recognized that they can do the problem and have "left the field." Others are copying and hoping to achieve the solution at a later time. Still others have mentally deserted because they understand none of it. The teacher or the teaching student is doing most of the work (Gorow, 1961). With the machine, each student is progressing at his own rate, and each is active. Learning, says Kilpatrick, involves two aspects, "one creative, in which a new response is contrived; the other conserving, in which this newly contrived response is added to the very structure of the organism." [7] Because the pupil does his own work (rather than watching the teacher) and progresses at his own rate (rather than being paced by others), he more closely fits the creative concept defined by Kilpatrick. This emphasis on activity is stressed by Lumsdaine (1964), who asserts that the major psychological focuses in programmed learning are active participation, immediate confirmation, and progression adapted to individual learners.

Robert E. Forshaw, a junior high school teacher in Connecticut, says that the machine gobbles material and saves time. The facts in physiology are learned thoroughly and much more quickly than they are in conventional instruction periods. With time on his hands, Forshaw has an "imagination period" in which students are encouraged to think adventurously (*Professional Growth for Teachers*, 1961). Drill sessions, manipulation of flash cards, grading papers, and quiz periods are replaced by a machine, and the pupil comes to the classroom with basic knowledge that can be discussed and amplified. The bright child who rushes through a program forces recognition of his ability, and his success makes him eager for new tasks (Galanter, 1961). Thus the creative role of the teacher is clarified; with the extra time and the background brought by the student, he can devote attention to divergent thinking.[8] This has always been a role assigned to teachers, but the machine, by

[7] William H. Kilpatrick, *A Reconstructed Theory of the Educative Process*, New York: Teachers College, Columbia University, 1935, p. 4.
[8] When one starts with familiar ideas and lets them branch out in various directions, he is involved in divergent thinking. When one starts with some precise data and seeks to focus them on a specific solution (as in solving a puzzle), he is engaged in convergent thinking.

reducing the routine and drudgery of teaching, now makes it increasingly possible for this role to become functional.

There is no guarantee that teaching machines will lead to creative thinking. Ultimately, creativity largely depends on teachers for the climate in which it may develop. Science has added a revolutionary dimension to teaching. It still remains the teacher's task to encourage imaginative faculties, love for excellence, and wisdom based on the proliferation of interrelationships (Riley, 1961). The truth appears to be that creativity may be enhanced when there is better balance between learning fundamental facts by programmed material and the proliferation and expansion of that material. The Carnegie Corporation is supporting experiments on the use of programs to foster creativity. There are programs that emphasize *how* to read poetry, but the programmers involved suggest that the analysis of a poem must be less confining than the limits imposed by the program (Klaw, 1961).

Machines versus Teachers   Unskilled laborers have been displaced by machines. But after temporary displacement, new jobs have appeared in larger numbers. As one looks at jobs entailing skills, the displacement is not even temporary. For example, machines have taken over many routine office functions in the U.S. National Bank in Portland, Oregon. But the experience there is that no workers have been displaced. Workers were simply reassigned to useful jobs elsewhere in the organization (Campbell, 1961). There is a strong belief on the part of some that machine teaching will not or, at least, need not reduce the total number of teachers. They will simply be freed to do more thoroughly the things that cannot be done by machines, which are sometimes neglected today (Flanagan, 1964). It is well to remember that the so-called "thinking machines" can produce no answers that were not originally put there by their human constructers.

> There is no reason why education should not be both as effective and as human as possible, and far from dehumanizing or mechanizing education, auto-instruction should provide much greater opportunity for the student to come under the influence of the skilled human teacher than is currently possible.[9]

Where programmed learning is taking place, the teacher's presence in the classroom is needed to reduce distractions, to provide occasional help, and to guide the selection of next steps upon the completion of a program. His help is needed when questions that are not included in the program arise. Dealing with these questions and being reinforced for asking the questions add to the possibility that the pupil will seek elaboration of what he is studying.

[9] William A. Deterline, *Programmed Instruction*, Englewood Cliffs, N.J.: Prentice-Hall, Inc., 1962, p. 78.

Group Processes and Programmed Learning   Among the stated objectives of education there is typically some reference to the need to learn how to function in groups. This objective implies that it is essential for individuals to deal effectively with interpersonal relations. Beyond educational objectives and into life philosophies, the need for effective action in groups is also emphasized: No matter what line of activity one pursues, his success is dependent, in large part, on his ability to get along with others; most failures are not due to lack of technique knowledge, but to lack of skill in interpersonal functioning.

> There is no way to learn this but to participate responsibly in group processes. Here is clearly an area where the teacher cannot be replaced. Any group activity—especially one that involves planning, division of labor, moderating conflicting value systems, taking of responsibility, cooperating and competing—is significant for the teaching of social process.[10]

Programmed instruction makes such group activity more probable than it is under ordinary teaching conditions. Attempting to teach thirty pupils in one class divides the group. Minds wander because of either boredom or lack of comprehension. With programs, some pursue their individually selected programs at their own speeds, while others who have completed certain programs can engage in discussion and exploration, but all will have some common background.

The more appropriate pacing that has just been indicated suggests another important use of programmed learning: individual enrichment. With programs available in science, mathematics, language, and literature, pupils can readily follow their own interests and develop their abilities. Teacher guidance and encouragement is necessary to prevent too much cursory sampling and insufficient follow-up on one program. But it is difficult to believe that enrichment will not remain one of the major advantages of programmed learning.

The Selection of Programs   One of the current problems in programmed learning is the hasty production of programs that do not make major use of the potential psychological advantages (step-by-step progress, reinforcement, individual suitability, exercise) that might be involved. This "beating the market" will teach some lessons, but some prospective users may become alienated in the meantime.

The typical teacher cannot be expected to be a judge of standardized tests, but he can review the evaluations of others on tests he is considering. Such review is also helpful to teachers in judging publishers of programs. A source of information is the Center for Programmed Instruction, Inc., in New York City, a nonprofit organization that publishes programs and should be able to give background information on many publications.

[10] Hilgard, *op. cit.*, p. 21.

Education periodicals carry reviews and evaluations of new programs just as they do of new books. Teachers have a responsibility for utilizing these evaluations.

Summary

A novel application, at least in terms of widened use, of certain principles of learning is called "auto-instruction and programmed learning." "Machine teaching" refers to the mechanical presentation of stimulus materials. With or without machines, programmed learning means the arrangement in short sequences of orderly, progressive educational material. The student responds to the material by checking multiple-choice items or selecting words to complete fill-in sentences.

The effectiveness of auto-instruction and programmed learning depends largely on the principle of reinforcement. Other learning principles that are particularly effective in the programmed context include the involvement of individual responsibility, the necessity for close and constant attention, and immediacy of response. Reinforcement occurs in several forms—prompt knowledge of results, the presentation of either corrective or new material, and the challenge of progressively more challenging material. Programs are constructed to capitalize on the principle that understanding of relationships facilitates retention. The sequence of panels calls for study at spaced intervals. The individuality of a program reduces tensions generated by interpersonal comparisons and the inappropriateness of material for certain learners.

Some concern has been expressed lest machine teaching dehumanize teaching. There is considerable opinion and some evidence that the opposite will occur. Auto-instruction will free both pupils and teachers to be more creative, to explore more widely, and to seek wider applications and generalizations. Pupils will continue to need the experience of group processes if their education is to be effective in achieving its final result—living most effectively.

Problems and exercises

1 Get hold of a programmed text (see Suggested Additional Readings) and spend an hour studying and responding to it. Do you find it challenging? Do you remember what the major messages were? What changes in its construction would you suggest?

2 Do you think that the linear or the branching program would be most advantageous for presenting material such as you study in educational psychology?

3 To what extent do you think the Hawthorne effect accounts for presently reported successes of programmed learning?

4 Do you agree or disagree that programmed learning will tend to increase the exercise and development of creativity?

5 What is your reaction to the statement: If a teacher can be replaced by a machine, he should be replaced.

6 How might the extensive use of various programs in a high school contribute to the improvement of group processes?

7 What are some subjects that probably should not be programmed, in addition to those mentioned in the text?

Suggested additional readings

Deterline, William A.: *An Introduction to Programmed Instruction,* Englewood Cliffs, N.J.: Prentice-Hall, Inc., 1962.
This book explains the theories upon which Skinner and Crowder have based their particular forms of programmed instruction. Experimental results are described, and the impact on teacher and pupils is discussed.

Galanter, Eugene: "The Mechanization of Learning," *National Education Association Journal,* 50 (8): 16–19, 1961.

Glaser, Robert, and A. Lumsdaine: *Teaching Machines and Programmed Learning: A Source Book,* Washington: National Education Association, 1960.
A description of various methods of machine teaching is presented. The authors discuss some of the advantages and disadvantages of the new approaches.

Holland, James G., and B. F. Skinner: *The Analysis of Behavior,* New York: McGraw-Hill Book Company, 1961.
The book not only illustrates a programmed text, but provides information regarding the way in which behavior is influenced. This will be helpful in providing background for the student of educational psychology.

Professional Growth for Teachers, "New Dimensions of Instruction," 7 (5): 4, 1961.

"Programmed Instruction," *Phi Delta Kappan,* 44: 241–298, March, 1963. (Special issue.)
The sixteen articles in this special issue deal with the utility, desirability, dangers, limitations, and prospects of programmed instruction.

Skinner, B. F.: "Teaching Machines," *Science,* 128: 969–976, Oct. 24, 1958.
One of the best single articles on the use of teaching machines and programmed learning. Bibliography suggests further readings.

Mental Hygiene as an Aspect
of Educational Psychology

19

Mental health is a growing concern of all persons, not just because of humanitarian orientation or because of increasing incidence of mental illness, but because it is realized that much of the waste caused by mental illness is avoidable. National leaders place it high on the action priority list for national strength (*National Education Improvement Act of 1963*, p. 34). Educators are increasingly recognizing questionable mental health as being involved in such persistent problems as underachievement, school dropouts, and personal and social maladjustment. Psychologists are adding a challenging new dimension by emphasizing the elevation and enhancement aspects of mental health to our previous largely curative and preventative emphases (Maslow, 1962; Combs and Snygg, 1959). The ramifications of the problems of mental health penetrate political action, industrial production, family and community life, and of course, educational problems and planning. Even though their concern is mainly academic learning, teachers must become involved in action for mental health. If their major orientation is pupil self-realization, their involvement in mental health and mental hygiene becomes all the more serious.

The meaning of mental health and mental hygiene

The Concept of Mental Hygiene The mental hygiene movement, which began in 1908, is attributed to the work of Clifford Beers, who was at one time committed to a mental institution. He was so disturbed by the inhuman treatment he received and by the misdirected efforts in such institutions in general that he determined to get better treatment for the mentally ill (Beers, 1917). Today mental hygiene is viewed in much the same light as physical hygiene; that is, the emphasis is on *health* rather than the prevention or cure of illness alone. Like physical hygiene, mental hygiene emphasizes better living conditions and regimes that will cure the afflicted, prevent illness, and bring the healthy to still higher levels of functioning. Thus we may say that mental hygiene is the program adopted to achieve adjustment to the

416

unavoidable and to improve conditions that are amenable to change. Mental hygiene involves the prevention of maladjustment in normal people as well as the curing of persons who already have become psychologically disorganized. It is the practical art of assisting oneself and others to the realization of a fuller, happier, more harmonious, and more effective life.[1]

For the classroom teacher, mental hygiene is being the kind of person and using the kinds of approaches that will help pupils realize a greater amount of their potential for well-rounded and constant growth and efficient living. It thus becomes increasingly clear that mental hygiene is a particular way of looking at educational problems. It involves the teacher's attitude toward his task and his pupils, his use of methods, his choice of objectives, his use of materials, and his individual influence on the personality development of pupils.

The Concept of Mental Health Mental health is not a passive acceptance of life and its conditions. It is a process of living that points to still better living. It is a life in which one's potentialities are coming to full development, in which one's inner nature expresses itself freely and is not warped, suppressed, or denied (Maslow, 1962, pp. 3–5). Herzberg and Hamlin (1961) distinguished between positive mental health and mental illness on the basis of job efficiency and satisfaction. In illness, the emphasis is on avoiding distressing conditions and searching for comfort; in positive mental health, the concern is with achievement, task responsibility, professional advancement, interest in work, and recognition for accomplishment. Karl Menninger (1953) states that mental health is not *just* efficiency or contentment or complacent abiding by the rules. It is an adjusting process that involves a maximum of effectiveness and happiness. It means an even temper, functional intelligence, and consideration of the social order. Reality is perceived and accepted. Problems are solved when possible and lived with when unsolved or unsolvable.

Mental health, like physical health, is a matter of degree. The dividing line between good and poor mental health is not clearly defined. On each side of the line are continuous gradations. The aim of mental hygiene is to strive toward better mental health, regardless of the position on the scale currently occupied. Hence we can say that mental health is a goal toward which to strive rather than a static condition that can be achieved. Thus mental health should be defined as a process of continuous adjustment on the part of the individual.

The Aims of Mental Hygiene As indicated above, mental hygiene has as its purpose helping individuals live a full, happy, harmonious, and effective life. It has also been indicated that the aims of mental hygiene are closely parallel to those of education; for example, the aims of educa-

[1] These points are expanded in Harold W. Bernard, *Toward Better Personal Adjustment,* 2d ed., New York: McGraw-Hill Book Company, 1957, pp. 20–21.

tion as formulated by the Educational Policies Commission (see Chapter 20, section on Behavioral Goals) lean heavily toward a mental health orientation.

1. *The objectives of self-realization* These objectives include speaking, reading, and writing effectively; listening and observing perceptively; understanding and protecting physical and mental health; engaging in wholesome leisure-time activities both as participant and as spectator; and giving responsible direction to one's life. Such objectives give explicit meaning to the phrase "fuller life"—a life in which many facets of the individual's personality are given expression.

2. *The objectives of human relationship* The Educational Policies Commission asserts that the educated person puts human relations first. He enjoys a varied social life; he works cooperatively with others, including his family; and he strives to maintain democratic group relationships. In brief, he strives for more harmonious living not only with others but also with himself—scaling his ambitions to his abilities, making decisions and sticking to them, and developing a degree of tension tolerance that will allow him to put up with inevitable frustrations.

3. *The objectives of economic efficiency* These objectives include two major goals: being an educated producer and being an educated consumer. Effective producers appreciate the value of quality workmanship. They appreciate the social value of work. They make wise selections of occupations, in which they will strive for constantly improving efficiency. Effective producers plan their economic life, scale expenditures to their resources, and are skilled and informed buyers. Secondary teachers have a specific responsibility in the area of educating consumers, but all teachers can play a part in educating pupils to take a pride in workmanship.

4. *The objectives of civic responsibility* Civic responsibility involves an interest in the welfare of all people and a sensitiveness to the disparities of human circumstances. It involves knowledge of propaganda, respect for the law, understanding and acceptance of civic duties, and unswerving loyalty to democratic ideals. Philosophers and mental hygienists have for a long time stressed the point that happiness cannot be obtained by direct pursuit. Happiness is most likely to ensue when the individual outgrows restrictive egocentricity. Teachers who stress the moral and democratic ideal of "What can I give?" rather than "What can I get?" are giving force to the aims of both mental hygiene and education.

These overlapping aims may be related to the field of educational psychology. Again, we learn what we do. These aims must be sought in school if they are to function in afterschool living. Teachers must seek to encourage self-realization in their pupils by providing many avenues of development to meet individual needs. They must seek to improve human relationships by providing opportunties for democratic procedures in academic work and student activities. They must seek to develop economic efficiency by stimulating habits of workmanship and economy in the use of school buildings and materials. They must encourage civic responsibility by stressing good citizenship in the school.

The Need for Mental Hygiene Emphasis　Mental illness has justifiably been called the nation's number one health problem. It is estimated that one out of sixteen persons is suffering currently from mental illness and that one out of ten children will at some time be hospitalized for mental illness (*Facts on Mental Health and Mental Illness*, 1957, p. 5). About half of the patients in all hospitals are there because of mental illness (*Action for Mental Health*, 1961, p. 4). The need for mental hygiene work is further emphasized by widespread social problems—delinquency, crime, suicide, alcoholism, drug addiction, prejudice, underachievement, and dropping out of school. The problem was recognized at the national level by the Mental Health Act of 1946, which provides:

> Federal support for the development of preventive mental health services in the States and communities, for research and for training of professional personnel. The goal of this program is to give every American the opportunity to achieve good mental health—to help him to live in peace with himself, his neighbors and the world.[2]

In view of the enormity of the problem, it is not possible for the schools to wait for an ideal time to work on it. We must realize that mental health springs from a social context—it is a *transaction* between the individual and his environment (Wedge, 1964)—and that the time to consider it is now.

The major concern of the teacher is not the person who may someday be hospitalized, but the maximum welfare of all children. The minor manifestations of poor mental health are prime considerations in educational psychology. These symptoms include shyness, laziness, frequent absences, lack of application, inability to get along with peers and teachers, withdrawal tendencies, transitory interests not appropriate to age, and failure to work at or near capacity. Mental hygiene in the school is concerned with the problem of more effective daily living—interest, cooperativeness, vitality, adaptability, friendliness, and the ability to bounce back after disappointment. This involves an emphasis on achieving greater humanness and more complete self-realization (Maslow, 1961).

The teacher's role in mental hygiene　Unfortunately, there is a dreadful lack of trained personnel (psychiatrists and psychologists) for the enormous task. Although teachers are not so highly trained, the incontrovertible fact remains that if school personnel do not provide help, some individuals will never get it (Arbuckle, 1962). Teachers must seriously study the meaning and principles of mental hygiene in order to

---

[2] Federal Security Agency, Public Health Service, *The National Mental Health Program*, Mental Health Series, no. 4, June, 1948, foreword.

function as adequately as possible in the job that is inevitably thrust upon them.

Teachers who have studied adjustment problems can help prevent mental ill health by working with individuals. They can try to supply the child's fundamental needs. They can work in accord with basic principles of growth instead of fighting against them. It should further be emphasized that the typical child has little need for specialized services. It will be to his advantage to have help in solving problems in normal, everyday situations. Teachers should, of course, recognize their limitations, and when they have any doubt that they are helping the child, they should seek the advice of experts.

> There are some who scoff at education for positive mental health, calling it religion, and asserting that it is not the function of a mental health association to help people achieve "the better life." Perhaps a closer examination would disclose that this is not at all related to religion, that this kind of education has as its goal the very same goal which psychotherapy has, and that is not only to free the patient of his immediate and disabling symptoms, but also to free him of residual infantile patterns of behavior which cripple his adequate functioning and which impede the development of his full capacity to lead a productive, contented, and even happy life.[3]

In recent years, there have been tremendous gains in physical health, because teachers have become aware of the symptoms of illness and have provided a first line of defense. Moreover, they have effectively taught the fundamental principles of health. Similar gains can be made in the area of mental health when teachers learn to work in accord with sound principles of psychology.

Some fundamentals of mental health

Among the many factors related to mental health is the degree to which one's basic needs are satisfied, approach satisfaction, or are denied. There are many lists of such needs, and they are often quite similar (Bernard, 1961, pp. 25–65). The following needs are selected for illustrative purposes because they suggest some practical steps that can be taken by teachers.

The Need for Acceptance   Some psychologists trace the need for acceptance back to the womb. They feel that the mother's acceptance or rejection of the unborn child affects his bodily chemistry and thereby establishes the basis for mental health or illness. Whether or not we wish to trace personality trends so far, the fact remains that wholesome accept-

[3] Harry Milt, "The Outlook for Mental Health Education," *Mental Hygiene*, 46: 31–40, 1962.

ance of the child is heavily emphasized by psychiatrists as a fundamental of mental health (Brammer and Shostrom, 1960, p. 158).

The ability of the teacher (or parent) to accept the child is an indication of the adult's maturity of personality. The study of psychology and mental hygiene can help one discern normal behavior. He will not then expect adult behavior and perspective from a child. He will know that the child's actions are not always synonymous with his intentions. He will regard deviations from desired behavior as indications of the fact that children are encountering difficulties in their growth. Acceptance means that a person's unique personality, interests, strong points, frailties, disposition, and temperament are recognized and respectfully evaluated. Accepting a pupil is a difficult task for the immature person or the teacher who wants pupils to be like him. Acceptance is illustrated by the teacher of the slum child who understands the child's attacks on other pupils and sometimes on the teacher himself. It is illustrated by the cheerful encouragement of the pupil who suddenly said, "Dem goddam peaches is burnin'" (Blake, 1964), although previously he had not said anything—certainly not a whole sentence. Genuine acceptance is truly the core of giving functional recognition to pupil differences. Acceptance means seeing through the behavior to the living individual. The idea of "I like you, Johnny, but I do not like what you do" must be conveyed to the child. A high school teacher looked at some discourteous boys and said, "You are too gentlemanly to act like that." The boys knew the teacher liked them and cared about what they did. They knew they were accepted despite their actions, and improvement was soon noted in their behavior.

There is need for acceptance in pupil-pupil relationships also. A particular child needs to be not only with the group but *of* the group. The teacher can help by encouraging class members to welcome newcomers. Friendliness can be practiced by asking a particular pupil to serve as a host or as a big brother during introductions. This responsibility also extends to members of minority groups. The teacher can do much by pointing out the contribution each pupil can make to the smooth-running behavior of the group.

The Need for Companionship This need, which is intimately related to the need for acceptance, is given particular emphasis by psychiatrists as they stress the seriousness of the symptoms of shyness or withdrawal (Hunter, 1957). It is of little value to say to the shy pupil, "You should be more friendly." He would be if he knew how. It is necessary to find the causes of the lack of companionship and take steps to correct them. Among the more important steps is encouragement in the development of skills. Almost any skill will help the pupil build the confidence that will allow him to participate more vigorously in personal contacts.

It is well to observe that not all pupils can be alike in social competence. If a pupil who has few intimate friends seems to be well adjusted, the teacher should not be too concerned. In short, the symptom of shyness takes on significance when it is accompanied by other symptoms of inadequate adjustment; it does not always indicate maladjustment. This would mean, for example, that the teacher should not insist that a high school boy get out on the dance floor with some attractive girl—this might add unnecessary burdens of adjustment, and it could be that he enjoys watching more than participation. However, the "loner" should be noticed. If his solitary nature is accompanied by other evidences of insecurity and maladjustment, the need for further investigation is indicated. The possible seriousness of lack of companionship is suggested by the remark of a superintendent of a school for delinquent girls, "These girls are just not joiners—they do not belong to choruses, pep squads, dance teams, or clubs." [4]

The Need for New Experiences It is a common experience of all people to be bored with routine and monotony. Satisfaction of the need for a variety of experiences can be met relatively easily in the school. New subject matter, new activities, new approaches, field trips, the use of teaching aids, and new responsibilities can help to satisfy this need. But the need for new experiences should not dim our view of the comfort of the routine and ordinary. We all like to have conditions upon which we can depend. It is therefore necessary that some of the details of schoolwork be kept much the same from day to day.

The need for new experiences is particularly important because other needs depend upon it for their satisfaction. For example, the need to develop feelings of security is dependent upon the pupil's ability to adjust to new situations; hence he needs the opportunity for experience in new areas if he is to develop a versatile competence. Everyone needs to be considered a growing personality and to satisfy curiosity; here again, the need for encountering unique circumstances is apparent. There is also the need for mastery; one needs to have new experiences in order to explore various avenues that may lead to mastery of his particular potentialities.

If the need for new experiences is not satisfied in the school, there is the distinct possibility that satisfaction will be sought by aberrant behavior, including delinquency. This, of course, does not occur only when new adventures are denied—lack of satisfaction or partial satisfaction of any of the fundamental needs creates tensions.

The Need for Success Success provides affirmation to the individual that he is a worthy, recognized, competent, autonomous individual. This

[4] Marjorie McBride, Superintendent of Hillcrest, Ore., School for Girls, "The School in the Life of Delinquent Girls," an address at the Portland Continuation Center, Oregon State System of Higher Education, Mar. 6, 1963.

need has been identified by various writers by the terms "achievement," "mastery," and "to be a cause" (see Chapter 11, section on Basic Needs of Children). Success is related to the need for recognition because, after babyhood and childhood, recognition is so largely dependent on one's competence. Success is related to one's self-concept because of the reflection of others' opinions and because one's autonomy depends so largely on the ability to perform independently.

School threats to satisfaction of the need for success are numerous. Autocratic regimes do not permit exploration and experimentation. Expectation of grade norms in writing, arithmetic, physics, and history is likely to deny genuine success to many—to the slow learner because the pace is too fast and to the able pupil because he has not been challenged and wins victory with what for him is mediocre performance. Success is denied to some pupils because their unique talents are not exercised in the academic curriculum. There is, for example, little chance for the budding mechanic, the would-be electrician, and the potential dress designer or dressmaker to be recognized as successful. The chances to satisfy the need for success are particularly limited for that one out of ten who is called an "exceptional" child—the retarded, the gifted, the physically handicapped, and the emotionally maladjusted individual (*Action for Mental Health*, 1961, p. 117).

It appears, therefore, that *school programs should be arranged for more equitable distribution of the experience of success so that every child may achieve some degree of it.* This means that teacher expectations will be scaled to indicated ability and the records of past performances, that school activities will be so varied as to call for the more extensive exercise of different capacities, and that pupils will judge their own performance on the basis of gain and growth rather than on interpersonal comparisons. This cannot be done when the academic program receives more than its just share of attention. Numerous and varied opportunities for emotional, physical, aesthetic, *and* intellectual achievements must be provided. Good teaching, which recognizes differences, illustrates acceptance, and challenges potentials, thus providing every pupil a chance to achieve success in effective learning, is a most positive approach to mental health. More teachers should realize that when they are teaching well, they are practicing mental hygiene.

The Need for Independence One sees the need for independence asserted very early in the life of the individual. Even before the baby begins to talk, he wants to feed himself. Later, even before he gains real competence, he wants to dress himself and to tie his own shoes. Goodenough and Tyler (1959, p. 399) state that one of the three most important needs of the child is opportunity for unhampered development and that permissive limits are considerably broader than many nervous people are inclined to think. It might be added that the permissive limits in school are probably much broader than many insecure teachers are able to admit. The teacher's role can best be executed by counseling with leaders, rather than by exercising authoritarian discipline. It may mean temporarily putting up with conditions one might wish to criticize. But it should be remembered, experience is a great teacher—even experience that is a failure.

Children need freedom of opportunity in order to develop. This does not mean a lack of restraint or guidance—as some parents and a few teachers seem to think. It does mean that restrictions should not be arbitrary or imposed for adult convenience. Independence will be developed as the individual is given freedom to cope with his own problems. Moreover, it is through freedom of opportunity to develop that one learns to live with the unavoidable.

A good many of the difficulties of adolescents stem from the desire to be independent—to be able to act without the prescription and direction of parents and teachers. This striving for independence is a main theme of adolescence. It involves not only the exercise of curiosity, but also the desire to test capacities and to make decisions (Stagner, 1961, p. 422). It is a wise parent or a perceptive teacher who recognizes in these strivings for independence the seeds of genuine psychological maturity.

Wise teachers recognize the need for independence in many of their methods of procedure. The following directives summarize much of the literature on independence and serve to review suggestions made elsewhere in this book:

1. Permit children a voice in the selection of activities.
2. Encourage a wide exploration of objects and ideas.
3. Accept children as they are and in spite of their undesirable behavior.
4. Be slow to interfere with the inevitable pupil conflicts.
5. Praise youngsters for acts that show evidence of independence.
6. Encourage performances that reveal creativity rather than demanding adherence to formalized patterns (in painting, drawing, and writing).
7. Challenge some of the statements made in textbooks and thus stimulate pupils to check the printed word against their own experience.
8. Help students to organize their own forms of homeroom and school-wide student government.

The Need to Develop Tension Tolerance   The author has often been asked whether there is not a danger of removing too many obstacles, too many tensions, from the developmental path of children. Theoretically, it is possible to make such an error. Practically, there is little danger that this will happen if the need for growth and independence is recognized. Of course, there are parents who are overprotective in dealing with their children, but it seems impossible to remove all obstacles from school or to make it so pleasant that growth will be prevented. Actually, one achieves the feelings of security that may be called "tension tolerance" by overcoming difficulties and enjoying success in physical and social activities. Disappointment and discouragement need not be thrust on growing children; they will encounter tension as they explore their world aggressively.

A big problem in the development of tension tolerance is motivation. If the individual is oriented toward achievement and growth, as contrasted to motivation toward the avoidance of stress, he can better cope with routine jobs, the routines of life, and other impediments to progress. The growth-oriented pupil focuses on long-term objectives, while the avoidance-oriented one focuses upon transitory comfort (Herzberg and Hamlin, 1961), which suggests that goals in school should alternate between the immediate (especially for younger pupils) and the more remote.

Tension tolerance depends also upon balance. A balanced program that permits alternation between challenge, success, and occasional defeat makes its contribution. An individual who views present circumstances in conjunction with long-term goals manifests a balanced orientation. A teacher who provides balance between direction and guidance and permits pupils to discover for themselves is diminishing the threat of present stress and preparing the pupil for future growth. Some general suggestions for the maintenance of balance can be given:

1. Teachers must avoid giving too much help, which is so easy to do in arithmetic, spelling, and geometry.

2. A task that is difficult but not impossible may warrant some help. When the job has been done, words of praise are not necessary, though they may help.

3. Goals should be attractive, i.e., understandable and important to the child.

4. Tension tolerance requires balance between help and no help, between the specific and the abstract, and between remote and immediate goals.

The development of tension tolerance may be likened to the acquisition of resistance to disease. Some resistance is gained through immunization and inoculation; in the area of mental hygiene and education, this might be exposure to planned experiences that are scaled to developmental levels. Some resistance is gained through the development of good health; the mental health parallel is encouragement of the development of skills and knowledge that will enable the individual to overcome obstacles. The policy of deliberate exposure to disease, which prevailed until recent years, is no longer accepted; similarly, in mental hygiene we seek to avoid unnecessary detrimental conditions (see next section).

Other Basic Needs The foregoing statement of needs should be regarded as tentative and representative. The teacher can easily translate the concept of needs into practical educational procedures that will be conducive to mental health. Thayer, Zachry, and Kotinsky (1939, p. 44) have form-

426

ulated a statement of the needs of adolescents that closely parallels some of the statements of the objectives of education. These needs are found in four areas: primary social relationships (home and school), community and civic relationships, vocational and financial relationships, and personal living (bound up with the others). Another formulation is the list of the imperative needs of youth (see Chapter 15).

Recognizing needs is only the point of beginning. It remains for teachers to devise methods and techniques that will, to the greatest extent possible, provide for their satisfaction.

Mental health hazards in the school

Certain conventional school practices are highly suspect as sources of genuine need satisfaction. In this section, we shall deal with certain of these practices with a view to their correction.

Lack of Friendliness It has been found that teachers use humor more often in a sarcastic than in a friendly manner (Brumbaugh, 1940) and that their own inner hostilities are attributed to others and thus create an unfriendly atmosphere (Symonds, 1954). It would be an exaggeration to say that there is a tradition of unfriendliness in the school. Yet the concept of the teacher as a stern disciplinarian and the attitude that "familiarity breeds contempt" tend to prevent a genuinely friendly atmosphere in the school, where mental health is so important. Ryan (1938, pp. 31ff), after spending a year visiting schools throughout the nation, announced that although simple friendliness was obviously desirable and seemingly easily obtainable, he found it in "shockingly" few places. Yet recognition, acceptance, approval, respect for differences, mutual support, and succourance are words and concepts found frequently in discussions of mental health.

Friendliness is too often lacking for many reasons. Citizens are often critical of the schools and teachers, and consequently teachers hesitate to depart from traditional concepts of the teacher as disciplinarian and undisputed leader. In addition, administrators find it impractical to establish friendly relations with teachers (Kvaraceus, 1951). Both factors are beyond the control of teachers, *except as matters of perception*. A factor within their control is the gradual removal of uncertainty regarding their role and task through improved understanding of children, professional study and growth, and participation in community affairs. Another factor within their control is improved self-understanding: As much as other individuals, teachers have unresolved problems and conflicts: those with modest talents as well as those with brilliant minds and distinguished careers are subject to anxiety (Kubie, 1954).

Teachers who are emotionally mature should be selected. But it should be remembered that emotional maturity is a process, not an achievement. It is therefore necessary that all teachers undertake the gratifying task of continual self-improvement. This was done by a number (over 200) of teachers in a study reported by Jersild and Lazar (1962). A control and an experimental group were questioned as to the nature and resolution of personal problems. The experimental group, whose problems were no more serious than those of the control group, underwent psychotherapy. In surprisingly high proportions, these teachers found that they could take a more realistic view of themselves, their work, and their pupils. They had an inner freedom they did not formerly possess. They were less fiercely competitive, more able to handle anger in themselves and pupils, more spontaneous in their friendships, and more accepting of self and others than they had been prior to therapy. Self-improvement was also sought in a continuing project conducted by Prescott. Working as a consultant in small groups with teachers in their own schools on real pupil cases, he sought to help them achieve deeper understandings of children's motivations, behavior, adjustment problems, and developmental tasks. Many of the teachers initially felt overwhelmed by the task—in fact, some withdrew from the plan—but most of them persisted in their efforts to become "professionals rather than craftsmen."

> Perhaps most meaningful of all for participants is the experience of working from day to day in the classroom with children whom they are coming to understand deeply. Among the more influential experiences of this sort reported by participants are discovering that their attitudes toward given children are changing from dislike to acceptance and from blaming to valuing as they gain insights into what situations mean to the children; having children change from avoiding the teacher to approaching the teacher with questions, comments, or proffers of help, or simply for informal conversation and companionship; and seeing children's behavior change from troublesome to cooperative and thoughtful. Interestingly enough, teachers report that these kinds of changes in the children's actions usually come shortly after the teacher has become aware of his own attitudinal changes toward the children.[5]

Advising the teacher to be friendly is suggesting that he lift himself by his bootstraps—like telling a pupil he should be happier. He would if he could and if he knew how. Teachers can help themselves in many ways. Psychotherapy is one way, and it involves self-help. In-service training is another way. Through the study of educational psychology, mental hygiene, and general psychology, teachers can seek a better understanding of their own childhood and adolescent experiences. They

[5] Daniel A. Prescott, *The Child in the Educative Process*, New York: McGraw-Hill Book Company, 1957, p. 469.

should examine critically various statements of the objectives of education and appraise the practices that purport to implement these objectives.

The lack of friendliness should probably be regarded as a symptom as well as a cause of hazardous school practices. It will be easier for teachers to become friendly as mental health hazards in the school are removed. It has been emphasized that subject matter *as a goal* is such a hazard. The "achievement tradition," in which the teacher focuses upon the child's learning certain facts and is irritated by anything that interferes with that goal, makes accomplishment primary and friendliness secondary. Grades and nonpromotion practices are other such hazards.

Psychiatrists and psychologists who use the words "security," "acceptance," "freedom," "permissiveness," "individual differences," and "understanding" are emphasizing the significance of friendly relations in achieving good mental health.

Competition We live in a competitive society, and a reasonable amount of competition in the school cannot be condemned. As stated previously, competition should take place between groups and individuals who all have the possibility of success or winning, and competition with one's own previous record is also a desirable source of motivation. Competition should be friendly and cooperative, the kind that minimizes jealousy and suspicion. If competition is between unequally matched individuals, it can become, and often is, a mental health hazard. Scholastic competition that pits slow learners against bright children, for example, makes for feelings of insecurity, inferiority, and frustration in some and unwarranted egotism and unjustified feelings of superiority in others. A sense of achievement can be realized by a group, and the teacher who wishes to provide motivation without the hazard of open competition can accent cooperative activities (Jenkins, Shacter, and Bauer, 1953, p. 248). The cooperative aspect of American life is just as basic as competition; in fact, it has been said to be our outstanding characteristic.

Uniform Grades Conventional grading systems can be criticized on much the same basis as unbridled competition. If the basis for grading is mastery of content, some youngsters will inevitably receive discouraging grades, and others will learn to get by with a minimum expenditure of effort.

Even if there were not wide individual differences among pupils, there would still be valid criticisms of uniform grading. One of these is unreliability. No two teachers give the same grade for work that is equivalent as judged by standardized achievement tests (Carter, 1952); experiments show that one paper graded by several teachers will receive scores that vary as much as 50 points on a 100-point scale. Moreover, a teacher may differ in scoring a paper when he grades it a second time. These conditions exist when teachers do not know which student's paper is being scored. When they do know whose paper is being marked, the matter is further complicated by the halo effect (see Glossary). The halo effect is particularly apparent in studies of grades in relation to social class. In one such study, upper-middle-class pupils received 343 A and B grades when their numbers in the total school population would have warranted 216 such marks. Lower-lower-class pupils received 48 A's and B's when their numbers would have indicated 147 such grades. Upper-middle-class pupils received 19 D and E grades when their proportionate number in the school group was 75. Lower-lower-class pupils received 136 D and E grades, while their numbers indicated their share as 51 (Sexton, 1961, p. 83). Even considering the cultural handicap exerted on intelligence test scores, this distribution is out of proportion, and we might conclude that the high dropout rate of lower-class pupils is in part due to their constant lack of reinforcement.

There has not been wide agreement on whether letter grades should mean academic achievement alone, whether they should indicate progress in achievement (personal growth rather than interpersonal comparison), or whether they should also include effort, attitude, social skills, and special interests and abilities. The lack of agreement on what a grade does and should mean probably explains in part why they are not strong incentives for most pupils. The few who can get good grades with reasonable effort are helped by them. Those who try and repeatedly fail to get recognition through grades do what they must do—adopt the defense mechanism of "I don't care." Page (1958) found that grades in junior and senior high school had little influence on subsequent effort. Pupils were much more responsive in terms of continued directed effort to teachers' written comments than to the letter grades.

Fortunately, the conventional grading systems are undergoing constant examination and evaluation. Increasingly, there is a trend toward reporting in various ways, with letter grades, conferences with parents, and conferences with pupils and parents used in various combinations. There is an attempt to consider individual capacity in relation to achievement, particularly in the elementary schools. In view of the fact that few parents (13 per cent in one study) are interested in how their child compares with others, more emphasis is being placed on work habits, attitudes, and social and emotional adjustments as items that should supplement academic evaluation ("Ten Criticisms of Public Education," 1957).

Promotion Practices Prior to the widespread practice of compulsory education, policies of promotion were less perplexing but nonetheless damaging. One either passed, repeated a grade, or quit school. Now the alternative of quitting school has been legally eliminated (even though the law is not uniformly enforced), and repeating a grade has experimentally been found to be unfruitful. Some adjustment to these facts has been made in the elementary school, and because of the philosophy that "the school is made for the child," practices that undermine the pupil's confidence and ego strength are not likely to be countenanced. At the college level it is presumed that prior guidance, choices in course selection, and wise evaluation will permit upholding the standards of professional schools without being undermined by permitting a pupil to move forward with his peer group regardless of the fact that his academic accomplishment is below average.

Many schools now practice so-called "block promotion," "nonfailure," or "uniform promotion." It is felt that if a youngster does as well as he can, he should not have the experience of failure forced upon him. Exceptions are made only on the basis of considered judgments involving many factors in the child's life. For example, if a child has started school at a very early age and has not yet attained the social, mental, and emotional age that will allow him to profit from first-grade experience, he may be held over for a year to great advantage. But retentions in later grades are much less likely to show positive results. It has been found that promoted low achievers usually do better than their nonpromoted counterparts. After a year, the repeaters showed less gain on achievement tests than did those who had been passed on to the next higher grade (Goodlad and Anderson, 1959, p. 35). Some experiments indicate that as many as 85 per cent of trial promotions are successful. Obviously, all who are retained are burdened by the sense of failure. An additional hazard to repeating a grade is that the youngster has to make an entirely new set of social adjustments—added to his perplexity in academic work, this makes repetition emotionally difficult.

Nonpromotion runs counter to what is now known about the nature and extent of individual differences and contradicts such aspects of mental hygiene as satisfaction of needs and the development of the whole child. The practice assumes that education consists of learning facts, but modern psychological and educational theory accents the idea that facts are only part of the educational enterprise. The encouraging outcome is emerging much faster than improved grading systems: Special classes are provided for those whose differences are marked; "streaming," or ability grouping, seeks to place the pupil where he can perform with some hope of success; remedial instruction seeks to correct academic deficiencies that are due to unfortunate school history; and the ungraded primary school helps get many young pupils off to a good start.

It is not realistic to hope that policy or organization will eliminate individual differences. No technique will automatically solve the academic problems of all pupils, provide for community demands, or satisfy the aspirations of all teachers. However, the ungraded school makes implementation of philosophical views and psychological insights somewhat easier. In this type of school, grade labels are not applied to students, and a pupil may be assigned to classes according to achievement and maturity. Thus, there may be several classes in an ungraded primary school. Some pupils may take four years and some only two years to complete what was formerly the first three grades. An intense effort is made to adapt instruction to individual needs and differences so that all are sure to get the fundamentals. Instead of having one grade and program to which all children must adjust, there is much overlapping—a nine-year-old child may be doing what was previously third, fourth, or fifth-grade work (see Table 7).

TABLE 7 *One of several ways in which an ungraded school may be organized in classes*

Age of pupils	Multiage class
Twelve-year-olds	6-7-8, plus advanced classes
Eleven-year-olds	5-6-7
Ten-year-olds	4-5-6
Nine-year-olds	3-4-5
Eight-year-olds	2-3-4
Seven-year-olds	1-2
Six-year-olds	K-K-1

The ungraded school began experimentally in the late 1940s, and by 1960, 18 per cent of elementary schools were using the "primary unit"—continuous progress for the first three years (Dean, 1960, p. 24). Perhaps one of the largest contributions of the ungraded school is that it calls other closely related problems—curriculum content, programs for the slow learner and the gifted, and procedures of evaluation—to the attention of school workers.

Survey respondents endorsed a variety of school practices which appear to have emerged as concomitants of recognizing individual differences through the creation of nongraded structures. Pressure from within sometimes leads to demand for several series of textbooks, more reference books, and materials designed for enrichment and for upward extension of more gifted learners. Available materials have been distributed on the basis of range of pupil interest and accomplishment within the class group rather than grade-level prescriptions. Efforts are made to evaluate and record pupil progress in relation to actual accomplishment, rather than in relation to some assumed grade-level standard. Nongrading apparently serves as a stimulus for a transition from report cards to conference methods of parent-teacher reporting as well as for organization of parent-teacher groups to study child development and modern educational practices. Teachers are brought together in the search for better ways of dealing with individual differences, in planning of curricular sequences, and in evaluative techniques for appraising learnings over and above the possession of subject-matter information.[6]

Regardless of class organization or promotion practices, it is still necessary for teachers to realize that pupil differences will continue to exist. Organization and policy lead to improvement only when teachers use them to promote the significant end of the individual pupil's development.

Homework   The policy of giving homework to pupils is no doubt carried out with the best of intentions. However, there are several reasons why assignment of uniform tasks to be performed at home must be questioned. For one thing (and a very minor point), homework is likely to increase the differences that plague teachers in grading, grouping, and promotion; that is, the child who already is advanced in relation to his peers is quite likely to have the home advantages (a room in which to study, library resources, and the help of interested adults) that will put him still further ahead. This is fine for him, but the less fortunate become more disheartened.

We talk of permitting the child to develop his resources, of encouraging him to enhance his uniqueness, of fostering his creativity. To assign uniform homework is to contradict these aspirations by limiting the free time requisite to their realization. It is not that many pupils will not respond—they do. Youngsters have readily responded to the national competition and emergency for scientific workers; but in so doing, they follow the crowd, and the free time needed for exploration of their unique personal interests is reduced. There is at least some probability that over-organization of the child's life, which uniform homework accentuates, has its harmful effects. Furthermore, there is no guarantee that additional work improves the quality of performance or knowledge of educational processes (Redl and Wattenberg, 1959, p. 338).

One must consider the effect of uniformly assigned homework on that approximately 50 per cent of pupils who come from the lower social classes. When homework is assigned, it is probable that lack of a place to study in a crowded home, household chores or part-time work, lack of interest or example on the part of parents, and unavailability of reference books and materials all contribute to putting the lower-class pupil further behind in comparison with his more fortunate companions. His defense is to quit school as soon as possible and contribute to the social dynamite of which Conant (1961) speaks.

As far as academic status is concerned, the value of prescribed homework is yet to be proved. Two equated groups were studied in New York

[6] John I. Goodlad, "Individual Differences and Vertical Organization of the School," *Individualizing Instruction,* Sixty-first Yearbook of the National Society for the Study of Education, Chicago: The University of Chicago Press, 1962, pp. 230–231.

City: One was given homework, and the other had none. In terms of academic achievement, there was no difference between the groups (Di-Napoli, 1937). In 1956, the Ministry of Education in France, after intensive social, medical, psychological, and educational study, decreed that homework should be abandoned in the elementary schools (Olson, 1959, p. 173).

The impact of uniformly assigned homework on mental health must be considered. The child needs time to develop his own resources, to engage in physical exercise, and to gain practice in social relationships. Play is important because it develops muscular coordination and social skills, and it is valuable in developing more aspects of the total personality than does homework.

> Excessive tension and a sense of pressure are often associated with homework. If a pupil is not able to resist the appeal of television or student activities, he may begin to think of himself as lacking in purpose and will power. Late hours spent in study and failure to complete assignments may make a conscientious pupil depressed and anxious.
>
> For mental health, children and young people need to engage in worthwhile out-of-school tasks suited to their individual capacities. Homework should supply such tasks and reasonable freedom in carrying them out. Whenever homework crowds out social experience, outdoor recreation, and creative activities, and whenever it usurps time that should be devoted to sleep, it is not meeting the basic needs of children and adolescents.[7]

Some agree with the foregoing as far as the elementary school is concerned, but believe that homework is desirable in high school and that it is good training for college work. However, the study skills necessary in college can probably be taught better in the school than at home—parents, though they may be expert teachers of other people's children, are among the world's poorest teachers of their own children because they become emotionally involved. In addition, the high school student tends to develop better work habits at school if he does not depend upon getting his work done at home. Moreover, the many pupils who do not intend to go to college anyway will not be stimulated by high school homework as preparation for higher education. If a student learns to capitalize on his time while he is in high school, he will be able to take on the additional hours of study required for college work when he is surrounded by others who are finding evening study advantageous.

Exceptions to the above generalizations can probably be made at both the elementary and high school levels. It must be remembered that the foregoing refers to "uniformly assigned" homework, not to varied assign-

[7] Ruth Strang, *Guided Study and Homework*, What Research Says to the Teacher, no. 8, Washington: National Education Association, 1955, p. 18.

ments that take into account individual differences in health, social adjustment, educational purpose, and home environment. Homework for those who are absent from school because of an untimely family vacation will not interfere with well-rounded development. Homework may also be desirable for children who are absent because of quarantine or illness, in which case a slow return to normal work is desirable. Home assignments for work that cannot be advantageously done in class may enrich school tasks. For example, interviewing a relative or friend who has had a unique experience or traveled in an unfamiliar land may have its place; building a model or setting up an experiment may enrich schoolwork for the entire class; preparing a set of 35-mm slides to illustrate a travel report can help both the individual and his classmates. But these are ways of meeting individual differences, not uniform prescriptions.

Eliminating Mental Health Hazards in the School   If teachers and administrators examine their practices in terms of the fundamental needs of human beings and the stated objectives of education, many mental health hazards can be eliminated, but correction of one or even all would not resolve the problems of mental health. The important thing is this: If a teacher focuses upon the reduction of any one hazard, he not only takes that one specific step toward mental health objectives, but he takes another by showing awareness of children's mental health needs.

Positive factors in mental health

Providing for Individual Differences   The recognition of individual differences is the foundation of our democratic society. Each person has a unique part to play in improving the life of all; each has a unique contribution to make. Youngsters differ widely in their interests, although apparently they may have equal ability. Some are interested in sports, while others are devoted to making model planes or doll dresses. Some find adventure in reading, while others are content to sit for hours before the television set. Some like to experiment with home chemistry sets, while others prefer to spend much time with their playmates. Of course, many —perhaps most—individuals can perform the tasks delegated by teachers, but the artful teacher will become aware of divergent motivations and suggest books and references that bridge the gap between school and out-of-school interests and activities.

There are differences in motivation too, and they may be explained on the basis of varying home and community backgrounds. For example, some parents regard education as a most important aspect of development, while others consider it an unnecessary delay to the child's becoming a wage earner. In some communities, it is customary for most youngsters to go to college after high school graduation; in others, only the exceptional youngster is concerned with such a future. Differences in motivation may also stem from the emotional tone of the pupil's home. He can hardly be expected to devote himself wholeheartedly to school tasks if his dominant thoughts are about the turmoil or hostility at home. However, the teacher can *help* compensate for emotional stress by implementing a varied and flexible class program that can be adjusted to the pupil's individual requirements.

Providing for Creative Expression   Teachers who provide opportunities for creative expression help to improve their students' mental health. Free and spontaneous play, writing, painting, and drawing are among the important media for such creative expression. Many teachers at all grade levels and in high school are using such media to enrich academic programs. It is felt that spontaneous expression gives the teacher and pupils the following advantages:

1. The teacher may regard creative expression as a projective technique (see Glossary). That is, what the child freely puts into his play, his writing, and his pictures is *himself*. He plays, writes, and draws what he feels and is sometimes unable to vocalize. The teacher uses his activities and his productions as *clues* to a better understanding of his unique personality (Powell, 1958).

2. Creative expression can provide variety in the school program, and creative activities often motivate pupils to do the more academic work. A sophomore boy who had taken little interest in class recitation was permitted to draw pictures of some prehistoric animals on the board to be used in connection with class studies. In order to make authentic pictures, he had to do some reading; his teacher noted that he gradually took a more active interest in his academic work as the studies progressed.

3. Students can work off tensions and frustrations through creative expression. A child who is jealous of a sibling may not attack his competitor, but he can with impunity draw a picture in which his brother or sister suffers chagrin or injury. A high school pupil may not wish to reveal feelings of hostility toward a parent or other family member, but he can write a story—presumably about other people. Dramatics are also becoming increasingly important as a mental hygiene technique for the classroom teacher (Boniface, 1958).

Making Schoolwork Meaningful   The things children like and spontaneously do and the goals they consider important are different from those of adults. For children, goals must be more immediate, and activities must be more specific and concrete. Teachers must ever be on the alert to make books and courses of study prepared by adults meaningful for children. For example, drill on word selection, sentence composition, and punctuation has been found to be relatively fruitless in terms of the amount of time spent (Burrows, 1959, p. 24), but if a letter requesting a speaker or materials is to be written and the teacher indicates that the best letter will be sent, real effort is usually expended, and good results are obtained. The goal is immediate, related to a need, and specific.

Democratic Procedures Some attitudes commonly considered democratic are faith in the worth of *each* child; confidence in the soundness of pooled opinion; belief in the ability of children to face and solve their own problems (especially a belief in their *good* intentions); and patience with the comparative slowness of democratic procedures. No teacher claims that democratic procedures are particularly easy, but those who have tried them know that there are dividends in terms of pupils' steady improvement in socially oriented conduct.

Some of the more common democratic procedures to be used in the classroom are:

1. Allowing pupils to discuss and decide (under direction) the activities and purposes of the class

2. Emphasizing freedom and flexibility rather than arbitrariness and indoctrination (Steinberg, 1962)

3. Permitting pupils to become increasingly self-directing in their behavior

4. Helping pupils understand the necessity for certain behavior rather than demanding conformity to imposed regulations

5. Providing opportunities in accord with the individual's ability to comprehend and profit from them

6. Working with pupils on a cooperative and congenial basis

7. Taking time to talk with and listen to those who wish to participate

8. Encouraging cooperative group work.

Democratic procedures are likely to go far in meeting such fundamental human needs as the desire for independence, the desire for companionship, the need for recognition, the need for security (security being dependent upon the person's ability to meet and solve problems), and the desire for new experiences. Democratic procedures are slow, but so too is growth toward better mental health, the reward of which is a richer life.

Teachers as Mental Health Influences There are many reasons why teachers are the focal point of mental health influences in the school. One is that children are with them constantly, and children learn much through imitation. They think more of themselves when a key person in their lives, such as their teacher, accepts them, gives affection, and shows confidence in their potential. Teachers help to remedy children's weaknesses, and they recognize children's strengths; they can help pupils solve troublesome everyday problems; they manipulate the pupils' physical and social environment to reduce mental health hazards. They can do such things as these most effectively when they realize the effect and implications of their classroom decisions. Teachers should not try to mold pupils into some preconceived form; their role is to nurture and prompt growth toward a uniquely creative and self-fulfilling life (Prescott, 1957, p. 48).

As mental health influences, teachers must consider not only what they do but what they are—actually, the two are inseparable. This implies that the teacher too must be involved in a continuing process of self-improvement; he must and will value objects, experiences, and goals that make for his own survival and growth and for the survival and growth of others (Rogers, 1961, p. 27).

The School and Community-wide Approaches to Mental Health   Teachers and schools influence and affect the lives of children, but there are other influences too; the most encouraging action for mental health occurs when the school and the wider community join forces. Those who recognize that there are many sources of strain in children's lives are prepared to see that community agencies work together. School workers can and, in some localities, do exchange information with juvenile workers on the police force. Social welfare workers who work intimately with certain families can warn the school of incipient problems and discuss cases with teacher and counselors. Ministers can be enlisted as partners in the work of understanding children and their parents. Recreation leaders can profit from the cooperation of teachers in both program development and utilization of physical resources. (One criticism of the expense of schools arises from the closing of gymnasiums, swimming pools, and playgrounds during vacation periods. Many schools today are encouraging use of these facilities by both children and parents and are even providing supervisory personnel.) Mental test and achievement test data provided by the school are useful in foster-child care and in adoptive procedures. Provisions for the handicapped are more effective when the school and community join forces. Some of the greatest gains from community-wide approaches are more widespread assumption of responsibility for mass media (radio, television, newspapers), provisions for the handicapped, and programs for the delinquent and predelinquent (Ojemann, 1955, pp. 125–141).

There are many opportunities for school-community cooperation. The first steps consist of communication—discussions, consultations, critical evaluation of the shortcomings of each agency, and explanations of the functions of each. The problem is often to utilize the existing agencies more effectively rather than to create new ones. Illustrative agencies and a possible way in which each might influence the lives of children are given in Table 8. The exchange of information on the extension of "possible function" would enhance the work of the agencies involved.

Mental health work is being done by many individuals and agencies, but the task remains for someone to take initiative and leadership in coordinating and improving action. "And in the process of helping to

TABLE 8

Agency	Possible function
Family casework agency	Reduction of family friction
Child guidance clinic	Specific suggestions for guiding children
Boy and Girl Scouts	Development of constructive interests
Church schools	Moral training and social experience
Mental health associations	Provision of literature and lecturers
Library association	Guidance of the curious and gifted
Art museum	Development of special talents
Dramatic clubs	Ego enhancement and social contact
Goodwill Industries	Easing of financial pressure on family
Recreation center	Development of skills; building of health
Junior baseball	Promotion of health and leisure interests

develop these resources, they will have to recognize and learn to live with their reliance on many other individuals who, by the force of circumstances, are involved in the treatment of mental and emotional disturbances." [8]

Summary

In addition to the prevention and remediation of mental illness, "mental health" is coming to refer to the more complete development of unique differences and potentialities. It is thus of intimate concern to everyone.

Because of the lack of trained mental health workers, because of the "becoming" emphasis, because the school is the one agency where children are most accessible, because borderline and incipient cases have nowhere else to turn, teachers cannot avoid playing an active role in the mental health emphasis. It is up to teachers to see, as best they can, that the child's basic needs for acceptance, companionship, new experiences, success, development of tension tolerance, among many other needs, are being met or on the way to being met.

There are mental health hazards in the school. Some of these are lack of friendliness, competition for grades between pupils of unequal background and ability, the threat of failure when faced by inappropriate tasks, and uniformly assigned homework. These hazards are partially compensated for by positive mental health factors in school. These include provisions for meeting individual differences, provisions for unique creative expression, the attempt to make schoolwork understandable and meaningful, and the increasing trend toward democratic procedures. Teachers are the most powerful school influences for mental health or, unfortunately, for maladjustment. But it is recognized that the problem of mental health is so vast that, in the final

[8] From *Action for Mental Health,* The Final Report of the Joint Commission on Mental Illness and Health, New York: Basic Books, Inc., 1961, p. 123.

analysis, really effective work is dependent upon community-wide action backed by national interest and support.

Problems and exercises

1 What are the similarities and what are the marked contrasts between remedial mental hygiene and mental hygiene that seeks maximum self-realization?

2 Discuss with three or four persons the advisability of the teacher's working with seriously disturbed children. How do the views you encounter accord with that presented in the chapter?

3 Describe, in terms of your own experience, some instances showing the teacher's role in the mental health of pupils.

4 Is it necessary for a youngster to fail a grade in order to learn that he is not "college material"?

5 What are some specific things that might be done to strengthen children's tension tolerance?

6 Which of the handicaps to mental health in the school do you consider to be most serious? Which do you consider to be least serious?

7 What is your conclusion about the effectiveness and advisability of using A, B, C, and D grades as motivational and evaluative techniques?

8 Are there any other hazards (e.g., authoritarianism, psychological distance between teachers and administrators, overload of teachers, limited facilities, or others) that you consider more serious than the ones listed?

9 Do you agree or disagree with the view of homework presented in the text?

10 What are some "possible" things that you, as a teacher, might do to enlist community-wide action for mental health?

Suggested additional readings

Allinsmith, Wesley, and George W. Goethals: *The Role of Schools in Mental Health,* New York: Basic Books, Inc., Publishers, 1962.
  This book focuses on curricular orientation (subject-matter or child-centered), instructional aims (life work or personality), and the extent to which schools should be involved in a mental health emphasis. Some incisive comments are made about teachers and their work attitudes.

Bernard, Harold W.: *Mental Hygiene for Classroom Teachers,* 2d ed., New York: McGraw-Hill Book Company, 1961.
  The chapters "The Mental Hygiene of Discipline," "Constructive Approaches to Mental Health," and other chapters on art, music, drama, free writing, and reading contain suggestions that may be of interest and help to the teacher.

Jersild, Arthur T., and Eve Lazar: *The Meaning of Psychotherapy in the Life* *and Work of Teachers,* New York: Bureau of Publications, Teachers College, Columbia University, 1962.

According to those who have experienced it—therapy works. Subjects in this study were performing well but felt that their lives could be improved. Changes in attitudes toward self, family, others; ability to handle anger, prejudice, jealousy; and performance on the job are among the items discussed.

Joint Commission on Mental Illness and Health, *Action for Mental Health: Final report,* New York: Basic Books, Inc., Publishers, 1961.

The need for, present efforts toward, and shortcomings of action for mental health are described as a prelude to proposing a nationwide program for improving our effectiveness.

Mental Health in Modern Education, Fifty-fourth Yearbook of the National Society for the Study of Education, Chicago: The University of Chicago Press, 1955, part II.

The problems of mental health are set forth, conditions of mental health in the classroom are described, and then focus is turned to mental hygiene programs at the preschool, primary, intermediate, high school, and college levels.

Evaluating for Future Growth

Educational practices are constantly improving, but it is certain that there is much to be done in implementing existing knowledge of psychological principles. Rote procedures, uniform curricula, stern disciplinary procedures, and primary emphasis upon subject matter (as contrasted to a pupil-centered emphasis) are currently being questioned. Grading and evaluation practices are also being modified, but the rate of change is less than gratifying in view of the dangers and the many unresolved dilemmas. A major hope for continued improvement resides in those who are about to enter the teaching field—those who are less encumbered by the habit of past action.

20

Just as machine teaching has recently become available, other as yet unsuspected areas of knowledge will be available to the next generation of teachers. The key to this yet undiscovered information and to the wise use of existing information lies primarily in our techniques of evaluation, which must be made an integral part of the total learning situation (e.g., feedback, reinforcement) rather than an end-product assessment. We must know the results of many measures of pupil behavior before we can decide whether to be "the first by whom the new is tried" or "the last by whom the old is set aside."

Evaluation is the attempt to see how sound our knowledge is and how well knowledge is applied. The symbols of evaluation are intended as communications between teachers and their pupils, and parents, and other current and subsequent teachers, and prospective employers. The relegation of evaluation to a final product—success in the grade or course—results in confusion. Thus appraisal techniques and symbols are some of the more knotty problems of education. In this chapter, an attempt is made to show how evaluation techniques can help to make more effective use of our knowledge of educational psychology and thus provide incentive for the pupil's present and future growth.

Purposes and concepts of appraisal

Purposes Much of the dissatisfaction with current techniques of appraisal stems from the fact that there is no clear and widely accepted conception of the purposes of grades. Some of the functions to be served are:

Informing the pupil about the progress he is making

Motivating the pupil to work more effectively

Showing the pupil specific faults that need correction

Identifying special individual talents and weaknesses

Informing parents about their child's status and progress

Providing data for teachers and counselors for pupil guidance

Providing data to principals to determine placement of transfer pupils and of pupils in their next year's class

Providing data on which to base educational plans—classes, curricula, choice of college, etc.

Providing data on which to base career plans—manual worker, technical worker, professional career

Aiding employers in the choice of employees

Establishing a school record of the pupil's performance

Even without adding a long list of items upon which grades might possibly be based, it can readily be seen that reducing all these purposes to a single letter or numerical grade is difficult—if not impossible.

Appraisal by Grades　In the past, the appraisal of pupil progress has been largely a matter of "measuring" status and growth in subject-matter areas, with perhaps more emphasis on status than on growth. Status was determined by the grades a pupil received, and many times the grade represented the teacher's opinion of how a particular pupil compared with his classmates. Formal "standardized" measures helped to objectify the teacher's opinion, but the measures are sometimes not fully comprehended. Grades may also be based on achievement tests and the degree to which age-grade standards or other norms are approximated.

Currently, there is much dissatisfaction with the concept of grading. A number of approaches are being tried, and there is evidence that substantial improvements are in the making (Rothney, 1955).

Appraisal by Evaluation　The word "evaluation" suggests that measurement by tests and examinations and estimates of progress or status and their reduction to grades are not enough. Only part of the evaluation of a house may be made by measuring the floor space, listing the cost of materials and labor, and citing the size and cost of the lot. The buyer's evaluation must also include style; utility of floor plan; age; neighborhood; proximity to schools, markets, and transportation; probably taxes; resale potential; and his own ability to pay. Similarly, many factors must be considered in school evaluation. Emphasis is placed on broad changes in personality, personal needs, and goals and on the achievement of *interrelated* major objectives of education (Rothney, Danielson, and

Heimann, 1959, p. 227). It has been said that measurement and grading are *atomistic*, whereas evaluation is *organismic* in scope. Grading focuses attention on minute and often independent elements of development; evaluation considers many interrelated facets of personality and has as an aim the integrating of the individual and the correlating of subject matter.

Awareness of the inaccuracy of tests, combined with the current emphasis upon emotional, social, and intellectual growth, emphasizes the importance of evaluation. Paper-and-pencil tests and simple letter or numerical grades cannot cover all the aspects of sound education that need attention. Evaluation capitalizes on tests; in addition, data from anecdotal records, interviews, questionnaires, pupil profiles, as well as examples of past work and reports from doctors and nurses, are utilized to obtain a complete view of the child. There is still a need for test results (achievement, ability, diagnostic, etc.), but it becomes clear that *test data must be interpreted.* An IQ score must be viewed in terms of age, sensory acuity, cultural background, emotional stability, type of test used, and recency of administration. An achievement test score must be interpreted in terms of ability, competing interests, past opportunity, and personality trends. These aspects are not likely to be overlooked by the teacher who has grasped the idea that Johnny Jones is to be evaluated, not graded.

Personality appraisal

Interviews It is important that objective data be used in evaluating the personality adjustment of the child, but it is no less important to know how he feels about the circumstances and conditions which surround him. An interview is helpful in obtaining this information, but the teacher must know what kinds of questions are most likely to bring results; in addition, there must be a high degree of rapport, so that the pupil will feel free to respond.

Questions that probe into relationships with parents, siblings, and out-of-school playmates may provide data on adjustment. Questions about the pupil's spare-time activities, his interests, and his vocational aims (in the upper grades and high school) will provide clues. Such information will suggest study materials for the pupil that can more quickly come to be continuing pursuits. Building on the interests discovered in interviews tends to make the pupil increasingly independent in his study and investigations. For example, a teacher who was concerned about the lackadaisical schoolwork of an eighth-grade boy discovered that he was interested in electricity. She made him responsible for the lighting effects in a stage production. He planned the arrangement of footlights, spotlights, and color lighting, and installed the necessary equipment under the supervision of an electrician. His interest spread to the construction of stage sets, and he learned the play thoroughly. Acceptance by the group and his own increased feeling of personal worth enabled him to apply himself more vigorously to academic work.

An interview is more than a verbal questionnaire. One should be aware of a smile, quickened verbal tempo, a change in voice or eyes that indicates a special interest. One should follow up the lead, be it verbal or nonverbal, that suggests something of unusual importance to the individual. Give him time—time to reflect, to form the answer he wants, to elaborate, or to wander. The silence one maintains often places considerble responsibility on the subject for contributing to the conversation.

The securing of rapport is, to a large extent, dependent upon the teacher. Some find one approach more effective than another. But it can be said that the following contribute to rapport: genuinely wanting to know the pupil, expressing interest in his interests, liking him despite objectionable behavior, avoiding the show of emotional or moral shock at some of his expressions, and seeing to it that he has an opportunity to make a contribution to the interchange. Above all, the teacher must be genuinely friendly (Farwell and Peters, 1960, p. 403).

Interviews should encourage the pupil to solve his own problems. Specifically, instead of launching immediately into "good, sound advice," the teacher should encourage the pupil to make his own suggestions for improvement of behavior. The evaluation that a pupil makes of his conduct has proved to be much more productive than the gratuitous advice of teachers. The word "interview" itself suggests this emphasis— a viewing between two persons (Fullmer and Bernard, 1964, p. 124).

Observation Teachers can learn a great deal about the personal and social orientation of pupils if they will take time to observe them carefully at work and at play. Instead of hastening to correct questionable behavior, they should permit children enough freedom to work out their own solutions. Observation does not give any answers, but it certainly provides clues for defining problems.

> The extent to which we understand him [the pupil in the school situation] depends on the extent and sensitivity of our seeing him as he works by himself, as he works with others, as he plays with others, as he is happy and moving forward or frustrated in attempting to solve his problem. We need to see how he reacts to success and to failure, how he relates himself to other individuals, to a group, how he expresses the dynamic process of growth, how he meets and attempts to deal with various kinds of problems in various contexts. We need to recognize the accumulated effect of previous experiences. By seeing characteristic ways of reacting to different kinds of situations, we can guess with considerable accuracy much about him, his

feelings about himself and about others and about his interaction with others.[1]

Observation leading to constructive evaluation is neither incidental nor accidental. Systematic notes on what has been seen serve a double purpose: They make the teacher increasingly aware of what is important, and they provide an inclusive record. An inexpensive card file for recording comments will soon become a valuable reference in suggesting avenues for future growth.

Objective Approaches to Personality Appraisal One approach to personality appraisal is the inventory or questionnaire. These inventories are mainly designed for the upper grades and beyond, though some can be used from the fourth grade up. Results are typically given in percentile ranks on such items as home adjustment, social adjustment, school adjustment, self-reliance, attitudes, beliefs, feelings of worth, etc. However, it must be observed that the score on such tests is *approximate* and *representative*. Thus interviews, observations, other teachers' reports, and supplementary test data should be used in connection with the formal inventory.

The user of personality inventories must be strongly warned against putting too much credence in them. The author believes that they provide a convenient point of orientation for an interview. That is, one can determine what area of a child's life is causing difficulty. The interview can then be directed toward this area. But taking and recording a score or percentile rank from the test is another matter. Actually, inventories have very low objective value, the scores have meaning only within a very limited situational range, and their diagnostic value is highly dependent on the specific training and knowledge of the administrator of the test.

> It seems that it [their wide use] must be a combination of amazing, psychometric innocence on the part of the users, naïveté in considering the counseling job as a "quickie" affair rather than a complex longitudinal problem, mistaken faith in statistics on the part of inventory producers and consumers, expediency, and a desire to keep up with the other fellow who uses them for any of the above reasons.[2]

Sociometry (see Chapter 12) is an easy and valuable approach to the evaluation of social adjustment. Said one teacher, trying the sociogram for the first time, "I was amazed at the results. I thought I knew my pupils very well, but I learned that some of the ones whom I thought would be frequently chosen were not very popular. Some whom I

[1] J. Murray Lee, and Dorris May Lee, *The Child and His Development*, New York: Appleton-Century-Crofts, Inc., 1958, p. 301.
[2] John W. M. Rothney, Paul J. Danielson, and Robert A. Heimann, *Measurement for Guidance*, New York: Harper & Row, Publishers, 1959, p. 283.

thought to be rather lonesome individuals were in reality quite attractive to their classmates." Her evaluation of the pupils became more realistic. She was able to group the pupils so that some of the disciplinary problems she had been encountering diminished or disappeared; it is likely that her evaluation made possible the organization of social experiences that were conducive to further personality growth.

Other formal techniques for personality evaluation include analysis through play activities and analysis of the child's art products. The Rorschach Ink Blot Test and Murray's Thematic Apperception Test are further techniques for understanding personality. However, these techniques must be used by carefully trained technicians; they are not ordinarily used by classroom teachers.

Evaluating school progress

Grading   Many youngsters in school today and nearly all teachers or students preparing to teach have had their school progress evaluated in terms of grades. Most of these grades are letter symbols which, on inspection, turn out to represent a numerical system. We would have thought that the older systems of percentages had been pretty well outmoded. For example, a report card of the year 1903 listed twelve subjects, and the student was rated in various subjects at 97, 91, 93, etc. Later, it was recognized that even a narrow range of subject matter could not be evaluated so accurately, and letter systems were started. An A grade

FIGURE 23.   *Providing opportunities to satisfy curiosity is a better means of motivation than are grades and marks.*

SOURCE: *Courtesy of Department of Instructional Materials, Portland, Ore., Public Schools.*

meant 90 to 100, B meant 80 to 89, etc. However, these letter grades are reconverted into grade-point averages that are accurate to three decimal places. And the third decimal place may make the difference between getting or not getting an honor! Apparently, little progress has been made in the last fifty years on the vexatious problem of evaluating school progress.

The absurdity of grading is widely recognized. Experiments have indicated that different teachers grade the same paper with scores ranging from 70 to 95 even in such subjects as algebra and arithmetic. It is reported that on one such experiment, the scoring key was inadvertently mixed in with the papers to be scored. It received grades from below failing to excellent. In addition to being unreliable, grades permit painful and unwarranted comparisons between unequals and thus make for traumatic discriminations. This is not the kind of evaluation that looks to future growth.

> Grades for course work are undesirable for many reasons: fear of failing or receiving a low grade can produce anxiety, and often hinders students rather than increasing their level of efficiency; grades often come to be perceived as the most important academic goals since honors, scholarships, "classroom fringe benefits" and many kinds of academic recognition seem to depend so much on a student's grade average; the teacher is forced to assign a single letter grade to a student, even though there are often many kinds of achievements that should be separately evaluated and recognized in a single course; and grades can also become the basis for a kind of reverse motivation in which the "gentlemen's grade" of C becomes not only a rationalization for many students, but also the cause of better students' lowering their sights and restricting their own level of achievement. Grades are considered to be, like heterogeneous groupings, a necessary evil accompanying mass education.[3]

Standardized Tests Standardized tests (see Chapter 9) have a valid place in a program of evaluation. They are usually carefully designed to ensure validity and reliability. Administration and scoring are precisely defined so that all pupils are tested and scored in the same manner—the halo effect is diminished, if not eliminated. Norms are available for guidance in the interpretation of scores. These are often expressed in percentile ranks, grade equivalents, age equivalents, or standard scores.[4]

Certain precautions must be observed in the use of standardized test results. For instance, standard scores must not be used to grade pupils,

---

[3] William A. Deterline, *An Introduction to Programmed Instruction*, Englewood Cliffs, N.J.: Prentice-Hall, Inc., 1962, p. 76.

[4] A standard score is based on the variability of a distribution of scores around the mean of the scores. The basic unit for expressing this variability is the standard deviation.

to judge a teacher's effectiveness, or to test the value of the curriculum. Scores should not be considered infallible.

The proper use of standardized instruments should be to give the teacher a more objective view of the child. They should help him to learn the child's present stage of development. Evaluation of the pupil should be *partially* in terms of his growth from a given point (the score on a test at the beginning of a term) to a given point (the score on an equivalent test at the end of the term). The pupil need not be judged in terms of the absolute score (grade equivalent of 5 in reading, etc.) or in comparison with other members of the class. The word "partially" means that the change of score from first test to retest is only part of the data upon which evaluation is based. A child who has experienced a prolonged illness, frequent change in residence, or an untoward event in his family or a child who is handicapped by some sensory defect should not be "graded down" because of his lack of accomplishment. Standardized tests can be additionally fruitful when they are used as motivating influences. A pupil well below average for his class may receive vigorous stimulation from knowing that he has made notable strides from where he was at a prior time. Since educational growth is characteristically slow, it is invigorating to have some objective indication of improvement.

The following kinds of standardized tests are of particular value in programs of evaluation that look toward the continuing growth of the individual pupil:

1. Intelligence tests give the teacher an *indication* of the potential with which he is working. Tests of mental ability translated into mental ages and grade equivalents, rather than intelligence quotients, provide the teacher with valuable clues. They *help* determine whether or not the pupil should be accomplishing at or near the norms for his grade.

2. Achievement tests are available for single subjects (arithmetic, English, reading, geography, etc.) and also in the form of batteries, in which several subjects are included in one test. They enable the teacher to estimate progress over a period of time. Each subject is scored in terms of an age or grade equivalent. This enables the teacher to evaluate pupils in terms of their potential and previous status.

3. Diagnostic tests are also valuable in evaluating for growth. These tests, available in such subjects as arithmetic, language, and reading, aid the teacher in locating specific areas of difficulty within subject areas. They do not tell what should be done by way of remediation. The tests do not diagnose. They give *indications* that narrow the search for difficulties.

4. Inventories of interest aid in the discovery of more productive approaches for individual pupils and provide tentative help in choosing the curricula and vocations that will be most stimulating to them.

5. Personality tests may help the pupil and teacher locate specific areas

of difficulty in personal and social adjustment, but they make no diagnosis.

A technique for using test scores Dr. Victor N. Phelps, Portland State College, has devised a means of plotting paired scores on standardized tests. It is a visual device to help teachers understand the accomplishment that might reasonably be expected of pupils in terms of their indicated capacity. MA scores are plotted on one axis, with the median MA being the center line. Achievement scores are plotted on the other axis, with the median grade score being the center line. Figure 24 shows the scores for a fourth-grade class at midyear. Each pair of scores is given one tally; thus pupil 1, having an MA of 132 and an achievement equivalent to third grade, is tallied at the intersection of the lines for these two scores.

After the sixteen paired scores are tallied, a line is drawn from the lower left-hand corner to the upper right-hand corner. Pupils whose paired scores are plotted close to this line (e.g., 9, 12, 16, 4, 3, 13, 2) should not be a serious concern to the teacher insofar as accomplishment is concerned. Even though some are below average for fourth grade, they are achieving in approximate accord with their capacity. Pupils in quadrant IV (15 and 6) are doing well despite below-average ability. The teacher's concern would be to see that they are not unduly worried and tense or sacrificing valuable play activities in order to study. Pupils above the diagonal, in quadrant I (8 and 14), may well receive some help. Possibly their retardation is due to too much previously applied pressure. Quadrant III indicates that pupils 1, 5, and 11 are retarded despite having average or better-than-average ability—special help for them may be quite fruitful. But it is possible that they suffer from some sensory difficulty, emotionally disturbed homes, tense sibling relationships, or lack of a sense of personal worth. Various remedial techniques can be tried after the specific difficulties are discovered. Pupil 10 (quadrant II) may profit from some encouragement; he could be told that he is not doing so well as he could and should, although he is above the class average.

This graphic representation of scores makes it easier for the teacher to see those who need special study. In the past, too often the teacher's major attention has been devoted to bringing pupils up to average, regardless of their potential.[5] Further, the child with high ability who was average or better in accomplishment (e.g., pupil 10, Figure 24) was neglected, despite the fact that he was not working in accord with his ability. Such a device as Figure 24 brings those who merit special attention into clear view.

Teacher-Pupil Evaluative Conferences One function of evaluation should be to clarify the pupil's responsibility for his educational growth, which

[5] It may help to remember that, by definition, 50 per cent of the pupils, in any item of measurement, are below average.

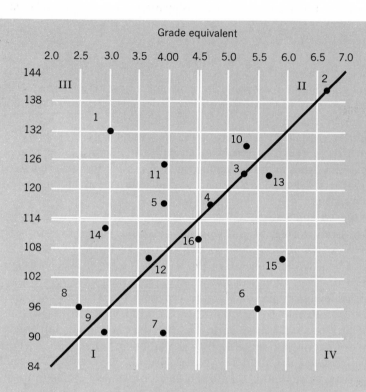

Pupil	Mental age	Achievement (grade equivalent)	Pupil	Mental age	Achievement (grade equivalent)
1	132	3.0	9	91	2.9
2	140	6.7	10	129	5.3
3	123	5.3	11	125	3.9
4	117	4.7	12	106	3.7
5	117	3.9	13	123	5.7
6	96	5.5	14	112	2.9
7	91	3.9	15	106	5.9
8	96	2.5	16	110	4.5

FIGURE 24. *Using standardized test scores in pupil evaluation*
SOURCE: *Courtesy of Victor N. Phelps, Portland State College.*

can be done in teacher-pupil evaluative conferences. The first step is to define objectives, *in terms that the pupil can understand* (Flanagan, 1964). Of necessity, there must be many objectives to fit the many activities of the school and the many variations between individuals, which indicates immediately that the outcomes of learning are many and varied—not single and isolated ("Reporting to Parents," 1961). A few representative items to be evaluated by the pupil and teacher might include (1) ability to carry out self-directed activities, (2) ability to solve problems in arithmetic appropriate to developmental level, (3) interest in varied pursuits, (4) skill in writing expression, (5) skill in oral expression, (6) manifestation of courtesy in dealing with others, (7) execution of assigned or accepted responsibilities, (8) respect for school property and the property of others, and (9) attention to personal appearance. Thus academic subjects, personal interests, social habits, and attitudes toward citizenship are involved.

An advantage of teacher-pupil evaluation is that the pupil understands the marking system and what it means exactly. He may not always agree with the teacher's evaluation, and the discussion that ensues will clarify misunderstandings on the part of both.

Teachers find that teacher-pupil conferences are no more time-consuming than is the attempt to grade accurately and conscientiously. Of course, if grades are assigned arbitrarily, teacher-pupil evaluation is comparatively time-consuming. The element of arbitrariness is reflected in one upper-grade student's remark: "You should not expect to get a good grade the first six weeks. If you did, then you could not show improvement in later periods. Just wait, next time you will have some grades that are higher than the ones you now have."

While it cannot be claimed that teacher-pupil evaluation answers all the questions that might be asked, these four advantages are worth considering.

1. Evaluation clarifies the pupil's concept of what he is working for.

2. Evaluation stimulates the child to ask questions that he feels are significant to him.

3. Evaluation makes possible the formulation of progressively higher objectives that are appropriate to the individual's present status and potentiality.

4. Evaluation helps the pupil to focus on growth rather than end-of-activity status.

Parent-Teacher Conferences Because the home and family constitute the greatest part of a child's psychological environment, bringing the school and parents together is good procedure, quite apart from evaluation (Ilioff, 1957). Three major advantages accrue. First, preparing for the conference helps the teacher obtain a better understanding of the human material with which he is working. Second, parents can come to a better appreciation of what teachers are attempting to do. Third, the pupil will profit from the positive view that the teacher is encouraged to take; that is, knowing that effective conferences start with remarks about favorable characteristics, the teacher looks more searchingly for the pupil's good points. Finally, there is the possibility that the teacher or the parent has perceived some attitude or pattern of behavior overlooked by the other that can be helpful; e.g., one of them knows that praise causes Craig to "rest on his oars" or that criticism causes Vicki to quit entirely.

It has been mentioned frequently that learning should be specific and that goals should be definite. Hence, it is advantageous for the teacher to take notes in a teacher-parent conference. The parent may be given a copy so that suggestions can be readily remembered and put into operation. In addition, written notes mitigate the disappointment at not having the customary report card. Some teachers use a prepared form for recording pertinent items in the interview.

Bringing parents and teachers together results in a type of evaluation that fosters vigorous child growth. Some feel that parent-teacher-pupil conferences would be a further improvement. There are, however, inherent shortcomings to the conference plan that makes the search for still better methods necessary. It is, of necessity, time-consuming. Unless conferences are a part of the regular teaching load, they impose too heavy a burden on teachers. Moreover, many parents are unwilling to give their time or find in the conference an opportunity to vent their resentments toward the child or the school. Conferences are not particularly advantageous unless the teacher has the child for all-day sessions. This limits its use in high school and in departmentalized systems in grade school.

Although research evidence is lacking that a way for reporting has been found, Rothney (1955, p. 30) asserts that it is common sense to share responsibilities. Despite the limitations and personal disadvantages, teachers who have experimented with the conference plan are enthusiastic. They feel that the increased motivation of the pupil and the greater understanding they have of him repays them many times for the effort involved. Said one such teacher, "It takes a lot of time; but it is time that pays dividends. The increased ability of pupils to accept the school and its challenges would be sufficient justification for its continued use. But, most of all, I now feel that the time previously spent in assigning marks was more than wasted. It hurt many of my pupils."

The essentials of evaluation

The Definition of Goals   The first step in evaluating teaching and learning is to define the purposes of instruction (Baron and Bernard, 1958,

p. 239). It is necessary to see these broad objectives *in terms of the particular pupil* one is teaching. For example, the objective of citizenship might include such subgoals as being responsible for school property, keeping the school grounds and classroom clean, executing assigned responsibilities, participating in group activities, observing rules and regulations, and voicing one's opinion in group discussion. Such considerations are known as the behavioral goals of education (French, 1957, pp. 58ff). The behavioral objectives of citizenship and other objectives of education depend on the maturity of the pupils being evaluated.

Because learning takes place in a wide context, it is advisable that many persons be involved in the process of formulating objectives. In some instances, those concerned have sat together in committee to formulate the statements of specific purposes. In some instances, the teacher has worked with pupils in such formulation. If pupils are not invited to define objectives, at least they should be allowed to discuss and modify them. Whatever the technique used in formulation, the following tests should be applied to the statements in order that they may be productive of good learning and helpful evaluation:

1. Can the pupil understand the statement of the goal? This can be easily determined by having pupils tell what the statement means to them.

2. Can the goal be stated in terms of pupil behavior? The objective should be to accomplish some desirable change in the actions of pupils.

3. Is the goal related to the needs of the pupil? If the objective does not have meaning for the individual, the result is likely to be learning only at the low level of memorization and verbalization.

4. Can the goal be achieved by the pupil? This suggests the need for *constant evaluation* to meet present level of ability.

5. Is it possible to devise techniques for evaluating progress toward the goal? Unless this can be answered affirmatively, the resulting evaluation will be vague.

6. Does the goal have both present and future reference for the pupil? This criterion will help in deciding which school activities are most desirable and least desirable. This is important in a society where the schools are called upon to perform more and more functions.

Behavioral Goals It has been indicated that translating broad objectives into behavioral goals is an important step in sound evaluation. It is felt that too often in the past goals were somewhat idealistically or even unrealistically stated. In order to make them meaningful and place them in a category where they can be evaluated, it is helpful to state them in terms of behavior. Thus in one study in which an objective was to promote the ability to do logical thinking, the aim of thinking was in part stated by the following:

a. Disposition to examine the logical structure of the arguments and to apply principles of logical reasoning to the study of these arguments.

b. Ability to distinguish between conclusions which do and ones which do not follow logically from a given set of assumptions.

c. Ability to isolate the significant elements in the logical structure of an argument as shown by distinguishing between statements of ideas which are relevant and statements of ideas which are irrelevant for explaining why a conclusion follows logically from given assumptions.[6]

The relationship between a broad objective of education and the description of behavior is illustrated by the Educational Policies Commission of the National Education Association. This committee stated four objectives: (1) the objectives of self-realization, (2) the objectives of human relationship, (3) the objectives of economic efficiency, and (4) the objectives of civic responsibility. Each of these is described in terms of several types of behavior—illustrative of which is the breakdown of the fourth:

The objectives of civic responsibilty:
The educated citizen
—is sensitive to the disparities of human circumstances.
—acts to correct unsatisfactory conditions.
—seeks to understand social structures.
—has defenses against propaganda.
—measures a scientific advance by its contribution to the general welfare.
—is a cooperating member of the world community.
—respects the law.
—is economically literate.
—accepts his civic duties.
—acts upon an unswerving loyalty to democratic ideals.[7]

Examination of the objectives listed above should reveal the need for continuity and specificity in the evaluation process. A step forward would be for each teacher to ask such questions as the following:

To which general objectives could and should the subject I am working with be primarily directed?

What specific behaviors (attitudes, habits, knowledges, ideals, etc.) should this subject contribute to the general objectives?

[6] Eugene R. Smith, Ralph W. Tyler, and the Evaluation Staff of the Commission on the Relation of School and College, *Adventure in American Education*, vol. 3, *Appraising and Recording Student Progress*, New York: Harper & Row, Publishers, 1942, p. 113.
[7] Educational Policies Commission, *The Purposes of Education in American Democracy*, Washington: National Education Association, 1938, p. 108.

What class and pupil activities will be likely to illustrate or indicate the behavior changes sought?

What teaching methods and teaching aids can contribute to an understanding of the objective on the part of the pupils?

What devices for evaluation will be most likely to help me and my pupils see the extent to which objectives are being realized?

The Instruments and Approaches Essential to an Evaluation Program

If our knowledge of educational psychology is brought to bear on evaluative processes, it must first be recognized that neither a single instrument nor a single symbol can suffice. Because the many instruments and approaches to evaluation have been mentioned in various places throughout the text, only a brief summary will be made here of the multiple approaches to comprehensive evaluation.

1. Teachers, together with their pupils and other teachers, should examine the broad statements of education to see which are particularly pertinent in the present situation.

2. Teachers, together with their pupils and other teachers, should translate the broad objectives into definable and achievable behaviors.

3. Intelligence tests should be used to give an indication of the pupil's present level of mental development and should be used to supplement other data in determining a profitable starting point for classroom procedures.

4. Standardized achievement tests should be used so that one has objective information regarding the pupil's growth in specific subject areas over a given period of time.

5. Diagnostic tests should be used to narrow the range of search for a specific area of difficulty for individual pupils.

6. Personality inventories should be used as clues to pertinent questions. Inventories may disclose felt difficulties that pupils are unable to express orally.

7. Case studies should be used for pupils who are manifesting unusual difficulties of adjustment.

8. Interviews should always be used in interpreting such data as are listed. *How the child feels* is no less important than the conditions that surround and impinge upon him.

9. Anecdotal records are valuable in describing behavior that is difficult to evaluate by means of test scores or case-study data. The anecdotal record is a picture of the child in his typical mood and action.

10. Sociometry provides a means of evaluating interpersonal relations and gives clues to the grouping of pupils that will lead to more harmonious social relations and to social growth.

11. Home visits by the teacher have the double advantage of helping the teacher see the child in terms of his environment and helping parents

arrive at a more objective evaluation of the school. Both have inherent value for the pupil.

12. Letters sent to the home by the teacher tend to get away from the stereotype of traditional report cards. Letters necessarily give attention to individual differences.

13. Teacher-made tests have their place in a comprehensive evaluation program. Such tests can be made to fit short units of study or brief periods of school. They can be made to fit the particular objectives that are dictated by the local situation.

14. Pupil diaries or logs can serve as a means of keeping the pupil informed of his progress. Teachers need but to indicate the items that are of educational significance. Diaries will help pupils become aware of the importance of radio listening, reading, informal visits, and leisure-time activities.

15. Rating scales and questionnaires can be used to supplement other bases for evaluation, such as personality inventories, objective test data, and anecdotal records. Rating scales that ask the pupil to evaluate himself are of special value. The scales help him look to the future rather than simply emphasizing his past and present status.

16. Cumulative records that summarize all the above data or contain representative samples of the pupil's work should be regarded as essential instruments of the evaluation program (Prescott, 1957, p. 427). Care must be taken so that material is not allowed to accumulate. Test results should be recorded in appropriate places and dates noted. Periodically, the material should be examined to see whether it contributes to an understanding of the child. If not, it should be destroyed. Too thick a folder discourages the teacher's use of it.

Emphasis on the Total Program   It has been emphasized throughout this book that the child as a learner has emotions, physical characteristics, and social relationships that influence the acquisition of intellectual information. The pupil cannot be separated from his home and family and community influences. Much of the recent progress in the field of educational psychology has resulted from recognition of this integrated wholeness of the pupil. Hence, the emphasis in evaluation must be upon the entire program of education (Horst, 1963). Evaluation is a *continuing* aspect of the learning process, and it involves the use of *all* the instruments available. If evaluation is made on the basis of one or two instruments, the result is likely to be grading rather than evaluation. An aim of educational psychology is to understand learners so well that better conditions for total growth may be obtained. The purpose of evaluation is to make specific some precise steps in further and continuing development.

Teachers should include themselves in the evaluative process. Some of this can be self-evaluation, using criteria selected or derived from professional reading. Some of it should be done by supervisors and principals, whose job is made easier and more effective if teachers express interest in their evaluation. It was shown in the chapter on habits (Chapter 5) that even the patterns of behavior that we consider rigid do change. Evaluation by self or others helps that change to become directed instead of drifting. Teachers should use evaluation throughout their entire careers to determine where they are weak and how they can improve. Evaluation gives them an incentive to continued professional and personal development; only through such continuous growth can teachers make their maximum contribution to the growth of children.

Summary

One of the more perplexing problems of formal education is that of pupil evaluation. The difficulty probably derives from the fact that evaluation is such an important aspect of so many phases of education. Not only are many items—together with complex interrelationships—to be considered in evaluation, but there are also widely varying purposes to be served.

Grading is still widely used, but there is much justifiable dissatisfaction with the attempt to reduce so much to a single letter or number. This is particularly true at the elementary level, where universal education brings such a diverse population together. Even at the professional level (e.g., prospective teachers or doctors), it is doubtful that grades are truly indicative of the global aspects of assessment.

Observations and interviews are at the high end of the scale in personality assessment. Tests and questionnaires are held in low esteem and must, for the most part, be used as points of orientation for further study and as supplementary and corroborative evidence.

In evaluating school progress, the psychologically sound system involves the use and interpretation of standardized test data. Evaluation should be an ongoing and essential aspect of the educative process—not just an end-of-period signing off. It should involve talking with pupils about specific aspects of learning activities. Because parents are important partners in the educational enterprise, teacher-pupil-parent conferences are growing in use and in esteem. With such conferences, grades of the conventional type may be used, but they are frequently discarded. Standardized tests are useful in providing objective data, but grades should not depend on their results.

Effective evaluation depends on the precise statement of goals, which can then be translated into behavioral objectives. These goals can then be accurately and meaningfully discussed in teacher-pupil and teacher-pupil-parent conferences.

Problems and exercises

1 Show specifically a number of ways in which basic tenets of educational psychology are involved in evaluation.

2 It is claimed that we are graded in our vocational activities. Is this true, or are we evaluated?

3 Let it be assumed that evaluation requires subjectivity on the part of the teacher. Would this be an argument against evaluation?

4 What are some of the more obvious errors the beginning teacher is likely to make as an interviewer?

5 Make a list of five or six things the teacher should look for while observing a pupil. Compare your list with that of other students and expand your list to include the best items.

6 Make a list of five precautions that must be observed in interpreting and using results from standardized tests.

7 What are the advantages and disadvantages of students' knowing their scores on an intelligence test? Would you favor telling pupils (or parents) what the score is?

8 Reflect on some conference you have had with a professor. Did that conference or the grade received in his course have more meaning to you as evaluation?

9 Make a list of goals and types of behavior that might well form objectives for evaluation in primary grades. Do the same for some subject that is commonly taught in high school.

10 Try to find a member of the class in educational psychology who can observe some teacher-pupil conferences. Ask for a description of what went on and how he rates it in terms of educational soundness.

11 What program of evaluation would you like to see your school adopt as the one most likely to promote pupil growth?

Suggested additional readings

Ahmann, J. S., and M. D. Glock: *Evaluating Pupil Growth*, Boston, Mass.: Allyn and Bacon, Inc., 1959.
   Chapter 17 contains a discussion of the many-sided approach that must be made to meaningful evaluation. Cooperative action is emphasized.

American Personnel and Guidance Association, *The Use of Multifactor Tests in Guidance*, Washington: No date. (A reprint series.)
   This collection of articles describes the uses, values, and limitations of intelligence tests that attempt to assess the various components (abstract, social, mathematical, linguistic, etc.) of intelligence. Inasmuch as some people have thought of intelligence as being some one thing, this booklet can serve to emphasize the complexity of evaluation.

Remmers, H. H., N. L. Gage, and J. F. Rummel: *A Practical Introduction to Measurement and Evaluation*, New York: Harper & Row, Publishers, 1960, pp. 265–281.
   This chapter describes the use and collation of test results into grades. The authors indicate shortcomings of grades and discuss precautions in their use.

Ricks, James H., Jr.: *On Telling Parents about Test Results,* Test Service Bulletin, no. 54, The Psychological Corporation, New York, December, 1959.
One of the many excellent pamphlets dealing with tests and their interpretation that may be obtained free from the organization. It gives specific and practical suggestions for explaining test scores to parents.

Rothney, John W. M.: *Evaluating and Reporting Pupil Progress,* What Research Says to the Teacher, no. 7, Washington: National Education Association, 1955.
This how-to-do-it booklet is based on research, and the recommendations are in terms of what is now taking place in some schools. Personality assessment, objectives, contacts with people, and the need for better evaluation are all considered.

Tyler, Leona E.: *Tests and Measurements,* Englewood Cliffs, N.J.: Prentice-Hall, Inc., 1963.
This paperback in the Foundations of Modern Psychology Series deals with some of the basic statistics involved in test making, selection, scoring, and interpretation. Intelligence tests, special ability tests, and personality assessment are also discussed.

Teacher Personality as a Factor in Learning

21

There is much truth in the statement: As the teacher, so is the school. Numerous experimental and observational studies confirm the fact that pupils learn what a teacher is as well as what he says. Pupils absorb his attitudes, they reflect his moods, they share his convictions, they imitate his behavior, and they quote his statements. The best buildings, the finest equipment, the soundest curriculum, and the most carefully written texts do not overshadow the importance of the teacher. Experience attests to the fact that such problems as motivation, discipline, social behavior, pupil achievement, and above all, the continuing thirst for knowledge all center around the personality of the teacher.

Personality is all that a person is and might be—it includes knowledge, skills, ideals, and attitudes, as well as the perceptions he has of other people. It is with these qualities, rather than personal appearance, that this chapter deals. Attention is directed to you as learner and teacher because in the helping professions the person who performs the service is important. Well prepared as some of you may already be, the dynamics of growth demand attention to the future, and this chapter contains suggestions for developing personal goals. It has been said that the prime requisite for the nation's mental health is a corps of properly trained and personally adequate teachers. Here we hope to take a small step in the indicated direction.

The role of the teacher in pupil behavior

Influence of Teacher Personality Mr. A., a sixth-grade teacher, was just under six feet tall, quite thin, had a large nose, and smiled easily but not effusively. He dressed neatly but informally. He exercised his sense of humor by telling jokes and laughing with his pupils. He spoke correctly and distinctly in a voice that was somewhat high-pitched for a man.

Alex, his largest and brightest pupil, was told three times within an hour to stop eating candy wafers—at the end of the period, there was a wafer in his mouth. There was some confusion in the room—pupils were moving about, jostling and giggling, but others were seriously engaged in work. Mr. A. worked with those who wanted to work and sought ways to stimulate the laggards. At recess, most of the pupils went outside in a somewhat orderly manner, but one girl insisted that she wanted to stay with Mr. A. She was urged to go out, but she insisted that she had some problems she wanted to talk over, so she stayed.

When the principal was asked why Mr. A. was so "easy" on pupils, he replied, "Easy? He's very effective with pupils over a period of time." The girl who stayed in was under the care of a psychiatrist. Another teacher had asked to be relieved of responsibility for her. The disobedient wafer chewer was accepted, and later tests showed that his achievement was appropriately high. Subsequent visits to this classroom showed a great improvement in orderly behavior, with most pupils seriously engaged in work.

Mr. A. was effective because of what he was and what he did. He liked children. *He genuinely accepted them as they were.* He expressed his appreciation of the attentive workers. He recognized that the emotionally disturbed "clinging-vine" girl needed support. He voluntarily spent Saturday mornings coaching a peewee baseball team. He transported the youngsters to ball games, movies, the dairy, and the art museum in his own car (some of the riders chose to ride with him rather than with their fathers). At the end of the year, the wafer eater had satisfied his appetite and was a staunch defender of Mr. A. and his excellence as a teacher; the girl's emotional condition had improved; and the hard workers continued to be diligent.

Mr. D., a high school teacher, presented a sharp contrast, but he too was effective in his own way. He was a stocky, red-faced, heavily bearded, sparse-haired athlete. His movements were quick, and his jaw was prominent and tight. He smiled rarely, talked rapidly, and barked orders like the proverbial sergeant. In fairness to him, it must be said that he was employed after the pupils had laughed another teacher out of the school in the first two weeks. No one laughed at or with Mr. D. When he spoke, pupils listened. Pupils were to be seen and not heard—even if they had a question. They studied algebra and general science earnestly. It is possible that some learned to like these subjects because they acquired some competence in them. But most of the pupils learned also to dislike Mr. D., and a junior who had a good bit of prestige as an up-and-coming middleweight at the time showed particular animosity. There was considerable verbal sparring, and pupils were relieved when it was announced that Mr. D. would continue his study of law the following year. Getting subject matter across is not always good teaching.

Mrs. Doe has a great zest for life. She is continually on the go. In addition to a busy social life, she is interested in art, music, drama, and politics. While she does not seem to be much concerned about clothes, she always appears to be neat and she keeps her iron-gray hair in a severe style. She has firm opinions about most subjects and will defend them vigorously with other adults; she tolerates no criticism of her pupils, always finding reasons, and sound ones, for interpreting misbehavior in an understanding manner.

Mrs. Doe's classroom conduct accords with her personality. Her room is virtually a three-ring circus, with something going on in every corner. Whether she is teaching the second grade, the fifth, or the eighth, it is the same story—except for content. Being truly creative, she finds ways to incorporate drawing, painting, drama, music, and dance into the various disciplines of arithmetic, writing, history, and geography. She listens to and respects the opinions of her pupils. Not all students respond with the same degree of enthusiasm; some appear to be confused by the variety of activities, and while they work diligently at the academic tasks, they do not participate in all activities. Most, however, are productive, and their pictures, poems, and science projects are frequently so outstanding that they well deserve the publicity that Mrs. Doe gets for them outside the classroom. A lad who had been a persistent problem to previous teachers was observed to be well on the way to finding himself. In Mrs. Doe's room, he was achieving at the level that was indicated by aptitude tests.

Miss R. was hardly ever observed in conversation with other teachers; she rarely found occasion to come to the principal's office. Her whole life appeared to center around school and her pupils. Achievement test data showed that her pupils consistently ranked above those in other sixth grades. Miss R. is with her pupils all the time. She takes no coffee break, she accompanies students to the playground, keeps them in the room for the lunch hour, though others in the school eat together in the cafeteria. If she has discipline problems, no one hears about them. Achievement-wise, there could be no criticism of her work. But one wonders about the development of the whole child. What is happening to his thrust for independence? Why is so little creativeness shown in writing, art, and student leadership? It must be concluded that a mother-hen personality in a teacher is not conducive to the development of the independence that is so much needed to get along in life.

Fortunately for the child and society, pupils meet many teachers in the course of formal education. Psychology teaches that pain is more readily forgotten than pleasure. Perhaps the errors made by some teachers will be erased by the next; or perhaps the strengths of one teacher will protect a child from the weakness of another. In addition, there is evidence that what makes one teacher good for certain pupils is the very thing that makes him less valuable for others; therefore, there is no one best teacher personality. The task for educational psychology is to diminish the obvious weakness by helping teachers in self-analysis and enabling them to offer effective instruction and wise supervision. Because the needs of pupils differ, *there should be no attempt to cast all teachers in the same mold.* The assumption here is the same as that underlying all education: "If you give a person the facts, then he will be in a much better position to think rationally and act reasonably about the situation to which the facts are related." [1]

Studies of Teacher Personality and Pupil Behavior All over the country, the attitudes, adjustments, and behavior of pupils are being influenced by the behavior, skills, methods, and attitudes of teachers. Children and adolescents who have experienced difficulty at home and in school have revealed improved ability to adjust when they encountered teachers who were capable of giving them responsibility (H. H. Anderson, 1959, p. 34). Boynton and his associates found, from a study of 70 teachers and over 1,000 fifth and sixth graders, that children begin to be affected by the characteristics of teachers in periods as short as two months. The pupils who had stable teachers showed markedly good mental health and emotional security; while those with tense and unstable teachers revealed poor mental health and instability on every measure (Boynton, Dugger, and Turner, 1934). It was found in New York City that the substantial differences in pupils' learning to read must be attributed to the effectiveness of teachers rather than to pupil differences in ability and previous experiences (Mitzel and Medley, 1956). Bassett compared three teachers, each of whom had about fifty-five pupils, and found marked differences in the incidence of reported misbehavior. Some teachers regularly had more disobedient, untruthful, discourteous, and disorderly behavior than others. This was attributed in part to the different ways in which each teacher viewed her pupils, but it was also concluded that many of the differences must be due to the different atmospheres created by the teachers themselves. (C. Bassett, 1931).

In a review of research on the causes of various kinds of discrimination and its reduction, Grambs (1960) found that teachers play a critical role. Without intending to do so, they often favor one group over another; for example, repeated studies show that more boys than girls receive failing grades. Because pupils reflect the attitudes of adults, teachers must be objective about the generalizations, clichés, and attitudes that enter into the total teaching situation. If schools are to be a place where differences are accepted and hostility and discrimination minimized, then *teachers must be informed and able to practice acceptance of all pupils, despite their differences in race, religion, color, and behavior.*

[1] Harry Milt, "The Outlook for Mental Health Education," *Mental Hygiene,* 46: 38, 1962.

One study—rare because of its long duration—provides a most significant example of the effect of teacher personality on pupil behavior. Fairbank (1933) found that a group of schoolchildren whose potentialities for adjustment had been very low revealed extremely satisfactory adjustment after a period of seventeen years. She attributed the fine records these students had in adult life mainly to their teachers—teachers who believed in their task and had faith in the "improvability" of their pupils.

What pupils learn, whether academic knowledge, social behavior, or personality traits, is a matter of slow accumulation. The effects of one teacher may be canceled by another, but there are at least temporary effects. In many cases, the impact of teacher personality persists for years. Fears, attitudes, ideals, and ambitions have been taught by and learned from teachers. The fact that a whole class does not respond in the same manner does not mean that individuals are not being affected. It has been frequently said that child behavior reflects parental handling. When we consider the number of waking hours the child spends with teachers, it can safely be remarked that *pupil behavior reflects teacher personality.* Let us examine some of the psychological explanations for this phenomenon.

The Dynamics of Teacher-Pupil Interaction   Pupil behavior reflects teacher behavior in many ways: Imitation, rejection of the role, and defenses against the teacher's attitude and action are most noticeable. Acting like the teacher is not simply a matter of modeling oneself after an ideal; it is also a matter of identifying with the teacher so that one perceives situations in the same manner. The imitation may be of specific mannerisms, modes of speech, or attitudes, but it is an *outcome of identification* (Peck, 1950, p. 147). We readily think of rejection of the role as determination never to be a teacher, but it goes further than that. It would be fortunate if pupils did reject authoritarianism, discourtesy, and intolerance, but these are not automatically replaced with positive models. The rejection may go so far as to stimulate repudiation of one's sex role or the pursuit of further education. Thus, in a study of dropouts, the central theme was to establish friendly relations between the pupil and his teachers and counselors (D. A. Davis, 1962). It is not surprising that humans should go to great lengths to avoid anxiety, insecurity, and lack of status in view of the great discomfort that these entail (Lindgren, 1959, p. 94).

Among the recent developments in the psychology of learning is an appreciation of the fact that *learning takes place within a total context that is more than the mere sum of the parts.* "There are specific content and skills to be learned which add to the store of competence; there are also the pervasive qualitative aspects of the learning situation which affect the self-feeling, the images of authority, the delineation of psychological planes of safety and adventure. These inevitably affect each other. [2] In addition to recognizing the role of the teacher as an important focus in the total learning situation, recent emphases stress the neglected and positive drives, which include curiosity, manipulation, activity, and achievement, rather than the negative drives from which escape is sought (Sears and Hilgard, 1964). It is well within the power of the teacher to learn to use these positive motives.

As the result of working with hundreds of teachers in their own schools, attempting to teach them the dynamics of teacher-pupil interaction, it can be stated that teachers make numerous daily decisions that constitute the fundamental bases of the educative process.

> These accumulating decisions create the conditions under which the pupils live and learn at school. For example, they determine the freedom or restriction of movement, of speech, of access to materials, of spontaneous inquiries or comments, of choice of experiences. They profoundly influence the kinds of relationships the children are able to establish and maintain with adults in the school and with each other in the classroom, on the playground, and everywhere about the school. These decisions often determine the actual learning experiences to which the children are exposed, the content upon which attention is focused, and the food for mental, social and spiritual growth that is offered each child. . . . They promote certain codes of conduct and imply the validity of certain attitudes and values for living in our times and in our society.[3]

Behavior Problems and Teacher Personality Articles appear frequently in magazines and newspapers about the state of discipline in the school —some assert that it is too lax and contributes to delinquency, while others say it is repressive and curbs creativity ("Ten Criticisms of Public Education, 1957). Most psychologists seem to agree that *methods of discipline must vary with the teacher and the individual pupils concerned.* A few pupils may temporarily need the security of rigid control. Others are restive under such a regime. The usual result of dictatorial control is that pupils ultimately break the boundaries and get into trouble. Their accumulated resentment may cause them to break windows, write on toilet-room walls, or deface books and materials. One supervisor summarized this problem by saying, "I think I can tell pretty accurately the kind of· teachers there are in a school by the number of windows we have to replace annually."

[2] Barbara Biber, Elizabeth Gilkeson, and Charlotte Winsor, "Teacher Education at Bank Street College," *Personnel and Guidance Journal,* 37: 550–568, April, 1959.
[3] Daniel A. Prescott, *The Child in the Educative Process,* New York: McGraw-Hill Book Company, 1957, pp. 6–7.

Some teachers, by virtue of their patience and understanding, motivate pupils constructively. In such a group, most of the pupils are working close to their capacity. Knowing and understanding pupils leads to acceptance of them. This, in turn, enables the teacher to give praise when it is appropriate or to prod when necessary. As for the child, acceptance stimulates him to concerted efforts. Rejection prompts the pupil to "leave the field." The teacher's range of knowledge and interests is also important in motivation. Knowing what book to recommend, to whom, and when is helpful. Knowing something about pupils' interests—horses, photography, philately, and popular music, for example—provides points of contact. Knowing when to admit ignorance (most easily done when one possesses a fundamental sense of security) is important, and the admission is sometimes stimulating. Pupils then feel that teacher and pupils are learners together; thus learning is stimulated by cooperation.

Similar relationships can be indicated for such problems as social adjustment of pupils. Teachers set the pattern. Pupil self-confidence is stimulated by teachers who have confidence in themselves and in their pupils. The influence of teacher personality on pupil behavior is a heavy professional responsibility, but it is also a rich opportunity for personal growth and development.

Characteristics of effective teachers

Variable Criteria of Teacher Effectiveness Your own initial impressions of different people and those with whom you ultimately form friendships indicate that the effectiveness of a person is in part dependent upon others' perceptions of him. A teacher does not impress school administrators and pupils in the same way. Teachers may have many combinations of personal qualities, and what appeals to one student and is effective provokes a negative response on the part of other students (F. P. Robinson, 1961). It is also obvious that teachers who are effective at one level may not be similarly effective at another because primary, elementary, and secondary pupils are at different stages in their mental and emotional development.

It is gratifying to see a young and beautiful teacher who was recently a campus queen or fraternity sweetheart. She welcomes the young misses and young men who flock around her to talk and ask questions. She is levelheaded, professionally well prepared, and an energetic worker. Most of the youngsters openly assert that she is wonderful. Her roommate and fellow teacher presents a marked contrast. She dresses well, is sincere, and is also well trained for her job. But she is somewhat shy and is not at all colorful. She does wear well, though it is difficult to become acquainted with her. This teacher has so-called "warm, friendly relations" with only a few pupils. But these pupils are not part of the throng that clusters about the former Miss Blankville. They are pupils who find in the quiet, reserved teacher a kindred spirit and a great stimulus for personal security. Without this teacher, these pupils would receive no help from an understanding adult. Each teacher has an important part to play in the balanced functioning of the school, and it is a real one.

The moral of this example is that you need not try to assume the personality traits of some other teacher in order to be effective. You need not attempt to develop all the characteristics named in any particular list. Pupils have different reactions to the same teacher-behavior pattern (Anderson and Hunka, 1963). There are, however, characteristics that can serve as a guide to personal improvement, some of which will be mentioned in the following paragraphs. The main point is that each teacher in his own unique way can contribute to the growth of pupils by being his own best self.

Criteria Stated for the U.S. Office of Education Rummell (1948) collected material on effective teachers by traveling throughout the country and talking with local teachers who had outstanding reputations. The teachers finally cited were called "distinguished examples of the best professional talent." The resulting descriptions may be summarized by five generalizations:

1. The best teachers are professionally alert. They do not live their lives in the tight confines of the classroom. They are attempting to make the community and the school better places for young people.

2. They are convinced of the worth of their job. Their ambition is to improve constantly in the work to which they have dedicated themselves.

3. They seem not to be irritated by the taboos on personal liberties that are said by some to characterize the teaching profession. Apparently they are so psychologically mature that the irritations are viewed as minor in comparison with their great opportunity.

4. They have an artistry in human relations that stems from observing the workings of psychology, biology, and cultural anthropology in the classroom.

5. They are humble about their own need for growth because they realize the magnitude of their responsibility. "They are poignantly aware that under their influence this raw material (human resources) may also change its very destiny."

This set of criteria makes two things clear. First, purpose, or motivation, is a basic feature of all behavior; *good teachers see their goals and work clearly and with conviction.* Second, coming back to the idea that teaching is the direction of learning, teachers should exemplify the learning habit; *good teachers give planned attention and effort to their own continuous growth through learning.*

Wisconsin Studies of Teacher Effectiveness Studies of effective teachers are made and reported periodically in education literature. There are some who object to trait-oriented and statistical approaches. They claim that good teachers or other workers in personnel fields are not identified by manipulating the console of an IBM machine (Jennings, 1962). We can readily agree that possession of many identified traits would not guarantee good teaching; we can also agree that some historically great teachers might have had very few of the identified traits. Nevertheless, until better approaches are found, the trait approach has value in setting goals. The desirable traits can be used by teachers in assessing their own merits and shortcomings.

Professional teacher educators in Wisconsin reviewed and analyzed many studies of teacher effectiveness. It was found that the following characteristics appeared over and over in various phraseology in the reports studied (Barr, 1961):

1. *Buoyancy*	7. *Verbal fluency*	12. *Objectivity*
2. *Considerateness*	8. *Flexibility*	13. *Personal magnetism*
3. *Cooperativeness*	9. *Forcefulness*	14. *Physical energy and*
4. *Dependability*	10. *Judgment*	*drive*
5. *Emotional stability*	11. *Mental alertness*	15. *Scholarliness*
6. *Ethicalness*		

American Council on Education Studies The Commission on Teacher Education of the American Council on Education published a report on effective teachers in 1944. It was pointed out that good teachers always vary in their combinations of traits; but that listed characteristics do indicate what teachers should strive for in terms of national well-being. Another study was completed in 1960, and it was again pointed out that "the qualities of good teachers are not absolute; they are, instead, interacting traits that vary in their merits, depending upon educational philosophy, pupil characteristics, course level and content, and other factors" (Ryans, 1960, p. vii). With full recognition that good teachers can more readily be recognized than described, the following characteristics are listed for women teachers in the elementary grades:

> Frequently give as reason for teaching, liking for children and interest in their development
> Express admiration of such qualities as friendliness, permissiveness, definiteness, and fairness in teachers
> Dislike in teachers such qualities as arrogance, intolerance, sarcasm, and partiality
> Typically appear to be "accepting" and generous in appraisals of other persons. See good points of a person rather than bad
> Express satisfaction with teaching (and also with teacher salaries); intend to continue teaching indefinitely

Frequently engaged in teaching activity as child (e.g., taking charge of class in absence of teacher)

Decision to become teacher frequently was made prior to college enrollment; had planned to be a teacher from relatively early age

Enjoyed school when they were students themselves

Showed superior accomplishment when in school

Report large number of teachers among parents and relatives

Report participation in religious activities

Enjoy activities with friends, but prefer small groups

Frequently are members and officers of clubs

Are married (85 per cent of group)

Interested and active in literary affairs (e.g., write poetry, have published books, etc.)

More emotionally stable than average adult (Guilford-Zimmerman)

More friendly than average adult (Guilford-Zimmerman)

More cooperative and agreeable than average adult (Guilford-Zimmerman)

More restrained than average adult (Guilford-Zimmerman)

More objective than average adult (Guilford-Zimmerman)

More tolerant than average adult (California Psychological Inventory)

More inclined to "try to give a good impression" than average adult (California Psychological Inventory)

More interested in social service than average adult (Kuder Preference Record)

Less interested than average adult in computational and clerical activities (Kuder Preference Record).[4]

Many of the above qualities point to the importance of the emotional climate in which learning takes place. Research studies show that pervasive parental attitudes and the overall atmosphere of the home, rather than specific training practices, count most in optimum child development (Bernard, 1962, p. 366). Study of the criteria of teachers point to a similar conclusion: *The emotional climate for learning is more important than the specific teaching procedures adopted.*

The Pupils' Viewpoints: Best-liked Teachers The ultimate criterion for teacher effectiveness is the teacher's impact upon pupils' learning. Being a pupil gives one an excellent vantage point in judging the qualities that make an effective teacher. Regardless of what parents think constitutes good teaching or what qualities administrators seek when they hire, the youngster is the final judge. If the objectives of education are to be realized, pupils should for some reason like learning, and teachers are

[4] David G. Ryans, *Characteristics of Teachers: A Research Study*, Washington: American Council on Education, 1960, pp. 365–366. The titles in parentheses for the last nine items refer to personality and interest inventories.

an important conditioning factor. To the degree that a pupil learns to dislike hard work, books, school, and the teacher, the enterprise of education must be considered a failure.

Pupils in the first to eighth grade wrote 14,000 letters about "The Teacher Who Helped Me Most." The letters were analyzed (Witty, 1950), and the following traits were mentioned in order of frequency:

1. Good teachers have a democratic and cooperative attitude.
2. They are kindly toward and considerate of individuals.
3. They are patient.
4. Their interests are varied.
5. They are pleasing in appearance and manner.
6. They are fair and impartial.
7. They have a sense of humor.
8. They are consistent in behavior and have good dispositions.
9. They take an interest in pupils' problems.
10. They are open-minded and flexible.
11. They make use of recognition and praise.
12. They are unusually capable in their subjects.

Despite differences in ages, high school seniors have quite similar perceptions of the teachers they like and from whom they can learn best (Hart, 1934, pp. 131ff). Their ten most desirable characteristics in teachers were:

1. Is helpful in schoolwork
2. Is cheerful and good humored
3. Is companionable
4. Is interested in and understands pupils
5. Stimulates interest
6. Has control of the class (Ultraprogressives, please note)
7. Is impartial
8. Avoids sarcasm and nagging
9. Is businesslike
10. Has a pleasing personality

Other studies from different grade levels show somewhat different listings; but all the traits indicated in the two lists above appear among the first twenty-five in all the lists. It should also be noted that the lists are very similar to those prepared by teacher educators. To you, the import of these lists is that many of the traits are susceptible to improvement with conscious effort and continuous attention.

National Teacher of the Year The U.S. Office of Education, the Council of Chief State School Officers, and *Look* magazine joined to make a National Teacher of the Year award. Teachers were nominated by state department of education officials, and the nominees were observed and rated by national leaders of education. Mrs. Marjorie French, of Topeka High School, Kansas, won the award in 1962. Mrs. French provides proof that such qualities as those listed in the foregoing sections are valued by pupils as well as by adults. She is buoyant, can communicate clearly, and is constantly on the search for new knowledge. At an early age she wanted to teach and played at teaching; she was elected to a national honorary society while she was in college. She is active in school and community affairs. She feels that teaching is an exciting way of life and is rewarded when she sees a student get "that sudden look" of comprehension.

Students appear early at Mrs. French's classes because they do not want to miss anything. Her pupils call her the best teacher they have ever had, as is attested to in the following evaluations:

> She understands kids and gets ideas over at our level, whether we are sophomores or seniors.
>
> She's the most intelligent, most understanding and most varied person that I have ever known.
>
> She's the finest teacher I ever had. We work very hard in her classes, but it's never drudgery.
>
> She has convinced me and many other kids that teaching is a wonderful life's work.[5]

The Criterion of Growth The philosophical tenet that one cannot stand still—he either grows or regresses—is confirmed by psychologists. Those who actively study do not so consistently suffer the mental decline that is characteristic of the average individual after the middle years. Studies of aging and senility indicate that the person who maintains physical and intellectual activity tends to live longer. The goal of adding years to one's life has been changed to the goal of adding life to one's years. Frailty of body and mind is not an entirely inevitable part of later life. Atrophy of body and mind can be retarded by physical care, mental activity, and emotional participation (Tibbitts and Donahue, 1957). It is perhaps too early to impress you with the import of these findings. But the implication is that you are now forming the intellectual, emotional, and physical habits that will condition both your present and your future. In listing traits of well-liked teachers, pupils have provided a stimulus: They value the teacher who himself has the habit of continuous growth.

Excellence in teaching is not inherent—teachers may be born, but they are also made. Competence in teaching is not a gift from your professors, nor is it a revelation from a textbook. It is the result of a clear goal that you, the future teacher, can help to set (Bryan, 1962). It is the outcome of many hours of work, more hours of reflection, many irritating failures,

[5] "Marjorie French: Teacher of the Year," *Look*, 26 (11): 76, 1962.

and a few gratifying successes. Both competence and confidence come from planned and purposeful work—both are qualities that make a successful and well-liked teacher.

Teachers as "helpers"

Occasional remarks in the preceding section indicate that the trait approach to describing and identifying teachers is not entirely satisfactory. Some pioneering psychologists have thought that a better approach would be to describe those in the helping professions in dynamic terms that relate to the personality of the helper as he tailors his behavior to the person he is helping. In some ways, it appears that this is much like the trait approach, but it does afford more opportunity for analysis of what lies beneath teacher behavior.

The Helping Relationship If we have a realistic concern for man's future, scientific discovery cannot be detached from philosophical values —nor can education. Education can serve many ends, and it has been used both to enslave [6] and to free man. It is here assumed that education in the United States is oriented to the freeing of pupils so that each can make his contribution to an evolving society. This society, it is further assumed, should be one in which people can become self-actualizing, using the optimum development of their capacities to enhance their own lives and the lives of others. To the extent that we are now falling short, there is an indication that the values of helpers have not been studiously determined and determinedly sought.

From psychological investigations, we know that *certain behaviors by helping persons probably will be followed by certain changes in personality and behavior on the part of the helped.* In studying the therapeutic relationship—and counseling is a helping profession from which inferences for teaching may be drawn—Rogers (1961) has found that if we want persons to become (1) more realistic in self-perceptions, (2) more confident and self-actualizing, (3) more mature and socialized, (4) less prone to be upset and quicker to recover from stress, and (5) more healthy, integrating, and effective, then the helper should have certain attitudes. These attitudes include some of the items cited for effective teachers: (1) they are genuinely and demonstrably sincere in their relationship with the helped; (2) they accept the person with whom they work as a separate, different, and worthwhile individual; and (3) they are empathic—able to see the person's private world of feelings and attitudes through his eyes. This kind of person, says Combs (1961, p. 55), does not behave in mechanical terms (by copying the traits of another);

[6] See Erika Mann, *School for Barbarians*, New York: Modern Age, Inc., 1938, for ways in which youth were enslaved by educational processes in Nazi Germany.

rather, he is more like a univac, taking many data, evaluating those data, and arriving at an answer in terms of all factors involved. The "formula" for achieving such answers resides in the perceptual field of the helper himself.

Two problems stem from the helper's perceptual field. One is the view he takes of the pupils with whom he works. Rogers (1961) found that "good" and "poor" teachers cannot be distinguished on the basis of what they know should be done; they can be distinguished on the basis of perceiving their pupils. Good teachers believe their pupils are capable of good work and can make them "work like crazy" because they *know* the pupils can do it. The second problem is how the helpers perceive themselves. The descriptions resemble those of mentally healthy people, and very briefly, some of the outstanding ones are as follows: They are identified with people, not apart from them. They see themselves as being adequate rather than inadequate. They feel that they are trustworthy, liked, wanted, and accepted. They feel certain of their roles rather than doubtful of and dissatisfied with them. They are sufficiently confident of themselves to be self-revealing rather than self-concealing (Combs, 1961, p. 56).

The Self-concept of the Helper It would be an extremely difficult task to trace the specific origins of fifteen traits such as those listed in the Wisconsin studies of teacher effectiveness. Results of such attempts have been ambiguous because what caused one person to become flexible might have rendered another quite rigid. Symonds (1939, pp. 104ff), for instance, found that dominant parents might rear either dominant or submissive children. This is but another way of saying that we cannot tell which specifics in a total milieu an individual will choose to give primary attention.

Because the self-concept admittedly derives from a variety of experiences, we can with some accuracy describe the *general* factors that tend to produce a robust self-concept. One's self-concept is significantly related to the attitudes he believes his parents hold toward him—what he believes is apparently more significant than their actual handling of him. In later childhood, many children select some glamorous figure as an ideal. Strength, good figure and features, and skills play a role in peer acceptance, although it is not always a crucial role. Altogether, we can say that acceptance by others, skills and knowledges that allow one to achieve status, and experiences that lead to feelings of security are conducive to a healthy self-concept.

It may appear that the adult is a victim of his childhood, and this is probably true for most persons. But therapeutic counseling for those in marked need of a stronger self-concept has proved that alteration is possible (Jersild, 1963). In effect, this is what forward-looking teacher preparation programs are attempting to do for those who do not need or have not received therapy. It is entirely possible that with the rapid forward movement of developmental counseling, such processes will become an integral part of teacher preparation programs. Self-analysis and self-understanding are part of some counselor-education programs. Similar procedures that lead to self-disclosure and improved perceptions of others are a distinct possibility and even a probability in teacher education. In the meantime, small, informal groups of teachers may be formed to discuss experiences, feelings, and perceptions that limit or enhance a healthy self-concept. To the extent that such groups can succeed in bringing about more tolerance and empathy for others, there will be direct contribution to the perceptions that undergird successful teaching.

Summary

The personality of the teacher has direct and cumulative impact on the lives and learning habits of pupils. It is neither expected nor desired that some ideal model of a teacher be established. Each teacher has his unique combination of experiences, interests, perceptions, and attitudes, and he must use them in ways most appropriate to him. Differences are desirable too from the standpoint of pupils—some respond to one kind of teacher, and others can work best with teachers who are quite different.

While differences among teachers are valued, common traits characterize the more effective ones. Many lists of traits have been prepared. It is to be expected that the lists would differ for elementary and secondary teachers, but they are surprisingly alike. Educators and pupils both see good teachers as people who are energetic, objective, fair-minded, cooperative, stable, flexible, and considerate. It is well worth special note that good teachers *all* have the habit of continuous learning. They study pupils, subject matter, and are involved in community affairs.

The trait approach to describing good teachers has defects, as research has frequently indicated. Attention has recently been focused upon the entire dynamics of the life patterns of those engaged in the helping professions. Here the object is to describe the attitudes that underlie the behaviors of successful teachers. The basic attitudes thus far discerned are acceptance of self and others. This enables teachers to see the potential of pupils and to know that pupils can do the work proposed. It enables teachers to inspire confidence in pupils because the teachers are confident of themselves.

Problems and exercises

1 Judging from your own experience, would you say that a teacher should be above average in appearance? In this context, evaluate the old saying that "beauty is as beauty does."

2 Discuss, pro and con, the statement that teacher personality has no permanent effect upon pupil personality.

3 Visit a classroom to see whether you can detect any relationships between teacher personality and the general behavior of the class as a whole.

4 Cite as many reasons as you can for the importance of the teacher's habit of continuous learning.

5 Study the lists of criteria of teacher effectiveness and pick out the three you consider most important. Compare your list with that of a classmate. Is the variation, if any, justifiable?

6 Talk with a number of teachers about their views of teaching. What effect do you think each would have on his pupils in terms of his views of teaching?

7 In a group of four or five of your classmates, start a discussion on the topic "What I Dislike about Teaching." Each participant should contribute his dislikes and evaluate others' presentations. Do you see how further discussions might alter one's perceptions of pupils?

8 Why is the teacher's self-concept so important in the development of pupils' self-concepts?

Suggested additional readings

Bernard, Harold W.: *Mental Hygiene for Classroom Teachers*, 2d ed., New York: McGraw-Hill Book Company, 1961, pp. 425–484.

Three chapters deal with the teacher's view of his profession, his responsibilities in the school, and a suggested program for living a more gratifying and effective life.

Jersild, Arthur T., and Eve Allina Lazar, in association with Adele B. Brodkin: *The Meaning of Psychotherapy in the Teacher's Life and Work*, New York: Bureau of Publications, Teachers College, Columbia University, 1962.

Because the teacher teaches what he is as well as what he says and does, it is important that he understand himself. The positive results reported in this book may help those who wish to "cross the threshold" to self-understanding through therapy.

Maslow, A. H.: *Motivation and Personality*, New York: Harper & Row, Publishers, 1954, pp. 199–234.

The author believes that individuals who have very good mental health are distinctly different from average people. In this chapter, he describes some of the attitudes of these "self-actualizing" persons.

Prescott, Daniel A.: *The Child and the Educative Process*, New York: McGraw-Hill Book Company, 1957, pp. 3–25.

The author describes the nature of the teaching task, some of the influences outside of school that condition his work, and the relationships (illustrated with case studies) of teachers and pupils.

Ryans, David G.: *Characteristics of Teachers*, Washington: American Council on Education, 1961, pp. 343–398.

The first of the chapters indicated summarizes the council's investigation of the characteristics of good teachers. The second relates teacher effectiveness to certain features, such as age, sex, civic participation, religious activities, etc.

Scott, C. Winfield, Clyde H. Hill, and Robert W. Burns (eds.): *The Great Debate: Our Schools in Crisis,* New York: McGraw-Hill Book Company, 1959, pp. 106–127.

The pages indicated present a number of short articles regarding pros and cons of the quality of today's teachers, certification policies, teacher preparation, and teacher shortages.

Appendix

The Concept of Correlation

The word "correlation" is a helpful one in psychology and education. It is a statistical term indicating *relationship*.

We frequently want to know whether two things have any connection. We may wish to know what effect a certain kind of home environment has on learning. We should like to have an answer to the question: Are athletes characteristically slow in academic work? Partial answers to such problems are phrased in terms of correlation. Thus the growth principle "Correlation rather than compensation is the general rule" means that there is a tendency for persons who are gifted in one area to be superior in other traits. If exacting measurements of the related traits are available, the degree of relationship may be expressed in terms of a "coefficient of correlation." This is a numerical expression of the amount of relationship between two factors.

If a number of individuals are measured in two things and the relative order, or comparative rank, of each individual is the same in both measures, the measures are said to be perfectly positively correlated. That is, the largest measure of one item (say, IQ) is found in the same person who has the largest measure of another item (say, vocabulary), and the next highest scores in both measures are found in the same person, etc., through the entire list, until the lowest scoring person in IQ has the lowest vocabulary score. This perfect positive correlation would be expressed as +1.00 (read "plus one, point, oh, oh"). This is *not* a percentage score. In some instances, it is conceivable that much of one thing would correspond to a lack (and to a corresponding amount of lack) of another. Thus, if the person scoring highest in IQ had the lowest vocabulary score, the next highest in IQ had the next lowest vocabulary score, etc., the correlation would be expressed as a perfect negative correlation, written as −1.00 (read "minus one, point, oh, oh"). Actually, such perfect correlations exist only in things subject to physical laws—not in terms of psychological measurement of traits now available.

Perfect positive correlation is shown in Charles's law: "The volume of a gas is directly proportional to the temperatures to which it is exposed—pressure remaining equal." That is, the greater the temperature, the greater the volume. There is a definite increase in the volume, which corresponds to each degree of rise in temperature. Perfect negative correlation is illustrated in Boyle's law: "The volume of a gas is inversely proportional to the pressure exerted upon it —temperature remaining constant." That is, the greater the pressure, the less the volume—the more you have of one thing, the less you have of another, and in proportionate amounts.

Human traits are less directly related than can be indicated by either a plus or minus 1.00. The relationship typically falls somewhere between no correlation (0.00) and a high positive, but not a perfect, correlation. Thus, there is no relationship between hair color and IQ. There is a slight positive correlation between size and intelligence (.10 to .25), but it is so slight that prediction for individuals would be foolish. The same thing may be said of correlations of good looks and intelligence—positive, but slight. Measures of school achievement and intelligence may be more highly correlated (.40 or thereabouts), but still one cannot say that the highest pupil in IQ should or will be the highest-ranking pupil on an achievement test. Two different tests of intelligence will correlate still more highly (.70 or so) than do achievement and IQ. Two forms of the same test will correlate still more highly (.85 or more). The meaning of coefficient of correlation may now be summarized roughly as follows:

1.00	Smoke drifts in the direction the wind blows and at the same rate.
.90	Two forms of a reliable test may correlate to this extent.
.80 ⎫	Different tests of the same trait may agree to this extent. Helpful
.70 ⎭	in predicting probable future of individuals (success in school, etc.)
.60 ⎫	
.50 ⎬	Various intellectual traits may agree to this extent.
.40 ⎭	
.30 ⎫	Just enough correlation to disprove stereotyped misconceptions, but
	of no value in individual prediction. Helpful in indicating a trend or
.20 ⎭	generalization.
.10 ⎫	
0.00 ⎬	No connection between the two traits or measures.
−.10 ⎭	

Human traits are so fluid that measurement of one trait will differ from day to day for one subject. The sum of the scores of thirty pupils in IQ or arithmetic achievement varies even if the measurements are taken on the same day (though individual fluctuations tend to cancel one another). Hence, a paired set of scores will not consistently show the same relationship. For this reason, the concept of probable error is usually used with the coefficient of correlation. For example, the relationship between a set of reading scores and a set of IQ scores may be .53 ± .12 (read "coefficient of correlation of point five three, plus or minus twelve"). It means that if other correlations were computed with similar tests and subjects, half the correlations could be expected to be between .65 (.53 + .12) and .41 (.53 − .12). The correlation is said to be significant if it is four or more times as large as its probable error.

In educational psychology, correlations are used to indicate the relationships between traits, between the results of two administrations of a test (coefficient of reliability), and between test results and other measures or estimates of the same trait (coefficient of validity).

Glossary

It has been indicated in the text that clarity of meaning in vocabulary usage is an aid to clear thinking. Attention to the terminology of educational psychology is therefore another step to a functional understanding of the subject. Of course, definitions are not enough. The student should try to form a concept of the word or term.

Some of the words in this glossary are familiar ones but may have a slightly different use from, or narrower concept than, the popular usage. Other words will probably be encountered only in educational or psychological literature. Whatever the category of a particular word, an understanding of it will contribute to improved thinking.

Ability Refers to what can actually be done as contrasted to capacity—which is the potential for developing an ability. Developed capacity is an ability.

Ability grouping A subdivision of students into groups so that the range of individual differences is narrowed. Ability grouping may be made on the basis of one kind of measure or may consider several correlated measures. Homogeneous grouping is *not* a good synonym.

Active recall Remembering or recalling without the use of aids or reminders. Remembering without specific and concrete clues.

Adolescence A phase of development that follows childhood and precedes maturity. Sometimes referred to as the "teen age." Roughly, the period between twelve and twenty years of age.

Adrenin One of the hormones secreted by the smooth (endocrine or ductless) glands called the "adrenals." Plays a major part in emotional manifestations.

Affective Relating to feelings or emotions. Frequently contrasted to "cognitive."

Anecdotal record A brief and usually periodic recording of typical, characteristic, or significant incidents in the child's school life. The objective is to observe and record facts and then (without judgment) try to understand feelings.

Aptitude Capacity, plus a probability that the individual will develop an ability. Aptitude usually refers to a rather narrow field of behavior, *e.g.*, musical or mechanical aptitude.

Attention Focusing of the sense organs upon a particular source of stimulation. Attention may be contrasted to interest, which is long-term or enduring. Attention may be brief.

Attitude A predisposition to act in a certain way. A state of readiness that influences a person to act in a given manner.

Atypical Deviation from the "normal" behavior or growth pattern.

Autonomy See *Functional autonomy.*

Behaviorism A viewpoint (or school) of psychology in which stress is placed on the primacy of external stimulation. The environment is considered to be prepotent. The phenomenon of "consciousness" is excluded from consideration.

Capacity Potential for development. That which one is potentially capable of doing or being. See also *Ability*.

Catharsis A process of cleaning out; specifically, a getting rid of unpleasant emotions or tensions through talking, writing, playing, drawing, etc. A means of emotional release.

Chronological age The actual length of time an individual has lived since birth. Usually expressed in years and months. Synonymous with "life age."

Cognitive Relating to the conscious life—knowing, remembering, judging, reasoning, etc. The contrasting aspect of "affective."

Compensation Making up for a real or imagined deficiency by stressing the development of a skill or ability. Indirect compensation is the development of skill other than the one that is weak. Direct compensation is the expenditure of more time and energy to overcome the particular real or felt defect. Also, the erroneous belief that a weakness in one aspect of the personality is offset by a balancing strength.

Concept The mental image of a thing or class of things formed by generalization from particulars. As used herein, the characterization of an idea that is broader and more inclusive than a definition.

Concomitant learning Knowledge or skill that is not specifically aimed at but accompanies the learning sought after.

Conditioning The process of getting the organism to respond to a substitute stimulus as though it were a natural stimulus for that behavior.

Configuration A gestalt term referring to the fact that stimuli occur in patterns rather than as isolated phenomena. Also connotes the fact that stimuli are not to be considered apart from the organism that is affected by the patterned stimuli.

Congenital Existing at the time of birth. A condition not due to heredity but to birth or prenatal conditions.

Constant IQ The theory that IQ does not change—that apparent changes in IQ are due to deficiencies in the instruments for evaluating intellectual growth.

Control group In an experimental situation, the group with which the experimental group is compared. All factors are held constant in the control group, while in the experimental group one factor is intentionally varied.

Correlation 1. Numerical: A statistical concept used to indicate the degree of relationship between two sets of paired phenomena. Correlation varies from a -1.00 through 0.0 to a $+1.00$. 2. Subject matter: Relating what is learned in one subject-matter area to that learned in another area, e.g., mathematics and science, science and social studies, social studies and literature.

Cramming An attempt to compress into one long learning period the study that should have been done over a period of days, weeks, or months. Cramming contrasts with spaced practice, which is short periods of regular study intermittently distributed over a prolonged period.

Decile   One of the nine points that divide a ranked distribution into ten parts, each containing one-tenth of all cases.

Defense mechanism   A kind of evasive behavior in which the individual seeks to avoid, or deny the existence of, conditions that make adjustment difficult.

Development   Change or increase in function due to experience and/or exercise. For *practical* purposes, no sharp line of distinction can be drawn between growth and development.

Deviate   One who departs from the wide band of what is called "normality" in any measured trait. One who would be placed at either extreme end of the normal curve of distribution. See also *Atypical.*

Differentiation   1. The process by which body parts and functions become increasingly distinct from other parts and functions. 2. The changed perception of a field of stimulation so the observer sees unique parts and values more clearly.

Discrete   Separate, distinct, or independent.

Education   The process by which behavior is changed and, ideally, improved through experience. Also, the formal situation in which the experiences are guided by an expert.

Educational psychology   The branch of applied psychology in which the facts, theories, and hypotheses of the science of psychology are studied, with particular reference to their application and implementation in schools.

Emergency theory   The theory which asserts that emotions are a means of preparing the individual for fight or flight. Also known as the "Cannon theory of emotion."

Emotion   A stirred-up state of the organism that involves mental, physical, physiological, situational, and habitual factors. Emotion embraces both strong and mild states and pleasant and unpleasant ones.

Empirical   Based on experience or observation; that which is known on the basis of what has been seen and experienced. Frequently contrasted with experimental evidence.

Endocrines   The glands of internal secretion, such as the thyroid, parathyroids, adrenals, pituitary, thymus, etc.

Enrichment   A means of providing stimulation to children (usually superior ones) by giving them more to do in the same subject-matter area in which other pupils of the class are working. May be contrasted with rapid promotion as a means of caring for individual differences.

Environment   An aspect of the "field" in which an individual functions, in contrast to that which resides within the individual. Environmental and internal factors are such inseparable parts of the field that distinctions between them are primarily matters of academic interest.

Equivalent test   A test that is equal to another in terms of length, difficulty, subject-matter area, and type of questions, but that is not a duplicate.

Euphoria   A feeling of well-being involving good mood and vitality, as contrasted to the emotional states of fear, anger, pain, etc.

Evaluation   The process of assessing the overall worth of an individual or activity. Many facets are investigated, and many measures are employed so that a broad or comprehensive assessment is achieved.

Experimental   Data or conclusions that are derived from the controlled conditions existing when factors causing behavior are artificially established.

Experimental group   The group in which one factor in teaching, learning, etc., is intentionally varied in order to evaluate the causal role of that one factor.

Exteroceptors   The group of sense organs that are sensitive to stimulating conditions outside of the body.

Extirpation   Removal of part of the brain, particularly of a laboratory animal. An experiment designed to determine how the brain functions.

Faculty psychology   The theory that the mind consists of separate compartments (faculties) for memory, reasoning, perception, etc.

Formal discipline   See *Mental discipline.*

Frustration   The act of blocking the needs or desires of the organism or individual. Sometimes means prolonged tension from which no relief is afforded.

Functional autonomy   A condition in which an act is carried on because of its *own* motivating power—outside incentives are no longer needed. For example, reading voluntarily because one has skill and developed interest, as contrasted to reading because one is required to.

Genetics   1. The study of genes in inheritance. 2. The phenomenon of growth in general, considering both inherited and environmental factors that influence progress toward more complete maturity.

Genius   An individual who has achieved eminence through unusual accomplishment that is esteemed by his social group. The term should not be used to denote giftedness—which is the potential for the development of genius.

Gestalt   Shape, form, or configuration. More specifically, the name given to a viewpoint in psychology that objects to simple cause-and-effect relations. The gestalt view criticizes atomistic (fragmented) interpretations.

Gifted child   One who is unusually bright—who has an IQ in excess of 135–140. May also refer to special talents in a person whose intellect is only average. Should not be confused with genius.

Goal   The end or object toward which behavior is directed and which tends to satisfy a particular need of an individual.

Grade equivalent   A score or scale expressed in terms of the school grade and month which indicates the average chronological age, mental age, achievement test score, or other characteristics of pupils classified at the given school grade.

Group test   A test that is administered to several subjects at one time.

Growth   Change and development as the result of the interaction of the organism with its environment. The word is sometimes restricted to mean increase in size as a result of multiplication of cells, i.e., maturation.

Guidance   A process of careful study of the pupil which precedes or accompanies an interview or a series of conferences with a pupil. The study and conferences are aimed at helping the pupil become capable of making his own choices with wisdom.

Halo effect   The influence of one trait or behavior on the evaluation of other traits or behaviors. Any pervasive impression of an individual that causes the rater's estimates of specific traits or abilities to be generally too high or too low; a bias.

Hawthorne effect   A condition of experimental situations which causes subjects to perform better, not because of experimental variables or external incentives, but because of the attention given them during the experiment.

Hereditary potential   The inborn possibility for development under favorable environmental conditions. The limits for development beyond which additional opportunity would be of no avail.

Homeostasis   The tendency of an organism to remain stable or seek to achieve balance or stability through its own regulatory action, as regards temperature, bodily chemistry, or psychological conditions.

Hypothesis   A tentative conclusion or guess. The basis for testing a particular procedure either by experiment or by observation.

Incentive   An external stimulus to action. Grades are thought by some persons to be a valuable incentive to learning.

Incidental learning   Information or skills acquired during the process of intentional learning, e.g., learning to use the dictionary, bibliographical aids, etc., while writing a paper on literature, psychology, etc.

Identification   Placing oneself in another's position, e.g., getting satisfactions from another's success or prestige. Acceptance of an action or goal as being significant to one's own self.

Individual test   A test administered by one examiner to one subject at a time.

Insight   The perception of a functional relationship between various factors or phenomena in a problem situation. Often thought to be sudden, but actually the result of a continuous growth and development.

Integration   A process of shaping facets of the personality into a harmoniously functioning whole. Sometimes used to indicate relationships between various subject-matter areas. The latter meaning is more frequently termed "correlation," thus leaving the word "integration" to refer to a condition of the organism in which subject matter has been functionally assimilated.

Intelligence   The developed ability of an individual to cope with his environment. The speed, facility, and appropriateness with which one does schoolwork and copes with the tasks of daily living.

Intelligence quotient (*IQ*)   The ratio of mental age to life age. Specifically, mental age divided by chronological age multiplied by 100.

Interest   A personal attitude or feeling involving identification with or concern about some person, situation, or object. A feeling of oneness between person and object.

Interoceptors   Internal sensory organs mediating the stimuli that give rise to hunger and internal pain.

Isolate   In sociometry, the rarely if ever chosen pupil.

Learning   The modification of behavior through activity and experience that alters modes of adjustment to the environment.

Level of aspiration   The degree of difficulty of response that an individual will attempt to overcome. The quality of goal which an individual desires to achieve.

Maladjustment Inadequate responses to the demands and problems of living in a particular environment.

Maturation The processes involved in progressive advancement toward maturity. Some references to the word imply growth from within (intrinsic), but increasingly it involves experience factors as well.

Maturity Used in two senses in psychology: 1. The full development of the individual, achievement of adult behavior and proportion—achievement of maximum growth. 2. Achievement of conduct or growth and development appropriate to one's age. (An immature child is one who acts below his age level—a mature child is still a child but "acts his age.")

Mean The sum of the scores divided by the number of cases. The average.

Median The midpoint of a series of scores. The point at which there are an equal number of cases (scores) below and above.

Mental age A numerical term used to express the level of intellectual ability an individual has achieved to date. A mental age of ten years means an intellectual ability that is equivalent to the average achieved by children who are ten years old chronologically.

Mental discipline The belief that "faculties" of the mind are stimulated to develop by exercise (usually rigorous). The belief that problem-solving ability in general is fostered by exercise in mathematics, that memory is cultivated by studying Latin, or that perseverance is generated by adversity.

Mental set A temporary preparedness to act in a certain direction at a given time, e.g., the disposition to study arithmetic at a given time—or resistance to such study. (Mental set is temporary, whereas readiness is a more or less permanent condition. A pupil may have achieved readiness for reading but not have the proper mental set for it.)

Molar A comprehensive approach to the study of behavior. The "world view" of a set of phenomena. ("Molar" and "molecular" are relative terms, not points of antagonism.)

Molecular An atomistic or fragmented approach to the study of behavior. The study of discrete bits of behavior. Analysis.

Morphology The study of body types or structures in relation to the effect these have on personality development and personality manifestations.

Motivation The process by which behavior is aroused or accelerated. Stimulation of activity toward a goal when previously there was little or no such behavior.

Need A lack (or requirement) which unless fulfilled or on the way to fulfillment leads to lack of self-realization, frustration, or maladjustment. See *Goals.*

Negative transfer A condition in which one learning hampers the acquisition of another learning.

Negativism The personality characteristic in which one chronically opposes reasonable requests and requirements (a normal and desirable phase of development in some circumstances).

Neurosis A minor mental or emotional disturbance. A condition in which the individual chronically falters and stumbles in the course of his daily living.

Neurotic One who suffers from minor mental or emotional illness.

Norm   An average or typical measure of a trait, level of development, or behavior.

Normal curve   A graphic representation of the distribution of a set of scores made by an unselected group showing a few cases at the extremes of the distribution and a clustering of cases at the center. The normal curve is often called the "bell-shaped" or Gaussian curve.

Objectivity   The characteristic of a test which indicates that it can be scored without danger of personal bias on the part of the scorer. A view in which opinion or wish has been eliminated.

Optimum   The most desirable or favorable degree, condition, or amount.

Organismic   Referring to the totality, or inclusiveness, of the individual. A view which considers the individual—his physical, mental, emotional, spiritual past and present status—and the situation in which he functions—his home, school, peer group, national setting, etc.

Overlearning   In memorizing, the repetition of a selection after it has been learned to the point of one successful reproduction. Applying oneself to the acquisition of a skill or knowledge beyond the point at which one can say it has been learned.

Percentile   One of the 99 point scores that divide a ranked distribution into groups, each of which contains $\frac{1}{100}$ of the scores. A pupil scoring 75 points out of a possible 100 on a test may have a percentile score of 90, which means that out of a theoretical group of 100 persons, he exceeds 90 of them with his score of 75. The score may also be interpreted to mean that 10 pupils out of 100 would equal or exceed this individual's performance.

Perception   The mental apprehension of that which is physically seen, heard, or felt. Psychological awareness.

Permissiveness   The practice of allowing children freedom to act, play, and develop freely. The placing of limitations on rules, prohibitions, scolding, punishment. Permissiveness must, in a practical sense, be limited to the child's developed ability to act with prudence.

Perseveration   1. The tendency for neural activities, once having been begun, to continue for a time. 2. The momentum one has to continue acting in a given direction. 3. The time, following learning, required for learning to be established.

Personality   The sum total of one's behavior and potential behavior in terms of physical, emotional, moral, social, aesthetic, and spiritual aspects of living as viewed and conditioned by one's fellow human beings.

Plateau   The level part of a learning curve, representing a time during which no measurable progress is being made in terms of the particular item being investigated.

Profile   The graphic representation of a set of test scores that shows an individual's comparative strengths and weaknesses in the various measured traits.

Projective technique   Any of a number of means by which inner personality trends are made known and/or released. Fundamentally, projective techniques consist of the subject's adding structure (or reading structure into) unstructured situations—painting and interpreting pictures or ink blots, playing with toys, finishing a story, etc.

Proprioceptors Sensory nerves located in muscles, tendons, and joints.

Psychological approach Introduction of a unit of schoolwork in terms of its meaning or interest to the pupils in a particular class, contrasted with the logical approach, which starts at the beginning and follows a series of events through to their ending.

Psychometrics Knowledge concerned with the development and application of mathematical and statistical concepts to psychological data; psychological testing.

Puberty The process during which the adolescent achieves sexual maturity.

Purposeful Action carried on because it has a definite purpose that is discernible to the behaving person.

Purposive Action that is directed toward satisfaction of certain needs, e.g., breathing, moving or exercise, the speeding up of heart action during a strong emotion, etc. The subject may be and often is unaware of the purpose of the behavior or action.

Rapport A feeling of oneness or identity that may exist between two persons. A feeling of mutual concern and warm, friendly regard.

Rationalization A process of false reasoning in which facts are twisted in order to justify a completed or contemplated act.

Readability The characteristic of a written selection that describes the ease with which it can be understood. Length and difficulty of words and length of sentence are among the determining factors of readability.

Reading readiness A stage of growth and development at which reading instruction will probably be effective and before which instruction will be relatively fruitless. Readiness for reading includes such factors as a mental age of 6.5 years, adequate sensory perception, emotional control commensurate with age, desire to read, and appropriate experiences.

Regression A phase of development in which the individual reverts to a less mature level of conduct after having apparently achieved a higher level. This is often a normal phenomenon, but it can become chronic.

Regressive eye movements Movements of the eyes back over a line of print to fixate upon a spot that is to the left (and on the same line) of a point that had previously been fixated. The eyes go back over material already once *visually* seen.

Reinforcement The effect of one process of mental excitation or activity in increasing the strength of a second activity. Immediate rewards tend to reinforce (strengthen) preceding behavior.

Reliability In terms of tests and measurement, the characteristics of a test that indicate that results will be consistent. A second administration of the test (or an equivalent form) on the same subject or group would yield highly similar results.

Retroactive inhibition The tendency for one experience to inhibit the recall of another; e.g., of two groups who learn a set of nonsense syllables, the one that rests between trials recalls more of the first set than does the group that learns a second set before attempting to recall the first set.

Saltatory Progressing suddenly—by leaps and bounds.

Socialization The process by which one makes himself an integral part of his living group.

Sociometry A schematic device for studying human relations or social attractions and/or repulsions. A mapping of interpersonal likes and dislikes.

Specificity The term refers to the fact that such character traits as honesty, dependability, truthfulness are different in various contexts or situations; that is, honesty is specific to a situation—one is not equally honest in all circumstances.

Standard deviation A statistic used to express the extent of deviation of a score from the mean of the total distribution. Approximately one-third of the scores are within one standard deviation above the mean and approximately one-third of the scores are within one standard deviation below the mean. Only about 27 per cent of the scores are within the next two standard deviations (13+ per cent on each side) above and below the first two standard deviations. About 99.7 per cent of all cases lie within the limits of three standard deviations above and below the mean.

Streaming Grouping pupils for classwork in terms of indicated ability and prior achievement.

Subjective Influenced by personal opinions or wishes. Personal bias.

Standardized test 1. A test for which norms have been established. (It has been given to large numbers of subjects and scores have definite expectancy values for given groups.) 2. A test for which uniform conditions of administering and scoring must be followed.

Standardizing population The group or groups used in determining the norms for a test.

Tachistoscope A device for controlling the illumination and duration of images, words, phrases, etc., that the subject must see in a brief unit of time in reading or in reacting to the stimuli presented.

Teacher's complex The tendency of a teacher to rephrase the answer to a question in the precise words that were in his mind before the pupil responded. An indication of the teacher's eagerness to answer all the questions that arise.

Teleological Directed toward a goal or purpose; behavior designed in accord with a definite pattern.

Tension tolerance The ability of an individual to withstand pressure, disappointment, and frustration. The capacity of an individual to bounce back after a rebuff or defeat.

Test battery A group or combination of psychometric tests. Several tests rather than one are thought to give a more comprehensive basis for evaluating an individual.

Track One of several terms used to indicate varying levels of difficulty in school learning tasks. Thus in a given school, pupils in the C track skip general science (unless experience indicates the wisdom of another approach) and take biology during their first year in high school, move into chemistry and physics the following year, and take a second year of chemistry or physics during their senior year.

Transfer of learning   The phenomenon of learning being facilitated in situation *B* by virtue of common elements, ideals, or generalizations that have been derived from first having learned in situation *A*.

Underachiever   A pupil whose academic accomplishment is at a level below that expected in terms of the predictive index yielded by general or specific aptitude tests.

Validity   The characteristic of a test which indicates that it measures that which it is supposed to measure.

Will power   A strengthened resolve resulting from clarified and increased motivation and a better understanding of and more conviction concerning advantages of the proposed course of action.

Worry   The process of turning a problem over and over in one's mind without arriving at a solution or hypothesis. A process of circular, as contrasted to straight-line, thinking.

Bibliography

A

Abercrombie, M. L. Johnson: *The Anatomy of Judgment*, New York: Basic Books, Inc., Publishers, 1960.

Adapting the Secondary-school Program to the Needs of Youth, Fifty-second Yearbook of the National Society for the Study of Education, Chicago: The University of Chicago Press, 1953.

Adkins, D. C.: "Measurement in Relation to the Educational Process," *Educational and Psychological Measurement*, 18: 221–240, 1958.

The Adolescent in Your Family, U.S. Children's Bureau Publication 347, 1954.

Aiken, James B.: "A High School Tries Community Development," *Phi Delta Kappan*, 44: 222–225, 1963.

Allport, Gordon W.: "Psychological Models for Guidance," *Harvard Educational Review*, 32: 373–381, 1963.

Allport, Gordon W.: *The Resolution of Intergroup Tensions*, New York: National Conference of Christians and Jews, 1952. (Pamphlet.)

Ames, Louise B., and Frances L. Ilg: "Developmental Trends in Writing Behavior," *Journal of Genetic Psychology*, 79: 42–45, 1951.

Anastasi, Anne: *Differential Psychology*, 3d ed., New York: The Macmillan Company, 1958.

Anderson, C. Arnold: "A Skeptical Note on the Relation of Vertical Mobility to Education," *American Journal of Sociology*, 66: 560–570, 1961.

Anderson, C. C., and S. M. Hunka: "Teacher Evaluation: Some Problems and a Proposal," *Harvard Educational Review*, 33: 74–95, 1963.

Anderson, H. H.: "Creativity in Perspective," in H. H. Anderson (ed.), *Creativity and Its Cultivation*, New York: Harper & Row, Publishers, 1959.

Anderson, H. H., J. E. Brewer, and M. F. Reid: *Studies of Teachers' Classroom Personalities: Part III. Follow-up Studies of the Effects of Dominative and Integrative Contacts of Children's Behavior*, Applied Psychology Monographs, no. 11, Stanford, Calif.; Stanford University Press, 1946.

Anderson, John E., and others: *A Survey of Children's Adjustment over Time*, Minneapolis: University of Minnesota, Institute of Child Development and Welfare, 1959.

Anderson, Robert H.: "Organizing Groups for Instruction," *Individualizing Instruction*, Sixty-first Yearbook of the National Society for the Study of Education, Chicago: The University of Chicago Press, 1962, part I.

Andrews, Thomas G., and Lee J. Cronbach: "Transfer of Training," in Judy F. Rosenblith and Wesley Allinsmith (eds.), *The Causes of Behavior*, Boston: Allyn and Bacon, Inc., 1962.

Angelino, Henry: "Characteristics of Superior and Talented Youth," in Bruce

Shertzer (ed.), *Working with Superior Students,* Chicago: Science Research Associates, Inc., 1960.

Angelino, Henry, and Charles L. Shedd: "An Initial Report of a Validation Study of the Davis-Eells Tests of General Intelligence or Problem-solving Ability," *Journal of Psychology,* 40: 35–38, 1955.

Arbuckle, Dugald S.: "A Semantic Excursion," *Personnel and Guidance Journal,* 41: 64–66, 1962.

Atkin, J. Myron: "A Study Formulating and Suggesting Tests for Hypotheses in Elementary School Science Learning Experiences," *Science Education,* 42: 414–422, 1958.

Ausubel, D. P., S. H. Schpoont, and Lillian Cukier: "Influence of Intention on Retention of School Materials," *Journal of Educational Psychology,* 48: 87–92, 1957.

B

Baer, Max F.: "Recent Labor Market Developments," *Personnel and Guidance Journal,* 29: 340, 1961.

Bagley, W. C.: *Educational Values,* New York: The Macmillan Company, 1911.

Baldwin, A. L., J. Kalhorn, and F. H. Breese: "Patterns of Parent Behavior," *Psychological Monographs,* 58 (3): 268, 1945.

Baldwin, Alfred L.: *Behavior and Development in Childhood,* New York: Holt, Rinehart and Winston, Inc., 1955.

Bales, Robert, and Fred Strodtbeck: in Dorwin Cartwright and Alvin Zander (eds.), *Group Dynamics: Research and Theory,* rev. ed., New York: Harper & Row, Publishers, 1960.

Barbe, Walter B., and Dorothy Norris: "Special Classes for Gifted Children in Cleveland," *Exceptional Children,* 21: 55–58, 1954.

Barker, Roger G.: "Success and Failure in the Classroom," *Progressive Education,* 19: 221–224, 1942.

Barker, Roger G., Tamara Dembo, and Kurt Lewin: *Frustration and Regression: An Experiment with Young Children,* University of Iowa Studies in Child Welfare, vol. 18, no. 1, 1941.

Baron, Denis, and Harold W. Bernard: *Evaluation Techniques for Classroom Teachers,* New York: McGraw-Hill Book Company, 1958.

Barzun, Jacques: "The Misbehavioral Sciences," in R. Thruelsen and John Kobler (eds.), *Adventures of the Mind,* First Series, New York: Alfred A. Knopf, Inc., 1961.

Basic Approaches to Mental Health in the Schools, Washington: American Personnel and Guidance Association, 1961. (A reprint series from *Personnel and Guidance Journal.*)

Bassett, Clara: *The School and Mental Health,* Cambridge, Mass.: Published for the Commonwealth Fund by Harvard University Press, 1931.

Bassett, Mildred, Vice-principal, Lincoln High School (Portland, Oregon): Personal interview, Nov. 20, 1962.

Baughman, E. Earl, and George Welsh: *Personality: A Behavioral Science,* Englewood Cliffs, N.J.: Prentice-Hall, Inc., 1962.

Bayley, N.: "Values and Limitations of Infant Testing," *Children,* 5: 129–133, 1958.

Beach, Leslie R.: "Sociability and Academic Achievement in Various Types of Learning Situations," *Journal of Educational Psychology,* 51: 208–212, 1960.

Beck, Robert H.: "Society and Individual Differences," *Individualizing Instruction,* Sixty-first Yearbook of the National Society for the Study of Education, Chicago: The University of Chicago Press, 1962, part I.

Beers, Clifford: *A Mind That Found Itself,* New York: Longmans, Green & Co., Inc., 1917.

Benne, Kenneth D.: "More Learning Takes Place When Teacher and Students Understand the Various Roles in the Classroom Group," *NEA Journal,* 42: 205–208, 1954.

Bennett, James V.: "A Cool Look at 'The Crime Crisis,'" *Harper's,* 228 (1367): 123–127, 1964.

Bennett, Margaret: *Getting the Most Out of College,* New York: McGraw-Hill Book Company, 1957.

Bernard, Harold W.: *Toward Better Personal Adjustment,* 2d ed., New York: McGraw-Hill Book Company, 1957.

Bernard, Harold W.: *Human Development in Western Culture,* Boston: Allyn and Bacon, Inc., 1962.

Bernard, Harold W.: *Mental Hygiene for Classroom Teachers,* 2d ed., New York: McGraw-Hill Book Company, 1961.

Bernard, Harold W.: "Some Relationships of Vocabulary to Scholarship," *School and Society,* 51: 494–496, 1940.

Bernard, Jessie: "Teen-age Culture: An Overview," *Annals of the American Academy of Political and Social Science,* 338: 1–12, 1961.

Bernays, Edward L.: *The Engineering of Consent,* Norman, Okla.: University of Oklahoma Press, 1955.

Bienstock, Herbert: "Realities of the Job Market," in Daniel Schreiber (ed.), *Guidance and the School Dropout,* Washington: National Education Association, 1964, pp. 84–108.

Bills, Robert E.: "Play Therapy with Well-adjusted Retarded Readers," *Journal of Consulting Psychology,* 14: 246–249, 1950.

Birkmaier, Emma M.: "Foreign Languages," *Review of Educational Research,* 28: 127–139, 1958.

Blackwood, Paul E.: *How Children Learn to Think,* U.S. Office of Education Bulletin no. 10, 1951.

Blair, Glenn M., and R. Stewart Jones: "Readiness," *Encyclopedia of Educational Research,* 3d ed., New York: The Macmillan Company, 1960, pp. 1081ff.

Blair, Glenn M., R. Stewart Jones, and R. H. Simpson: *Educational Psychology,* 2d ed., New York: The Macmillan Company, 1962.

Blake, Patricia: "A Big Break for Poverty's Children," *Life,* 56 (14): 89, 1964.

Bobbitt, Franklin: *How to Make a Curriculum,* Boston: Houghton Mifflin Company, 1924.

Bond, Guy L., and Stanley B. Kegler: "Reading Instruction in the Senior High School." *Development in and through Reading,* Sixtieth Yearbook of the

National Society for the Study of Education, Chicago: The University of Chicago Press, 1961, part I, pp. 320–335.

Bongers, H.: "Teaching Modern Languages to the Elementary School Child," *Educational Research Bulletin,* 32 (6): 144–150, 1953.

Boniface, Jenore: "Role-playing in the Kindergarten," *Grade Teacher,* 76: 31, October, 1958.

Boynton, P. L., H. Dugger, and M. Turner: "The Emotional Stability of Teachers and Pupils," *Journal of Juvenile Research,* 18: 223–232, 1934.

Bradway, K. P., C. W. Thompson, and R. B. Cravens: "Preschool IQs after Twenty-five Years," *Journal of Educational Psychology,* 49: 278–281, 1958.

Brammer, Lawrence M., and Everett L. Shostrom: *Therapeutic Psychology,* Englewood Cliffs, N.J.: Prentice-Hall, Inc., 1960.

Bristow, William H.: "Curriculum Problems of Special Import for Early School Leavers," in Daniel Schreiber (ed.), *Guidance and the School Dropout,* Washington: National Education Association, 1964, pp. 144–158.

Bronfenbrenner, Urie: "Developmental Theory in Transition," *Child Psychology,* Sixty-second Yearbook of the National Society for the Study of Education, Chicago: The University of Chicago Press, 1963, part I.

Broudy, Harry S., B. Othanel Smith, and Joe R. Burnett: *Democracy and Excellence in American Secondary Education,* Chicago: Rand McNally & Company, 1964.

Brown, B. Frank: "The Non-graded High School," *Phi Delta Kappan,* 44: 206–209, 1963.

Brown, Francis: "Knowledge of Results as an Incentive in Schoolroom Practice," *Journal of Educational Psychology,* 23: 532–552, 1932.

Brown, Marcus: "Knowing and Learning," *Harvard Educational Review,* 31: 1–20, 1961.

Brownstein, Samuel C., and Mitchell Weiner: *How to Prepare for College Entrance Examinations,* rev. and enlarged, Great Neck, N.Y.: Barron's Educational Series, Inc., 1958.

Brumbaugh, F. N.: "Laughter and Teachers," *Educational Method,* 20: 69–70, 1940.

Bruner, Jerome S.: "The Act of Discovery," *Harvard Educational Review,* 31: 21–32, Winter, 1961.

Bruner, Jerome S.: *The Process of Education,* Cambridge, Mass.: Harvard University Press, 1963.

Bryan, R. C.: "Student Reaction to Teachers," *Clearing House,* 36: 353–360, 1962.

Buhler, Charlotte: *Childhood Problems and the Teacher,* New York: Holt, Rinehart and Winston, Inc., 1952.

Bullock, Robert P.: "Some Cultural Implications of Year-round Schools," *Theory into Practice,* 1: 154–161, 1962.

Burrell, Anne P.: "Facilitating Learning through Emphasis on Meeting Children's Basic Needs: An In-service Training Program," *Journal of Educational Sociology,* 24: 381–393, 1951.

Burrows, Alvina T.: *Teaching Composition,* What Research Says to the Teacher, no. 18, Washington: National Education Association, 1959.

Burton, William H.: "Education and Social Class in the United States," *Harvard Educational Review*, 23: 243–256, 1953.

Buswell, Guy T.: "Arithmetic," *Encyclopedia of Educational Research*, 3d ed., New York: The Macmillan Company, 1960, pp. 63ff.

Butler, John, M.D.: Psychiatrist, Consultant to Counseling and Guidance Training Institute (NDEA-sponsored), Portland Continuation Center, Oregon State System of Higher Education, 1959–1963. Lecture, May 27, 1963.

C

Caldwell, Edson: *Group Techniques for the Classroom Teacher*, Chicago: Science Research Associates, Inc., 1960.

Campbell, Floyd: American Data Services, Inc., Portland, Ore., Personal interview, January, 1961.

Cannon, W. B: *Bodily Changes in Pain, Hunger, Fear, and Rage*, 2d ed., New York: Appleton-Century-Crofts, Inc., 1929.

Cannon, W. B.: "The Role of Chance in Discovery," *Scientific Monthly*, 50: 204–209, 1940.

Cantril, H., and W. A. Hunt: "Emotional Effects Produced by the Injection of Adrenalin," *American Journal of Psychology*, 44: 300–307, 1932.

Capehart, Bertis E.: "Illustrative Courses and Programs in Selected Secondary Schools," *The Integration of Educational Experiences*, Fifty-seventh Yearbook of the National Society for the Study of Education, Chicago: The University of Chicago Press, 1958, part III.

Capoferi, A.: "How Can a Junior High School Mathematics Teacher Strengthen the Science Course?" *School Science and Mathematics*, 56: 233–236, 1956.

Carlsmith, Lyn: "Effect of Early Father Absence on Scholastic Aptitude," *Harvard Educational Review*, 34: 3–21, 1964.

Carpenter, Regan: "Creativity: Its Nature and Nurture," *Education*, 82: 391–395, 1962.

Carroll, Herbert A.: *Genius in the Making*, New York: McGraw-Hill Book Company, 1940.

Carrow, M. A.: "Linguistic Functioning of Bilingual and Monolingual Children," *Journal of Speech and Hearing Disorders*, 22: 371–380, 1957.

Carsley, J. D.: "The Interests of Children (Aged 10–11) in Books," *British Journal of Educational Psychology*, 27: 13–23, 1957.

Carter, R. S.: "How Invalid Are Marks Assigned by Teachers?" *Journal of Educational Psychology*, 43: 218–228, 1952.

Castaneda, A., D. S. Palermo, and B. R. McCandless: "Complex Learning and Performance as a Function of Anxiety in Children and Task Difficulty," *Child Development*, 27: 327–332, 1956.

The Challenge of Jobless Youth, Washington: U.S. Department of Labor, April, 1963.

Chaplin, J. P., and T. S. Krawiec: *Systems and Theories of Psychology*, New York: Holt, Rinehart and Winston, Inc., 1960.

Chase, W. Linwood: "Individual Differences in Classroom Learning," *Social Studies in the Elementary School*, Fifty-sixth Yearbook of the National

Society for the Study of Education, Chicago: The University of Chicago Press, 1957, part II.

Christensen, C. M.: "Relationships between Pupil Achievement, Pupil Affect-need, Teacher Warmth, and Teacher Permissiveness," *Journal of Educational Psychology*, 51: 169–174, 1960.

Cleghorn, R. A.: "Endocrinology and Psychiatry Symposium," *International Record of Medicine and General Practice Clinics*, 166: 177ff., 1953.

Coch, Lester, and John R. P. French, Jr.: "Overcoming Resistance to Change," *Journal of Human Relations*, 1: 4, 1948.

Coleman, James S.: *Personality Dynamics and Effective Behavior*, Chicago: Scott, Foresman and Company, 1960.

Combs, Arthur W.: "The Myth of Competition," *Childhood Education*, 33: 264–269, 1957.

Combs, Arthur W.: "A Perceptual View of the Nature of 'Helpers,'" *Personality Theory and Counseling Practice*, Gainesville, Fla.: University of Florida, January, 1961.

Combs, Arthur W., and Donald Snygg: *Individual Behavior*, rev. ed., New York: Harper & Row, Publishers, 1959.

Conant, James B.: *The American High School Today*, New York: McGraw-Hill Book Company, 1959.

Conant, James B.: *Slums and Suburbs*, New York: McGraw-Hill Book Company, 1961.

Cook, Desmond L.: "Teaching Machine Terms," *Audiovisual Instruction*, 6: 152–153, 1961.

Costar, J. K.: "Some Characteristics of High School Pupils from Three Income Groups," *Journal of Educational Psychology*, 59: 55–62, 1959.

Coughlin, William J.: "The Great *Mokusatsu* Mistake," *Harper's*, 206: 31–40, March, 1953.

Craig, Gerald S.: *Science in the Elementary Schools*, What Research Says to the Teacher, no. 12, Washington: National Education Association, 1957.

Crandall, Vaughn J.: "Achievement," *Child Psychology*, Sixty-second Yearbook of the National Society for the Study of Education, Chicago: The University of Chicago Press, 1963, part I.

Cronbach, Lee J.: *Educational Psychology*, New York: Harcourt, Brace & World, Inc., 1954.

Cronbach, Lee J.: *Educational Psychology*, 2d ed., New York: Harcourt, Brace & World, Inc., 1963.

Crowder, Norman A.: "On the Differences between Linear and Intrinsic Programing," *Phi Delta Kappan*, 44: 250–254, 1963.

D

Dahlberg, C. C., F. Roswell, and Jeanne Chall: "Psychotherapeutic Principles as Applied to Remedial Reading," *Elementary School Journal*, 53: 211–217, 1952.

Dansereau, H. Kirk: "Work and the Teen-ager," *Annals of the American Academy of Political and Social Science*, 338: 44–52, 1961.

Davids, Anthony, and Augustus A. White: "Effects of Success, Failure, and

Social Facilitation on Level of Aspiration in Emotionally Disturbed and Normal Children," *Journal of Personality*, 26: 77–93, 1958.

Davie, James S.: "Social Class Factors and School Attendance," *Harvard Educational Review*, 23: 175–185, 1953.

Davis, Allison, and Kenneth Eells: *Davis-Eells Test of General Intelligence or Problem-solving Ability*, New York: Harcourt, Brace & World, Inc., 1963.

Davis, Donald A.: "An Experimental Study of Potential Dropouts," *Personnel and Guidance Journal*, 40: 899–906, 1962.

Dean, Stuart E.: *Elementary School Administration and Organization*, U.S. Office of Education Bulletin no. 11, 1960.

De Angeli, Marguerite: *The Door in the Wall*, Garden City, N.Y.: Doubleday & Company, Inc., 1949.

DeBoer, John J., and Gertrude Whipple: "Reading Development in Other Curriculum Areas," *Development in and through Reading*, Sixtieth Yearbook of the National Society for the Study of Education, Chicago: The University of Chicago Press, 1961, part I.

Deese, James: *The Psychology of Learning*, 2d ed., New York: McGraw-Hill Book Company, 1958.

DeProspo, Nicholas: "Developing Scientific Attitudes by Responding Actively to Motion Pictures," *Dissertation Abstracts*, 18 (2): 521–522, 1958.

Deterline, William A.: *An Introduction to Programmed Instruction*, Englewood Cliffs, N.J.: Prentice-Hall, Inc., 1962.

Deutsch, Morton: "A Theory of Cooperation and Competition," *Journal of Human Relations*, 2: 2, 1949.

D'Evelyn, Katherine E.: *Meeting Children's Emotional Needs*, Englewood Cliffs, N.J.: Prentice-Hall, Inc., 1957.

Dewey, John: *Democracy and Education*, New York: The Macmillan Company, 1928.

Dewey, John: *How We Think*, Boston: D. C. Heath and Company, 1933.

Dicarlo, Louis M.: "The Deaf and Hard of Hearing," *Review of Educational Research*, 29: 497–519, 1959.

Dimock, H. S.: "A Research in Adolescence: I. Pubescence and Physical Growth," *Child Development*, 6: 177–195, 1935.

DiNapoli, P. J.: *Homework in the New York City Elementary Schools*, Contributions to Education, no. 719, New York: Bureau of Publications, Teachers College, Columbia University, 1937.

Di Vesta, Francis J.: "Meaningful Learning: Motivational, Personality, Interpersonal, and Social Variables," *Review of Educational Research*, 31: 511–521, 1961.

Dodson, Dan W.: "Schools in Our Rural Slums," *Saturday Review*, 46 (16): 75, 1963.

Dollard, John, and Neal E. Miller: *Personality and Psychotherapy*, New York: McGraw-Hill Book Company, 1950.

Donahue, Wilma, and Clark Tibbitts: *Aging in the Modern World*, Ann Arbor, Mich.: University of Michigan, 1957.

Dressel, Paul L.: "The Meaning and Significance of Integration," *The Integration of Educational Experiences*, Fifty-seventh Yearbook of the

National Society for the Study of Education, Chicago: The University of Chicago Press, 1958, part III.

Drever, James: *A Dictionary of Psychology,* Baltimore: Penguin Books, Inc., 1952.

Drucker, Peter F.: *Landmarks of Tomorrow,* New York: Harper & Row, Publishers, 1959.

Duel, Henry J.: "Effect of Periodical Self-evaluation on Student Achievement," *Journal of Educational Psychology,* 49: 197–199, 1958.

Dugdale, R. L.: *The Jukes,* New York: G. P. Putnam's Sons, 1877.

Dunn, Lloyd M. (ed.): *Exceptional Children in the Schools,* New York: Holt, Rinehart and Winston, Inc., 1963.

E

Educational Policies Commission: *Moral and Spiritual Values in the Public Schools,* Washington: National Education Association, 1951.

Educational Policies Commission: *The Purposes of Education in American Democracy,* Washington: National Education Association, 1938.

Eells, K., A. Davis, R. J. Havighurst, V. E. Herrick, and R. W. Tyler: *Intelligence and Cultural Differences,* Chicago: The University of Chicago Press, 1951.

Eicholz, G., and R. Barbe: "Vocabulary Development," *Elementary School Journal,* 61: 414, 1961.

Eichorn, Dorothy H.: "Biological Correlates of Behavior," *Child Psychology,* Sixty-second Yearbook of the National Society for the Study of Education, Chicago: The University of Chicago Press, 1963, part I, pp. 4–61.

Eigen, Lewis D.: "High-school Student Reactions to Programed Instruction," *Phi Delta Kappan,* 44: 282–285, 1963.

Elsbree, W. S.: "School Practices That Help and Hurt Personality," *Teachers College Record,* 43: 24–34, 1941.

Espenschade, Anna S.: *Physical Education in the Elementary Schools,* What Research Says to the Teacher, no. 27, Washington: National Education Association, 1963.

Ewers, Dorothea: "How Do You Interpret IQ Test Scores?" *Illinois Education,* 44: 182, 1956.

F

Facts on Mental Health and Mental Illness, Bethesda, Md.: U.S. Department of Health, Education, and Welfare, Public Health Service, 1957.

Fairbank, Ruth E.: "The Subnormal Child—Seventeen Years After," *Mental Hygiene,* 17: 177–208, 1933.

Faison, Edmund W. J.: "Readability of Children's Textbooks," *Journal of Educational Psychology,* 42: 43–51, 1951.

Farnham, Marynia: *The Adolescent,* New York: Harper & Row, Publishers, 1952.

Farwell, Gail F., and Herman J. Peters (eds.): *Guidance Readings for Counselors,* Chicago: Rand McNally & Company, 1960.

Fawcett, H. P.: *The Nature of Proof,* New York: Bureau of Publications, Teachers College, Columbia University, 1938.

Feinberg, M. R., Max Smith, and Robert Schmidt: "An Analysis of Expressions Used by Adolescents at Varying Economic Levels to Describe Accepted and Rejected Peers," *Journal of Genetic Psychology*, 93: 133–148, 1958.

Filbin, Robert L.: "Teaching Reading," *Atlantic Monthly*, 204: 125–126, November, 1959.

Fischer, John: "Why Nobody Can't Write Good," *Harper's*, 228 (1365): 16–26, 1964.

Fisher, S., and S. E. Cleveland: *Body Image and Personality*, Princeton, N.J.: D. Van Nostrand Company, Inc., 1958.

Flanagan, John C.: "The Implications of Recent Research for the Improvement of Secondary Education," *American Educational Research Journal*, 1: 1–9, 1964.

Flanders, Ned A.: "Diagnosing and Utilizing Social Structures in Classroom Learning," *The Dynamics of Instructional Groups*, Fifty-ninth Yearbook of the National Society for the Study of Education, Chicago: The University of Chicago Press, 1960, part III.

Flexner, Abraham: "Usefulness of Useless Knowledge," *Harper's*, 179: 544–552, October, 1939.

Ford, Donald H.: "Group and Individual Counseling in Modifying Behavior," *Personnel and Guidance Journal*, 40: 770–773, 1962.

Frandsen, Arden N.: *Educational Psychology*, New York: McGraw-Hill Book Company, 1961.

Frank, Lawrence K.: *The Fundamental Needs of the Child*, New York: National Association for Mental Health, Inc., 1952.

Frank, Lawrence K.: *Nature and Human Nature*, New Brunswick, N.J.: Rutgers University Press, 1951.

Frankel, Edward: "A Comparative Study of Achieving and Under-achieving High School Boys of High Intellectual Ability," *Journal of Educational Research*, 53: 172–180, 1960.

Frazier, A., and L. K. Lisonbee: "Adolescent Concerns with Physique," *School Review*, 58: 397–405, 1950.

Frederiksen, Norman B., and Arthur C. F. Gilbert: "Replication of a Study of Differential Predictability," *Educational and Psychological Measurement*, 20: 759–767, 1960.

Freeman, Frank N.: *Teaching Handwriting*, What Research Says to the Teacher, no. 4, Washington: National Education Association, 1954.

French, John R. P., Jr.: *Organized and Unorganized Groups under Fear and Frustration*, University of Iowa Studies in Child Welfare, Studies in Vector and Topological Psychology, vol. 20, 1944.

French, Joseph L. (ed.): *Educating the Gifted*, New York: Holt, Rinehart and Winston, Inc., 1959.

French, Will, and others: *Behavioral Goals of General Education in High School*, New York: Russell Sage Foundation, 1957.

Freud, Sigmund: *The Problem of Anxiety*, New York: W. W. Norton & Company, Inc., 1936.

Froehlich, Clifford P.: "Must Counseling Be Individual?" *Educational and Psychological Measurement*, 18: 681–689, 1958.

Fullmer, Daniel W., and Harold W. Bernard: *Counseling: Content and Process,* Chicago: Science Research Associates, Inc., 1964.

G

Gates, Arthur I.: *Teaching Reading,* What Research Says to the Teacher, no. 1, Washington: National Education Association, 1953.

Gates, Arthur I.: "Teaching of Reading: Objective Evidence *versus* Opinion," *Phi Delta Kappan,* 43: 197–205, 1962.

Gerard, Ralph W.: "Aging and Organizations," in James E. Birren (ed.), *Handbook of Aging and the Individual,* Chicago: The University of Chicago Press, 1959.

Getzels, Jacob W., and Philip W. Jackson: *Creativity and Intelligence,* New York: John Wiley & Sons, Inc., 1962.

Gewirtz, H. B.: "Generalization of Children's Preferences as a Function of Reinforcement and Task Similarity," *Journal of Abnormal and Social Psychology,* 58: 111–118, 1959.

Gibb, E. Geraldine, John R. Mayer, and Edith Treuenfels: "Mathematics," *Encyclopedia of Educational Research,* 3d ed., New York: The Macmillan Company, 1960, pp. 796–804.

Gibson, E. J.: "Improvements in Perceptual Judgments as a Function of Controlled Practice," *Psychological Bulletin,* 50: 401–431, 1953.

Gibson, E. J.: "Retroactive Inhibition as a Function of Degree of Generalization between Tasks," *Journal of Experimental Psychology,* 28: 93–115, 1941.

Gies, Joseph: "The Real Causes of Illegitimacy," *This Week Magazine,* Nov. 4, 1962, pp. 4–5.

Glanz, Edward C.: *Groups in Guidance,* Boston: Allyn and Bacon, Inc., 1962.

Goertzen, Stanley M.: "Factors Relating to Opinions of Seventh Grade Children regarding the Acceptability of Certain Behaviors in the Peer Group," *Journal of Genetic Psychology,* 94: 29–34, 1959.

Goffman, Erving: *The Presentation of Self in Everyday Life,* Garden City, N.Y.: Doubleday & Company, Inc., 1959.

Goldberg, Arthur: "Juvenatrics: Study of Prolonged Adolescence," *The Clearing House,* 38: 488–492, 1964.

Goldstein, K., P. Hoch, R. May, K. Horney, F. A. Weiss, and H. Gershman: "Neurotic Anxiety: A Panel Discussion," *American Journal of Psychoanalysis,* 12: 89–95, 1952.

Goldstein, M., and C. H. Rittenhouse: "Knowledge of Results in the Acquisition and Transfer of a Gunnery Skill," *Journal of Experimental Psychology,* 48: 187–196, 1954.

Good, Carter V. (ed.): *Dictionary of Education,* 2d ed., New York: McGraw-Hill Book Company, 1959.

Goodenough, Florence L., and Leona E. Tyler: *Developmental Psychology,* 3d ed., New York: Appleton-Century-Crofts, Inc., 1959.

Goodlad, John I.: "Illustrative Programs and Procedures in Elementary Schools," *The Integration of Educational Experiences,* Fifty-seventh Yearbook of the National Society for the Study of Education, Chicago: The University of Chicago Press, 1958, part III.

Goodlad, John I.: "Individual Differences and Vertical Organization of the School," *Individualizing Instruction,* Sixty-first Yearbook of the National Society for the Study of Education, Chicago: The University of Chicago Press, 1962, part I.

Goodlad, John I., and Robert H. Anderson: *The Nongraded Elementary School,* New York: Harcourt, Brace & World, Inc., 1959.

Goodson, Max R.: "The 'Person' and the 'Group' in American Culture and Education," *The Dynamics of Instructional Groups,* Fifty-ninth Yearbook of the National Society for the Study of Education, Chicago: The University of Chicago Press, 1960, part II.

Goratos, L. A.: "Relationships and Age Differences in Growth Measures and Motor Skills," *Child Development,* 30: 333–340, 1959.

Gordon, H.: *Mental and Scholastic Tests among Retarded Children,* Educational Pamphlets, no. 44, London: Bureau of Education, 1923.

Gordon, Ira J., and Arthur W. Combs: "The Learner: Self and Perception," *Review of Educational Research,* 28: 433–444, 1958.

Gorow, Frank F.: "I Wrote a Scrambled Book," *Audiovisual Instruction,* 6: 136–137, 1961.

Gowan, J. C.: "Summary of the Intensive Study of Twenty Highly Selected Women Teachers," *Journal of Experimental Education,* 26: 115–124, 1957.

Grambs, Jean D.: *Understanding Intergroup Relations,* What Research Says to the Teacher, no. 21, Washington: National Education Association, 1960.

Greenleaf, Walter J.: *Occupations and Careers,* New York: McGraw-Hill Book Company, 1955.

Grossack, M. M.: "Some Effects of Cooperation and Competition upon Small Group Behavior," *Journal of Abnormal and Social Psychology,* 49: 341–348, 1954.

Growing Up in an Anxious Age, Yearbook of the Association for Supervision and Curriculum Development, Washington: National Education Association, 1952.

Guilford, J. P.: "Factors That Aid and Hinder Creativity," *Teachers College Record,* 63: 380–392, 1962.

Guilford, J. P., R. C. Wilson, P. R. Christensen, and D. J. Lewis: *A Factor-analytic Study of Creative Thinking: I. Hypothesis and Description of Tests,* Los Angeles: University of Southern California, 1951.

Guthrie, E. R.: "Conditioning: A Theory of Learning in Terms of Stimulus, Response, and Association," *The Psychology of Learning,* Forty-first Yearbook of the National Society for the Study of Education, Chicago: The University of Chicago Press, 1942, part II.

H

Hamblen, A. A.: *The Extent to Which the Effect of the Study of Latin upon a Knowledge of English Derivations Can Be Increased,* Philadelphia: University of Pennsylvania, 1925. Dissertation.

Harcleroad, Fred: "Theoretical Formulations in Audiovisual Communications," *Review of Educational Research,* 32: 119–126, 1962.

Haring, Norris G., and E. Lakin Phillips: *Educating Emotionally Disturbed Children,* New York: McGraw-Hill Book Company, 1962.

Harlow, H. F.: "The Formation of Learning Sets," *Psychological Review*, 56: 51–65, 1949.

Harrell, R. F.: "Mental Response to Added Thiamine," *Journal of Nutrition*, 31: 283–298, 1946.

Harris, Albert J.: "Reading and Human Development," *Development in and through Reading*, Sixtieth Yearbook of the National Society for the Study of Education, Chicago: The University of Chicago Press, 1961, part I.

Harris, Dale B.: "Sex Differences in the Life Problems and Interests of Adolescents, 1935 and 1957," *Child Development*, 30: 453–459, 1959.

Harris, Theodore L.: "Handwriting," *Encyclopedia of Educational Research*, 3d ed., New York: The Macmillan Company, 1960, pp. 616ff.

Hart, F. W.: *Teachers and Teaching, by Ten Thousand High School Seniors*, New York: The Macmillan Company, 1934.

Haselrud, G. M., and Shirley Meyers: "The Transfer Value of Given and Individually Derived Principles," *Journal of Educational Psychology*, 49: 293–298, 1958.

Havighurst, Robert J.: *Human Development and Education*, New York: Longmans, Green & Co., Inc., 1953.

Havighurst, Robert J.: "Social-class Influences on American Education," *Social Forces Influencing American Education*, Sixtieth Yearbook of the National Society for the Study of Education, Chicago: The University of Chicago Press, 1961, part II.

Havighurst, Robert J., P. H. Bowman, G. P. Liddle, C. V. Matthews, and James V. Pierce: *Growing Up in River City*, New York: John Wiley & Sons, Inc., 1962.

Havighurst, Robert J, and Bernice L. Neugarten: *Society and Education*, 2d ed., Boston: Allyn and Bacon, Inc., 1962.

Hayakawa, S. I.: "How Words Change Our Lives," in Richard Thruelsen and John Kobler (eds.), *Adventures of the Mind*, First Series, New York: Alfred A. Knopf, Inc., 1959.

Heaton, Margaret M.: *Feelings Are Facts*, New York: National Conference of Christians and Jews, 1952.

Hebb, D. O.: *A Textbook of Psychology*, Philadelphia: W. B. Saunders Company, 1958.

Hechinger, Fred M.: "Foreign Languages Stage a Comeback," *Saturday Review*, 44 (7): 64–66, 1963.

Heffernan, Helen (ed.): *Guiding the Young Child*, Boston: D. C. Heath and Company, 1961.

Hendrickson, G., and W. H. Schroeder: "Transfer of Training in Learning to Hit a Submerged Target," *Journal of Educational Psychology*, 32: 205–213, 1941.

Henry, William G., Jr.: "What Makes a Teaching Machine Teach?" *Audiovisual Instruction*, 6: 126–129, 1961.

Herge, Henry Curtis: "Teacher Certification, Supply, and Demand," *Review of Educational Research*, 28: 185–197, 1958.

Herriott, Robert E.: "Some Social Determinants of Educational Aspiration," *Harvard Educational Review*, 33: 157–177, 1963.

Herzberg, Frederick, and Roy M. Hamlin: "A Motivation-hygiene Concept of Mental Health," *Mental Hygiene,* 45: 394–401, 1961.

"High School Drop-outs," *NEA Research Bulletin,* 38: 11–14, February, 1960.

Higher Horizons, New York: Syracuse University, Youth Development Center, 1961. (A booklet of newspaper clippings.)

Hildreth, Gertrude: "Comparative Speed of Joined and Unjoined Writing Strokes," *Journal of Educational Psychology,* 36: 81–102, 1945.

Hilgard, Ernest R.: *Introduction to Psychology,* 3d ed., New York: Harcourt, Brace & World, Inc., 1962.

Hilgard, Ernest R.: *Theories of Learning,* 2d ed., New York: Appleton-Century-Crofts, Inc., 1956.

Hilgard, Ernest R.: "What Support from the Psychology of Learning?" *NEA Journal,* 50 (8): 20–21, 1961.

Hilgard, Josephine R.: "Learning and Maturation in Preschool Children," *Journal of Genetic Psychology,* 41: 40–53, 1932.

Hillson, Henry T.: *Demonstration Guidance Project at George Washington High School, Part I,* New York: Board of Education of the City of New York, 1961.

Hodgkinson, H. L.: *Education in Social and Cultural Perspectives,* Englewood Cliffs, N.J.: Prentice-Hall, Inc., 1962.

Hoffman, Lois W., and Ronald Lippitt: "The Measurement of Family Life Variables," in Paul H. Mussen (ed.), *Handbook of Research Methods in Child Development,* New York: John Wiley & Sons, Inc., 1960, pp. 945–1013.

Holland, James G., and Douglas Porter: "The Influence of Repetition of Incorrectly Answered Items in a Teaching-machine Program," paper presented to the American Psychological Association, Harvard University, Cambridge, Mass., 1960. 4 pp. (Mimeographed.)

Holland, James G., and B. F. Skinner: *The Analysis of Behavior,* New York: McGraw-Hill Book Company, 1961.

Holland, John L.: "Creative and Academic Performance among Talented Adolescents," *Journal of Educational Psychology,* 52: 136–147, 1961.

Hollingshead, August B.: *Elmtown's Youth: The Impact of Social Classes on Adolescents,* New York: John Wiley & Sons, Inc., 1949.

Hollister, Hal: "An Ex-convict's Scheme for More Practical Prisons," *Harper's,* 225 (1347): 14–20, 1962.

Hone, Elizabeth: "Centers of Infection," *Phi Delta Kappan,* 44: 138–140, 1962.

Honzik, M. P.: "Developmental Studies of Parent-Child Resemblance in Intelligence," *Child Development,* 28: 215–222, 1957.

Horney, Karen: *Our Inner Conflicts,* New York: W. W. Norton & Company, Inc., 1945.

Horrocks, John E.: *The Psychology of Adolescence,* 2d ed., Boston: Houghton Mifflin Company, 1962.

Horst, Paul: "The Statewide Testing Program," *Personnel and Guidance Journal,* 41: 394–402, 1963.

Hottel, John V.: *An Evaluation of the Tennessee Day Class Program for Severely Mentally Retarded Trainable Children,* Nashville: Tennessee State Department of Education, 1958.

Hovland, C. I.: "Human Learning and Retention," in S. S. Stevens (ed.), *Handbook of Experimental Psychology*, New York: John Wiley & Sons, Inc., 1951, pp. 613–689.

Hoyt, Kenneth: Guest lecturer, University of Oregon, Eugene, Ore., May, 1964.

Hudgins, Bryce B.: "Effects of Group Experience on Individual Problem Solving," *Journal of Educational Psychology*, 51: 37–42, 1960.

Hull, Clark R.: *Principles of Behavior*, New York: Appleton-Century-Crofts, Inc., 1943.

Hull, J. Dan, and Howard Cummings: "Discovering the Extent to Which Youth Needs Are Being Met," *Adapting the Secondary-school Program to the Needs of Youth*, Fifty-second Yearbook of the National Society for the Study of Education, Chicago: The University of Chicago Press, 1953, part I.

Hunt, J. McV.: "Experience and the Development of Motivation: Some Reinterpretations," *Child Development*, 31: 489–504, 1960.

Hunt, J. McV.: *Intelligence and Experience*, New York: The Ronald Press Company, 1961.

Hunter, E. C.: "Changes in Teachers' Attitudes toward Children's Behavior over the Last Thirty Years," *Mental Hygiene*, 41: 3–11, 1957.

Hurlock, Elizabeth B.: "The Use of Group Rivalry as an Incentive," *Journal of Abnormal and Social Psychology*, 22: 278–290, 1927.

Hutt, Max L., and Robert G. Gibby: *Patterns of Abnormal Behavior*, Boston: Allyn and Bacon, Inc., 1957.

Huxley, Aldous: "Can We Be Well Educated?" *Esquire*, 47: 112, December, 1956.

Huxley, Julian: *Evolution in Action*, New York: Harper & Row, Publishers, 1953.

Hymes, James L., Jr.: *Behavior and Misbehavior*, Englewood Cliffs, N.J.: Prentice-Hall, Inc., 1955.

I

Ilg, Frances, and Louise B. Ames: "Developmental Trends in Arithmetic," *Journal of Genetic Psychology*, 79: 3–28, 1951.

Ilioff, Louie B.: "The Effect of Certain Teaching Practices Involving Systematic Home-School Cooperation upon the Achievement of Eighth Grade Pupils in Mathematics," *Dissertation Abstracts*, 17 (12): 29–35, 1957.

Impellizzeri, Irene H.: in Leonard M. Miller (ed.), *Guidance for the Underachiever with Superior Ability*, U.S. Office of Education Bulletin no. 25, 1961.

J

Jack, Lois M.: "An Experimental Study of Ascendant Behavior in Preschool Children," *University of Iowa Studies in Child Welfare*, 9 (3): 7–65, 1934.

James, Donald: *An Investigation of Teachers' Attitudes concerning Children's Behavior*, unpublished bachelor's thesis, Reed College, Portland, Ore., 1950.

James, William: *Habit*, New York: Holt, Rinehart and Winston, Inc., 1914.

James, William: *Talks to Teachers on Psychology,* new ed., New York: Holt, Rinehart and Winston, Inc., 1939.

Jenkins, David H.: "Counseling through Group Activities," *Clearing House,* 23: 488–493, 1949.

Jenkins, Gladys G., Helen Shacter, and William W. Bauer: *These Are Your Children,* rev. and enlarged, Chicago: Scott, Foresman and Company, 1953.

Jennings, F. G.: "Great Teachers," *Teachers College Record,* 63: 308–312, 1962.

Jensen, Gale: "Introduction: The Newcomer," *The Dynamics of Instructional Groups,* and "The Sociopsychological Structure of the Instructional Group," Fifty-ninth Yearbook of the National Society for the Study of Education, Chicago: The University of Chicago Press, 1960, part II.

Jersild, Arthur T.: *Child Psychology,* 5th ed., Englewood Cliffs, N.J.: Prentice-Hall, Inc., 1960.

Jersild, Arthur T.: "What Teachers Say about Psychotherapy," *Phi Delta Kappan,* 44: 313–317, 1963.

Jersild, Arthur T., and Eve A. Lazar: *The Meaning of Psychotherapy in the Teacher's Life and Work,* New York: Bureau of Publications, Teachers College, Columbia University, 1962.

Johnson, Granville B.: "The Relationship Existing between Bilingualism and Racial Attitude," *Journal of Educational Psychology,* 42: 357–365, 1951.

Johnson, Lyndon B.: Message to Congress, Jan. 8, 1964.

Johnson, Wendell: *People in Quandaries,* New York: Harper & Row, Publishers, 1946.

Joint Commission on Mental Health: *Action for Mental Health: Final Report,* New York: Basic Books, Inc., Publishers, 1961.

Jones, Ayrlene McGahey: "Teaching of Trigonometry on Closed-circuit T.V.," *American Mathematical Monthly,* 65: 536, 1959. (Abstract.)

Jones, Harold E.: "Intelligence and Problem Solving," in James E. Birren (ed.), *Handbook of Aging and the Individual,* Chicago: The University of Chicago Press, 1959.

Jones, Harold E.: *Motor Performance and Growth,* Berkeley, Calif.: University of California, 1949.

Jones, Mary Cover: "The Later Careers of Boys Who Were Early- or Late-maturing," *Child Development,* 28: 113–128, 1957.

Juul, Kristen D.: "The Positive Promotion of Learning," *Journal of Teacher Education,* 12: 342–347, 1961.

K

Kagan, Jerome: "The Choice of Models," paper presented at the Conference to Strengthen the Bridge between Scientific Knowledge and Its Application to Guidance, Columbia University, Arden House, New York, Jan. 7, 1963.

Kagan, Jerome, L. W. Sontag, C. T. Baker, and V. L. Nelson: "Personality and I.Q. Change," *Journal of Abnormal and Social Psychology,* 56: 261–266, 1958.

Kahl, Joseph A.: "Educational and Occupational Aspirations of 'Common Man' Boys," *Harvard Educational Review,* 23: 183–203, 1953.

Kaiser, George M., and Joann Timmer: "Teen-agers with a Looking Glass," *Personnel and Guidance Journal*, 42: 608–609, 1964.

Kammett, Pauline H.: "Parents' Attitudes toward 'Special Classes' for Mentally Retarded Children," *Understanding the Child*, 29: 110–115, 1951.

Kaplan, Oscar J.: "Psychological Aspects of Aging," *Annals of the American Academy of Political and Social Science*, 279: 39–42, 1952.

Katona, G.: *Organizing and Memorizing*, New York: Columbia University Press, 1940.

Katona, G.: "The Role of Order of Presentation in Learning," *American Journal of Psychology*, 55: 328–353, 1942.

Katz, Elias: "Success on Stanford-Binet Intelligence Scale Test Items of Children with Cerebral Palsy as Compared to Non-handicapped," *Cerebral Palsy Review*, 16: 17–18, 1955.

Kaufmann, Margaret A.: "High-level Wellness: A Pertinent Concept for the Health Professions," *Mental Hygiene*, 47: 57–62, 1963.

Kaulfers, Walter V.: "Earmarks of a Good Foreign Language Program," *California Journal of Secondary Education*, 31: 4–13, 1956.

Kausler, Donald H.: "A Study of the Relationship between Ego-involvement and Learning," *Journal of Psychology*, 32: 225–230, 1951.

Keister, Mary E.: "The Behavior of Young Children in Failure," in R. G. Barker, J. S. Kounin, and H. F. Wright (eds.), *Child Behavior and Development*, New York: McGraw-Hill Book Company, 1943.

Kelley, Earl C.: *In Defense of Youth*, Englewood Cliffs, N.J.: Prentice-Hall, Inc., 1962.

Kephart, N. C.: *The Slow Learner in the Classroom*, Englewood Cliffs, N.J.: Charles E. Merrill, Inc., 1960.

Kersh, Bert Y.: "The Adequacy of Meaning as an Explanation for the Superiority of Learning by Inadequate Discovery," *Journal of Educational Psychology*, 49: 282–292, 1958.

Kilpatrick, William H.: *A Reconstructed Theory of the Educative Process*, New York: Bureau of Publications, Teachers College, Columbia University, 1935.

Kirk, Samuel A., and G. Orville Johnson: *Educating the Retarded Child*, Boston: Houghton Mifflin Company, 1951.

Kittell, Jack E.: "Experimental Study of the Effect of External Direction during Learning on Transfer and Retention of Principles," *Journal of Educational Psychology*, 48: 391–405, 1957.

Klausmeier, H. J.: *Principles and Practices of Secondary School Teaching*, New York: Harper & Row, Publishers, 1953.

Klaw, Spencer: "What Can We Learn from the Teaching Machines?" *The Reporter*, 27 (2): 19–26, 1962.

Kluckhohn, Florence R.: "Dominant and Variant Value Orientations," in Clyde Kluckhohn and Henry R. Murray (eds.), *Personality in Nature, Society, and Culture*, 2d ed., New York: Alfred A. Knopf, Inc., 1953.

Klugman, Samuel: "Cooperative *vs.* Individual Efficiency in Problem-solving," *Journal of Educational Psychology*, 35: 91–100, 1944.

Knapp, C. G., W. R. Dixon, and M. Lazier: "Learning to Juggle: III. A Study of Performance by Two Different Age Groups," *Research Quarterly*, 29: 32–36, 1958.

Knott, John R., Robert E. Correll, and Jean N. Shepherd: "Frequency Analysis of Electroencephalograms of Stutterers and Nonstutterers," *Journal of Speech and Hearing Research,* 2: 74–80, 1959.

Koestler, Arthur: *The Sleepwalkers,* New York: The Macmillan Company, 1959.

Kohlberg, Lawrence: "Moral Development and Identification," *Child Psychology,* Sixty-second Yearbook of the National Society for the Study of Education, Chicago: The University of Chicago Press, 1963, part I.

Kolesnik, Walter B.: *Mental Discipline in Modern Education,* Madison, Wis.: The University of Wisconsin Press, 1958.

Krathwohl, William C.: "Effects of Industrious and Indolent Work Habits on Grade Prediction in College Mathematics," *Journal of Educational Research,* 43: 32–40, 1949.

Krueger, W. C. F.: "The Effect of Overlearning on Retention," *Journal of Experimental Psychology,* 12: 71–78, 1929.

Kubala, Albert L., and M. M. Katz: "Nutritional Factors in Psychological Test Behavior," *Journal of Genetic Psychology,* 96: 343–352, 1960.

Kubie, Lawrence S.: "Hidden Brain Power," *Saturday Review,* 39: 26, Oct. 13, 1956.

Kubie, Lawrence S.: "Some Unresolved Problems of the Scientific Career," *American Scientist,* 42: 104–122, 1954.

Kuhlen, Raymond G.: "Aging and Life Adjustment," in James E. Birren (ed.), *Handbook of Aging and the Individual,* Chicago: The University of Chicago Press, 1959.

Kuhlen, Raymond G.: *The Psychology of Adolescent Development,* New York: Harper & Row, Publishers, 1952.

Kupferman, Saul C., and Raymond A. Ulmer: "An Experimental Total Push Program for Emotionally Disturbed Adolescents," *Personnel and Guidance Journal,* 42: 894–898, 1964.

Kvaraceus, W. C.: "Delinquency: A By-product of the School," *School and Society,* 59: 450–451, 1944.

Kvaraceus, W. C.: *Juvenile Delinquency,* What Research Says to the Teacher, no. 15, Washington: National Education Association, 1958.

Kvaraceus, W. C.: "Mental Health Hazards Facing Teachers," *Phi Delta Kappan,* 32: 349, 1951.

Kvaraceus, W. C., and others: *Delinquent Behavior: I. Culture and the Individual,* Washington: National Education Association, 1959.

L

LaBrant, Lou: "Mental-health Practices in the High School Grades," *Mental Health in Modern Education,* Fifty-fourth Yearbook of the National Society for the Study of Education, Chicago: The University of Chicago Press, 1955, part II.

Lambert, Wallace E.: "Developmental Aspects of Second-language Acquisition: I. Associational Fluency, Stimulus Provocativeness, and Word-order Influence," *Journal of Social Psychology,* 43: 83–89, 1956.

Lambert, William W., and Wallace E. Lambert: *Social Psychology,* Englewood Cliffs, N.J.: Prentice-Hall, Inc., 1964.

Landsman, Ted: "The Facilitation of Individual Fulfillment," address at the University of Wisconsin, Madison, Wis., Mar. 13, 1962.

Lange, Patricia: "Frustration Reaction of Physically Handicapped Children," *Exceptional Children,* 25: 355–357, 1959.

LaRiviere, Lee: Librarian, Portland Continuation Center and Portland State College: Personal interview, Mar. 15, 1963.

Lazarus, Richard S.: *Adjustment and Personality,* New York: McGraw-Hill Book Company, 1961.

Leese, Joseph: "Creativity and Academic Excellence: Incompatible?" *Bulletin of the National Association of Secondary-school Principals,* 45: 113–120, December, 1961.

Leuba, Clarence J.: *Man: A General Psychology,* New York: Holt, Rinehart and Winston, Inc., 1961.

Levinson, Boris M.: "Quo Vadis I.Q.?" *Mental Hygiene,* 48: 108–113, 1964.

Levitt, E. E.: "Effect of a 'Causal' Teacher Training Program on Authoritarianism and Responsibility in Grade School Children," *Psychological Reports,* 1: 449–458, 1955.

Lewin, Kurt: "Field Theory and Experiment in Social Psychology," *American Journal of Sociology,* 44: 868–897, 1939.

Lewin, Kurt: "Field Theory and Learning," *The Psychology of Learning,* Forty-first Yearbook of the National Society for the Study of Education, Bloomington, Ill.: Public School Publishing Company, 1942.

Lewin, Kurt: *Resolving Social Conflicts,* New York: Harper & Row, Publishers, 1948.

Lewin, Kurt, Ronald Lippitt, and Ralph K. White: "Patterns of Aggressive Behavior in Experimentally Created Social Climates," *Journal of Social Psychology,* 10: 271–299, 1939.

Lewis, Claudia: *Children of the Cumberland,* New York: Columbia University Press, 1946.

Lewis, W. D.: "Some Characteristics of Very Superior Children," *Journal of Genetic Psychology,* 62: 301–309, 1943.

Lindgren, Henry Clay: *Psychology of Personal and Social Adjustment,* 2d ed., New York: American Book Company, 1959.

Lipson, Shirley: "The Dilemma of the Year-round School," *Theory into Practice,* 1: 121–124, 1962.

Logan, Frank A.: "Micromolar Behavior Theory and Performance Speed in Education," *Harvard Educational Review,* 33: 178–185, 1963.

Loree, M. Ray, and Margaret B. Koch: "Use of Verbal Reinforcement in Developing Group Discussion Skills," *Journal of Educational Psychology,* 51: 164–168, 1960.

Lorge, Irving, and others: "A Survey of Studies Contrasting the Quality of Group Performance and Individual Performance," *Psychological Bulletin,* 55: 337–372, 1958.

Luchins, A. S., and E. H. Luchins: "Rigidity of Behavior: A Variational Approach to the Effect of Einstellung," *Studies in Psychology,* University of Oregon Monographs, no. 3, Eugene, Ore., 1959.

Lumsdaine, A. A.: "Educational Technology, Programed Learning, and Instructional Science," *Theories of Learning and Instruction,* Sixty-third

Yearbook of the National Society for the Study of Education, Chicago: The University of Chicago Press, 1964, part I.

Lynn, R.: "Individual Differences in Introversion-Extroversion, Reactive Inhibition, and Reading Attainment," *Journal of Educational Psychology*, 51: 318–321, 1960.

Lynton, R. P.: *The Tide of Learning: The Aloka Experience*, London: Routledge & Kegan Paul, Ltd., 1960.

M

Macfarlane, J. W.: "Uses and Predictive Limitations of Intelligence Tests in Infants and Young Children," *Bulletin of the World Health Organization*, 9: 409–415, 1953.

Maltzman, I.: "Thinking: From a Behavioristic Point of View," *Psychological Review*, 62: 275–286, 1955.

Maltzman, I., Eugene Eisman, and Lloyd O. Brooks: "Some Relationships between Methods of Instruction, Personality Variables, and Problem Solving Behavior," *Journal of Educational Psychology*, 47: 71–78, 1956.

Mann, J. H., and C. H. Mann: "The Importance of a Group Task in Producing Group-member Personality and Behavior Change," *Human Relations*, 12: 75–80, 1959.

Manpower Challenge of the 1960s, U.S. Department of Labor, Washington, 1960.

Marksheffel, N. D.: "Reading Readiness at the High School and College Levels," *Education*, 81: 269–272, 1961.

Marshall, Helen R.: "Relations between Home Experiences and Children's Use of Language in Play Interactions with Peers," *Psychological Monographs*, 75 (5): 77 pp., 1961.

Marvel, John A.: "Acquisition and Retention of Reading Performance on Two Response Dimensions as Related to 'Set' and Tachistoscope Training," *Journal of Educational Research*, 52: 232–237, 1959.

Maslow, A. H.: *Motivation and Personality*, New York: Harper & Row, Publishers, 1954.

Maslow, A. H.: "Some Frontier Problems in Psychological Health," *Personality Theory and Counseling Practice*, Gainesville, Fla.: University of Florida, 1961.

Maslow, A. H.: "A Theory of Motivation," *Psychological Review*, 50: 370–396, 1943.

Maslow, A. H.: *Toward a Psychology of Being*, Princeton, N.J.: D. Van Nostrand Company, Inc., 1962.

May, Rollo: "Freedom and Responsibility Reexamined," Conference to Strengthen the Bridge between Scientific Knowledge and Its Application in Guidance, Columbia University, Arden House, New York, Jan. 8, 1963.

Mayer, Frederick: *Philosophy of Education for Our Time*, New York: The Odyssey Press, Inc., 1958.

Mayer, Kurt B.: *Class and Society*, Garden City, N.Y.: Doubleday & Company, Inc., 1955.

Mayer, W. E.: "Why Did Many GI Captives Cave In?" *U.S. News & World Report*, 40: 56–62, Feb. 24, 1956.

Mays, John B.: "Teen-age Culture in Contemporary Britain and Europe," *Annals of the American Academy of Political and Social Science,* 338: 22–32, 1961.

McCandless, Boyd R.: "Should a Bright Child Start to School before He's Five?" *Education,* 77: 1–7, 1957.

McGeoch, John A., and Arthur L. Irion: *The Psychology of Human Learning,* 2d ed., New York: Longmans, Green & Co., Inc., 1952.

McGrath, Earl J.: "Language Study and World Affairs," *Phi Delta Kappan,* 34: 144–148, 1953.

McGraw, Myrtle: "Later Development of Children Specially Trained during Infancy," *Child Development,* 10: 1–19, 1939.

McGuigan, F. J.: "Variations of Whole-Part Methods of Learning," *Journal of Educational Psychology,* 51: 213–216, 1960.

McLendon, Jonathon C.: *Teaching the Social Studies,* What Research Says to the Teacher, no. 20, Washington: National Education Association, 1960.

McNeil, John D.: "Programmed Instruction versus Usual Classroom Procedures in Teaching Boys to Read," *American Educational Research Journal,* 1: 113–119, 1964.

McNemar, Quinn: "A Critical Examination of the University of Iowa Studies of Environmental Influences upon the I.Q." *Psychological Bulletin,* 37: 63–92, 1940.

Mead, Margaret: *Growing Up in New Guinea,* New York: William Morrow and Company, Inc., 1930.

Mead, Margaret: "Problems of the Late Adolescent and Young Adult," *Children and Youth in the 1960s,* Golden Anniversary White House Conference on Children and Youth.

Mead, Margaret: *From the South Seas: Studies of Adolescence and Sex in Primitive Societies,* New York: William Morrow and Company, Inc., 1939.

Meadow, A., S. J. Parnes, and H. Reese: "Influence of Brainstorming Instructions and Problem Sequence on Creative Problem Solving Test," *Journal of Applied Psychology,* 43: 413–416, 1959.

Mech, E. V., F. M. Hurst, J. D. Auble, and N. A. Fattu: "An Experimental Analysis of Differential Verbal Reinforcement in Classroom Situations," *Bulletin of the School of Education of Indiana University,* 29 (5): 1953.

Megroth, E. J., and V. Z. Washburne: "Integration in Education," *Journal of Educational Research,* 43: 81–92, 1949.

Menninger, Karl A.: Quotation in "Keeping Abreast in Education," *Phi Delta Kappan,* 34: 156, 1953.

Mental Efficiency Clinic Service Bulletin, no. 1, Detroit, Mich.: University of Detroit, no date.

Metcalf, Lawrence E.: "The Reflective Teacher," *Phi Delta Kappan,* 44: 17–21, 1962.

Meyer, William J., and George G. Thompson: "Sex Differences in the Distribution of Teacher Approval and Disapproval among Sixth-grade Children," *Journal of Educational Psychology,* 47: 385–396, 1956.

Millard, Cecil V.: *Child Growth and Development,* rev. ed., Boston: D. C. Heath and Company, 1958.

Miller, D. R., and G. E. Swanson: *The Changing American Parent*, New York: John Wiley & Sons, Inc., 1958.

Miller, Leonard M. (ed.): *Guidance for the Underachiever with Superior Ability*, U.S. Office of Education Bulletin no. 25, 1961.

Miller, Robert V.: "Social Status and Socioempathic Differences among Mentally Superior, Mentally Typical and Mentally Retarded Children," *Exceptional Children*, 23: 114–119, 1956.

Mingoia, Edwin: "Can Creativity Be Harnessed?" *Journal of Educational Sociology*, 35: 152–158, 1961.

Mitzel, Harold E., and Donald M. Medley: *Studies of Teacher Behavior: Pupil Growth in Reading*, New York: Board of Higher Education of the City of New York, 1956.

Morgan, C. D., and H. A. Murray: "A Method for Investigating Fantasies: The Thematic Apperception Test," *Archives of Neurological Psychiatry*, 34: 289–306, 1935.

Morgan, Elmer F., Jr., and Gerald R. Stucker: "The Joplin Plan of Reading *vs.* a Traditional Method," *Journal of Educational Psychology*, 51: 69–73, 1960.

Morton, R. L.: *Teaching Arithmetic*, What Research Says to the Teacher, no. 2, Washington: National Education Association, 1953.

Mowrer, O. H.: "On the Dual Nature of Learning: A Reinterpretation of 'Conditioning' and 'Problem Solving,'" *Harvard Educational Review*, 17: 102–148, 1947.

Mowrer, O. H.: *Learning Theory and Behavior*, New York: John Wiley & Sons, Inc., 1960.

Mowrer, O. H.: *Learning Theory and the Symbolic Processes*, New York: John Wiley & Sons, Inc., 1960.

Muehl, Siegmar: "The Relationship of Recall Ability between Different Tasks with the Effects of Learning Held Constant," *Dissertation Abstracts*, 19 (12): 3217, 1959.

Mueller, Theodore, and George P. Borglum: "Language Laboratory and Target Language," *French Review*, 29: 322–331, 1956.

Mummery, D. V.: "An Analytical Study of Ascendant Behavior of Preschool Children," *Child Development*, 18: 40–81, 1947.

Murphy, Gardner: "Symposium," in *Creative Thinking and the Common Man*, Washington: National Education Association, Association for Supervision and Curriculum Development, 1956.

Murray, H. A.: *Explorations in Personality*, Fair Lawn, N.J.: Oxford University Press, 1938.

Mursell, James L.: *Psychology for Modern Education*, New York: W. W. Norton & Company, Inc., 1952.

Mussen, Paul H.: *The Psychological Development of the Child*, Englewood Cliffs, N.J.: Prentice-Hall, Inc., 1963.

N

National Education Improvement Act of 1963, 88th Cong., 1st Sess., Committee Print, 1963.

Nelson, Dale B.: "Studies of Transfer of Learning in Gross Motor Skills," *Research Quarterly*, 28: 364–373, 1957.

Newman, H. H., F. N. Freeman, and K. H. Holzinger: *Twins: A Study of Heredity and Environment*, Chicago: The University of Chicago Press, 1937.

Newman, Joseph: "Psychological Problems of Children and Youth with Chronic Medical Disorders," in William M. Cruickshank (ed.), *Psychology of Exceptional Children and Youth*, Englewood Cliffs, N.J.: Prentice-Hall, Inc., 1955.

Nimmo, Hazel T.: "Values of a Pupil Activities Program," *School Activities*, 29: 249–250, 1958.

O

Ojemann, Ralph H.: "The Role of the Community in the Mental-health Program of the Schools," *Mental Health in Modern Education*, Fifty-fourth Yearbook of the National Society for the Study of Education, Chicago: The University of Chicago Press, 1955, part II.

Olson, Willard C.: *Child Development*, 2d ed., Boston: D. C. Heath and Company, 1959.

Olson, Willard C.: "Implications of the Dynamics of Instructional Groups," *The Dynamics of Instructional Groups*, Fifty-ninth Yearbook of the National Society for the Study of Education, Chicago: The University of Chicago Press, 1960, part II.

Oseas, L., and B. J. Underwood: "Studies of Distributed Practice: V. Learning and Retention of Concepts," *Journal of Experimental Psychology*, 43: 143–148, 1952.

P

Page, Ellis B.: "Teacher Comment and Student Performance," *Journal of Educational Psychology*, 49: 173–181, 1958.

Panlasigui, I., and F. B. Knight: *Research in Mathematics*, Twenty-ninth Yearbook of the National Society for the Study of Education, Chicago: The University of Chicago Press, 1930, part II, pp. 611–621.

Parsons, Talcott: "Youth in the Context of American Society," in Henry Borow (ed.), *Man in a World at Work*, Boston: Houghton Mifflin Company, 1964, pp. 237–255.

Patrick, Catherine: *What Is Creative Thinking?* New York: Philosophical Library, Inc., 1955.

Patrick, D.: "Creative Thought in Poets," *Archives of Psychology*, no. 178, p. 30, 1935.

Patterson, C. H.: "The Classroom Teacher and the Emotional Problems of Children," *Understanding the Child*, 21: 67–72, 1952.

Pavlov, Ivan P.: *Conditioned Reflexes*, London: Oxford University Press, 1927. (Translated by G. V. Anrep.)

Peck, Robert F.: "Family Patterns Correlated with Adolescent Personality Structure," *Journal of Abnormal and Social Psychology*, 57: 347–350, 1958.

Peck, Robert F.: *Fostering Mental Health in Our Schools*, 1950 Yearbook of the Association for Supervision and Curriculum Development, Washington: National Education Association, 1950.

Penfield, Wilder, and Lamar Roberts: *Speech and Brain Mechanisms*, Princeton, N.J.: Princeton University Press, 1959.

Pennington, D. F., F. Haravey, and B. M. Bass: "Some Effects of Decision and Discussion on Coalescence, Change, and Effectiveness," *Journal of Applied Psychology*, 42: 404–408, 1959.

Perkins, H. V.: "Climate Influences Group Learning," *Journal of Educational Research*, 45: 115–119, 1951.

Peterson, H. A.: "Recitation or Recall as a Factor in the Learning of Long Prose Selections," *Journal of Educational Psychology*, 35: 220–228, 1944.

Piaget, Jean: *The Origins of Intelligence in Children*, New York: International Universities Press, Inc., 1952.

Pines, Maya: "How Three-year-olds Teach Themselves to Read—and Love It," *Harper's*, 226: 58–64, May, 1963.

Pinneau, Samuel R., and Harold E. Jones: "Development of Mental Abilities," *Review of Educational Research*, 28: 392–400, 1958.

Pooley, Robert C.: "Reading and the Language Arts," *Development in and through Reading*, Sixtieth Yearbook of the National Society for the Study of Education, Chicago: The University of Chicago Press, 1961, part I.

Poull, L. E.: "The Effect of Improvement in Nutrition on the Mental Capacity of Young Children," *Child Development*, 9: 123–126, 1938.

Powell, Eleanor A.: "Improving Classroom Atmosphere through the Use of Projective Techniques," unpublished manuscript, Portland, Ore., Spring, 1958.

Prescott, Daniel A.: *The Child in the Educative Process*, New York: McGraw-Hill Book Company, 1957.

Prescott, Daniel A.: *Emotion and the Educative Process*, Washington: American Council on Education, 1938.

Proff, Fred C.: "Non-verbal Clues in Counseling," lecture given at Portland Continuation Center, Oregon State System of Higher Education, July 26, 1962.

"Pupil Failure and Nonpromotion," *NEA Research Bulletin*, 37 (1): 16–17, 1959.

Q

"Quotients of Creativity," *The London Times Educational Supplement*, 2240: 346, Feb. 23, 1962.

R

Redl, Fritz, and William W. Wattenberg: *Mental Hygiene in Teaching*, 2d ed., New York: Harcourt, Brace & World, Inc., 1959.

Reed, Horace B., Jr.: "Anxiety: The Ambivalent Variable," *Harvard Educational Review*, 30: 141–153, 1960.

Remmers, H. H., and R. D. Franklin: "Sweet Land of Liberty," *Phi Delta Kappan*, 44: 22–27, 1962.

"Reporting to Parents," *NEA Research Bulletin*, 39: 24–25, 1961.

Rhine, R. J.: "The Effect on Problem Solving of Success or Failure as a Function of Cue Specificity," *Journal of Experimental Psychology,* 53: 121–125, 1957.

Riley, Susan B.: "Mr. Gradgrind and Girl Number Twenty," *NEA Journal,* 50 (8): 22–25, 1961.

Robinson, D. W.: "Who Is a Good Teacher?" *Clearing House,* 35: 323–325, 1961.

Robinson, Francis P.: *Effective Study,* rev. ed., New York: Harper & Row, Publishers, 1961.

Roethlisberger, F. J.: *Management and Morale,* Cambridge, Mass.: Harvard University Press, 1941.

Rogers, Carl R.: "The Developing Values of the Growing Person," *Personality Theory and Counseling Practice,* Gainesville, Fla.: University of Florida, 1961.

Rogers, Carl R.: "The Place of the Person in the New World of the Behavioral Sciences," *Personnel and Guidance Journal,* 39: 442–451, 1961.

Rorschach, Hermann: *Psychodiagnostik,* 3d ed., Bern, Switzerland: Hans Huber, 1937.

Rosen, Bernard C.: "Race, Ethnicity, and the Achievement Syndrome," *American Sociological Review,* 24: 47–60, 1959.

Rosenzweig, Mark R., and Leo Postman: "Frequency of Usage and the Perception of Words," *Science,* 127: 263–266, 1958.

Rothney, John W. M.: *Evaluating and Reporting Pupil Progress,* What Research Says to the Teacher, no. 7, Washington: National Education Association, 1955.

Rothney, John W. M., Paul Danielson, and Robert A. Heimann: *Measurement for Guidance,* New York: Harper & Row, Publishers, 1959.

Rowlett, John D.: "An Experimental Comparison of Teaching Methods in Mechanical Drawing," *Industrial Education Teacher,* 20: 14–15, 1960.

Rubenstein, H., and M. Aborn: "Immediate Recall as a Function of Degree of Organization and Length of Study Period," *Journal of Experimental Psychology,* 48: 146–152, 1954.

Rubinfeld, William A.: "The School Counselor and the Emotionally Disturbed," *The School Counselor,* 9: 66–69, 1961.

Rummell, Frances V.: "What Are Good Teachers Like?" *School Life,* 30: 7–11, July, 1948.

Ryan, W. Carson: *Mental Health through Education,* New York: The Commonwealth Fund, 1938.

Ryans, David G.: *Characteristics of Teachers,* Washington: American Council on Education, 1960.

S

Sarason, Irwin G.: "Effects on Verbal Learning of Anxiety, Reassurance, and Meaningful Material," *Journal of Experimental Psychology,* 56: 472–477, 1958.

Sarbin, T. R., and B. G. Rosenberg: "Contributions to Role Taking Theory: IV. A Method for Obtaining a Quantitative Estimate of Self," *Journal of Social Psychology,* 42: 71–81, 1955.

Sarnoff, I., and D. Katz: "The Motivational Bases of Attitude Change," *Journal of Abnormal and Social Psychology,* 49: 115–124, 1954.

Sarnoff, I., F. Lighthall, R. Waite, K. Davidson, and S. Sarason: "A Cross-cultural Study of Anxiety among American and English School Children," *Journal of Educational Psychology,* 49: 129–136, 1958.

Saslow, George, M.D., Head, Psychiatric Division, University of Oregon Medical School: Lecture at the Portland Continuation Center, Jan. 17, 1963.

Scheier, I. H.: "The Method of Natural Variation in Applied Educational Research," *Journal of Educational Research,* 52: 167–170, 1959.

Schill, William J.: "Education and Occupational Success," *Personnel and Guidance Journal,* 41: 442–444, 1963.

Schmidt, H. O.: "The Effects of Praise and Blame as Incentives to Learning," *Psychological Monographs,* 53 (240), 1941.

Scholckow, O., and C. H. Judd: "The Relation of Special Training to General Intelligence," *Educational Review,* 36: 28–42, 1908.

Schorr, Alvin L.: "Families on Wheels," *Harper's,* 216: 71–76, January, 1958.

Schreiber, Daniel: "The Dropout and the Delinquent: Promising Practices Gleaned from a Year of Study," *Phi Delta Kappan,* 44: 215–221, 1963.

Schreiber, Daniel: *The Higher Horizons Program: First Annual Progress Report,* New York: Board of Education of the City of New York, 1960. (Pamphlet.)

Schreiber, Daniel: "A School's Work with Urban Disadvantaged Pupils," *College Admissions: 7. The Search for Talent,* New York: College Entrance Examination Board, 1960. 10 pp.

Schukart, Janice: *Achieving a Better Understanding of Adolescent Problems through Creative Writing,* master's thesis, Reed College, Portland, Ore., 1950.

The Shape of Education for 1964, Washington: National Education Association, 1964.

Scott, C. Winfield, Clyde M. Hill, and Hobart W. Burns: *The Great Debate: Our Schools in Crisis,* Englewood Cliffs, N.J.: Prentice-Hall, Inc., 1959.

Sears, Pauline S., and Ernest R. Hilgard: "The Teacher's Role in the Motivation of the Learner," *Theories of Learning and Instruction,* Sixty-third Yearbook of the National Society for the Study of Education, Chicago: The University of Chicago Press, 1964, part II, pp. 182–209.

Seidler, M. B., and M. J. Ravitz: "A Jewish Peer Group," *American Journal of Sociology,* 61: 11–15, 1955.

Sexton, Patricia C.: *Education and Income,* New York: The Viking Press, Inc., 1961.

Shaffer, Laurance F., and Edward J. Shoben, Jr., *The Psychology of Adjustment,* 2d ed., Boston: Houghton Mifflin Company, 1956.

Shane, Harold G.: "The School and Individual Differences," *Individualizing Instruction,* Sixty-first Yearbook of the National Society for the Study of Education, Chicago: The University of Chicago Press, 1962, part I.

Shaw, Merville C., Kenneth Edson, and Hugh M. Bell: "The Self-concept of Bright Underachieving High School Students as Revealed by an Adjective Check List," *Personnel and Guidance Journal,* 39: 193–196, 1960.

Sheldon, W. H., and others: *Atlas of Men,* New York: Harper & Row, Publishers, 1954.

Sheldon, W. H., and S. S. Stevens: *The Varieties of Temperament,* New York: Harper & Row, Publishers, 1942.

Sherman, Mandel, and Cora B. Key: "The Intelligence of Isolated Mountain Children," *Child Development,* 3: 279–290, 1932.

Sheviakov, George V., and Fritz Redl: *Discipline for Today's Children and Youth,* new revision by Sybil K. Richardson, Washington: National Education Association, Association for Supervision and Curriculum Development, 1956.

Siggins, C. M.: "Motivation in Teaching," *Education,* 82: 115–117, 1961.

Skinner, B. F.: "Reinforcement Today," *The American Psychologist,* 13: 94–99, 1958.

Skinner, B. F.: "The Science of Learning and the Art of Teaching," *Harvard Educational Review,* 24: 86–97, 1954.

Slavson, S. R.: *Child-centered Group Guidance of Parents,* New York: International Universities Press, Inc., 1958.

Smith, Louis M., and Bryce B. Hudgins: *Educational Psychology,* New York: Alfred A. Knopf, Inc., 1964.

Sontag, L. W., C. T. Baker, V. L. Nelson: *Mental Growth and Personality Development: A Longitudinal Study,* Monograph of the Society for Research in Child Development, 23 (2): ser. no. 68, 1958.

Sperry, R. W.: "The Growth of Nerve Circuits," *Scientific American,* 20: 46, 68–75, November, 1959.

Stagner, Ross: *Psychology of Personality,* 3d ed., New York: McGraw-Hill Book Company, 1961.

Stagner, Ross, and T. F. Karwoski: *Psychology,* New York: McGraw-Hill Book Company, 1952.

Steinberg, Ira S.: "Indoctrination and Ideals of Democracy," *Phi Delta Kappan,* 44: 66–68, 1962.

Stendler, C., D. Damrin, and A. C. Haines: "Studies in Cooperation and Competition: I. The Effects of Working for Group and Individual Rewards on the Social Climates of Children's Groups," *Journal of Genetic Psychology,* 79: 173–197, 1951.

Stephens, George D.: "Needed: A Declaration of Dependence," *Educational Forum,* 23: 61–68, 1958.

Stephens, J. M.: "Educational Psychology," in Paul R. Farnsworth (ed.), *Annual Review of Psychology,* vol. 10, Palo Alto, Calif.: Annual Reviews, Inc., 1959.

Stephens, J. M.: *Educational Psychology: The Study of Educational Growth,* New York: Holt, Rinehart and Winston, Inc., 1951.

Stern, Helen G.: "Guidance for the Gifted Underachiever in High School," *NEA Journal,* 51 (8): 24–26, 1962.

Stevenson, H. W., M. W. Weir, and E. F. Zigler: "Discrimination Learning in Children as a Function of Motive-incentive Conditions," *Psychological Reports,* 5: 95–98, 1959.

Stevenson, Ian: "Why People Change," *Harper's,* 207: 55–60, December, 1953.

Stoddard, George D.: "On the Meaning of Intelligence," *Psychological Review*, 48: 250–260, 1941.

Stolz, Lois Meek: "Youth: The Gesell Institute and Its Latest Study," *Contemporary Psychology*, 3: 10–15, 1958.

Stone, L. Joseph, and Joseph Church: *Childhood and Adolescence*, New York: Random House, Inc., 1957.

Stuart, Harold C.: "Normal Growth and Development during Adolescence," in Jerome M. Seidman (ed.), *The Adolescent: A Book of Readings*, rev. ed., New York: Holt, Rinehart and Winston, Inc., 1958.

Sullivan, H. S.: *The Meaning of Anxiety in Psychiatry and in Life*, New York: William Alanson White Institute of Psychiatry, 1948.

Suppes, Patrick: "Modern Learning Theory and the Elementary-school Curriculum," *American Educational Research Journal*, 1: 79–93, 1964.

Swanson, J. Chester: "Education for Occupational Competence," *Phi Delta Kappan*, 44: 322–325, 1963.

Swenson, Esther J.: "Application of Learning Principles to the Improvement of Teaching in the Early Elementary Grades," *Learning and Instruction*, Forty-ninth Yearbook of the National Society for the Study of Education, Chicago: The University of Chicago Press, 1950, part I.

Symonds, P. M.: *The Ego and the Self*, New York: Appleton-Century-Crofts, Inc., 1951.

Symonds, P. M.: "The Organization of Educational Research in the United States," *Harvard Educational Review*, 27: 159–167, 1957.

Symonds, P. M.: *The Psychology of Parent-Child Relationships*, New York: Appleton-Century-Crofts, Inc., 1939.

Symonds, P. M.: "Teaching as a Function of the Teacher's Personality," *Journal of Teacher Education*, 5: 79–83, 1954.

T

Tapfer, William: "A Prediction of Potential Male Drop-outs in Grade Eleven and an Attempt to Prevent this Action through Extensive Counseling," unpublished master's study, Oregon State System of Higher Education, Portland Center, June, 1962.

Taylor, C. W.: "Effects of Instructional Media on Creativity," *Educational Leadership*, 19: 453–458, 1962.

Taylor, C. W.: "A Tentative Description of the Creative Individual," in *Human Variability and Learning*, Washington: National Education Association, Association for Supervision and Curriculum Development, 1961.

Taylor, M., and others: "Assessing Emerging Leadership Behavior in Small Discussion Groups," *Journal of Educational Psychology*, 52: 12–18, 1961.

"Teacher Supply and Demand in Public Schools," *NEA Research Bulletin*, 40: 93–95, October, 1962.

Teachers for Our Times, Washington: American Council on Education, 1944.

Tead, Ordway: "Crisis on Campus: Standards of Quality," *Survey Graphic*, 36: 598–602, 1947.

"Ten Criticisms of Public Education," *NEA Research Bulletin*, 35 (4): 131–174, 1957.

Terman, Lewis M.: *Genetic Studies of Genius: I. Mental and Physical Traits of a Thousand Gifted Children*, Stanford, Calif.: Stanford University Press, 1925.

Terman, Lewis M., and Maud A. Merrill: *Stanford-Binet Intelligence Scale, Manual for Third Revision, Form L-M*, Boston: Houghton Mifflin Company, 1960.

Terrell, Glenn, Jr., Kathryn Durkin, and Melvin Wiesley: "Social Class and the Nature of the Incentive in Discrimination Learning," *Journal of Abnormal and Social Psychology*, 59: 270–272, 1959.

Thayer, V. T., Caroline B. Zachry, and Ruth Kotinsky: *Reorganizing Secondary Education*, New York: Appleton-Century-Crofts, Inc., 1939.

Thibault, J., and others: "Communication, Task Demands, and Group Effectiveness," *Journal of Personality*, 28: 156–166, 1960.

Thompson, George G.: *Child Psychology*, 2d ed., Boston: Houghton Mifflin Company, 1962.

Thompson, George G., E. F. Gardner, F. J. Di Vesta: *Educational Psychology*, New York: Appleton-Century-Crofts, Inc., 1959.

Thompson, George G., and C. W. Hunnicutt: "The Effects of Repeated Praise or Blame on the Work Achievement of Introverts and Extroverts," *Journal of Educational Psychology*, 35: 257–266, 1944.

Thorndike, E. L.: *Educational Psychology: Briefer Course*, New York: Bureau of Publications, Teachers College, Columbia University, 1924.

Thorndike, E. L.: *Fundamentals of Learning*, New York: Bureau of Publications, Teachers College, Columbia University, 1932.

Thorndike, E. L.: *Human Learning*, New York: Appleton-Century-Crofts, Inc., 1931.

Thorndike, E. L., and others: *The Measurement of Intelligence*, New York: Bureau of Publications, Teachers College, Columbia University, 1927.

Thorpe, Louis P., and Allen M. Schmuller: *Contemporary Theories of Learning*, New York: The Ronald Press Company, 1954.

Tibbitts, Clark, and Wilma Donahue: *Aging in the Modern World*, Ann Arbor, Mich.: University of Michigan, 1957.

Tiedeman, David V., and Frank L. Field: "Guidance: The Science of Purposeful Action Applied through Education," *Harvard Educational Review*, 32: 483–501, 1962.

Tiller, Marguerite: "How Confused Can Teachers Be?" *NEA Journal*, 51 (8): 49, 1962.

Torrance, E. P.: *Guiding Creative Talent*, Englewood Cliffs, N.J.: Prentice-Hall, Inc., 1962.

Torrance, E. P.: "Problem of Creative Children," *Educational Digest*, 27: 40–42, November, 1961.

Travers, Robert M. W.: *Essentials of Learning*, New York: The Macmillan Company, 1963.

Trenholme, A. K.: "New Media Contribute to Classroom Instructional Programs," *The School Bulletin*, 47 (4): 13–15, 1962. (Portland Public Schools.)

Trillingham, C. C. (ed.): *Guiding Today's Youth*, Monterey, Calif.: California Test Bureau, 1962.

Trow, William C.: "Role Functions of the Teacher in the Instructional Group," *The Dynamics of Instructional Groups,* Fifty-ninth Yearbook of the National Society for the Study of Education, Chicago: The University of Chicago Press, 1960, part II.

Trow, William C., Alvin F. Zander, William C. Morse, and David H. Jenkins: "Psychology of Group Behavior: The Class as a Group," *Journal of Educational Psychology,* 41: 322–338, 1950.

V

Voelker, Paul H., and Frances A. Mullen: "Organization, Administration, and Supervision of Special Education," *Review of Educational Research,* 33: 5–19, 1963.

Vroom, V. H.: "Projection, Negation, and Self-concept," *Human Relations,* 12: 335–344, 1959.

W

Wallas, Graham: *The Art of Thought,* New York: Harcourt, Brace & World, Inc., 1926.

Wallen, Norman E.: "Creativity: Fantasy and Fact," *Elementary School Journal,* 64: 438–443, 1964.

Walter, L. M., and S. S. Marzolf: "The Relation of Sex, Age, and School Achievement to Levels of Aspiration," *Journal of Educational Psychology,* 42: 285–292, 1951.

Wann, Kenneth D., M. S. Dorn, and E. A. Liddle: *Fostering Intellectual Development in Young Children,* New York: Bureau of Publications, Teachers College, Columbia University, 1962.

Warburton, F. W.: "Educational Psychology," in Quinn McNemar (ed.), *Annual Review of Psychology,* vol. 13, Palo Alto, Calif.: Annual Reviews, Inc., 1962.

Warner, W. Lloyd: *American Life: Dream and Reality,* Chicago: The University of Chicago Press, 1953.

"Wasted Talent," *Time,* Nov. 21, 1960, pp. 53–56.

Wattenberg, William: "Social Origin and Teaching Role: Some Typical Patterns," in Lindley J. Stiles (ed.), *The Teacher's Role in American Society,* New York: Harper & Row, Publishers, 1957.

Wedge, Bryant: "Changing Conceptions of Mental Health," *Mental Hygiene,* 48: 22–31, 1964.

Wellman, Beth L.: *Intelligence: Its Nature and Nurture,* Thirty-ninth Yearbook of the National Society for the Study of Education, Chicago: The University of Chicago Press, 1940, part II.

Wellman, Beth L., and E. L. Pegram: "Binet I.Q. Changes of Orphanage Preschool Children: A Re-analysis," *Journal of Genetic Psychology,* 65: 239–263, 1944.

Wenar, C.: "The Effects of a Motor Handicap on Personality: I. The Effect on Level of Aspiration," *Child Development,* 24: 123–130, 1953.

Wenkart, A.: "Self-acceptance," *American Journal of Psychoanalysis,* 15: 135–143, 1955.

Wesman, A. G.: "A Study of Transfer of Training from High School Subjects to Intelligence," *Journal of Educational Research*, 39: 254–264, 1945.

Wetzler, W. F.: "Brainstorming in the College Classroom," *Improving College and University Teaching*, 10: 34–36, 1962.

Wheeler, Raymond H.: *The Science of Psychology*, 2d ed., New York: Thomas Y. Crowell Company, 1940.

White, Sheldon H.: "Learning," *Child Psychology*, Sixty-second Yearbook of the National Society for the Study of Education, Chicago: The University of Chicago Press, 1963, part I.

Whiting, John W. M.: "Theories of Learning and Behavior," in Judy F. Rosenblith and Wesley Allinsmith (eds.), *The Causes of Behavior*, Boston: Allyn and Bacon, Inc., 1962.

Whitla, Dean K.: "Effect of Tutoring on Scholastic Aptitude Test Scores," *Personnel and Guidance Journal*, 41: 32–37, 1962.

Wickman, E. K.: *Children's Behavior and Teachers' Attitudes*, Cambridge, Mass.: Published for the Commonwealth Fund by Harvard University Press, 1928.

Wiener, Gerald: "The Interaction among Anxiety, Stress Instructions and Difficulty," *Journal of Consulting Psychology*, 23: 324–328, 1959.

Wiggins, Sam P.: *The Student Teacher in Action*, Boston: Allyn and Bacon, Inc., 1957.

Wilhelms, Fred T.: "The Curriculum and Individual Differences," *Individualizing Instruction*, Sixty-first Yearbook of the National Society for the Study of Education, Chicago: The University of Chicago Press, 1962, part I.

Williams, Frankwood W : *Adolescence*, New York: Holt, Rinehart and Winston, Inc., 1930.

Wilson, Alan B.: "Residential Segregation of Social Classes and Aspirations of High School Boys," *American Sociological Review*, 24: 836–845, 1959.

Wingo, G. Max: "Implications for Improving Instruction in the Upper Elementary Grades," *Learning and Instruction*, Forty-ninth Yearbook of the National Society for the Study of Education, Chicago: The University of Chicago Press, 1950, part I.

Wisconsin Improvement Program, 1959–1961: *Making Teaching and Learning Better*, Madison, Wis.: The University of Wisconsin, 1962. (Booklet.)

Witty, Paul A.: "Some Characteristics of the Effective Teacher," *Educational Administration and Supervision*, 36: 193–208, 1950.

Witty, Paul A., and R. A. Sizemore: "Phonics in the Reading Program: A Review and an Evaluation," *Elementary English*, 32: 355–371, 1955.

Wohlwill, Joachim: "A Study of the Development of the Number Concept by Scalogram Analysis," *Journal of Genetic Psychology*, 97: 345–377, 1960.

Wolfe, Don M.: *Creative Ways to Teach English*, New York: The Odyssey Press, Inc., 1958.

Wolfle, Dael L.: "Diversity of Talent," *American Psychologist*, 15: 536, 1960.

Wolfle, Dael L.: Introduction in C. Gilbert Wrenn, *The Counselor in a Changing World*, Washington: American Personnel and Guidance Association, 1962.

Woodring, M. N.: *A Study of the Quality of English in Latin Translation*, Contributions to Education, no. 187, New York: Bureau of Publications, Teachers College, Columbia University, 1925.

Worell, Leonard: "Level of Aspiration and Academic Success," *Journal of Educational Psychology,* 50: 47–54, 1959.

Wrenn, C. Gilbert: *The Counselor in a Changing World,* Washington: American Personnel and Guidance Association, 1962.

Y

Yamamoto, Kaoru: "Creative Thinking: Some Thoughts on Research," *Exceptional Children,* 30: 403–410, 1964.

Young, F. M.: "Response of Juvenile Delinquents to the Thematic Apperception Test," *Journal of Genetic Psychology,* 88: 251–264, 1956.

Z

Zander, Alvin: "Resistance to Change: Its Analysis and Prevention," *Advanced Management,* 15: 9–12, 1950.

Zander, Alvin, and A. R. Cohen: "Attributed Social Power and Group Acceptance: A Classroom Experimental Demonstration," *Journal of Abnormal and Social Psychology,* 51: 490–492, 1955.

Zander, Alvin, and others: "Unity of Group, Identification with Group, and Self-esteem of Members," *Journal of Personality,* 28: 463–478, 1960.

Ziller, R. C.: "Vocational Choice and Utility for Risk," *Journal of Consulting Psychology,* 4: 61–64, 1957.

Ziller, R. C., and R. D. Behringer: "Assimilation of the Knowledgeable Newcomer under Conditions of Success and Failure," *Journal of Abnormal and Social Psychology,* 60: 288–291, 1960.

Ziller, R. C., and others: "Group Creativity under Conditions of Success or Failure and Variations in Group Stability," *Journal of Applied Psychology,* 46: 43–49, 1962.

Zimmerman, Donald W.: "Durable Secondary Reinforcement: Method and Theory," *Psychological Review,* 64: 373–383, 1957.

Name Index

Subject Index